Nissan Maxima Automotive Repair Manual

by Ken Freund and John H Haynes
Member of the Guild of Motoring Writers

Models covered:
All Nissan Maxima models
1985 through 1992

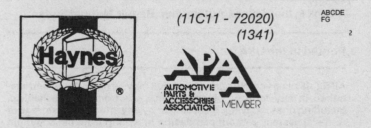

(11C11 - 72020)
(1341)

ABCDE
FG

2

AUTOMOTIVE PARTS & ACCESSORIES ASSOCIATION MEMBER

Haynes Publishing Group
Sparkford Nr Yeovil
Somerset BA22 7JJ England

Haynes North America, Inc
861 Lawrence Drive
Newbury Park
California 91320 USA

Acknowledgements

We are grateful for the help and cooperation of Nissan Motor Company, Ltd., for assistance with technical information, certain illustrations and vehicle photos. Technical writers who contributed to this project include Jon LaCourse and Robert Maddox.

A book in the **Haynes Automotive Repair Manual Series**

Printed in the USA

ISBN 1 56392 365 3

Library of Congress Catalog Card Number 99-68982

Contents

Introductory pages

About this manual	5
Introduction to the Nissan Maxima	5
Vehicle identification numbers	6
Buying parts	8
Maintenance techniques, tools and working facilities	8
Booster battery (jump) starting	15
Jacking and towing	15
Automotive chemicals and lubricants	17
Safety first!	18
Conversion factors	19
Troubleshooting	20

Chapter 1
Tune-up and routine maintenance 28 — 1

Chapter 2 Part A
Engine 63 — 2A

Chapter 2 Part B
General engine overhaul procedures 93 — 2B

Chapter 3
Cooling, heating and air conditioning systems 121 — 3

Chapter 4
Fuel and exhaust systems 136 — 4

Chapter 5
Engine electrical systems 163 — 5

Chapter 6
Emissions control systems 174 — 6

Chapter 7 Part A
Manual transaxle 185 — 7A

Chapter 7 Part B
Automatic transaxle 191 — 7B

Chapter 8
Clutch and driveaxles 197 — 8

Chapter 9
Brakes 212 — 9

Chapter 10
Suspension and steering systems 233 — 10

Chapter 11
Body 256 — 11

Chapter 12
Chassis electrical system 270 — 12

Wiring diagrams 290

Index 300

A 1986 Nissan Maxima 4-door sedan

About this manual

Its purpose

The purpose of this manual is to help you get the best value from your vehicle. It can do so in several ways. It can help you decide what work must be done, even if you choose to have it done by a dealer service department or a repair shop; it provides information and procedures for routine maintenance and servicing; and it offers diagnostic and repair procedures to follow when trouble occurs.

We hope you use the manual to tackle the work yourself. For many simpler jobs, doing it yourself may be quicker than arranging an appointment to get the vehicle into a shop and making the trips to leave it and pick it up. More importantly, a lot of money can be saved by avoiding the expense the shop must pass on to you to cover its labor and overhead costs. An added benefit is the sense of satisfaction and accomplishment that you feel after doing the job yourself.

Using the manual

The manual is divided into Chapters. Each Chapter is divided into numbered Sections, which are headed in bold type between horizontal lines. Each Section consists of consecutively numbered paragraphs.

At the beginning of each numbered section you will be referred to any illustrations which apply to the procedures in that section. The reference numbers used in illustration captions pinpoint the pertinent Section and the Step within that section. That is, illustration 3.2 means the illustration refers to Section 3 and Step (or paragraph) 2 within that Section.

Procedures, once described in the text, are not normally repeated. When it's necessary to refer to another Chapter, the reference will be given as Chapter and Section number. Cross references given without use of the word "Chapter" apply to Sections and/or paragraphs in the same Chapter. For example, "see Section 8" means in the same Chapter.

References to the left or right side of the vehicle assume you are sitting in the driver's seat, facing forward.

Even though we have prepared this manual with extreme care, neither the publisher nor the author can accept responsibility for any errors in, or omissions from, the information given.

NOTE

A **Note** provides information necessary to properly complete a procedure or information which will make the procedure easier to understand.

CAUTION

A **Caution** provides a special procedure or special steps which must be taken while completing the procedure where the **Caution** is found. Not heeding a **Caution** can result in damage to the assembly being worked on.

WARNING

A **Warning** provides a special procedure or special steps which must be taken while completing the procedure where the **Warning** is found. Not heeding a **Warning** can result in personal injury.

Introduction to the Nissan Maxima

Nissan Maxima models are available in 4-door sedan and station wagon body styles.

The transversely mounted V6 engine used in these models is equipped with electronic fuel injection.

The engine drives the front wheels through either a 5-speed manual or 4-speed automatic transaxle via independent driveaxles.

Independent suspension, featuring coil spring/strut damper units, is used on all four wheels. The power assisted rack and pinion steering unit is mounted behind the engine.

The brakes are disc at the front with either drum or discs at the rear, depending on model, with power assist standard.

Vehicle identification numbers

Modifications are a continuing and unpublicized process in vehicle manufacturing. Since spare parts manuals and lists are compiled on a numerical basis, the individual vehicle numbers are essential to correctly identify the component required.

Vehicle Identification Number (VIN)

This very important identification number is stamped on the firewall in the engine compartment and on a plate attached to the dashboard inside the windshield on the driver's side of the vehicle **(see illustration)**. The

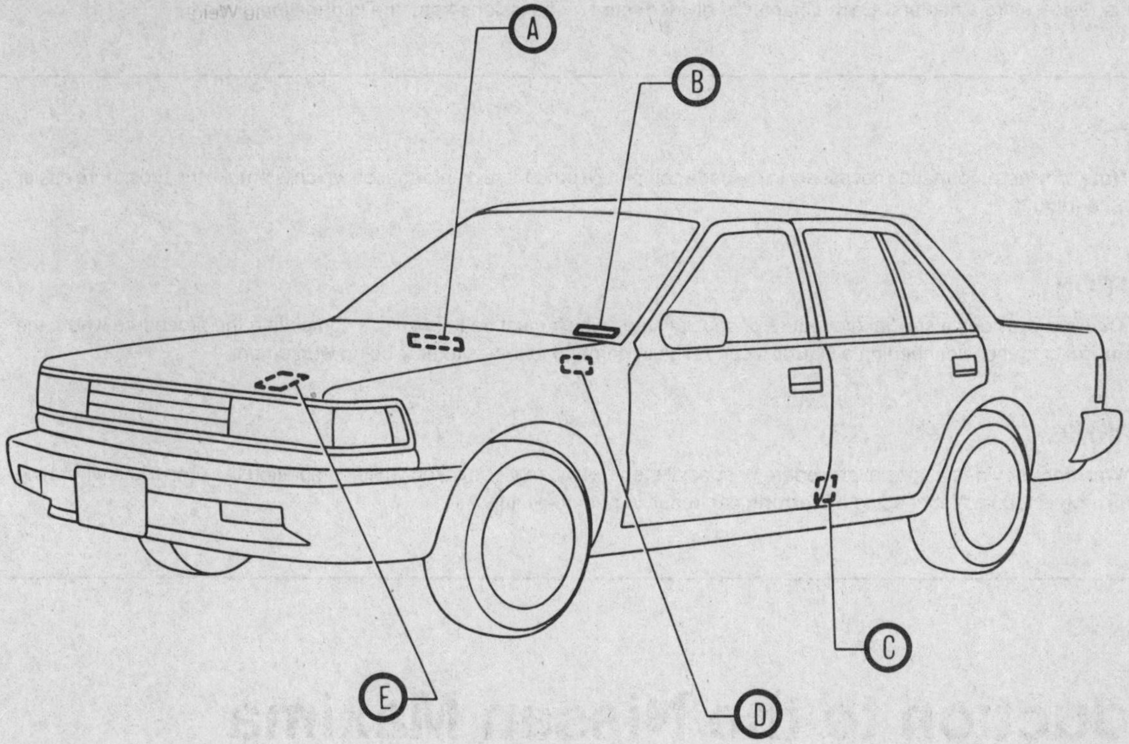

Important ID numbers and other information can be found in several locations on the vehicle

A Vehicle Identification Number (stamped on firewall)
B Vehicle Identification Number (visible through the driver's side windshield)
C Certification regulation plate
D Manufacturer's plate
E Vehicle Emission Control Information (VECI) label

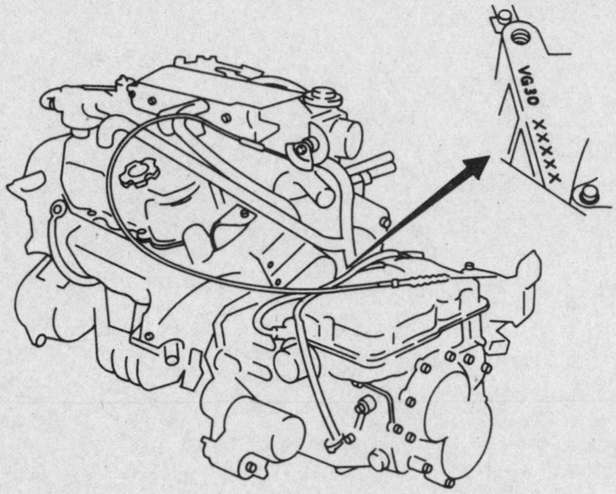

Location of the engine serial number

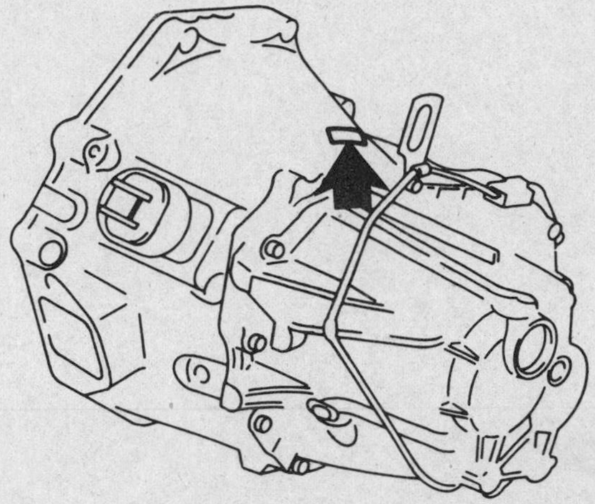

Location of the manual transaxle serial number

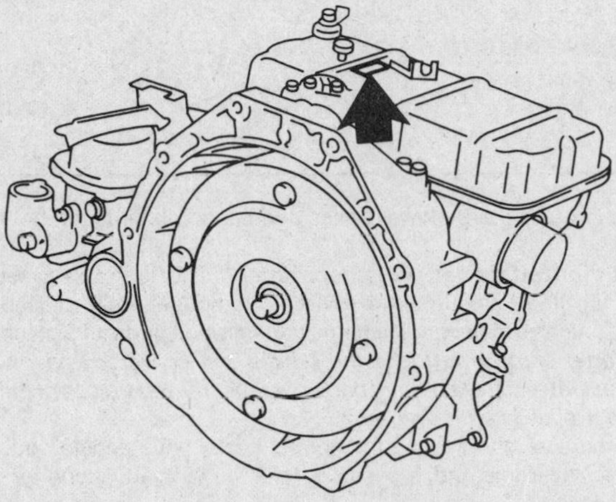

Location of the automatic transaxle serial number

VIN also appears on the Vehicle Certificate of Title and Registration. It contains information such as where and when the vehicle was manufactured, the model year and the body style.

Vehicle identification plate

The vehicle identification plate is attached to the firewall in the engine compartment **(see illustration)**. The plate contains the name of the manufacturer, the month and year of production, the Gross Vehicle Weight Rating (GVWR), the Gross Axle Weight Rating (GAWR) and the certification statement.

Engine number

The engine serial number is located on the left (driver's) end of the engine block, near the transaxle **(see illustration)**.

Transaxle numbers

The transaxle serial numbers are located on the bellhousing (manual transaxle) or on the top of the transaxle on the control valve cover (automatic transaxle) **(see illustration)**.

Buying parts

Replacement parts are available from many sources, which generally fall into one of two categories – authorized dealer parts departments and independent retail auto parts stores. Our advice concerning these parts is as follows:

Retail auto parts stores: Good auto parts stores will stock frequently needed components which wear out relatively fast, such as clutch components, exhaust systems, brake parts, tune-up parts, etc. These stores often supply new or reconditioned parts on an exchange basis, which can save a considerable amount of money. Discount auto parts stores are often very good places to buy materials and parts needed for general vehicle maintenance such as oil, grease, filters, spark plugs, belts, touch-up paint, bulbs, etc. They also usually sell tools and general accessories, have convenient hours, charge lower prices and can often be found not far from home.

Authorized dealer parts department: This is the best source for parts which are unique to the vehicle and not generally available elsewhere (such as major engine parts, transmission parts, trim pieces, etc.).

Warranty information: *If the vehicle is still covered under warranty, be sure that any replacement parts purchased – regardless of the source – do not invalidate the warranty!*

To be sure of obtaining the correct parts, have engine and chassis numbers available and, if possible, take the old parts along for positive identification.

Maintenance techniques, tools and working facilities

Maintenance techniques

There are a number of techniques involved in maintenance and repair that will be referred to throughout this manual. Application of these techniques will enable the home mechanic to be more efficient, better organized and capable of performing the various tasks properly, which will ensure that the repair job is thorough and complete.

Fasteners

Fasteners are nuts, bolts, studs and screws used to hold two or more parts together. There are a few things to keep in mind when working with fasteners. Almost all of them use a locking device of some type, either a lockwasher, locknut, locking tab or thread adhesive. All threaded fasteners should be clean and straight, with undamaged threads and undamaged corners on the hex head where the wrench fits. Develop the habit of replacing all damaged nuts and bolts with new ones. Special locknuts with nylon or fiber inserts can only be used once. If they are removed, they lose their locking ability and must be replaced with new ones.

Rusted nuts and bolts should be treated with a penetrating fluid to ease removal and prevent breakage. Some mechanics use turpentine in a spout-type oil can, which works quite well. After applying the rust penetrant, let it work for a few minutes before trying to loosen the nut or bolt. Badly rusted fasteners may have to be chiseled or sawed off or removed with a special nut breaker, available at tool stores.

If a bolt or stud breaks off in an assembly, it can be drilled and removed with a special tool commonly available for this purpose. Most automotive machine shops can perform this task, as well as other repair procedures, such as the repair of threaded holes that have been stripped out.

Flat washers and lockwashers, when removed from an assembly, should always be replaced exactly as removed. Replace any damaged washers with new ones. Never use a lockwasher on any soft metal surface (such as aluminum), thin sheet metal or plastic.

Fastener sizes

For a number of reasons, automobile manufacturers are making wider and wider use of metric fasteners. Therefore, it is important to be able to tell the difference between standard (sometimes called U.S. or SAE) and metric hardware, since they cannot be interchanged.

All bolts, whether standard or metric, are sized according to diameter, thread pitch and length. For example, a standard 1/2 – 13 x 1 bolt is 1/2 inch in diameter, has 13 threads per inch and is 1 inch long. An M12 – 1.75 x 25 metric bolt is 12 mm in diameter, has a thread pitch of 1.75 mm (the distance between threads) and is 25 mm long. The two bolts are nearly identical, and easily confused, but they are not interchangeable.

In addition to the differences in diameter, thread pitch and length, metric and standard bolts can also be distinguished by examining the bolt heads. To begin with, the distance across the flats on a standard bolt head is measured in inches, while the same dimension on a metric bolt is sized in millimeters (the same is true for nuts). As a result, a standard wrench should not be used on a metric bolt and a metric wrench should not be used on a standard bolt. Also, most standard bolts have slashes radiating out from the center of the head to denote the grade or strength of the bolt, which is an indication of the amount of torque that can be applied to it. The greater the number of slashes, the greater the strength of the bolt. Grades 0 through 5 are commonly used on automobiles. Metric bolts have a property class (grade) number, rather than a slash, molded into their heads to indicate bolt strength. In this case, the higher the number, the stronger the bolt. Property class numbers 8.8, 9.8 and 10.9 are commonly used on automobiles.

Strength markings can also be used to distinguish standard hex nuts from metric hex nuts. Many standard nuts have dots stamped into one side, while metric nuts are marked with a number. The greater the number of dots, or the higher the number, the greater the strength of the nut.

Metric studs are also marked on their ends according to property class (grade). Larger studs are numbered (the same as metric bolts), while smaller studs carry a geometric code to denote grade.

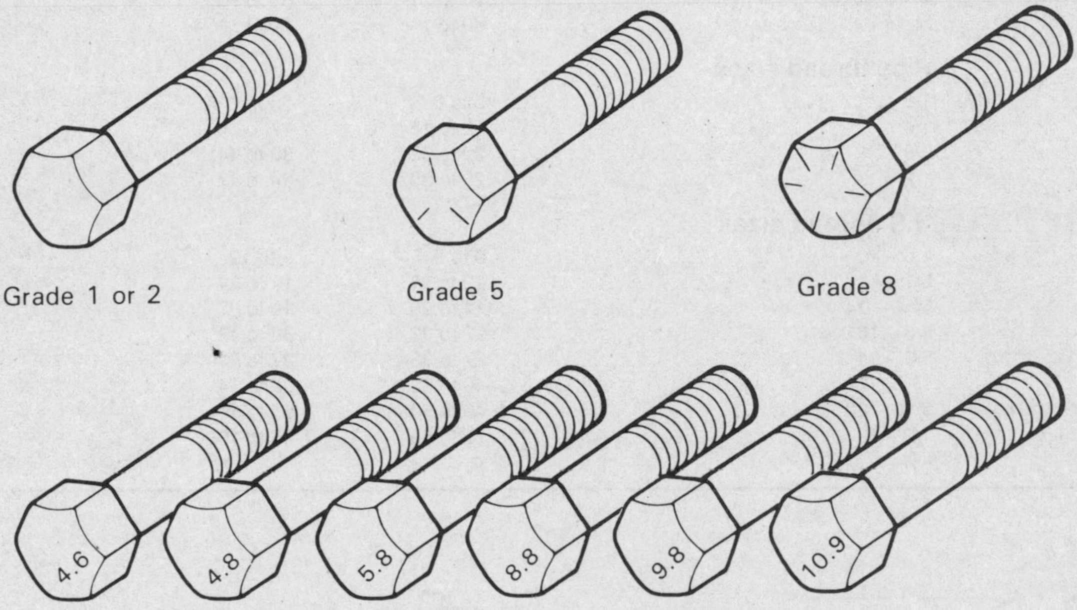

Bolt strength markings (top – standard/SAE/USS; bottom – metric)

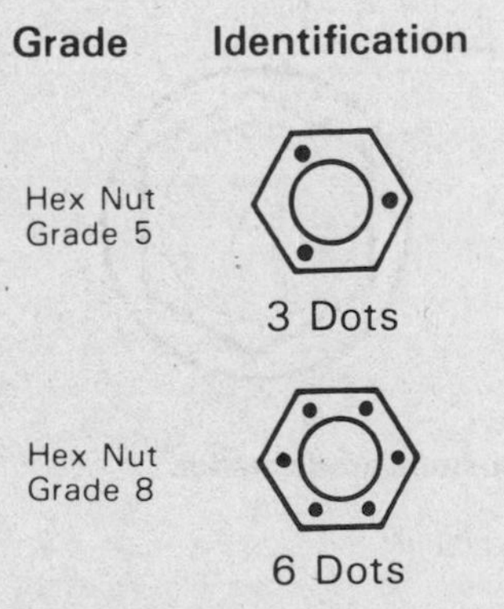

Standard hex nut strength markings

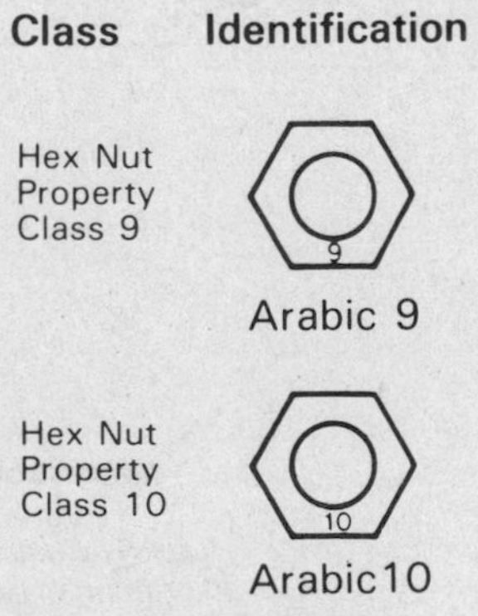

Metric hex nut strength markings

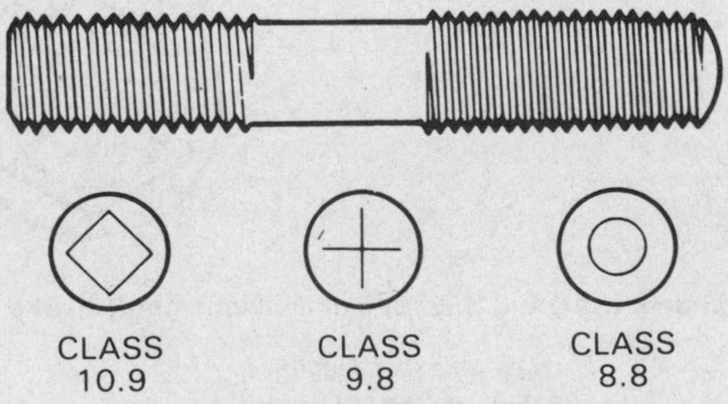

Metric stud length markings

It should be noted that many fasteners, especially Grades 0 through 2, have no distinguishing marks on them. When such is the case, the only way to determine whether it is standard or metric is to measure the thread pitch or compare it to a known fastener of the same size.

Standard fasteners are often referred to as SAE, as opposed to metric. However, it should be noted that SAE technically refers to a non-metric *fine thread* fastener only. Coarse thread non-metric fasteners are referred to as USS sizes.

Since fasteners of the same size (both standard and metric) may have different strength ratings, be sure to reinstall any bolts, studs or nuts removed from your vehicle in their original locations. Also, when replacing a fastener with a new one, make sure that the new one has a strength rating equal to or greater than the original.

Tightening sequences and procedures

Most threaded fasteners should be tightened to a specific torque value (torque is the twisting force applied to a threaded component such as a nut or bolt). Overtightening the fastener can weaken it and cause it to break, while undertightening can cause it to eventually come loose. Bolts, screws and studs, depending on the material they are made of and their thread diameters, have specific torque values, many of which are noted in the Specifications at the beginning of each Chapter. Be sure to follow the torque recommendations closely. For fasteners not assigned a specific torque, a general torque value chart is presented here as a guide. These torque values are for dry (unlubricated) fasteners threaded into steel or cast iron (not aluminum). As was previously mentioned, the size and grade of a fastener determine the amount of torque that can safely

Metric thread sizes	**Ft-lbs**	**Nm**
M-6	6 to 9	9 to 12
M-8	14 to 21	19 to 28
M-10	28 to 40	38 to 54
M-12	50 to 71	68 to 96
M-14	80 to 140	109 to 154
Pipe thread sizes		
1/8	5 to 8	7 to 10
1/4	12 to 18	17 to 24
3/8	22 to 33	30 to 44
1/2	25 to 35	34 to 47
U.S. thread sizes		
1/4 – 20	6 to 9	9 to 12
5/16 – 18	12 to 18	17 to 24
5/16 – 24	14 to 20	19 to 27
3/8 – 16	22 to 32	30 to 43
3/8 – 24	27 to 38	37 to 51
7/16 – 14	40 to 55	55 to 74
7/16 – 20	40 to 60	55 to 81
1/2 – 13	55 to 80	75 to 108

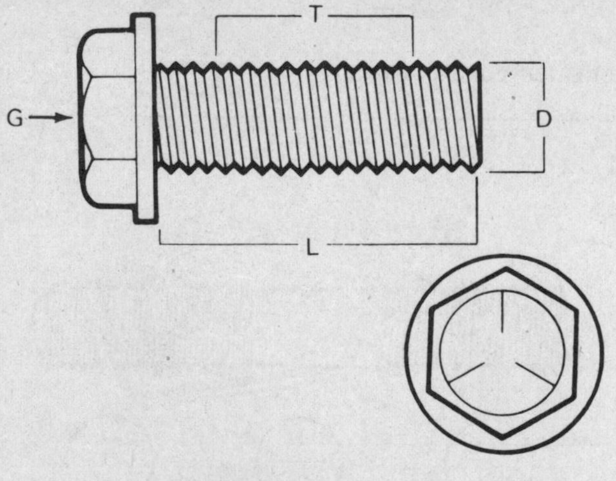

Standard (SAE and USS) bolt dimensions/grade marks

- *G* *Grade marks (bolt length)*
- *L* *Length (in inches)*
- *T* *Thread pitch (number of threads per inch)*
- *D* *Nominal diameter (in inches)*

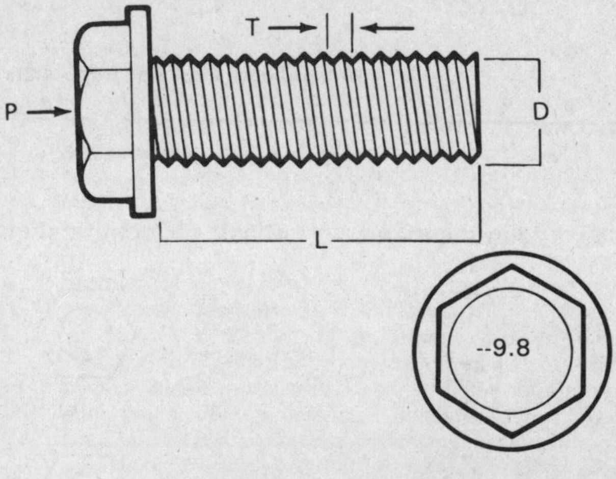

Metric bolt dimensions/grade marks

- *P* *Property class (bolt strength)*
- *L* *Length (in millimeters)*
- *T* *Thread pitch (distance between threads in millimeters)*
- *D* *Diameter*

be applied to it. The figures listed here are approximate for Grade 2 and Grade 3 fasteners. Higher grades can tolerate higher torque values.

Fasteners laid out in a pattern, such as cylinder head bolts, oil pan bolts, differential cover bolts, etc., must be loosened or tightened in sequence to avoid warping the component. This sequence will normally be shown in the appropriate Chapter. If a specific pattern is not given, the following procedures can be used to prevent warping.

Initially, the bolts or nuts should be assembled finger-tight only. Next, they should be tightened one full turn each, in a criss-cross or diagonal pattern. After each one has been tightened one full turn, return to the first one and tighten them all one-half turn, following the same pattern. Finally, tighten each of them one-quarter turn at a time until each fastener has been tightened to the proper torque. To loosen and remove the fasteners, the procedure would be reversed.

Component disassembly

Component disassembly should be done with care and purpose to help ensure that the parts go back together properly. Always keep track of the sequence in which parts are removed. Make note of special characteristics or marks on parts that can be installed more than one way, such as a grooved thrust washer on a shaft. It is a good idea to lay the disassembled parts out on a clean surface in the order that they were removed. It may also be helpful to make sketches or take instant photos of components before removal.

When removing fasteners from a component, keep track of their locations. Sometimes threading a bolt back in a part, or putting the washers and nut back on a stud, can prevent mix-ups later. If nuts and bolts cannot be returned to their original locations, they should be kept in a compartmented box or a series of small boxes. A cupcake or muffin tin is ideal for this purpose, since each cavity can hold the bolts and nuts from a particular area (i.e. oil pan bolts, valve cover bolts, engine mount bolts, etc.). A pan of this type is especially helpful when working on assemblies with very small parts, such as the carburetor, alternator, valve train or interior dash and trim pieces. The cavities can be marked with paint or tape to identify the contents.

Whenever wiring looms, harnesses or connectors are separated, it is a good idea to identify the two halves with numbered pieces of masking tape so they can be easily reconnected.

Gasket sealing surfaces

Throughout any vehicle, gaskets are used to seal the mating surfaces between two parts and keep lubricants, fluids, vacuum or pressure contained in an assembly.

Many times these gaskets are coated with a liquid or paste-type gasket sealing compound before assembly. Age, heat and pressure can sometimes cause the two parts to stick together so tightly that they are very difficult to separate. Often, the assembly can be loosened by striking it with a soft-face hammer near the mating surfaces. A regular hammer can be used if a block of wood is placed between the hammer and the part. Do not hammer on cast parts or parts that could be easily damaged. With any particularly stubborn part, always recheck to make sure that every fastener has been removed.

Avoid using a screwdriver or bar to pry apart an assembly, as they can easily mar the gasket sealing surfaces of the parts, which must remain smooth. If prying is absolutely necessary, use an old broom handle, but keep in mind that extra clean up will be necessary if the wood splinters.

After the parts are separated, the old gasket must be carefully scraped off and the gasket surfaces cleaned. Stubborn gasket material can be soaked with rust penetrant or treated with a special chemical to soften it so it can be easily scraped off. A scraper can be fashioned from a piece of copper tubing by flattening and sharpening one end. Copper is recommended because it is usually softer than the surfaces to be scraped, which reduces the chance of gouging the part. Some gaskets can be removed with a wire brush, but regardless of the method used, the mating surfaces must be left clean and smooth. If for some reason the gasket surface is gouged, then a gasket sealer thick enough to fill scratches will have to be used during reassembly of the components. For most applications, a non-drying (or semi-drying) gasket sealer should be used.

Hose removal tips

Warning: *If the vehicle is equipped with air conditioning, do not disconnect any of the A/C hoses without first having the system depressurized by a dealer service department or a service station.*

Hose removal precautions closely parallel gasket removal precautions. Avoid scratching or gouging the surface that the hose mates against or the connection may leak. This is especially true for radiator hoses. Because of various chemical reactions, the rubber in hoses can bond itself to the metal spigot that the hose fits over. To remove a hose, first loosen the hose clamps that secure it to the spigot. Then, with slip-joint pliers, grab the hose at the clamp and rotate it around the spigot. Work it back and forth until it is completely free, then pull it off. Silicone or other lubricants will ease removal if they can be applied between the hose and the outside of the spigot. Apply the same lubricant to the inside of the hose and the outside of the spigot to simplify installation.

As a last resort (and if the hose is to be replaced with a new one anyway), the rubber can be slit with a knife and the hose peeled from the spigot. If this must be done, be careful that the metal connection is not damaged.

If a hose clamp is broken or damaged, do not reuse it. Wire-type clamps usually weaken with age, so it is a good idea to replace them with screw-type clamps whenever a hose is removed.

Tools

A selection of good tools is a basic requirement for anyone who plans to maintain and repair his or her own vehicle. For the owner who has few tools, the initial investment might seem high, but when compared to the spiraling costs of professional auto maintenance and repair, it is a wise one.

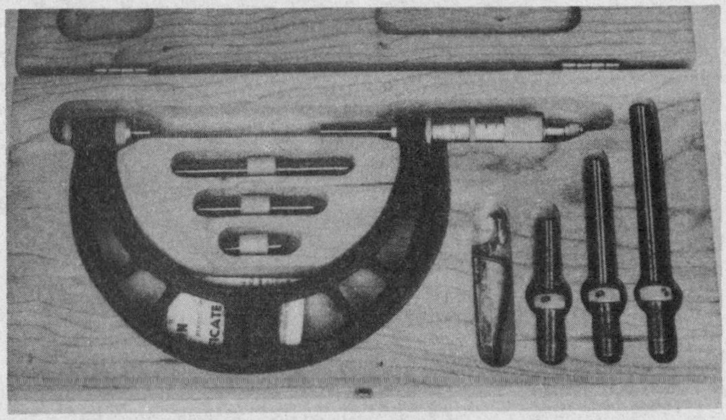

Micrometer set

Dial indicator set

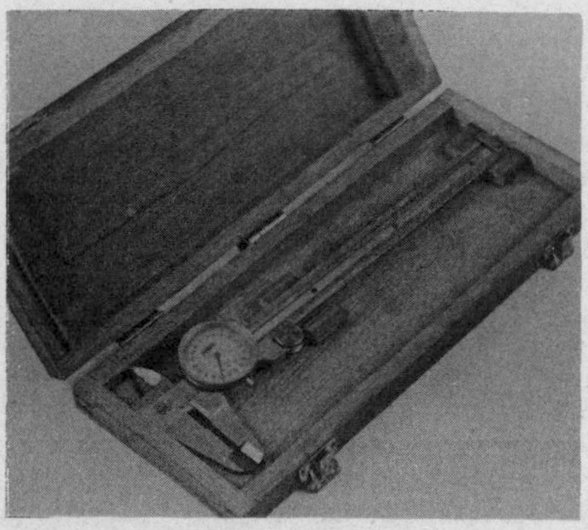
Dial caliper

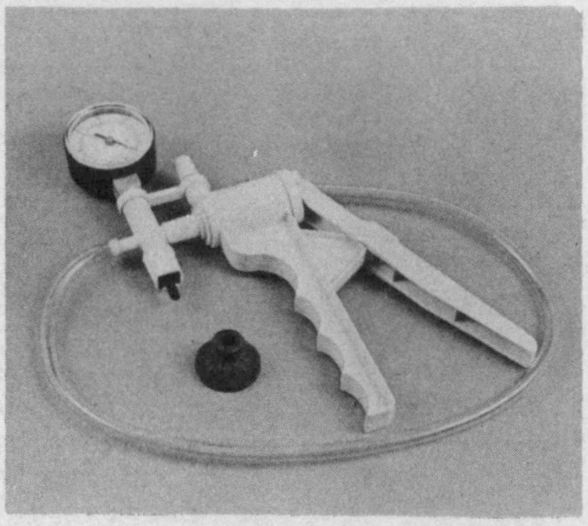
Hand-operated vacuum pump

Timing light

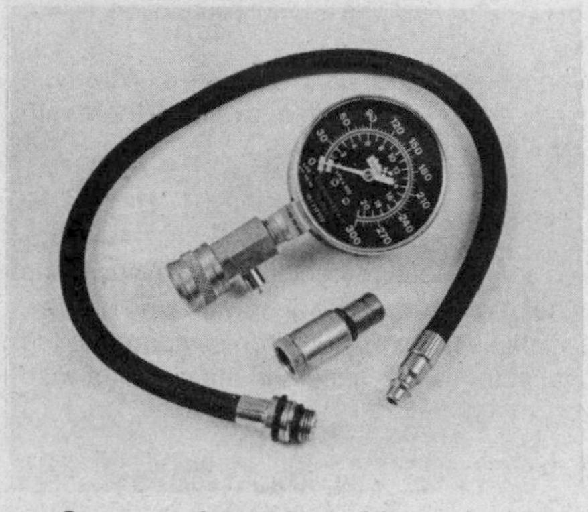
Compression gauge with spark plug hole adapter

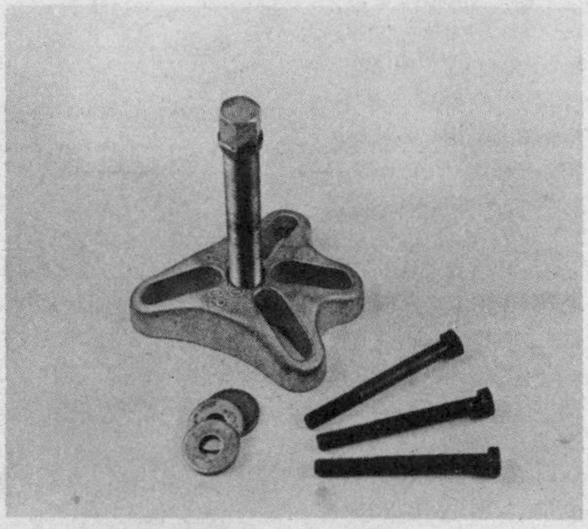
Damper/steering wheel puller

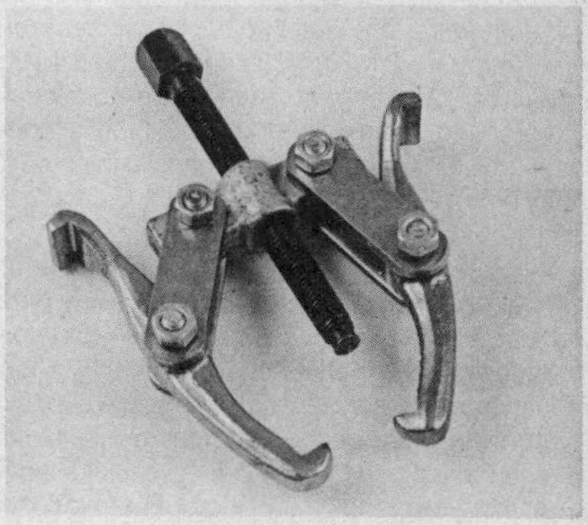
General purpose puller

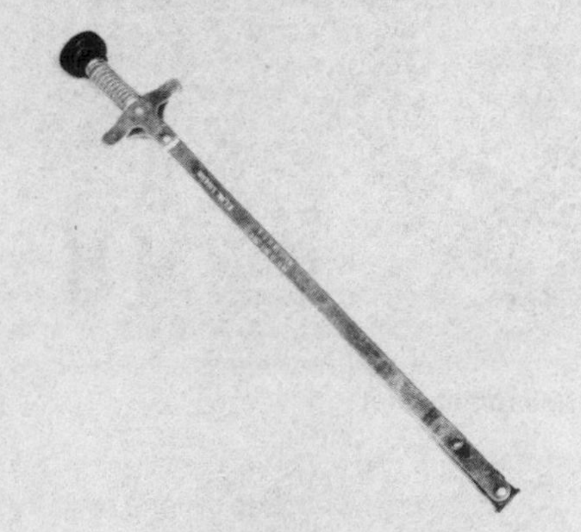
Hydraulic lifter removal tool

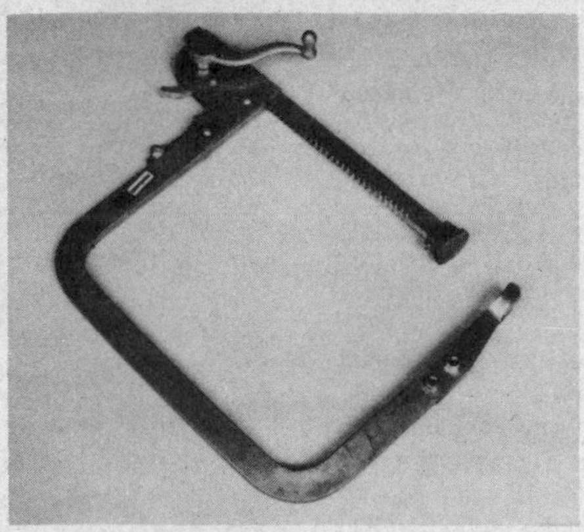
Valve spring compressor

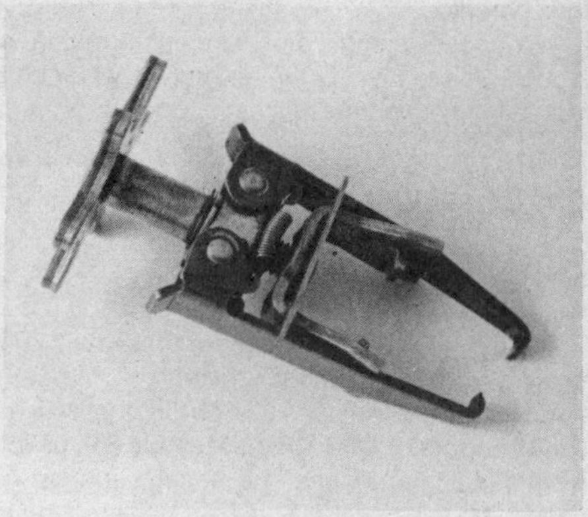
Valve spring compressor

Ridge reamer

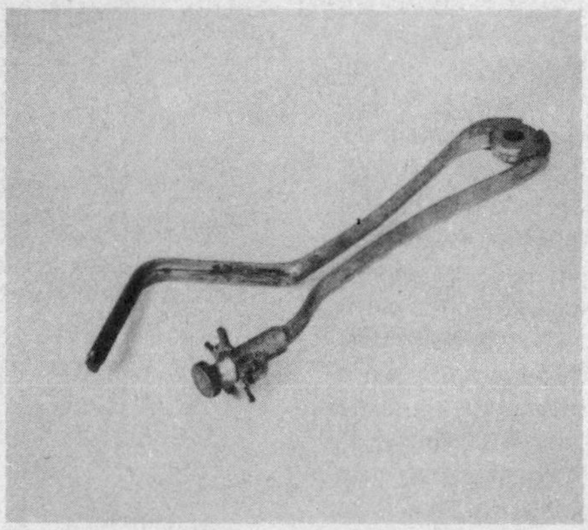
Piston ring groove cleaning tool

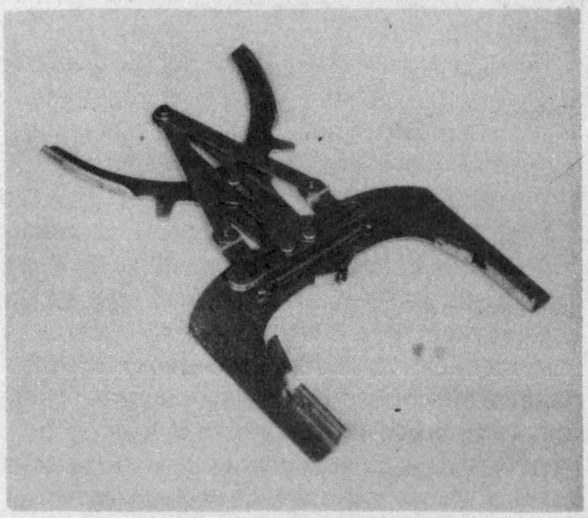
Ring removal/installation tool

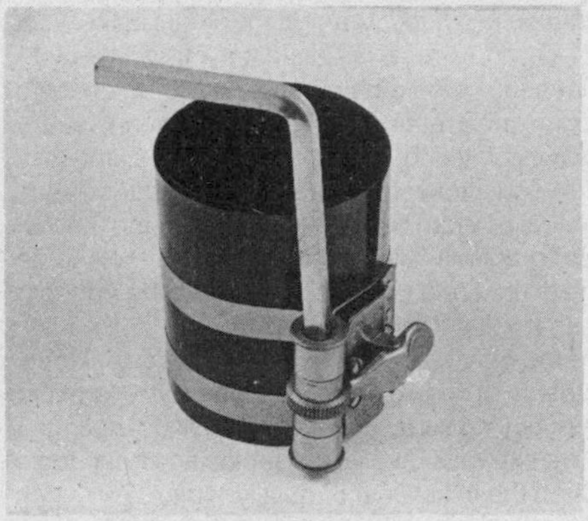

Ring compressor

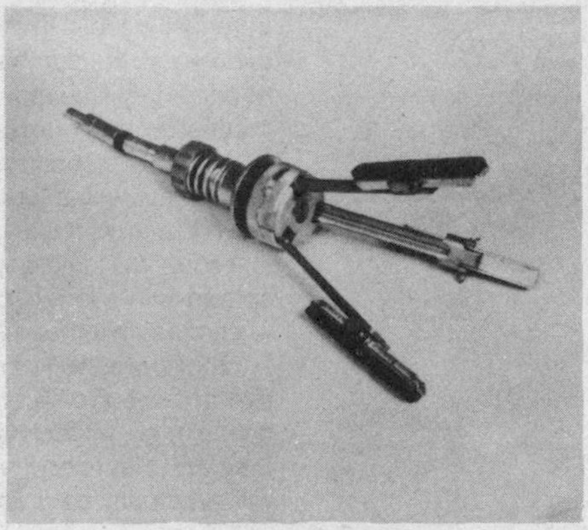

Cylinder hone

Brake hold-down spring tool

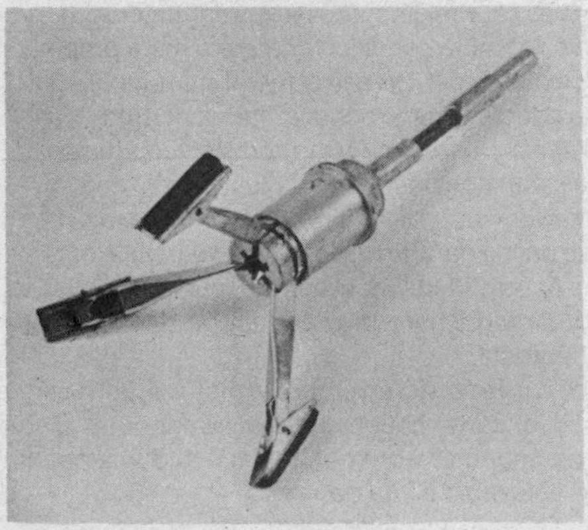

Brake cylinder hone

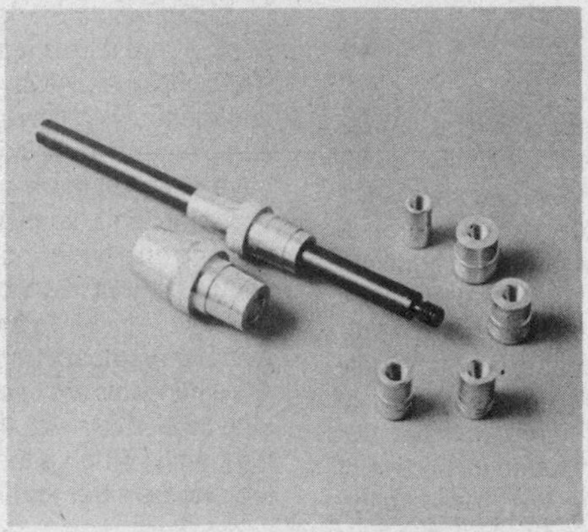

Clutch plate alignment tool

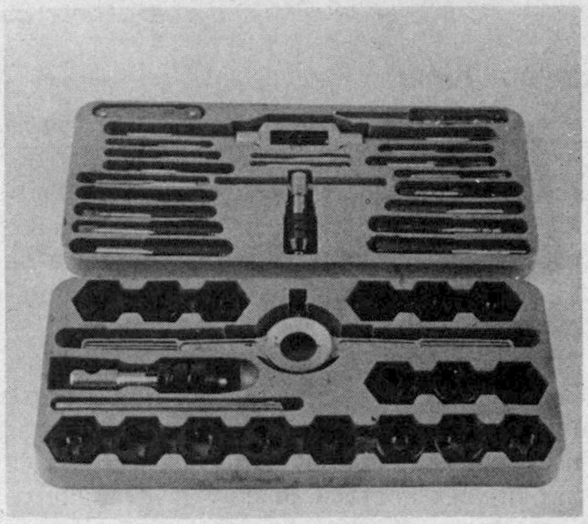

Tap and die set

To help the owner decide which tools are needed to perform the tasks detailed in this manual, the following tool lists are offered: *Maintenance and minor repair, Repair/overhaul and Special.*

The newcomer to practical mechanics should start off with the maintenance and minor repair tool kit, which is adequate for the simpler jobs performed on a vehicle. Then, as confidence and experience grow, the owner can tackle more difficult tasks, buying additional tools as they are needed. Eventually the basic kit will be expanded into the repair and overhaul tool set. Over a period of time, the experienced do-it-yourselfer will assemble a tool set complete enough for most repair and overhaul procedures and will add tools from the special category when it is felt that the expense is justified by the frequency of use.

Maintenance and minor repair tool kit

The tools in this list should be considered the minimum required for performance of routine maintenance, servicing and minor repair work. We recommend the purchase of combination wrenches (box-end and open-end combined in one wrench). While more expensive than open end wrenches, they offer the advantages of both types of wrench.

Combination wrench set (1/4-inch to 1 inch or 6 mm to 19 mm)
Adjustable wrench, 8 inch
Spark plug wrench with rubber insert
Spark plug gap adjusting tool
Feeler gauge set
Brake bleeder wrench
Standard screwdriver (5/16-inch x 6 inch)
Phillips screwdriver (No. 2 x 6 inch)
Combination pliers – 6 inch
Hacksaw and assortment of blades
Tire pressure gauge
Grease gun
Oil can
Fine emery cloth
Wire brush
Battery post and cable cleaning tool
Oil filter wrench
Funnel (medium size)
Safety goggles
Jackstands(2)
Drain pan

Note: *If basic tune-ups are going to be part of routine maintenance, it will be necessary to purchase a good quality stroboscopic timing light and combination tachometer/dwell meter. Although they are included in the list of special tools, it is mentioned here because they are absolutely necessary for tuning most vehicles properly.*

Repair and overhaul tool set

These tools are essential for anyone who plans to perform major repairs and are in addition to those in the maintenance and minor repair tool kit. Included is a comprehensive set of sockets which, though expensive, are invaluable because of their versatility, especially when various extensions and drives are available. We recommend the 1/2-inch drive over the 3/8-inch drive. Although the larger drive is bulky and more expensive, it has the capacity of accepting a very wide range of large sockets. Ideally, however, the mechanic should have a 3/8-inch drive set and a 1/2-inch drive set.

Socket set(s)
Reversible ratchet
Extension – 10 inch
Universal joint
Torque wrench (same size drive as sockets)
Ball peen hammer – 8 ounce
Soft-face hammer (plastic/rubber)
Standard screwdriver (1/4-inch x 6 inch)
Standard screwdriver (stubby – 5/16-inch)
Phillips screwdriver (No. 3 x 8 inch)
Phillips screwdriver (stubby – No. 2)

Pliers – vise grip
Pliers – lineman's
Pliers – needle nose
Pliers – snap-ring (internal and external)
Cold chisel – 1/2-inch
Scribe
Scraper (made from flattened copper tubing)
Centerpunch
Pin punches (1/16, 1/8, 3/16-inch)
Steel rule/straightedge – 12 inch
Allen wrench set (1/8 to 3/8-inch or 4 mm to 10 mm)
A selection of files
Wire brush (large)
Jackstands (second set)
Jack (scissor or hydraulic type)

Note: *Another tool which is often useful is an electric drill motor with a chuck capacity of 3/8-inch and a set of good quality drill bits.*

Special tools

The tools in this list include those which are not used regularly, are expensive to buy, or which need to be used in accordance with their manufacturer's instructions. Unless these tools will be used frequently, it is not very economical to purchase many of them. A consideration would be to split the cost and use between yourself and a friend or friends. In addition, most of these tools can be obtained from a tool rental shop on a temporary basis.

This list primarily contains only those tools and instruments widely available to the public, and not those special tools produced by the vehicle manufacturer for distribution to dealer service departments. Occasionally, references to the manufacturer's special tools are included in the text of this manual. Generally, an alternative method of doing the job without the special tool is offered. However, sometimes there is no alternative to their use. Where this is the case, and the tool cannot be purchased or borrowed, the work should be turned over to the dealer service department or an automotive repair shop.

Valve spring compressor
Piston ring groove cleaning tool
Piston ring compressor
Piston ring installation tool
Cylinder compression gauge
Cylinder ridge reamer
Cylinder surfacing hone
Cylinder bore gauge
Micrometers and/or dial calipers
Hydraulic lifter removal tool
Balljoint separator
Universal-type puller
Impact screwdriver
Dial indicator set
Stroboscopic timing light (inductive pick-up)
Hand operated vacuum/pressure pump
Tachometer/dwell meter
Universal electrical multimeter
Cable hoist
Brake spring removal and installation tools
Floor jack

Buying tools

For the do-it-yourselfer who is just starting to get involved in vehicle maintenance and repair, there are a number of options available when purchasing tools. If maintenance and minor repair is the extent of the work to be done, the purchase of individual tools is satisfactory. If, on the other hand, extensive work is planned, it would be a good idea to purchase a modest tool set from one of the large retail chain stores. A set can usually be bought at a substantial savings over the individual tool prices, and they often come with a tool box. As additional tools are needed, add–on sets, individual tools and a larger tool box can be purchased to expand the tool selection. Building a tool set gradually allows the cost of the tools to be spread over a longer period of time and gives the mechanic the freedom to choose only those tools that will actually be used.

Tool stores will often be the only source of some of the special tools that are needed, but regardless of where tools are bought, try to avoid cheap ones, especially when buying screwdrivers and sockets, because they won't last very long. The expense involved in replacing cheap tools will eventually be greater than the initial cost of quality tools.

Care and maintenance of tools

Good tools are expensive, so it makes sense to treat them with respect. Keep them clean and in usable condition and store them properly when not in use. Always wipe off any dirt, grease or metal chips before putting them away. Never leave tools lying around in the work area. Upon completion of a job, always check closely under the hood for tools that may have been left there so they won't get lost during a test drive.

Some tools, such as screwdrivers, pliers, wrenches and sockets, can be hung on a panel mounted on the garage or workshop wall, while others should be kept in a tool box or tray. Measuring instruments, gauges, meters, etc. must be carefully stored where they cannot be damaged by weather or impact from other tools.

When tools are used with care and stored properly, they will last a very long time. Even with the best of care, though, tools will wear out if used frequently. When a tool is damaged or worn out, replace it. Subsequent jobs will be safer and more enjoyable if you do.

Working facilities

Not to be overlooked when discussing tools is the workshop. If anything more than routine maintenance is to be carried out, some sort of suitable work area is essential.

It is understood, and appreciated, that many home mechanics do not have a good workshop or garage available, and end up removing an engine or doing major repairs outside. It is recommended, however, that the overhaul or repair be completed under the cover of a roof.

A clean, flat workbench or table of comfortable working height is an absolute necessity. The workbench should be equipped with a vise that has a jaw opening of at least four inches.

As mentioned previously, some clean, dry storage space is also required for tools, as well as the lubricants, fluids, cleaning solvents, etc. which soon become necessary.

Sometimes waste oil and fluids, drained from the engine or cooling system during normal maintenance or repairs, present a disposal problem. To avoid pouring them on the ground or into a sewage system, pour the used fluids into large containers, seal them with caps and take them to an authorized disposal site or recycling center. Plastic jugs, such as old antifreeze containers, are ideal for this purpose.

Always keep a supply of old newspapers and clean rags available. Old towels are excellent for mopping up spills. Many mechanics use rolls of paper towels for most work because they are readily available and disposable. To help keep the area under the vehicle clean, a large cardboard box can be cut open and flattened to protect the garage or shop floor.

Whenever working over a painted surface, such as when leaning over a fender to service something under the hood, always cover it with an old blanket or bedspread to protect the finish. Vinyl covered pads, made especially for this purpose, are available at auto parts stores.

Booster battery (jump) starting

Observe these precautions when using a booster battery to start a vehicle:

a) Before connecting the booster battery, make sure the ignition switch is in the Off position.
b) Turn off the lights, heater and other electrical loads.
c) Your eyes should be shielded. Safety goggles are a good idea.
d) Make sure the booster battery is the same voltage as the dead one in the vehicle.
e) The two vehicles MUST NOT TOUCH each other!
f) Make sure the transmission is in Neutral (manual) or Park (automatic).
g) If the booster battery is not a maintenance-free type, remove the vent caps and lay a cloth over the vent holes.

Connect the red jumper cable to the positive (+) terminals of each battery.

Connect one end of the black jumper cable to the negative (–) terminal of the booster battery. The other end of this cable should be connected to a good ground on the vehicle to be started, such as a bolt or bracket on the engine block **(see illustration)**. Make sure the cable will not come into contact with the fan, drivebelts or other moving parts of the engine.

Start the engine using the booster battery, then, with the engine running at idle speed, disconnect the jumper cables in the reverse order of connection.

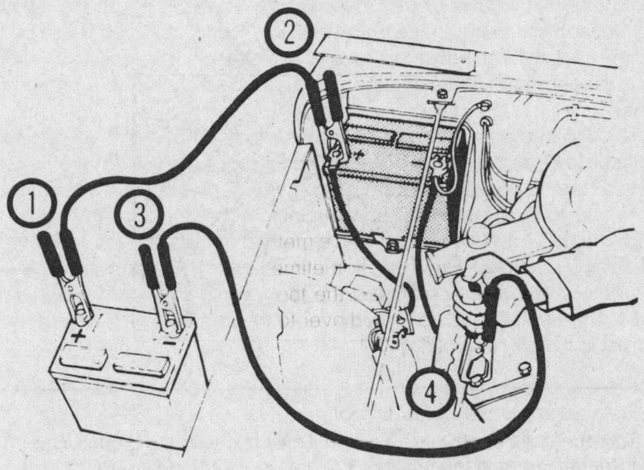

Make the booster battery cable connections in the numerical order shown (note that the negative cable of the booster battery is NOT attached to the negative terminal of the dead battery)

Jacking and towing

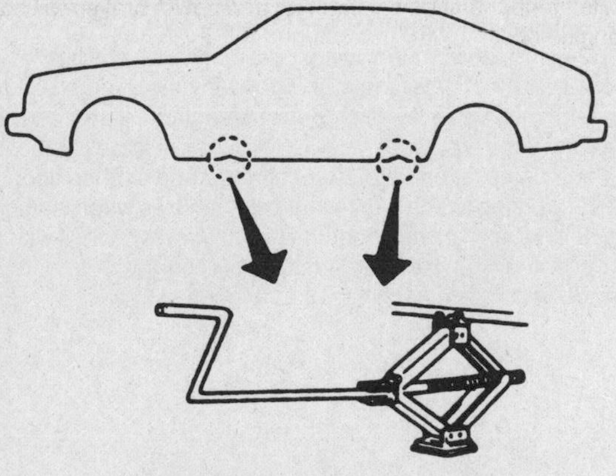

Jacking points (for vehicle jack)

Jacking

Warning: *The jack supplied with the vehicle should only be used for changing a tire or placing jackstands under the frame. Never work under the vehicle or start the engine while this jack is being used as the only means of support.*

The vehicle should be on level ground. Place the shift lever in Park, if you have an automatic, or Reverse if you have a manual transaxle. Block the wheel diagonally opposite the wheel being changed. Set the parking brake.

Remove the spare tire and jack from stowage. Remove the wheel cover and trim ring (if so equipped) with the tapered end of the lug nut wrench by inserting and twisting the handle and then prying against the back of the wheel cover. Loosen, but do not remove, the lug nuts (one-half turn is sufficient).

Place the scissors-type jack under the side of the vehicle and adjust the jack height until it fits between the notches in the vertical rocker panel flange nearest the wheel to be changed. There is a front and rear jacking point on each side of the vehicle **(see illustration)**.

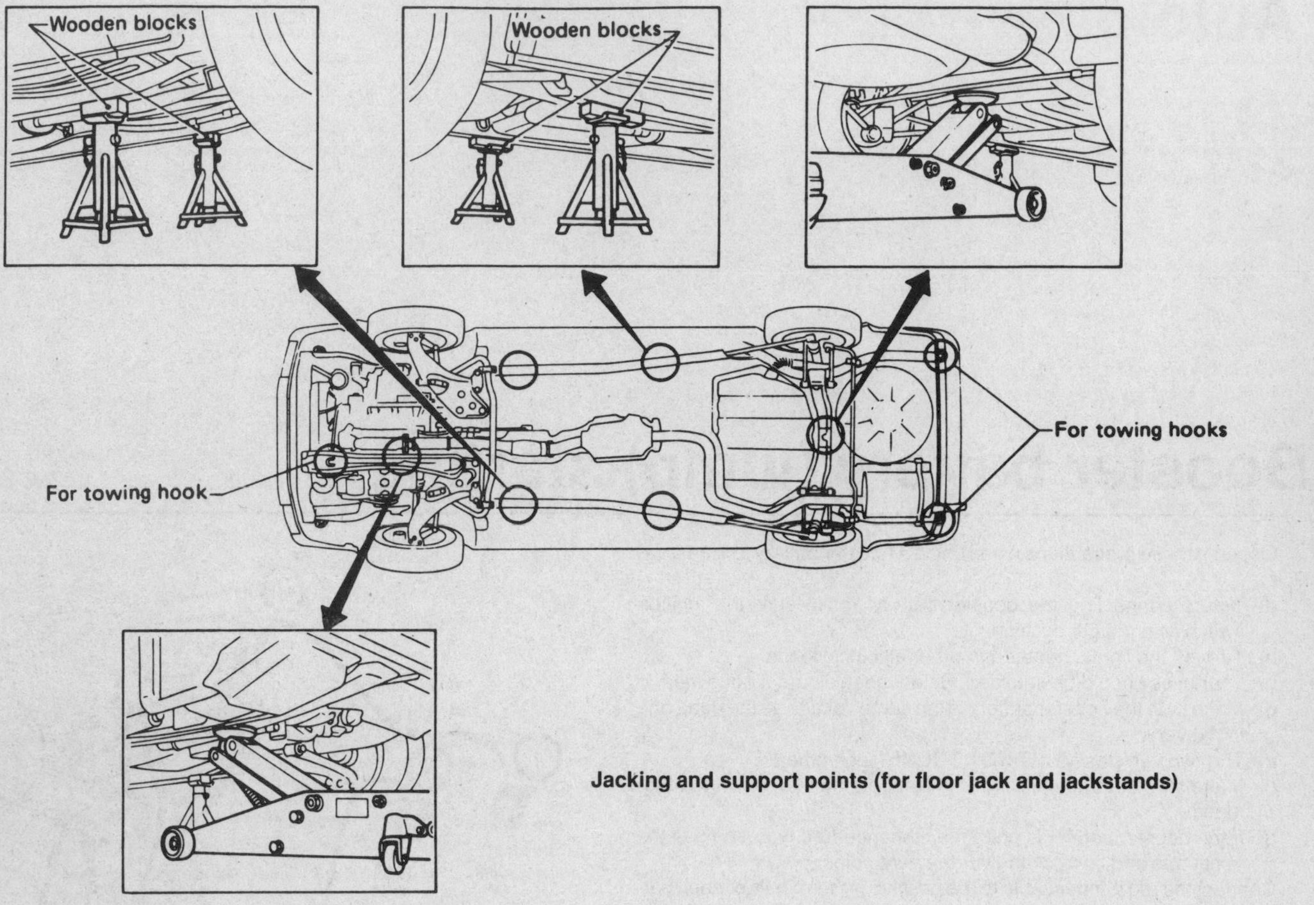

Jacking and support points (for floor jack and jackstands)

Turn the jack handle clockwise until the tire clears the ground. Remove the lug nuts and pull the wheel off. Replace it with the spare.

Replace the lug nuts with the beveled edges facing in. Tighten them snugly. Don't attempt to tighten them completely until the vehicle is lowered or it could slip off the jack. Turn the jack handle counterclockwise to lower the vehicle. Remove the jack and tighten the lug nuts in a criss-cross pattern.

Stow the tire, jack and wrench. Unblock the wheels.

Towing

As a general rule, the vehicle should be towed with the front (drive) wheels off the ground. If they can't be raised, place them on a dolly. The ignition key must be in the Acc position, since the steering lock mechanism isn't strong enough to hold the front wheels straight while towing.

Vehicles equipped with an automatic transaxle should be towed with the front wheels off the ground, but they can be towed from the front with all four wheels on the ground, provided that speeds don't exceed 30 mph and the distance is not over 40 miles. Before towing, check the transmission fluid level (see Chapter 1). If the level is below the Hot line on the dipstick, add fluid or use a towing dolly. Release the parking brake, put the transaxle in Neutral and place the ignition key in the Acc position. **Caution:** *Never tow a vehicle with an automatic transaxle from the rear with the front wheels on the ground.*

Equipment specifically designed for towing should be used. It should be attached to the tow hooks of the vehicle, not the tie-down hooks, bumpers or brackets.

Safety is a major consideration when towing and all applicable state and local laws must be obeyed. A safety chain system must be used at all times. Remember that power steering and power brakes will not work with the engine off.

Automotive chemicals and lubricants

A number of automotive chemicals and lubricants are available for use during vehicle maintenance and repair. They include a wide variety of products ranging from cleaning solvents and degreasers to lubricants and protective sprays for rubber, plastic and vinyl.

Cleaners

Carburetor cleaner and choke cleaner is a strong solvent for gum, varnish and carbon. Most carburetor cleaners leave a dry-type lubricant film which will not harden or gum up. Because of this film it is not recommended for use on electrical components.

Brake system cleaner is used to remove grease and brake fluid from the brake system, where clean surfaces are absolutely necessary. It leaves no residue and often eliminates brake squeal caused by contaminants.

Electrical cleaner removes oxidation, corrosion and carbon deposits from electrical contacts, restoring full current flow. It can also be used to clean spark plugs, carburetor jets, voltage regulators and other parts where an oil-free surface is desired.

Demoisturants remove water and moisture from electrical components such as alternators, voltage regulators, electrical connectors and fuse blocks. They are non-conductive, non-corrosive and non-flammable.

Degreasers are heavy-duty solvents used to remove grease from the outside of the engine and from chassis components. They can be sprayed or brushed on and, depending on the type, are rinsed off either with water or solvent.

Lubricants

Motor oil is the lubricant formulated for use in engines. It normally contains a wide variety of additives to prevent corrosion and reduce foaming and wear. Motor oil comes in various weights (viscosity ratings) from 5 to 80. The recommended weight of the oil depends on the season, temperature and the demands on the engine. Light oil is used in cold climates and under light load conditions. Heavy oil is used in hot climates and where high loads are encountered. Multi-viscosity oils are designed to have characteristics of both light and heavy oils and are available in a number of weights from 5W-20 to 20W-50.

Gear oil is designed to be used in differentials, manual transmissions and other areas where high-temperature lubrication is required.

Chassis and wheel bearing grease is a heavy grease used where increased loads and friction are encountered, such as for wheel bearings, balljoints, tie-rod ends and universal joints.

High-temperature wheel bearing grease is designed to withstand the extreme temperatures encountered by wheel bearings in disc brake equipped vehicles. It usually contains molybdenum disulfide (moly), which is a dry-type lubricant.

White grease is a heavy grease for metal-to-metal applications where water is a problem. White grease stays soft under both low and high temperatures (usually from –100 to +190-degrees F), and will not wash off or dilute in the presence of water.

Assembly lube is a special extreme pressure lubricant, usually containing moly, used to lubricate high-load parts (such as main and rod bearings and cam lobes) for initial start-up of a new engine. The assembly lube lubricates the parts without being squeezed out or washed away until the engine oiling system begins to function.

Silicone lubricants are used to protect rubber, plastic, vinyl and nylon parts.

Graphite lubricants are used where oils cannot be used due to contamination problems, such as in locks. The dry graphite will lubricate metal parts while remaining uncontaminated by dirt, water, oil or acids. It is electrically conductive and will not foul electrical contacts in locks such as the ignition switch.

Moly penetrants loosen and lubricate frozen, rusted and corroded fasteners and prevent future rusting or freezing.

Heat-sink grease is a special electrically non-conductive grease that is used for mounting electronic ignition modules where it is essential that heat is transferred away from the module.

Sealants

RTV sealant is one of the most widely used gasket compounds. Made from silicone, RTV is air curing, it seals, bonds, waterproofs, fills surface irregularities, remains flexible, doesn't shrink, is relatively easy to remove, and is used as a supplementary sealer with almost all low and medium temperature gaskets.

Anaerobic sealant is much like RTV in that it can be used either to seal gaskets or to form gaskets by itself. It remains flexible, is solvent resistant and fills surface imperfections. The difference between an anaerobic sealant and an RTV-type sealant is in the curing. RTV cures when exposed to air, while an anaerobic sealant cures only in the absence of air. This means that an anaerobic sealant cures only after the assembly of parts, sealing them together.

Thread and pipe sealant is used for sealing hydraulic and pneumatic fittings and vacuum lines. It is usually made from a teflon compound, and comes in a spray, a paint-on liquid and as a wrap-around tape.

Chemicals

Anti-seize compound prevents seizing, galling, cold welding, rust and corrosion in fasteners. High-temperature anti-seize, usually made with copper and graphite lubricants, is used for exhaust system and exhaust manifold bolts.

Anaerobic locking compounds are used to keep fasteners from vibrating or working loose and cure only after installation, in the absence of air. Medium strength locking compound is used for small nuts, bolts and screws that may be removed later. High-strength locking compound is for large nuts, bolts and studs which aren't removed on a regular basis.

Oil additives range from viscosity index improvers to chemical treatments that claim to reduce internal engine friction. It should be noted that most oil manufacturers caution against using additives with their oils.

Gas additives perform several functions, depending on their chemical makeup. They usually contain solvents that help dissolve gum and varnish that build up on carburetor, fuel injection and intake parts. They also serve to break down carbon deposits that form on the inside surfaces of the combustion chambers. Some additives contain upper cylinder lubricants for valves and piston rings, and others contain chemicals to remove condensation from the gas tank.

Miscellaneous

Brake fluid is specially formulated hydraulic fluid that can withstand the heat and pressure encountered in brake systems. Care must be taken so this fluid does not come in contact with painted surfaces or plastics. An opened container should always be resealed to prevent contamination by water or dirt.

Weatherstrip adhesive is used to bond weatherstripping around doors, windows and trunk lids. It is sometimes used to attach trim pieces.

Undercoating is a petroleum-based, tar-like substance that is designed to protect metal surfaces on the underside of the vehicle from corrosion. It also acts as a sound-deadening agent by insulating the bottom of the vehicle.

Waxes and polishes are used to help protect painted and plated surfaces from the weather. Different types of paint may require the use of different types of wax and polish. Some polishes utilize a chemical or abrasive cleaner to help remove the top layer of oxidized (dull) paint on older vehicles. In recent years many non-wax polishes that contain a wide variety of chemicals such as polymers and silicones have been introduced. These non-wax polishes are usually easier to apply and last longer than conventional waxes and polishes.

Safety first!

Regardless of how enthusiastic you may be about getting on with the job at hand, take the time to ensure that your safety is not jeopardized. A moment's lack of attention can result in an accident, as can failure to observe certain simple safety precautions. The possibility of an accident will always exist, and the following points should not be considered a comprehensive list of all dangers. Rather, they are intended to make you aware of the risks and to encourage a safety conscious approach to all work you carry out on your vehicle.

Essential DOs and DON'Ts

DON'T rely on a jack when working under the vehicle. Always use approved jackstands to support the weight of the vehicle and place them under the recommended lift or support points.
DON'T attempt to loosen extremely tight fasteners (i.e. wheel lug nuts) while the vehicle is on a jack — it may fall.
DON'T start the engine without first making sure that the transmission is in Neutral (or Park where applicable) and the parking brake is set.
DON'T remove the radiator cap from a hot cooling system — let it cool or cover it with a cloth and release the pressure gradually.
DON'T attempt to drain the engine oil until you are sure it has cooled to the point that it will not burn you.
DON'T touch any part of the engine or exhaust system until it has cooled sufficiently to avoid burns.
DON'T siphon toxic liquids such as gasoline, antifreeze and brake fluid by mouth, or allow them to remain on your skin.
DON'T inhale brake lining dust — it is potentially hazardous (see *Asbestos* below)
DON'T allow spilled oil or grease to remain on the floor — wipe it up before someone slips on it.
DON'T use loose fitting wrenches or other tools which may slip and cause injury.
DON'T push on wrenches when loosening or tightening nuts or bolts. Always try to pull the wrench toward you. If the situation calls for pushing the wrench away, push with an open hand to avoid scraped knuckles if the wrench should slip.
DON'T attempt to lift a heavy component alone — get someone to help you.
DON'T rush or take unsafe shortcuts to finish a job.
DON'T allow children or animals in or around the vehicle while you are working on it.
DO wear eye protection when using power tools such as a drill, sander, bench grinder, etc. and when working under a vehicle.
DO keep loose clothing and long hair well out of the way of moving parts.
DO make sure that any hoist used has a safe working load rating adequate for the job.
DO get someone to check on you periodically when working alone on a vehicle.
DO carry out work in a logical sequence and make sure that everything is correctly assembled and tightened.
DO keep chemicals and fluids tightly capped and out of the reach of children and pets.
DO remember that your vehicle's safety affects that of yourself and others. If in doubt on any point, get professional advice.

Asbestos

Certain friction, insulating, sealing, and other products — such as brake linings, brake bands, clutch linings, torque converters, gaskets, etc. — contain asbestos. *Extreme care must be taken to avoid inhalation of dust from such products since it is hazardous to health.* If in doubt, assume that they *do* contain asbestos.

Fire

Remember at all times that gasoline is highly flammable. Never smoke or have any kind of open flame around when working on a vehicle. But the risk does not end there. A spark caused by an electrical short circuit, by two metal surfaces contacting each other, or even by static electricity built up in your body under certain conditions, can ignite gasoline vapors, which in a confined space are highly explosive. Do not, under any circumstances, use gasoline for cleaning parts. Use an approved safety solvent.

Always disconnect the battery ground (–) cable *at the battery* before working on any part of the fuel system or electrical system. Never risk spilling fuel on a hot engine or exhaust component.

It is strongly recommended that a fire extinguisher suitable for use on fuel and electrical fires be kept handy in the garage or workshop at all times. Never try to extinguish a fuel or electrical fire with water.

Fumes

Certain fumes are highly toxic and can quickly cause unconsciousness and even death if inhaled to any extent. Gasoline vapor falls into this category, as do the vapors from some cleaning solvents. Any draining or pouring of such volatile fluids should be done in a well ventilated area.

When using cleaning fluids and solvents, read the instructions on the container carefully. Never use materials from unmarked containers.

Never run the engine in an enclosed space, such as a garage. Exhaust fumes contain carbon monoxide, which is extremely poisonous. If you need to run the engine, always do so in the open air, or at least have the rear of the vehicle outside the work area.

If you are fortunate enough to have the use of an inspection pit, never drain or pour gasoline and never run the engine while the vehicle is over the pit. The fumes, being heavier than air, will concentrate in the pit with possibly lethal results.

The battery

Never create a spark or allow a bare light bulb near the battery. The battery normally gives off a certain amount of hydrogen gas, which is highly explosive.

Always disconnect the battery ground (–) cable *at the battery* before working on the fuel or electrical systems.

If possible, loosen the filler caps or cover when charging the battery from an external source. Do not charge at an excessive rate or the battery may burst.

Take care when adding water and when carrying a battery. The electrolyte, even when diluted, is very corrosive and should not be allowed to contact clothing or skin.

Always wear eye protection when cleaning the battery to prevent the caustic deposits from entering your eyes.

Household current

When using an electric power tool, inspection light, etc., which operates on household current, always make sure that the tool is correctly connected to its plug and that, where necessary, it is properly grounded. Do not use such items in damp conditions and, again, do not create a spark or apply excessive heat in the vicinity of fuel or fuel vapor.

Secondary ignition system voltage

A severe electric shock can result from touching certain parts of the ignition system (such as the spark plug wires) when the engine is running or being cranked, particularly if components are damp or the insulation is defective. In the case of an electronic ignition system, the secondary system voltage is much higher and could prove fatal.

Conversion factors

Length (distance)

Inches (in)	X	25.4	= Millimetres (mm)	X	0.0394	= Inches (in)
Feet (ft)	X	0.305	= Metres (m)	X	3.281	= Feet (ft)
Miles	X	1.609	= Kilometres (km)	X	0.621	= Miles

Volume (capacity)

Cubic inches (cu in; in^3)	X	16.387	= Cubic centimetres (cc; cm^3)	X	0.061	= Cubic inches (cu in; in^3)
Imperial pints (Imp pt)	X	0.568	= Litres (l)	X	1.76	= Imperial pints (Imp pt)
Imperial quarts (Imp qt)	X	1.137	= Litres (l)	X	0.88	= Imperial quarts (Imp qt)
Imperial quarts (Imp qt)	X	1.201	= US quarts (US qt)	X	0.833	= Imperial quarts (Imp qt)
US quarts (US qt)	X	0.946	= Litres (l)	X	1.057	= US quarts (US qt)
Imperial gallons (Imp gal)	X	4.546	= Litres (l)	X	0.22	= Imperial gallons (Imp gal)
Imperial gallons (Imp gal)	X	1.201	= US gallons (US gal)	X	0.833	= Imperial gallons (Imp gal)
US gallons (US gal)	X	3.785	= Litres (l)	X	0.264	= US gallons (US gal)

Mass (weight)

Ounces (oz)	X	28.35	= Grams (g)	X	0.035	= Ounces (oz)
Pounds (lb)	X	0.454	= Kilograms (kg)	X	2.205	= Pounds (lb)

Force

Ounces-force (ozf; oz)	X	0.278	= Newtons (N)	X	3.6	= Ounces-force (ozf; oz)
Pounds-force (lbf; lb)	X	4.448	= Newtons (N)	X	0.225	= Pounds-force (lbf; lb)
Newtons (N)	X	0.1	= Kilograms-force (kgf; kg)	X	9.81	= Newtons (N)

Pressure

Pounds-force per square inch (psi; lbf/in^2; lb/in^2)	X	0.070	= Kilograms-force per square centimetre (kgf/cm^2; kg/cm^2)	X	14.223	= Pounds-force per square inch (psi; lbf/in^2; lb/in^2)
Pounds-force per square inch (psi; lbf/in^2; lb/in^2)	X	0.068	= Atmospheres (atm)	X	14.696	= Pounds-force per square inch (psi; lbf/in^2; lb/in^2)
Pounds-force per square inch (psi; lbf/in^2; lb/in^2)	X	0.069	= Bars	X	14.5	= Pounds-force per square inch (psi; lbf/in^2; lb/in^2)
Pounds-force per square inch (psi; lbf/in^2; lb/in^2)	X	6.895	= Kilopascals (kPa)	X	0.145	= Pounds-force per square inch (psi; lbf/in^2; lb/in^2)
Kilopascals (kPa)	X	0.01	= Kilograms-force per square centimetre (kgf/cm^2; kg/cm^2)	X	98.1	= Kilopascals (kPa)

Torque (moment of force)

Pounds-force inches (lbf in; lb in)	X	1.152	= Kilograms-force centimetre (kgf cm; kg cm)	X	0.868	= Pounds-force inches (lbf in; lb in)
Pounds-force inches (lbf in; lb in)	X	0.113	= Newton metres (Nm)	X	8.85	= Pounds-force inches (lbf in; lb in)
Pounds-force inches (lbf in; lb in)	X	0.083	= Pounds-force feet (lbf ft; lb ft)	X	12	= Pounds-force inches (lbf in; lb in)
Pounds-force feet (lbf ft; lb ft)	X	0.138	= Kilograms-force metres (kgf m; kg m)	X	7.233	= Pounds-force feet (lbf ft; lb ft)
Pounds-force feet (lbf ft; lb ft)	X	1.356	= Newton metres (Nm)	X	0.738	= Pounds-force feet (lbf ft; lb ft)
Newton metres (Nm)	X	0.102	= Kilograms-force metres (kgf m; kg m)	X	9.804	= Newton metres (Nm)

Power

Horsepower (hp)	X	745.7	= Watts (W)	X	0.0013	= Horsepower (hp)

Velocity (speed)

Miles per hour (miles/hr; mph)	X	1.609	= Kilometres per hour (km/hr; kph)	X	0.621	= Miles per hour (miles/hr; mph)

*Fuel consumption**

Miles per gallon, Imperial (mpg)	X	0.354	= Kilometres per litre (km/l)	X	2.825	= Miles per gallon, Imperial (mpg)
Miles per gallon, US (mpg)	X	0.425	= Kilometres per litre (km/l)	X	2.352	= Miles per gallon, US (mpg)

Temperature

Degrees Fahrenheit = (°C x 1.8) + 32

Degrees Celsius (Degrees Centigrade; °C) = (°F - 32) x 0.56

****It is common practice to convert from miles per gallon (mpg) to litres/100 kilometres (l/100km), where mpg (Imperial) x l/100 km = 282 and mpg (US) x l/100 km = 235***

Troubleshooting

Contents

Symptom *Section*

Engine

Engine backfires 15
Engine diesels (continues to run) after switching off 18
Engine hard to start when cold 3
Engine hard to start when hot 4
Engine lacks power 14
Engine lopes while idling or idles erratically 8
Engine misses at idle speed 9
Engine misses throughout driving speed range 10
Engine rotates but will not start 2
Engine runs with oil pressure light on 17
Engine stalls 13
Engine starts but stops immediately 6
Engine stumbles on acceleration 11
Engine surges while holding accelerator steady 12
Engine will not rotate when attempting to start 1
Oil puddle under engine 7
Pinging or knocking engine sounds during acceleration or uphill 16
Starter motor noisy or excessively rough in engagement 5

Engine electrical system

Alternator light fails to go out 20
Battery will not hold a charge 19
Alternator light fails to come on when key is turned on 21

Fuel system

Excessive fuel consumption 22
Fuel leakage and/or fuel odor 23

Cooling system

Coolant loss 28
External coolant leakage 26
Internal coolant leakage 27
Overcooling 25
Overheating 24
Poor coolant circulation 29

Clutch

Clutch pedal stays on floor 39
Clutch slips (engine speed increases with no increase in vehicle speed) 35
Fluid in area of master cylinder dust cover and on pedal 31
Fluid on release cylinder 32
Grabbing (chattering) as clutch is engaged 36
High pedal effort 40
Noise in clutch area 38
Pedal feels spongy when depressed 33
Pedal travels to floor – no pressure or very little resistance 30
Transaxle rattling (clicking) 37
Unable to select gears 34

Manual transaxle

Clicking noise in turns 44
Clunk on acceleration or deceleration 43

Symptom *Section*

Knocking noise at low speeds 41
Leaks lubricant 50
Locked in Second gear 51
Noise most pronounced when turning 42
Noisy in all gears 48
Noisy in Neutral with engine running 46
Noisy in one particular gear 47
Slips out of gear 49
Vibration 45

Automatic transaxle

Engine will start in gears other than Park or Neutral 56
Fluid leakage 52
General shift mechanism problems 54
Transaxle fluid brown or has a burned smell 53
Transaxle slips, shifts roughly, is noisy or has no drive in forward or reverse gears 57
Transaxle will not downshift with accelerator pedal pressed to the floor 55

Driveaxles

Clicking noise in turns 58
Shudder or vibration during acceleration 59
Vibration at highway speeds 60

Brakes

Brake pedal feels spongy when depressed 68
Brake pedal travels to the floor with little resistance 69
Brake roughness or chatter (pedal pulsates) 63
Dragging brakes 66
Excessive brake pedal travel 65
Excessive pedal effort required to stop vehicle 64
Grabbing or uneven braking action 67
Noise (high-pitched squeal when the brakes are applied) 62
Parking brake does not hold 70
Vehicle pulls to one side during braking 61

Suspension and steering systems

Abnormal or excessive tire wear 72
Abnormal noise at the front end 77
Cupped tires 82
Erratic steering when braking 79
Excessive pitching and/or rolling around corners or during braking 80
Excessive play or looseness in steering system 86
Excessive tire wear on inside edge 84
Excessive tire wear on outside edge 83
Hard steering 75
Poor returnability of steering to center 76
Rattling or clicking noise in rack and pinion 87
Shimmy, shake or vibration 74
Suspension bottoms 81
Tire tread worn in one place 85
Vehicle pulls to one side 71
Wander or poor steering stability 78
Wheel makes a thumping noise 73

This section provides an easy reference guide to the more common problems which may occur during the operation of your vehicle. These problems and their possible causes are grouped under headings denoting various components or systems, such as *Engine, Cooling system,* etc. They also refer you to the Chapter and/or Section which deals with the problem.

Remember that successful troubleshooting is not a mysterious black art practiced only by professional mechanics. It is simply the result of the right knowledge combined with an intelligent, systematic approach to the problem. Always work by a process of elimination, starting with the simplest solution and working through to the most complex - and never overlook the obvious. Anyone can run the gas tank dry or leave the lights on overnight, so don't assume that you are exempt from such oversights.

Finally, always establish a clear idea of why a problem has occurred and take steps to ensure that it doesn't happen again. If the electrical system fails because of a poor connection, check the other connections in the system to make sure that they don't fail as well. If a particular fuse continues to blow, find out why – don't just replace one fuse after another. Remember, failure of a small component can often be indicative of potential failure or incorrect functioning of a more important component or system.

Engine

1 Engine will not rotate when attempting to start

1 Battery terminal connections loose or corroded (Chapter 1).
2 Battery discharged or faulty (Chapter 1).
3 Automatic transmission not completely engaged in Park (Chapter 7) or clutch not completely depressed (Chapter 8).
4 Broken, loose or disconnected wiring in the starting circuit (Chapters 5 and 12).
5 Starter motor pinion jammed in flywheel ring gear (Chapter 5).
6 Starter solenoid faulty (Chapter 5).
7 Starter motor faulty (Chapter 5).
8 Ignition switch faulty (Chapter 12).
9 Starter pinion or flywheel teeth worn or broken (Chapter 5).

2 Engine rotates but will not start

1 Fuel tank empty.
2 Battery discharged (engine rotates slowly) (Chapter 5).
3 Battery terminal connections loose or corroded (Chapter 1).
4 Leaking fuel injector(s), faulty cold start valve, fuel pump, pressure regulator, etc. (Chapter 4).
5 Fuel not reaching fuel rail, or other fuel injection problem (Chapter 4).
6 Ignition components damp or damaged (Chapter 5).
7 Worn, faulty or incorrectly gapped spark plugs (Chapter 1).
8 Broken, loose or disconnected wiring in the starting circuit (Chapter 5).
9 Faulty crank angle sensor (Chapter 5).
10 Broken, loose or disconnected wires at the ignition coil or faulty coil (Chapter 5).

3 Engine hard to start when cold

1 Battery discharged or low (Chapter 1).
2 Malfunctioning fuel system (Chapter 4).
3 Faulty cold start injector (Chapter 4).
4 Injector(s) leaking (Chapter 4).
5 Crank angle sensor rotor carbon tracked (Chapter 5).

4 Engine hard to start when hot

1 Air filter clogged (Chapter 1).
2 Fuel not reaching the fuel injection system (Chapter 4).
3 Corroded battery connections, especially ground (Chapter 1).
4 Worn starter motor (Chapter 5).

5 Starter motor noisy or excessively rough in engagement

1 Pinion or flywheel gear teeth worn or broken (Chapter 5).
2 Starter motor mounting bolts loose or missing (Chapter 5).

6 Engine starts but stops immediately

1 Loose or faulty electrical connections at crank angle sensor, coil or alternator (Chapter 5).
2 Insufficient fuel reaching the fuel injector(s) (Chapters 1 and 4).
3 Vacuum leak at the gasket between the intake manifold/plenum and throttle body (Chapters 1 and 4).

7 Oil puddle under engine

1 Oil pan gasket and/or oil pan drain bolt washer leaking (Chapter 2).
2 Oil pressure sending unit leaking (Chapter 2).
3 Cylinder head covers leaking (Chapter 2).
4 Engine oil seals leaking (Chapter 2).
5 Oil pump housing leaking (Chapter 2).

8 Engine lopes while idling or idles erratically

1 Vacuum leakage (Chapters 2 and 4).
2 Leaking EGR valve (Chapter 6).
3 Air filter clogged (Chapter 1).
4 Fuel pump not delivering sufficient fuel to the fuel injection system (Chapter 4).
5 Leaking head gasket (Chapter 2).
6 Timing belt and/or sprockets worn (Chapter 2).
7 Camshaft lobes worn (Chapter 2).
8 Throttle body ports clogged (Chapter 4).

9 Engine misses at idle speed

1 Spark plugs worn or not gapped properly (Chapter 1).
2 Faulty spark plug wires (Chapter 1).
3 Vacuum leaks (Chapter 1).
4 Incorrect ignition timing (Chapter 1).
5 Uneven or low compression (Chapter 2).

10 Engine misses throughout driving speed range

1 Fuel filter/injectors clogged and/or impurities in the fuel system (Chapter 1).
2 Low fuel output at the injector(s) (Chapter 4).
3 Faulty or incorrectly gapped spark plugs (Chapter 1).
4 Incorrect ignition timing (Chapter 5).
5 Cracked distributor cap or damaged crank angle sensor components (Chapters 1 and 5).

6 Leaking spark plug wires (Chapters 1 or 5).
7 Faulty emission system components (Chapter 6).
8 Low or uneven cylinder compression pressures (Chapter 2).
9 Weak or faulty ignition system (Chapter 5).
10 Vacuum leak in fuel injection system, intake manifold, air regulator valve or vacuum hoses (Chapter 4).

11 Engine stumbles on acceleration

1 Spark plugs fouled (Chapter 1).
2 Fuel injection system needs adjustment or repair (Chapter 4).
3 Fuel filter clogged (Chapters 1 and 4).
4 Incorrect ignition timing (Chapter 5).
5 Intake manifold air leak (Chapters 2 and 4).

12 Engine surges while holding accelerator steady

1 Intake air leak (Chapter 4).
2 Fuel pump faulty (Chapter 4).
3 Loose fuel injector wire harness connectors (Chapter 4).
4 Defective ECU (Chapter 6).
5 Damaged air flow meter (Chapter 4).

13 Engine stalls

1 Idle speed incorrect (Chapter 1).
2 Fuel filter clogged and/or water and impurities in the fuel system (Chapters 1 and 4).
3 Crank angle sensor components damp or damaged (Chapter 5).
4 Faulty emissions system components (Chapter 6).
5 Faulty or incorrectly gapped spark plugs (Chapter 1).
6 Faulty spark plug wires (Chapter 1).
7 Vacuum leak in the fuel injection system, intake manifold or vacuum hoses (Chapters 2 and 4).

14 Engine lacks power

1 Incorrect ignition timing (Chapter 5).
2 Excessive play in distributor shaft (Chapter 5).
3 Worn rotor, distributor cap or wires (Chapters 1 and 5).
4 Faulty or incorrectly gapped spark plugs (Chapter 1).
5 Fuel injection system out of adjustment or excessively worn (Chapter 4).
6 Faulty coil (Chapter 5).
7 Brakes binding (Chapter 9).
8 Automatic transaxle fluid level incorrect (Chapter 1).
9 Clutch slipping (Chapter 8).
10 Fuel filter clogged and/or impurities in the fuel system (Chapters 1 and 4).
11 Emission control system not functioning properly (Chapter 6).
12 Low or uneven cylinder compression pressures (Chapter 2).

15 Engine backfires

1 Emission control system not functioning properly (Chapter 6).
2 Ignition timing incorrect (Chapter 5).
3 Faulty secondary ignition system (cracked spark plug insulator, faulty plug wires, distributor cap and/or rotor) (Chapters 1 and 5).
4 Fuel injection system in need of adjustment or worn excessively (Chapter 4).
5 Vacuum leak at fuel injector(s), intake manifold, air regulator valve or vacuum hoses (Chapters 2 and 4).

16 Pinging or knocking engine sounds during acceleration or uphill

1 Incorrect grade of fuel.
2 Ignition timing incorrect (Chapter 5).
3 Fuel injection system in need of adjustment (Chapter 4).
4 Improper or damaged spark plugs or wires (Chapter 1).
5 Worn or damaged distributor components (Chapter 5).
6 Faulty emission system (Chapter 6).
7 Vacuum leak (Chapters 2 and 4).

17 Engine runs with oil pressure light on

1 Low oil level (Chapter 1).
2 Idle rpm below specification (Chapter 1).
3 Short in wiring circuit (Chapter 12).
4 Faulty oil pressure sending unit (Chapter 2).
5 Worn engine bearings and/or oil pump (Chapter 2).

18 Engine diesels (continues to run) after switching off

1 Idle speed too high (Chapter 1).
2 Excessive engine operating temperature (Chapter 3).

Engine electrical system

19 Battery will not hold a charge

1 Alternator drivebelt defective or not adjusted properly (Chapter 1).
2 Battery electrolyte level low (Chapter 1).
3 Battery terminals loose or corroded (Chapter 1).
4 Alternator not charging properly (Chapter 5).
5 Loose, broken or faulty wiring in the charging circuit (Chapter 5).
6 Short in vehicle wiring (Chapter 12).
7 Internally defective battery (Chapters 1 and 5).

20 Alternator light fails to go out

1 Faulty alternator or charging circuit (Chapter 5).
2 Alternator drivebelt defective or out of adjustment (Chapter 1).
3 Alternator voltage regulator inoperative (Chapter 5).

21 Alternator light fails to come on when key is turned on

1 Warning light bulb defective (Chapter 12).
2 Fault in the printed circuit, dash wiring or bulb holder (Chapter 12).

Fuel system

22 Excessive fuel consumption

1 Dirty or clogged air filter element (Chapter 1).
2 Incorrectly set ignition timing (Chapter 5).

3 Emissions system not functioning properly (Chapter 6).
4 Fuel injection internal parts excessively worn or damaged (Chapter 4).
5 Low tire pressure or incorrect tire size (Chapter 1).

23 Fuel leakage and/or fuel odor

1 Leaking fuel feed or return line (Chapters 1 and 4).
2 Tank overfilled.
3 Evaporative canister filter clogged (Chapters 1 and 6).
4 Fuel injector internal parts excessively worn (Chapter 4).
5 Leaking fuel injectors (Chapter 4).

Cooling system

24 Overheating

1 Insufficient coolant in system (Chapter 1).
2 Water pump drivebelt defective or out of adjustment (Chapter 1).
3 Radiator core blocked or grille restricted (Chapter 3).
4 Thermostat faulty (Chapter 3).
5 Electric coolant fan blades broken or cracked (Chapter 3).
6 Radiator cap not maintaining proper pressure (Chapter 3).
7 Ignition timing incorrect (Chapter 5).

25 Overcooling

1 Faulty thermostat (Chapter 3).
2 Inaccurate temperature gauge sending unit (Chapter 3).

26 External coolant leakage

1 Deteriorated/damaged hoses; loose clamps (Chapters 1 and 3).
2 Water pump seal defective (Chapter 3).
3 Leakage from radiator core or coolant reservoir (Chapter 3).
4 Engine drain or water jacket core plugs leaking (Chapter 2).

27 Internal coolant leakage

1 Leaking cylinder head gasket (Chapter 2).
2 Cracked cylinder bore or cylinder head (Chapter 2).

28 Coolant loss

1 Too much coolant in system (Chapter 1).
2 Coolant boiling away because of overheating (Chapter 3).
3 Internal or external leakage (Chapter 3).
4 Faulty radiator cap (Chapter 3).

29 Poor coolant circulation

1 Inoperative water pump (Chapter 3).
2 Restriction in cooling system (Chapters 1 and 3).
3 Water pump drivebelt defective/out of adjustment (Chapter 1).
4 Thermostat sticking (Chapter 3).

Clutch

30 Pedal travels to floor – no pressure or very little resistance

1 Master or release cylinder faulty (Chapter 8).
2 Hose/pipe burst or leaking (Chapter 8).
3 Connections leaking (Chapter 8).
4 No fluid in reservoir (Chapter 1).
5 If fluid level in reservoir rises as pedal is depressed, master cylinder center valve seal is faulty (Chapter 8).
6 If there is fluid on dust seal at master cylinder, piston primary seal is leaking (Chapter 8).
7 Broken release bearing or fork (Chapter 8).
8 Collapsed diaphragm spring in clutch pressure plate (Chapter 8).

31 Fluid in area of master cylinder dust cover and on pedal

Rear seal failure in master cylinder (Chapter 8).

32 Fluid on release cylinder

Release cylinder plunger seal faulty (Chapter 8).

33 Pedal feels spongy when depressed

Air in system (Chapter 8).

34 Unable to select gears

1 Faulty transaxle (Chapter 7).
2 Faulty clutch disc (Chapter 8).
3 Fork and bearing not assembled properly (Chapter 8).
4 Faulty pressure plate (Chapter 8).
5 Pressure plate-to-flywheel bolts loose (Chapter 8).

35 Clutch slips (engine speed increases with no increase in vehicle speed)

1 Clutch plate worn (Chapter 8).
2 Clutch plate is oil soaked by leaking rear main seal (Chapter 8).
3 Clutch plate not seated. It may take 30 or 40 normal starts for a new one to seat.
4 Warped pressure plate or flywheel (Chapter 8).
5 Weak diaphragm spring (Chapter 8).
6 Clutch plate overheated. Allow to cool.

36 Grabbing (chattering) as clutch is engaged

1 Oil on clutch plate lining, burned or glazed linings (Chapter 8).
2 Worn or loose engine or transaxle mounts (Chapters 2 and 7).
3 Worn splines on clutch plate hub (Chapter 8).
4 Warped pressure plate or flywheel (Chapter 8).
5 Burned or smeared resin on flywheel or pressure plate (Chapter 8).

37 Transaxle rattling (clicking)

1 Release fork loose (Chapter 8).
2 Clutch plate damper spring failure (Chapter 8).
3 Low engine idle speed (Chapter 1).

38 Noise in clutch area

1 Fork shaft improperly installed (Chapter 8).
2 Faulty bearing (Chapter 8).

39 Clutch pedal stays on floor

1 Piston binding in bore (Chapter 8).
2 Broken release bearing or fork (Chapter 8).

40 High pedal effort

1 Piston binding in bore (Chapter 8).
2 Pressure plate faulty (Chapter 8).
3 Incorrect size master or release cylinder (Chapter 8).

Manual transaxle

41 Knocking noise at low speeds

1 Worn driveaxle constant velocity (CV) joints (Chapter 8).
2 Worn side gear shaft counterbore in differential case (Chapter 7A).*

42 Noise most pronounced when turning

Differential gear noise (Chapter 7A).*

43 Clunk on acceleration or deceleration

1 Loose engine or transaxle mounts (Chapters 2 and 7A).
2 Worn differential pinion shaft in case.*
3 Worn side gear shaft counterbore in differential case (Chapter 7A).*
4 Worn or damaged driveaxle inner CV joints (Chapter 8).

44 Clicking noise in turns

Worn or damaged outer CV joint (Chapter 8).

45 Vibration

1 Rough wheel bearing (Chapters 1 and 10).
2 Damaged driveaxle (Chapter 8).
3 Out-of-round tires (Chapter 1).
4 Tire out-of-balance (Chapters 1 and 10).
5 Worn CV joint (Chapter 8).

46 Noisy in Neutral with engine running

1 Damaged input gear bearing (Chapter 7A).*
2 Damaged clutch release bearing (Chapter 8).

47 Noisy in one particular gear

1 Damaged or worn constant mesh gears (Chapter 7A).*
2 Damaged or worn synchronizers (Chapter 7A).*
3 Bent reverse fork (Chapter 7A).*
4 Damaged Fourth speed gear or output gear (Chapter 7A).*
5 Worn or damaged Reverse idler gear or idler bushing (Chapter 7A).*

48 Noisy in all gears

1 Insufficient lubricant (Chapter 7A).
2 Damaged or worn bearings (Chapter 7A).*
3 Worn or damaged input gear shaft and/or output gear shaft (Chapter 7A).*

49 Slips out of gear

1 Worn or improperly adjusted linkage (Chapter 7A).
2 Transaxle loose on engine (Chapter 7A).
3 Shift linkage does not work freely, binds (Chapter 7A).
4 Input gear bearing retainer broken or loose (Chapter 7A).*
5 Dirt between clutch cover and engine housing (Chapter 7A).
6 Worn shift fork (Chapter 7A).*

50 Leaks lubricant

1 Side gear shaft seals worn (Chapter 8).
2 Excessive amount of lubricant in transaxle (Chapters 1 and 7A).
3 Loose or broken input gear shaft bearing retainer (Chapter 7A).*
4 Input gear bearing retainer O-ring and/or lip seal damaged (Chapter 7A).*

51 Locked in Second gear

Lock pin or interlock pin missing (Chapter 7A).*

* Although the corrective action necessary to remedy the symptoms described is beyond the scope of the home mechanic, the above information should be helpful in isolating the cause of the condition so the owner can communicate clearly with a professional mechanic.

Automatic transaxle

Note: *Due to the complexity of the automatic transaxle, it is difficult for the home mechanic to properly diagnose and service this component. For problems other than the following, the vehicle should be taken to a dealer or transmission shop.*

52 Fluid leakage

1 Automatic transmission fluid is a deep red color. Fluid leaks should not be confused with engine oil, which can easily be blown onto the transaxle by air flow.
2 To pinpoint a leak, first remove all built-up dirt and grime from the transaxle housing with degreasing agents and/or steam cleaning. Then drive the vehicle at low speeds so air flow will not blow the leak far from its source. Raise the vehicle and determine where the leak is coming from. Common areas of leakage are:
a) Control valve cover (Chapters 1 and 7)
b) Dipstick tube (Chapters 1 and 7)

c) Transaxle oil lines (Chapter 7)
d) Speed sensor (Chapter 7)

53 Transaxle fluid brown or has a burned smell

Transaxle fluid burned (Chapter 1).

54 General shift mechanism problems

1 Chapter 7, Part B, deals with checking and adjusting the shift linkage on automatic transaxles. Common problems which may be attributed to poorly adjusted linkage are:

a) Engine starting in gears other than Park or Neutral.
b) Indicator on shifter pointing to a gear other than the one actually being used.
c) Vehicle moves when in Park.

2 Refer to Chapter 7B for the shift linkage adjustment procedure.

55 Transaxle will not downshift with accelerator pedal pressed to the floor

Throttle valve cable out of adjustment (Chapter 7B).

56 Engine will start in gears other than Park or Neutral

Neutral start switch malfunctioning (Chapter 7B).

57 Transaxle slips, shifts roughly, is noisy or has no drive in forward or reverse gears

There are many probable causes for the above problems, but the home mechanic should be concerned with only one possibility – fluid level. Before taking the vehicle to a repair shop, check the level and condition of the fluid as described in Chapter 1. Correct the fluid level as necessary or change the fluid and filter if needed. If the problem persists, have a professional diagnose the cause.

Driveaxles

58 Clicking noise in turns

Worn or damaged outer CV joint (Chapter 8).

59 Shudder or vibration during acceleration

1 Excessive toe-in (Chapter 10).
2 Incorrect spring heights (Chapter 10).
3 Worn or damaged CV joints (Chapter 8).
4 Sticking inner CV joint assembly (Chapter 8).

60 Vibration at highway speeds

1 Out-of-balance front wheels and/or tires (Chapters 1 and 10).
2 Out-of-round front tires (Chapters 1 and 10).
3 Worn CV joint(s) (Chapter 8).

Brakes

Note: *Before assuming that a brake problem exists, make sure that:*

a) The tires are in good condition and properly inflated (Chapter 1).
b) The front end alignment is correct (Chapter 10).
c) The vehicle is not loaded with weight in an unequal manner.

61 Vehicle pulls to one side during braking

1 Incorrect tire pressures (Chapter 1).
2 Front end out of line (have the front end aligned).
3 Front, or rear, tires not matched to one another.
4 Restricted brake lines or hoses (Chapter 9).
5 Malfunctioning drum brake or caliper assembly (Chapter 9).
6 Loose suspension parts (Chapter 10).
7 Loose calipers (Chapter 9).
8 Excessive wear of brake shoe or pad material or disc/drum on one side.

62 Noise (high-pitched squeal when the brakes are applied)

Front and/or rear disc brake pads worn out. The noise comes from the wear sensor rubbing against the disc (does not apply to all vehicles). Replace pads with new ones immediately (Chapter 9).

63 Brake roughness or chatter (pedal pulsates)

1 Excessive lateral runout (Chapter 9).
2 Uneven pad wear (Chapter 9).
3 Defective rotor (Chapter 9).

64 Excessive pedal effort required to stop vehicle

1 Malfunctioning power brake booster (Chapter 9).
2 Partial system failure (Chapter 9).
3 Excessively worn pads or shoes (Chapter 9).
4 Piston in caliper or wheel cylinder stuck or sluggish (Chapter 9).
5 Brake pads or shoes contaminated with oil or grease (Chapter 9).
6 New pads or shoes installed and not yet seated. It will take a while for the new material to seat against the rotor or drum.

65 Excessive brake pedal travel

1 Partial brake system failure (Chapter 9).
2 Insufficient fluid in master cylinder (Chapters 1 and 9).
3 Air trapped in system (Chapters 1 and 9).

66 Dragging brakes

1 Incorrect adjustment of brake light switch (Chapter 9).
2 Master cylinder pistons not returning correctly (Chapter 9).
3 Restricted brakes lines or hoses (Chapters 1 and 9).
4 Incorrect parking brake adjustment (Chapter 9).

67 Grabbing or uneven braking action

1 Malfunction of proportioning valve (Chapter 9).
2 Malfunction of power brake booster unit (Chapter 9).
3 Binding brake pedal mechanism (Chapter 9).

68 Brake pedal feels spongy when depressed

1 Air in hydraulic lines (Chapter 9).
2 Master cylinder mounting bolts loose (Chapter 9).
3 Master cylinder defective (Chapter 9).

69 Brake pedal travels to the floor with little resistance

1 Little or no fluid in the master cylinder reservoir caused by leaking caliper or wheel cylinder piston(s) (Chapter 9).
2 Loose, damaged or disconnected brake lines (Chapter 9).

70 Parking brake does not hold

Parking brake linkage improperly adjusted (Chapters 1 and 9).

Suspension and steering systems

Note: *Before attempting to diagnose the suspension and steering systems, perform the following preliminary checks:*

a) *Tires for wrong pressure and uneven wear.*
b) *Steering universal joints from the column to the rack and pinion for loose connectors or wear.*
c) *Front and rear suspension and the rack and pinion assembly for loose or damaged parts.*
d) *Out-of-round or out-of-balance tires, bent rims and loose and/or rough wheel bearings.*

71 Vehicle pulls to one side

1 Mismatched or uneven tires (Chapter 10).
2 Broken or sagging springs (Chapter 10).
3 Wheel alignment incorrect (Chapter 10).
4 Front brake dragging (Chapter 9).

72 Abnormal or excessive tire wear

1 Wheel alignment (Chapter 10).
2 Sagging or broken springs (Chapter 10).
3 Tire out-of-balance (Chapter 10).
4 Worn strut damper (Chapter 10).
5 Overloaded vehicle.
6 Tires not rotated regularly.

73 Wheel makes a thumping noise

1 Blister or bump on tire (Chapter 10).
2 Improper strut damper action (Chapter 10).

74 Shimmy, shake or vibration

1 Tire or wheel out-of-balance or out-of-round (Chapter 10).
2 Loose or worn wheel bearings (Chapters 1, 8 and 10).
3 Worn tie-rod ends (Chapter 10).
4 Worn lower balljoints (Chapters 1 and 10).
5 Excessive wheel runout (Chapter 10).
6 Blister or bump on tire (Chapter 10).

75 Hard steering

1 Lack of lubrication at balljoints, tie-rod ends and rack and pinion assembly (Chapter 10).
2 Front wheel alignment incorrect (Chapter 10).
3 Low tire pressure(s) (Chapters 1 and 10).

76 Poor returnability of steering to center

1 Lack of lubrication at balljoints and tie-rod ends (Chapter 10).
2 Binding in balljoints (Chapter 10).
3 Binding in steering column (Chapter 10).
4 Lack of lubricant in rack and pinion assembly (Chapter 10).
5 Front wheel alignment incorrect (Chapter 10).

77 Abnormal noise at the front end

1 Lack of lubrication at balljoints and tie-rod ends (Chapters 1 and 10).
2 Damaged strut mounting (Chapter 10).
3 Worn control arm bushings or tie-rod ends (Chapter 10).
4 Loose stabilizer bar (Chapter 10).
5 Loose wheel nuts (Chapters 1 and 10).
6 Loose suspension bolts (Chapter 10).

78 Wander or poor steering stability

1 Mismatched or uneven tires (Chapter 10).
2 Lack of lubrication at balljoints and tie-rod ends (Chapters 1 and 10).
3 Worn strut assemblies (Chapter 10).
4 Loose stabilizer bar (Chapter 10).
5 Broken or sagging springs (Chapter 10).
6 Wheel alignment (Chapter 10).

79 Erratic steering when braking

1 Wheel bearings worn (Chapter 10).
2 Broken or sagging springs (Chapter 10).
3 Leaking wheel cylinder or caliper (Chapter 10).
4 Warped discs or drums (Chapter 10).

80 Excessive pitching and/or rolling around corners or during braking

1 Loose stabilizer bar (Chapter 10).
2 Worn strut dampers or mountings (Chapter 10).
3 Broken or sagging springs (Chapter 10).
4 Overloaded vehicle.

81 Suspension bottoms

1 Overloaded vehicle.
2 Worn strut dampers (Chapter 10).
3 Incorrect, broken or sagging springs (Chapter 10).

82 Cupped tires

1 Front or rear wheel alignment incorrect (Chapter 10).
2 Worn strut dampers (Chapter 10).

3 Wheel bearings worn (Chapter 10).
4 Excessive tire or wheel runout (Chapter 10).
5 Worn balljoints (Chapter 10).

83 Excessive tire wear on outside edge

1 Inflation pressures incorrect (Chapter 1).
2 Excessive speed in turns.
3 Front end alignment incorrect (excessive toe-in). Have professionally aligned.
4 Suspension arm bent or twisted (Chapter 10).

84 Excessive tire wear on inside edge

1 Inflation pressures incorrect (Chapter 1).
2 Front end alignment incorrect (toe-out). Have professionally aligned.
3 Loose or damaged steering components (Chapter 10).

85 Tire tread worn in one place

1 Tires out-of-balance.
2 Damaged or buckled wheel. Inspect and replace if necessary.
3 Defective tire (Chapter 1).

86 Excessive play or looseness in steering system

1 Wheel bearing(s) worn (Chapter 10).
2 Tie-rod end loose (Chapter 10).
3 Rack and pinion loose (Chapter 10).
4 Worn or loose steering intermediate shaft (Chapter 10).

87 Rattling or clicking noise in rack and pinion

1 Insufficient or improper lubricant in steering gear (Chapter 10).
2 Steering gear attachment loose (Chapter 10).
3 Internal steering gear problem (Chapter 10).

Chapter 1 Tune-up and routine maintenance

Contents

Air filter replacement ... 16
Automatic transaxle fluid change ... 31
Automatic transaxle fluid level check ... 9
Battery check and maintenance ... 10
Brake check ... 13
Brake pedal height adjustment ... 19
Chassis and body lubrication and maintenance ... 15
Clutch pedal height and freeplay check and adjustment ... 18
Cooling system check ... 11
Cooling system servicing (draining, flushing and refilling) ... 30
Cylinder compression check ... See Chapter 2
Driveaxle boot check ... 20
Drivebelt check, adjustment and replacement ... 12
Engine oil and filter change ... 8
Evaporative emissions control system check ... 36
Exhaust Gas Recirculation (EGR) valve check ... 33
Exhaust gas sensor (1985 through 1987 models) servicing ... 28
Exhaust system check ... 21
Fluid level checks ... 4
Fuel filter replacement ... 25
Fuel system check ... 29
Fuel tank cap gasket replacement ... 35
Ignition timing check and adjustment ... 37
Introduction ... 1
Maintenance schedule ... 3
Manual transaxle lubricant change ... 32
Manual transaxle lubricant level check ... 23
Positive Crankcase Ventilation (PCV) valve check and replacement ... 34
Power steering fluid level check ... 5
Seatbelt check ... 14
Spark plug replacement ... 27
Spark plug wire, distributor cap and rotor check and replacement ... 26
Suspension and steering check ... 22
Tire and tire pressure checks ... 6
Tire rotation ... 24
Tune-up general information ... 2
Underhood hose check and replacement ... 17
Warning lights general information ... 38
Wiper blade inspection and replacement ... 7

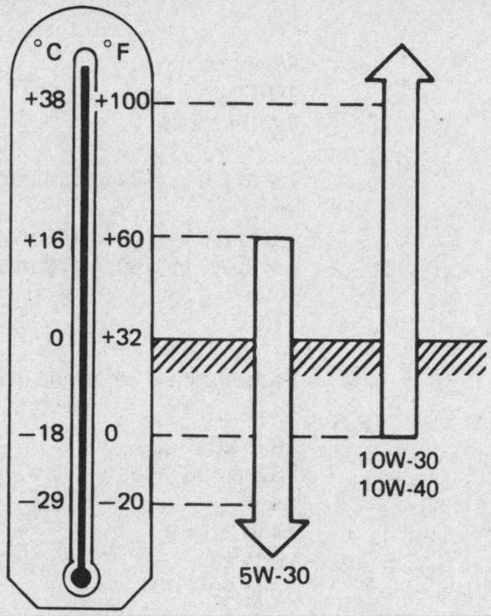

Engine oil viscosity chart

Specifications

Recommended lubricants and fluids

Engine oil	
Type	API grade SF or SF/CC multigrade and fuel efficient oil
Viscosity	See accompanying chart
Fuel	Unleaded gasoline, 87 octane or higher
Automatic transaxle fluid type	Dexron II automatic transmission fluid
Manual transaxle lubricant type	API GL-4 SAE 75W90W or 80W90W gear oil
Brake fluid type	DOT 3 brake fluid
Clutch fluid type	DOT 3 brake fluid
Power steering system fluid	Dexron II automatic transmission fluid

Capacities

Engine coolant	9 qts
Engine oil	
With oil filter change	4.5 qts
Without filter change	4.0 qts
Transaxle (approximate)	
Manual	5.0 qts
Automatic	
Dry fill	7.0 qts
Drain and refill	3.5 qts

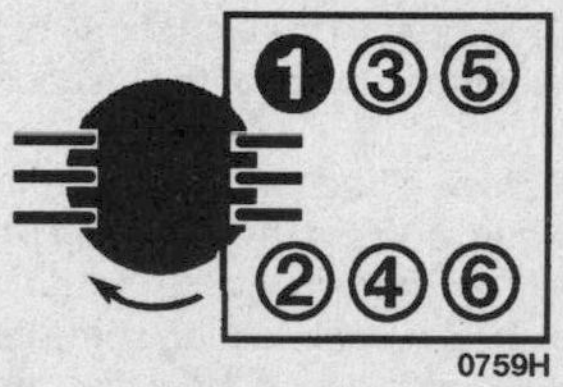

Cylinder location and distributor rotation

Ignition system

Spark plug type and gap	
1985 through 1988	NGK BCPR6ES-11 or equivalent @ 0.044 inch*
1989 and later	NGK BKR6ES-11 or equivalent @ 0.044 inch*
Spark plug wire resistance	Less than 25000 ohms
Ignition timing	
Manual transaxle	15-degrees BTDC*
Automatic transaxle	20-degrees BTDC*
Cylinder locations (drivebelt end-to-transaxle end)	
Rear (firewall side)	1-3-5
Front (radiator side)	2-4-6
Firing order	1-2-3-4-5-6

**Refer to the Emission Control Information label in the engine compartment (it supersedes the information printed here)*

Thermostat rating

Starts to open	170-degrees F (76-degrees C)
Fully open	212-degrees F (100-degrees C)

Clutch

Pedal freeplay	0.04 to 0.12 in (1 to 3 mm)
Pedal height	
1985 through 1988 models	6.7 to 7.2 in (171 to 181 mm)
1989 and later models	6.5 to 6.9 in (165 to 175 mm)

Brakes

Disc brake pad lining thickness (minimum)	5/64-inch
Drum brake shoe lining thickness (minimum)	1/16-inch
Parking brake adjustment	9 to 11 clicks
Brake pedal free height	
1985 through 1988 models	7.2 to 7.6 in (184 to 194 mm)
1989-on models	
Manual transaxle	6.3 to 6.6 in (159 to 169 mm)
Automatic transaxle	6.7 to 7.0 in (169 to 179 mm)

Torque specifications

	Ft-lbs (unless otherwise indicated)
Automatic transaxle drain plug	
1985 through 1991	18 to 25
1992	132 to 168 in-lbs
Manual transaxle drain and filler plugs	14
Spark plugs	14 to 22
Engine oil drain plug	22 to 29
Cylinder block drain cock/plug	16 to 20
Wheel lug nuts	
1986 and earlier	58 to 72
1987 on	72 to 87

1 Introduction

This Chapter is designed to help the home mechanic maintain the Nissan Maxima with the goals of maximum performance, economy, safety and reliability in mind.

Included is a master maintenance schedule (page 34), followed by procedures dealing specifically with each item on the schedule. Visual checks, adjustments, component replacement and other helpful items are included. Refer to the accompanying illustrations of the engine compartment and the underside of the vehicle for the locations of various components.

Servicing your vehicle in accordance with the planned mileage/time maintenance schedule and the step-by-step procedures should result in maximum reliability and extend the life of your vehicle. Keep in mind that it's a comprehensive plan – maintaining some items but not others at the specified intervals will not produce the same results.

As you perform routine maintenance procedures, you'll find that many can, and should, be grouped together because of the nature of the procedures or because of the proximity of two otherwise unrelated components or systems.

For example, if the vehicle is raised for chassis lubrication, you should inspect the exhaust, suspension, steering and fuel systems while you're under the vehicle. When you're rotating the tires, it makes good sense to check the brakes since the wheels are already removed. Finally, let's suppose you have to borrow or rent a torque wrench. Even if you only need it to tighten the spark plugs, you might as well check the torque of as many critical fasteners as time allows.

The first step in this maintenance program is to prepare yourself before the actual work begins. Read through all the procedures you're planning to do, then gather up all the parts and tools needed. If it looks like you might run into problems during a particular job, seek advice from a mechanic or experienced do-it-yourselfer.

2 Tune-up general information

The term tune-up is used in this manual to represent a combination of individual operations rather than one specific procedure.

If, from the time the vehicle is new, the routine maintenance schedule is followed closely and frequent checks are made of fluid levels and high wear items, as suggested throughout this manual, the engine will be kept in relatively good running condition and the need for additional work will be minimized.

More likely than not, however, there will be times when the engine is running poorly due to lack of regular maintenance. This is even more likely if a used vehicle, which has not received regular and frequent maintenance checks, is purchased. In such cases, an engine tune-up will be needed outside of the regular routine maintenance intervals.

The first step in any tune-up or diagnostic procedure to help correct a poor running engine is a cylinder compression check. A compression check (see Chapter 2 Part B) will help determine the condition of internal engine components and should be used as a guide for tune-up and repair procedures. If, for instance, a compression check indicates serious internal engine wear, a conventional tune-up will not improve the performance of the engine and would be a waste of time and money. Because of its importance, the compression check should be done by someone with the right equipment and the knowledge to use it properly.

The following procedures are those most often needed to bring a generally poor running engine back into a proper state of tune.

Minor tune-up

Check all engine related fluids (Section 4)
Clean, inspect and test the battery (Section 10)
Check and adjust the drivebelts (Section 12)
Replace the spark plugs (Section 27)
Check the cylinder compression (Chapter 2)
Replace the air filter (Section 16)
Inspect the distributor cap and rotor (Section 26)
Inspect the spark plug and coil wires (Section 26)
Check and adjust the ignition timing (Section 37)
Replace the fuel filter (Section 25)
Check the PCV valve (Section 34)
Check the cooling system (Section 11)
Check all underhood hoses (Section 17)

Major tune-up

All items listed under Minor tune-up plus . . .
Check the EGR valve and system (Section 33 and Chapter 6)
Check the ignition system (Chapter 5)
Check the charging system (Chapter 5)
Check the fuel system (Section 29 and Chapter 4)
Replace the spark plug wires, distributor cap and rotor (Section 26)

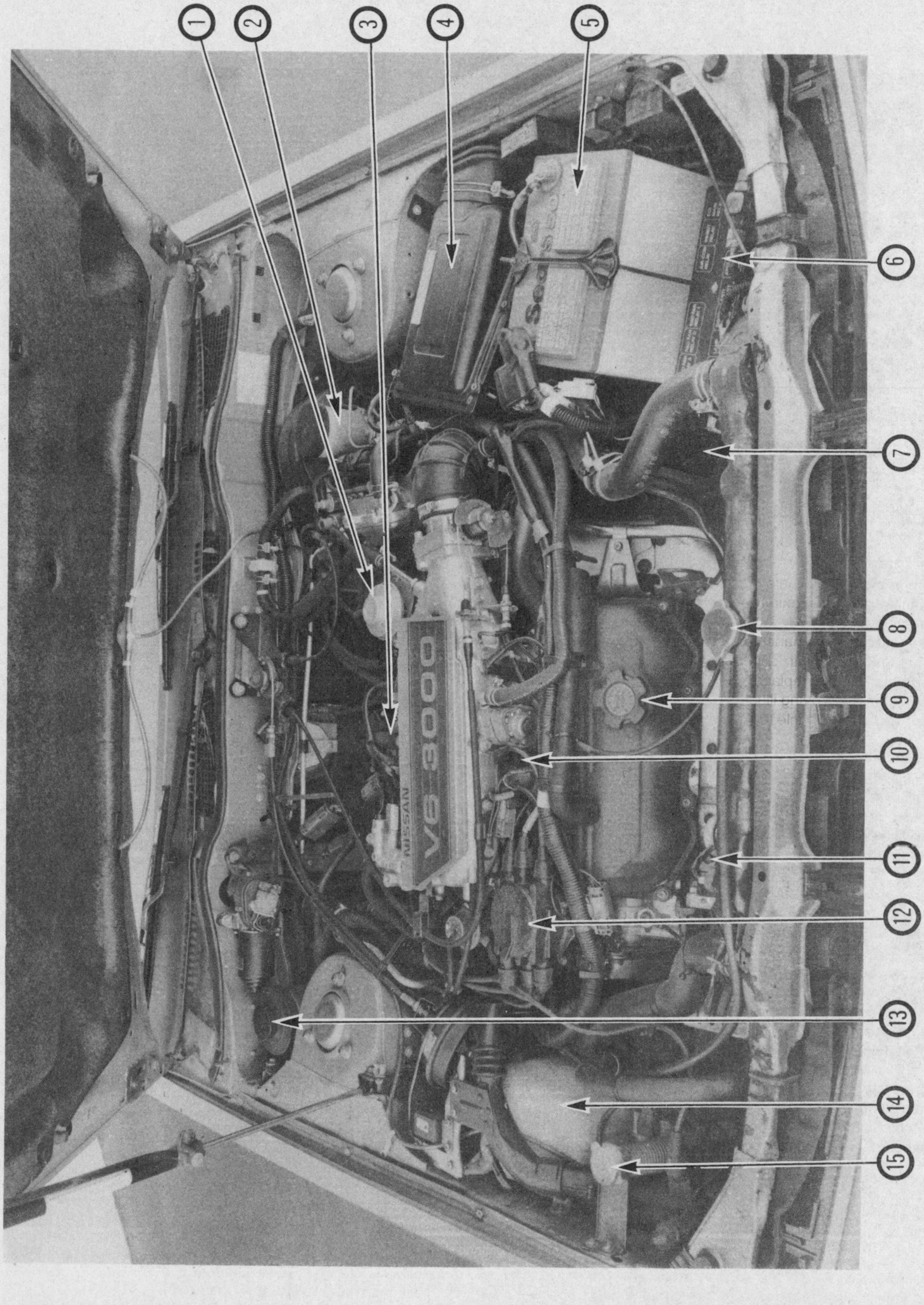

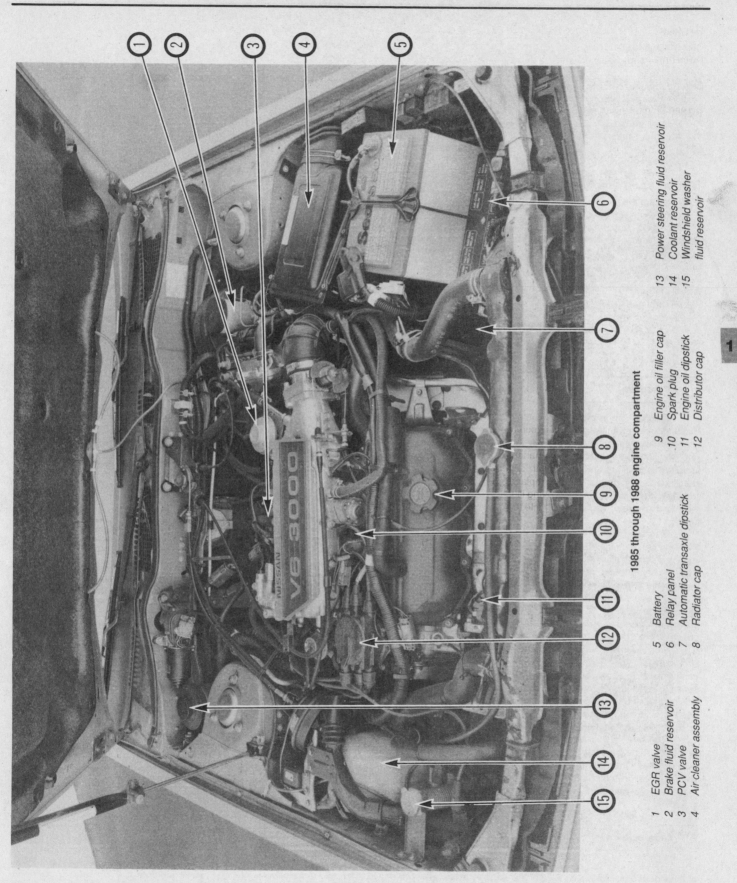

1985 through 1988 engine compartment

1 EGR valve
2 Brake fluid reservoir
3 PCV valve
4 Air cleaner assembly
5 Battery
6 Relay panel
7 Automatic transaxle dipstick
8 Radiator cap
9 Engine oil filler cap
10 Spark plug
11 Engine oil dipstick
12 Distributor cap
13 Power steering fluid reservoir
14 Coolant reservoir
15 Windshield washer fluid reservoir

1

Typical engine compartment underside components

1. Brake caliper
2. Charcoal canister
3. Automatic transaxle drain plug
4. Exhaust pipe
5. Crossmember
6. Power steering gear boot
7. Engine oil drain plug
8. Drivebelt
9. Brake hose
10. Driveaxle boot

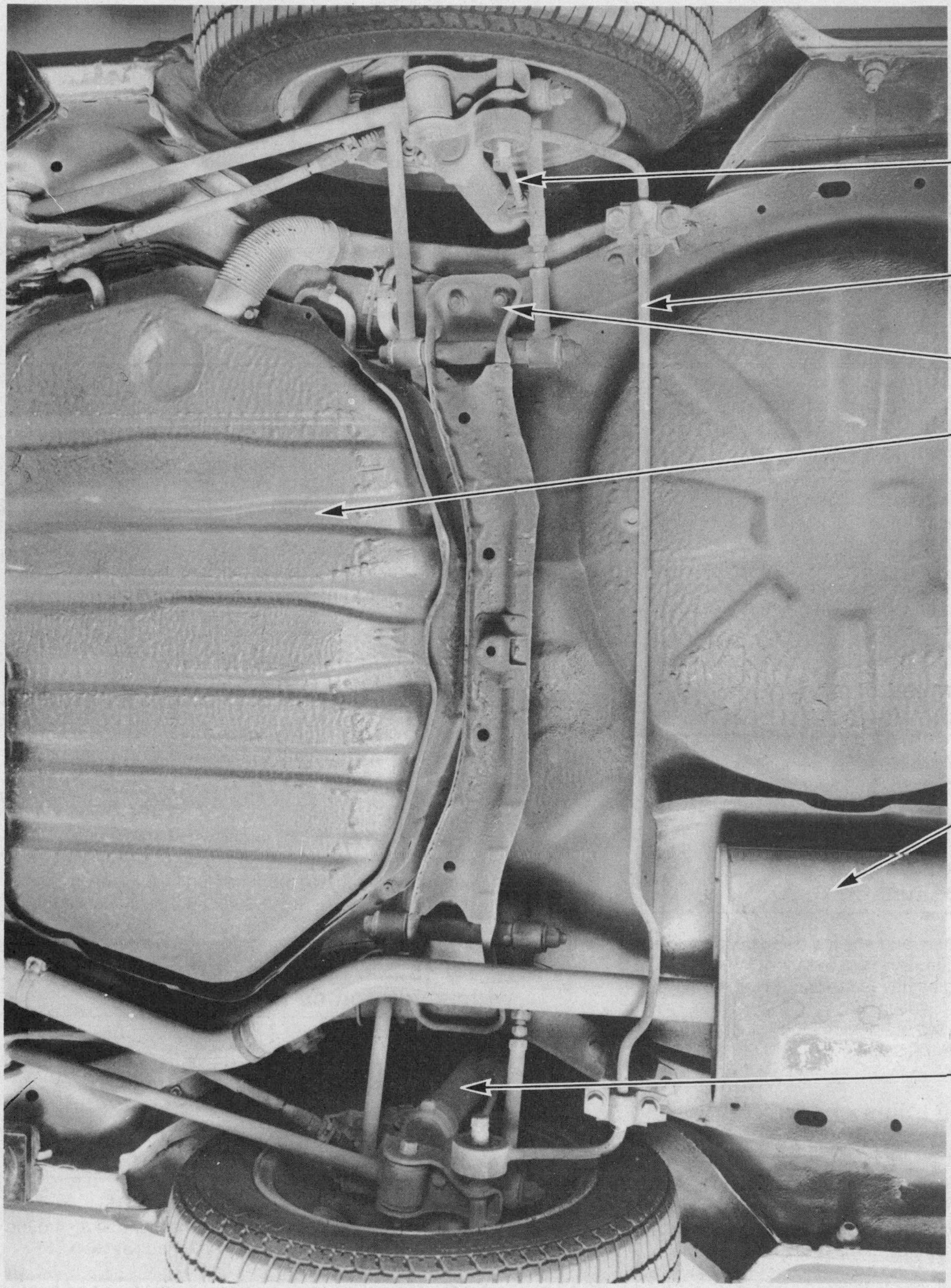

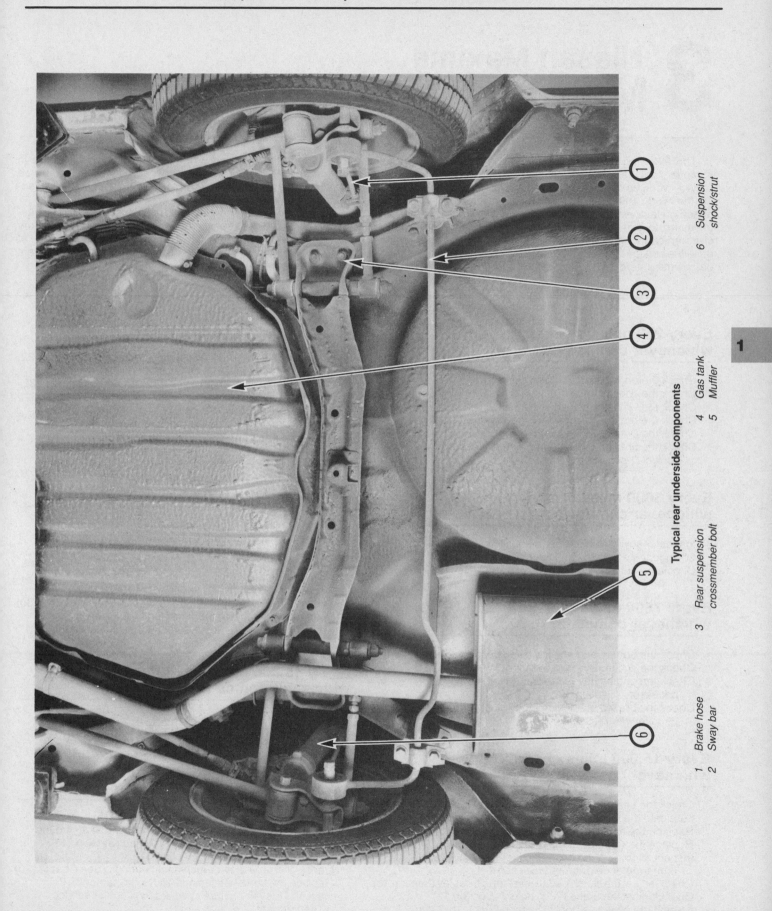

Typical rear underside components

1 *Brake hose*
2 *Sway bar*
3 *Rear suspension crossmember bolt*
4 *Gas tank*
5 *Muffler*
6 *Suspension shock/strut*

3 Nissan Maxima Maintenance schedule

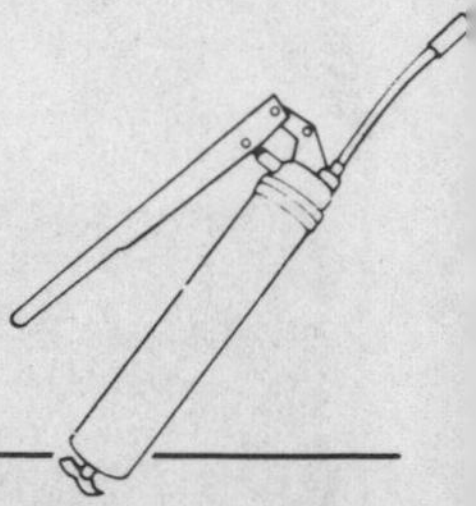

The following maintenance intervals are based on the assumption that the vehicle owner will be doing the maintenance or service work, as opposed to having a dealer service department do the work. Although the time/mileage intervals are loosely based on factory recommendations, most have been shortened to ensure, for example, that such items as lubricants and fluids are checked/changed at intervals that promote maximum engine/driveline service life. Also, subject to the preference of the individual owner interested in keeping his or her vehicle in peak condition at all times, and with the vehicle's ultimate resale in mind, many of the maintenance procedures may be performed more often than recommended in the following schedule. We encourage such owner initiative.

When the vehicle is new it should be serviced initially by a factory authorized dealer service department to protect the factory warranty. In many cases the initial maintenance check is done at no cost to the owner (check with your dealer service department for more information).

Every 250 miles or weekly, whichever comes first

Check the engine oil level (Section 4)
Check the coolant level (Section 4)
Check the windshield washer fluid level (Section 4)
Check the brake and clutch fluid levels (Section 4)
Check the power steering fluid level (Section 5)
Check the tires and make sure the tire pressures are correct (Section 6)

Every 3000 miles or 3 months, whichever comes first

Inspect the windshield wiper blades (Section 7)
Change the engine oil and filter (Section 8)
Check the automatic transaxle fluid level (Section 9)

Every 7500 miles or 6 months, whichever comes first

Check the battery and service it if necessary (Section 10)
Check the cooling system (Section 11)
Check the engine drivebelts and adjust them if necessary (Section 12)
Check the brakes (particularly the front brake pads for wear) (Section 13)

Every 15,000 miles or 12 months, whichever comes first

Check the seatbelts and related components (Section 14)
Lubricate the locks, hinges and latches (Section 15)
Replace the air filter element (Section 16)
Replace the windshield wiper blades (Section 7)
Inspect all underhood hoses and replace any that are damaged or deteriorated (Section 17)
Check/adjust the clutch pedal height and freeplay (Section 18)
Check/adjust the brake pedal height (Section 19)
Inspect the driveaxle boots (Section 20)
Inspect the exhaust system (Section 21)
Inspect the brake lines and hoses (Section 13)
Inspect the steering and suspension components (Section 22)
Inspect the power steering lines and hoses (Section 22)
Check the manual transmission lubricant level (Section 23)
Rotate the tires (Section 24)
Replace the fuel filter (Section 25)
Have the engine idle speed checked by a dealer service department

Every 30,000 miles or 24 months, whichever comes first

Check the spark plug wires, distributor cap and rotor; replace damaged and deteriorated parts (Section 26)
Replace the spark plugs (Section 27)
Inspect the exhaust gas sensor (1985 through 1987 models only) (Section 28)
Inspect the fuel lines and vapor hoses (Section 29)
Service the cooling system (drain, flush and refill) (Section 30)
Change the automatic transmission fluid (Section 31)
Change the manual transmission lubricant (Section 32)

Every 45,000 miles or 24 months, whichever comes first

Check the EGR system (Section 33)
Replace the PCV valve (Section 34)

Every 60,000 miles or 24 months, whichever comes first

Replace the fuel tank cap gasket (Section 35)
Check the charcoal canister for leaks and make sure the vacuum hoses are securely attached (Section 36)
Check the ignition timing (Section 37)
Check and repack the rear wheel bearings (See Chapter 10)
Replace the camshaft timing belt (See Chapter 2)
Have the fuel/air mixture checked by a dealer service department

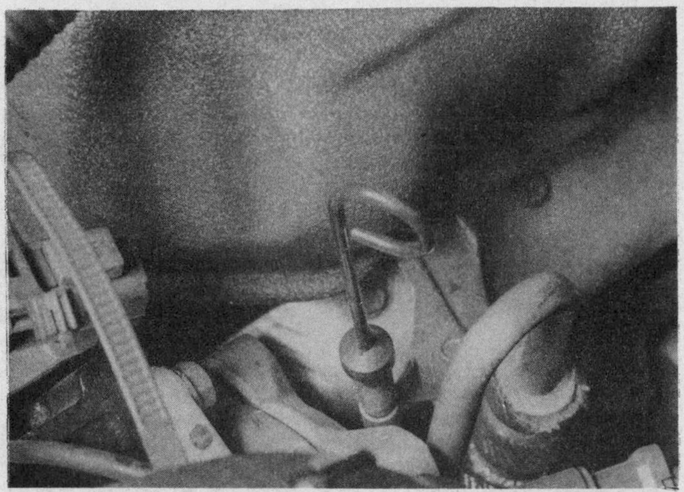

4.2 The dipstick is located on the front of the engine

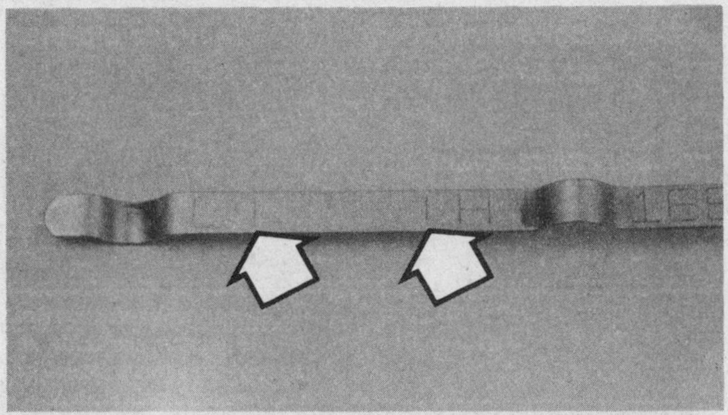

4.4 The engine oil level must be maintained between the marks at all times – it takes one quart of oil to raise the level from the L mark to the H mark (arrows)

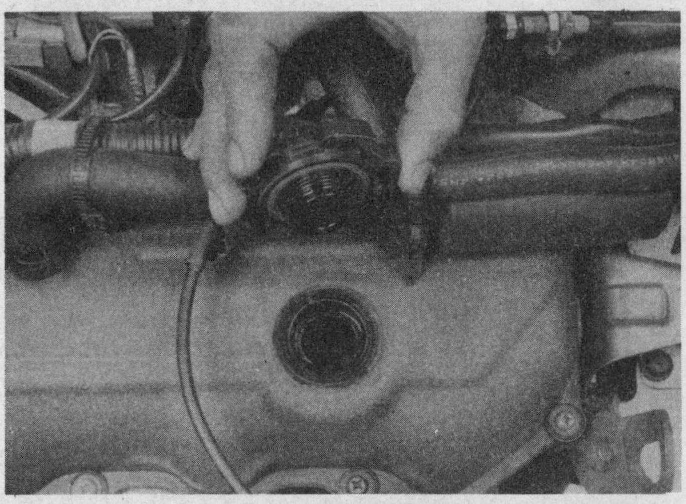

4.6 Oil is added to the engine after removing the cap from the front rocker arm cover

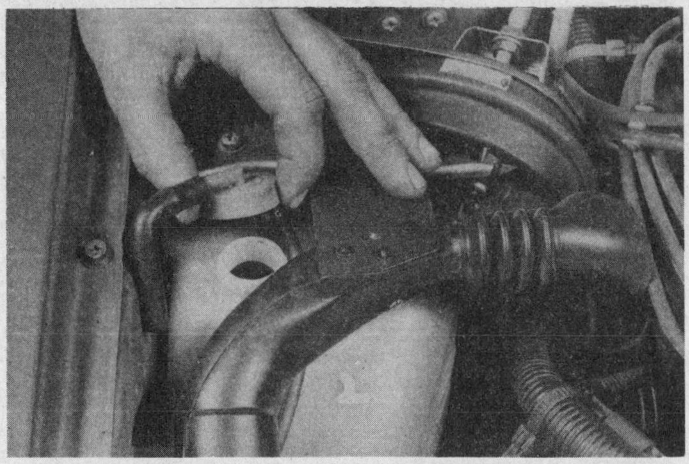

4.8 The coolant reservoir is located on the right (passenger) side inner fender panel

4 Fluid level checks

Refer to illustrations 4.2, 4.4, 4.6, 4.8, 4.14 and 4.19

Note: *The following are fluid level checks to be done on a 250 mile or weekly basis. Additional fluid level checks can be found in specific maintenance procedures which follow. Regardless of intervals, be alert to fluid leaks under the vehicle which would indicate a fault to be corrected immediately.*

1 Fluids are an essential part of the lubrication, cooling, brake, clutch and windshield washer systems. Because the fluids gradually become depleted and/or contaminated during normal operation of the vehicle, they must be periodically replenished. See *Recommended lubricants and fluids* at the beginning of this Chapter before adding fluid to any of the following components. **Note:** *The vehicle must be on level ground when fluid levels are checked.*

Engine oil

2 The engine oil level is checked with a dipstick that extends through a tube and into the oil pan at the bottom of the engine **(see illustration)**.

3 The oil level should be checked before the vehicle has been driven, or about 15 minutes after the engine has been shut off. If the oil is checked immediately after driving the vehicle, some of the oil will remain in the upper engine components, resulting in an inaccurate reading on the dipstick.

4 Pull the dipstick from the tube and wipe all the oil from the end with a clean rag or paper towel. Insert the clean dipstick all the way back into the tube, then pull it out again. Note the oil at the end of the dipstick. Add oil as necessary to keep the level between the L (low) mark and the H (high) mark on the dipstick **(see illustration)**.

5 Do not overfill the engine by adding too much oil since this may result in oil fouled spark plugs, oil leaks or oil seal failures.

6 Oil is added to the engine after unscrewing the filler cap **(see illustration)**. An oil can spout or funnel may help to reduce spills.

7 Checking the oil level is an important preventive maintenance step. A consistently low oil level indicates oil leakage through damaged seals, defective gaskets or past worn rings or valve guides. If the oil looks milky in color or has water droplets in it, the cylinder head gasket(s) may be blown or the head(s) or block may be cracked. The engine should be checked immediately. The condition of the oil should also be checked. Whenever you check the oil level, slide your thumb and index finger up the dipstick before wiping off the oil. If you see small dirt or metal particles clinging to the dipstick, the oil should be changed (Section 8).

Engine coolant

Warning: *Do not allow antifreeze to come in contact with your skin or painted surfaces of the vehicle. Flush contaminated areas immediately with plenty of water. Don't store new coolant or leave old coolant lying around where it's accessible to children or pets - they're attracted by its sweet taste. Ingestion of even a small amount of coolant can be fatal! Wipe up garage floor and drip pan coolant spills immediately. Keep antifreeze containers covered and repair leaks in the cooling system immediately.*

8 All vehicles covered by this manual are equipped with a pressurized coolant recovery system. A white plastic coolant reservoir located in the engine compartment is connected by a hose to the radiator filler neck **(see illustration)**. If the engine overheats, coolant escapes through a valve in

4.14 In cold climates, use *windshield washer* antifreeze

4.19 The brake fluid level is easily checked by looking through the clear reservoir

the radiator cap and travels through the hose into the reservoir. As the engine cools, the coolant is automatically drawn back into the cooling system to maintain the correct level.

9 The coolant level in the reservoir should be checked regularly. **Warning:** *Do not remove the radiator cap to check the coolant level when the engine is warm.* The level in the reservoir varies with the temperature of the engine. When the engine is cold, the coolant level should be at or slightly above the FULL COLD mark on the reservoir. Once the engine has warmed up, the level should be at or near the FULL HOT mark. If it isn't, allow the engine to cool, then remove the cap from the reservoir and add a 50/50 mixture of ethylene glycol-based antifreeze and water.

10 Drive the vehicle and recheck the coolant level. If only a small amount of coolant is required to bring the system up to the proper level, water can be used. However, repeated additions of water will dilute the antifreeze and water solution. In order to maintain the proper ratio of antifreeze and water, always top up the coolant level with the correct mixture. An empty plastic milk jug or bleach bottle makes an excellent container for mixing coolant. Do not use rust inhibitors or additives.

11 If the coolant level drops consistently, there may be a leak in the system. Inspect the radiator, hoses, filler cap, drain plugs and water pump (see Section 11). If no leaks are noted, have the radiator cap pressure tested by a service station.

12 If you have to remove the radiator cap, wait until the engine has cooled, then wrap a thick cloth around the cap and turn it to the first stop. If coolant or steam escapes, let the engine cool down longer, then remove the cap.

13 Check the condition of the coolant as well. It should be relatively clear. If it's brown or rust colored, the system should be drained, flushed and refilled. Even if the coolant appears to be normal, the corrosion inhibitors wear out, so it must be replaced at the specified intervals.

Windshield washer fluid

14 Fluid for the windshield washer system is located in a plastic reservoir in the engine compartment **(see illustration)**.

15 In milder climates, plain water can be used in the reservoir, but it should be kept no more than 2/3 full to allow for expansion if the water freezes. In colder climates, use windshield washer system antifreeze, available at any auto parts store, to lower the freezing point of the fluid. Mix the antifreeze with water in accordance with the manufacturer's directions on the container. **Caution:** *Don't use cooling system antifreeze – it will damage the vehicle's paint.*

16 To help prevent icing in cold weather, warm the windshield with the defroster before using the washer.

Battery electrolyte

17 All vehicles with which this manual is concerned are equipped with a battery which is permanently sealed (except for vent holes) and has no filler caps. Water doesn't have to be added to these batteries at any time. If a maintenance-type battery is installed, the caps on the top of the battery should be removed periodically to check for a low water level. This check is most critical during the warm summer months.

Brake and clutch fluid

18 The brake master cylinder is mounted on the front of the power booster unit in the engine compartment. The clutch cylinder used on manual transmissions is mounted adjacent to it on the firewall.

19 The fluid inside is readily visible. The level should be above the MIN marks on the reservoirs **(see illustration)**. If a low level is indicated, be sure to wipe the top of the reservoir cover with a clean rag to prevent contamination of the brake and/or clutch system before removing the cover.

20 When adding fluid, pour it carefully into the reservoir to avoid spilling it onto surrounding painted surfaces. Be sure the specified fluid is used, since mixing different types of brake fluid can cause damage to the system. See *Recommended lubricants and fluids* at the front of this Chapter or your owner's manual. **Warning:** *Brake fluid can harm your eyes and damage painted surfaces, so use extreme caution when handling or pouring it. Do not use brake fluid that has been standing open or is more than one year old. Brake fluid absorbs moisture from the air. Excess moisture can cause a dangerous loss of braking effectiveness.*

21 At this time the fluid and master cylinder can be inspected for contamination. The system should be drained and refilled if deposits, dirt particles or water droplets are seen in the fluid.

22 After filling the reservoir to the proper level, make sure the cover is on tight to prevent fluid leakage.

23 The brake fluid level in the master cylinder will drop slightly as the pads and the brake shoes at each wheel wear down during normal operation. If the master cylinder requires repeated additions to keep it at the proper level, it's an indication of leakage in the brake system, which should be corrected immediately. Check all brake lines and connections (see Section 13 for more information).

24 If, upon checking the master cylinder fluid level, you discover one or both reservoirs empty or nearly empty, the brake system should be bled (Chapter 9).

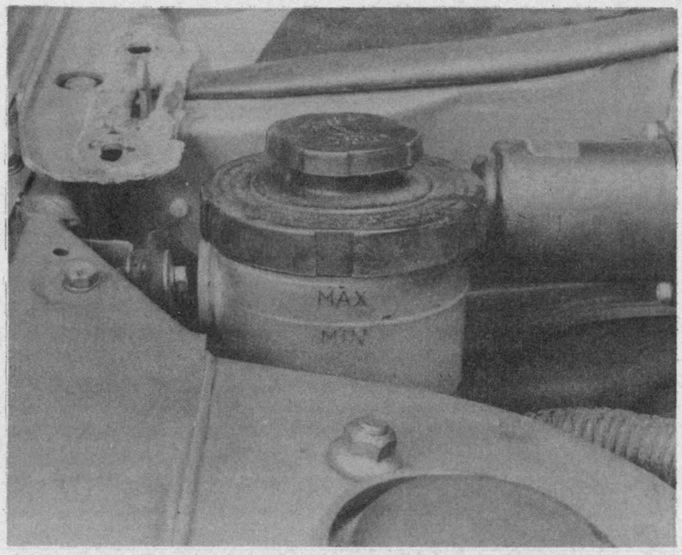

5.2a The power steering fluid reservoir is located in the rear corner of the engine compartment near the windshield wiper motor (1985 through 1988 models)

5.2b On 1989 and later models, the power steering fluid reservoir is located on the right-side strut tower

5 Power steering fluid level check

Refer to illustrations 5.2a and 5.2b

1 Unlike manual steering, the power steering system relies on fluid which may, over a period of time, require replenishing.
2 The fluid reservoir for the power steering pump is located in the rear corner of the engine compartment near the windshield wiper motor, or on the right-side strut tower **(see illustrations)**.
3 For the check, the front wheels should be pointed straight ahead and the engine should be off.
4 Use a clean rag to wipe off the reservoir cap and the area around the cap. This will help prevent any foreign matter from entering the reservoir during the check.
5 Twist off the cap and check the temperature of the fluid with your finger.
6 On models with a see-through reservoir, check to see that the fluid is between the MIN and MAX lines. On models with a dipstick, wipe off the fluid with a clean rag, reinsert the dipstick, then withdraw it and read the fluid level. The level should be at the HOT, or upper mark if the fluid was hot to the touch. It should be at the COLD, or lower mark if the fluid was cool to the touch. Never allow the fluid level to drop below the lower mark.
7 If additional fluid is required, pour the specified type directly into the reservoir, using a funnel to prevent spills.
8 If the reservoir requires frequent fluid additions, all power steering hoses, hose connections and the power steering pump should be carefully checked for leaks.

6 Tire and tire pressure checks

Refer to illustrations 6.2, 6.3, 6.4a, 6.4b and 6.8

1 Periodic inspection of the tires may spare you the inconvenience of being stranded with a flat tire. It can also provide you with vital information regarding possible problems in the steering and suspension systems before major damage occurs.
2 The original tires on this vehicle are equipped with 1/2-inch side bands that will appear when tread depth reaches 1/16-inch, but they don't appear until the tires are worn out. Tread wear can be monitored with a simple, inexpensive device known as a tread depth indicator **(see illustration)**.

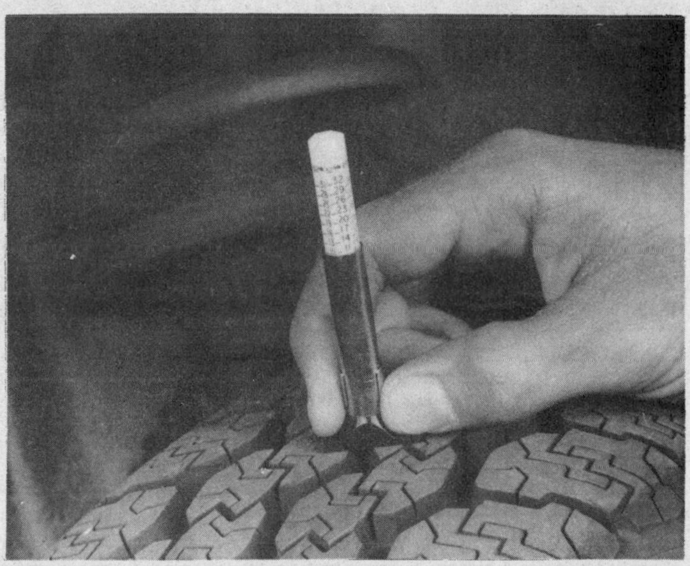

6.2 A tire tread depth indicator should be used to monitor tire wear – they are available at auto parts stores and service stations and cost very little

3 Note any abnormal tread wear **(see illustration on next page)**. Tread pattern irregularities such as cupping, flat spots and more wear on one side than the other are indications of front end alignment and/or balance problems. If any of these conditions are noted, take the vehicle to a tire shop or service station to correct the problem.
4 Look closely for cuts, punctures and embedded nails or tacks. Sometimes a tire will hold air pressure for a short time or leak down very slowly after a nail has embedded itself in the tread. If a slow leak persists, check

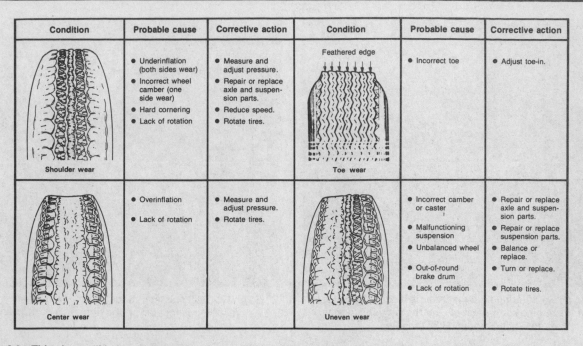

Condition	Probable cause	Corrective action	Condition	Probable cause	Corrective action
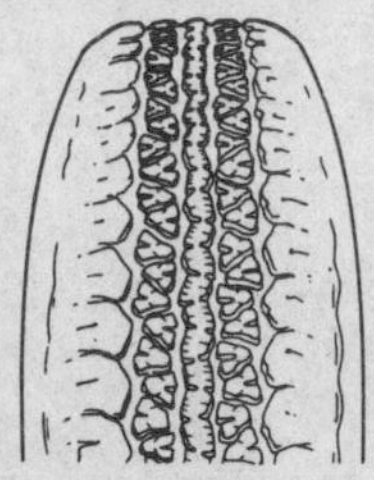 Shoulder wear	• Underinflation (both sides wear) • Incorrect wheel camber (one side wear) • Hard cornering • Lack of rotation	• Measure and adjust pressure. • Repair or replace axle and suspension parts. • Reduce speed. • Rotate tires.	Feathered edge  Toe wear	• Incorrect toe	• Adjust toe-in.
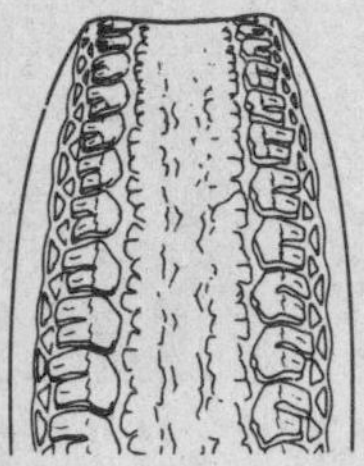 Center wear	• Overinflation • Lack of rotation	• Measure and adjust pressure. • Rotate tires.	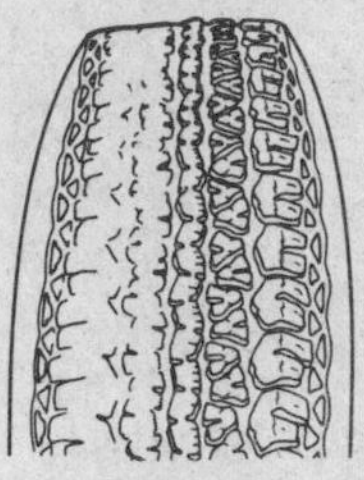 Uneven wear	• Incorrect camber or caster • Malfunctioning suspension • Unbalanced wheel • Out-of-round brake drum • Lack of rotation	• Repair or replace axle and suspension parts. • Repair or replace suspension parts. • Balance or replace. • Turn or replace. • Rotate tires.

6.3 This chart will help you determine the condition of the tires, the probable cause(s) of abnormal wear and the corrective action necessary

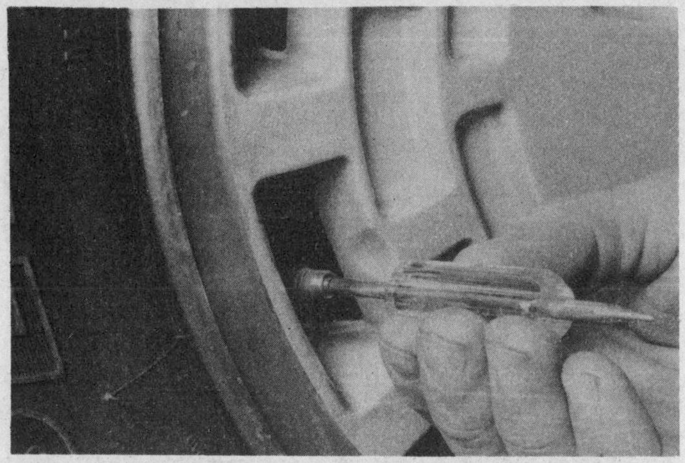

6.4a If a tire loses air on a steady basis, check the valve core first to make sure it's snug (special inexpensive wrenches are commonly available at auto parts stores)

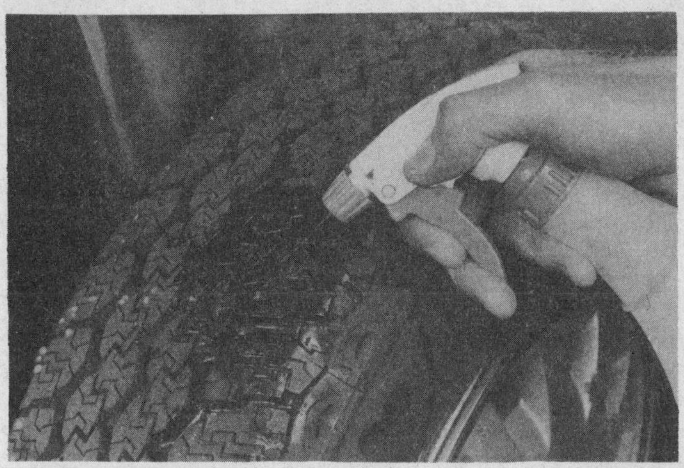

6.4b If the valve core is tight, raise the corner of the vehicle with the low tire and spray a soapy water solution onto the tread as the tire is turned slowly – leaks will cause small bubbles to appear

the valve stem core to make sure it's tight **(see illustration)**. Examine the tread for an object that may have embedded itself in the tire or for a "plug" that may have begun to leak (radial tire punctures are repaired with a plug that's installed in a puncture). If a puncture is suspected, it can be easily verified by spraying a solution of soapy water onto the puncture area **(see illustration)**. The soapy solution will bubble if there's a leak. Unless the puncture is unusually large, a tire shop or service station can usually repair the tire.

5 Carefully inspect the inner sidewall of each tire for evidence of brake fluid leakage. If you see any, inspect the brakes immediately.

6 Correct air pressure adds miles to the lifespan of the tires, improves mileage and enhances overall ride quality. Tire pressure cannot be accurately estimated by looking at a tire, especially if it's a radial. A tire pressure gauge is essential. Keep an accurate gauge in the vehicle. The pressure gauges attached to the nozzles of air hoses at gas stations are often inaccurate.

7 Always check tire pressure when the tires are cold. Cold, in this case, means the vehicle has not been driven over a mile in the three hours preceding a tire pressure check. A pressure rise of four to eight pounds is not uncommon once the tires are warm.

8 Unscrew the valve cap protruding from the wheel or hubcap and push the gauge firmly onto the valve stem **(see illustration)**. Note the reading on the gauge and compare the figure to the recommended tire pressure shown on the placard on the driver's side door pillar. Be sure to reinstall the valve cap to keep dirt and moisture out of the valve stem mechanism. Check all four tires and, if necessary, add enough air to bring them up to the recommended pressure.

9 Don't forget to keep the spare tire inflated to the specified pressure (refer to your owner's manual or the tire sidewall). Note that the pressure recommended for the compact spare is higher than for the tires on the vehicle.

6.8 To extend the life of the tires, check the air pressure at least once a week with an accurate gauge (don't forget the spare!)

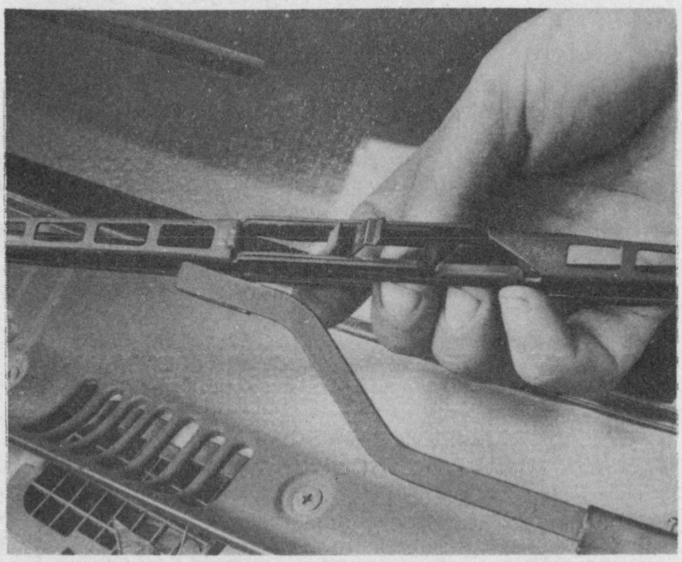

7.6 Depress the blade connector and slide the wiper blade off the arm

7 Wiper blade inspection and replacement

Refer to illustration 7.6

1 The windshield wiper and blade assembly should be inspected periodically for damage, loose components and cracked or worn blade elements.

2 Road film can build up on the wiper blades and affect their efficiency, so they should be washed regularly with a mild detergent solution.

3 The action of the wiping mechanism can loosen the bolts, nuts and fasteners, so they should be checked and tightened, as necessary, at the same time the wiper blades are checked.

4 If the wiper blade elements (sometimes called inserts) are cracked, worn or warped, they should be replaced with new ones.

5 Pull the wiper blade/arm assembly away from the glass.

6 Depress the blade-to-arm connector and slide the blade assembly off the wiper arm and over the retaining stud **(see illustration)**.

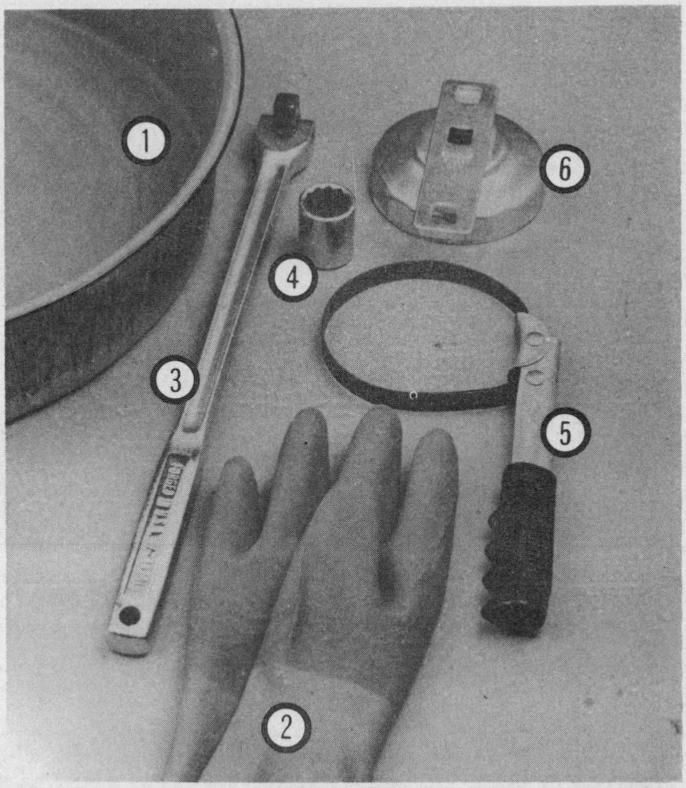

8.3 These tools are required when changing the engine oil and filter

1 ***Drain pan*** *– It should be fairly shallow in depth, but wide to prevent spills*
2 ***Rubber gloves*** *– When removing the drain plug and filter, you will get oil on your hands (the gloves will prevent burns)*
3 ***Breaker bar*** *– Sometimes the oil drain plug is tight and a long breaker bar is needed to loosen it*
4 ***Socket*** *– To be used with the breaker bar or a ratchet (must be the correct size to fit the drain plug – 6-point preferred)*
5 ***Filter wrench*** *– This is a metal band-type wrench, which requires clearance around the filter to be effective*
6 ***Filter wrench*** *– This type fits on the bottom of the filter and can be turned with a ratchet or breaker bar (different size wrenches are available for different types of filters)*

7 Pinch the tabs at the end, then slide the element out of the blade assembly.

8 Compare the new element with the old for length, design, etc.

9 Slide the new element into place. It will automatically lock at the correct location.

10 Reinstall the blade assembly on the arm, wet the windshield and check for proper operation.

8 Engine oil and filter change

Refer to illustrations 8.3, 8.9, 8.14a, 8.14b and 8.18

1 Frequent oil changes are the most important preventive maintenance procedures that can be done by the home mechanic. As engine oil ages, it becomes diluted and contaminated, which leads to premature engine wear.

2 Although some sources recommend oil filter changes every other oil change, we feel that the minimal cost of an oil filter and the relative ease with which it is installed dictate that a new filter be installed every time the oil is changed.

3 Gather together all necessary tools and materials before beginning this procedure **(see illustration)**.

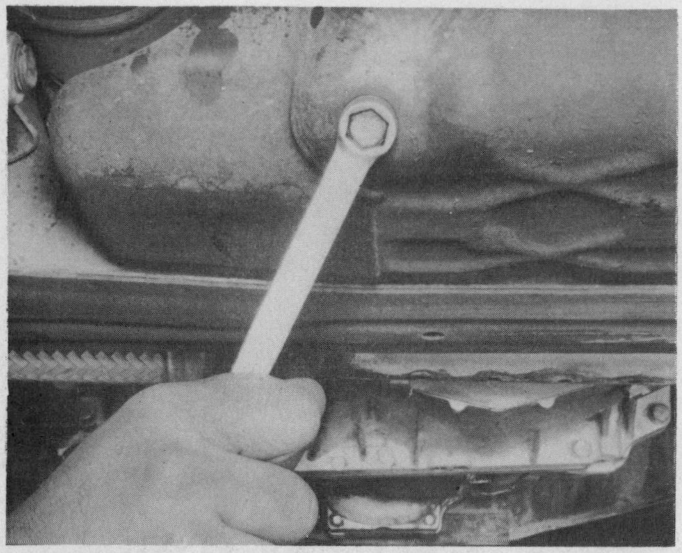

8.9 The oil drain plug is located at the bottom of the pan and should be removed with a socket or box-end wrench – DO NOT use an open end wrench as the corners on the bolt can be easily rounded off

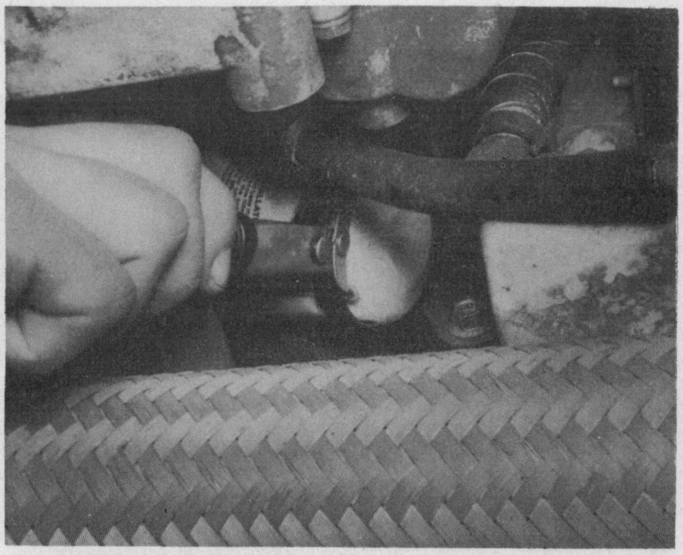

8.14a Use a strap type oil filter wrench to loosen the filter – if access makes removal difficult, other types of filter wrenches are available (1985 through 1988 models)

8.14b Remove the oil filter from above (near the transaxle) on 1989 models

4 You should have plenty of clean rags and newspapers handy to mop up any spills. Access to the underside of the vehicle is greatly improved if the vehicle can be lifted on a hoist, driven onto ramps or supported by jackstands. **Warning:** *Do not work under a vehicle which is supported only by a bumper, hydraulic or scissors-type jack.*

5 If this is your first oil change, get under the vehicle and familiarize yourself with the locations of the oil drain plug and the oil filter. The engine and exhaust components will be warm during the actual work, so note how they are situated to avoid touching them when working under the vehicle.

6 Warm the engine to normal operating temperature. If the new oil or any tools are needed, use this warm-up time to gather everything necessary for the job. The correct type of oil for your application can be found in *Recommended lubricants and fluids* at the beginning of this Chapter.

7 With the engine oil warm (warm engine oil will drain better and more built-up sludge will be removed with it), raise and support the vehicle. Make sure it's safely supported!

8 Move all necessary tools, rags and newspapers under the vehicle. Set the drain pan under the drain plug. Keep in mind that the oil will initially flow from the pan with some force; position the pan accordingly.

9 Being careful not to touch any of the hot exhaust components, use a wrench to remove the drain plug near the bottom of the oil pan **(see illustration)**. Depending on how hot the oil is, you may want to wear gloves while unscrewing the plug the final few turns.

10 Allow the old oil to drain into the pan. It may be necessary to move the pan as the oil flow slows to a trickle.

11 After all the oil has drained, wipe off the drain plug with a clean rag. Small metal particles may cling to the plug and would immediately contaminate the new oil.

12 Clean the area around the drain plug opening and reinstall the plug. Tighten the plug securely with the wrench. If a torque wrench is available, use it to tighten the plug.

13 Move the drain pan into position under the oil filter.

14 Use the filter wrench to loosen the oil filter **(see illustrations)**. Chain or metal band filter wrenches may distort the filter canister, but it doesn't matter since the filter will be discarded anyway.

15 Completely unscrew the old filter. Be careful; it's full of oil. Empty the oil inside the filter into the drain pan.

16 Compare the old filter with the new one to make sure they're the same type.

17 Use a clean rag to remove all oil, dirt and sludge from the area where the oil filter mounts to the engine. Check the old filter to make sure the rubber gasket isn't stuck to the engine. If the gasket is stuck to the engine (use a flashlight if necessary), remove it.

18 Apply a light coat of clean oil to the rubber gasket on the new oil filter **(see illustration)**.

19 Attach the new filter to the engine, following the tightening directions printed on the filter canister or packing box. Most filter manufacturers recommend against using a filter wrench due to the possibility of overtightening and damage to the seal.

20 Remove all tools, rags, etc. from under the vehicle, being careful not to spill the oil in the drain pan, then lower the vehicle.

21 Move to the engine compartment and locate the oil filler cap.

22 If an oil can spout is used, push the spout into the top of the oil can and pour the fresh oil through the filler opening. A funnel may also be used.

23 Pour four quarts of fresh oil into the engine. Wait a few minutes to allow the oil to drain into the pan, then check the level on the oil dipstick (see Section 4 if necessary). If the oil level is above the ADD mark, start the engine and allow the new oil to circulate.

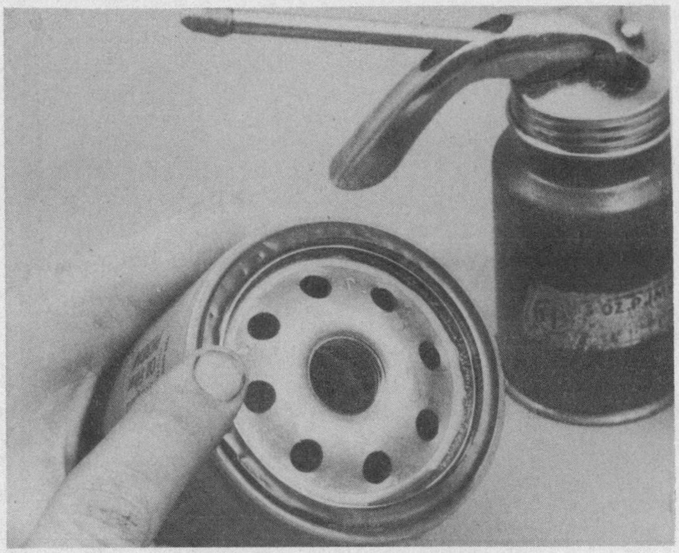

8.18 **Lubricate the oil filter gasket with clean engine oil before installing the filter on the engine**

9.4 **The automatic transaxle fluid dipstick is located on the driver's end of the engine, below and just to the left of the battery**

24 Run the engine for only about a minute and then shut it off. Immediately look under the vehicle and check for leaks at the oil pan drain plug and around the oil filter. If either is leaking, tighten with a bit more force.
25 With the new oil circulated and the filter now completely full, recheck the level on the dipstick and add more oil as necessary.
26 During the first few trips after an oil change, make it a point to check frequently for leaks and proper oil level.
27 The old oil drained from the engine cannot be reused in its present state and should be disposed of. Oil reclamation centers, auto repair shops and gas stations will normally accept the oil, which can be refined and used again. After the oil has cooled it can be drained into a suitable container (capped plastic jugs, topped bottles, milk cartons, etc.) for transport to one of these disposal sites.

9 Automatic transaxle fluid level check

Refer to illustrations 9.4 and 9.6

Warning: *The electric cooling fan can activate at any time, even when the ignition is in the Off position. Disconnect the fan motor or negative battery cable when working in the vicinity of the fan.*

1 The level of the automatic transaxle fluid should be carefully maintained. Low fluid level can lead to slipping or loss of drive, while overfilling can cause foaming, loss of fluid and transaxle damage.
2 The transaxle fluid level should only be checked when the engine is at normal operating temperature. **Caution:** *If the vehicle has just been driven for a long time at high speed or in city traffic in hot weather, or if it has been pulling a trailer, an accurate fluid level reading cannot be obtained. Allow the fluid to cool down for about 30 minutes.*
3 Park on level ground, apply the parking brake and start the engine. While the engine is idling, depress the brake pedal and move the selector lever through all the gear ranges, beginning and ending in Park.
4 With the engine still idling, remove the dipstick **(see illustration)**.
5 Wipe the fluid off the dipstick with a clean rag and reinsert it until the cap seats.
6 Pull the dipstick out again. The fluid level should be in the HOT range **(see illustration)**. If the level is at the low side of the range, add the specified automatic transmission fluid through the dipstick tube with a funnel.
7 Add the fluid a little at a time and keep checking the level until it's correct.
8 The condition of the fluid should also be checked along with the level. If the fluid at the end of the dipstick is black or a dark reddish-brown color, or if it smells burned, the fluid should be changed (see Section 31). If you're in doubt about the condition of the fluid, purchase some new fluid and compare the two for color and odor.

10 Battery check and maintenance

Refer to illustrations 10.1 and 10.6

Warning: *Certain precautions must be followed when checking and servicing the battery. Hydrogen gas, which is highly flammable, is always present in the battery cells, so keep lighted tobacco and all other open flames and sparks away from the battery. The electrolyte inside the battery is actually dilute sulfuric acid, which will cause injury if splashed on your skin or in your eyes. It will also ruin clothes and painted surfaces. When removing the battery cables, always detach the negative cable first and hook it up last!*

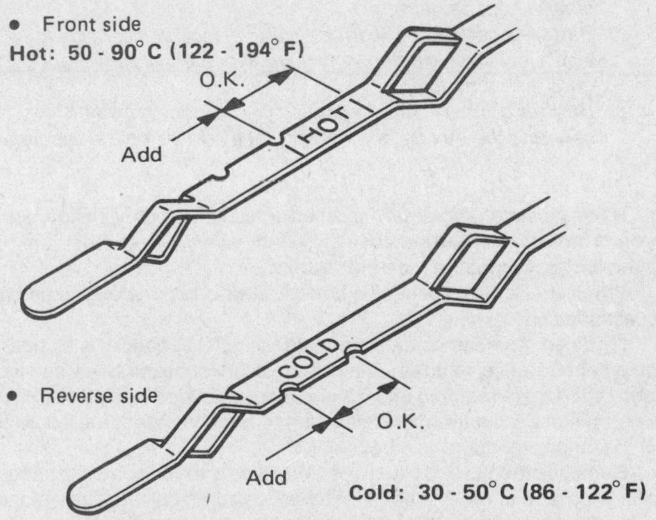

9.6 **Keep the fluid at the proper level – overfilling may blow out the fluid and/or damage the transaxle**

10.1 Tools and materials required for battery maintenance

1 ***Face shield/safety goggles*** – *When removing corrosion with a brush, the acidic particles can easily fly up into your eyes*
2 ***Baking soda*** – *A solution of baking soda and water can be used to neutralize corrosion*
3 ***Petroleum jelly*** – *A layer of this on the battery posts will help prevent corrosion*
4 ***Battery post/cable cleaner*** – *This wire brush cleaning tool will remove all traces of corrosion from the battery posts and cable clamps*
5 ***Treated felt washers*** – *Placing one of these on each post, directly under the cable clamps, will help prevent corrosion*
6 ***Puller*** – *Sometimes the cable clamps are very difficult to pull off the posts, even after the nut/bolt has been completely loosened. This tool pulls the clamp straight up and off the post without damage.*
7 ***Battery post/cable cleaner*** – *Here is another cleaning tool which is a slightly different version of number 4 above, but it does the same thing*
8 ***Rubber gloves*** – *Another safety item to consider when servicing the battery; remember that's acid inside the battery!*

1 Battery maintenance is an important procedure which will help ensure that you are not stranded because of a dead battery. Several tools are required for this procedure **(see illustration)**.
2 When checking/servicing the battery, always turn the engine and all accessories off.
3 A sealed (sometimes called maintenance-free) battery is standard equipment on these vehicles. The cell caps cannot be removed, no electrolyte checks are required and water cannot be added to the cells. However, if a standard aftermarket battery has been installed, the following maintenance procedure can be used.
4 Remove the caps and check the electrolyte level in each of the battery cells. It must be above the plates. There's usually a split-ring indicator in each cell to indicate the correct level. If the level is low, add distilled water only, then reinstall the cell caps. **Caution:** *Overfilling the cells may cause electrolyte to spill over during periods of heavy charging, causing corrosion and damage to nearby components.*

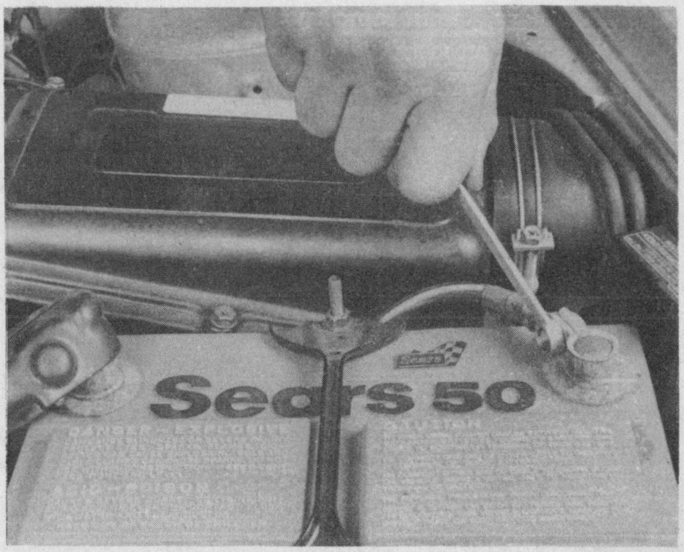

10.6 Make sure the battery terminal bolts are tight

5 The external condition of the battery should be checked periodically. Look for damage such as a cracked case.
6 Check the tightness of the battery cable bolts **(see illustration)** to ensure good electrical connections. Inspect the entire length of each cable, looking for cracked or abraded insulation and frayed conductors.
7 If corrosion (visible as white, fluffy deposits) is evident, remove the cables from the terminals, clean them with a battery brush and reinstall them. Corrosion can be kept to a minimum by applying a layer of petroleum jelly or grease to the bolt threads.
8 Make sure the battery carrier is in good condition and the hold-down clamp is tight. If the battery is removed (see Chapter 5 for the removal and installation procedure), make sure that no parts remain in the bottom of the carrier when it's reinstalled. When reinstalling the hold-down clamp, don't overtighten the bolt.
9 Corrosion on the carrier, battery case and surrounding areas can be removed with a solution of water and baking soda. Apply the mixture with a small brush, let it work, then rinse it off with plenty of clean water.
10 Any metal parts of the vehicle damaged by corrosion should be coated with a zinc-based primer, then painted.
11 Additional information on the battery, charging and jump starting can be found in the front of this manual and in Chapter 5.

11 Cooling system check

Refer to illustration 11.4

1 Many major engine failures can be attributed to a faulty cooling system. If the vehicle is equipped with an automatic transmission, the cooling system also cools the transmission fluid and thus plays an important role in prolonging transmission life.
2 The cooling system should be checked with the engine cold. Do this before the vehicle is driven for the day or after it has been shut off for at least three hours.
3 Remove the radiator cap by turning it to the left until it reaches a stop. If you hear a hissing sound (indicating there is still pressure in the system), wait until this stops. Now press down on the cap with the palm of your hand and continue turning to the left until the cap can be removed. Thoroughly clean the cap, inside and out, with clean water. Also clean the filler neck on the radiator. All traces of corrosion should be removed. The coolant inside the radiator should be relatively transparent. If it is rust colored, the system should be drained and refilled (see Section 30). If the coolant level is not up to the top, add additional antifreeze/coolant mixture (see Section 4).

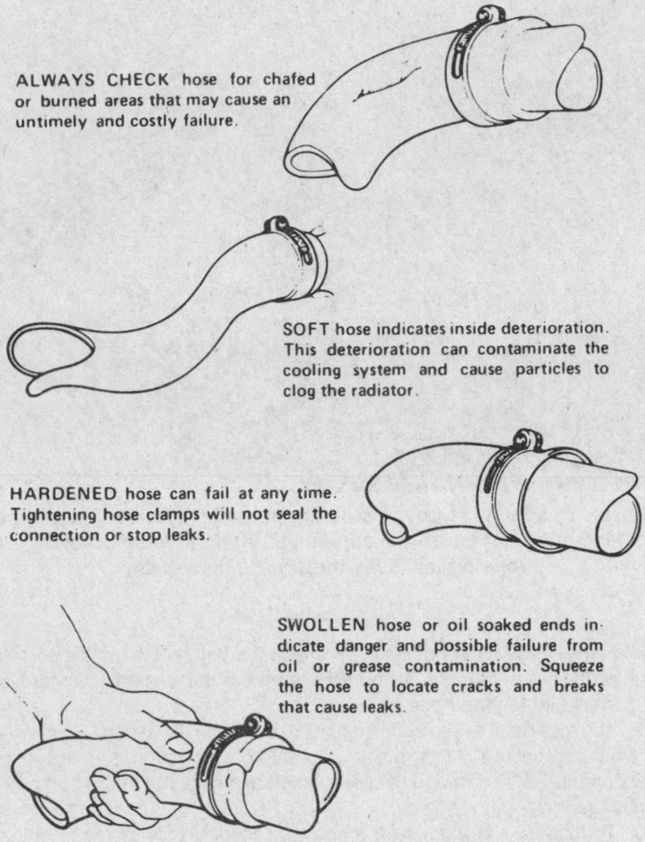
ALWAYS CHECK hose for chafed or burned areas that may cause an untimely and costly failure.
SOFT hose indicates inside deterioration. This deterioration can contaminate the cooling system and cause particles to clog the radiator.
HARDENED hose can fail at any time. Tightening hose clamps will not seal the connection or stop leaks.
SWOLLEN hose or oil soaked ends indicate danger and possible failure from oil or grease contamination. Squeeze the hose to locate cracks and breaks that cause leaks.

11.4 Hoses, like drivebelts, have a habit of failing at the worst possible time – to prevent the inconvenience of a blown radiator or heater hose, inspect them carefully as shown here

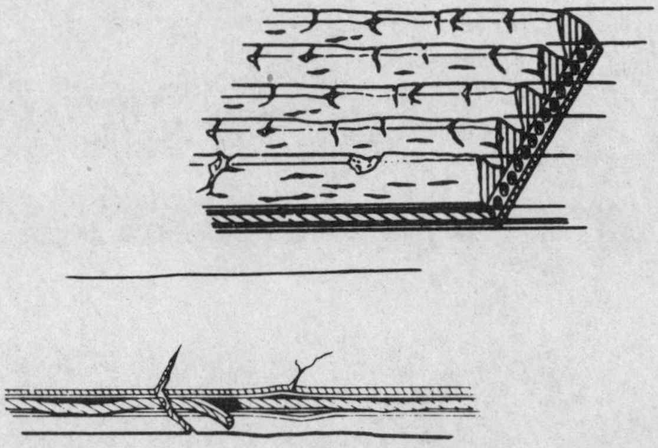

12.3 Check the V-ribbed belt for signs of wear like these – if it looks worn, replace it

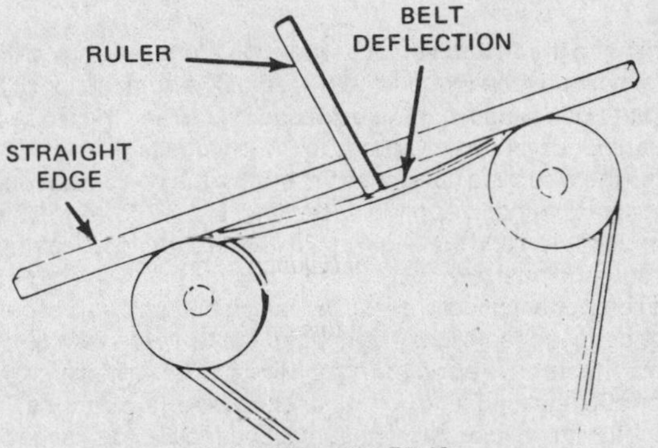
RULER
BELT DEFLECTION
STRAIGHT EDGE
MAKE SURE RULER IS PERPENDICULAR TO STRAIGHT EDGE

12.4 Drivebelt tension can be checked with a straightedge and ruler

4 Carefully check the large upper and lower radiator hoses along with the smaller diameter heater hoses which run from the engine to the firewall. On some models the heater return hose runs directly to the radiator. Inspect each hose along its entire length, replacing any hose which is cracked, swollen or shows signs of deterioration. Cracks may become more apparent if the hose is squeezed **(see illustration)**. Regardless of condition, it's a good idea to replace hoses with new ones every two years.
5 Make sure that all hose connections are tight. A leak in the cooling system will usually show up as white or rust colored deposits on the areas adjoining the leak. If wire-type clamps are used at the ends of the hoses, it may be a good idea to replace them with more secure screw-type clamps.
6 Use compressed air or a soft brush to remove bugs, leaves, etc. from the front of the radiator or air conditioning condenser. Be careful not to damage the delicate cooling fins or cut yourself on them.
7 Every other inspection, or at the first indication of cooling system problems, have the cap and system pressure tested. If you don't have a pressure tester, most gas stations and repair shops will do this for a minimal charge.

12 Drivebelt check, adjustment and replacement

Refer to illustrations 12.3, 12.4, 12.5, 12.7a, 12.7b and 12.7c

1 The drivebelts are located at the front of the engine and play an important role in the overall operation of the engine and accessories. Due to their function and material makeup, the belts are prone to failure after a period of time and should be inspected and adjusted periodically to prevent major engine damage.
2 The number of belts used on a particular vehicle depends on the accessories installed. Drivebelts are used to turn the alternator, power steering pump, water pump and air conditioning compressor. Depending on the pulley arrangement, more than one of the components may be driven by a single belt.
3 With the engine off, locate the drivebelts at the front of the engine. Using your fingers (and a flashlight, if necessary), move along the belts checking for cracks and separation of the belt plies. Also check for fraying and glazing, which gives the belt a shiny appearance **(see illustration)**. Both sides of each belt should be inspected, which means you'll have to twist each belt to check the underside. Check the pulleys for nicks, cracks, distortion and corrosion.
4 The tension of each belt is checked by pushing on it at a distance halfway between the pulleys. Push firmly with your thumb and see how much the belt moves (deflects) **(see illustration)**. A rule of thumb is that if the distance from pulley center-to-pulley center is between 7 and 11 inches, the belt should deflect 1/4-inch. If the belt travels between pulleys spaced 12-to-16 inches apart, the belt should deflect 1/2-inch.
5 If adjustment is needed, either to make the belt tighter or looser, it's

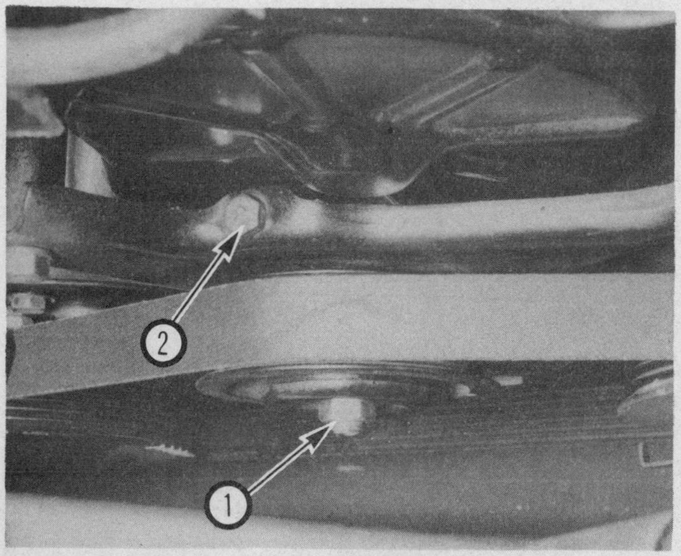

12.5 To adjust the ribbed belt, loosen the pulley locking nut (1) and turn the adjusting bolt (2) to raise or lower the idler pulley

12.7a To adjust the power steering pump belt, loosen the pulley locking nut (1) and turn the adjusting bolt (2) to raise or lower the idler pulley (1985 through 1988 models)

done by moving the belt-driven accessory on the bracket **(see illustration)**. the main drivebelt (ribbed belt) is adjusted from the top of the engine compartment. Remove the injector cooling fan and the cruise control servo (if equipped) for easier access to the drivebelts.

6 Loosen the wheel lug nuts, raise the front of the vehicle and support it securely on jackstands. Apply the parking brake. Remove the front wheels, fender apron and the engine splash shield for access to the drivebelts and components.

7 Each component usually has an adjusting bolt and a pivot bolt. Both bolts must be loosened slightly to enable you to move the component. Some components have an adjusting bolt that can be turned to change the belt tension after the mounting bolt is loosened **(see illustrations)**. Others are equipped with an idler pulley that must be moved to change the belt tension.

8 After the two bolts have been loosened, move the component away from the engine to tighten the belt or toward the engine to loosen the belt. Hold the accessory in position and check the belt tension. If it's correct, tighten the two bolts until just snug, then recheck the tension. If the tension is correct, tighten the bolts.

9 You may have to use some sort of pry bar to move the accessory while the belt is adjusted. If this must be done to gain the proper leverage, be very careful not to damage the component being moved or the part being pried against.

10 To replace a belt, follow the above procedures for drivebelt adjustment but slip the belt off the pulleys and remove it. Since belts tend to wear out more or less at the same time, it's a good idea to replace all of them at the same time. Mark each belt and the corresponding pulley grooves so the replacement belts can be installed properly.

11 Take the old belts with you when purchasing new ones in order to make a direct comparison for length, width and design.

12 Adjust the belts as described earlier in this Section.

12.7b Location of the alternator pivot bolt (arrow) (1985 through 1988 models)

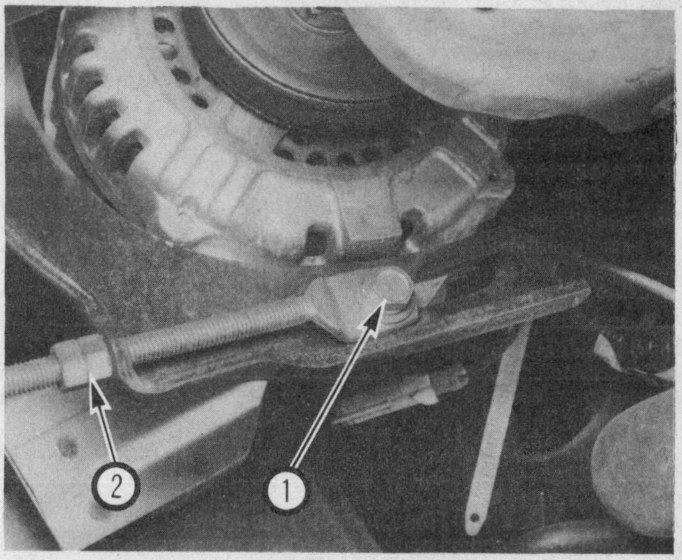

12.7c To adjust the alternator belt, loosen the adjusting bolt (1) and tighten the adjuster nuts (2) until the desired tension is obtained (1985 through 1988 models)

13.6a Inspect the brake pad thickness through the opening in the caliper (arrow)

13.6b On rear calipers, remove the caliper assembly to check brake pad thickness

13.8 Check all brake hoses and fittings for cracks, splits and leakage

13 Brake check

Refer to illustrations 13.6a, 13.6b and 13.8

Note: *For detailed photographs of the brake system, refer to Chapter 9.*

Warning: *Brake system dust may contain asbestos, which is hazardous to your health. DO NOT blow it out with compressed air and DO NOT inhale it. DO NOT use gasoline or solvents to remove the dust. Use brake system cleaner only.*

1 In addition to the specified intervals, the brakes should be inspected every time the wheels are removed or whenever a defect is suspected.

2 To check the brakes, raise the vehicle and place it securely on jackstands. Remove the wheels (see *Jacking and towing* at the front of the manual, if necessary).

Disc brakes

3 Disc brakes are used on the front wheels on all models and on the rear wheels of most models covered by this manual. Extensive disc damage can occur if the pads are not replaced when needed.

4 These vehicles are equipped with a wear sensor attached to the inner pad. This is a small, bent piece of metal which is visible from the inner side of the brake caliper. When the pad wears to the specified limit, the metal sensor rubs against the disc and makes a squealing sound.

5 The disc brake calipers, which contain the pads, are visible with the wheels removed. There is an outer pad and an inner pad in each caliper. All pads should be inspected.

6 Each front caliper has a "window" to inspect the pads. Check the thickness of the pad lining by looking into the caliper at each end and down through the inspection window at the top of the housing **(see illustration)**. If the wear sensor is very close to the disc or the pad material has worn to about 1/8-inch or less, the pads should be replaced. To check the rear brake pads, unbolt the caliper and remove it (Chapter 9) **(see illustration)**.

7 If you're unsure about the exact thickness of the remaining lining material, remove the pads for further inspection or replacement (refer to Chapter 9).

8 Before installing the wheels, check for leakage and/or damage (cracks, splitting, etc.) around the brake hose connections **(see illustration)**. Replace the hose or fittings as necessary, referring to Chapter 9.

9 Check the condition of the disc. Look for score marks, deep scratches and burned spots. If these conditions exist, the disc should be removed for servicing.

Drum brakes

10 Remove the brake drum/hub assembly (see Chapter 10).

11 With the drum removed, do not touch any brake dust (see the Warning at the beginning of this Section).

12 Note the thickness of the lining material on both the front and rear brake shoes. If the material has worn away to within 1/16-inch of the recessed rivets or metal backing, the shoes should be replaced. The shoes should also be replaced if they're cracked, glazed (shiny surface) or contaminated with brake fluid.

13 Make sure that all the brake assembly springs are connected and in good condition.

14 Check the brake components for any signs of fluid leakage. With your finger, carefully pry back the rubber cups on the wheel cylinders located at the top of the brake shoes. Any leakage is an indication that the wheel cylinders should be overhauled immediately (see Chapter 9). Also check brake hoses and connections for signs of leakage.

15 Clean the inside of the drum with brake cleaner. Again, be careful not to breath the asbestos dust.

16.2 Remove the screws and detach the cover from the housing . . .

16.3 . . . then carefully lift the filter out of the housing

16 Check the inside of the drum for cracks, score marks, deep scratches and hard spots, which will appear as small discolorations. If these imperfections cannot be removed with emery cloth or sandpaper, the drum must be taken to a machine shop equipped to resurface the drums.
17 If after the inspection process all parts are in good working condition, reinstall the brake drum.
18 Install the wheels and lower the vehicle.

Parking brake

19 The parking brake operates from a hand lever and locks the rear brake system. The easiest, and perhaps most obvious method of periodically checking the operation of the parking brake assembly is to park the vehicle on a steep hill with the parking brake set and the transmission in Neutral. If the parking brake cannot prevent the vehicle from rolling, it's in need of adjustment (see Chapter 9).

14 Seatbelt check

1 Check the seatbelts, buckles, latch plates and guide loops for any obvious damage or signs of wear.
2 Make sure the seatbelt reminder light comes on when the key is turned on.
3 The seatbelts are designed to lock up during a sudden stop or impact, yet allow free movement during normal driving. The retractors should hold the belt against your chest while driving and rewind the belt when the buckle is unlatched.
4 If any of the above checks reveal problems with the seatbelt system, replace parts as necessary.

15 Chassis and body lubrication and maintenance

Note: *The steering and suspension connections are "sealed-for-life" and require no lubrication. However, they should still be periodically checked for leaks, cracks and other obvious signs of wear.*
1 For easier access to the underside of the vehicle, raise it and place jackstands under the frame. Make sure the vehicle is securely supported by the jackstands.
2 From underneath the car, inspect the rear axle and suspension components for looseness, wear or damage.
3 Rock each front wheel sideways and listen for rattles indicating loose components.
4 Tighten all steering and suspension nuts and bolts.
5 Check the struts (shock absorbers) for oil leakage or damage. If any damage is apparent, replace the struts.
6 Check the balljoints for grease leakage or other damage.
7 Check the rear wheels for looseness by shaking them from side to side. Adjust the wheel bearing preload if necessary (Chapter 10).
8 While you are under the vehicle, clean and lubricate the parking brake cable, along with the cable guides and levers. Smear multi-purpose grease onto the cable and its guides with your fingers.
9 Lubricate the transmission shift linkage rods and swivels with a few drops of engine oil.
10 Lower the vehicle to lubricate the body components.
11 Open the hood and lubricate the hood latch mechanism with a few drops of oil. The hood has an inside release, so have an assistant pull the release knob from inside the vehicle as you lubricate the cable at the latch.
12 Lubricate all the hinges – door, hood, hatch – with a few drops of engine oil to keep them in proper working order.
13 The key lock cylinders can be lubricated with spray-on graphite, which is available at auto parts stores.

16 Air filter replacement

Refer to illustrations 16.2 and 16.3
1 The air filter is located inside the air cleaner housing on the left-hand side of the engine compartment.
2 To remove the filter, unscrew the four retaining screws at the top of the housing and lift off the cover **(see illustration)**.
3 Carefully lift the air filter out of the housing **(see illustration)**.
4 The paper type air filter cannot be washed. If it is slightly dirty, you can blow it out with compressed air. If that doesn't restore it, replace it with a new unit.
5 Reverse the removal procedure for installation.

17 Underhood hose check and replacement

General

1 **Caution:** *Replacement of air conditioning hoses must be left to a dealer service department or air conditioning shop that has the equipment to depressurize the system safely. Never remove air conditioning components or hoses until the system has been depressurized.*
2 High temperatures in the engine compartment can cause the deterioration of the rubber and plastic hoses used for engine, accessory and emission systems operation. Periodic inspection should be made for cracks, loose clamps, material hardening and leaks. Information specific to the cooling system hoses can be found in Section 11.
3 Some, but not all, hoses are secured to the fittings with clamps. Where clamps are used, check to be sure they haven't lost their tension, allowing the hose to leak. If clamps aren't used, make sure the hose has

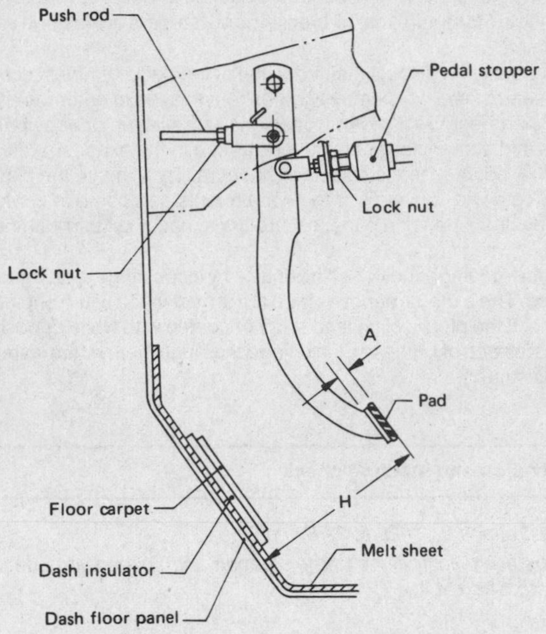

18.2 Clutch pedal adjustment details
H Pedal height A Freeplay

not expanded and/or hardened where it slips over the fitting, allowing it to leak.

Vacuum hoses

4 It's quite common for vacuum hoses, especially those in the emissions system, to be color coded or identified by colored stripes molded into them. Various systems require hoses with different wall thicknesses, collapse resistance and temperature resistance. When replacing hoses, be sure the new ones are made of the same material.

5 Often the only effective way to check a hose is to remove it completely from the vehicle. If more than one hose is removed, be sure to label the hoses and fittings to ensure correct installation.

6 When checking vacuum hoses, be sure to include any plastic T-fittings in the check. Inspect the fittings for cracks and the hose where it fits over the fitting for distortion, which could cause leakage.

7 A small piece of vacuum hose (1/4-inch inside diameter) can be used as a stethoscope to detect vacuum leaks. Hold one end of the hose to your ear and probe around vacuum hoses and fittings, listening for the "hissing" sound characteristic of a vacuum leak. **Warning:** *When probing with the vacuum hose stethoscope, be very careful not to come into contact with moving engine components such as the drivebelt, cooling fan, etc.*

Fuel hose

Warning: *There are certain precautions which must be taken when inspecting or servicing fuel system components. Work in a well ventilated area and do not allow open flames (cigarettes, appliance pilot lights, etc.) or bare light bulbs near the work area. Don't work in a garage if a natural gas type appliance such as a water heater or clothes dryer is present. Mop up any spills immediately and do not store fuel soaked rags where they could ignite. The fuel system is under pressure, so if any fuel lines are to be disconnected, the pressure in the system must be relieved first (see Chapter 4 for more information).*

8 Check all rubber fuel lines for deterioration and chafing. Check especially for cracks in areas where the hose bends and just before fittings, such as where a hose attaches to the fuel filter.

9 High quality fuel line, usually identified by the word Fluroelastomer printed on the hose, should be used for fuel line replacement. Never, under any circumstances, use unreinforced vacuum line, clear plastic tubing or water hose for fuel lines.

10 Spring-type clamps are commonly used on fuel lines. These clamps often lose their tension over a period of time, and can be "sprung" during removal. Replace all spring-type clamps with screw clamps whenever a hose is replaced.

Metal lines

11 Sections of metal line are often used for fuel line between the fuel pump and fuel injection unit. Check carefully to be sure the line has not been bent or crimped and that cracks have not started in the line.

12 If a section of metal fuel line must be replaced, only seamless steel tubing should be used, since copper and aluminum tubing don't have the strength necessary to withstand normal engine vibration.

13 Check the metal brake lines where they enter the master cylinder and brake proportioning unit (if used) for cracks in the lines or loose fittings. Any sign of brake fluid leakage calls for an immediate thorough inspection of the brake system.

18 Clutch pedal height and freeplay check and adjustment

Refer to illustration 18.2

1 On vehicles with a manual transaxle, the clutch pedal height and freeplay must be correctly adjusted.

2 The height of the clutch pedal is the distance the pedal sits off the floor **(see illustration)**. The distance should be as listed in this Chapter's Specifications. If the pedal height isn't within the specified range, loosen the locknut on the pedal stopper or switch located to the rear of the clutch pedal and turn the stopper or switch in or out until the pedal height is correct. Retighten the locknut.

3 The freeplay is the pedal slack, or the distance the pedal can be depressed before it begins to have any effect on the clutch (dimension "A" in illustration 18.2). The distance should be as listed in this Chapter's Specifications. If it isn't, loosen the locknut on the clutch master cylinder pushrod, turn the pushrod until the freeplay is correct, then retighten the locknut.

19 Brake pedal height adjustment

Refer to illustrations 19.1 and 19.2

1 Remove the carpet directly below the brake pedal and measure the distance (H) from the floor to the top of the brake pad **(see illustration)**. The free height should be as listed in this Chapter's Specifications.

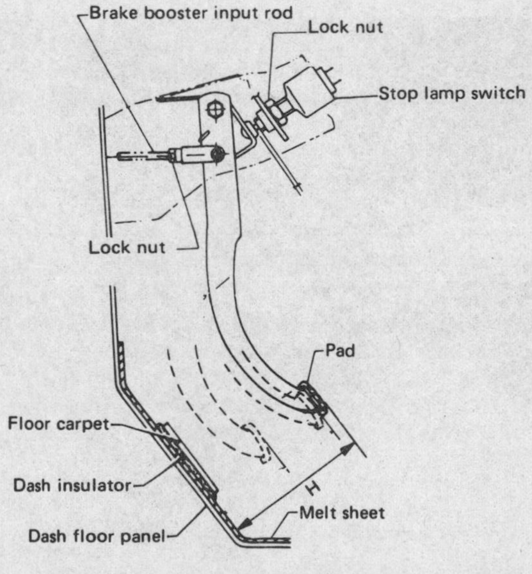

19.1 Adjust the brake pedal free height (H) on the brake booster input rod

1

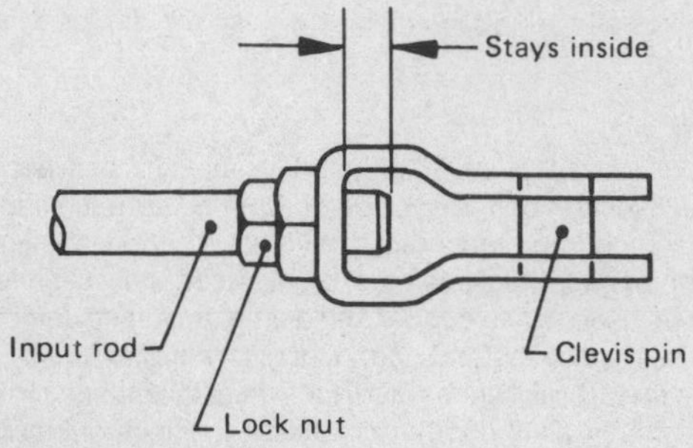

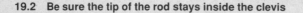

19.2 Be sure the tip of the rod stays inside the clevis

2 Adjust the pedal free height on the brake booster input rod. Be sure the tip of the rod stays inside the clevis **(see illustration)**. Tighten the lock nut securely.

20 Driveaxle boot check

Refer to illustration 20.2

1 The driveaxle boots are very important because they prevent dirt, water and foreign material from entering and damaging the constant velocity (CV) joints.

2 Inspect the boots for tears and cracks as well as loose clamps **(see illustration)**. If there is any evidence of cracks or leaking lubricant, they must be replaced as described in Chapter 8.

21 Exhaust system check

1 With the engine cold (at least three hours after the vehicle has been driven), check the complete exhaust system from the manifold to the tailpipe. If a hoist isn't available, raise the vehicle and support it securely on jackstands.

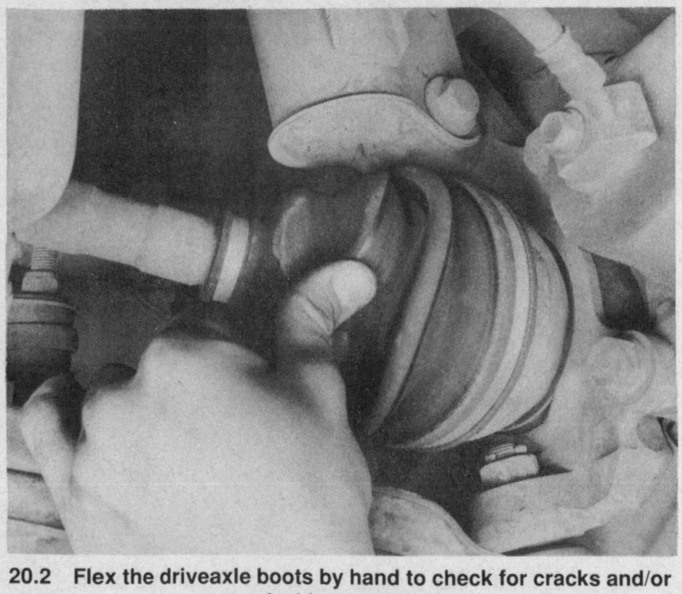

20.2 Flex the driveaxle boots by hand to check for cracks and/or leaking grease

2 Check the pipes and connections for evidence of leaks, severe corrosion or damage. Make sure that all brackets and hangers are in good condition and tight.

3 At the same time, inspect the underside of the body for holes, corrosion, open seams, etc. which may allow exhaust gases to enter the passenger compartment. Seal all body openings with silicone or body putty.

4 Rattles and other noises can often be traced to the exhaust system, especially the mounts, heat shields and hangers. Try to move the pipes, muffler and catalytic converter. If the components can come in contact with the body or suspension parts, secure the exhaust system with new mounts.

5 Check the running condition of the engine by inspecting inside the end of the tailpipe. The exhaust deposits here are an indication of the engine's state-of-tune. If the pipe is black and sooty or coated with white deposits, the engine is in need of a tune-up, including a thorough fuel system inspection and adjustment.

22 Suspension and steering check

Refer to illustrations 22.1, 22.6, 22.8 and 22.9

Note: *For detailed illustrations of the steering and suspension components, refer to Chapter 10.*

With the wheels on the ground

1 With the vehicle stopped and the front wheels pointed straight ahead, rock the steering wheel gently back and forth. If freeplay **(see illustration)** is greater than 1-3/8 inch (measured at the steering wheel), a front wheel bearing, main shaft yoke, intermediate shaft yoke, lower arm balljoint or steering system joint is worn or the steering gear is out of adjustment or broken. Refer to Chapter 10 for the appropriate repair procedure.

2 Other symptoms, such as excessive vehicle body movement over rough roads, swaying (leaning) around corners and binding as the steering wheel is turned, may indicate faulty steering and/or suspension components.

3 Check the shock absorbers by pushing down and releasing the vehicle several times at each corner. If the vehicle does not come back to a level position within one or two bounces, the shocks/struts are worn and must be replaced. When bouncing the vehicle up and down, listen for squeaks and noises from the suspension components. Additional information on suspension components can be found in Chapter 10.

4 Measure the front and rear chassis clearance (the height of the vehicle above the ground) by measuring the distance from the ground to the center of the control arm bolts. Also note whether the vehicle looks canted to one side or corner. If the clearance of the vehicle is not as specified or if it

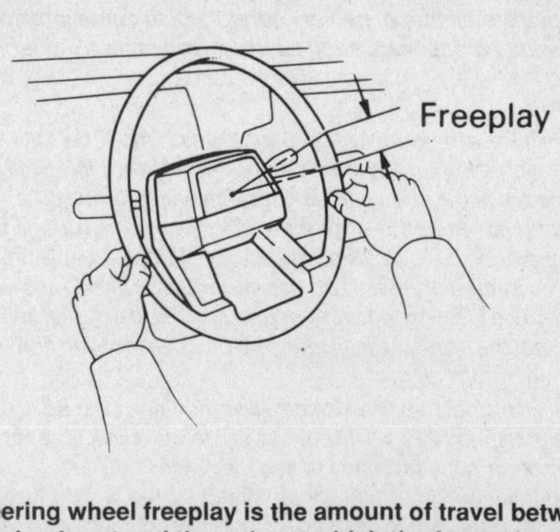

22.1 Steering wheel freeplay is the amount of travel between an initial steering input and the point at which the front wheels begin to turn (indicated by a slight resistance)

is canted to one side or corner, try to level it by rocking it down. If this doesn't work, look for bad springs or worn or loose suspension parts.

Under the vehicle

5 Raise the vehicle with a floor jack and support it securely on jackstands. See *Jacking and towing* at the front of this book for the proper jacking points.

6 Check the tires for irregular wear patterns (see Section 6) and proper inflation. If you have a dial gauge and base, check the lateral runout of the wheels **(see illustration)**. If lateral runout is greater than 0.012-inch (aluminum wheels)/0.031-inch (steel wheels), the wheels are bent or the wheel bearings are loose or worn. See Section 6 in this chapter for information regarding tire wear and Chapter 10 for the wheel bearing replacement procedures.

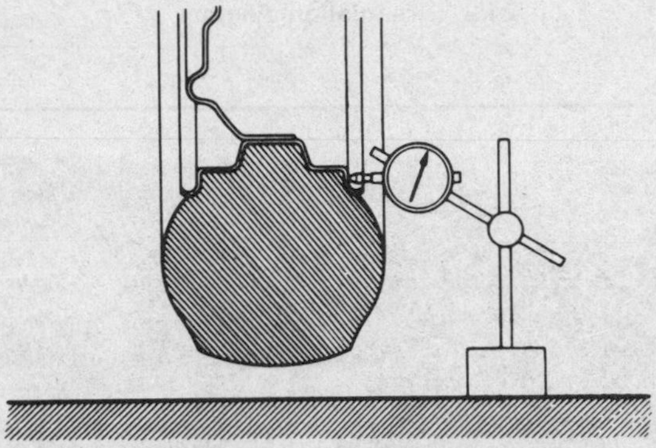

22.6 If you have a dial gauge, you can easily pinpoint lateral wheel runout – set it up like this with the pointer against the bead flange of the wheel, then slowly spin the wheel

7 Inspect the universal joint between the steering shaft and the steering gear housing. Check the steering gear housing for grease leakage or oozing. Make sure that the dust seals and boots are not damaged and that the boot clamps are not loose. Check the steering linkage for looseness or damage. Check the tie-rod ends for excessive play. Look for loose bolts, broken or disconnected parts and deteriorated rubber bushings on all suspension and steering components. While an assistant turns the steering wheel from side to side, check the steering components for free movement, chafing and binding. If the steering components do not seem to be reacting with the movement of the steering wheel, try to determine where the slack is located

8 Check the balljoints for wear by prying the control arm up and down. Make sure the front wheels are in a straight forward position and block the wheel with chocks. Move each control arm up and down with a pry bar **(see illustration)** to ensure that its balljoint has no play. If either balljoint has play, replace it. Refer to Chapter 10 for the balljoint replacement procedure.

9 Inspect the balljoint boots for damage and leaking grease **(see illustration)**. Replace the balljoints with new ones if they are damaged (see Chapter 10).

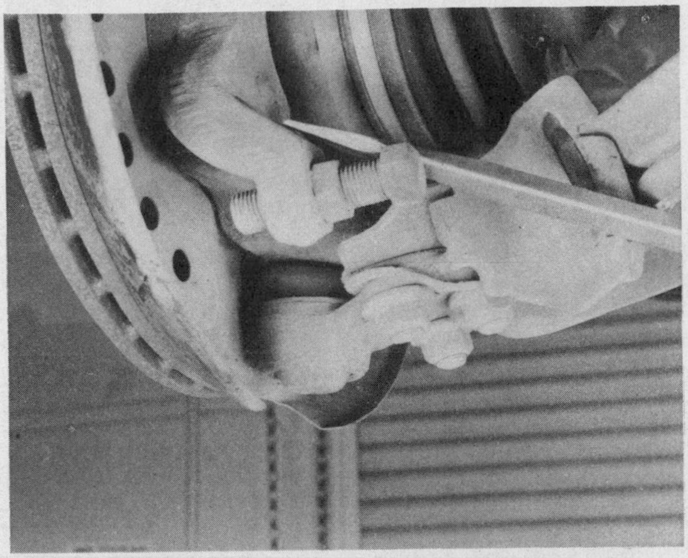

22.8 Use a pry bar to force the control arm up and down to check for excessive play in the balljoint

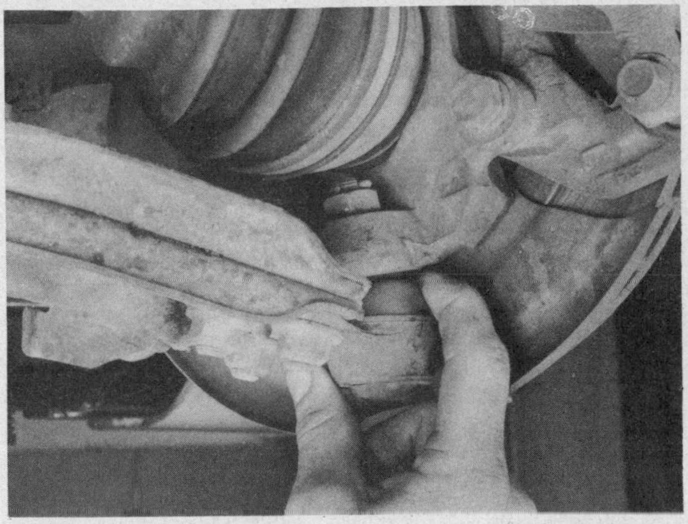

22.9 Inspect the balljoint boots for cracks, leaks or damage

23 Manual transaxle lubricant level check

Refer to illustrations 23.1a and 23.1b

1 The manual transaxle does not have a dipstick. To check the lubricant level, raise the vehicle and support it securely on jackstands. On the lower rear side of the transaxle housing, you will see the speedometer cable **(see illustration)**. Remove the hold-down bolt and pull out the speedometer pinion assembly. Use the pinion gear as a dipstick. If the lubricant level

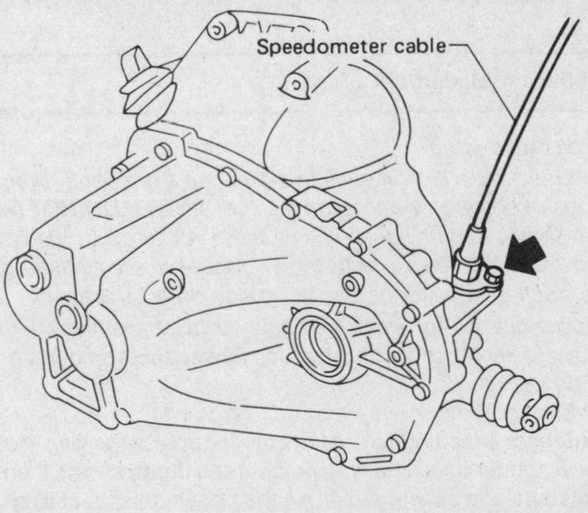

23.1a Check the lubricant level by removing the speedometer drive pinion at the transaxle case

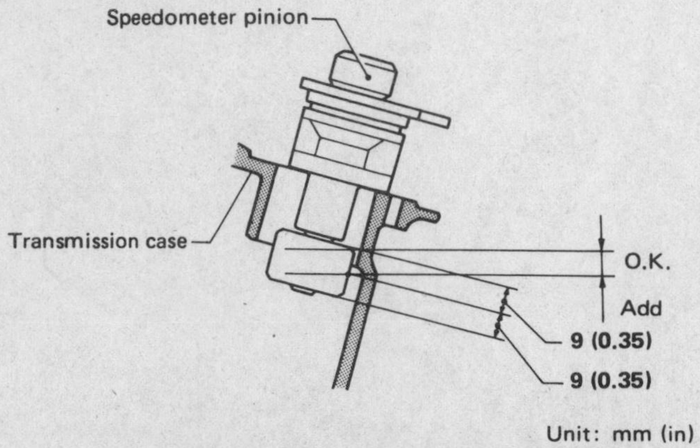

23.1b Use the drive pinion gear as a dipstick – a film of oil should be visible in the range indicated – if not, add the recommended lubricant until it is

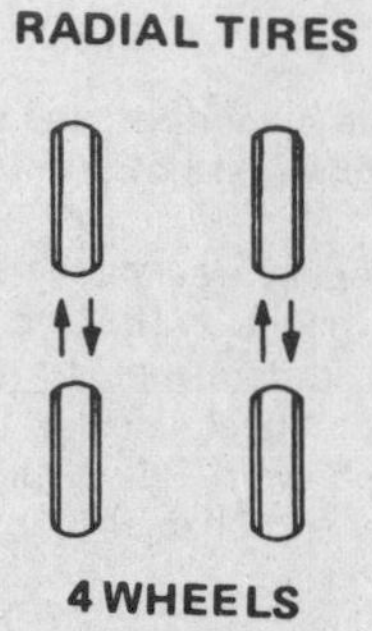

24.2 Tire rotation diagram

is correct, a film of oil should be apparent halfway up the gear **(see illustration)**.

2 If the transaxle needs more lubricant, use a funnel and add a little at a time until the level is half way up the gear.

3 Install the speedometer pinion and clamp, tightening the bolt securely.

24 Tire rotation

Refer to illustration 24.2

1 The tires should be rotated at the specified intervals and whenever uneven wear is noticed.

2 Refer to the accompanying illustration for the preferred tire rotation pattern.

3 Refer to the information in *Jacking and towing* at the front of this manual for the proper procedures to follow when raising the vehicle and changing a tire. If the brakes are to be checked, don't apply the parking brake as stated. Make sure the tires are blocked to prevent the vehicle from rolling as it's raised.

4 Preferably, the entire vehicle should be raised at the same time. This can be done on a hoist or by jacking up each corner and then lowering the vehicle onto jackstands placed under the frame rails. Always use four jackstands and make sure the vehicle is safely supported.

5 After rotation, check and adjust the tire pressures as necessary and be sure to check the lug nut tightness.

6 For additional information on the wheels and tires, refer to Chapter 10.

25 Fuel filter replacement

Refer to illustration 25.3

Warning: *Gasoline is extremely flammable, so extra safety precautions must be observed when working on the fuel system. DO NOT smoke or allow open flames or bare light bulbs near the vehicle. Also, don't perform fuel system maintenance procedures in a garage where a natural gas type appliance, such as a water heater or clothes dryer, is present.*

1 This job should be done with the engine cold (after sitting at least three hours). Place a metal container, rags or newspapers under the filter to catch spilled fuel.

2 Depressurize the fuel system (see Chapter 4).

3 The fuel filter is located on the firewall. To replace the filter, loosen the clamp screw and remove it from its holder **(see illustration)**, then loosen the hose clamps and slide them down the hoses, past the fittings on the filter.

4 Note how the filter is installed (which end is facing up) so the new filter doesn't get installed backwards (most fuel filters have an arrow indicating

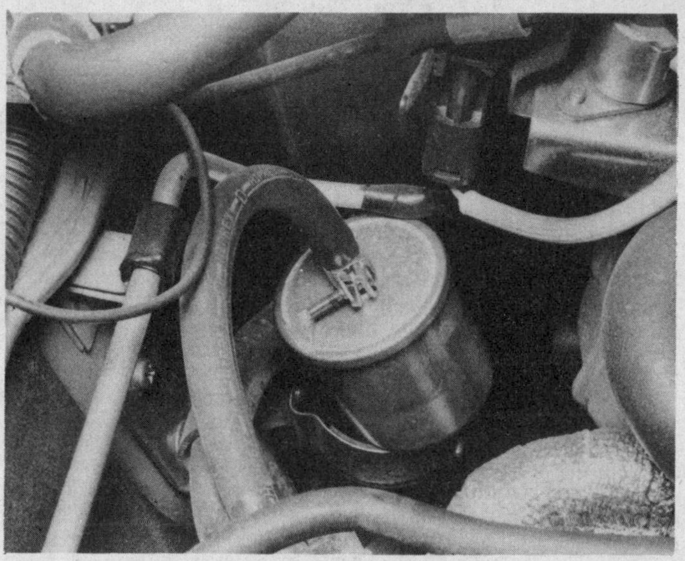

25.3 Loosen the clamp screw and remove the fuel filter from the holder for easy access to the hose clamps

the direction of fuel flow). Carefully twist and pull on the hoses to separate them from the filter. If the hoses are in bad shape, now would be a good time to replace them with new ones.

5 Connect the hoses to the new filter and tighten the clamps securely.

6 Install the new filter in the clamp and tighten the screw.

7 Start the engine and check carefully for leaks at the filter hose connections.

26 Spark plug wire, distributor cap and rotor check and replacement

Refer to illustrations 26.11, 26.12 and 26.13

1 The spark plug wires should be checked whenever new spark plugs are installed.

2 Begin this procedure by making a visual check of the spark plug wires while the engine is running. In a darkened garage (make sure there is ventilation) start the engine and observe each plug wire. Be careful not to come into contact with any moving engine parts. If there is a break in the wire, you will see arcing or a small spark at the damaged area. If arcing is noticed, make a note to obtain new wires, then allow the engine to cool and check the distributor cap and rotor.

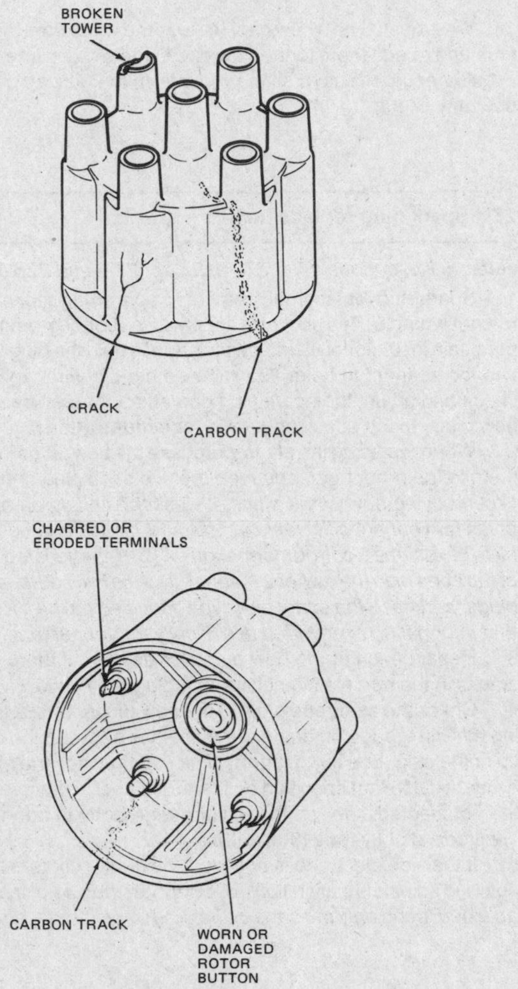

26.11 Shown here are some of the common defects to look for when inspecting the distributor cap (if in doubt about its condition, install a new one)

3 The spark plug wires should be inspected one at a time to prevent mixing up the order, which is essential for proper engine operation. Each original plug wire should be numbered to help identify its location. If the number is illegible, a piece of tape can be marked with the correct number and wrapped around the plug wire.

4 Disconnect the plug wire from the spark plug. A removal tool can be used for this purpose or you can grasp the rubber boot, twist the boot half a turn and pull the boot free **(see illustration 27.6)**. Do not pull on the wire itself.

5 Check inside the boot for corrosion, which will look like a white crusty powder.

6 Push the wire and boot back onto the end of the spark plug. It should fit tightly onto the end of the plug. If it doesn't, remove the wire and use pliers to carefully crimp the metal connector inside the wire boot until the fit is snug.

7 Using a clean rag, wipe the entire length of the wire to remove built-up dirt and grease. Once the wire is clean, check for burns, cracks and other damage. Do not bend the wire sharply, because the conductor within the wire might break.

8 Disconnect the wire from the distributor. Again, pull only on the rubber boot. Check for corrosion and a tight fit. Press the wire back into the distributor.

9 Inspect the remaining spark plug wires, making sure that each one is securely fastened at the distributor and spark plug when the check is complete.

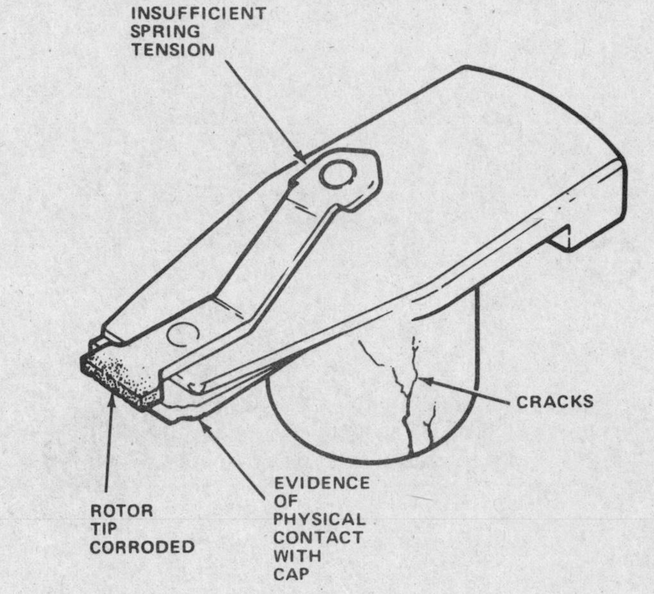

26.12 The ingnition rotor should be checked for wear and corrosion as indicated here (if in doubt about its condition, buy a new one)

10 If new spark plug wires are required, purchase a set for your specific engine model. Pre-cut wire sets with the boots already installed are available. Remove and replace the wires one at a time to avoid mix-ups in the firing order.

11 Detach the distributor cap by removing the two screws. Look inside it for cracks, carbon tracks and worn, burned or loose contacts **(see illustration)**.

12 Remove the small set screw, then pull the rotor off the distributor shaft and examine it for cracks and carbon tracks **(see illustration)**. Replace the cap and rotor if any damage or defects are noted.

13 It is common practice to install a new cap and rotor whenever new spark plug wires are installed, but if you wish to continue using the old cap, check the resistance between the spark plug wires and the cap first **(see illustration)**. If the indicated resistance is more than the specified value (for spark plug wires), replace the cap and/or wires.

26.13 Measure the resistance value of the distributor cap and the spark plug wires – if it is excessive, replace either the cap, the wires, or both

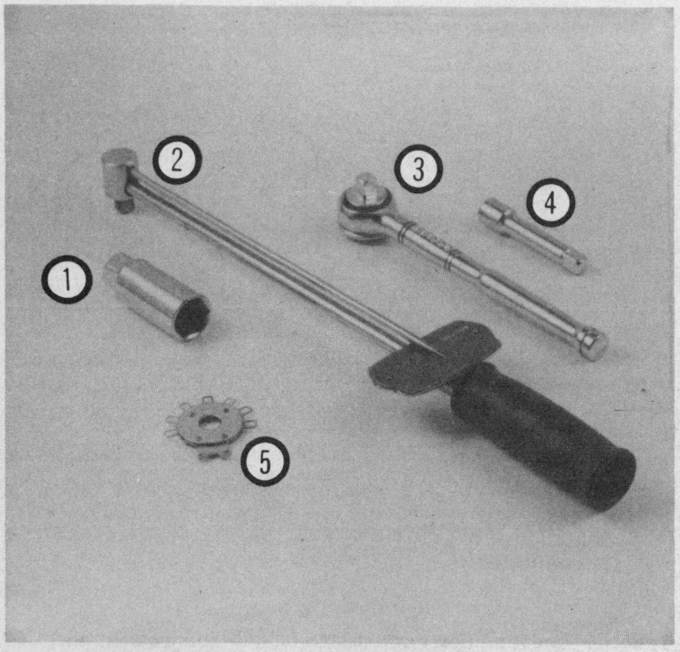

27.1 Tools required for changing spark plugs

1 ***Spark plug socket*** – *This will have special padding inside to protect the spark plug's porcelain insulator*
2 ***Torque wrench*** – *Although not mandatory, using this tool is the best way to ensure the plugs are tightened properly*
3 ***Ratchet*** – *Standard hand tool to fit the spark plug socket*
4 ***Extension*** – *Depending on model and accessories, you may need special extensions and universal joints to reach one or more of the plugs*
5 ***Spark plug gap gauge*** – *This gauge for checking the gap comes in a variety of styles. Make sure the gap for your engine is included.*

14 When installing a new cap, remove the wires from the old cap one at a time and attach them to the new cap in the exact same location – do not simultaneously remove all the wires from the old cap or firing order mix-ups may occur.

27 Spark plug replacement

Refer to illustrations 27.1, 27.4a, 27.4b, 27.6 and 27.10

1 Spark plug replacement requires a spark plug socket which fits onto a ratchet wrench. This socket is lined with a rubber grommet to protect the porcelain insulator of the spark plug and to hold the plug while you insert it into the spark plug hole. You will also need a wire-type feeler gauge to check and adjust the spark plug gap and a torque wrench to tighten the new plugs to the specified torque **(see illustration)**.

2 When replacing the plugs, purchase the new plugs in advance, adjust them to the proper gap and then replace each plug one at a time. **Note:** *When buying new spark plugs, it's essential that you obtain the correct plugs for your specific vehicle. This information can be found on the Vehicle Emissions Control Information (VECI) label located on the underside of the hood or in the owner's manual. If these two sources specify different plugs, purchase the spark plug type specified on the VECI label because that information is provided specifically for your engine.*

3 Inspect each of the new plugs for defects. If there are any signs of cracks in the porcelain insulator of a plug, don't use it.

4 Check the electrode gaps of the new plugs. Check the gap by inserting the wire gauge of the proper thickness between the electrodes at the tip of the plug **(see illustration)**. The gap between the electrodes should be identical to that specified on the VECI label. If the gap is incorrect, use the notched adjuster on the feeler gauge body to bend the curved side electrode slightly **(see illustration)**.

5 If the side electrode is not exactly over the center electrode, use the notched adjuster to align them. **Caution:** *If the gap of a new plug must be adjusted, bend only the base of the ground electrode; do not touch the tip.*

27.4a Spark plug manufacturers recommend using a wire-type gauge when checking the gap – if the wire does not slide between the electrodes with a slight drag, adjustment is required

27.4b To change the gap, bend the side electrode only, as indicated by the arrows, and be very careful not to crack or chip the porcelain insulator surrounding the center electrode

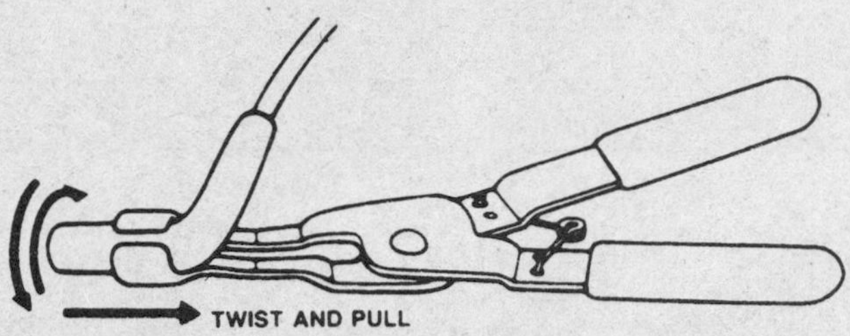

27.6 When removing the spark plug wires, pull only on the boot and use a twisting/pulling motion

Removal

6 To prevent the possibility of mixing up spark plug wires, work on one spark plug at a time. Remove the wire and boot from one spark plug. Grasp the boot – not the cable – as shown, give it a half twisting motion and pull it off **(see illustration)**.

7 If compressed air is available, blow any dirt or foreign material away from the spark plug area before proceeding (a common bicycle pump will also work).

8 Remove the spark plug.

9 Compare each old spark plug with those shown on the inside back cover of this manual to determine the overall running condition of the engine.

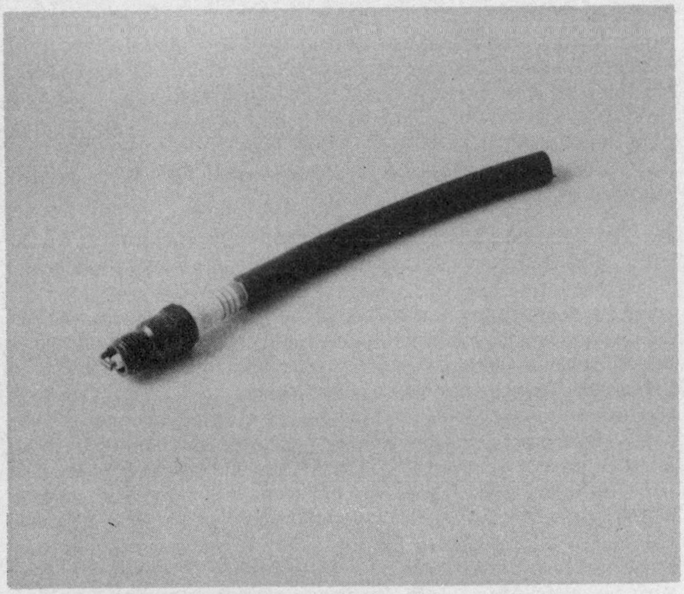

27.10 A length of 5/16-inch ID rubber hose will save time and prevent damaged threads when installing the spark plugs

Installation

10 It's often difficult to insert spark plugs into their holes without cross-threading them. To avoid this possibility, fit a short piece of 5/16-inch ID rubber hose over the end of the spark plug **(see illustration)**. The flexible hose acts as a universal joint to help align the plug with the plug hole. Should the plug begin to cross-thread, the hose will slip on the spark plug, preventing thread damage. Tighten the plug securely.

11 Attach the plug wire to the new spark plug, again using a twisting motion on the boot until it is firmly seated on the end of the spark plug.

12 Follow the above procedure for the remaining spark plugs, replacing them one at a time to prevent mixing up the spark plug wires.

28 Exhaust gas sensor (1985 through 1987 models) servicing

Refer to illustrations 28.2, 28.5, 28.9 and 28.10

1 The exhaust gas sensor warning light will come on at 30,000 miles (48,000 Km on Canadian models), whether the sensor has been replaced during that service interval or not, to let you know that the sensor should be inspected and, if necessary, replaced. The exhaust gas sensor is a screw-in unit located in the exhaust manifold. The sensor should be inspected at the specified intervals but shouldn't be replaced unless it's faulty.

2 The electronic control unit (ECU) is equipped with a self diagnostic system for checking the sensor. To reach the ECU, remove the ECU mounting screws from under the passenger seat and pull the unit out **(see illustration)**.

3 Start the engine and warm it to normal operating temperature.

4 Run the engine at about 2000 rpm for about two minutes.

5 Verify that the diagnosis mode selector on the ECU is turned counterclockwise as far as possible **(see illustration)**.

6 With the engine running at 2000 rpm, check the green inspection light on the bottom of the ECU. It should blink on and off more than five times during a 10-second period (with the engine running at 2000 rpm).

7 If the control unit inspection light is operating as described, the exhaust gas sensor is functioning properly. If it isn't, the Mixture Ratio Feedback system should be checked by a Nissan dealer. Chapter 4 contains a procedure for checking the sensor.

8 Shut off the engine and replace the control unit by reversing the removal procedure.

28.2 On 1985 through 1988 models, the ECU is located under the passenger seat

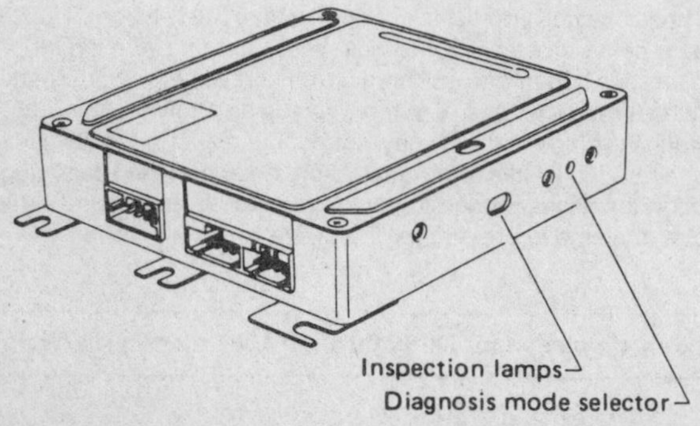

28.5 Location of the ECU mode selector

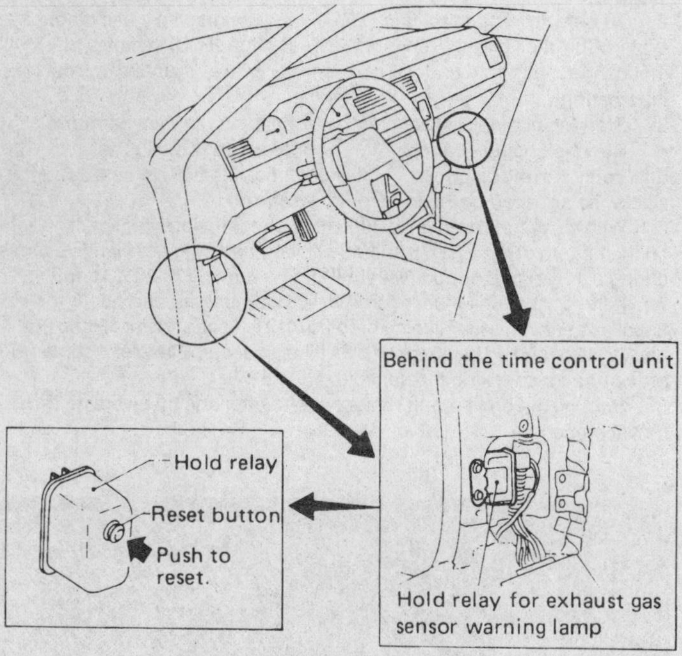

28.10 The reset button for the sensor warning light is located on a relay behind the driver's side kick panel (1985-1986) or the passenger side kick panel (1987)

9 If the exhaust gas sensor must be replaced, it may be difficult to remove when the engine is cold, so the operation is best done with the engine at operating temperature.

a) Disconnect the electrical connector from the sensor **(see illustration)**.
b) Squirt some penetrating oil around the sensor threads and allow it to soak in for a few minutes. Carefully unscrew the sensor and remove it. Be careful not to damage the threads in the exhaust manifold while doing this.

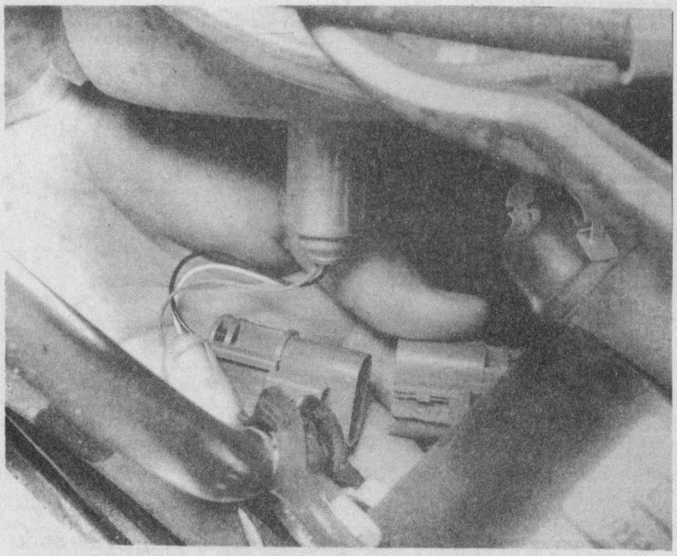

28.9 Disconnect the electrical connector from the sensor

c) Coat the threads of the new sensor with anti-seize compound and install it.
d) Tighten the sensor securely.
e) Reconnect the electrical connector to the sensor.

10 To turn off the warning light and reset the time control unit, remove the driver's side kick panel on 1985-1986 models, or the passenger side kick panel on 1987 models. Turn the ignition switch to the On position and depress the reset button on the backside of the hold relay **(see illustration)**. The light will go out and will not come on again until the next 30,000 mile interval is reached.

29 Fuel system check

Warning: *There are certain precautions to take when inspecting or servicing the fuel system components. Work in a well ventilated area and don't allow open flames (cigarettes, appliance pilot lights, etc.) in the work area. Mop up spills immediately and don't store fuel soaked rags where they could ignite. Don't work in a garage if a natural gas type appliance, such as a water heater or clothes dryer, is present. The fuel system is under pressure. No components should be disconnected until the pressure has been relieved (see Chapter 4).*

1 The fuel system should be checked with the vehicle raised on a hoist so the components underneath the vehicle are readily visible and accessible.

2 If the smell of gasoline is noticed while driving or after the vehicle has been in the sun, the system should be thoroughly inspected immediately.

3 Remove the gas tank cap and check for damage, corrosion and an unbroken sealing imprint on the gasket. Replace the cap with a new one if necessary.

4 With the vehicle raised, check the gas tank and filler neck for punctures, cracks and other damage. The connection between the filler neck and the tank is especially critical. Sometimes a rubber filler neck will leak due to loose clamps or deteriorated rubber, problems a home mechanic can usually rectify. **Warning:** *Do not, under any circumstances, try to repair a fuel tank yourself (except rubber components). A welding torch or any open flame can easily cause the fuel vapors to explode if the proper precautions are not taken!*

5 Carefully check all rubber hoses and metal lines leading away from the fuel tank. Look for loose connections, deteriorated hoses, crimped

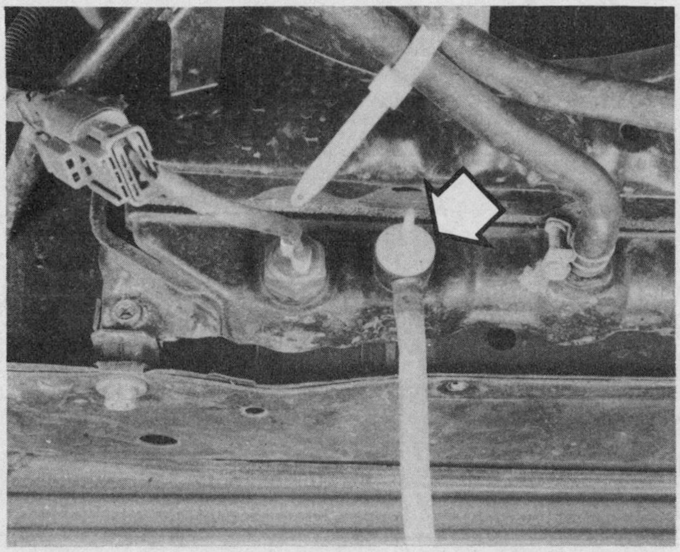

30.4 If the drain cock is too tight to turn by hand, use a pair of pliers

30.5 Use a socket and an extension to loosen the engine block drain cock (arrow)

lines and other damage. Follow the lines to the front of the vehicle, carefully inspecting them all the way. Repair or replace damaged sections as necessary.

6 If a fuel odor is still evident after the inspection, refer to Chapter 6 and check the EEC system.

30 Cooling system servicing (draining, flushing and refilling)

Refer to illustrations 30.4, 30.5, 30.12a and 30.12b

Warning: *Antifreeze is a corrosive and poisonous solution, so be careful not to spill any of the coolant mixture on the vehicle's paint or your skin. If you do, rinse it off immediately with plenty of clean water. NEVER leave antifreeze lying around in an open container or in a puddle in the driveway or on the garage floor. Children and pets are attracted by it's sweet smell. Antifreeze is fatal if ingested. Consult local authorities regarding proper disposal of antifreeze before draining the cooling system. In many areas, reclamation centers have been established to collect used oil and coolant mixtures.*

1 Periodically, the cooling system should be drained, flushed and refilled to replenish the antifreeze mixture and prevent formation of rust and corrosion, which can impair the performance of the cooling system and cause engine damage. When the cooling system is serviced, all hoses and the radiator cap should be checked and replaced if necessary.

2 Apply the parking brake and block the wheels. Raise the vehicle and support it securely on jackstands. If the vehicle has just been driven, wait several hours to allow the engine to cool down before beginning this procedure.

3 Once the engine is completely cool, remove the radiator cap. Place the heater temperature control in the maximum heat position.

4 Move a large container under the radiator drain to catch the coolant, then unscrew the drain cock a few turns **(see illustration)**. A pair of pliers may be required to turn it.

5 After the coolant stops flowing out of the radiator, move the container under the engine block drain cocks (one of them is located at the right-front corner of the block, behind the alternator) **(see illustration)**. Remove the plug and allow the coolant in the block to drain. The other drain cock is in a similar location on the other side of the block. Some models use drain plugs (bolts) instead of drain cocks – if this is the case, remove the bolts completely.

6 While the coolant is draining, check the condition of the radiator hoses, heater hoses and clamps (refer to Section 11 if necessary).

7 Replace any damaged clamps or hoses.

8 Once the system is completely drained, flush the radiator with fresh water from a garden hose until it runs clear at the drain. The flushing action of the water will remove sediments from the radiator but will not remove rust and scale from the engine and cooling tube surfaces.

9 These deposits can be removed with a chemical cleaner. Follow the procedure outlined in the manufacturer's instructions. If the radiator is severely corroded, damaged or leaking, it should be removed (see Chapter 3) and taken to a radiator repair shop.

10 Remove the overflow hose from the coolant recovery reservoir. Drain the reservoir and flush it with clean water, then reconnect the hose.

11 Tighten the radiator and cylinder block drain cocks (or install the drain plugs).

12 On 1988 and earlier models, loosen the air bleed bolt, located on the rear cylinder bank next to the EGR valve **(see illustration)** and slowly add new coolant (a 50/50 mixture of water and antifreeze) to the radiator until it's full. Coolant should begin to seep from the air bleed bolt – at this point, tighten the bolt securely. On 1989 models, the air bleed bolt is located on

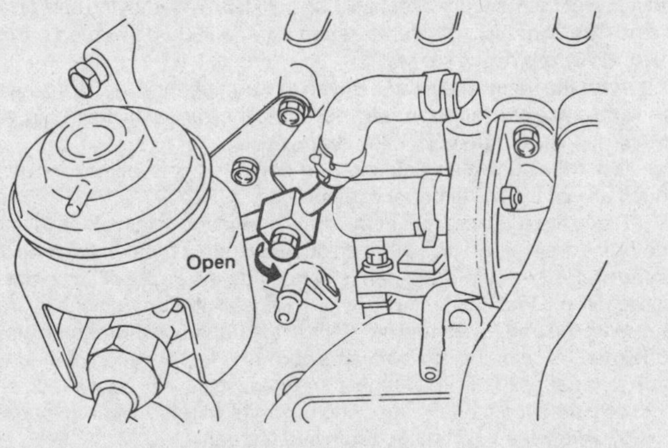

30.12a Loosen the air bleed bolt while filling the cooling system in order to bleed the air from the system (1988 and earlier model shown)

1

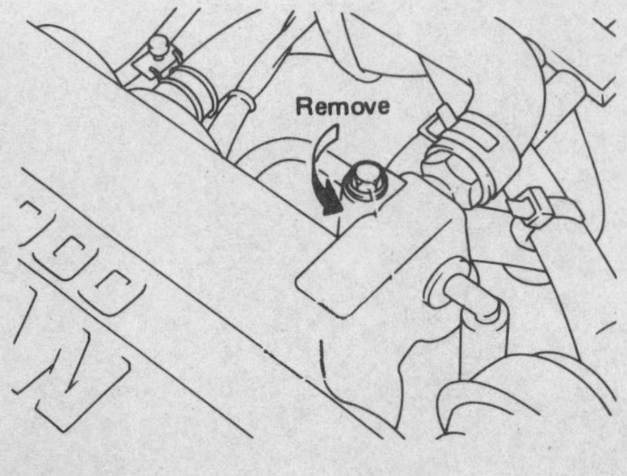

30.12b On 1989 models, the air bleed bolt is located on the top of the intake air collector

top of the intake air collector **(see illustration)**. Also, add the coolant mixture to the reservoir up to the lower mark.

13 Leave the radiator cap off and run the engine in a well-ventilated area until the thermostat opens (coolant will begin flowing through the radiator and the upper radiator hose will become hot).

14 Turn the engine off and let it cool. Add more coolant mixture to bring the level back up to the lip on the radiator filler neck.

15 Squeeze the upper radiator hose to expel air, then add more coolant mixture if necessary. Install the radiator cap.

16 Start the engine, allow it to reach normal operating temperature and check for leaks.

31 Automatic transaxle fluid change

Refer to illustration 31.7

1 At the specified time intervals, the automatic transaxle/differential fluid should be drained and replaced. The oil strainer is not serviceable.

2 Before beginning work, purchase the specified transmission fluid (see *Recommended lubricants and fluids* at the front of this chapter).

3 Other tools necessary for this job include jackstands to support the vehicle in a raised position, a drain pan capable of holding at least eight pints, newspapers and clean rags.

4 The fluid should be drained immediately after the vehicle has been driven. Hot fluid is more effective than cold fluid at removing built up sediment. **Caution:** *Fluid temperature can exceed 350-degrees in a hot transaxle. Wear protective gloves.*

5 After the vehicle has been driven to warm up the fluid, raise the front end and place it on jackstands for access to the transaxle drain plug. Apply the parking brake and block the rear wheels.

6 Move the necessary equipment under the vehicle, being careful not to touch any of the hot exhaust components.

7 Place the drain pan under the drain plug in the transaxle case and remove the drain plug with a 3/8-inch drive ratchet or breaker bar **(see illustration)**. Be sure the drain pan is in position, as fluid will come out with some force. Once the fluid is drained, reinstall the drain plug securely.

8 With the engine off, add new fluid to the transaxle through the dipstick tube (see *Recommended lubricants and fluids* for the recommended fluid type and capacity). Use a funnel to prevent spills. It is best to add a little fluid at a time, continually checking the level with the dipstick (see Section 9). Allow the fluid time to drain into the pan.

9 Start the engine and shift the selector into all positions, then shift into Park and apply the parking brake.

10 With the engine idling, check the fluid level. Add fluid up to the Cold level on the dipstick.

31.7 Use a 3/8-inch drive ratchet or breaker bar to loosen the automatic transaxle drain plug

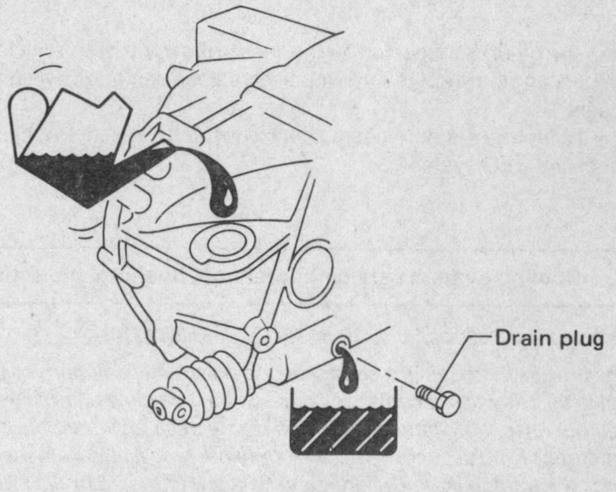

32.2 The manual transaxle drain plug is located on the lower rear portion of the case – after the lubricant has been drained, reinstall the plug, remove the speedometer cable drive pinion and add lubricant through the opening

32 Manual transaxle lubricant change

Refer to illustration 32.2

1 Raise the front of the vehicle and support it securely on jackstands. Apply the parking brake and block the rear wheels.

2 Remove the drain plug and drain the lubricant **(see illustration)**.

3 Reinstall the drain plug securely.

4 Remove the speedometer drive pinion from the transaxle and add lubricant through the hole. Use the drive pinion gear as a dipstick (see Section 23).

33 Exhaust Gas Recirculation (EGR) valve check

Refer to illustrations 33.2 and 33.5

1 Open the hood and locate the EGR valve at the right rear of the engine (as you are standing in front of the vehicle, facing it).

Common spark plug conditions

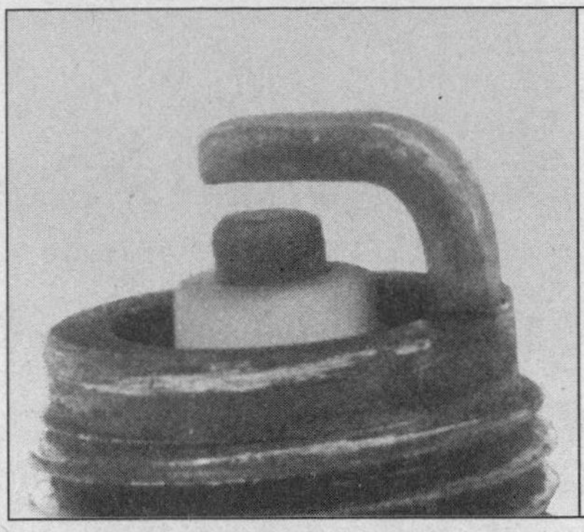

NORMAL

Symptoms: Brown to grayish-tan color and slight electrode wear. Correct heat range for engine and operating conditions.
Recommendation: When new spark plugs are installed, replace with plugs of the same heat range.

WORN

Symptoms: Rounded electrodes with a small amount of deposits on the firing end. Normal color. Causes hard starting in damp or cold weather and poor fuel economy.
Recommendation: Plugs have been left in the engine too long. Replace with new plugs of the same heat range. Follow the recommended maintenance schedule.

CARBON DEPOSITS

Symptoms: Dry sooty deposits indicate a rich mixture or weak ignition. Causes misfiring, hard starting and hesitation.
Recommendation: Make sure the plug has the correct heat range. Check for a clogged air filter or problem in the fuel system or engine management system. Also check for ignition system problems.

ASH DEPOSITS

Symptoms: Light brown deposits encrusted on the side or center electrodes or both. Derived from oil and/or fuel additives. Excessive amounts may mask the spark, causing misfiring and hesitation during acceleration.
Recommendation: If excessive deposits accumulate over a short time or low mileage, install new valve guide seals to prevent seepage of oil into the combustion chambers. Also try changing gasoline brands.

OIL DEPOSITS

Symptoms: Oily coating caused by poor oil control. Oil is leaking past worn valve guides or piston rings into the combustion chamber. Causes hard starting, misfiring and hesitation.
Recommendation: Correct the mechanical condition with necessary repairs and install new plugs.

GAP BRIDGING

Symptoms: Combustion deposits lodge between the electrodes. Heavy deposits accumulate and bridge the electrode gap. The plug ceases to fire, resulting in a dead cylinder.
Recommendation: Locate the faulty plug and remove the deposits from between the electrodes.

TOO HOT

Symptoms: Blistered, white insulator, eroded electrode and absence of deposits. Results in shortened plug life.
Recommendation: Check for the correct plug heat range, over-advanced ignition timing, lean fuel mixture, intake manifold vacuum leaks, sticking valves and insufficient engine cooling.

PREIGNITION

Symptoms: Melted electrodes. Insulators are white, but may be dirty due to misfiring or flying debris in the combustion chamber. Can lead to engine damage.
Recommendation: Check for the correct plug heat range, over-advanced ignition timing, lean fuel mixture, insufficient engine cooling and lack of lubrication.

HIGH SPEED GLAZING

Symptoms: Insulator has yellowish, glazed appearance. Indicates that combustion chamber temperatures have risen suddenly during hard acceleration. Normal deposits melt to form a conductive coating. Causes misfiring at high speeds.
Recommendation: Install new plugs. Consider using a colder plug if driving habits warrant.

DETONATION

Symptoms: Insulators may be cracked or chipped. Improper gap setting techniques can also result in a fractured insulator tip. Can lead to piston damage.
Recommendation: Make sure the fuel anti-knock values meet engine requirements. Use care when setting the gaps on new plugs. Avoid lugging the engine.

MECHANICAL DAMAGE

Symptoms: May be caused by a foreign object in the combustion chamber or the piston striking an incorrect reach (too long) plug. Causes a dead cylinder and could result in piston damage.
Recommendation: Repair the mechanical damage. Remove the foreign object from the engine and/or install the correct reach plug.

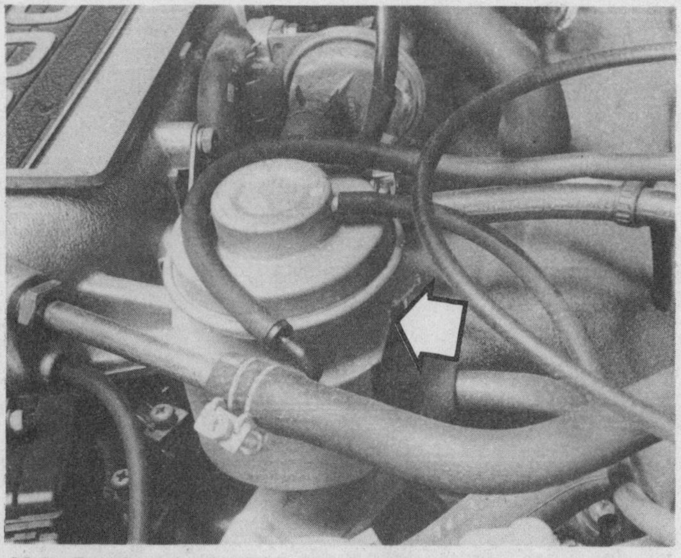

33.2 Reach under the EGR diaphragm with a finger and push up – the diaphragm should move freely (be careful, it may be hot)

33.5 With vacuum applied to the EGR valve, the engine should run roughly and/or stall

34.1 The PCV valve is threaded into the rear side of the intake air collector

2 Reach under the EGR valve and push the valve diaphragm up with a finger to make sure that the valve isn't stuck **(see illustration)**. It should spring back when released. **Warning:** *If the engine is warm, wear gloves – the EGR valve can become extremely hot!*

3 Start the engine and warm it to operating temperature.

4 With the engine still running, disconnect the vacuum hose attached to the EGR valve.

5 Connect a hand held vacuum pump to the nipple where the vacuum hose was removed **(see illustration)**.

6 Apply vacuum to the valve. The diaphragm inside the valve should open and the engine should cough and stumble badly, or stall. If it does, the valve works.

7 If the engine doesn't stall or run poorly when vacuum is applied to the EGR valve, the valve is defective. Remove it and look for blockage or carbon buildup. If there is no apparent cause for valve malfunction, replace it (see Chapter 6).

34 Positive Crankcase Ventilation (PCV) valve check and replacement

Refer to illustration 34.1

1 On all models the PCV valve threads into the intake air collector and is connected by a rubber hose and metal tube to the crankcase **(see illustration)**.

Check

2 With the engine running at idle speed, remove the ventilation hose from the PCV valve. If the valve is working properly, a hissing noise will be heard as air passes through it. Place your finger over the valve inlet and feel for vacuum. If no noise is heard or no vacuum is felt, replace the valve.

Replacement

3 When purchasing a replacement PCV valve, make sure it's the correct one for your vehicle.

4 Loosen the clamp securing the hose to the PCV valve and disconnect the hose from the valve (if not already done).

5 Unscrew the valve from the intake air collector **(see illustration 34.1)**.

6 Compare the old valve with the new one to make sure they're the same.

7 Screw the new valve into the intake air collector and connect the hose to it.

8 More information on the PCV system can be found in Chapter 6.

35 Fuel tank cap gasket replacement

1 Obtain a new gasket.

2 Remove the tank cap and carefully pry the old gasket out of the recess. Be very careful not to damage the sealing surface inside the cap.

3 Work the new gasket into the cap recess.

4 Install the cap, then remove it and make sure the gasket seals all the way around.

36.2 Remove the relay panel retaining screws and lift it up to gain access to the charcoal canister

36.3 Check the canister and all the hoses for damage and deterioration

36 Evaporative emissions control system check

Refer to illustrations 36.2 and 36.3

1 The function of the evaporative emissions control system is to draw fuel vapors from the gas tank and fuel system, store them in a charcoal canister and route them to the intake manifold during normal engine operation.

2 The most common symptom of a fault in the evaporative emissions control system is a strong fuel odor in the engine compartment. If a fuel odor is detected, inspect the charcoal canister. To gain access to the canister, remove the relay panel, located in front of the battery **(see illustration)**.

3 Check the canister and all hoses for damage and deterioration **(see illustration)**.

4 The evaporative emissions control system is explained in more detail in Chapter 6.

37 Ignition timing check and adjustment

Refer to illustrations 37.2, 37.6, 37.8 and 37.9

1 The ignition timing setting for your car is printed on the VECI label located on the underside of the hood.

2 Locate the timing marks – a series of notches on the edge of the crankshaft pulley. With the engine turning in its normal clockwise operating direction (as you look at it from the front), the first mark to approach the stationary pointer attached to the oil pump housing is the 30-degree mark **(see illustration)**. Each subsequent mark is in 5-degree increments. The last mark to approach the pointer is the 0-degree mark.

3 Locate the timing notch on the pulley specified for your vehicle and mark it with a dab of paint or chalk so it will be visible under the timing light.

4 Connect a tachometer in accordance with the manufacturer's instructions.

5 Allow the engine to reach normal operating temperature. Be sure the air conditioner and other electrical accessories are off.

6 Turn the ignition off. Connect the pick-up lead of the timing light to the number one spark plug wire **(see illustration)**. Use either a jumper lead between the spark plug wire and plug or an inductive-type pickup. Do not pierce the spark plug wire or attempt to insert a wire between the boot and the spark plug wire.

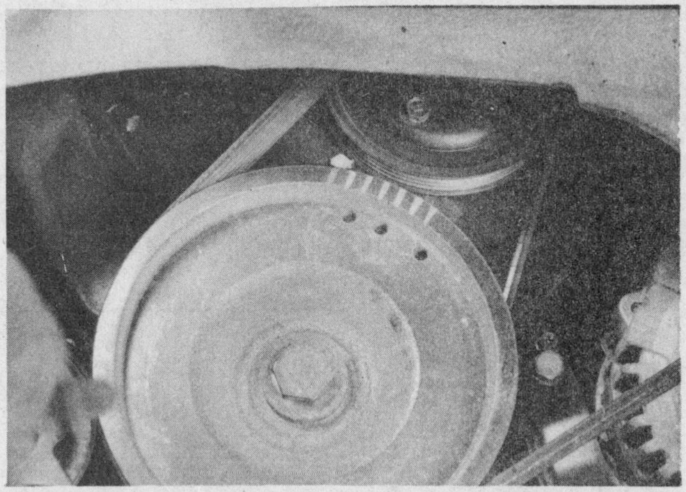

37.2 The timing marks are located on the crankshaft pulley – it's a good idea to highlight the marks and the pointer with white paint or chalk

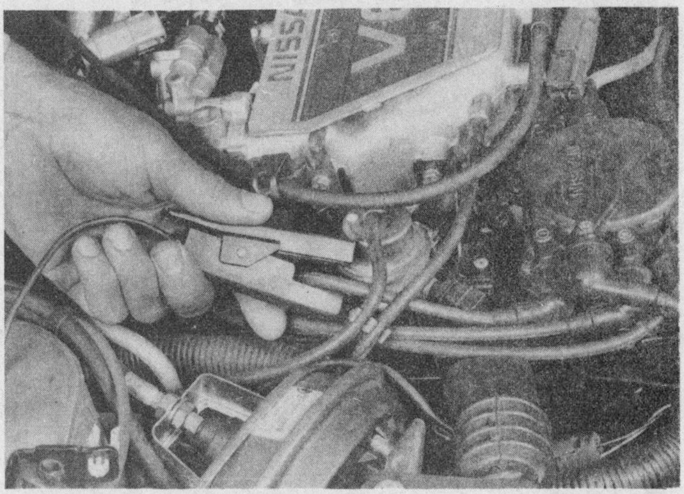

37.6 Clip the timing light pickup lead to the number one spark plug wire

37.8 **Point the timing light at the timing marks making sure the leads don't touch the fan or exhaust manifold**

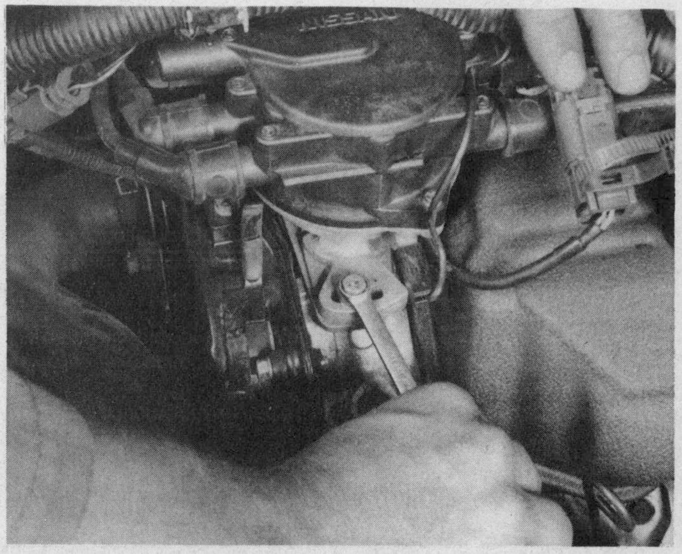

37.9 **Loosen the adjusting bolt at the base of the distributor and rotate the distributor to adjust the timing**

7 Make sure that the wires of the timing light are clear of all moving engine components, then start the engine.
8 Point the timing light at the timing marks **(see illustration)**, again being careful to avoid entanglement with hot or moving parts. The notch that you painted should appear stationary and should be in alignment with the stationary pointer. If the notch and pointer are not in alignment, or if the painted notch appears blurry or jumpy, you must adjust the timing.
9 If the timing marks do not line up, turn off the engine and loosen the adjusting nut at the base of the distributor **(see illustration)** just enough to rotate the distributor body.
10 Start the engine and slowly turn the distributor either left or right until the painted notch and the pointer coincide.
11 Shut off the engine and tighten the distributor adjusting nut, being careful not to move the distributor body.
12 Start the engine and recheck the timing to make sure the notch and pointer are still in alignment.

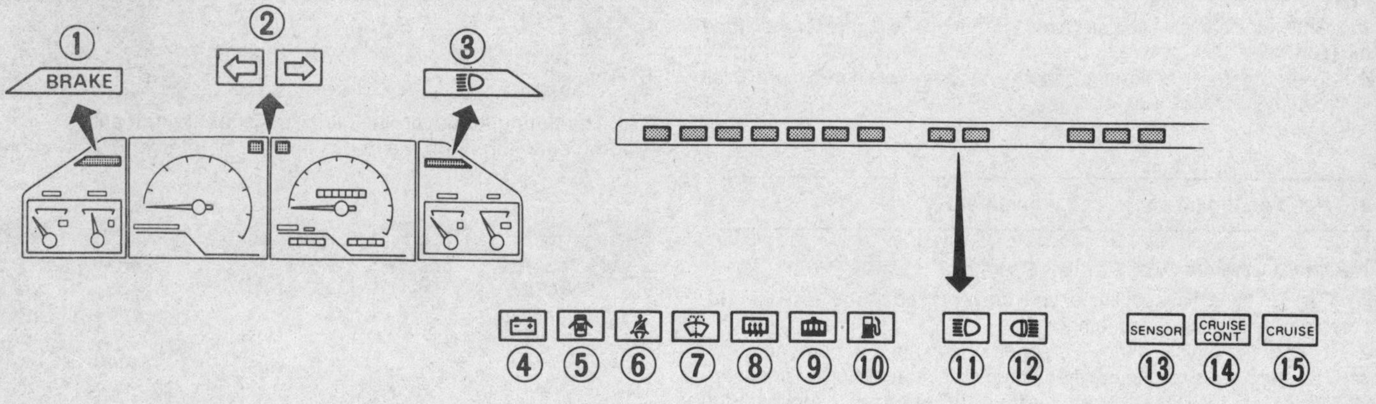

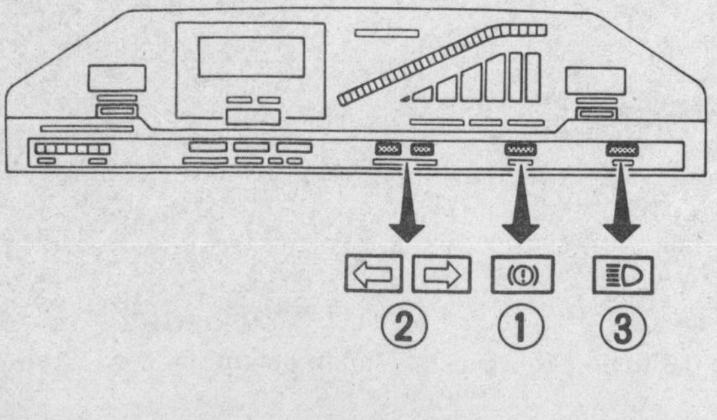

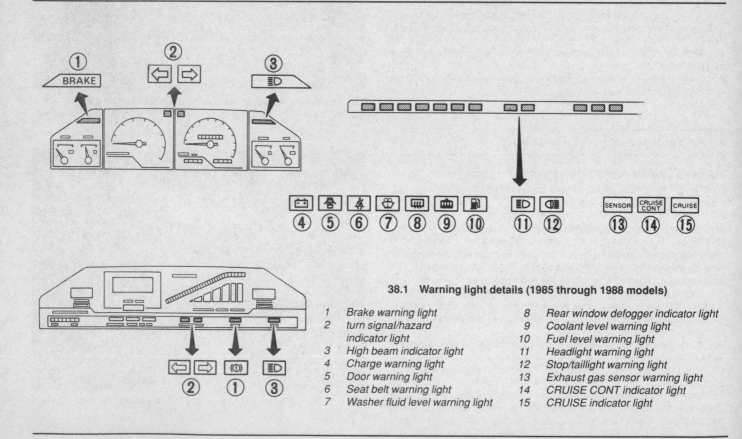

38.1 Warning light details (1985 through 1988 models)

1 Brake warning light
2 turn signal/hazard indicator light
3 High beam indicator light
4 Charge warning light
5 Door warning light
6 Seat belt warning light
7 Washer fluid level warning light
8 Rear window defogger indicator light
9 Coolant level warning light
10 Fuel level warning light
11 Headlight warning light
12 Stop/taillight warning light
13 Exhaust gas sensor warning light
14 CRUISE CONT indicator light
15 CRUISE indicator light

13 Disconnect the timing light.
14 Race the engine two or three times and then allow it to run at idle. Recheck the idle speed with the tachometer. If it is not correct, have it adjusted by a dealer service department or other repair shop that has the necessary equipment.

38 Warning lights general information

Refer to illustration 38.1

1 The vehicles covered by this manual are equipped with several dash mounted warning lights **(see illustration)** and a voice warning system to inform you of the operating condition of your vehicle. Many times the warning is something simple, such as a door ajar or the headlights on. The system also warns of vital engine functions such as engine oil pressure loss, low coolant level, brake system failure and low electrical charging rate. When one of these lights comes on, it is a sign that the problem must be dealt with immediately.

Oil pressure warning light

2 The oil pressure warning light indicates that the engine oil pressure is low. Should the light flicker on and off or stay on during normal driving speeds you should pull off the road immediately and stop the engine until the cause is found and corrected (see Chapter 2). **Caution:** *Continued operation of the engine when the oil pressure warning light is on may damage the engine.*

Charge (alternator) warning light

3 The charge warning light indicates an alternator or electrical wiring harness malfunction.
4 This light should glow only when the ignition switch is in the ON" position (engine off), indicating the bulb itself and the electrical system are satisfactory. It should go out when the engine is started.
5 Should the light come on during normal engine operation the alternator and electrical system should be checked as soon as possible (see Chapter 5).

Fuel level warning light

6 This light serves as a fuel reserve warning system. When it comes on, 2-1/8 US gallons of fuel remain in the tank. **Note:** *Generally speaking, it's good practice to keep the gas tanks of fuel injected automobiles full, especially in moist climates, because it helps to ward off moisture caused by condensation.*

Exhaust gas sensor warning light

7 This light, which comes on every 30,000 miles, means that the exhaust gas sensor should be inspected. The exhaust gas sensor warning light also comes on when the ignition switch is turned to the ON position before the engine starts.

Brake warning light

8 The brake warning light serves both the foot brake system and the parking brake.
9 The light glows when the ignition switch is turned to ON before the engine is started.
10 Should the light fail to come on when the ignition switch is turned to ON, check the electrical system for a burned-out bulb or look for an open circuit in the wiring for the brake light system (see Chapter 12).
11 The light will continue to glow when the parking brake is set with the engine running.
12 If the warning light comes on while you are driving, it's an indication that the brake fluid level is lower than the prescribed level. Pull over and check the brake fluid level immediately. If the reservoir is low, fill it to the specified level.
13 **Warning:** *If these checks cannot be made immediately, pull off the road and stop carefully. Remember that your stopping distance may be longer and the pedal may go down farther than normal and be more difficult to operate. Test the brakes by carefully starting and stopping the vehicle on the shoulder of the road. If you judge it to be safe, drive carefully to the nearest service station for repairs. Otherwise, have your car towed. Driving the vehicle with the brake warning light on may be dangerous.*

Seat belt warning light and chime

14 The driver's seat is equipped with a seat belt warning light and chime system. When the ignition switch is turned to the ON position, the seat belt warning light will come on and remain on for about six seconds. The chime will also sound for about six seconds any time the ignition switch is turned to ON but it will be deactivated sooner if the driver's seat belt is securely fastened.

Lights "ON" warning chime/voice

15 When the key is removed from the ignition and the driver's door is opened, a chime and/or voice warning will alert you if the headlight switch is still turned on. Both warnings cancel as soon as the headlights are turned off.

Key warning chime

16 A warning chime tells the driver that the key is in the ignition. The chime will sound any time the driver's door is open when the ignition key is in the ACC, OFF or LOCK position.

1

Door warning light

17 The door warning light comes on if one of the doors or the rear hatch is not closed securely when the engine is running. It also glows when the ignition switch is turned ON and the engine is not running.

Check engine light (California models)

18 If the check engine light comes on while the engine is running, a problem with the engine or the engine control system has been detected. Have it inspected at a dealer service department or other repair shop as soon as possible.

Headlight warning light

19 This light comes on when the headlight switch is in the ON position with the engine off, or if a headlight bulb is burned out.

Talllight warning light

20 This light comes on with the light switch in the ON position with the engine off or when a tail light bulb is burned out.

High beam indicator light

21 With the headlights on, the high beam indicator glows whenever the high beams are in use and goes out when the driver switches to low beams. If it fails to come on when the lights are switched to the high beam, check the headlights for a burned out high beam filament. If the headlights are both good, check the high beam indicator bulb itself (see Chapter 12).

Turn signal/hazard indicator lights

22 The green indicator light on the dash panel should flash when the exterior turn signal lights flash. If it doesn't, check the flasher module, the wiring and the turn signal lights (see Chapter 12).

Theft warning indicator light

23 The theft warning light is indicated by the word Security on the dash panel. Once the key is removed from the ignition and all the doors are locked the indicator will come on for 30 seconds.
24 Once the light goes off the theft alarm system remains armed until one of the doors is opened with a key. If the theft warning indicator light fails to come on for any reason, the theft warning system should be checked (see Chapter 12).

Cruise control indicator light

25 When the cruise control unit is in operation, the green light on the combination meter panel will glow.
26 Once the desired speed is set by pushing the Coast set switch, a blue light will light up on an analog (needle type) dashboard and the set speed

will light up in the graphic display on a digital dashboard. If either light fails to come on when the system is in use, inspect the dashboard bulbs and the cruise control wiring (see Chapter 12).

Voice warning

27 A voice warning is sounded to warn the driver of an open left or right door, a low fuel level or a parking brake left on when the ignition switch is in the ON position. Each warning will continue until the condition is corrected, except the low fuel level warning, which repeats two or three times, then stops.

28 The voice warning will sound once the vehicle is moving over 5 mph if one of the doors is open or if the parking brake is on.

29 A voice warning indicating the lights are still on will sound if the driver's door is opened and the ignition switch is not in the ON position.

Chapter 2 Part A Engine

Contents

Camshaft oil seal – replacement 12
Camshaft, lifters and bearing surfaces/rocker arms and shafts – inspection 16
Camshaft – removal and installation 15
Crankshaft front oil seal – replacement 11
Crankshaft pulley – removal and installation 9
Crankshaft rear oil seal – replacement 20
Cylinder compression check .... See Chapter 2B
Cylinder head(s) – removal and installation 14
Drivebelt check, adjustment and replacement .... See Chapter 1
Engine mounts – check and replacement 21
Engine oil and filter change .... See Chapter 1
Engine overhaul – general information .... See Chapter 2B
Engine – removal and installation .... See Chapter 2B
Exhaust manifolds – removal and installation 8
Flywheel/driveplate – removal and installation 19
General information 1
Intake manifold – removal and installation 7
Lifters – removal and installation 6
Oil pan – removal and installation 17
Oil pump – removal, inspection and installation 18
Repair operations possible with the engine in the vehicle 2
Rocker arm components – removal and installation 5
Rocker arm covers – removal and installation 4
Spark plug replacement .... See Chapter 1
Thermostat – check and replacement .... See Chapter 3
Timing belt – removal, installation and adjustment 10
Top Dead Center (TDC) for number one piston – locating 3
Valve spring, retainer and seals – replacement 13
Water pump – replacement .... See Chapter 3

Specifications

General

Displacement	181 cu in (2960 cc)
Compression ratio	9.0:1
Firing order	1-2-3-4-5-6
Cylinder numbers (drivebelt end-to-transaxle end)	
Rear (firewall side)	1-3-5
Front (radiator side)	2-4-6

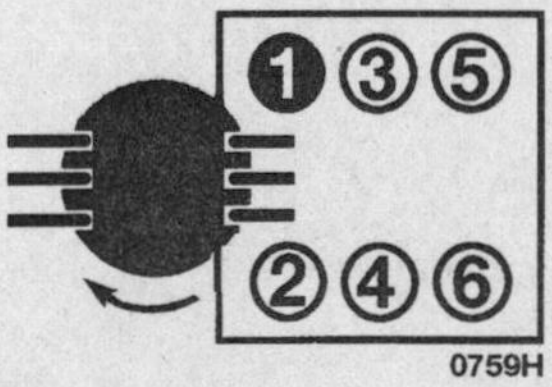

Cylinder location and distributor rotation

Camshaft and related components

Lifters	
Outside diameter	0.6278 to 0.6282 in (15.947 to 15.957 mm)
Guide bore diameter	0.6299 to 0.6304 in (16.000 to 16.013 mm)
Lifter-to-guide clearance	0.0017 to 0.0026 in (0.043 to 0.066 mm)
Lifter movement limit	0.040 in (1.0 mm)

Camshaft and related components (continued)

Rocker arms and shafts	
Shaft outside diameter	
1985 through 1988	0.7078 to 0.7087 in (17.979 to 18.000 mm)
1989 on	0.7082 to 0.7087 in (17.988 to 18.000 mm)
Rocker arm bore diameter	0.7089 to 0.7098 in (18.007 to 18.028 mm)
Rocker arm-to-shaft clearance	0.0003 to 0.0019 in (0.007 to 0.049 mm)
Camshaft	
Bearing inside diameter	
1985 through 1987	1.8504 to 1.8514 in (47.00 to 47.025 mm)
1988 on	
Front bearing (timing belt end)	1.8898 to 1.8907 in (48.000 to 48.025 mm)
Rear bearing	1.6732 to 1.6742 in (42.500 to 42.525 mm)
All others	1.8504 to 1.8512 in (47.000 to 47.025 mm)
Camshaft journal outside diameter	
1985 through 1987	1.8478 to 1.8486 in (46.935 to 46.955 mm)
1988-on	
Front journal (timing belt end)	1.8866 to 1.8874 in (47.920 to 47.940 mm)
Rear journal	1.6701 to 1.6709 in (42.420 to 42.440 mm)
All others	1.8472 to 1.8480 in (46.920 to 46.940 mm)
Bearing oil clearance (journal-to-bearing clearance)	
1985 through 1987	
Standard	0.0018 to 0.0035 in (0.045 to 0.090 mm)
Limit	0.0059 in (0.15 mm)
1988-on	
Standard	0.0024 to 0.0041 in (0.060 to 0.105 mm)
Limit	0.0059 in (0.15 mm)
Camshaft runout limit (total indicator reading)	0.004 in (0.10 mm)
Camshaft end play	0.0012 to 0.0024 in (0.03 to 0.06 mm)
Lobe height	1.5566 to 1.5641 in (39.537 to 39.727 mm)
Lobe wear limit	0.0059 in (0.15 mm)
Thrust plate available thickness	See illustration 15.11

Oil pump

Housing-to-outer gear clearance	0.0043 to 0.0079 in (0.11 to 0.20 mm)
Inner gear-to-crescent clearance	0.0047 to 0.0091 in (0.12 to 0.23 mm)
Outer gear-to-crescent clearance	0.0083 to 0.0126 in (0.21 to 0.32 mm)
Cover-to-inner gear end clearance	0.0020 to 0.0035 in (0.05 to 0.09 mm)
Cover-to-outer gear end clearance	0.0020 to 0.0043 in (0.05 to 0.11 mm)

Torque specifications

	Ft-lbs (unless otherwise indicated)
Rocker arm cover screws	8.4 to 26.4 in-lbs
Rocker arm shaft bolts	13 to 16
Intake manifold	
Bolts	12 to 14
Nuts	17 to 20
Exhaust manifold nuts	13 to 16
Crankshaft pulley bolt	90 to 98
Camshaft sprocket bolt	58 to 65
Timing belt tensioner locking nut	32 to 43
Camshaft retaining bolt	58 to 65
Cylinder head bolts	
Step 1	22
Step 2	43
Step 3	Loosen all bolts
Step 4	22
Step 5	40 to 47
Flywheel/driveplate mounting bolts*	72 to 80
Oil pan mounting bolts	61 to 70 in-lbs
Oil pump mounting bolts	
6 mm	52 to 61 in-lbs
8 mm	108 to 144 in-lbs
Oil pump regulator cap	29 to 36
Oil pick-up tube-to-pump bolts	12 to 15
Oil pick-up tube bracket bolts	36 to 78 in-lbs

** Apply a thread locking compound to the threads prior to installation*

1 General information

This Part of Chapter 2 is devoted to in-vehicle repair procedures for the engine. All information concerning engine removal and installation and engine block and cylinder head overhaul can be found in Part B of this Chapter.

The following repair procedures are based on the assumption that the engine is installed in the vehicle. If the engine has been removed from the vehicle and mounted on a stand, many of the steps outlined in this Part of Chapter 2 will not apply.

The Specifications included in this Part of Chapter 2 apply only to the procedures contained in this Part. Part B of Chapter 2 contains the Specifications necessary for cylinder head and engine block rebuilding.

The 60-degree V6 has a cast iron block and aluminum crossflow heads with a camshaft in each head. The block has thin walled sections for light weight. A "cradle frame" main bearing casting – the main bearing caps are cast as a unit, with a bridge, or truss, connecting them – supports the cast ductile iron crankshaft.

Both camshafts are driven off the crankshaft by a cog belt. A spring loaded tensioner, adjusted by an eccentric type locknut, maintains belt tension. Each camshaft actuates two valves per cylinder through hydraulic lifters and shaft-mounted forged aluminum rocker arms.

Each cast aluminum three-ring piston has two compression rings and a three-piece oil control ring. The piston pins are pressed into forged steel connecting rods. The flat-topped pistons produce a 9.0:1 compression ratio.

The distributor (also called the crank angle sensor), which is mounted on the drivebelt end of the front cylinder head, is driven by a helical gear on the camshaft. The water pump, which is bolted to the timing belt end of the block, is driven off the crankshaft by a drivebelt and pulley. The gear type oil pump is mounted on the crankshaft adjacent to the timing belt.

From the oil pump, oil travels through the filter to the main oil gallery, from which it is routed either directly to the main bearings, crankshaft, connecting rod bearings and pistons and cylinder walls or to the cylinder heads.

2 Repair operations possible with the engine in the vehicle

Many major repair operations can be accomplished without removing the engine from the vehicle.

Clean the engine compartment and the exterior of the engine with some type of degreaser before any work is done. It will make the job easier and help keep dirt out of the internal areas of the engine.

Depending on the components involved, it may be helpful to remove the hood to improve access to the engine as repairs are performed (refer to Chapter 11 if necessary). Cover the fenders to prevent damage to the paint. Special pads are available, but an old bedspread or blanket will also work.

If vacuum, exhaust, oil or coolant leaks develop, indicating a need for gasket or seal replacement, the repairs can generally be made with the engine in the vehicle. The intake and exhaust manifold gaskets, oil pan gasket, camshaft and crankshaft oil seals and cylinder head gaskets are all accessible with the engine in place.

Exterior engine components, such as the intake and exhaust manifolds, the oil pan (and the oil pump), the water pump, the starter motor, the alternator, the distributor and the fuel system components can be removed for repair with the engine in place.

Since the cylinder heads can be removed without pulling the engine, camshaft and valve component servicing can also be accomplished with the engine in the vehicle. Replacement of the timing belt and sprockets is also possible with the engine in the vehicle.

In extreme cases caused by a lack of necessary equipment, repair or replacement of piston rings, pistons, connecting rods and rod bearings is possible with the engine in the vehicle. However, this practice is not recommended because of the cleaning and preparation work that must be done to the components involve.

3 Top Dead Center (TDC) for number one piston – locating

Refer to illustrations 3.5, 3.6 and 3.8

Note: *The following procedure is based on the assumption that the spark plug wires and distributor are correctly installed. If you are trying to locate TDC to install the distributor correctly, piston position must be determined by feeling for compression at the number one spark plug hole as the crankshaft is slowly turned clockwise, then aligning the ignition timing marks as described in Step 8.*

1 Top Dead Center (TDC) is the highest point in the cylinder that each piston reaches as it travels up-and-down when the crankshaft turns. Each piston reaches TDC on the compression stroke and again on the exhaust stroke, but TDC generally refers to piston position on the compression stroke.

2 Positioning the piston(s) at TDC is an essential part of many procedures such as camshaft and timing belt/sprocket removal and distributor removal.

3 Before beginning this procedure, be sure to place the transmission in Neutral and apply the parking brake or block the rear wheels. Also, disable the ignition system by detaching the coil wire from the terminal marked "C" on the distributor cap and grounding it on the block with a jumper wire. Remove the spark plugs (see Chapter 1).

4 In order to bring any piston to TDC, the crankshaft must be turned using one of the methods outlined below. When looking at the drivebelt end of the engine, normal crankshaft rotation is clockwise.

a) The preferred method is to turn the crankshaft with a socket and ratchet attached to the bolt threaded into the front of the crankshaft.
b) A remote starter switch, which may save some time, can also be used. Follow the instructions included with the switch. Once the piston is close to TDC, use a socket and ratchet as described in the previous paragraph.
c) If an assistant is available to turn the ignition switch to the Start position in short bursts, you can get the piston close to TDC without a remote starter switch. Make sure your assistant is out of the vehicle, away from the ignition switch, then use a socket and ratchet as described in Paragraph a) to complete the procedure.

5 Note the position of the terminal for the number one spark plug wire on the distributor cap **(see illustration)**. If the terminal isn't marked, follow the plug wire from the number one cylinder spark plug to the cap.

3.5 The inner post for the number one spark plug is offset from the outer terminal and is located at about the 12 o'clock position (arrow) – turn the cap over to verify the exact location

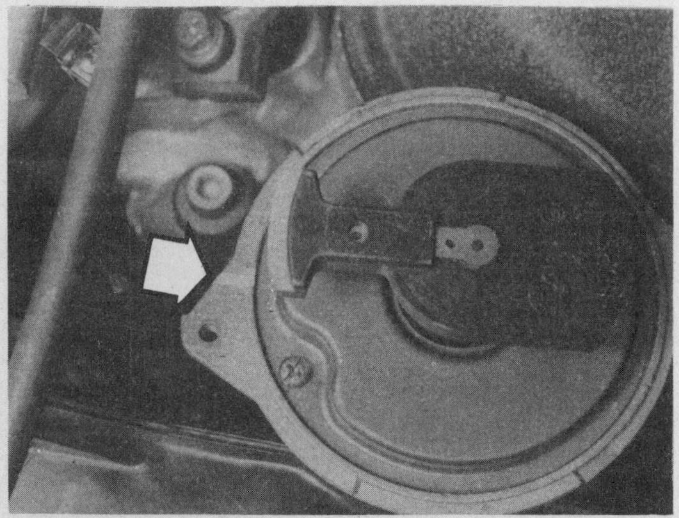

3.6 **Make a mark on the distributor housing (arrow) below the number one post *inside* the distributor cap**

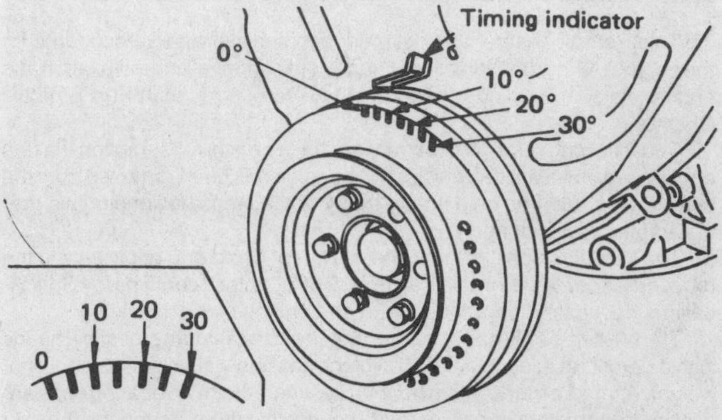

3.8 Align the zero notch with the timing indicator

6 Use a felt-tip pen or chalk to make a mark on the distributor body directly under the terminal **(see illustration)**.

7 Detach the cap from the distributor and set it aside (see Chapter 1 if necessary).

8 Turn the crankshaft (see Paragraph 3 above) until the "O" notch in the crankshaft pulley is aligned with the timing indicator (located at the front of the engine) **(see illustration)**.

9 Look at the distributor rotor – it should be pointing directly at the mark you made on the distributor body. If it is, go to Step 12.

10 If the rotor is 180-degrees off, the number one piston is at TDC on the exhaust stroke, go to Step 11.

11 To get the piston to TDC on the compression stroke, turn the crankshaft one complete turn (360-degrees) clockwise. The rotor should now be pointing at the mark on the distributor. When the rotor is pointing at the number one spark plug wire terminal inside the distributor cap and the ignition timing marks are aligned, the number one piston is at TDC on the compression stroke.

12 After the number one piston has been positioned at TDC on the compression stroke, TDC for any of the remaining pistons can be located by turning the crankshaft and following the firing order. Mark the remaining spark plug wire terminal locations on the distributor body just like you did for the number one terminal, then number the marks to correspond with the cylinder numbers. As you turn the crankshaft, the rotor will also turn. When it's pointing directly at one of the marks on the distributor, the piston for that particular cylinder is at TDC on the compression stroke.

4 Rocker arm covers – removal and installation

Refer to illustrations 4.3, 4.8 and 4.11

1 Relieve the fuel system pressure (see Chapter 4).

2 Disconnect the negative cable from the battery.

Removal

Front (radiator side) cover

3 Remove the breather hose by sliding the hose clamp back and pulling the hose off the fitting on the rocker arm cover **(see illustration)**. On 1989 models, remove the throttle chamber and air intake collector (see Chapter 4).

4 Remove the number 2, 4 and 6 spark plug wires from the spark plugs. Mark them clearly with pieces of masking tape to prevent confusion during installation. **Note**: *On 1989 and later models, remove the distributor (see Chapter 5).*

5 Remove the wires and hoses attached to the rocker arm cover.

6 Remove the rocker arm cover screws and washers.

7 Detach the rocker arm cover. **Caution:** *If the cover is stuck to the head, bump one end with a block of wood and a hammer to jar it loose. If that doesn't work, try to slip a flexible putty knife between the head and cover to break the gasket seal. Don't pry at the cover-to-head joint or damage to the sealing surfaces may occur (leading to oil leaks in the future).*

Rear (firewall side) cover

8 Remove the breather hose from the cover **(see illustration)**.

9 Tag and detach the spark plug wires.

10 Release the wiring retainers. Label and move the wiring and hoses aside.

11 Remove the rocker arm cover screws and washers and lift off the rocker arm cover **(see illustration)**. Read the **Caution** in Step 7.

4.3 Remove the breather hose and release the retaining straps by pinching the clamps and sliding the straps out

1 Breather hose *2 Retaining straps*

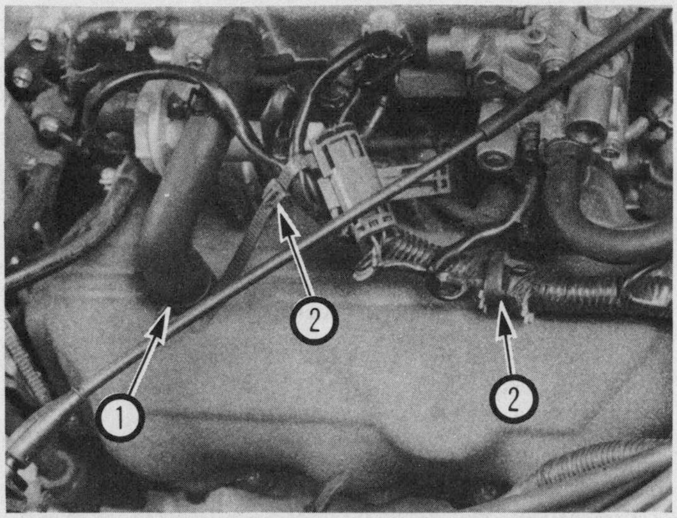

4.8 Detach the breather hose and release the wiring retainers (1986 model shown – others similar)

1 Breather hose *2 Wiring retainers*

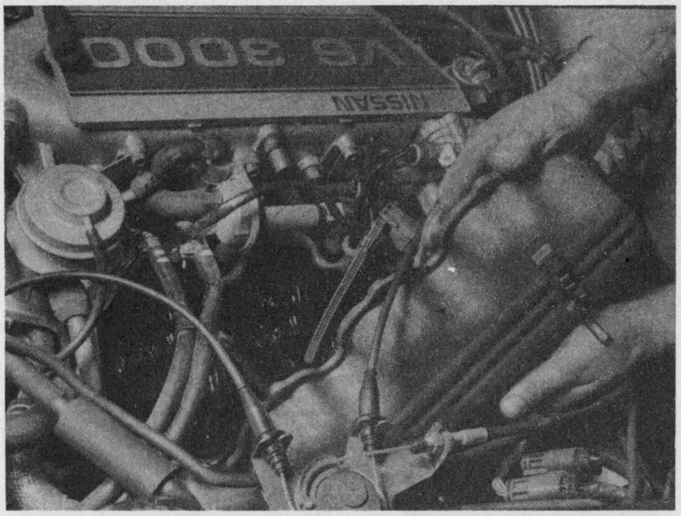

4.11 The rear rocker arm cover may be slipped between the cables if care is taken (1986 model shown – others similar)

Installation

12 The mating surfaces of each cylinder head and rocker arm cover must be perfectly clean when the covers are installed. Use a gasket scraper to remove all traces of sealant and old gasket material, then clean the mating surfaces with lacquer thinner or acetone. If there's sealant or oil on the mating surfaces when the cover is installed, oil leaks may develop.
13 If necessary, clean the mounting screw threads with a die to remove any corrosion and restore damaged threads. Make sure the threaded holes in the head are clean – run a tap into them to remove corrosion and restore damaged threads.
14 The gaskets should be mated to the covers before the covers are installed. Apply a thin coat of RTV sealant to the cover groove, then position the gasket inside the cover and allow the sealant to set up so the gasket adheres to the cover. If the sealant isn't allowed to set, the gasket may fall out of the cover as it's installed on the engine.
15 Carefully position the cover on the head and install the screws.
16 Tighten the screws in three or four steps to the specified torque.
17 The remaining installation steps are the reverse of removal.
18 Start the engine and check carefully for oil leaks as the engine warms up.

5 Rocker arm components – removal and installation

Refer to illustrations 5.2, 5.3 and 5.4

1 Remove the rocker arm cover (see Section 4).
2 Loosen the rocker arm shaft retaining bolts **(see illustration)** in two or three stages, working your way from the ends toward the middle of the shafts. **Caution**: *Some of the valves will be open when you loosen the rocker arm shaft bolts and the rocker arm shafts will be under a certain amount of valve spring pressure. Therefore, the bolts must be loosened gradually. Loosening a bolt all at once near a rocker arm under spring pressure could distort the rocker arm shaft.*
3 Prior to removal, scribe or paint identifying marks on the rockers to ensure they will be installed in their original locations **(see illustration)**.

5.2 Loosen the rocker arm shaft bolts (arrows) a little at a time to avoid bending the shaft

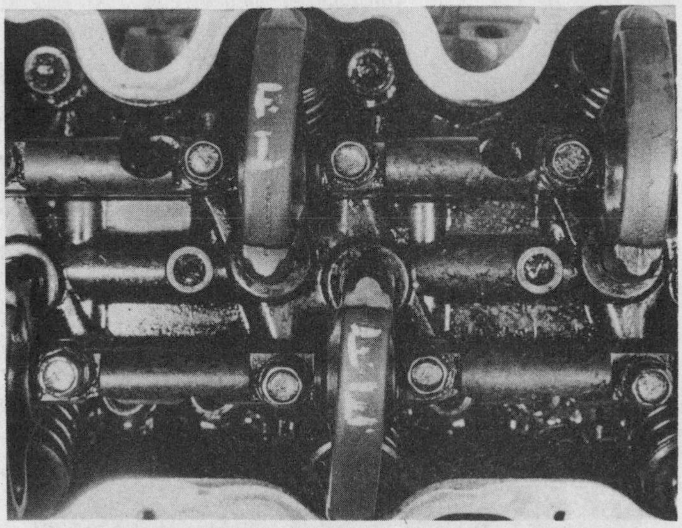

5.3 Mark the rockers to identify their locations – these are marked FI for Front Intake and FE for Front Exhaust

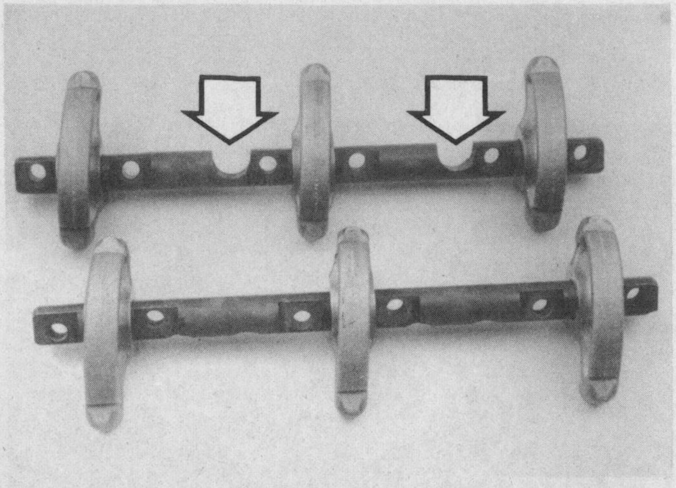

5.4 The rocker arm shaft assemblies are installed with the large notches (arrows) on the intake manifold side – the small notches on the other shaft must face the exhaust manifold

6.2 Wrap each lifter with a rubber band so it can't fall out of the lifter guide

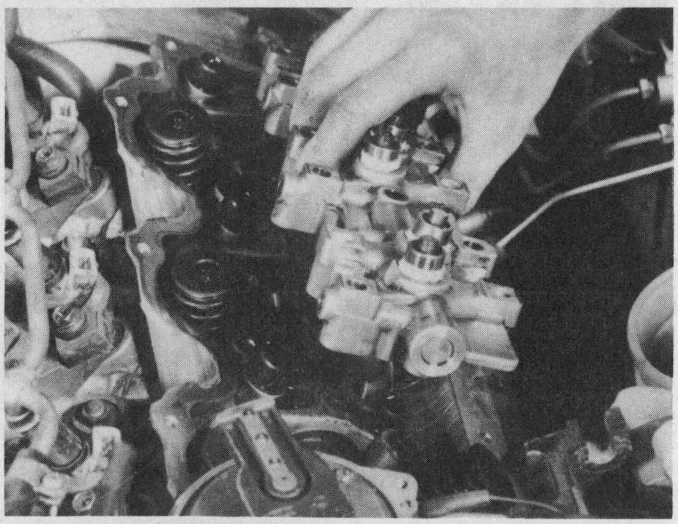

6.3 With the lifters retained by rubber bands, the lifter guide assembly can be removed from the cylinder head

4 Remove the bolts and lift off the rocker arm shaft assemblies one at a time. Lay them down on a nearby workbench in the same relationship to each other that they're in when installed. They must be reinstalled on the same cylinder head. Note that the shafts with the larger notches go on the intake manifold side **(see illustration)**. Refer to Section 16 for the inspection procedure.

5 Installation is the reverse of the removal procedure. Tighten the rocker arm shaft retaining bolts, in several steps, to the torque listed in this Chapter's Specifications. Work from the ends of the shafts toward the middle.

6 Lifters – removal and installation

Refer to illustrations 6.2, 6.3 and 6.5

1 Remove the rocker arm cover (see Section 4) and the rocker arm shaft assemblies (see Section 5).

2 Secure the lifters by raising them slightly and wrapping a rubber band around each one to prevent them from falling out of the guides **(see illustration)**. **Note**: *If a lifter should fall out of the guide, immediately put it back in its original location.*

3 Remove the lifter guide assembly **(see illustration)**.

4 Remove the lifters from the bores one at a time. Keep them in order. Each lifter must be reinstalled in its original bore. **Caution**: *Try to avoid turning the lifters upside down. If you turn a lifter upside down, air can become trapped inside and the lifter will have to be bled as follows.*

5 With the lifter in its bore, push down on it **(see illustration)**. If it moves more than 0.040-inch (1 mm), air may be trapped inside the lifter.

6 If you think air is trapped inside a valve lifter, reinstall the rocker arm shaft assemblies and rocker arm cover.

7 Bleed air from the lifters by running the engine at 1,000 rpm under no load for about 10 minutes.

8 Remove the rocker arm cover and rocker arm shaft assemblies again. Repeat the procedure in Step 5 once more. If there's still air in the lifter, replace it with a new one.

9 While the lifters are out of the engine, inspect them for wear. Refer to Section 16 for inspection procedures.

10 Installation is the reverse of removal. Be sure to lubricate each lifter with liberal amounts of clean engine oil prior to installation.

7 Intake manifold – removal and installation

Removal

Refer to illustrations 7.7, 7.9, 7.11 and 7.12

1 Relieve the fuel system pressure (see Chapter 4).

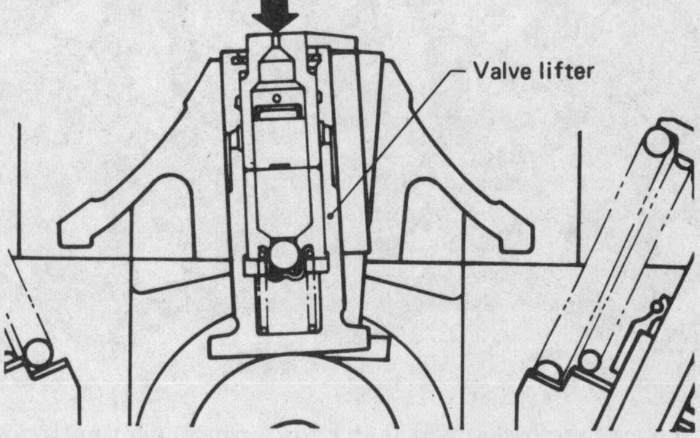

6.5 Depress the valve lifter by hand to see how far it moves

7.7 Pull the coolant hose off the fitting and set it aside, then remove the two bolts and detach the housing

7.9 Remove the bolts (arrows) and detach the coolant tube from the intake manifold

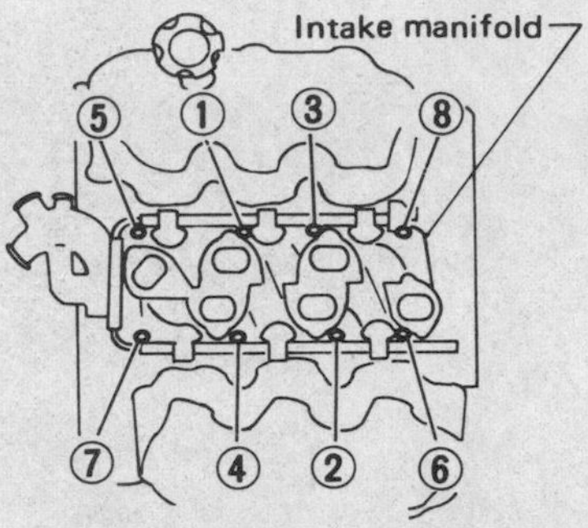

7.11 Intake manifold bolt/nut *loosening* sequence

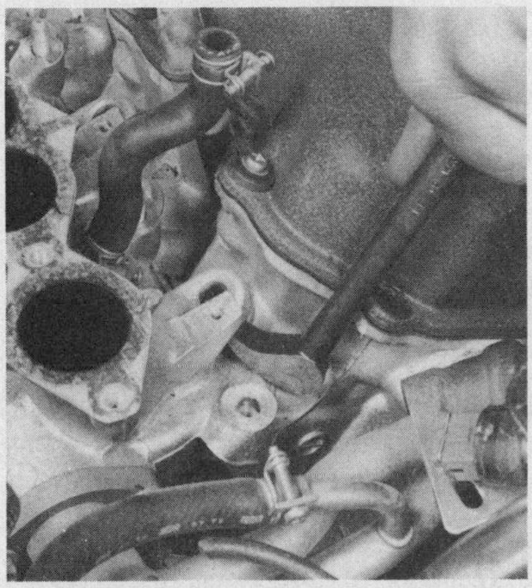

7.12 Pry against casting protrusions – don't pry between the gasket surfaces

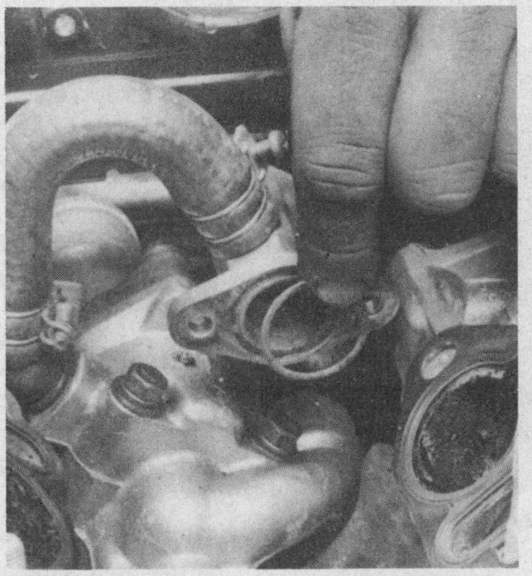

7.15a Install a new O-ring in the coolant outlet on the timing belt end of the manifold

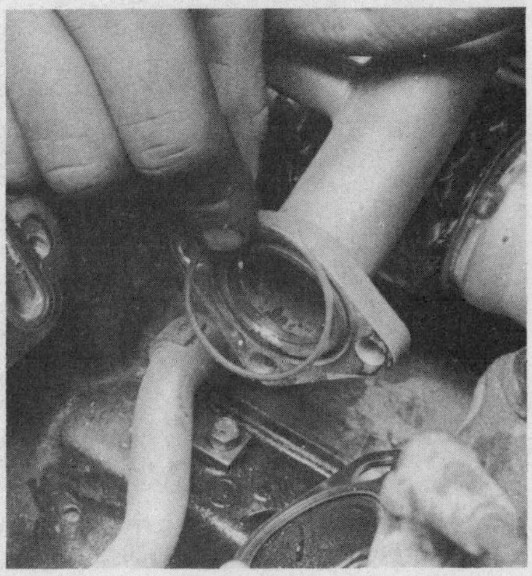

7.15b Install a new O-ring in the coolant tube on the transaxle end of the manifold

2 Disconnect the cable from the negative terminal of the battery.
3 Drain the cooling system (don't forget to drain the cylinder block) (see Chapter 1).
4 Remove the EGR valve (see Chapter 6).
5 Remove the spark plug wires and distributor cap. Be sure to mark the spark plug wires for proper reinstallation.
6 Remove the fuel injectors, throttle body and air intake collector (see Chapter 4).
7 Loosen the hose clamp and pry the hose off the coolant hose fitting **(see illustration)**.
8 Remove the bolts securing the coolant hose fitting to the intake manifold.
9 Remove the coolant tube from the transaxle end of the intake manifold **(see illustration)**.
10 Label and remove any remaining hoses, wires or cables attached to the intake manifold or its components.
11 Loosen the manifold mounting bolts/nuts in 1/4-turn increments until they can be removed by hand. Follow the recommended sequence **(see illustration)**.
12 The manifold will probably be stuck to the cylinder heads and force may be required to break the gasket seal **(see illustration)**. **Caution**: *Don't pry between the manifold and the heads or damage to the gasket sealing surfaces may occur, leading to vacuum leaks.*

Installation

Refer to illustrations 7.15a, 7.15b, 7.16 and 7.19

Note: *The mating surfaces of the cylinder heads and manifold must be perfectly clean when the manifold is installed. Gasket removal solvents in aerosol cans are available at most auto parts stores and may be helpful when removing old gasket material that's stuck to the heads and manifold (since they're made of aluminum, aggressive scraping can cause damage). Be sure to follow the directions printed on the container.*

13 Use a gasket scraper to remove all traces of sealant and old gasket material, then clean the mating surfaces with lacquer thinner or acetone. If there's old sealant or oil on the mating surfaces when the manifold is installed, oil or vacuum leaks may develop. Use a vacuum cleaner to remove any material that falls into the intake ports in the heads.
14 Use a tap of the correct size to chase the threads in the bolt holes, then use compressed air (if available) to remove the debris from the holes. **Warning**: *Wear safety glasses or a face shield to protect your eyes when using compressed air!*
15 Install new O-rings in the grooves of the coolant flanges at both ends of the manifold **(see illustrations)**. Apply a thin coating of sealant to the O-rings before seating them in the grooves.

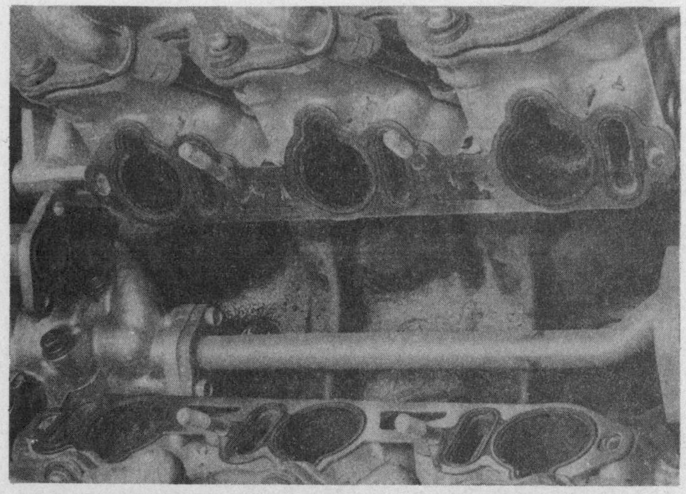

7.16 Position the new intake manifold gaskets as shown

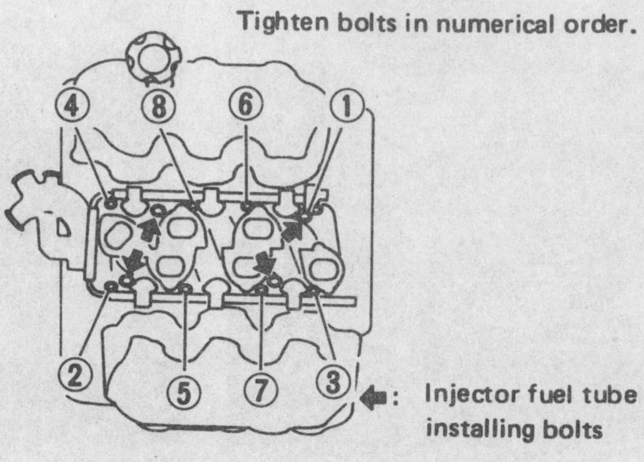

7.19 Intake manifold bolt/nut *tightening* sequence

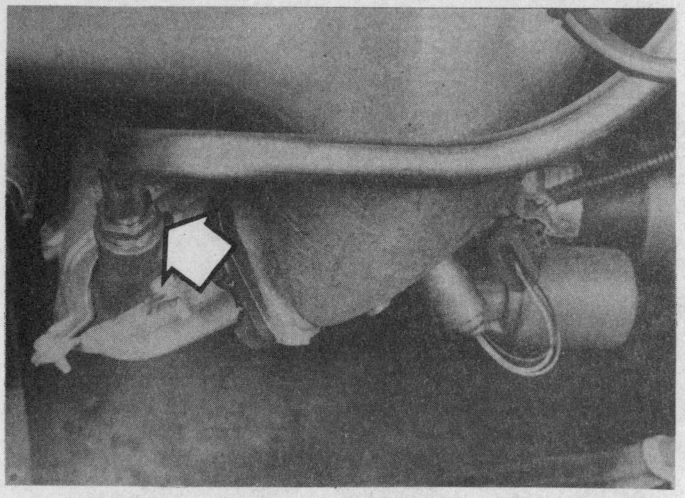

8.3a Remove the EGR tube (arrow) from the front manifold (1985 through 1988 shown, 1989 and later models similar)

16 Position the gaskets on the cylinder heads **(see illustration)**. No sealant is required; however, follow the instructions included with the new gaskets.

17 Make sure all intake port openings, coolant passage holes and bolt holes are aligned correctly.

18 Carefully set the manifold in place. **Caution**: *Don't disturb the gaskets.*

19 Install the bolts/nuts and tighten them to the torque listed in this Chapter's Specifications following the recommended sequence **(see illustration)**. Work up to the final torque in two steps.

20 The remaining installation steps are the reverse of removal. Start the engine and check carefully for oil and coolant leaks at the intake manifold joints.

8 Exhaust manifolds – removal and installation

Refer to illustrations 8.3a, 8.3b, 8.4a, 8.4b, 8.5a, 8.5b, 8.6, 8.7a, 8.7b and 8.12

Note: *The engine must be completely cool when this procedure is done.*

1 Disconnect the negative cable from the battery and support the vehicle on jackstands.

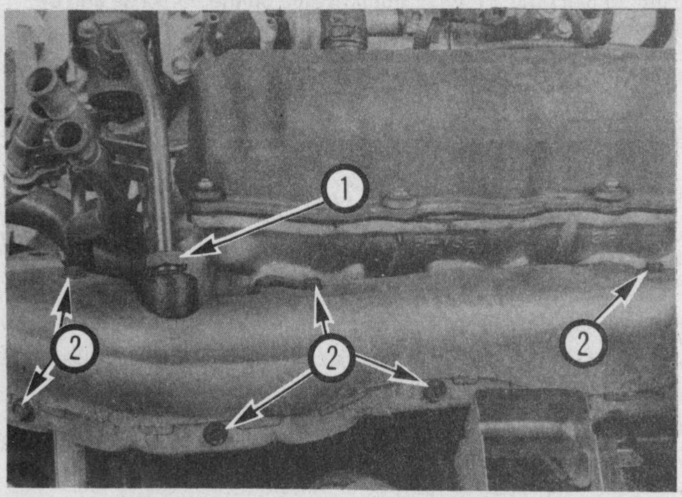

8.3b View of rear (firewall side) manifold on 1985 through 1988 models (engine removed for clarity)

1 *EGR pipe* 2 *Heat insulator bolts*

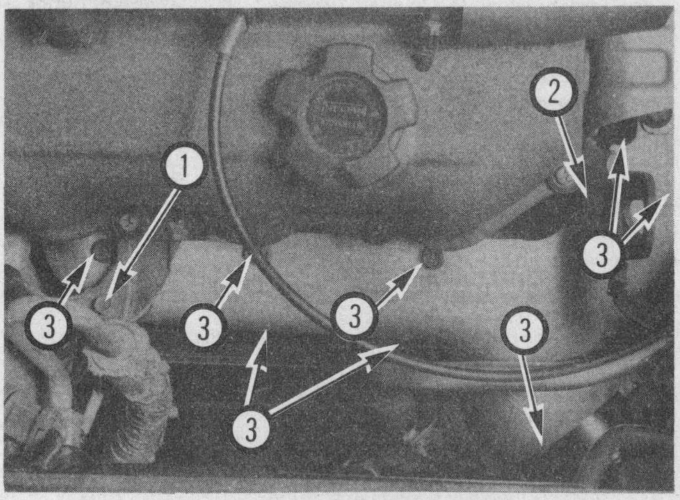

8.4a Rear manifold mounting details – 1985 through 1988 models

1 *Dipstick tube bracket bolt*
2 *Engine lifting bracket bolt*
3 *Heat insulator bolts*

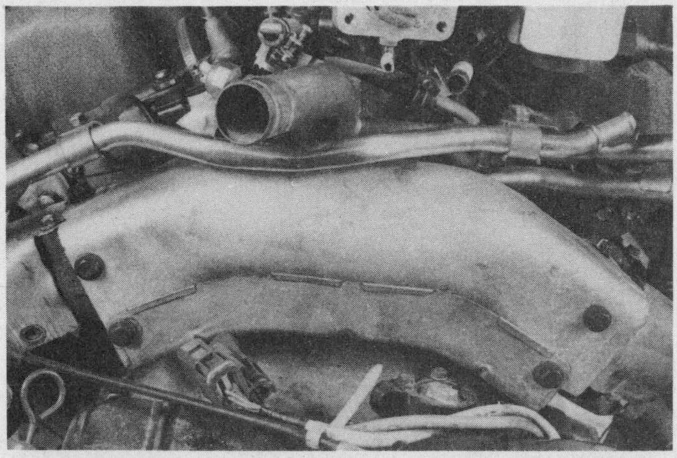

8.4b On 1985 through 1988 models, remove the three exhaust crossover pipe nuts/bolts on each end (air flow meter and air filter housing removed for clarity)

2 Spray penetrating oil on the exhaust manifold fasteners and allow it to soak in.
3 Remove the EGR pipes from the manifold(s) being removed **(see illustrations)**. **Note:** *Beginning with 1989 models, the rear manifold has no EGR pipe.*
4 Unbolt the heat insulators from the crossover pipe and manifold(s) being removed **(see illustrations)**. To access the exhaust crossover pipe on 1985 through 1988 models, it may be necessary to remove the air inlet tube, air flow meter and air filter housing (see Chapter 4).
5 Disconnect the exhaust crossover pipe **(see illustrations)**.

Front (radiator side) manifold only

6 Detach the exhaust pipe and oxygen sensor from the exhaust manifold **(see illustration)**.

Both manifolds

7 Remove the nuts retaining the manifold to the cylinder head and slip it off the mounting studs **(see illustrations)**. **Note**: *The manifolds on 1989 models are shaped differently but fastener locations are the same.*

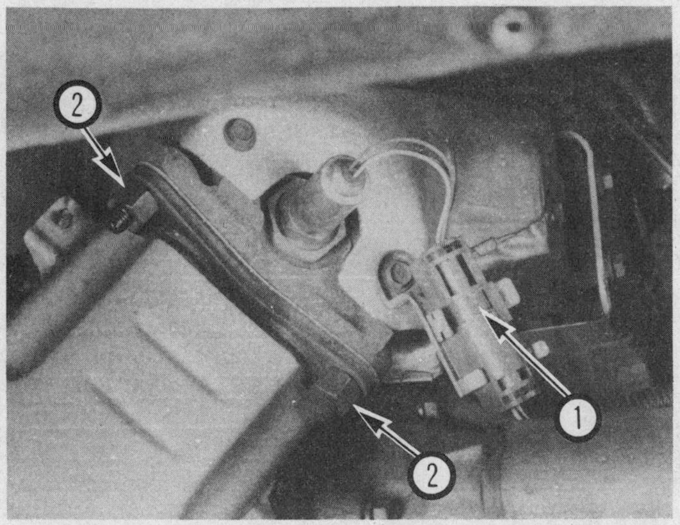

8.6 Disconnect the oxygen sensor electrical connector and remove the manifold-to-exhaust pipe nuts – note that the rear one is obscured (1985 through 1988 model shown)

1 Oxygen sensor connector 2 Mounting nuts

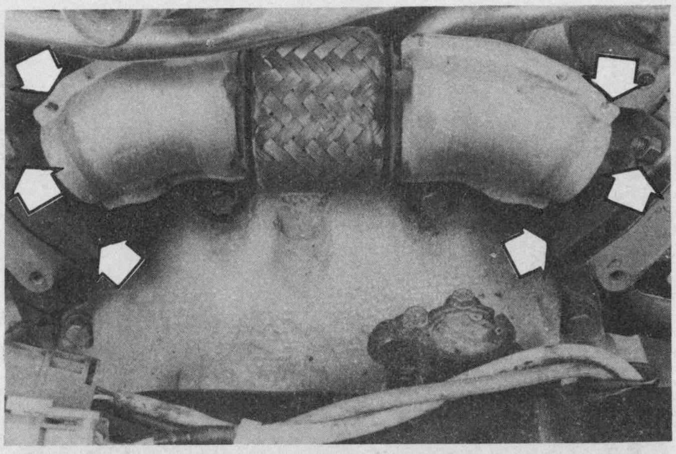

8.5a The exhaust crossover pipe on 1985 through 1988 models is attached to the manifolds at each end with three nuts/bolts (arrows)

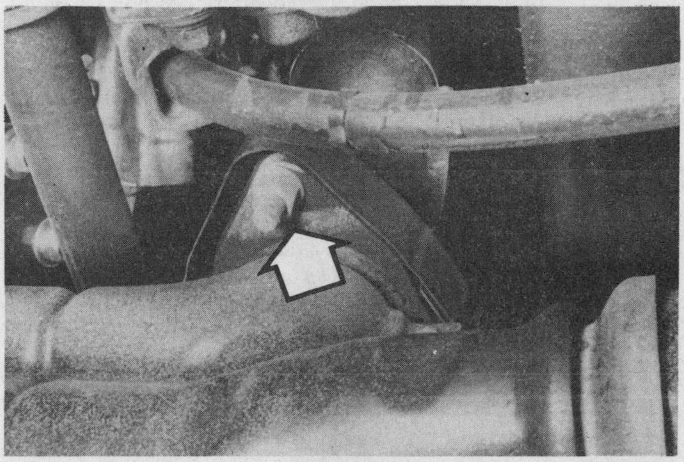

8.5b Beginning with 1989 models, the crossover pipe runs below the engine – this view shows the location of the rear manifold connection (arrow)

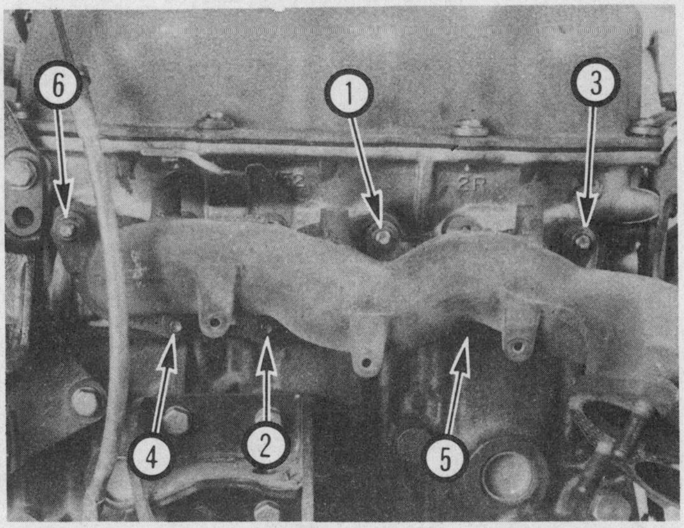

8.7a Loosen the front manifold retaining nuts in the numerical order shown (engine removed for clarity)

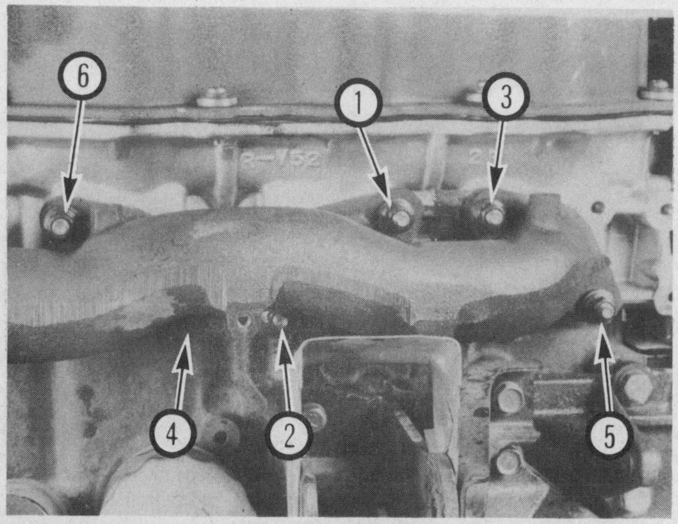

8.7b Loosen the rear manifold retaining nuts in the numerical order shown (engine removed for clarity)

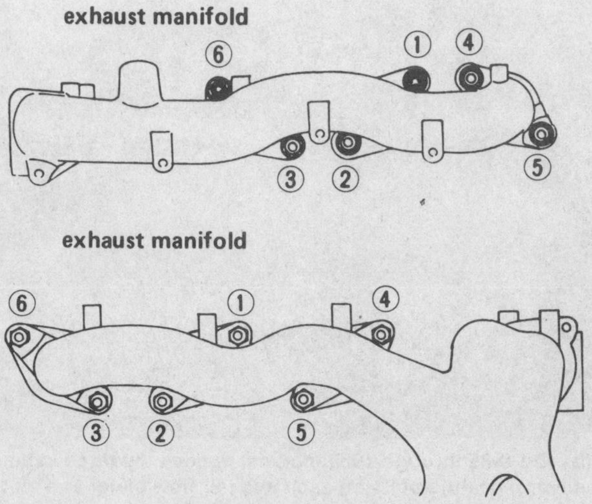

8.12 Tighten the exhaust manifold nuts in the sequence shown

8 Carefully inspect the manifolds and fasteners for cracks and damage.
9 Use a scraper to remove all traces of old gasket material and carbon deposits from the manifold and cylinder head mating surfaces. If the gasket was leaking, have the manifold checked for warpage at an automotive machine shop and resurfaced if necessary.
10 Position new gaskets over the cylinder head studs.
11 Install the manifold and thread the mounting nuts into place.
12 Working from the center out **(see illustration)**, tighten the nuts to the torque listed in this Chapter's Specifications in three or four equal steps.
13 Reinstall the remaining parts in the reverse order of removal. Use new gaskets when connecting the exhaust pipes.
14 Run the engine and check for exhaust leaks.

9 Crankshaft pulley – removal and installation

Refer to illustrations 9.4, 9.5 and 9.6

Removal

1 Disconnect the negative cable from the battery.
2 Loosen the lug nuts of the right front wheel, raise the front of the vehicle and support it securely on jackstands. Apply the parking brake. Remove the wheel.
3 Remove the drivebelts (see Chapter 1).
4 Wrap a cloth around the pulley to protect the belt surface and attach a chain wrench to the pulley. Hold the crankshaft from turning and use a socket and ratchet to loosen the bolt **(see illustration)**.
5 With the bolt installed loosely to prevent the pulley from falling, attempt to wiggle it off the crankshaft. If it is stuck, it may be necessary to pry it off **(see illustration)** or use a jaw-type puller.

Installation

6 Before installing the pulley, make sure the timing belt plate is positioned properly **(see illustration)**. To install the pulley, lightly lubricate the seal contact surface with engine oil and position it on the nose of the crankshaft. Align the keyway in the pulley with the key in the crankshaft and push the pulley into place by hand.
7 Hold the crankshaft from turning as described in Step 4, then install the bolt and tighten it to the torque listed in this Chapter's Specifications.
8 Reinstall the remaining parts in the reverse order of removal.

9.4 Clamp a chain wrench around the pulley to hold the crankshaft and loosen the bolt with a socket and ratchet

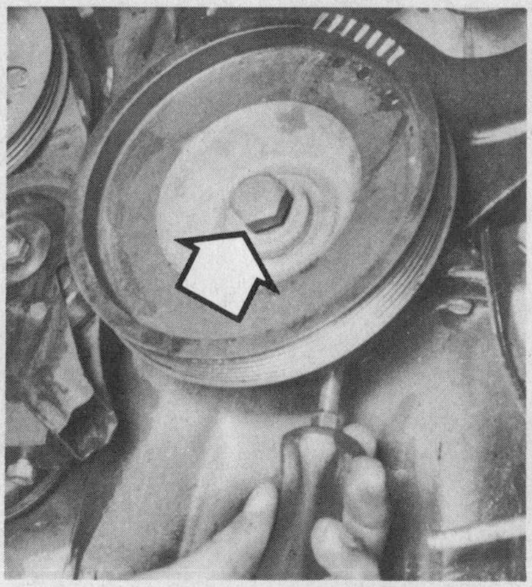

9.5 With the bolt (arrow) loosened, work the pulley off the crankshaft

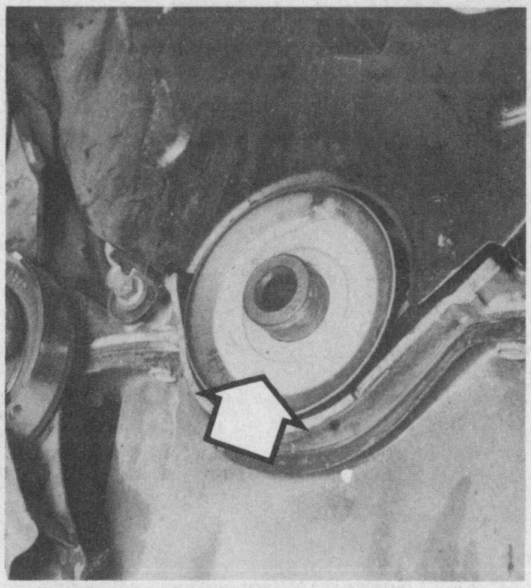

9.6 Be sure to install the timing belt plate (arrow) with the curved lip facing away from the belt

10.2a Remove the injector fan duct and cruise control servo screws (arrows) – 1985 through 1988 models

10.2b Cruise control servo mounting screw locations (arrows) – 1989 and later models

10 Timing belt – removal, installation and adjustment

Removal

Refer to illustrations 10.2a, 10.2b, 10.11a, 10.11b, 10.13a, 10.13b, 10.14a, 10.14b, 10.15, 10.16a and 10.16b

1 Disconnect the cable from the negative terminal of the battery.

2 Remove the injector fan duct, if equipped **(see illustration)**. Unbolt the cruise control servo and set it aside, without disconnecting the wires or cables **(see illustration)**.

3 Remove the coolant reservoir (see Chapter 3).

4 Loosen the lug nuts on the right front wheel.

5 Raise the front of the vehicle and support it securely on jackstands. Apply the parking brake.

6 Remove the right front wheel and detach the splash shield from the inner fenderwell.

7 Remove the splash pan and drain the cooling system (see Chapter 1).

8 Position the number one piston at TDC on the compression stroke (see Section 3). Remove the spark plugs (see Chapter 1).

9 Remove the drivebelts (see Chapter 1).

10 Disconnect the radiator hose from the thermostat and detach the water pump pulley.

11 Remove the air conditioning compressor idler pulley and bracket **(see illustrations)**.

12 Remove the crankshaft pulley (see Section 9). **Note**: *Don't allow the crankshaft to rotate during removal of the pulley. If the crankshaft moves, the number one piston will no longer be at TDC.*

13 Remove the bolts securing the timing belt upper and lower covers **(see illustrations)**. Note that various types and sizes of bolts are used. They must be reinstalled in their original locations. Mark each bolt or make a sketch to help remember where they go.

14 Confirm that the number one piston is still at TDC on the compression stroke by verifying that the timing marks on all three timing belt sprockets are aligned with their respective stationary alignment marks **(see illustrations)**.

15 Relieve tension on the timing belt by loosening the nut in the middle of the timing belt tensioner **(see illustration)**.

16 Check to see if the timing belt is marked with an arrow indicating which side faces out **(see illustration)**. If there isn't a mark, paint one on (only if the same belt will be reinstalled). Slide the timing belt off the sprockets.

2A

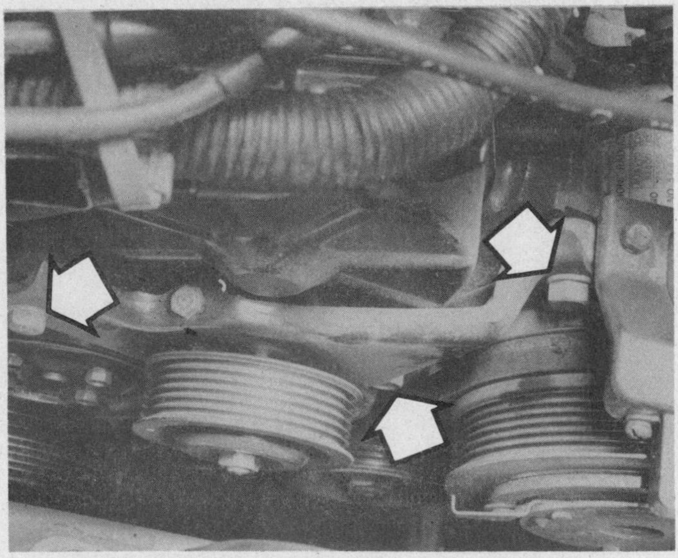

10.11a Remove the idler pulley bracket bolts (arrows)

10.11b Note the locations of the various length bolts for reinstallation (1985 through 1988 shown, newer models similar)

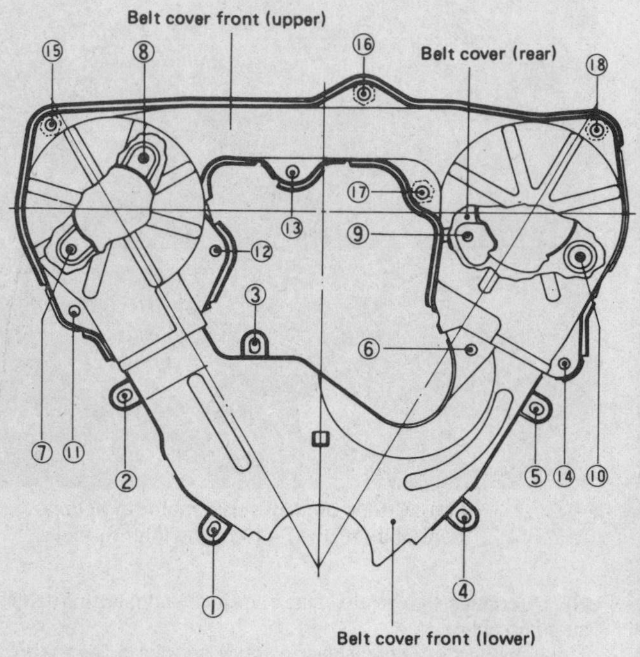

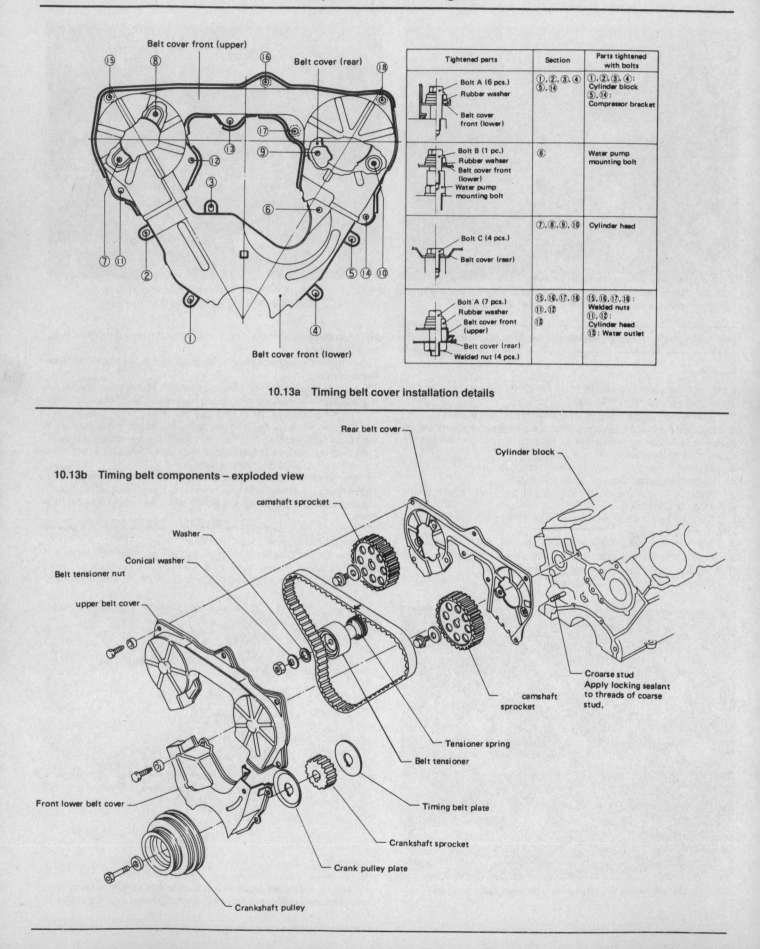

Tightened parts	Section	Parts tightened with bolts
Bolt A (6 pcs.), Rubber washer, Belt cover front (lower)	①, ②, ③, ④, ⑤, ⑭	①, ②, ③, ④: Cylinder block; ⑤, ⑭: Compressor bracket
Bolt B (1 pc.), Rubber wahser, Belt cover front (lower), Water pump mounting bolt	⑥	Water pump mounting bolt
Bolt C (4 pcs.), Belt cover (rear)	⑦, ⑧, ⑨, ⑩	Cylinder head
Bolt A (7 pcs.), Rubber washer, Belt cover front (upper), Belt cover (rear), Welded nut (4 pcs.)	⑮, ⑯, ⑰, ⑱, ⑪, ⑫, ⑬	⑮, ⑯, ⑰, ⑱: Welded nuts; ⑪, ⑫: Cylinder head; ⑬: Water outlet

10.13a Timing belt cover installation details

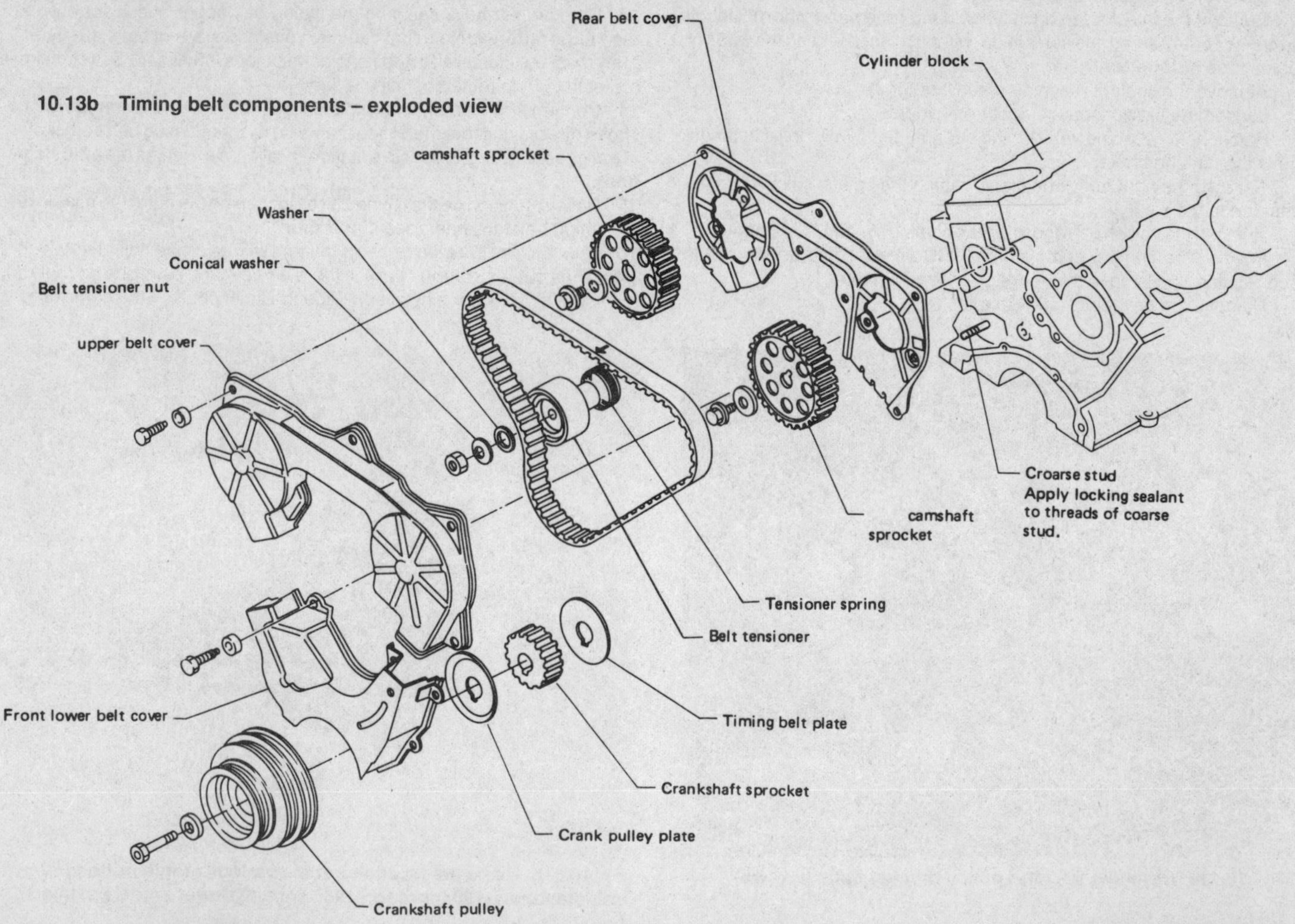

10.13b Timing belt components – exploded view

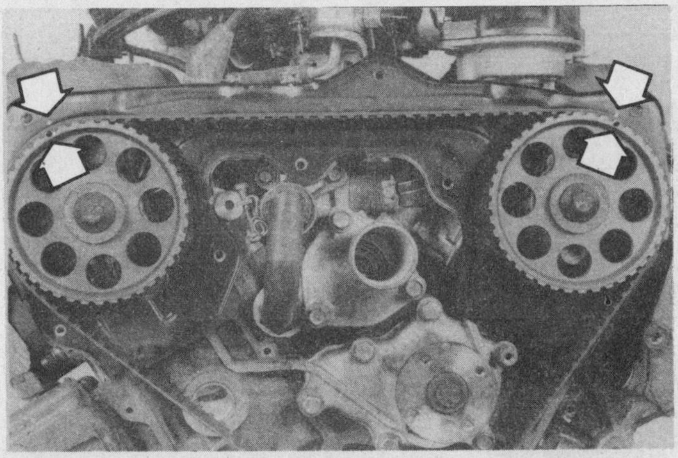

10.14a Make sure the marks on the camshaft sprockets align with the marks on the timing belt rear cover (arrows)

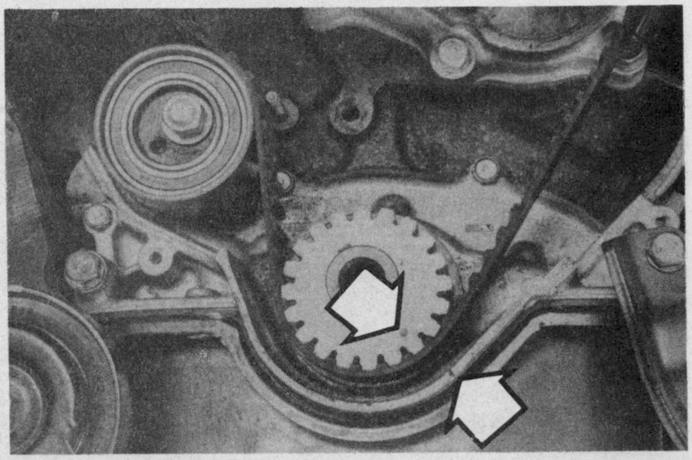

10.14b Working from below, be sure the mark on the crankshaft sprocket aligns with the mark on the oil pump housing (arrows)

10.15 Loosen the locking nut (arrow) in the middle of the timing belt tensioner

10.16a The timing belt should be marked (arrow) to indicate which side faces out – if not, use chalk to make an arrow on the belt before removal

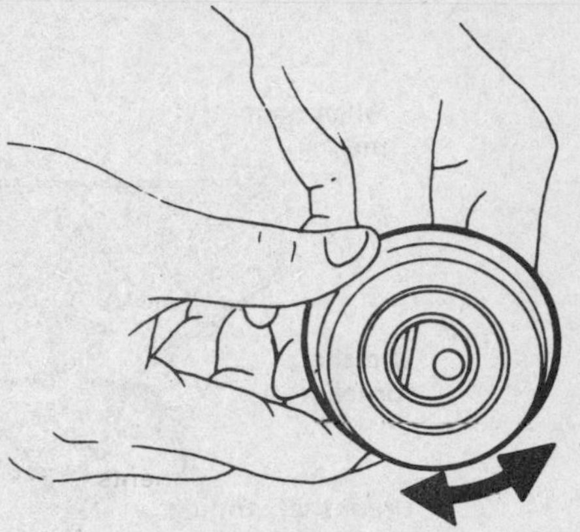

10.16b Check the belt tensioner and spring for wear and damage – the pulley should rotate smoothly

2A

Caution: *After removing the timing belt, DO NOT turn the camshafts or crankshaft separately - the valves will hit the pistons if you do. If the belt is cracked, worn or contaminated with oil or coolant, replace it with a new one.* Check the condition of the tensioner **(see illustration)**. Make sure the camshaft and crankshaft sprockets are in good condition - if they're worn or damaged, replace them (see Sections 11 and 12). Also at this time, check the water pump for leakage and replace if necessary (see Chapter 3).

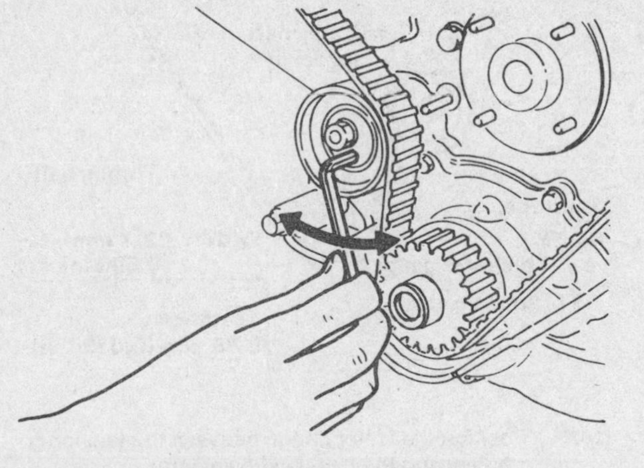

10.17 Turn the tensioner with an Allen wrench to vary timing belt tension

Installation

Refer to illustrations 10.17, 10.19a and 10.19b

17 Prepare to install the timing belt by turning the tensioner clockwise with an Allen wrench and temporarily tightening the locking nut **(see illustration)**.

18 Install the timing belt with the directional arrow pointing away from the engine.

19 Align the factory white lines on the timing belt with the punch mark on each of the camshaft sprockets **(see illustration)** and the crankshaft sprocket. Make sure all three sets of timing marks are properly aligned **(see illustration)**.

Adjustment

Refer to illustrations 10.20, 10.21, 10.24, 10.25 and 10.29

20 If the tensioner was removed, reinstall it and make sure the spring is positioned properly **(see illustration)**. Keep the tensioner steady with the Allen wrench and loosen the locking nut.

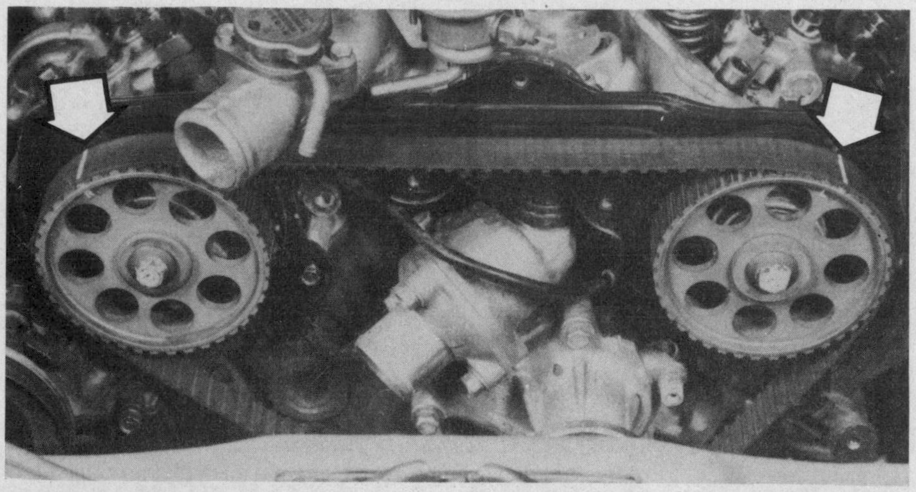

10.19a Align the white marks on the belt (arrows) with the punch marks on the camshaft sprockets and the rear timing belt cover to ensure correct valve timing – this is extremely important – don't continue with belt installation until you're sure it's correct!

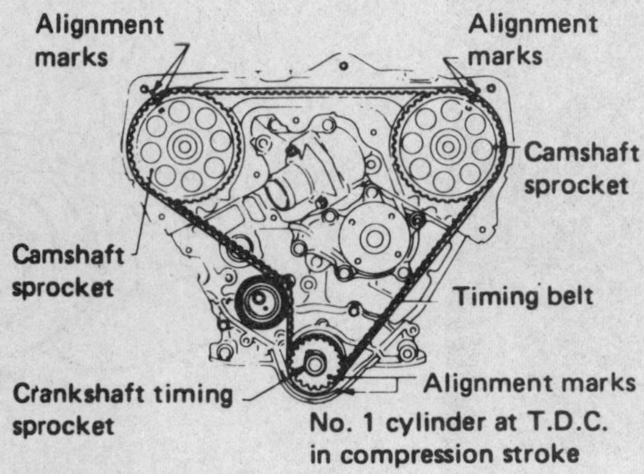

10.19b Make sure all the marks are aligned

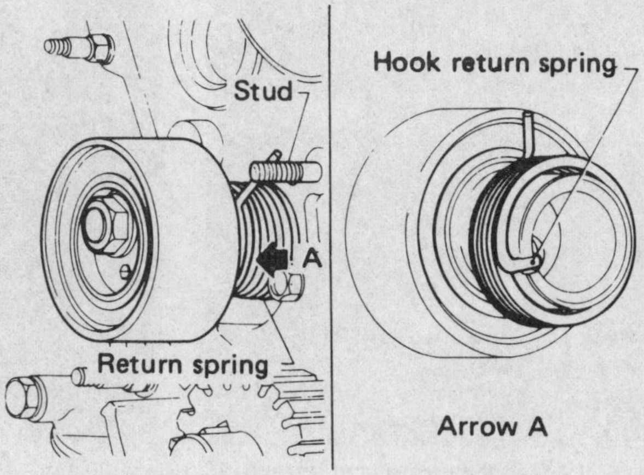

10.20 Belt tensioner spring mounting details (if the stud is removed, use a thread locking compound on the threads during installation)

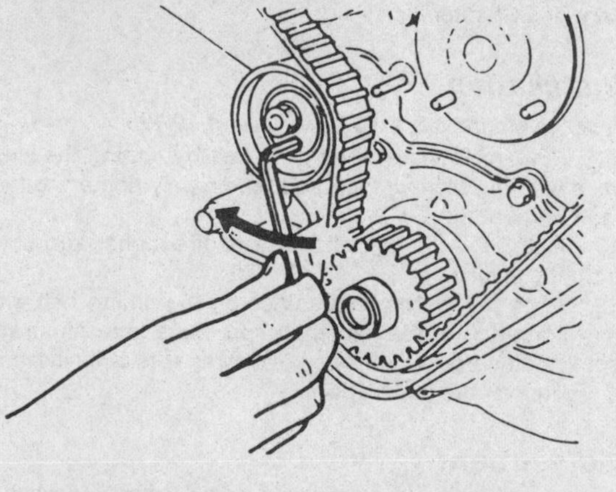

10.21 Use an Allen wrench to turn the tensioner pulley 70 to 80-degrees in a CLOCKWISE direction

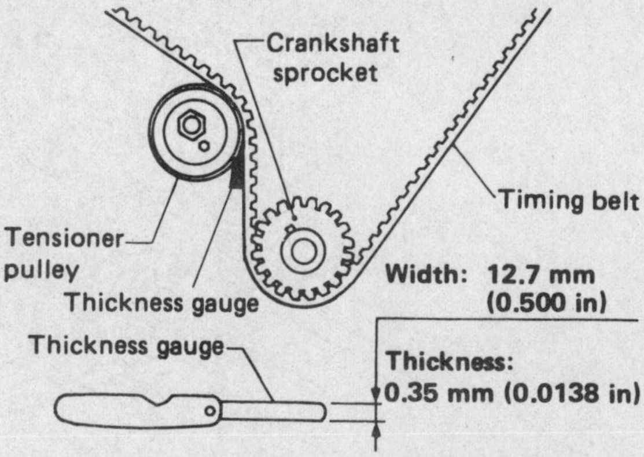

10.24 Position the feeler gauge between the tensioner pulley and the belt as shown here . . .

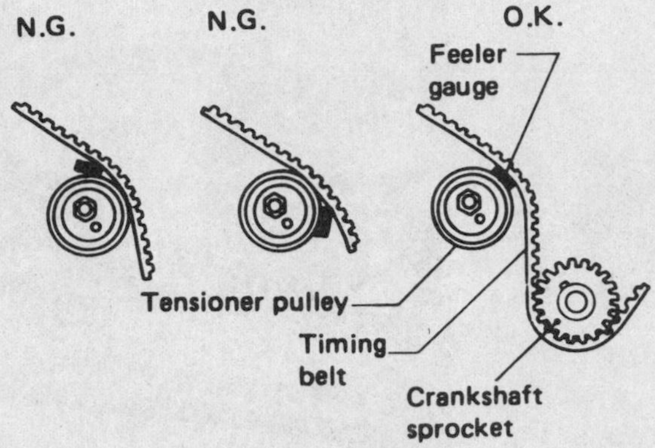

10.25 . . . then turn the crankshaft to move the feeler gauge to the point shown here (it must be exact, so work carefully)

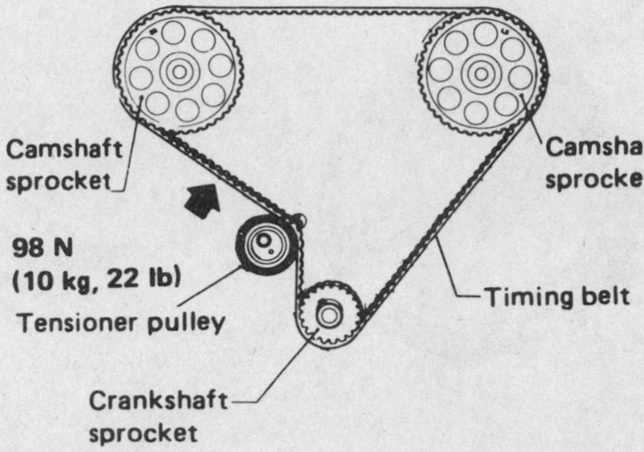

10.29 The deflection of the timing belt is checked exactly half-way between the rear camshaft sprocket and the tensioner pulley

21 Using the Allen wrench, swing the tensioner 70 to 80-degrees in a clockwise direction and temporarily tighten the locking nut **(see illustration)**.

22 Slowly turn the crankshaft clockwise two full revolutions, returning the number one piston to TDC on the compression stroke. **Caution**: *If excessive resistance is felt while turning the crankshaft, it's an indication that the pistons are coming into contact with the valves. Go back over the procedure to correct the situation before proceeding.*

23 Loosen the tensioner locking nut while keeping the tensioner steady with the Allen wrench.

24 Place a 0.0138-inch thick feeler gauge (or a combination of gauges to obtain this thickness) adjacent to the tensioner pulley **(see illustration)**.

25 Slowly turn the crankshaft clockwise until the feeler gauge is between the belt and the tensioner pulley **(see illustration)**.

26 Tighten the tensioner locking nut, keeping the tensioner steady with the Allen wrench.

27 Turn the crankshaft to remove the feeler gauge.

28 Slowly turn the crankshaft two revolutions and return the number one piston to TDC.

29 Check the deflection of the timing belt by applying 22 pounds of force midway between the rear camshaft sprocket and the tensioner pulley **(see illustration)**. The belt should deflect 0.512 to 0.571-inch (13 to 14.5 mm). Readjust the belt if necessary.

30 Install the various components removed during disassembly, referring to the appropriate Sections as necessary.

2A

11 Crankshaft front oil seal – replacement

Refer to illustrations 11.3, 11.4, 11.6, 11.7, 11.8a and 11.8b

1 Disconnect the negative cable from the battery.

2 Remove the drivebelts (see Chapter 1), pulley and timing belt (see Section 10).

3 Wedge two screwdrivers behind the crankshaft sprocket **(see illustration)**. Carefully pry the sprocket off the crankshaft. Some timing belt sprockets can be pried off easily with screwdrivers. Others are more difficult to remove because corrosion fuses them onto the nose of the crankshaft. If the pulley on your engine is difficult to pry off, don't damage the oil pump with the screwdrivers.

4 If the sprocket won't come loose, drill and tap two holes into the face of the sprocket and use a bolt-type puller to slip it off the crankshaft **(see illustration)**. **Caution**: *Do not reuse a drilled sprocket – replace it.*

11.3 Use two screwdrivers to pry the crankshaft sprocket off

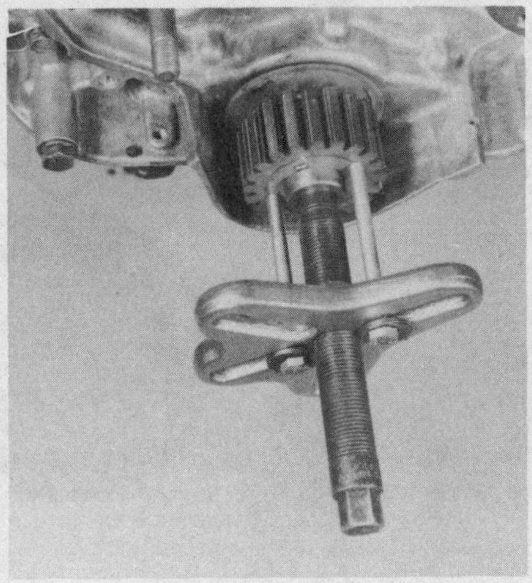

11.4 If it's stuck, drill and tap two holes and remove it with a bolt-type puller

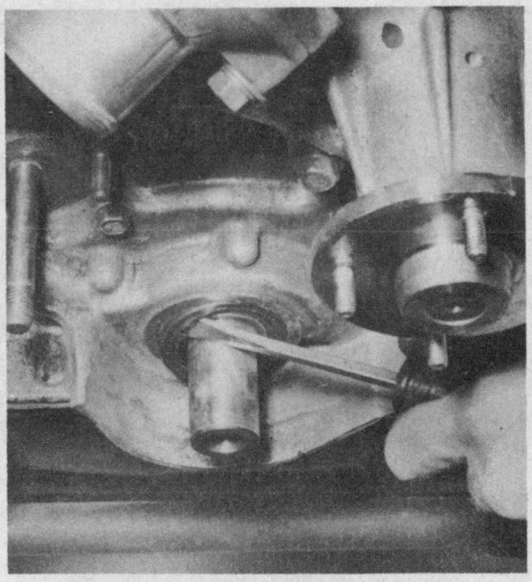

11.6 Pry the seal out very carefully with a screwdriver – if the crankshaft is nicked or otherwise damaged, the new seal will leak!

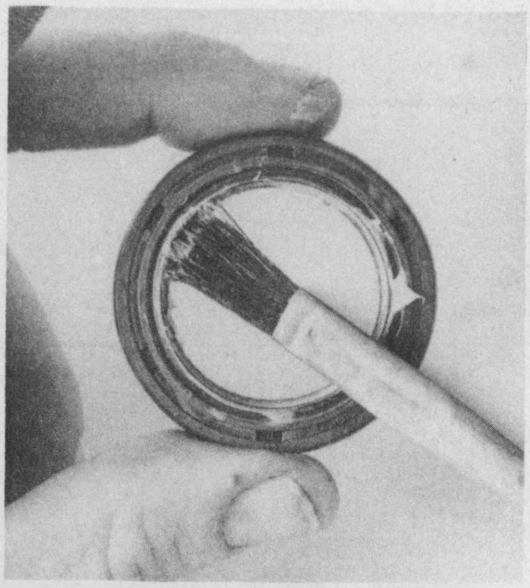

11.7 Apply moly-base grease or assembly lube to the lips of the new seal before installing it (if you apply a small amount of grease to the outer edge, it will be easier to push into the bore)

11.8a Fabricate a seal installation tool from a piece of pipe and a large washer . . .

11.8b . . . to push the seal into the bore – the pipe must bear against the outer edge of the seal as the bolt is tightened

5 Turn the bolt of the puller until the pulley comes off. Remove the timing belt plate.

6 Carefully pry the oil seal out with a screwdriver **(see illustration)**. Don't scratch or nick the crankshaft in the process!

7 Before installation, apply a thin coat of assembly lube to the inside of the seal **(see illustration)**.

8 Fabricate a seal installation tool with a short length of pipe of equal or slightly smaller outside diameter than the seal itself. File the end of the pipe that will bear down on the seal until it's free of sharp edges. You'll also need a large washer, slightly larger in diameter than the pipe, on which the bolt head can seat **(see illustration)**. Install the oil seal by pressing it into position with the seal installation tool **(see illustration)**. When you see and feel the seal stop moving, don't turn the bolt any more or you'll damage the seal.

9 Slide the timing belt plate onto the nose of the crankshaft.

10 Make sure the Woodruff key is in place in the crankshaft.

11 Apply a thin coat of assembly lube to the inside of the timing belt sprocket and slide it onto the crankshaft.

12 Installation of the remaining components is the reverse of removal. Be sure to refer to Section 10 for the timing belt installation and adjustment procedure. Tighten all bolts to the torque listed in this Chapter's Specifications.

12 Camshaft oil seal – replacement

Refer to illustrations 12.3, 12.4, 12.5a, 12.5b and 12.6

1 Disconnect the negative battery cable from the battery.

2 Remove the drivebelts (see Chapter 1), crankshaft pulley (see Section 9) and timing belt (see Section 10).

3 Insert a screwdriver through a hole in the camshaft sprocket to lock it in place while loosening the mounting bolt **(see illustration)**.

4 Once the bolt is out, the sprocket can be removed by hand. **Note:** *Each sprocket is marked with either an R or L* **(see illustration)**. *If you're removing both camshaft sprockets, don't mix them up. They must be installed on the same cam they were removed from, R on the rear and L on the front.*

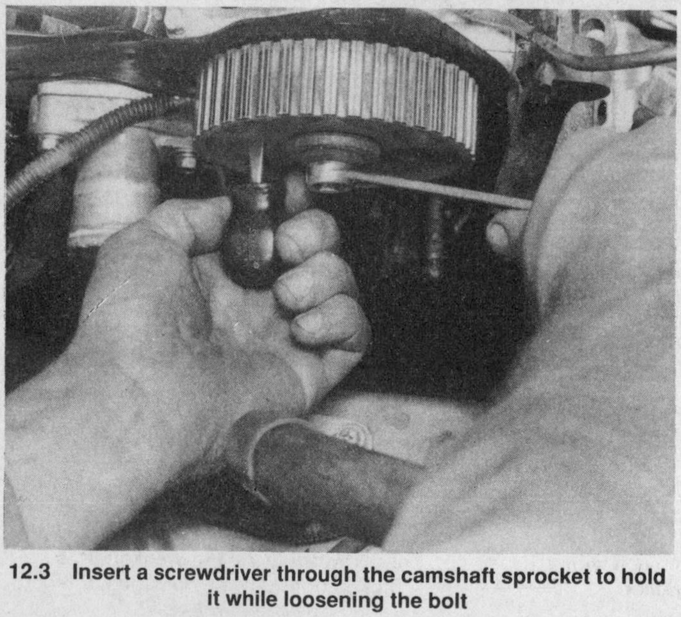

12.3 Insert a screwdriver through the camshaft sprocket to hold it while loosening the bolt

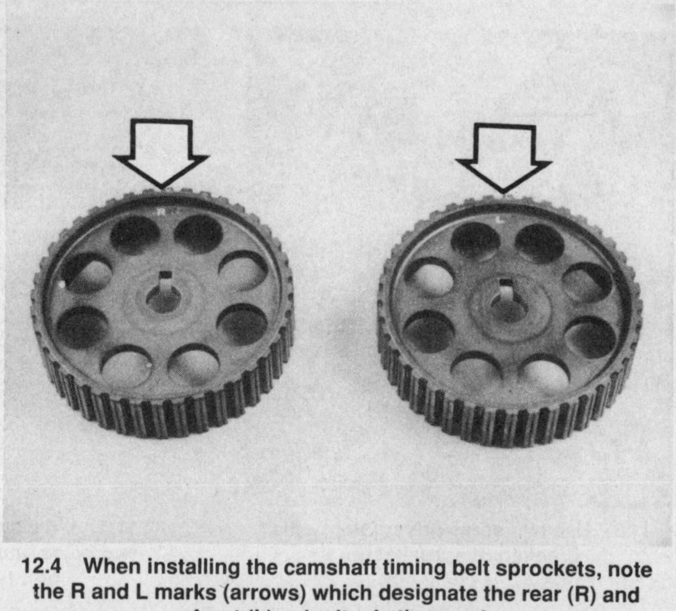

12.4 When installing the camshaft timing belt sprockets, note the R and L marks (arrows) which designate the rear (R) and front (L) – don't mix them up!

12.5a Pry the seal out very carefully with a screwdriver (if the camshaft is nicked or scratched, the new seal will leak!

12.5b The tool described in the previous Section may be used for camshaft seal installation

5 Carefully remove the old oil seal with a screwdriver. Don't nick or scratch the camshaft in the process **(see illustration)**. Refer to Steps 6, 7 and 8 in Section 11. The same seal installation tool used for the crankshaft seal can be used for both camshaft seals **(see illustration)**.
6 Install the sprocket. Make sure the R or L mark faces out! The side of the sprocket with the deep recess must face the engine, which means the shallow recess must face out **(see illustration)**.
7 Insert a screwdriver through the top hole in the camshaft sprocket to lock it in place while you tighten the bolt to the torque listed in this Chapter's Specifications.
8 Installation of the remaining components is the reverse of removal.

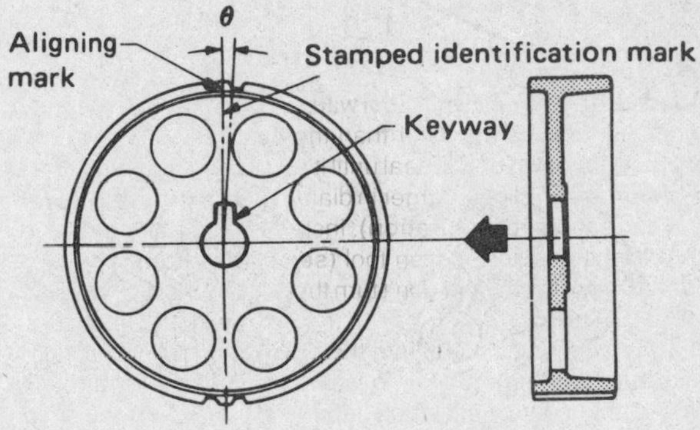

12.6 Make sure the camshaft sprocket is installed with the marked side facing OUT!

13 Valve spring, retainer and seals – replacement

Refer to illustrations 13.4, 13.9a, 13.9b, 13.15a, 13.15b, 13.16 and 13.17

Note: *Broken valve springs and defective valve stem seals can be replaced without removing the cylinder heads. Two special tools and a compressed air source are normally required to perform this operation, so read through this Section carefully and rent or buy the tools before beginning the job. If compressed air isn't available, a length of nylon rope can be used to keep the valves from falling into the cylinder during this procedure.*

1 Refer to Section 4 and remove the rocker arm cover from the affected cylinder head. If all of the valve stem seals are being replaced, remove both rocker arm covers.
2 Remove the spark plug from the cylinder which has the defective component. If all of the valve stem seals are being replaced, all of the spark plugs should be removed.
3 Turn the crankshaft until the piston in the affected cylinder is at top dead center on the compression stroke (refer to Section 3 for instructions). If you're replacing all of the valve stem seals, begin with cylinder number one and work on the valves for one cylinder at a time. Move from cylinder-to-cylinder following the firing order sequence (see the Specifications Section in this Chapter).
4 Thread an adapter into the spark plug hole **(see illustration)** and connect an air hose from a compressed air source to it. Most auto parts stores can supply the air hose adapter. **Note**: *Many cylinder compression gauges utilize a screw-in fitting that may work with your air hose quick-disconnect fitting.*
5 Remove the rocker arm assembly for the valve with the defective part. If all of the valve stem seals are being replaced, the rocker arm assemblies on both heads should be removed (refer to Section 5).
6 Apply compressed air to the cylinder. **Warning**: *The piston may be forced down by compressed air, causing the crankshaft to turn suddenly. If*

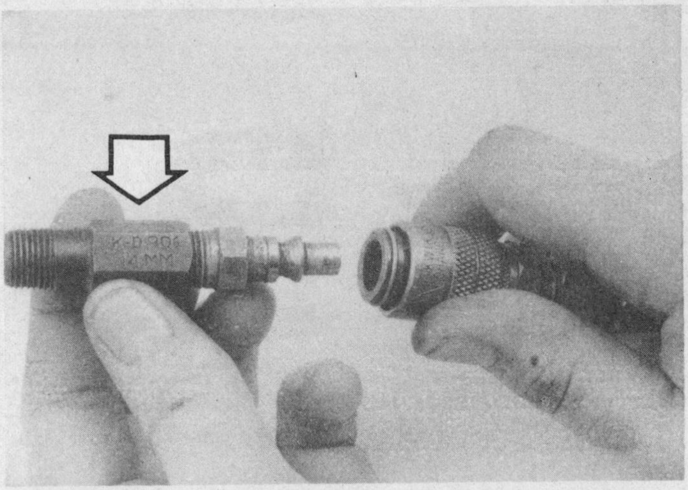

13.4 This is what the air hose adapter that threads into the spark plug hole looks like – they're commonly available from auto parts stores

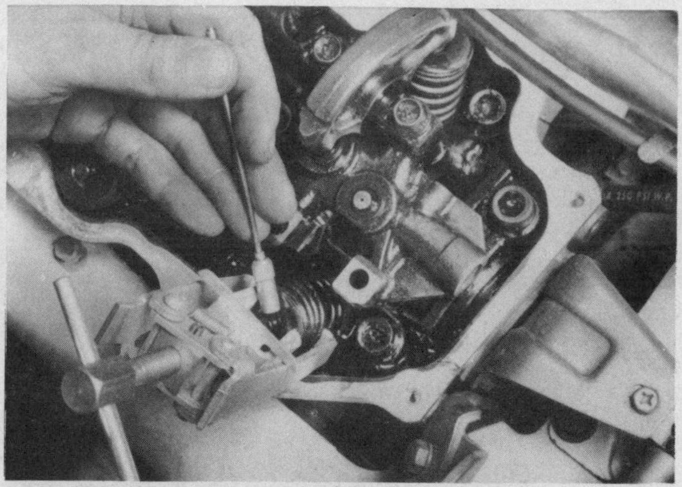

13.9a Compress the valve spring enough to release the keepers and lift them out with a magnet or needle-nose pliers

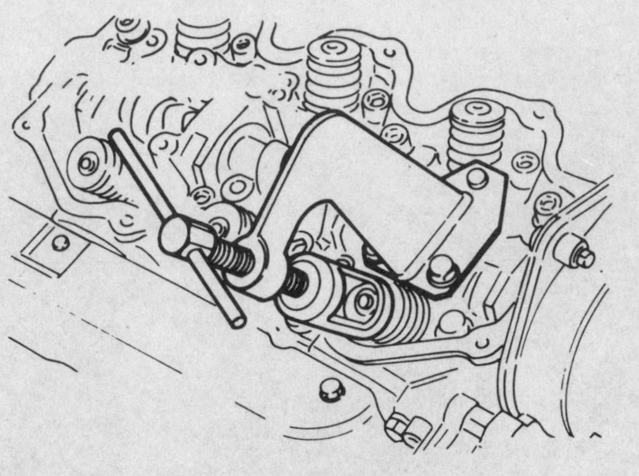

13.9b A special tool KV10110600 is available from your Nissan dealer for compressing valve springs

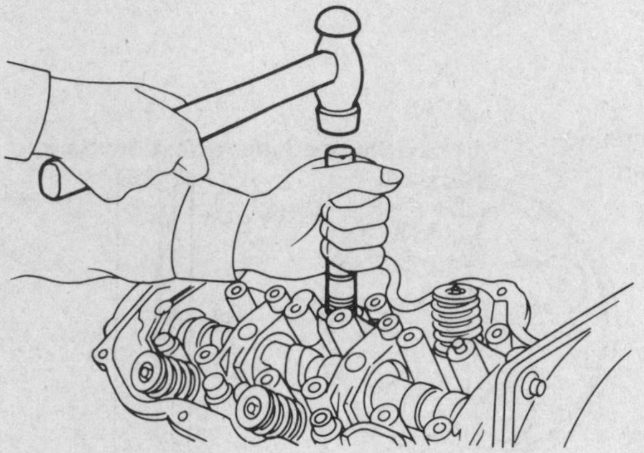

13.15a Special tool KV10107501 is recommended for intake valve seal installation – if this tool isn't available, an appropriately-sized deep socket can be used – don't hammer on the seals once they're seated!

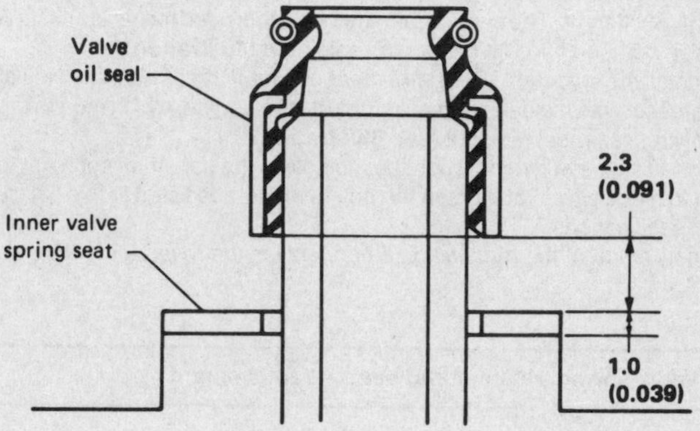

13.15b The exhaust valve seals should be installed until the seal-to-spring seat clearance is 0.091-inch

13.16 Make sure each outer valve spring (right) is installed with the narrow pitch end (arrow) against the cylinder head

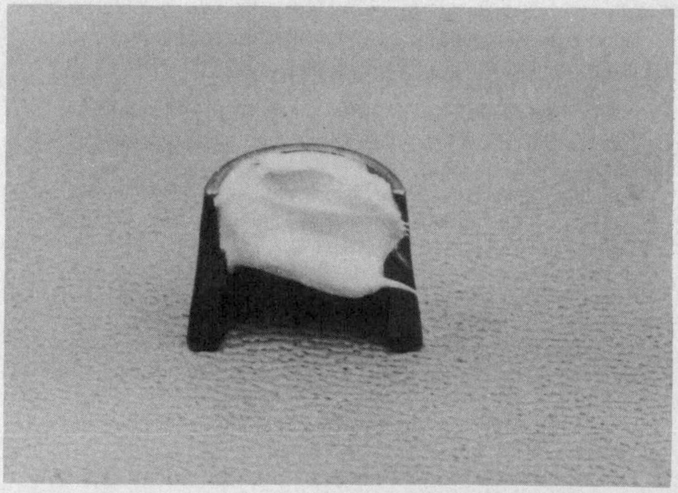

13.17 Apply a small dab of grease to each keeper as shown here before installation – it will hold them in place on the valve stem as the spring is released

the wrench used when positioning the number one piston at TDC is still attached to the bolt in the crankshaft nose, it could cause damage or injury when the crankshaft moves.

7 The valves should be held in place by the air pressure. If the valve faces or seats are in poor condition, leaks may prevent air pressure from retaining the valves – refer to the alternative procedure below.

8 If you don't have access to compressed air, an alternative method can be used. Position the piston a few degrees before TDC on the compression stroke, then feed a long piece of nylon rope through the spark plug hole until it fills the combustion chamber. Be sure to leave the end of the rope hanging out of the engine so it can be removed easily. Use a large ratchet and socket to rotate the crankshaft in the normal direction of rotation until *slight* resistance is felt.

9 Stuff shop rags into the cylinder head holes above and below the valves to prevent parts and tools from falling into the engine, then use a valve spring compressor to compress the spring **(see illustrations)**. Remove the keepers with small needle-nose pliers or a magnet.

10 Remove the spring retainer and valve springs, then remove the guide seal. **Note**: *If air pressure fails to hold the valve in the closed position during this operation, the valve face and/or seat is probably damaged. If so, the cylinder heads will have to be removed for additional repair operations.*

11 Wrap a rubber band or tape around the top of the valve stem so the valve won't fall into the combustion chamber, then release the air pressure. **Note**: *If a rope was used instead of air pressure, turn the crankshaft slightly counterclockwise.*

12 Inspect the valve stem for damage. Rotate the valve in the guide and check the end for eccentric movement, which would indicate that the valve is bent.

13 Move the valve up-and-down in the guide and make sure it doesn't bind. If the valve stem binds, either the valve is bent or the guide is damaged. In either case, the head will have to be removed for repair.

14 Reapply air pressure to the cylinder to retain the valve in the closed position, then remove the tape or rubber band from the valve stem. If a rope was used instead of air pressure, rotate the crankshaft in the normal direction of rotation until slight resistance is felt.

15 Lubricate the valve stem with engine oil and install a new guide seal **(see illustrations)**.

16 Install the springs in position over the valve **(see illustration)**.

17 Install the valve spring retainer. Compress the valve spring and carefully position the keepers in the groove. Apply a small dab of grease to the inside of each keeper to hold it in place if necessary **(see illustration)**.

18 Remove the pressure from the spring tool and make sure the keepers are seated.

19 Disconnect the air hose and remove the adapter from the spark plug hole. If a rope was used in place of air pressure, pull it out of the cylinder.

20 Refer to Section 5 and install the rocker arm(s).

21 Install the spark plug(s) and hook up the wire(s).

22 Refer to Section 4 and install the rocker arm cover(s).

23 Start and run the engine, then check for oil leaks and unusual sounds coming from the rocker arm cover area.

14 Cylinder head(s) – removal and installation

Note: *Allow the engine to cool completely before beginning this procedure.*

Removal

1 Remove the timing belt, camshaft sprocket(s) and rear timing cover (see Sections 10 and 12).

2 Remove the intake manifold (see Section 7).

3 Remove the rocker arm components (see Section 5) and lifters (see Section 6).

4 Remove the exhaust manifold(s) as described in Section 8. **Note**: *If desired, each manifold may remain attached to the cylinder head until after the head is removed from the engine, however, the manifold must still be disconnected from the exhaust system and/or crossover pipe.*

Front (radiator side) cylinder head

Refer to illustration 14.7

5 Remove the distributor (crank angle sensor) and alternator (see Chapter 5).

6 Remove the air conditioning compressor from the bracket without disconnecting any hoses (see Chapter 3) and set it aside. It may be helpful to secure the compressor to the vehicle with rope or wire to make sure it doesn't hang by its hoses.

7 Remove the compressor and alternator bracket **(see illustration)**.

Rear (firewall side) cylinder head

8 Detach the heater hoses and brackets from the transaxle end of the head.

Both sides

Refer to illustrations 14.9, 14.10 and 14.11

9 Loosen the cylinder head bolts with a 10 mm hex drive tool in 1/4-turn increments until they can be removed by hand. Be sure to follow the proper numerical sequence **(see illustration)**.

2A

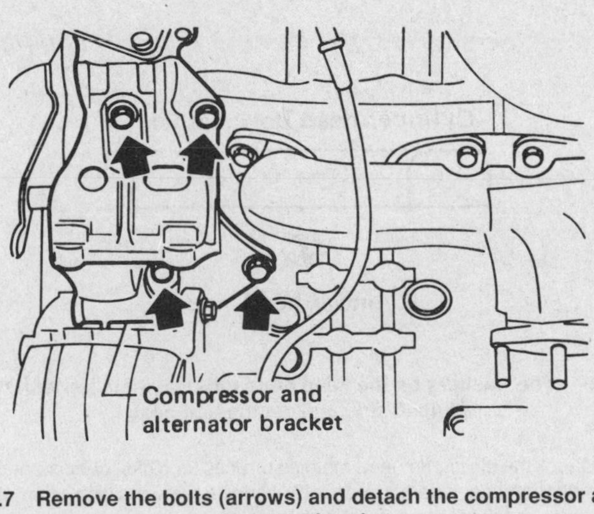

14.7 Remove the bolts (arrows) and detach the compressor and alternator bracket

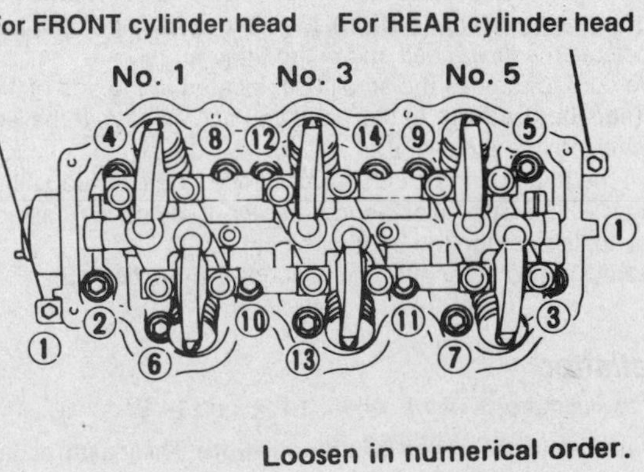

14.9 Cylinder head bolt LOOSENING sequence (loosen the bolts 1/4-turn at a time until they can be removed by hand)

14.10 To avoid mixing up the head bolts, use a new gasket to transfer the hole pattern to a piece of cardboard, punch holes to accept the bolts and push each bolt through the matching hole in the cardboard

14.11 Don't overlook the small bolt at the end of both cylinder heads (front cylinder head shown)

14.14 Peel off the old gaskets and clean the block and head mating surfaces thoroughly

14.18 Position the gasket over the dowel pins (arrows) so that all the holes line up

10 Head bolts must be reinstalled in their original locations. To keep them from getting mixed up, store them in cardboard holders marked to indicate the bolt pattern **(see illustration)**. Mark the holders F (front) and R (rear) and indicate the timing belt end of the engine.
11 Be sure to remove the small bolt, located at the end of the cylinder head **(see illustration)**. At this point you should have removed 13 large bolts plus the one small one.
12 Lift the head off the block. If resistance is felt, dislodge the head by striking it with a wood block and hammer. If prying is required, be very careful not to damage the head or block!
13 Remove the camshaft(s) as described in Section 15.

Installation

Refer to illustrations 14.14, 14.18, 14.20 and 14.21

14 Peel the old gaskets off **(see illustration)**. The mating surfaces of the cylinder heads and block must be perfectly clean when the heads are installed.
15 Use a gasket scraper to remove all traces of carbon and old gasket material, then clean the mating surfaces with lacquer thinner or acetone. If there's oil on the mating surfaces when the heads are installed, the gaskets may not seal correctly and leaks may develop. Use a vacuum cleaner to remove any debris that falls into the cylinders.

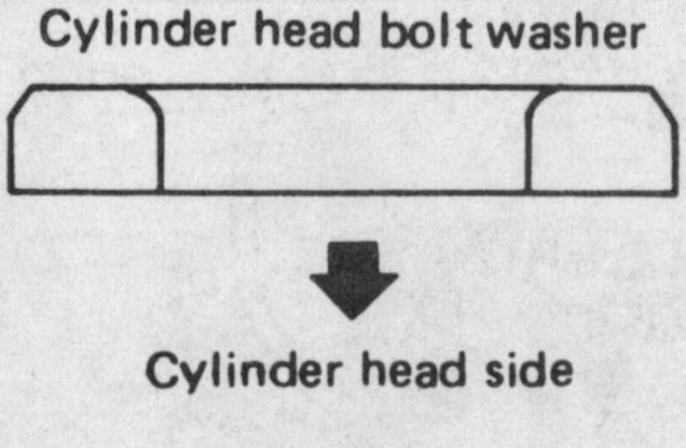

14.20 The washers on the head bolts must be installed with the radiused side against the bolt head

16 Check the block and head mating surfaces for nicks, deep scratches and other damage. If damage is slight, it can be removed with a file – if it's excessive, machining may be the only alternative.
17 Use a tap of the correct size to chase the threads in the head bolt holes. Mount each bolt in a vise and run a die down the threads to remove

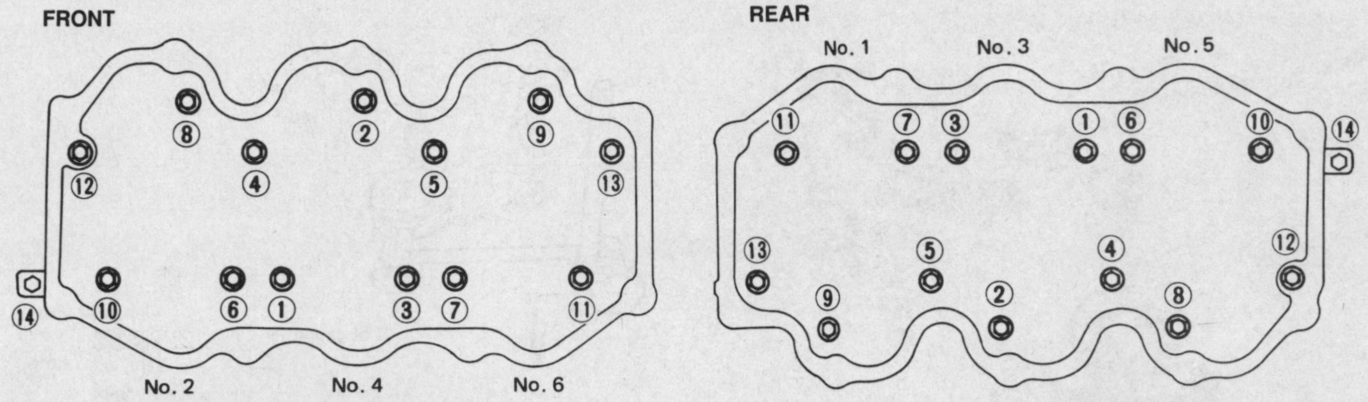

14.21 Cylinder head bolt tightening sequence (note that bolts 4, 5, 12 and 13 in the sequence are longer than the rest)

corrosion and restore the threads. Dirt, corrosion, sealant and damaged threads will affect torque readings. Ensure that the threaded holes in the block are clean and dry.

18 Position the new gaskets over the dowel pins in the block **(see illustration)**.

19 Carefully position the heads on the block without disturbing the gaskets.

20 Lightly oil the threads and install the bolts in their original locations. Tighten them finger tight. Make sure the washers are in place on the bolts – the radiused side of the washer must be against the bolt head, which means the flat side must be against the cylinder head surface **(see illustration)**.

21 Follow the recommended sequence and tighten the bolts in five steps to the torque specified in this Chapter **(see illustration)**. **Caution**: *Bolts 4, 5, 12 and 13 in the sequence are longer than the others – be sure all bolts are in their original installed locations!*

22 The remaining installation steps are the reverse of removal.

23 Add coolant and change the engine oil and filter (see Chapter 1), then start the engine and check carefully for oil and coolant leaks.

15 Camshaft – removal and installation

Removal

Refer to illustrations 15.2, 15.3a, 15.3b, 15.4 and 15.5

1 Remove the cylinder heads from the engine (see Section 14).

2 Remove the bolts **(see illustration)** and gently pry off the camshaft cover plate.

3 Use the holding lugs **(see illustration)** to secure the camshaft while loosening the retaining bolt **(see illustration)**. Remove the bolt and the thrust (locate) plate.

4 Carefully pry the camshaft oil seal out of the head with a small screwdriver **(see illustration)**. Don't scratch or nick the camshaft in the process!

5 Carefully pull the camshaft out the front of the head using a twisting motion **(see illustration)**. **Caution:** *Don't scratch the bearing surfaces with the cam lobes.* Camshaft and bearing inspection is covered in Section 16.

15.2 Remove the cover plate bolts (arrows) and gently pry off the cover (front head shown, rear head similar)

15.3a Hold the camshaft lug (arrow) . . .

15.3b . . . with pliers or a wrench to prevent the camshaft from moving while loosening the bolt

15.4 Carefully pry the camshaft oil seal out with a small screwdriver

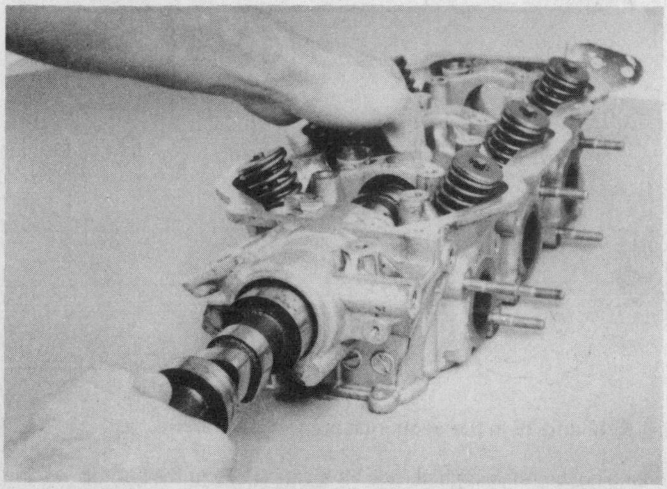

15.5 Pull the camshaft out the front of the head, using both hands to support it to avoid damage to the bearing surfaces in the head

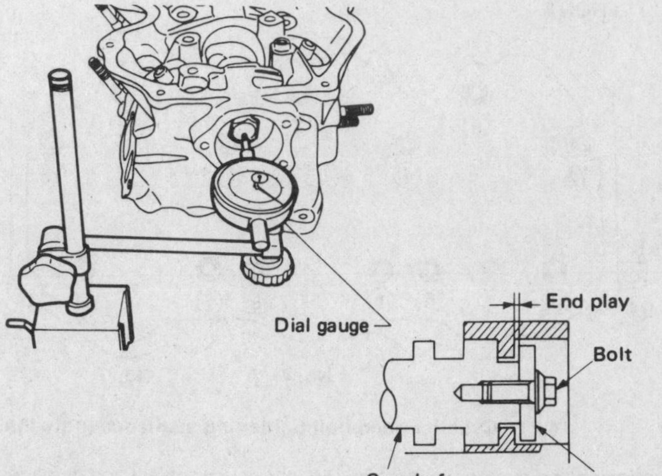

15.8 A dial indicator is needed to check camshaft end play

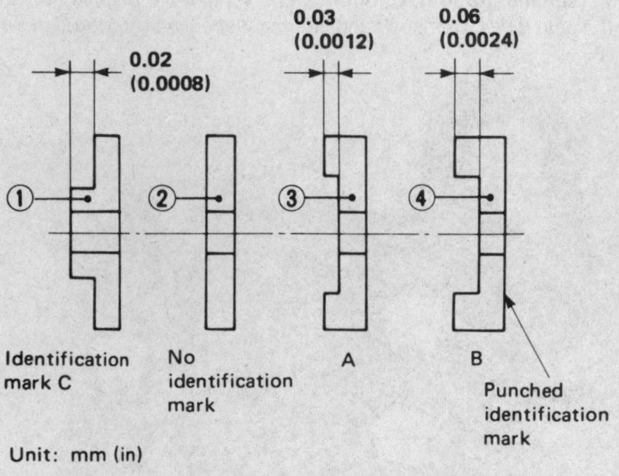

15.11 If the camshaft end play exceeds the specified limit, select a different thrust plate to bring the end play within specification

Installation

Refer to illustrations 15.8 and 15.11

6 Lubricate the camshaft bearing journals and lobes with moly-base grease or engine assembly lube, then install it carefully in the head. Don't scratch the bearing surfaces with the cam lobes!

7 Install the camshaft thrust (locate) plate and retaining bolt and tighten it to the torque specified in this Chapter.

8 With the camshaft installed in the head, mount a dial indicator to check the end play **(see illustration)**.

9 Move the camshaft as far as possible to the rear of the head.

10 Zero the dial indicator. Move the cam forward as far as possible. Compare the results to the Specifications in this Chapter.

11 End play outside the specified range requires thrust plate replacement. Measure the old plate **(see illustration)** and obtain a new one from your dealer that will produce end play as close to the specification as possible.

16 Camshaft, lifters and bearing surfaces/rocker arms and shafts – inspection

Refer to illustrations 16.1, 16.2, 16.3, 16.4, 16.5, 16.6, 16.7, 16.10 and 16.11

1 Visually check the camshaft bearing surfaces for pitting, score marks, galling and abnormal wear. If the bearing surfaces are damaged, the head will have to be replaced **(see illustration)**.

2 Measure the outside diameter of each camshaft bearing journal and record your measurements **(see illustration)**. Compare them to the journal outside diameter specified in this Chapter, then measure the inside diameter of each corresponding camshaft bearing and record the measurements. Compare them to the specified camshaft bearing inside diameter. Subtract each cam journal outside diameter from its respective cam bearing bore inside diameter to determine the oil clearance for each bearing. Compare the results to the specified journal-to-bearing clearance. If any of the measurements fall outside the standard specified wear limits in this Chapter, either the camshaft or the head, or both, must be replaced.

3 Check camshaft runout by placing the camshaft between two V-blocks and set up a dial indicator on the center journal **(see illustration)**. Zero the dial indicator. Turn the camshaft slowly and note the dial indicator readings. Record your readings and compare them with the specified runout in this Chapter. If the measured runout exceeds the runout specified in this Chapter, replace the camshaft.

4 Check the camshaft lobe height by measuring each lobe with a micrometer **(see illustration)**. Compare the measurement to the cam lobe height specified in this Chapter. Then subtract the measured cam lobe height from the specified height to compute wear on the cam lobes. Compare it to the specified wear limit. If it's greater than the specified wear limit, replace the camshaft.

5 Inspect the contact and sliding surfaces of each lifter for wear and scratches **(see illustration)**. **Note**: *If the lifter pad is worn, it's a good idea to check the corresponding camshaft lobe, because it will probably be worn too.* **Caution**: *Don't turn the lifters upside down – air can enter and become trapped inside (see Section 6).*

6 Measure the outside diameter of each lifter with a micrometer **(see illustration)** and compare it to the Specifications in this Chapter. If any lifter is worn beyond the specified limit, replace it.

7 Check each lifter bore diameter in the lifter guide assembly **(see illustration)** and compare the results to the Specifications in this Chapter. If any lifter bore is worn beyond the specified limit, the lifter guide assembly must be replaced.

8 Subtract the outside diameter of each lifter from the inside diameter of the lifter bore and compare the difference to the clearance specified in this Chapter. If both the lifter and the bore are within acceptable limits, this measurement should fall within tolerance as well. However, if you buy a new set of lifters alone, or a lifter guide assembly by itself, you may find that this clearance no longer falls within the specified limit.

9 Check the rocker arms and shafts for abnormal wear, pits, galling, score marks and rough spots. Don't attempt to restore rocker arms by grinding the pad surfaces.

10 Measure the outside diameter of the rocker arm shaft at each rocker arm journal **(see illustration)**. Compare the measurements to the rocker

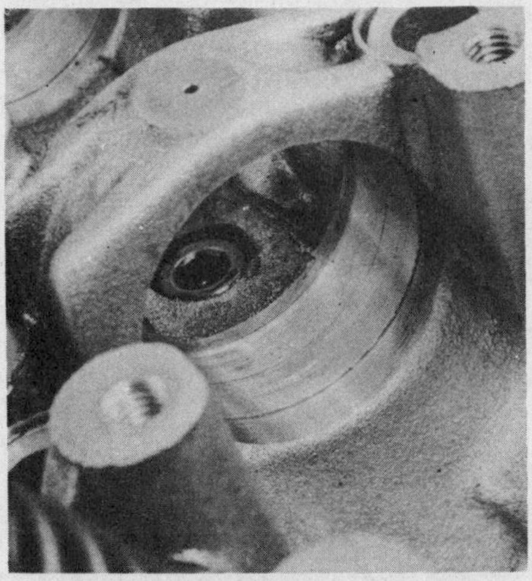

16.1 Inspect the cam bearing surfaces in each head for pits, score marks and abnormal wear – if wear or damage is noted, the head must be replaced

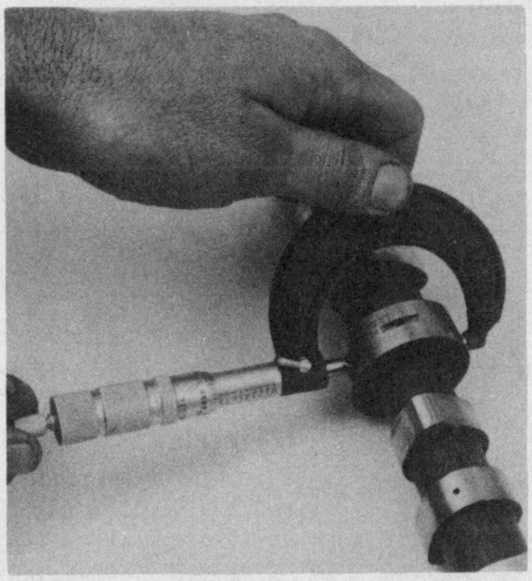

16.2 Measure the outside diameter of each camshaft journal and the inside diameter of each bearing to determine the clearances

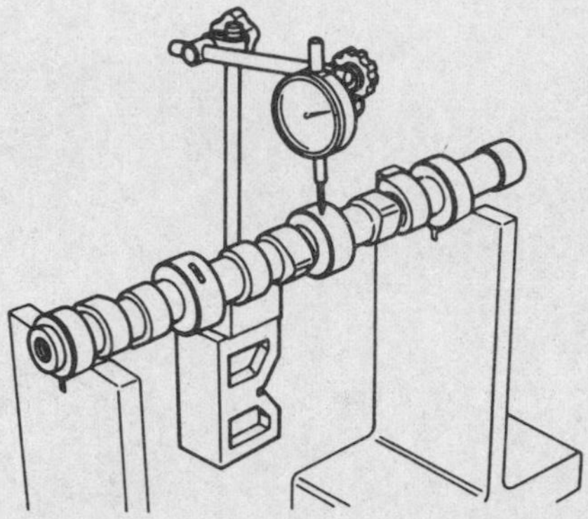

16.3 A dial indicator and V-blocks are needed to check camshaft runout

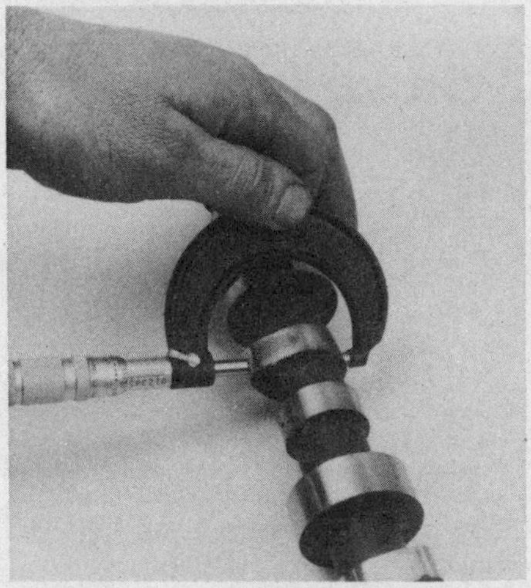

16.4 Measuring cam lobe height with a micrometer

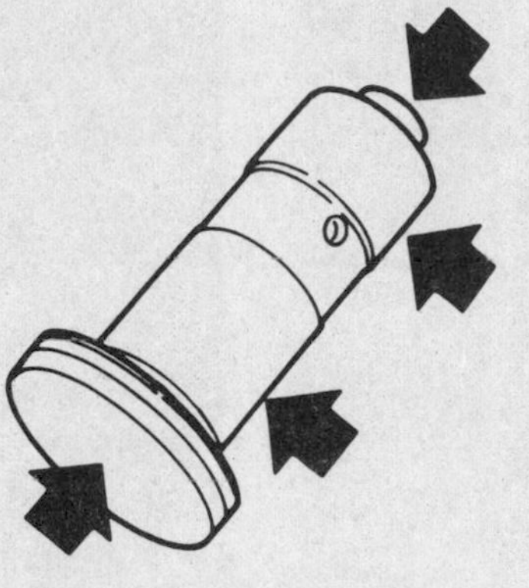

16.5 Check the contact and sliding surfaces of each lifter (arrows) for wear and damage

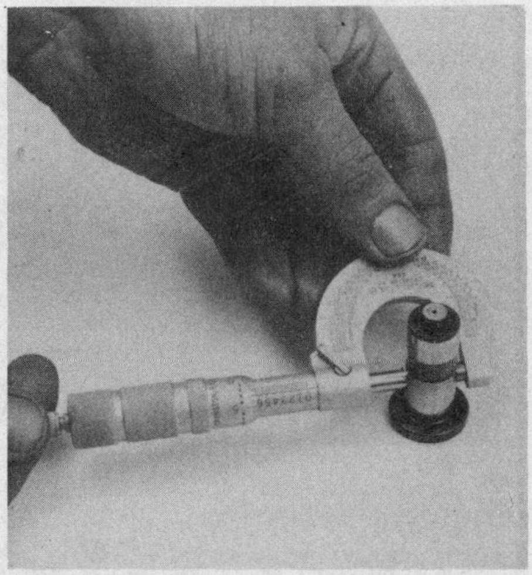

16.6 Measure the outside diameter of each lifter with a micrometer . . .

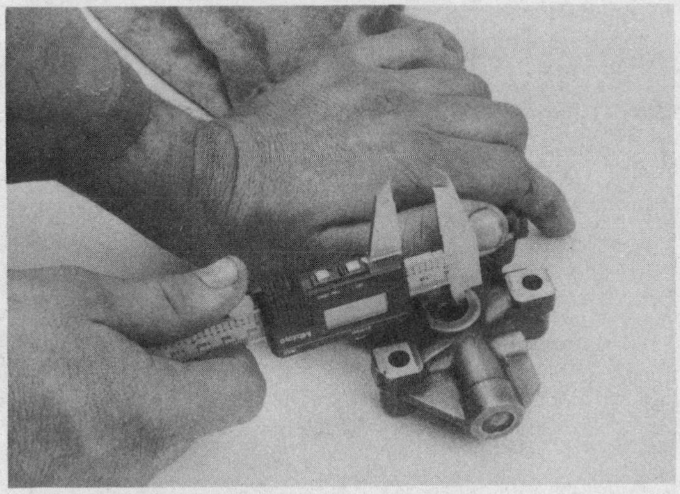

16.7 . . . and the inside diameter of each lifter bore, then subtract the lifter diameter to find the lifter-to-guide clearance (compare the results to the Specifications)

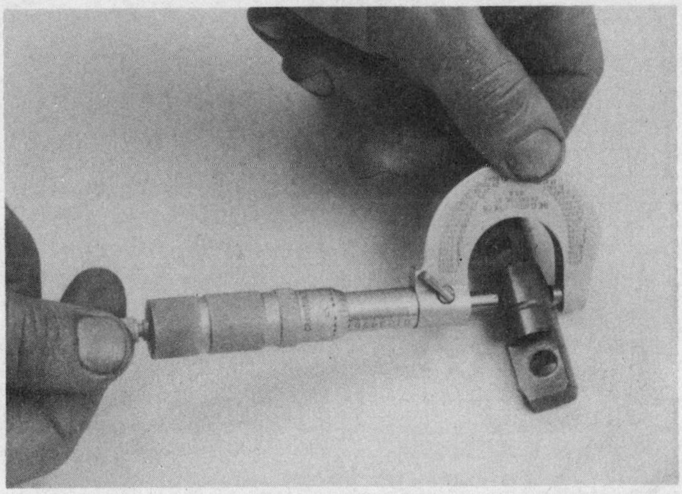

16.10 Measure the rocker arm shaft diameter at each journal where a rocker arm rides on the shaft

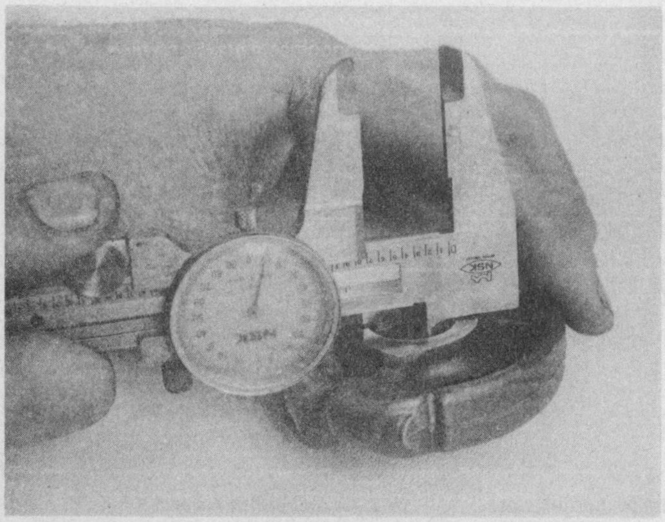

16.11 Measure the inside diameter of each rocker arm bore, subtract the corresponding rocker arm shaft diameter to get the clearance and compare the results to the Specifications

arm shaft outside diameter specified in this Chapter.

11 Measure the inside diameter of each rocker arm with either an inside micrometer or a dial caliper **(see illustration)**. Compare the measurements to the rocker arm bore diameter specified in this Chapter.

12 Subtract the outside diameter of each rocker arm shaft journal from the corresponding rocker arm bore diameter to compute the clearance between the rocker arm shaft and the rocker arm. Compare the measurements to the clearance specified in this Chapter. If any of them fall outside the specified limits, replace either the rocker arms or the shaft, or both.

17 Oil pan – removal and installation

Removal

Refer to illustrations 17.6a, 17.6b, 17.9, 17.11, 17.12 and 17.14

1 Disconnect the negative cable from the battery.

2 Raise the vehicle and support it securely on jackstands.

3 Remove the under-vehicle splash pan.

4 Drain the engine oil and install a new oil filter (see Chapter 1).

5 Unbolt the exhaust pipe from the front manifold (see Section 8).

6 Remove the gussets joining the engine to the bellhousing **(see illustration)** and on automatic transaxle models, detach the bellhousing cover **(see illustration)**.

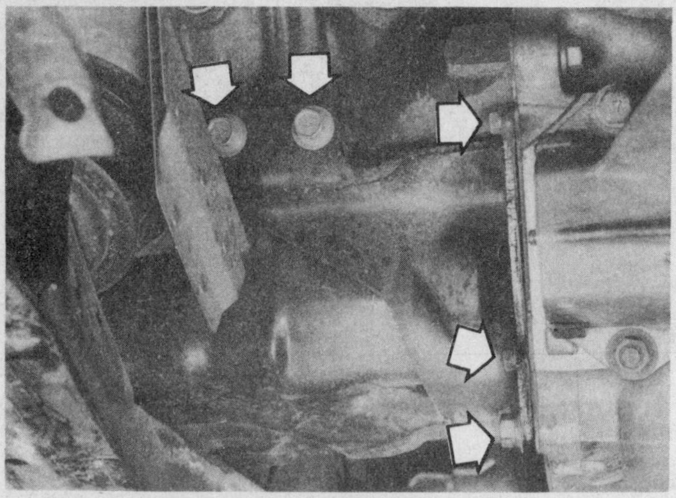

17.6a Remove the bolts (arrows) and detach the gusset on the radiator side (shown) – the gusset on the firewall side of the engine is similar

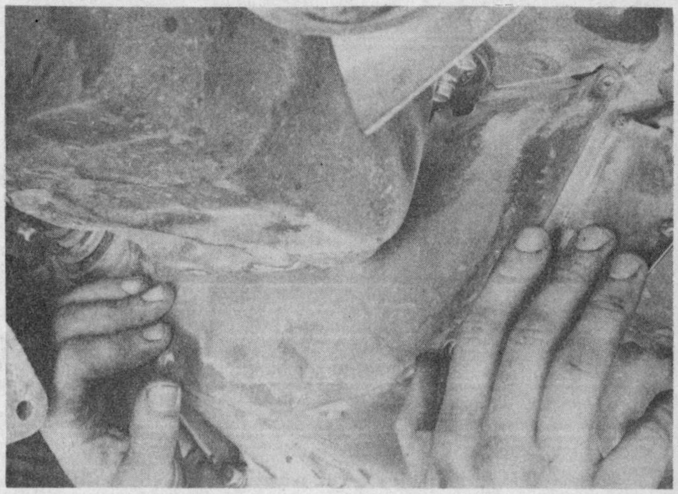

17.6b Once the gussets are removed, the bellhousing cover will drop free (automatic transaxle models)

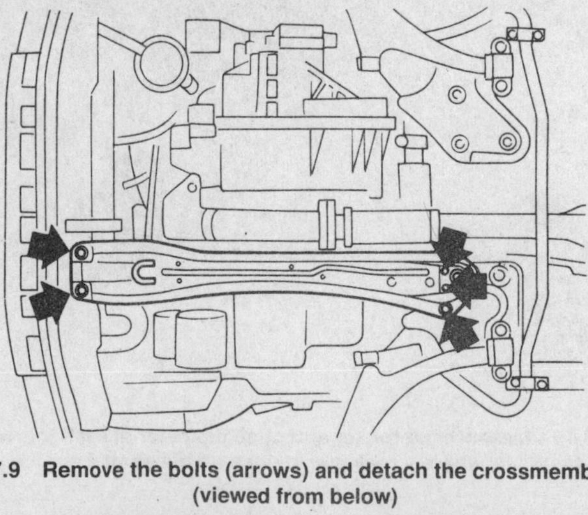

17.9 Remove the bolts (arrows) and detach the crossmember (viewed from below)

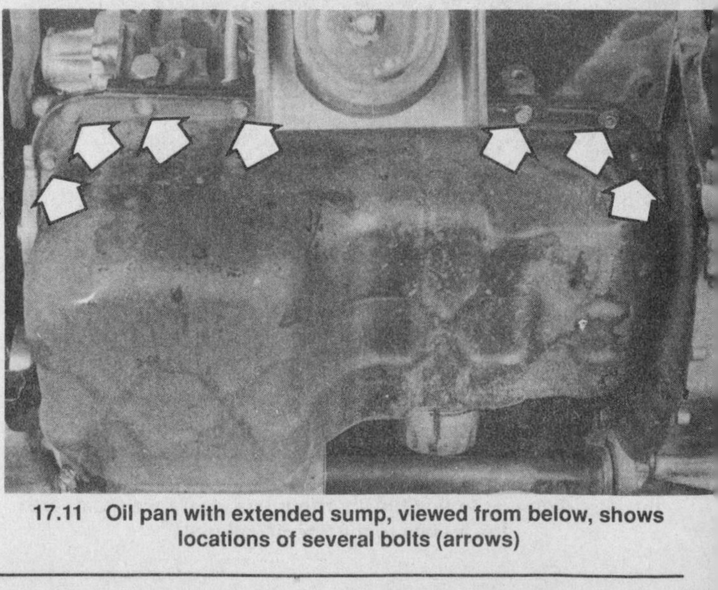

17.11 Oil pan with extended sump, viewed from below, shows locations of several bolts (arrows)

7 Support the engine/transaxle securely with a hoist from above or a jack under the bellhousing. Protect the bellhousing by placing a wood block on the jack pad. **Warning**: *Be absolutely certain the engine/transaxle is securely supported! DO NOT place any part of your body under the engine/transaxle – it could crush you if the jack or hoist fails!*

8 Unbolt the engine mounts from the crossmember (see Section 21).

9 Remove the front suspension crossmember from beneath the oil pan **(see illustration)**.

10 Remove the alternator (see Chapter 5).

11 Remove the oil pan bolts **(see illustration)**. **Note**: *On models with extended sumps, bolts six and ten in the tightening sequence* **(see illustration 17.21)** *may be removed with a 10 mm swivel socket, extension and ratchet.*

12 Detach the oil pan. Don't pry between the pan and block or damage to the sealing surfaces may result and oil leaks could develop. If the pan is stuck, dislodge it with a soft-face hammer **(see illustration)**.

13 Use a gasket scraper to remove all traces of old gasket material and sealant from the block and pan. Clean the mating surfaces with lacquer thinner or acetone.

14 Unbolt the oil pick-up tube and screen assembly **(see illustration)**.

Installation

Refer to illustrations 17.15, 17.17, 17.19, 17.20 and 17.21

15 Replace the O-ring on the flange of the oil pick-up tube **(see illustration)** and reinstall the tube. Tighten the pick-up tube bolts to the torque listed in this Chapter's Specifications.

16 Ensure that the threaded holes in the block are clean (use a tap to remove any sealant or corrosion from the threads).

Models with a one-piece gasket

17 Apply a small amount of Nissan Liquid Sealant (or equivalent RTV sealant) to the oil pump-to-block and rear seal retainer-to-block junctions **(see illustration)** and apply a thin continuous bead to the oil pan flange. **Note**: *Install the oil pan within five minutes of sealant application.*

18 Apply sealant to the engine-side of the gasket and position the gasket in the groove in the block.

Models with end seals

19 Apply Nissan Liquid Sealant (or equivalent RTV sealant) to the ends of the seals **(see illustration)** and position them on the oil pump and rear seal housings.

17.12 Once the bolts are removed, break the oil pan loose with a soft-face hammer

17.14 Remove the oil pick-up tube bolts (arrows)

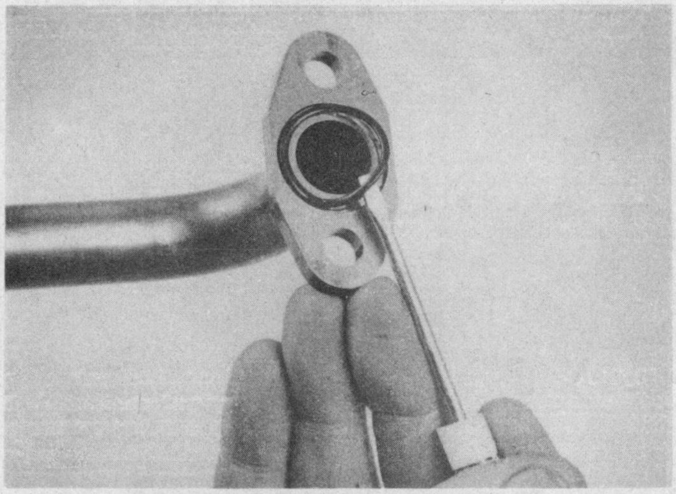

17.15 Before installing the oil pick-up tube, replace the rubber O-ring

17.17 On models with a one-piece gasket, apply sealant to the engine block at the oil pump and rear main oil seal retainer junctions (arrows)

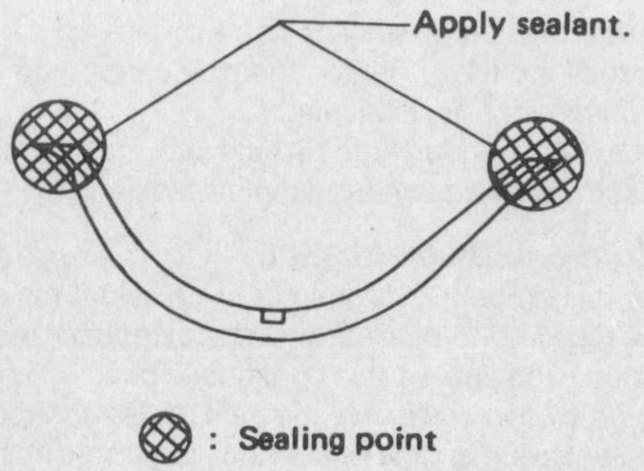

17.19 On models with end seals, apply sealant to the points shown here

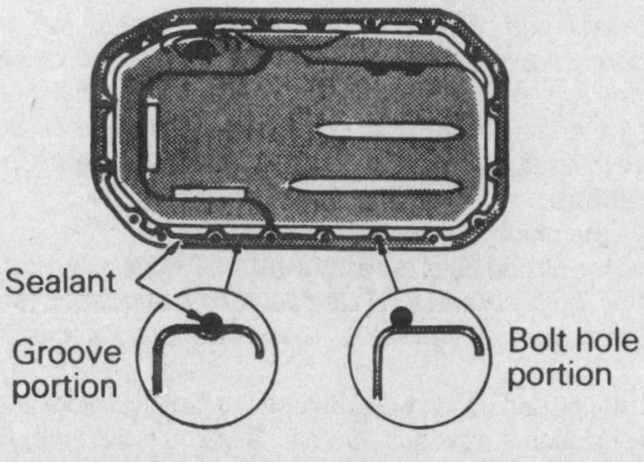

17.20 If the oil pan was sealed with RTV sealant only, apply sealant in the groove and to the inside of the bolt holes

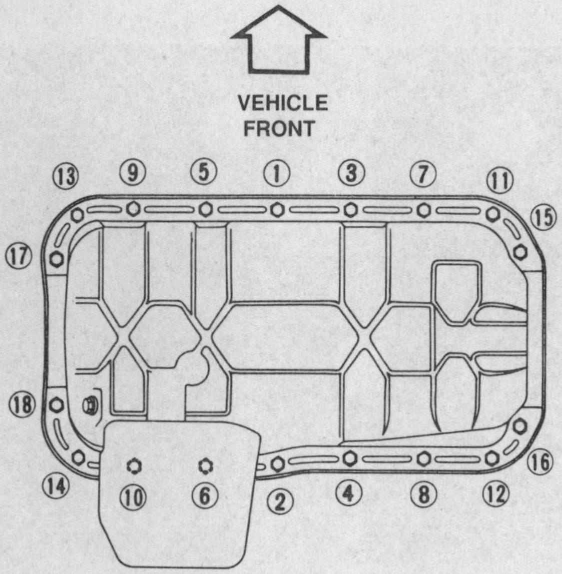

17.21 Oil pan bolt tightening sequence

20 Apply a continuous 5/32-inch (3.5 mm) bead of Nissan Liquid Sealant (or equivalent RTV sealant) to the inner sealing surface of the oil pan **(see illustration)**. **Note**: *Install the oil pan within five minutes of sealant application.*

All models

21 Install the oil pan and tighten the bolts in three or four steps following the sequence shown **(see illustration)** to the torque specified in this Chapter.

22 The remaining installation steps are the reverse of removal.

23 Allow at least 30 minutes for the sealant to dry, add oil, start the engine and check for oil pressure and leaks.

18 Oil pump – removal, inspection and installation

Removal

Refer to illustrations 18.2, 18.3 and 18.4

1 Remove the timing belt and the crankshaft sprocket (see Sections 10 and 11). Remove the oil pan and pick-up tube (Section 17).

2 Unbolt the power steering pump (see Chapter 10) without disconnecting the hoses. Remove the power steering pump bracket **(see illustration)**.

3 Remove the oil pump-to-engine block bolts from the front of the engine **(see illustration)**.

18.2 Remove the power steering pump bracket bolts (arrows) – engine removed for clarity

18.3 Remove the oil pump mounting bolts (arrows) and detach the pump from the engine

4 Use a block of wood and a hammer to break the oil pump gasket seal **(see illustration)**.
5 Pull out on the oil pump to remove it from the engine block.
6 Use a scraper to remove old gasket material and sealant from the oil pump and engine block mating surfaces. Clean the mating surfaces with lacquer thinner or acetone.

Inspection

Refer to illustrations 18.7, 18.8, 18.10a, 18.10b, 18.10c and 18.10d

7 Use a large Phillips screwdriver to remove the seven screws holding the rear cover on the oil pump **(see illustration)**.
8 Clean all components **(see illustration)** with solvent, then inspect them for wear and damage.
9 Remove the oil pressure regulator cap, washer, spring and valve. Check the oil pressure regulator valve sliding surface and valve spring. If either the spring or the valve is damaged, they must be replaced as a set.
10 Check the following clearances with a feeler gauge **(see illustrations)** and compare the measurements to the specified clearances:
Housing-to-outer gear
Inner gear-to-crescent
Outer gear-to-crescent
Cover-to-inner gear
Cover-to-outer gear
If any of the clearances are excessive, replace the entire oil pump assembly.
11 **Note**: *Pack the pump with petroleum jelly to prime it.* Assemble the oil pump and tighten the screws securely. Install the oil pressure regulator valve, spring and washer, then tighten the oil pressure regulator valve cap.

Installation

Refer to illustration 18.13

12 Apply RTV sealant to the oil pump mounting surface.

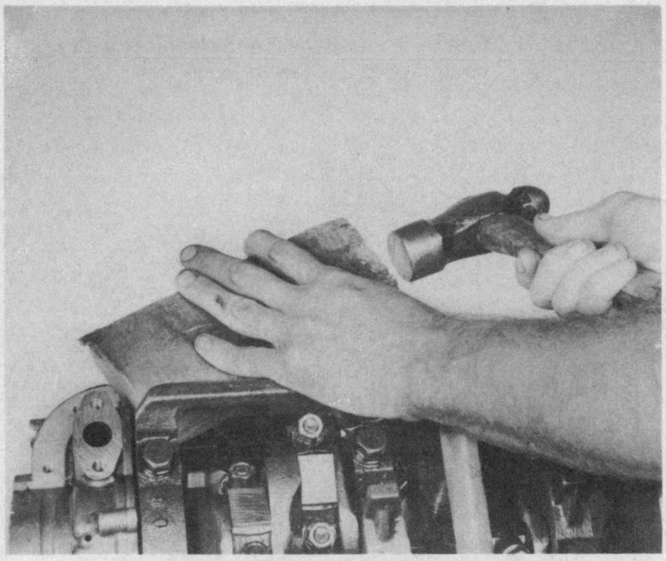

18.4 Use a block of wood and a hammer to gently break the oil pump gasket seal – don't strike the pump body with a steel hammer!

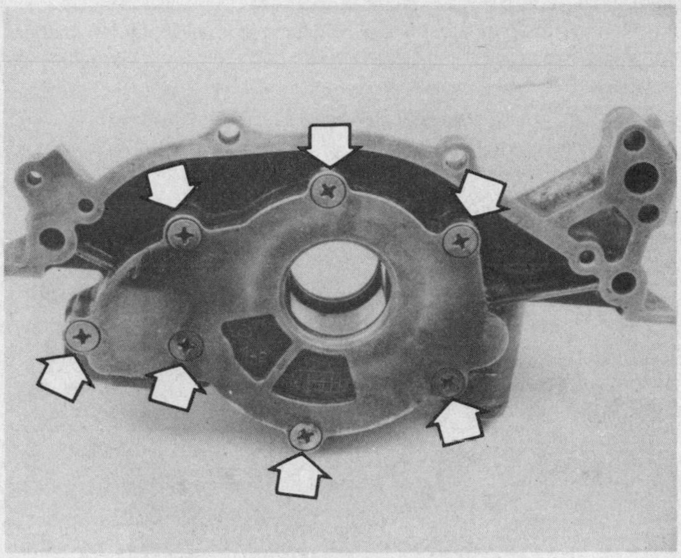

18.7 Remove the screws and lift the cover off

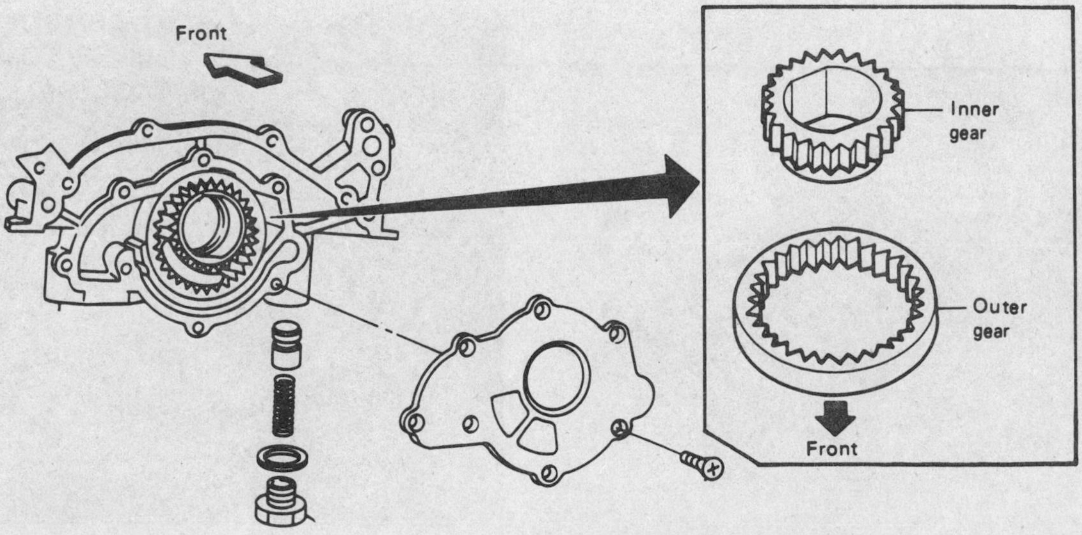

18.8 Oil pump components – exploded view

13 Use new gaskets on all disassembled parts and reverse the removal procedure for installation. Align the flats on the crankshaft **(see illustration)** with the flats on the oil pump gear. Tighten all fasteners to the torque specified in this Chapter. **Note**: *Before installing the oil pump pick-up, replace the rubber O-ring* **(see illustration 17.15)**.

19 Flywheel/driveplate – removal and installation

Refer to illustrations 19.3, 19.4 and 19.7

Note: *On automatic transaxle equipped models, you must remove the engine and transaxle as a unit and separate them outside the vehicle for access to the driveplate. See Chapter 2 Part B for the engine removal procedure.*

1 Raise the vehicle and support it securely on jackstands, then refer to Chapter 7 and remove the transaxle. If it's leaking, now would be a very good time to replace the front pump seal/O-ring (automatic transaxle only).

2 Remove the pressure plate and clutch disc (see Chapter 8) (manual transmission equipped vehicles). Now is a good time to check/replace the clutch components.

18.10a Measure the cover-to-gear end clearance with a straightedge and feeler gauge

18.10b Measuring the housing-to-outer gear clearance with a feeler gauge

18.10c Measuring outer gear-to-crescent clearance

18.10d Measuring inner gear-to-crescent clearance

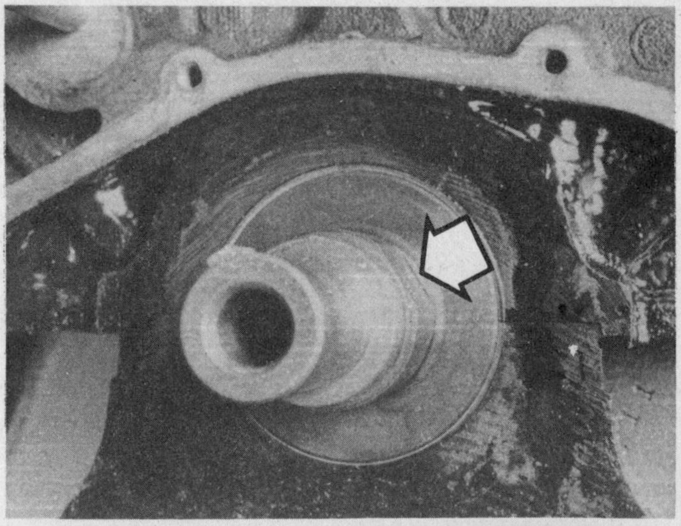

18.13 There is a flat surface (arrow) on each side of the crankshaft – align them with the flats on the gear

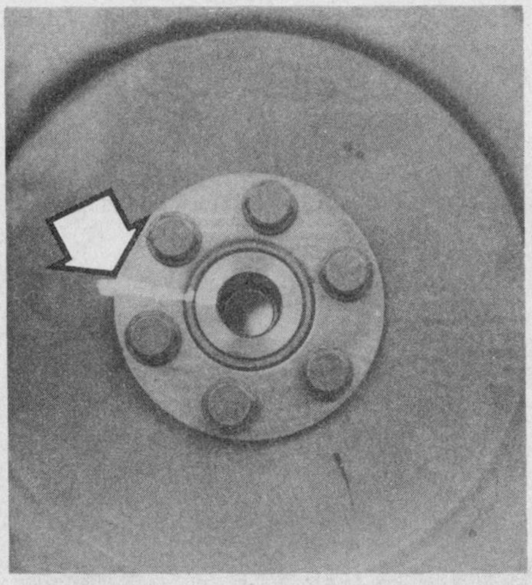

19.3 Make alignment marks (arrow) on the flywheel/driveplate and crankshaft

19.4 On automatic transaxle models (shown), hold a lever against a casting protrusion on the engine block – on manual transaxle models, use the ring gear teeth to keep the flywheel/driveplate from turning

19.7 The engine rear plate must be positioned over the locating dowels (arrow)

3 Once the transaxle is removed, use paint or a center punch to make alignment marks on the flywheel/driveplate and crankshaft to ensure correct alignment during reinstallation **(see illustration)**.

4 Remove the bolts that secure the flywheel/driveplate to the crankshaft **(see illustration)**. If the crankshaft turns, slip a small lever through a bolt hole and hold it against a casting protrusion on automatic transaxle models or wedge a screwdriver against the ring gear to jam the flywheel on manual transaxle models.

5 Remove the flywheel/driveplate from the crankshaft. Since the flywheel is fairly heavy, be sure to support it while removing the last bolt.

6 Clean the flywheel to remove grease and oil. Inspect the surface for cracks, rivet grooves, burned areas and score marks. Light scoring can be removed with emery cloth. Check for cracked and broken ring gear teeth. Lay the flywheel on a flat surface and use a straightedge to check for warpage.

7 Clean and inspect the mating surfaces of the flywheel/driveplate and the crankshaft. If the crankshaft rear seal is leaking, replace it before reinstalling the flywheel/driveplate. Make sure the engine rear plate **(see illustration)** is positioned over the locating dowels.

8 Position the flywheel/driveplate against the crankshaft. Be sure to align the marks made during removal. Note that some engines have an alignment dowel to ensure correct installation. On automatic transaxle models, install the washer plate and align the holes. Before installing the bolts, apply thread locking compound to the threads.

9 Keep the flywheel/driveplate from turning as described in Step 4 while you tighten the bolts to the torque specified in this Chapter.

10 The remainder of installation is the reverse of the removal procedure.

20 Crankshaft rear oil seal – replacement

Refer to illustrations 20.2 and 20.5

1 Remove the flywheel/driveplate (see Section 19).

2 Insert a screwdriver between the oil seal and crankshaft, then pry the seal out of the retainer **(see illustration)**. Be very careful not to nick or scratch the crankshaft in the process!

3 Apply moly-base grease to the outer edge and the lips of the new seal.

4 Push the seal onto the crankshaft and gently tap it into the bore with a soft-face hammer.

5 Once the seal face is flush with the seal retainer and the crankshaft flange, very carefully drive the seal the rest of the way into the retainer with the blunt end of a punch. A brass punch is best **(see illustration)**. **Cau-**

20.2 Pry the seal out very carefully with a screwdriver – if the crankshaft is damaged, the new seal will leak!

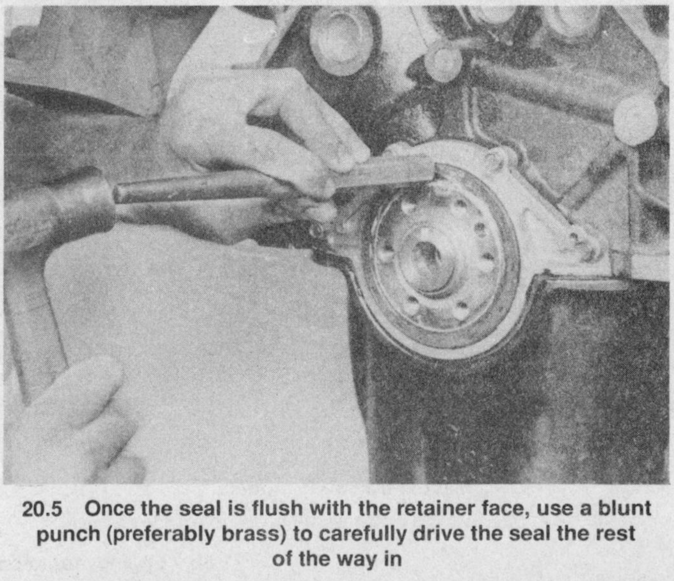

20.5 Once the seal is flush with the retainer face, use a blunt punch (preferably brass) to carefully drive the seal the rest of the way in

tion: *Be extremely careful. Take your time and drive the seal gently and evenly into place. Damaging a new seal will result in an oil leak.*
6 The rest of installation is the reverse of removal.

21 Engine mounts – check and replacement

Refer to illustrations 21.8a and 21.8b

1 Engine mounts seldom require attention, but broken or deteriorated mounts should be replaced immediately or the added strain placed on the driveline components may cause damage or wear.

Check

2 During the check, the engine must be raised slightly to remove the weight from the mounts.
3 Raise the vehicle and support it securely on jackstands, then position a jack under the engine oil pan. Place a large block of wood between the jack head and the oil pan, then carefully raise the engine just enough to take the weight off the mounts. **Warning**: *DO NOT place any part of your body under the engine when it's supported only by a jack!*
4 Check the mounts to see if the rubber is cracked, hardened or separated from the metal plates. Sometimes the rubber will split right down the center.
5 Check for relative movement between the mount plates and the engine or frame (use a large screwdriver or pry bar to attempt to move the mounts). If movement is noted, lower the engine and tighten the mount fasteners.
6 Rubber preservative should be applied to the mounts to slow deterioration.

Replacement

7 Disconnect the negative battery cable from the battery, then raise the vehicle and support it securely on jackstands (if not already done).
8 Support the engine with a hoist from above or a jack under the oil pan. **Caution**: *Use a block of wood to avoid damaging the oil pan. Remove the fasteners and detach the mount from the crossmember bracket* **(see illustrations)**.
9 Remove the mount-to-bracket bolts/nuts and detach the mount. Raise the engine slightly to remove the mount, if necessary.
10 Installation is the reverse of removal. Use thread locking compound on the mount nuts/bolts and be sure to tighten them securely.

21.8a The front mount on automatic transaxle models has a nut on the top (arrow) and a nut on the bottom

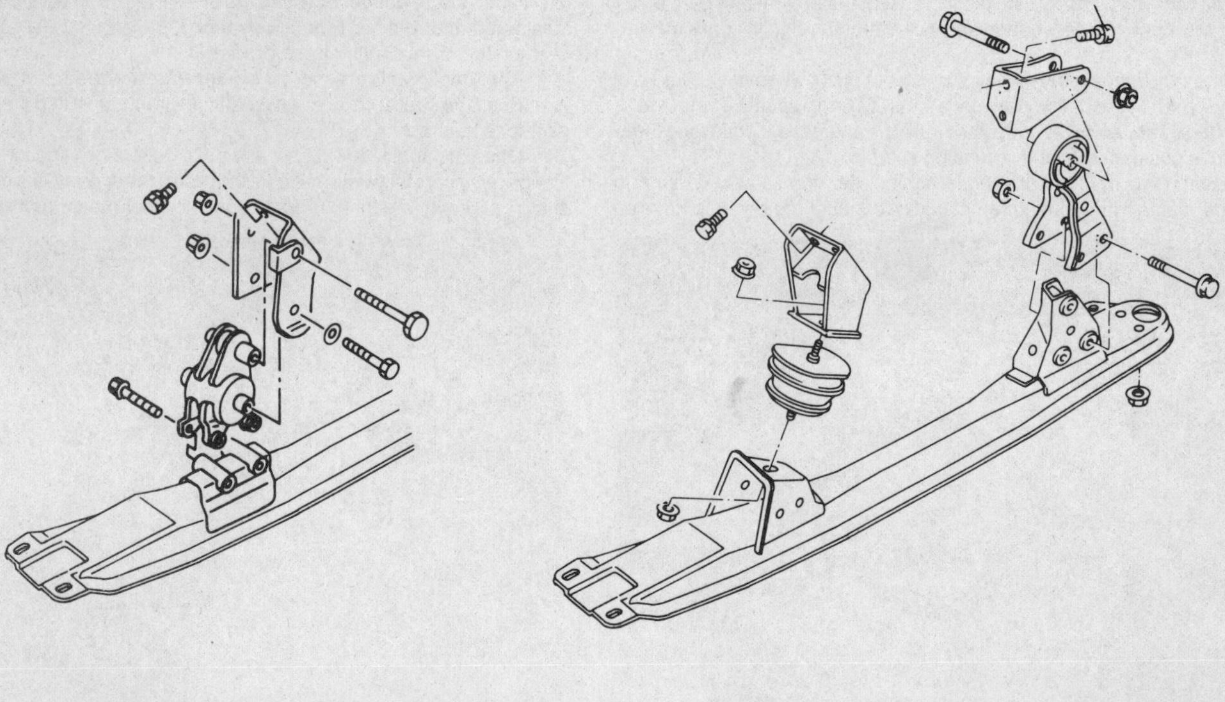

Manual transaxle models

Automatic transaxle models

21.8b Engine mount components – exploded view

Chapter 2 Part B
General engine overhaul procedures

Contents

Crankshaft – inspection	18
Crankshaft – installation and main bearing oil clearance check	22
Crankshaft – removal	13
Cylinder compression check	3
Cylinder head – cleaning and inspection	9
Cylinder head – disassembly	8
Cylinder head – reassembly	11
Cylinder honing	16
Engine block – cleaning	14
Engine block – inspection	15
Engine overhaul – disassembly sequence	7
Engine overhaul – general information	2
Engine overhaul – reassembly sequence	20
Engine rebuilding alternatives	6
Engine – removal and installation	5
Engine removal – methods and precautions	4
General information	1
Initial start-up and break-in after overhaul	25
Main and connecting rod bearings – inspection and main bearing selection	19
Pistons/connecting rods – inspection	17
Pistons/connecting rods – installation and rod bearing oil clearance check	24
Pistons/connecting rods – removal	12
Piston rings – installation	21
Rear main oil seal installation	23
Valves – servicing	10

2B

Specifications

General

Oil pressure	
1985 through 1987	
At 1200 rpm	28 psi
At 4000 rpm	57 psi
1988 on	
At idle	More than 9 psi
At 3200 rpm	53 to 65 psi
Cylinder compression pressure (at 300 rpm)	
Standard	173 psi
Minimum	128 psi
Maximum difference between cylinders	14 psi

Cylinder head

Warpage limit	0.004 in (0.1 mm)

Valves and related components

Valve stem diameter	
Intake	0.2742 to 0.2748 in (6.965 to 6.980 mm)
Exhaust	0.3136 to 0.3138 in (7.965 to 7.970 mm)
Valve margin	
Intake	0.051 in (1.3 mm)
Exhaust	0.059 in (1.5 mm)
Valve margin limit	Not less than 0.020 in (0.5 mm)
Valve spring free length	
Outer	2.016 in (51.2 mm)
Inner	1.736 in (44.1 mm)
Valve spring pressure/height	
Outer	1.181 in @ 117.7 lb (3.0 mm @ 53.4 kg)
Inner	0.984 in @ 57.3 lb (25.0 mm @ 26.0 kg)
Valve spring installed height	
Outer	1.575 in @ 56.2 lb (4.0 mm @ 25.5 kg)
Inner	1.378 in @ 24.3 lb (35.0 mm @ 11.0 kg)
Valve spring out of square limit	
Outer	0.087 in (2.2 mm)
Inner	0.075 in (1.9 mm)

Valves and related components (continued)

Valve stem to guide clearance	
Intake	
Standard	0.0008 to 0.0021 in (0.020 to 0.053 mm)
Maximum	0.004 in (0.10 mm)
Exhaust	
Standard	0.0016 to 0.0029 in (0.040 to 0.073 mm)
Maximum	0.004 in (0.10 mm)
Rocker arm shaft outer diameter	
1985 through 1988	0.7078 to 0.7087 in (17.979 to 18.000 mm)
1989 on	0.7082 to 0.7087 in (17.988 to 18.000 mm)
Rocker arm bore diameter	0.7089 to 0.7098 in (18.007 to 18.028 mm)
Clearance between rocker arm and shaft	0.0003 to 0.0019 in (0.007 to 0.049 mm)
Hydraulic valve lifters	
Lifter outside diameter	0.6278 to 0.6282 in (15.947 to 15.957 mm)
Lifter guide inside diameter	0.6299 to 0.6304 in (16.000 to 16.013 mm)

Camshaft

Journal to bearing clearance	0.0024 to 0.0041 in (0.060 to 0.105 mm)
Standard	
1985	0.0018 to 0.0035 in (0.045 to 0.090 mm)
1986 on	0.0024 to 0.0041 in (0.060 to 0.105 mm)
Maximum (all)	0.0059 in (0.15 mm)
Inner diameter of camshaft bearing	1.8504 to 1.8514 in (47.00 to 47.025 mm)
Outer diameter of camshaft journal	1.8478 to 1.8486 in (46.935 to 46.955 mm)
Camshaft runout – total indicator reading	0.004 in (0.01 mm) max
Camshaft end play	0.0012 to 0.0024 in (0.03 to 0.06 mm)
Cam lobe height	1.5566 to 1.5640 in (39.537 to 39.725 mm)
Cam lobe wear limit	0.0059 in (0.15 mm)

Engine block

Deck warpage limit	0.0039 in (0.10 mm) max
Cylinder bore diameter	
Standard	3.4252 to 3.4272 in (87.000 to 87.050 mm)
Wear limit	0.0079 in (0.20 mm)
Out-of-round limit	Less than 0.0006 in (0.015 mm)
Taper limit	Less than 0.0006 in (0.015 mm)
Main journal bore diameter	
Grade no. 0	2.6238 to 2.6242 in (66.645 to 66.654 mm)
Grade no. 1	2.6242 to 2.6245 in (66.654 to 66.663 mm)
Grade no. 2	2.6245 to 2.6249 in (66.663 to 66.672 mm)

Pistons and rings

Piston skirt diameter	
Grade no. 1	3.4238 to 3.4242 in (86.965 to 86.975 mm)
Grade no. 2	3.4242 to 3.4246 in (86.975 to 86.985 mm)
Grade no. 3	3.4246 to 3.4250 in (86.985 to 86.995 mm)
Grade no. 4	3.4250 to 3.4254 in (86.995 to 87.005 mm)
Grade no. 5	3.4254 to 3.4258 in (87.005 to 87.015 mm)
Piston-to-cylinder clearance	
1985 through 1988	0.0010 to 0.0018 in (0.025 to 0.045 mm)
1989 on	0.0006 to 0.0014 in (0.015 to 0.035 mm)
Piston rings	
Side clearance	
Top comprssion ring	
Standard	0.0016 to 0.0029 in (0.040 to 0.073 mm)
Maximum	0.004 in (0.10 mm)
Second compression ring	
Standard	0.0012 to 0.0025 in (0.030 to 0.063 mm)
Maximum	0.04 in (1.0 mm)
Oil rail	
Standard	0.0006 to 0.0075 in (0.015 to 0.190 mm)
Maximum	0.04 in (1.0 mm)
Ring end gap	
Top compression ring	0.0083 to 0.0173 in (0.21 to 0.44 mm)
Second compression ring	0.0071 to 0.0173 in (0.18 to 0.44 mm)
Oil rail	0.0079 to 0.0299 in (to .76 mm)
Limit (all)	0.039 in (1.0 mm)

Crankshaft

Main journal diameter	
Grade no. 0	2.4790 to 2.4793 in (62.967 to 62.975 mm)
Grade no. 1	2.4787 to 2.4790 in (62.959 to 62.967 mm)
Grade no. 2	2.4784 to 2.4787 in (62.951 to 62.959 mm)
Rod journal diameter	
1985 through 1987	1.9670 to 1.9675 in (49.961 to 49.974 mm)
1988 on	1.9667 to 1.9675 (49.955 to 49.974 mm)
Crankshaft journal out-of-round limit	Less than 0.0002 in (0.005 mm)
End play	
Standard	0.0020 to 0.0067 in (0.05 to 0.17 mm)
Maximum	0.0118 in (0.30 mm)
Main bearing oil clearance	
Standard	0.0011 to 0.0022 in (0.028 to 0.055 mm)
Maximum	0.0035 in (0.090 mm)
Rod bearing oil clearance	
Standard	
1985 through 1987	0.0004 to 0.0020 in (0.010 to 0.052 mm)
1988 on	0.0006 to 0.0021 in (0.014 to 0.054 mm)
Maximum (all)	0.0035 in (0.090 mm)
Connecting rod side clearance (end play)	
Standard	0.0079 to 0.0138 in (0.20 to 0.35 mm)
Limit	0.0157 in (0.40 mm)

Torque specifications*

	Ft-lbs (unless otherwise indicated)
Rear main oil seal retainer bolts	48 to 64 in-lbs
Connecting rod nuts	
1985 through 1987	33 to 40
1988 on	
Step one	10 to 12
Step two	28 to 33
Main bearing cap bolts	67 to 74

**Refer to Part A for additional torque specifications*

1 General information

Included in this portion of Chapter 2 are the general overhaul procedures for the cylinder heads and internal engine components.

The information ranges from advice concerning preparation for an overhaul and the purchase of replacement parts to detailed, step-by-step procedures covering removal and installation of internal engine components and the inspection of parts.

The following Sections have been written based on the assumption that the engine has been removed from the vehicle. For information concerning in-vehicle engine repair, as well as removal and installation of the external components necessary for the overhaul, see Part A of this Chapter and Section 7 of this Part.

The Specifications included in this Part are only those necessary for the inspection and overhaul procedures which follow. Refer to Part A for additional Specifications.

2 Engine overhaul – general information

Refer to illustrations 2.4a and 2.4b

It's not always easy to determine when, or if, an engine should be completely overhauled, as a number of factors must be considered.

High mileage is not necessarily an indication that an overhaul is needed, while low mileage doesn't preclude the need for an overhaul. Frequency of servicing is probably the most important consideration. An engine that's had regular and frequent oil and filter changes, as well as other required maintenance, will most likely give many thousands of miles of reliable service. Conversely,a neglected engine may require an overhaul very early in its life.

Excessive oil consumption is an indication that piston rings, valve seals and/or valve guides are in need of attention. Make sure that oil leaks aren't responsible before deciding that the rings and/or guides are bad. Perform a cylinder compression check to determine the extent of the work required (see Section 3).

Check the oil pressure with a gauge installed in place of the oil pressure sending unit **(see illustrations)** and compare it to the Specifications. If it's extremely low, the bearings and/or oil pump are probably worn out.

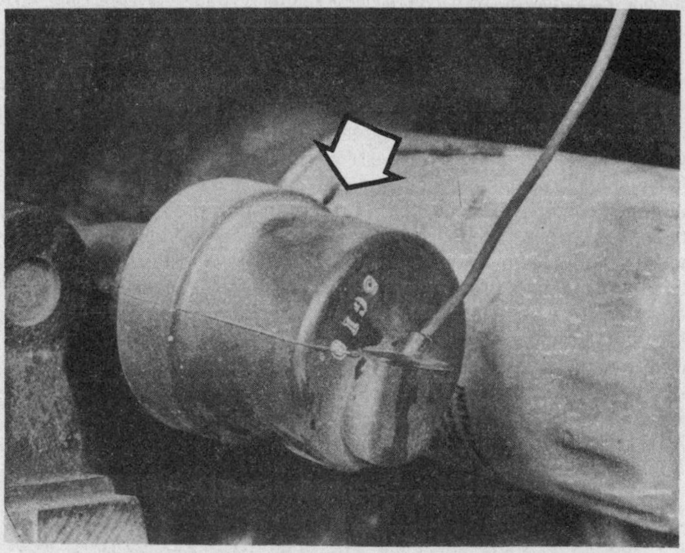

2.4a Remove the oil pressure sending unit (arrow) located on the firewall-side of the engine adjacent to the transaxle . . .

2.4b . . . and connect a gauge to check oil pressure

3.6 A compression gauge with a threaded fitting for the spark plug hole is preferred over the type that requires hand pressure to maintain the seal

Loss of power, rough running, knocking or metallic engine noises, excessive valve train noise and high fuel consumption rates may also point to the need for an overhaul, especially if they're all present at the same time. If a complete tune-up doesn't remedy the situation, major mechanical work is the only solution.

An engine overhaul involves restoring the internal parts to the specifications of a new engine. During an overhaul, the piston rings are replaced and the cylinder walls are reconditioned (rebored and/or honed). If a rebore is done by an automotive machine shop, new oversize pistons will also be installed. The main bearings, connecting rod bearings and camshaft bearings are generally replaced with new ones and, if necessary, the crankshaft may be reground to restore the journals. Generally, the valves are serviced as well, since they're usually in less-than-perfect condition at this point. While the engine is being overhauled, other components, such as the distributor, starter and alternator, can be rebuilt as well. The end result should be a like new engine that will give many trouble free miles. **Note:** *Critical cooling system components such as the hoses, drivebelts, thermostat and water pump MUST be replaced with new parts when an engine is overhauled. The radiator should be checked carefully to ensure that it isn't clogged or leaking (see Chapter 3). Also, we don't recommend overhauling the oil pump – always install a new one when an engine is rebuilt.*

Before beginning the engine overhaul, read through the entire procedure to familiarize yourself with the scope and requirements of the job. Overhauling an engine isn't difficult if you follow all of the instructions carefully, have the necessary tools and equipment and pay close attention to all specifications; however, it can be time consuming. Plan on the vehicle being tied up for a minimum of two weeks, especially if parts must be taken to an automotive machine shop for repair or reconditioning. Check on availability of parts and make sure that any necessary special tools and equipment are obtained in advance. Most work can be done with typical hand tools, although a number of precision measuring tools are required for inspecting parts to determine if they must be replaced. Often an automotive machine shop will handle the inspection of parts and offer advice concerning reconditioning and replacement. **Note:** *Always wait until the engine has been completely disassembled and all components, especially the engine block, have been inspected before deciding what service and repair operations must be performed by an automotive machine shop. Since the block's condition will be the major factor to consider when determining whether to overhaul the original engine or buy a rebuilt one, never purchase parts or have machine work done on other components until the block has been thoroughly inspected.* As a general rule, time is the primary cost of an overhaul, so it doesn't pay to install worn or substandard parts.

As a final note, to ensure maximum life and minimum trouble from a rebuilt engine, everything must be assembled with care in a spotlessly clean environment.

3 Cylinder compression check

Refer to illustration 3.6

1 A compression check will tell you what mechanical condition the upper end (pistons, rings, valves, head gaskets) of the engine is in. Specifically, it can tell you if the compression is down due to leakage caused by worn piston rings, defective valves and seats or a blown head gasket. **Note:** *The engine must be at normal operating temperature and the battery must be fully charged for this check.*

2 Begin by cleaning the area around the spark plugs before you remove them (compressed air should be used, if available, otherwise a small brush or even a bicycle tire pump will work). The idea is to prevent dirt from getting into the cylinders as the compression check is being done.

3 Remove all of the spark plugs from the engine (see Chapter 1).

4 Block the throttle wide open.

5 Detach the coil wire from the "C" terminal of the distributor cap and ground it on the engine block. Use a jumper wire with alligator clips on each end to ensure a good ground. The fuel pump circuit should also be disabled (see Chapter 4).

6 Install the compression gauge in the number one spark plug hole **(see illustration)**.

7 Crank the engine over at least seven compression strokes and watch the gauge. The compression should build up quickly in a healthy engine. Low compression on the first stroke, followed by gradually increasing pressure on successive strokes, indicates worn piston rings. A low compression reading on the first stroke, which doesn't build up during successive strokes, indicates leaking valves or a blown head gasket (a cracked head could also be the cause). Deposits on the undersides of the valve heads can also cause low compression. Record the highest gauge reading obtained.

8 Repeat the procedure for the remaining cylinders and compare the results to the Specifications in this Chapter.

9 Add some engine oil (about three squirts from a plunger-type oil can) to each cylinder, through the spark plug hole, and repeat the test.

10 If the compression increases after the oil is added, the piston rings are definitely worn. If the compression doesn't increase significantly, the leakage is occurring at the valves or head gasket. Leakage past the valves

may be caused by burned valve seats and/or faces or warped, cracked or bent valves.

11 If two adjacent cylinders have equally low compression, there's a strong possibility that the head gasket between them is blown. The appearance of coolant in the combustion chambers or the crankcase would verify this condition.

12 If one cylinder is about 20 percent lower than the others, and the engine has a slightly rough idle, a worn lobe on the camshaft could be the cause.

13 If the compression is unusually high, the combustion chambers are probably coated with carbon deposits. If that's the case, the cylinder heads should be removed and decarbonized.

14 If compression is way down or varies greatly between cylinders, it would be a good idea to have a leak-down test performed by an automotive repair shop. This test will pinpoint exactly where the leakage is occurring and how severe it is.

4 Engine removal – methods and precautions

If you've decided that an engine must be removed for overhaul or major repair work, several preliminary steps should be taken.

Locating a suitable place to work is extremely important. Adequate work space, along with storage space for the vehicle, will be needed. If a shop or garage isn't available, at the very least a flat, level, clean work surface made of concrete or asphalt is required.

Cleaning the engine compartment and engine before beginning the removal procedure will help keep tools clean and organized.

An engine hoist or A-frame will also be necessary. Make sure the equipment is rated in excess of the combined weight of the engine and transaxle. Safety is of primary importance, considering the potential hazards involved in lifting the engine out of the vehicle.

If the engine is being removed by a novice, a helper should be available. Advice and aid from someone more experienced would also be helpful. There are many instances when one person cannot simultaneously perform all of the operations required when lifting the engine out of the vehicle.

Plan the operation ahead of time. Arrange for or obtain all of the tools and equipment you'll need prior to beginning the job. Some of the equipment necessary to perform engine removal and installation safely and with relative ease are (in addition to an engine hoist) a heavy duty floor jack, complete sets of wrenches and sockets as described in the front of this manual, wooden blocks and plenty of rags and cleaning solvent for mopping up spilled oil, coolant and gasoline. If the hoist must be rented, make sure that you arrange for it in advance and perform all of the operations possible without it beforehand. This will save you money and time.

Plan for the vehicle to be out of use for quite a while. A machine shop will be required to perform some of the work which the do-it-yourselfer can't accomplish without special equipment. These shops often have a busy schedule, so it would be a good idea to consult them before removing the engine in order to accurately estimate the amount of time required to rebuild or repair components that may need work.

Always be extremely careful when removing and installing the engine. Serious injury can result from careless actions. Plan ahead, take your time and a job of this nature, although major, can be accomplished successfully.

5 Engine – removal and installation

Refer to illustrations 5.2, 5.6, 5.12, 5.15a, 5.15b, 5.17, 5.18a and 5.18b

Note: *Read through the entire Section before beginning this procedure. The engine and transaxle are removed as a unit and then separated outside the vehicle.*

Removal

1 Relieve the fuel system pressure (see Chapter 4).

2 Remove the battery (see Chapter 5) and the battery tray **(see illustration)**.

3 Place protective covers on the fenders and cowl and remove the hood (see Chapter 11).

4 Remove the air cleaner assembly (see Chapter 4).

2B

5 Raise the vehicle and support it securely on jackstands. Drain the cooling system, transaxle and engine oil and remove the drivebelts (see Chapter 1).

6 Clearly label, then disconnect all vacuum lines, coolant and emissions hoses, wiring harness connectors, ground straps and fuel lines. Masking tape and/or a touch up paint applicator work well for marking items **(see illustration)**. Take instant photos or sketch the locations of components and brackets.

7 Remove the cooling fans and radiator (see Chapter 3).

8 Release the residual fuel pressure in the tank by removing the gas cap, then disconnect the fuel lines from the fuel rail (see Chapter 4). Plug or cap all open fittings.

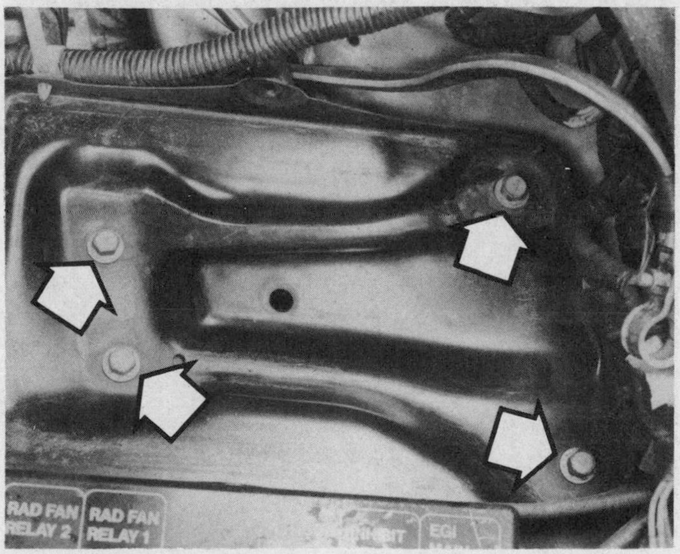

5.2 Remove the battery tray bolts (arrows) and remove the tray (also remove the relay box screws on some models)

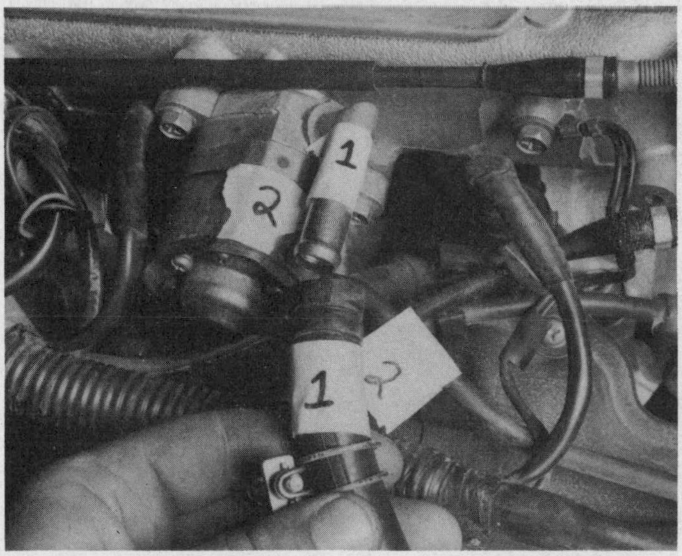

5.6 Label the hoses and wires to ensure proper assembly

5.12 Unbolt the air conditioning compressor and tie it to the radiator support so it clears the mounting bracket (arrow) – 1986 model shown, others similar

9 On 1985 through 1988 models, remove the air inlet tube and vacuum chamber (see Chapter 4).
10 Disconnect the throttle linkage (and TV cable and speed control cable, when equipped) from the engine (see Chapter 4).
11 Unbolt the power steering pump. Tie the pump aside without disconnecting the hoses (see Chapter 10).
12 Unbolt the air conditioning compressor (see Chapter 3) and set it aside **(see illustration)**. Do not disconnect the refrigerant hoses.
13 Detach the exhaust pipe from the front manifold (see Chapter 4).
14 Remove the driveaxles and on manual transaxle models, the clutch release cylinder (see Chapter 8). Disconnect the wire harness, shift linkage and speedometer cable from the transaxle (see Chapter 7).
15 Attach a lifting sling or chain to the brackets on the engine. Position a hoist and connect the sling to it. **Note:** *On some models it may be necessary to remove the throttle body for sling clearance.* Take up the slack until there is slight tension on the hoist **(see illustrations)**.
16 Recheck to be sure nothing except the mounts are still connecting the engine/transaxle to the vehicle. Disconnect anything still remaining.
17 Support the transaxle with a floor jack. Place a block of wood on the jack head to prevent damage to the transaxle. Remove the through-bolt from the rear engine mount **(see illustration)**. Unbolt the front transaxle mount from the transaxle and also from the body **(see illustration 5.17)**. Unbolt the rear transaxle mount from the body only. **Warning:** *Do Not place any part of your body under the engine/transaxle when it's supported only by a hoist or other lifting device.*
18 Slowly lift the engine/transaxle out of the vehicle **(see illustrations)**. It may be necessary to pry the mounts away from the frame brackets.
19 Move the engine/transaxle away from the vehicle and carefully lower the hoist until the transaxle is supported in a level position.
20 Separate the engine from the transaxle (see Chapter 7).
21 Place the engine on the floor or remove the flywheel/driveplate and mount the engine on an engine stand.

Installation

22 Check the engine/transaxle mounts. If they're worn or damaged, replace them.
23 On manual transaxle equipped models, inspect the clutch components (see Chapter 8) and on automatic models inspect the converter seal and bushing.
24 On automatic transaxle equipped models, apply a dab of grease to the nose of the converter and to the seal lips.
25 Carefully guide the transaxle into place, following the procedure outlined in Chapter 7. **Caution:** *Do Not use the bolts to force the engine and transaxle into alignment. It may crack or damage major components.*
26 Install the engine-to-transaxle bolts and tighten them securely.
27 Attach the hoist to the engine and carefully lower the engine/transaxle assembly into the engine compartment.
28 Install the mount bolts and tighten them securely.
29 Reinstall the remaining components and fasteners in the reverse order of removal.
30 Add coolant, oil, power steering and transmission fluids as needed (see Chapter 1).
31 Run the engine and check for proper operation and leaks. Shut off the engine and recheck the fluid levels.

6 Engine rebuilding alternatives

The do-it-yourselfer is faced with a number of options when performing an engine overhaul. The decision to replace the engine block, piston/connecting rod assemblies and crankshaft depends on a number of factors, with the number one consideration being the condition of the block. Other

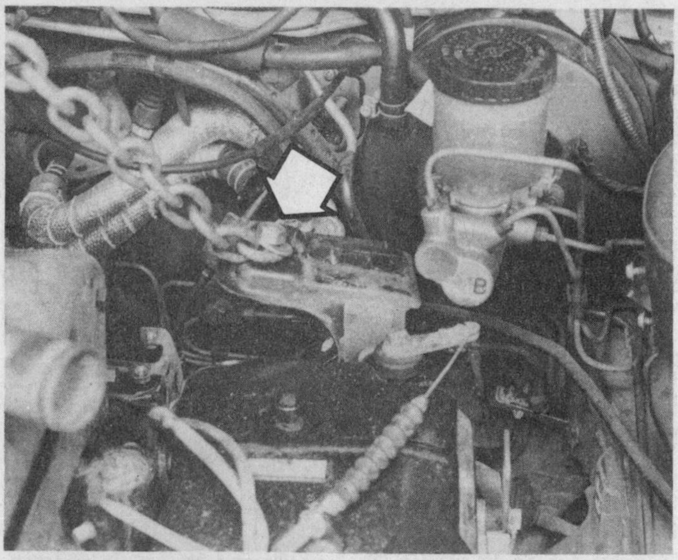

5.15a Attach a lifting sling to the rear transaxle mount (arrow) or a lifting eye – use care when raising the engine/transaxle to avoid hitting the master cylinder (1986 model shown, others similar)

5.15b Attach the sling diagonally and take up the slack

5.17 Engine mounting details (1986 model shown, others similar)

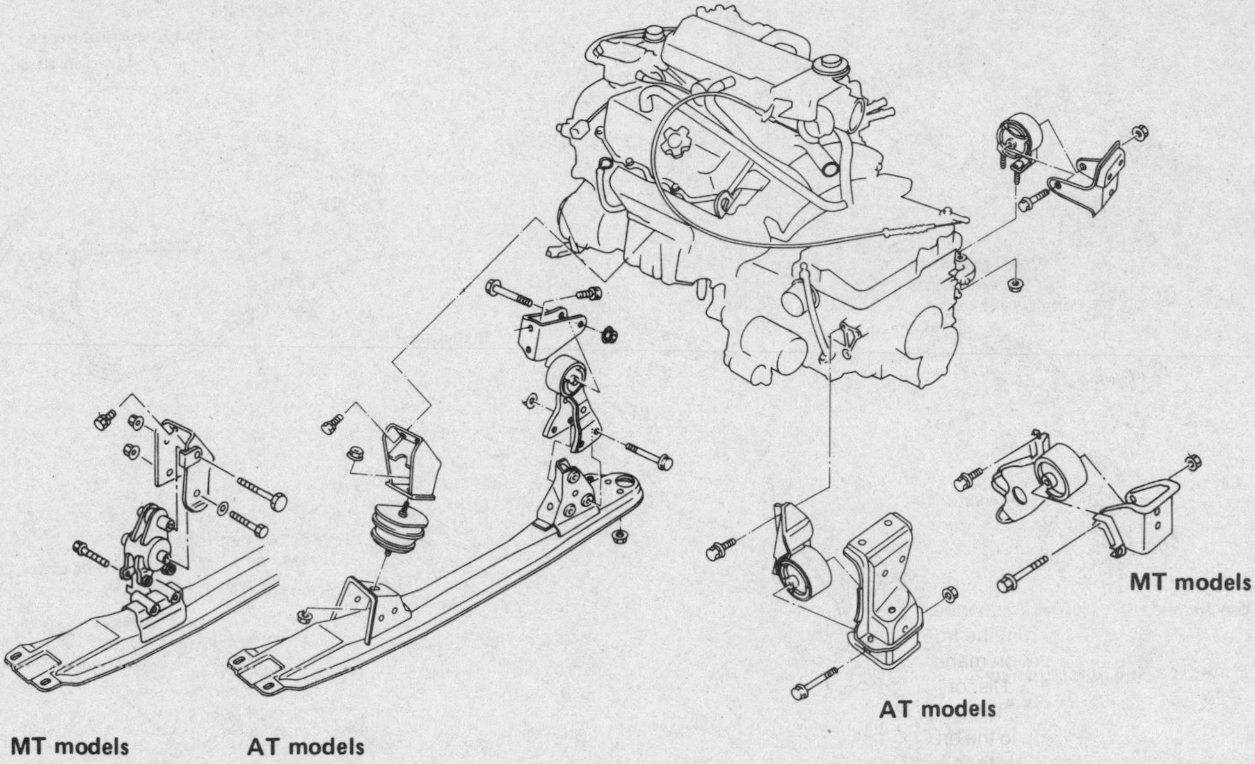

5.18a Lift the engine/transaxle off the mounts, taking care to clear obstructions such as the master cylinder

5.18b Raise the engine/transaxle high enough to clear the front of the vehicle

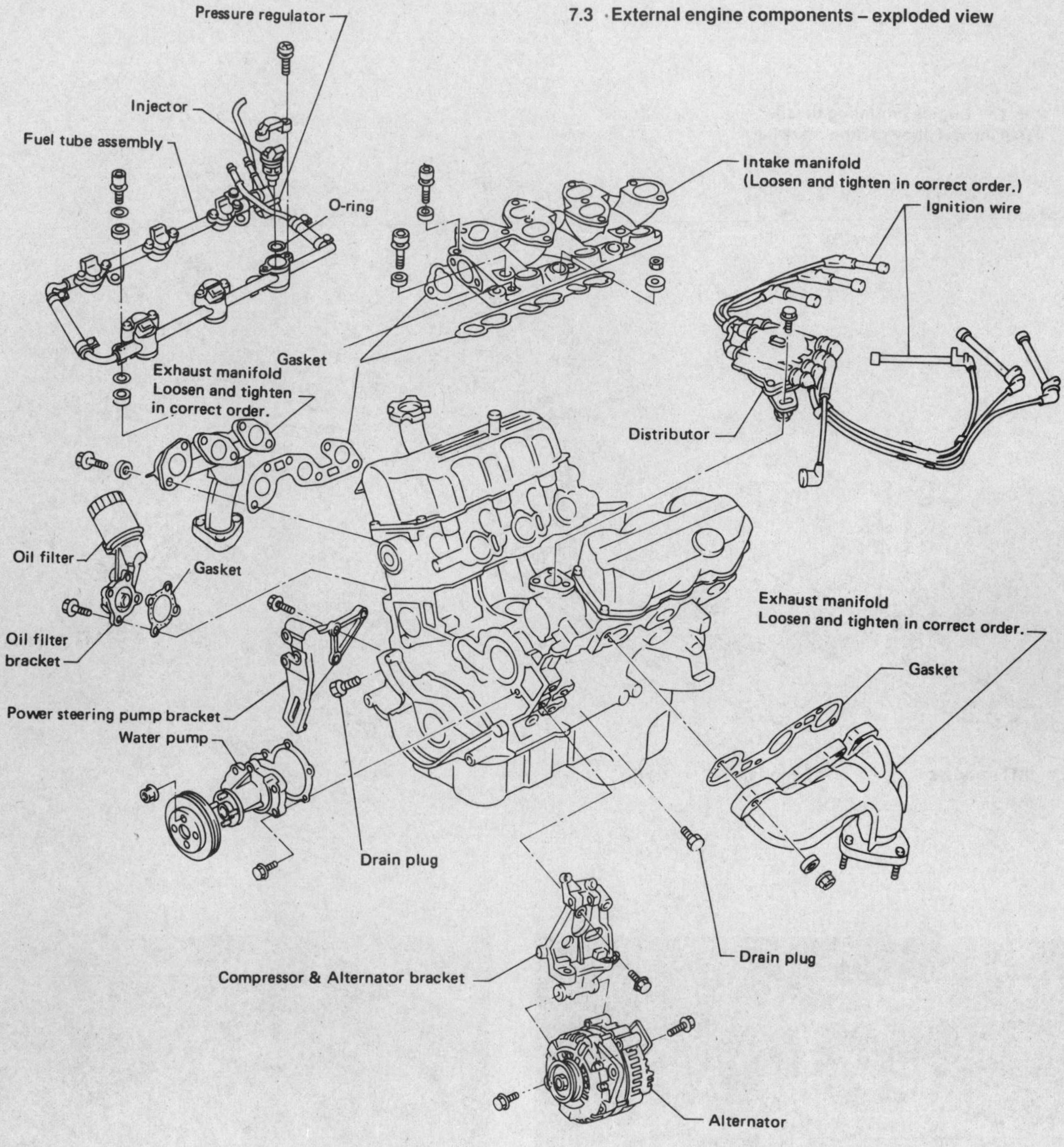

7.3 External engine components – exploded view

considerations are cost, access to machine shop facilities, parts availability, time required to complete the project and the extent of prior mechanical experience on the part of the do-it-yourselfer.

Some of the rebuilding alternatives include:

Individual parts – If the inspection procedures reveal that the engine block and most engine components are in reusable condition, purchasing individual parts may be the most economical alternative. The block, crankshaft and piston/connecting rod assemblies should all be inspected carefully. Even if the block shows little wear, the cylinder bores should be surface honed.

Short block – A short block consists of an engine block with a crankshaft and piston/connecting rod assemblies already installed. All new bearings are incorporated and all clearances will be correct. The existing camshafts, valve train components, cylinder heads and external parts can be bolted to the short block with little or no machine shop work necessary.

Long block – A long block consists of a short block plus an oil pump, oil pan, cylinder heads, rocker arm covers, camshafts and valve train components, timing sprockets, belt and timing cover. All components are in-

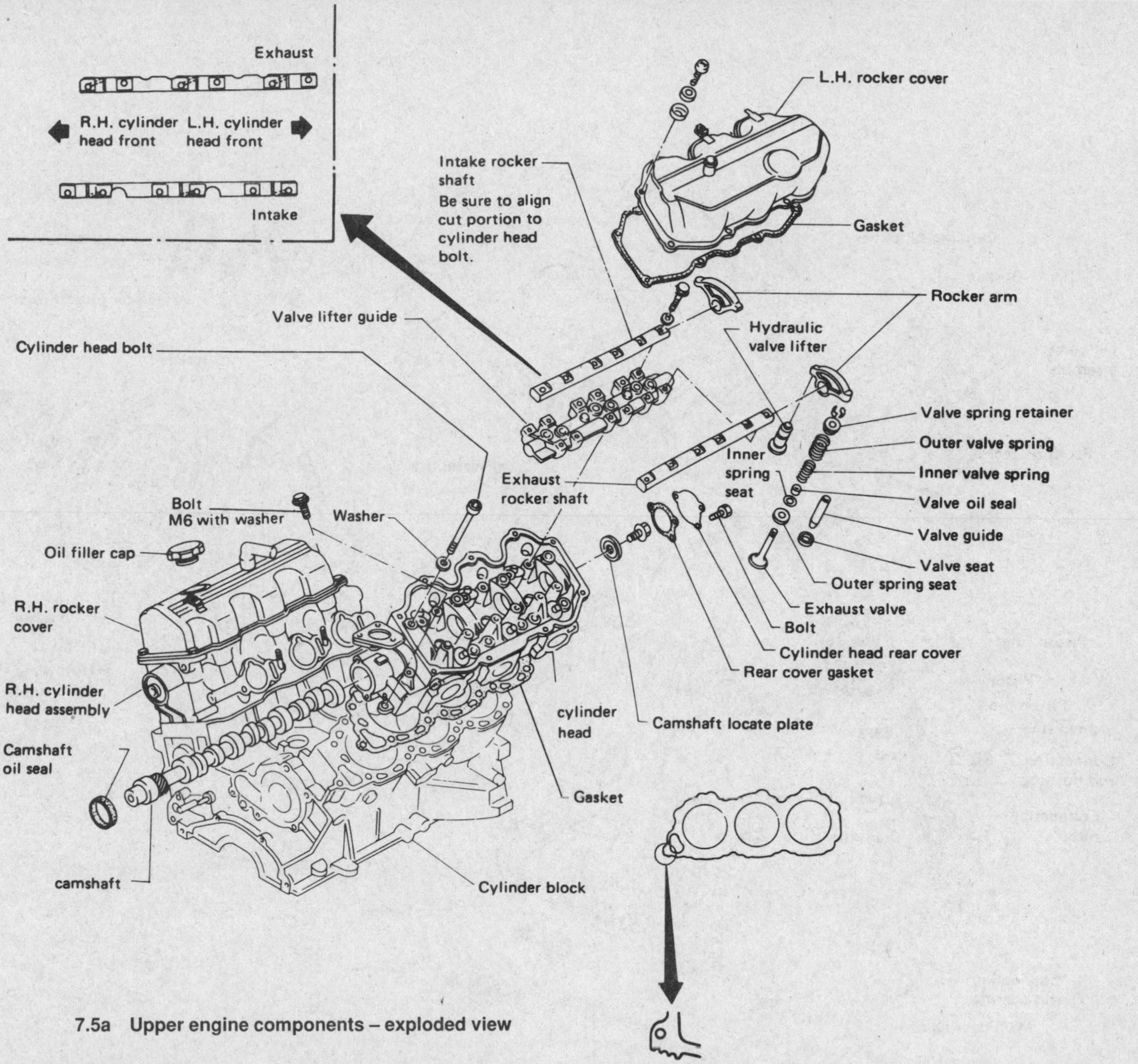

7.5a Upper engine components – exploded view

stalled with new bearings, seals and gaskets incorporated throughout. The installation of manifolds and external parts is all that's necessary.

Give careful thought to which alternative is best for you and discuss the situation with local automotive machine shops, auto parts dealers and experienced rebuilders before ordering or purchasing replacement parts.

7 Engine overhaul – disassembly sequence

Refer to illustrations 7.3, 7.5a and 7.5b

1 It's much easier to disassemble and work on the engine if it's mounted on a portable engine stand. A stand can often be rented quite cheaply from an equipment rental yard. Before the engine is mounted on a stand, the flywheel/driveplate and engine rear plate should be removed from the engine.

2 If a stand isn't available, it's possible to disassemble the engine with it blocked up on the floor. Be extra careful not to tip or drop the engine when working without a stand.

3 If you're going to obtain a rebuilt engine, all external components **(see illustration)** must come off first, to be transferred to the replacement engine, just as they will if you're doing a complete engine overhaul yourself. These include:

Alternator and brackets
Emissions control components
Distributor (crank angle sensor), spark plug wires and spark plugs
Thermostat and housing cover
Water pump
EFI components
Intake/exhaust manifolds
Oil filter
Engine mounts
Clutch and flywheel/driveplate
Engine rear plate

Note: *When removing the external components from the engine, pay close attention to details that may be helpful or important during installation. Note the installed position of gaskets, seals, spacers, pins, brackets, washers, bolts and other small items.*

4 If you're obtaining a short block, which consists of the engine block, crankshaft, pistons and connecting rods all assembled, then the cylinder heads, oil pan and oil pump will have to be removed as well. See *Engine rebuilding alternatives* for additional information regarding the different possibilities to be considered.

5 If you're planning a complete overhaul, the engine must be disassembled and the internal components **(see illustrations)** removed in the

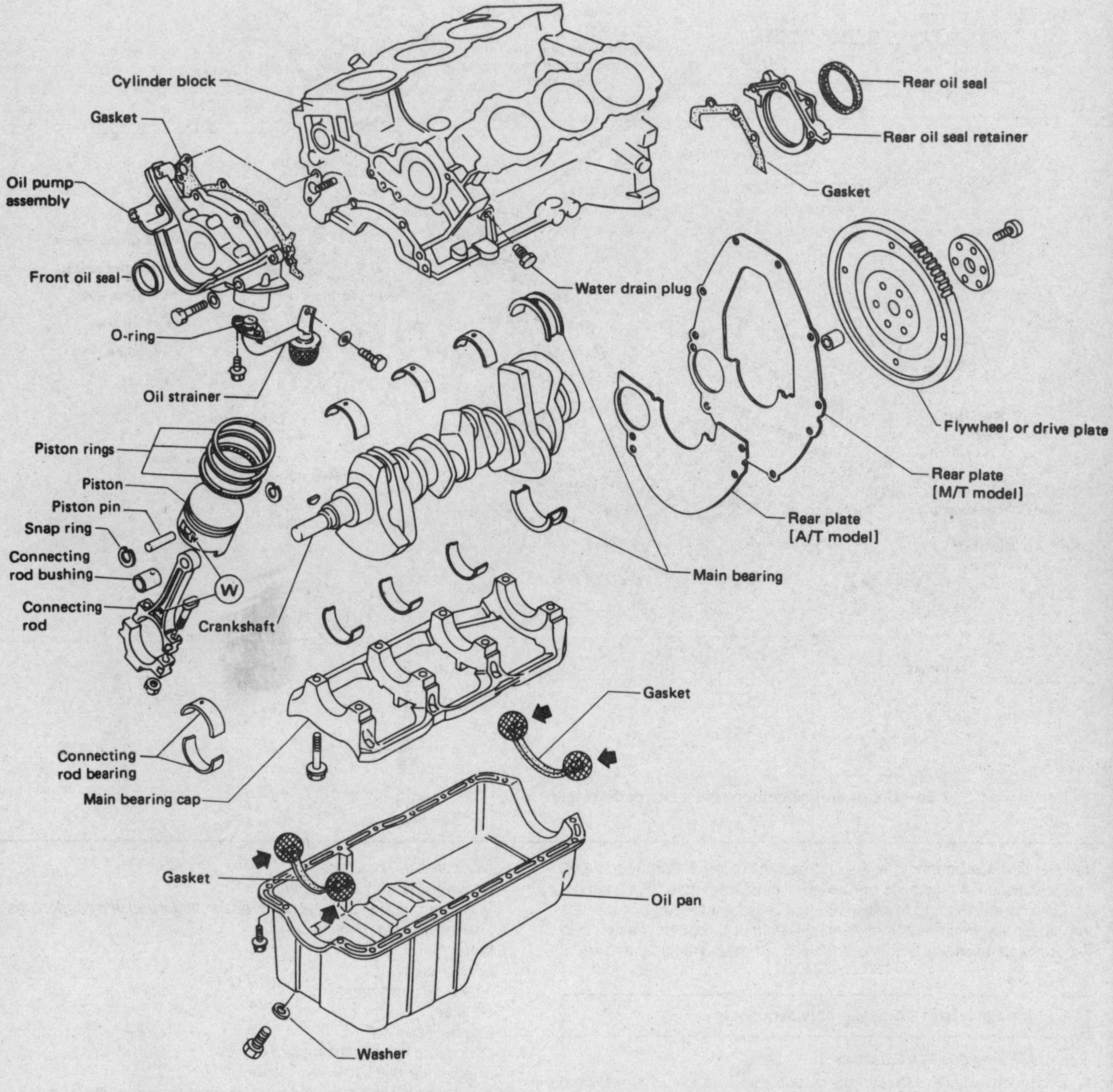

7.5b Lower engine components – exploded view

following general order:

Rocker arm covers
Intake and exhaust manifolds
Rocker arm assemblies
Valve lifters
Cylinder heads
Timing cover
Timing belt and sprockets
Camshafts
Oil pan and pick-up
Oil pump
Piston/connecting rod assemblies
Rear main oil seal and retainer
Crankshaft and main bearings

6 Before beginning the disassembly and overhaul procedures, make sure the following items are available. Also, refer to *Engine overhaul – reassembly sequence* for a list of tools and materials needed for engine reassembly.

Common hand tools
Small cardboard boxes or plastic bags for storing parts
Gasket scraper
Ridge reamer
Vibration damper puller
Micrometers
Telescoping gauges
Dial indicator set
Valve spring compressor
Cylinder surfacing hone
Piston ring groove cleaning tool
Electric drill motor
Tap and die set
Wire brushes
Oil gallery brushes
Cleaning solvent

8 Cylinder head – disassembly

Refer to illustrations 8.2, 8.3 and 8.4

Note: *New and rebuilt cylinder heads are commonly available for most engines at dealerships and auto parts stores. Due to the fact that some specialized tools are necessary for the disassembly and inspection procedures, and replacement parts may not be readily available, it may be more practical and economical for the home mechanic to purchase replacement heads rather than taking the time to disassemble, inspect and recondition the originals.*

1 Cylinder head disassembly involves removal of the intake and exhaust valves and related components. If they're still in place, remove the rocker arms and lifters (see Chapter 2A) from the cylinder head. Label the parts or store them separately so they can be reinstalled in their original locations.

2 Before the valves are removed, arrange to label and store them, along with their related components, so they can be kept separate and reinstalled in the same valve guides they are removed from **(see illustration)**.

3 Compress the springs on the first valve with a spring compressor and remove the keepers **(see illustration)**. Carefully release the valve spring compressor and remove the retainer, the spring and the spring seat (if used).

4 Pull the valve out of the head, then remove the oil seal from the guide. If the valve binds in the guide (won't pull through), push it back into the head and deburr the area around the keeper groove with a fine file or whetstone **(see illustration)**.

8.2 A small plastic bag, with an appropriate label, can be used to store the valve train components so they can be kept together and reinstalled in the correct guide

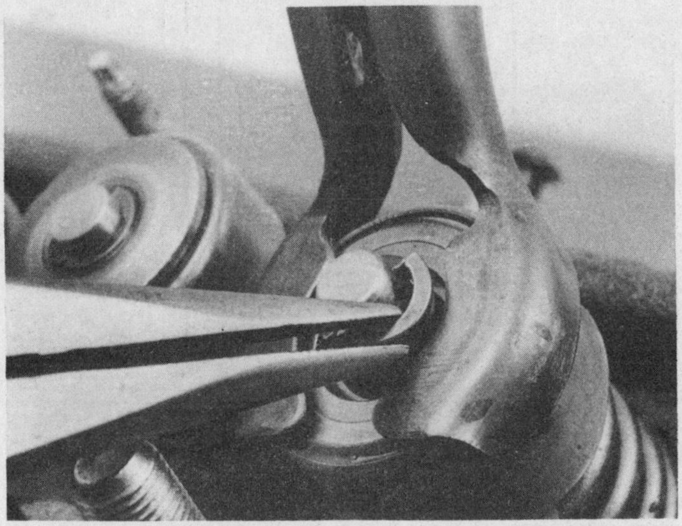

8.3 Use a valve spring compressor to compress the spring, then remove the keepers from the valve stem

8.4 If the valve won't pull through the guide, deburr the edge of the stem end and the area around the top of the keeper groove with a fine file or whetstone

2B

5 Repeat the procedure for the remaining valves. Remember to keep all the parts for each valve together so they can be reinstalled in the same locations.

6 Once the valves and related components have been removed and stored in an organized manner, the head should be thoroughly cleaned and inspected. If a complete engine overhaul is being done, finish the engine disassembly procedures before beginning the cylinder head cleaning and inspection process.

9 Cylinder head – cleaning and inspection

Refer to illustrations 9.12, 9.14, 9.15, 9.16, 9.17 and 9.18

1 Thorough cleaning of the cylinder heads and related valve train components, followed by a detailed inspection, will enable you to decide how much valve service work must be done during the engine overhaul. **Note:** *If the engine was severely overheated, the cylinder heads are probably warped (see Step 12).*

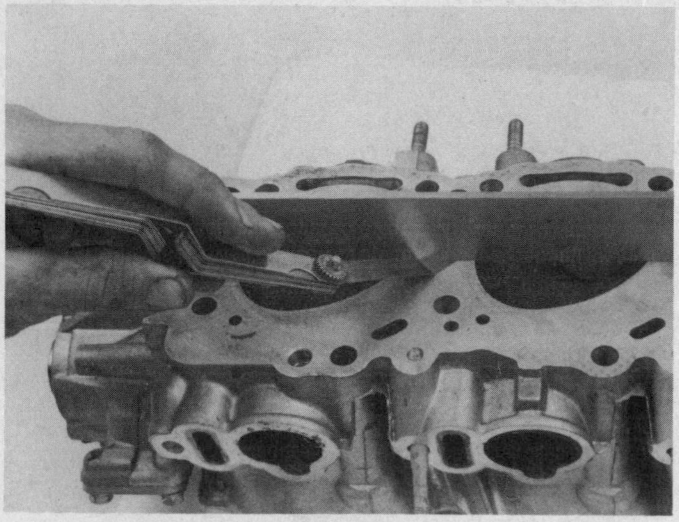

9.12 Check the cylinder head gasket surface for warpage by trying to slip a feeler gauge under the straightedge (see the Specifications for the maximum warpage allowed and use a feeler gauge of that thickness)

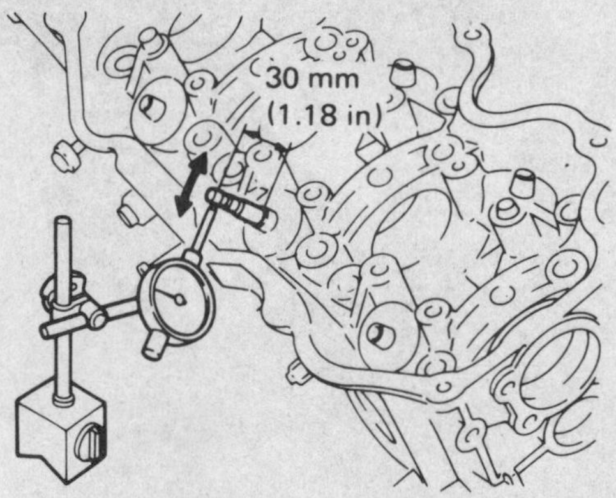

9.14 A dial indicator can be used to determine the valve stem-to-guide clearance (move the valve stem as indicated by the arrows)

Cleaning

2 Scrape all traces of old gasket material and sealing compound off the head gasket, intake manifold and exhaust manifold sealing surfaces. Be very careful not to gouge the cylinder head. Special gasket removal solvents that soften gaskets and make removal much easier are available at auto parts stores.

3 Remove all built up scale from the coolant passages.

4 Run a stiff wire brush through the various holes to remove deposits that may have formed in them.

5 Run an appropriate size tap into each of the threaded holes to remove corrosion and thread sealant that may be present. If compressed air is available, use it to clear the holes of debris produced by this operation. **Warning:** *Wear eye protection when using compressed air!*

6 Clean the combustion chambers with a wire brush if carbon has accumulated.

7 Clean the cylinder head with solvent and dry it thoroughly. Compressed air will speed the drying process and ensure that all holes and recessed areas are clean. **Note:** *Decarbonizing chemicals are available and may prove very useful when cleaning cylinder heads and valve train components. They are very caustic and should be used with caution. Be sure to follow the instructions on the container.*

8 Clean the rocker arms and shafts with solvent and dry them thoroughly (don't mix them up during the cleaning process). Compressed air will speed the drying process and can be used to clean out the oil passages.

9 Clean all the valve springs, spring seats, keepers and retainers with solvent and dry them thoroughly. Do the components from one valve at a time to avoid mixing up the parts.

10 Scrape off any heavy deposits that may have formed on the valves, then use a motorized wire brush to remove deposits from the valve heads and stems. Again, make sure the valves don't get mixed up.

Inspection

Note: *Be sure to perform all of the following inspection procedures before concluding that machine shop work is required. Make a list of the items that need attention.*

Cylinder head

11 Inspect the heads very carefully for cracks, evidence of coolant leakage and other damage. If cracks are found, check with an automotive ma-

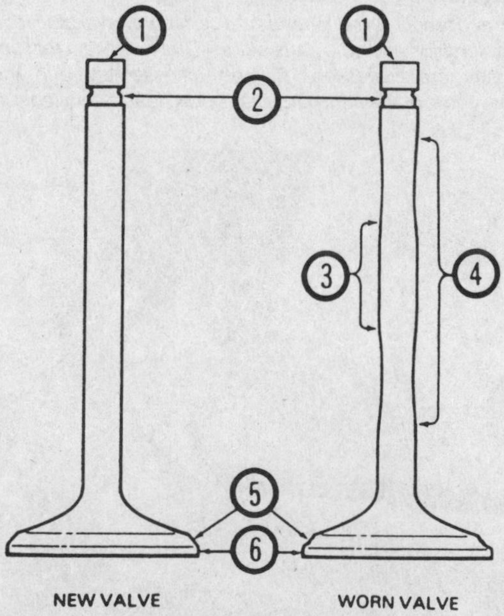

9.15 Check for valve wear at the points shown here

1 *Valve tip*
2 *Keeper groove*
3 *Stem (least worn area)*
4 *Stem (most worn area)*
5 *Valve face*
6 *Margin*

chine shop concerning repair. If repair isn't possible, a new cylinder head should be obtained.

12 Using a straightedge and feeler gauge, check the head gasket mating surface for warpage **(see illustration)**. If the warpage exceeds the limit specified in this Chapter, it can be resurfaced at an automotive machine shop. **Note:** *If the heads are resurfaced, the intake manifold flanges will also require machining.*

13 Examine the valve seats in each of the combustion chambers. If they're pitted, cracked or burned, the head will require valve service that's beyond the scope of the home mechanic.

14 Check the valve stem-to-guide clearance by measuring the lateral movement of the valve stem with a dial indicator attached securely to the head **(see illustration)**. The valve must be in the guide and approximately 1/16-inch off the seat. The total valve stem movement indicated by the gauge needle must be divided by two to obtain the actual clearance. After this is done, if there's still some doubt regarding the condition of the valve guides they should be checked by an automotive machine shop (the cost should be minimal).

Valves

15 Carefully inspect each valve face for uneven wear, deformation, cracks, pits and burned areas **(see illustration)**. Check the valve stem for scuffing and galling and the neck for cracks. Rotate the valve and check for any obvious indication that it's bent. Look for pits and excessive wear on the end of the stem. The presence of any of these conditions indicates the need for valve service by an automotive machine shop.

16 Measure the margin width on each valve **(see illustration)**. Any valve with a margin narrower than specified in this Chapter will have to be replaced with a new one.

Valve components

17 Check each valve spring for wear (on the ends) and pits. Measure the free length and compare it to the Specifications in this Chapter **(see illustration)**. Any springs that are shorter than specified have sagged and should not be reused. The tension of all springs should be checked with a special fixture before deciding that they're suitable for use in a rebuilt engine (take the springs to an automotive machine shop for this check).

18 Stand each spring on a flat surface and check it for squareness **(see illustration)**. If any of the springs are distorted or sagged, replace all of them with new parts.

19 Check the spring retainers and keepers for obvious wear and cracks. Any questionable parts should be replaced with new ones, as extensive damage will occur if they fail during engine operation.

Camshaft, lifters, rocker arms and shafts

20 Refer to Part A (Section 16) for the inspection procedures.

21 Any damaged or excessively worn parts must be replaced with new ones.

22 If the inspection process indicates that the valve components are in generally poor condition and worn beyond the limits specified, which is usually the case in an engine that's being overhauled, reassemble the valves in the cylinder head and refer to Section 10 for valve servicing recommendations.

10 Valves – servicing

1 Because of the complex nature of the job and the special tools and equipment needed, servicing of the valves, the valve seats and the valve guides, commonly known as a valve job, should be done by a professional.

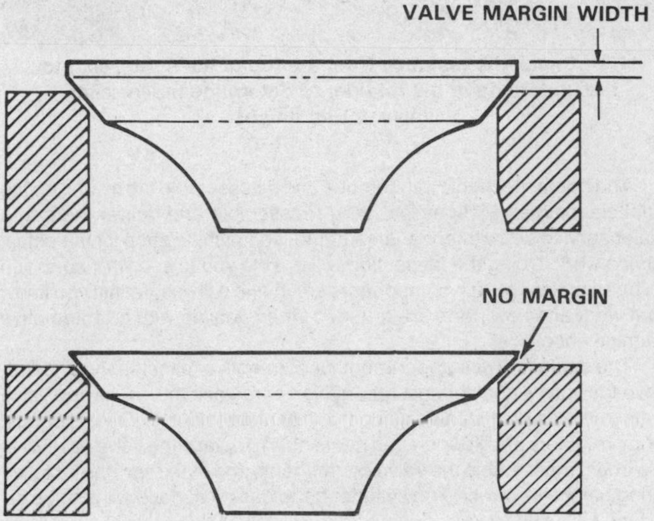

9.16 The margin width on each valve must be as specified (if no margin exists, the valve cannot be reused)

2B

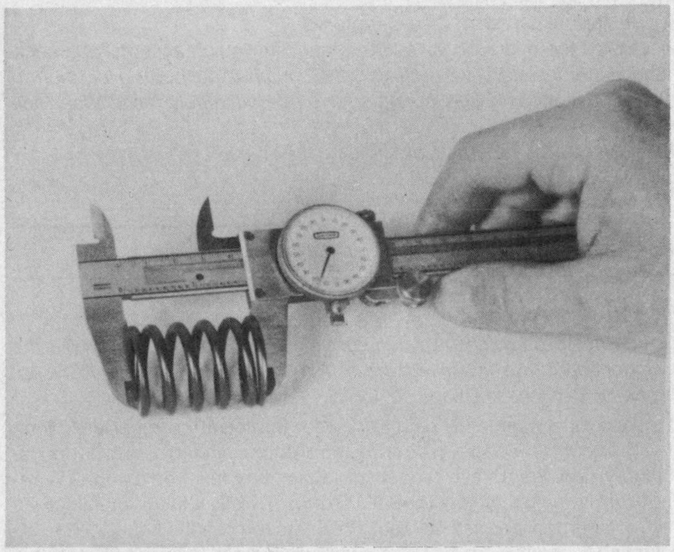

9.17 Measure the free length of each valve spring with a dial or vernier caliper

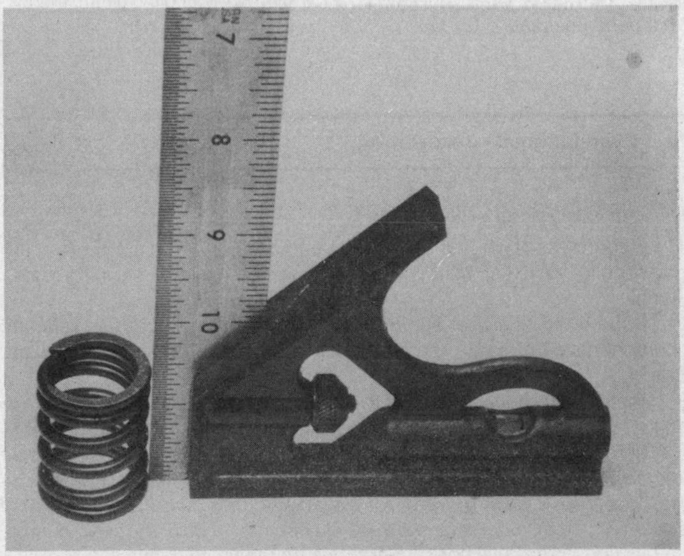

9.18 Check each valve spring for squareness

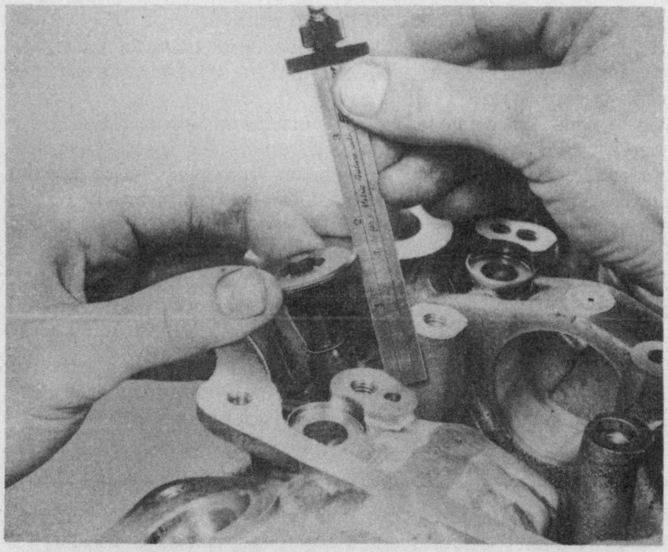

11.4 Check the distance from the top of the spring seat to the underside of the retainer to determine the installed valve spring height

11.7 Double-check the height with the valve springs installed (do this for each valve)

2 The home mechanic can remove and disassemble the heads, do the initial cleaning and inspection, then reassemble and deliver them to a dealer service department or an automotive machine shop for the actual service work. Doing the inspection will enable you to see what condition the head and valvetrain components are in and will ensure that you know what work and new parts are required when dealing with an automotive machine shop.
3 The dealer service department, or automotive machine shop, will remove the valves and springs, recondition or replace the valves and valve seats, recondition the valve guides, check and replace the valve springs, spring retainers and keepers (as necessary), replace the valve seals with new ones, reassemble the valve components and make sure the installed spring height is correct. The cylinder head gasket surface will also be resurfaced if it's warped.
4 After the valve job has been performed by a professional, the head will be in like new condition. When the head is returned, be sure to clean it again before installation on the engine to remove any metal particles and abrasive grit that may still be present from the valve service or head resurfacing operations. Use compressed air, if available, to blow out all the oil holes and passages.

11 Cylinder head – reassembly

Refer to illustrations 11.4 and 11.7

1 Regardless of whether or not the head was sent to an automotive repair shop for valve servicing, make sure it is clean before beginning reassembly.
2 If the head was sent out for valve servicing, the valves and related components will already be in place. Begin the reassembly procedure with Step 7.
3 Install new seals on each of the valve guides. To install the intake oil seals, you will need a seal installation tool (Nissan part number KV10107501) or an appropriate size deep socket. Gently tap each seal into place until it is properly seated onto the guide (see illustration 13.15a in Chapter 2A). **Caution:** *Do not hammer on the guide seal once it is seated or you may damage the seal. Do not twist or cock the seals during installation or they will not seal properly on the valve stems.*
4 Install the valves, taking care not to damage the new valve guide oil seals. Slip the valve seat over the valve guide boss and set the keepers and retainer in place. Measure the installed spring height by lifting up on the retainer until the valve is seated. Measure the distance between the top of the spring seat and the underside of the retainer **(see illustration)**. Compare your measurement to the installed height specified in this Chapter. Add shims under the seat to bring the height within specifications.
5 Once the correct height is established, remove the keepers and retainer and install the valve springs. **Note:** *The outer spring has a graduated pitch. Install it with the narrow pitch end toward the cylinder head (see illustration 13.16 in Chapter 2A).*
6 Compress the springs and retainer with a valve compressor and slip the keepers into place. Release the compressor, making sure the keepers are seated properly in the valve stem upper groove. If necessary, grease can be used to hold the keepers in place as the compressor is released (see illustration 13.17 in Chapter 2A).
7 Double-check the installed valve spring height for each valve. Measure the installed spring height with a small ruler and compare it to the specified installed height **(see illustration)**. If it was correct prior to reassembly, it should still be within the limits specified in this Chapter. If it is not, you must install additional valve spring shim(s) to bring the height within the specified limits.
8 Install the camshaft (see Chapter 2A).
9 Install the hydraulic valve lifters and lifter guide assembly on each head. **Note:** *Install the valve lifters in their original lifter bores. Hold them in place with rubber bands during lifter guide assembly installation (see Chapter 2A).*
10 Remove the rubber bands holding the lifters.

12 Pistons/connecting rods – removal

Refer to illustrations 12.1, 12.3 and 12.6

Note: *Prior to removing the piston/connecting rod assemblies, remove the cylinder heads, the oil pan and the oil pump pick-up by referring to the appropriate Sections in Chapter 2A.*

1 Use your fingernail to feel if a ridge has formed at the upper limit of ring travel (about 1/4-inch down from the top of each cylinder). If carbon deposits or cylinder wear have produced ridges, they must be completely removed with a special tool **(see illustration)**. Follow the manufacturer's instructions provided with the tool. Failure to remove the ridges before attempting to remove the piston/connecting rod assemblies may result in piston breakage.
2 After the cylinder ridges have been removed, turn the engine upside-down so the crankshaft is facing up.

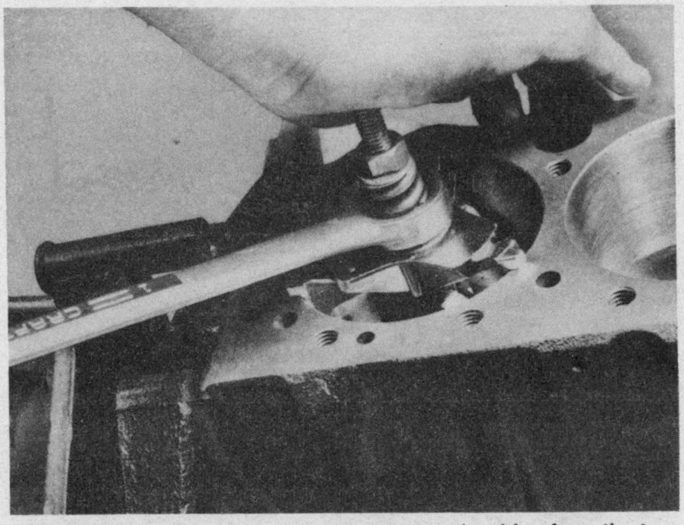

12.1 . A ridge reamer is required to remove the ridge from the top of each cylinder – do this before removing the pistons!

3 Before the connecting rods are removed, check the side clearance with feeler gauges. Slide them between the first connecting rod and the crankshaft throw until the play is removed **(see illustration)**. The side clearance is equal to the thickness of the feeler gauge(s). If the side clearance exceeds the service limit, new connecting rods will be required. If new rods (or a new crankshaft) are installed, the side clearance may fall under the specified minimum (if it does, the rods will have to be machined to restore it – consult an automotive machine shop for advice if necessary). Repeat the procedure for the remaining connecting rods.

4 Check the connecting rods and caps for identification marks. If they aren't plainly marked, use a small center punch to make the appropriate number of indentations on each rod and cap (1, 2, 3, etc.).

5 Loosen each of the connecting rod cap nuts 1/2-turn at a time until they can be removed by hand. Remove the number one connecting rod cap and bearing insert. Don't drop the bearing insert out of the cap.

6 Slip a short length of plastic or rubber hose over each connecting rod cap bolt to protect the crankshaft journal and cylinder wall as the piston is removed **(see illustration)**.

7 Remove the bearing insert and push the connecting rod/piston assembly out through the top of the engine. Use a wooden hammer handle to push on the upper bearing surface in the connecting rod. If resistance is felt, double-check to make sure that all of the ridge was removed from the cylinder.

8 Repeat the procedure for the remaining cylinders.

9 After removal, reassemble the connecting rod caps and bearing inserts in their respective connecting rods and install the cap nuts finger tight. Leaving the old bearing inserts in place until reassembly will help prevent the connecting rod bearing surfaces from being accidentally nicked or gouged.

10 Don't separate the pistons from the connecting rods (see Section 17 for additional information).

13 Crankshaft – removal

Refer to illustrations 13.1, 13.3 and 13.4

Note: *The crankshaft can be removed only after the engine has been removed from the vehicle. It's assumed that the flywheel or driveplate, crankshaft pulley, timing belt, sprocket, oil pan, oil pump and piston/connecting rod assemblies have already been removed. The rear main oil seal retainer must be unbolted and separated from the block before proceeding with crankshaft removal.*

1 Before the crankshaft is removed, check the end play. Mount a dial indicator with the stem in line with the crankshaft and just touching one of the crank throws **(see illustration)**.

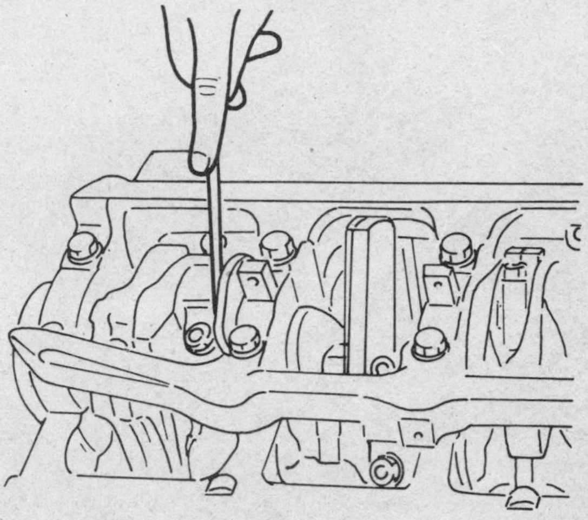

12.3 Check the connecting rod side clearance with a feeler gauge as shown

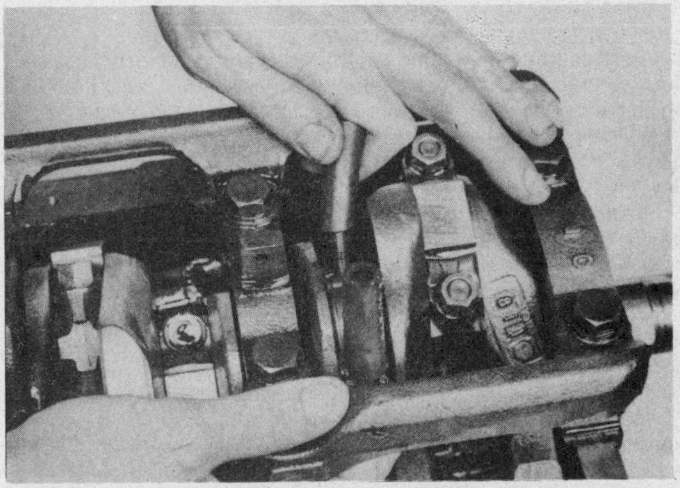

12.6 To prevent damage to the crankshaft journals and the cylinder walls, slip sections of hose over the rod bolts before removing the pistons

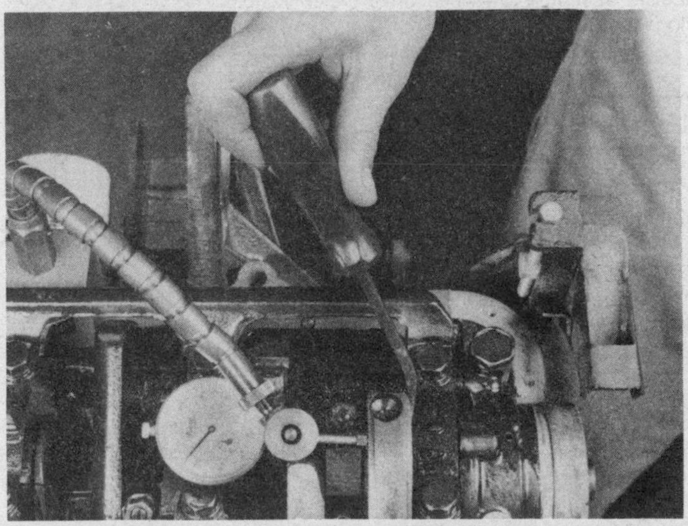

13.1 Crankshaft end play can be checked with a dial indicator on the front counterweight

13.3 Crankshaft end play can also be measured with a feeler gauge at the number four main bearing

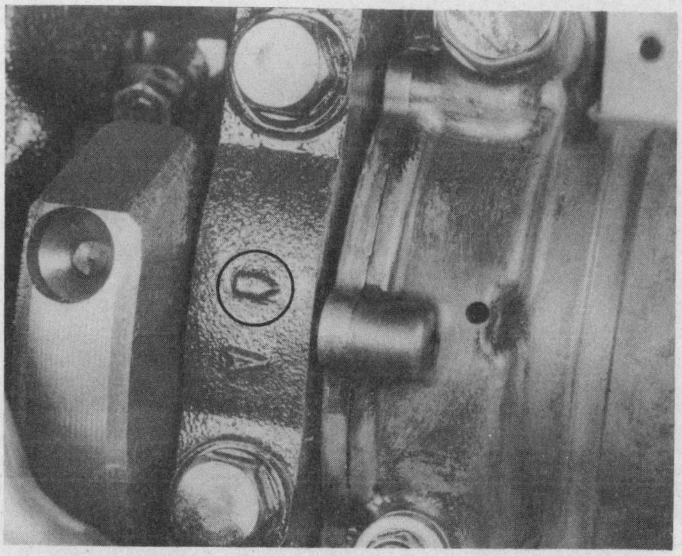

13.4 The main bearing cap assembly has a cast-in arrow which points toward the timing belt end of the engine

2 Push the crankshaft all the way to the rear and zero the dial indicator. Next, pry the crankshaft to the front as far as possible and check the reading on the dial indicator. The distance that it moves is the end play. If it's greater than specified in this Chapter, check the crankshaft thrust surfaces for wear. If no wear is evident, new main bearings should correct the end play.

3 If a dial indicator isn't available, feeler gauges can be used. Gently pry or push the crankshaft all the way to the front of the engine. Slip feeler gauges between the crankshaft and the front face of the rear (thrust) main bearing to determine the clearance **(see illustration)**.

4 The main bearing cap assembly has a cast-in arrow, which points to the timing belt end of the engine **(see illustration)**. Loosen the main bearing cap bolts 1/4-turn at a time each, until the assembly can be removed by hand.

5 Gently tap the cap assembly with a soft-face hammer, then separate it from the engine block. If necessary, use the bolts as levers to remove the cap assembly. Try not to drop the bearing inserts if they come out with the cap assembly.

6 Carefully lift the crankshaft out of the engine. It may be a good idea to have an assistant available, since the crankshaft is quite heavy. With the bearing inserts in place in the engine block and main bearing caps, return the cap assembly to it's location on the engine block and tighten the bolts finger tight.

14 Engine block – cleaning

Refer to illustrations 14.1, 14.8 and 14.10

Caution: *The core plugs (also known as freeze or soft plugs) may be difficult or impossible to retrieve if they're driven into the block coolant passages.*

1 Drill a small hole in the center of each core plug and pull them out with an auto body type dent puller **(see illustration)**.

2 Using a gasket scraper, remove all traces of gasket material from the engine block. Be very careful not to nick or gouge the gasket sealing surfaces.

3 Remove the main bearing caps and separate the bearing inserts from the caps and the engine block. Tag the bearings, indicating which cylinder they were removed from and whether they were in the cap or the block, then set them aside.

4 Remove all of the threaded oil gallery plugs from the block. The plugs are usually very tight – they may have to be drilled out and the holes retapped. Use new plugs when the engine is reassembled.

5 If the engine is extremely dirty it should be taken to an automotive machine shop to be steam cleaned or hot tanked.

6 After the block is returned, clean all oil holes and oil galleries one more time. Brushes specifically designed for this purpose are available at most auto parts stores. Flush the passages with warm water until the water runs clear, dry the block thoroughly and wipe all machined surfaces with a light, rust preventive oil. If you have access to compressed air, use it to speed the drying process and to blow out all the oil holes and galleries. **Warning:** *Wear eye protection when using compressed air!*

7 If the block isn't extremely dirty or sludged up, you can do an adequate cleaning job with hot soapy water and a stiff brush. Take plenty of time and do a thorough job. Regardless of the cleaning method used, be sure to clean all oil holes and galleries very thoroughly, dry the block completely and coat all machined surfaces with light oil.

8 The threaded holes in the block must be clean to ensure accurate torque readings during reassembly. Run the proper size tap into each of the holes to remove rust, corrosion, thread sealant or sludge and restore damaged threads **(see illustration)**. If possible, use compressed air to clear the holes of debris produced by this operation. Now is a good time to clean the threads on the head bolts and the main bearing cap bolts as well.

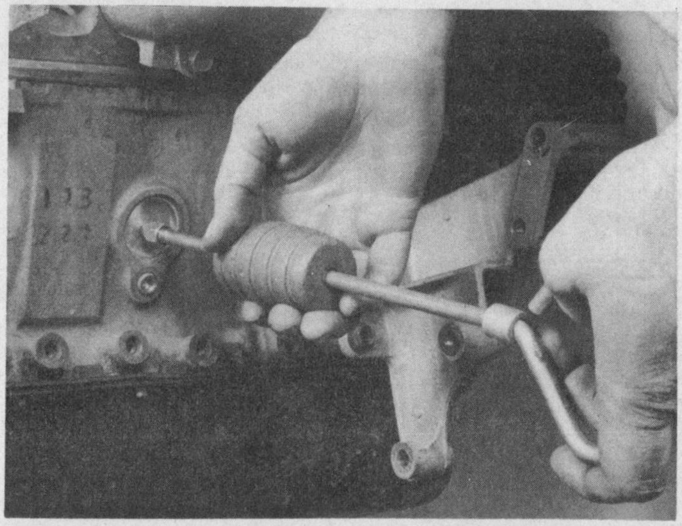

14.1 The core plugs should be removed with a puller – if they're driven into the block, they may be impossible to retrieve

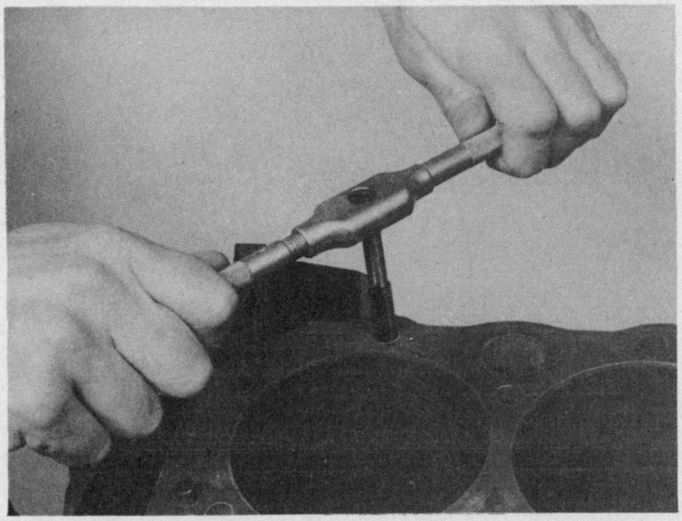

14.8 All bolt holes in the block – particularly the main bearing cap and head bolt holes – should be cleaned and restored with a tap (be sure to remove debris from the holes after this is done)

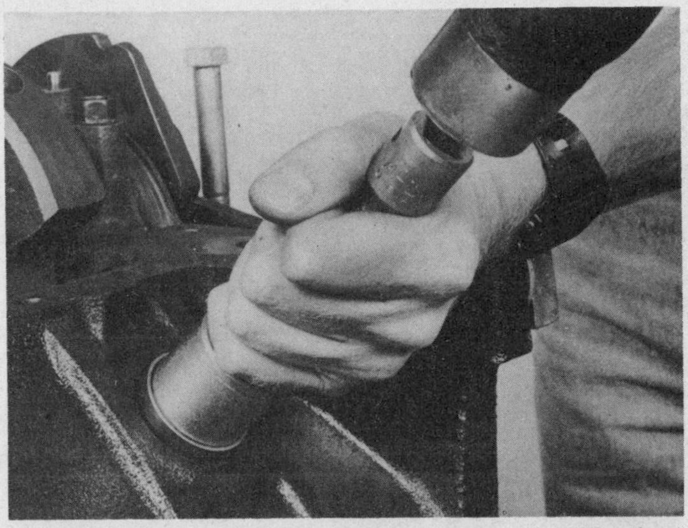

14.10 A large socket on an extension can be used to drive the new core plugs into the bores

9 Reinstall the main bearing caps and tighten the bolts finger tight.

10 After coating the sealing surfaces of the new core plugs with Permatex no. 2 sealant (or equivalent), install them in the engine block **(see illustration)**. Make sure they're driven in straight and seated properly or leakage could result. Special tools are available for this purpose, but a large socket, with an outside diameter that will just slip into the core plug, a 1/2-inch drive extension and a hammer will work just as well.

11 Apply non-hardening sealant (such as Permatex no. 2 or Teflon pipe sealant) to the new oil gallery plugs and thread them into the holes in the block. Make sure they're tightened securely.

12 If the engine isn't going to be reassembled right away, cover it with a large plastic trash bag to keep it clean.

15 Engine block – inspection

Refer to illustrations 15.4a, 15.4b and 15.4c

1 Before the block is inspected, it should be cleaned as described in Section 14.

2 Visually check the block for cracks, rust and corrosion. Look for stripped threads in the threaded holes. It's also a good idea to have the block checked for hidden cracks by an automotive machine shop that has the special equipment to do this type of work. If defects are found, have the block repaired, if possible, or replaced.

3 Check the cylinder bores for scuffing and scoring.

4 Measure the diameter of each cylinder at the top (just under the ridge area), center and bottom of the cylinder bore, parallel to the crankshaft axis **(see illustrations)**.

5 Next, measure each cylinder's diameter at the same three locations across the crankshaft axis. Compare the results to the Specifications in this Chapter.

6 If the required precision measuring tools aren't available, the piston-to-cylinder clearances can be obtained, though not quite as accurately, using feeler gauge stock. Feeler gauge stock comes in 12-inch lengths and various thicknesses and is generally available at auto parts stores.

7 To check the clearance, select a feeler gauge and slip it into the cylinder along with the matching piston. The piston must be positioned exactly

2B

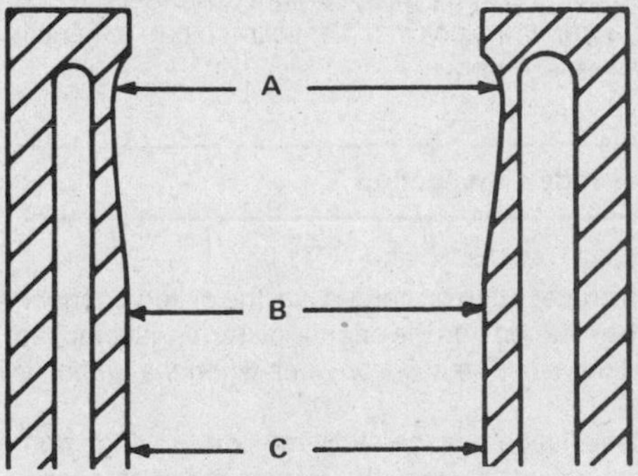

15.4a Measure the diameter of each cylinder just under the wear ridge (A), at the center (B) and at the bottom (C)

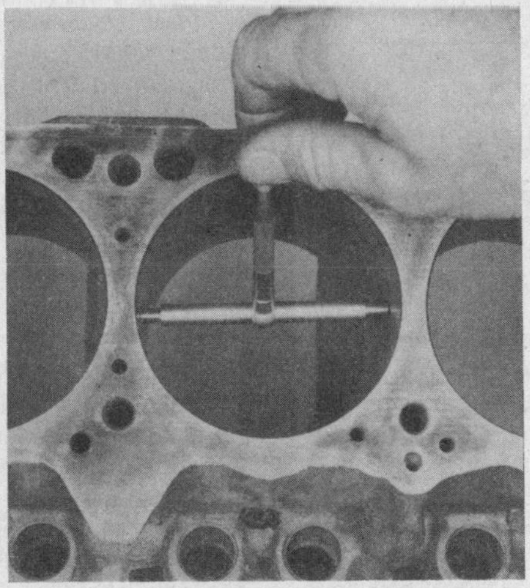

15.4b The ability to "feel" when the telescoping gauge is at the correct point will be developed over time, so work slowly and repeat the check until you're satisfied the bore measurement is accurate

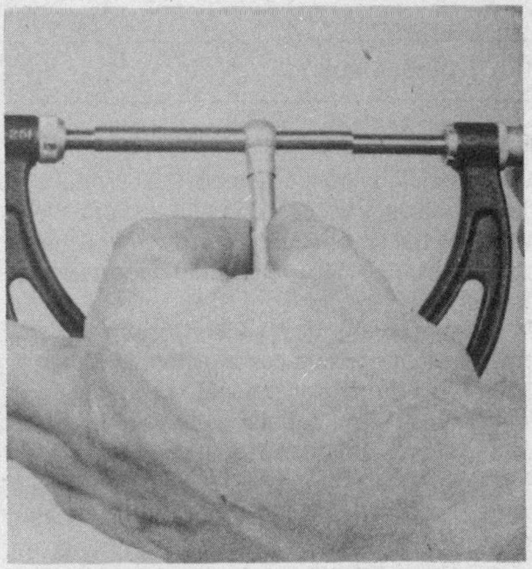

15.4c The gauge is then measured with a micrometer to determine the bore size

16.3a A "bottle brush" hone will produce better results if you've never done cylinder honing before

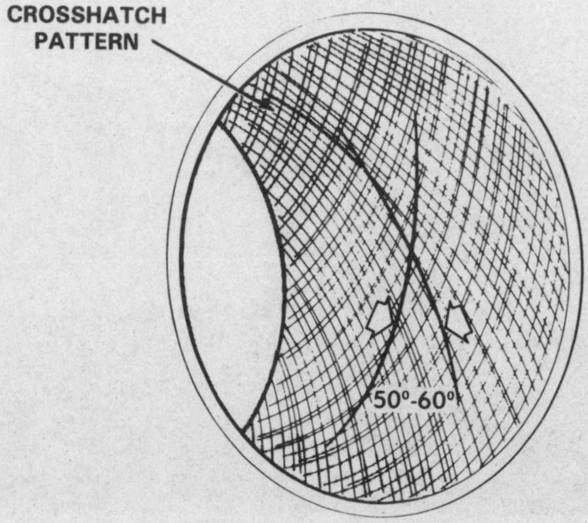

16.3b The cylinder hone should leave a smooth, crosshatch pattern with the lines intersecting at approximately a 60-degree angle

as it normally would be. The feeler gauge must be between the piston and cylinder on one of the thrust faces (90-degrees to the piston pin bore).
8 The piston should slip through the cylinder (with the feeler gauge in place) with moderate pressure.
9 If it falls through or slides through easily, the clearance is excessive and a new piston will be required. If the piston binds at the lower end of the cylinder and is loose toward the top, the cylinder is tapered. If tight spots are encountered as the piston/feeler gauge is rotated in the cylinder, the cylinder is out-of-round.
10 Repeat the procedure for the remaining pistons and cylinders.
11 If the cylinder walls are badly scuffed or scored, or if they're out-of-round or tapered beyond the limits given in the Specifications in this Chapter, have the engine block rebored and honed at an automotive machine shop. If a rebore is done, oversize pistons and rings will be required.
12 If the cylinders are in reasonably good condition and not worn to the outside of the limits, and if the piston-to-cylinder clearances can be maintained properly, then they don't have to be rebored. Honing is all that's necessary (see Section 16).

16 Cylinder honing

Refer to illustrations 16.3a and 16.3b

1 Prior to engine reassembly, the cylinder bores must be honed so the new piston rings will seat correctly and provide the best possible combustion chamber seal. **Note:** *If you don't have the tools or don't want to tackle the honing operation, most automotive machine shops will do it for a reasonable fee.*
2 Before honing the cylinders, install the main bearing caps and tighten the bolts to the torque specified in this Chapter.
3 Two types of cylinder hones are commonly available – the flex hone or "bottle brush" type and the more traditional surfacing hone with spring-loaded stones. Both will do the job, but for the less experienced mechanic the "bottle brush" hone will probably be easier to use. You'll also need some kerosene or honing oil, rags and an electric drill motor. Proceed as follows:

a) Mount the hone in the drill motor, compress the stones and slip it into the first cylinder **(see illustration)**. Be sure to wear safety goggles or a face shield!
b) Lubricate the cylinder with plenty of honing oil, turn on the drill and move the hone up-and-down in the cylinder at a pace that will produce a fine crosshatch pattern on the cylinder walls. Ideally, the crosshatch lines should intersect at approximately a 60-degree angle **(see illustration)**. Be sure to use plenty of lubricant and don't take off any more material than is absolutely necessary to produce the desired finish. **Note:** *Piston ring manufacturers may specify a smaller crosshatch angle than the traditional 60-degrees – read and follow any instructions included with the new rings.*
c) Don't withdraw the hone from the cylinder while it's running. Instead, shut off the drill and continue moving the hone up-and-down in the cylinder until it comes to a complete stop, then compress the stones and withdraw the hone. If you're using a "bottle brush" type hone, stop the drill motor, then turn the chuck in the normal direction of rotation while withdrawing the hone from the cylinder.
d) Wipe the oil out of the cylinder and repeat the procedure for the remaining cylinders.

4 After the honing job is complete, chamfer the top edges of the cylinder bores with a small file so the rings won't catch when the pistons are installed. Be very careful not to nick the cylinder walls with the end of the file.
5 The entire engine block must be washed again very thoroughly with warm, soapy water to remove all traces of the abrasive grit produced during the honing operation. **Note:** *The bores can be considered clean when a lint-free white cloth – dampened with clean engine oil – used to wipe them out doesn't pick up any more honing residue, which will show up as gray areas on the cloth. Be sure to run a brush through all oil holes and galleries and flush them with running water.*
6 After rinsing, dry the block and apply a coat of light rust preventive oil to all machined surfaces. Wrap the block in a plastic trash bag to keep it clean and set it aside until reassembly.

17 Pistons/connecting rods – inspection

Refer to illustrations 17.4a, 17.4b, 17.10 and 17.11

1 Before the inspection process can be carried out, the piston/connecting rod assemblies must be cleaned and the original piston rings removed from the pistons. **Note:** *Always use new piston rings when the engine is reassembled.*
2 Using a piston ring installation tool, carefully remove the rings from the pistons. Be careful not to nick or gouge the pistons in the process.
3 Scrape all traces of carbon from the top of the piston. A handheld wire brush or a piece of fine emery cloth can be used once the majority of the deposits have been scraped away. Do not, under any circumstances, use a wire brush mounted in a drill motor to remove deposits from the pistons. The piston material is soft and may be eroded away by the wire brush.
4 Use a piston ring groove cleaning tool to remove carbon deposits from the ring grooves. If a tool isn't available, a piece broken off the old ring

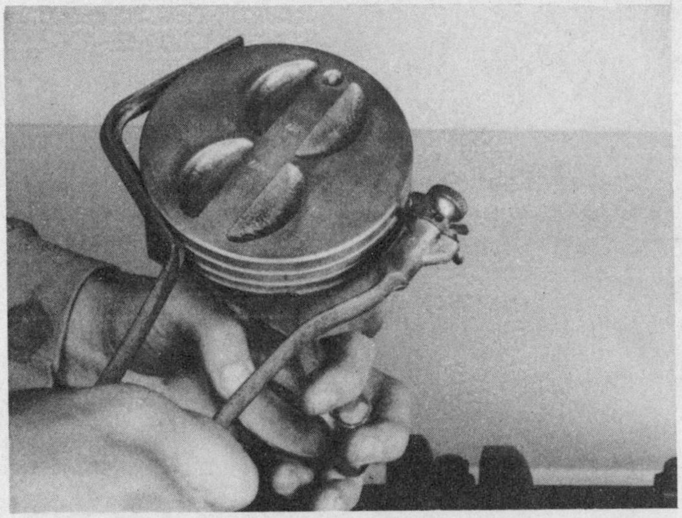

17.4a The piston ring grooves can be cleaned with a special tool, as shown here, . . .

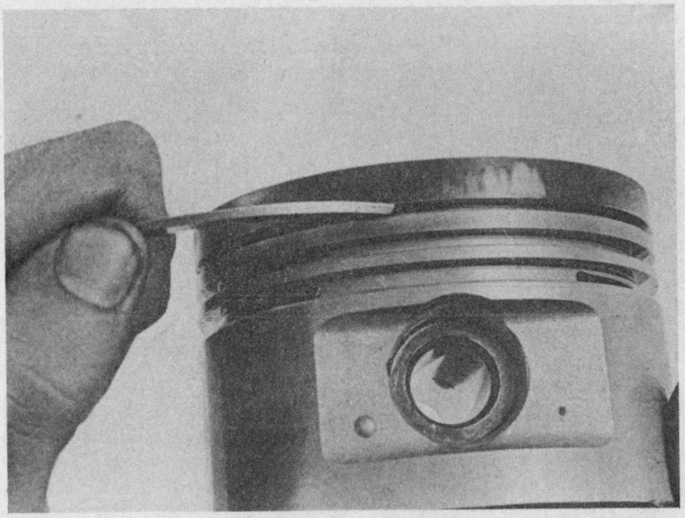

17.4b . . . or a section of broken ring

will do the job. Be very careful to remove only the carbon deposits – don't remove any metal and do not nick or scratch the sides of the ring grooves **(see illustrations)**.

5 Once the deposits have been removed, clean the piston/rod assemblies with solvent and dry them with compressed air (if available). Make sure the oil return holes in the back sides of the ring grooves are clear.

6 If the pistons and cylinder walls aren't damaged or worn excessively, and if the engine block is not rebored, new pistons won't be necessary. Normal piston wear appears as even vertical wear on the piston thrust surfaces and slight looseness of the top ring in its groove. New piston rings, however, should always be used when an engine is rebuilt.

7 Carefully inspect each piston for cracks around the skirt, at the pin bosses and at the ring lands.

8 Look for scoring and scuffing on the thrust faces of the skirt, holes in the piston crown and burned areas at the edge of the crown. If the skirt is scored or scuffed, the engine may have been suffering from overheating and/or abnormal combustion, which caused excessively high operating temperatures. The cooling and lubrication systems should be checked thoroughly. A hole in the piston crown is an indication that abnormal combustion (preignition) was occurring. Burned areas at the edge of the piston crown are usually evidence of spark knock (detonation). If any of the above problems exist, the causes must be corrected or the damage will occur again. The causes may include intake air leaks, incorrect fuel/air mixture, incorrect ignition timing and EGR system malfunctions.

9 Corrosion of the piston, in the form of small pits, indicates that coolant is leaking into the combustion chamber and/or the crankcase. Again, the cause must be corrected or the problem may persist in the rebuilt engine.

10 Measure the piston ring side clearance by laying a new piston ring in each ring groove and slipping a feeler gauge in beside it **(see illustration)**. Check the clearance at three or four locations around each groove. Be sure to use the correct ring for each groove – they are different. If the side clearance is greater than specified in this Chapter, new pistons will have to be used.

11 Check the piston-to-bore clearance by measuring the bore (see Section 15) and the piston diameter. Make sure the pistons and bores are correctly matched. Measure the piston across the skirt, at a 90-degree angle to the piston pin, 3/4-inch from the bottom of the skirt **(see illustration)**. Subtract the piston diameter from the bore diameter to obtain the clearance. If it's greater than specified in this Chapter, the block will have to be rebored and new pistons and rings installed.

17.10 Check the ring side clearance with a feeler gauge at several points around the groove

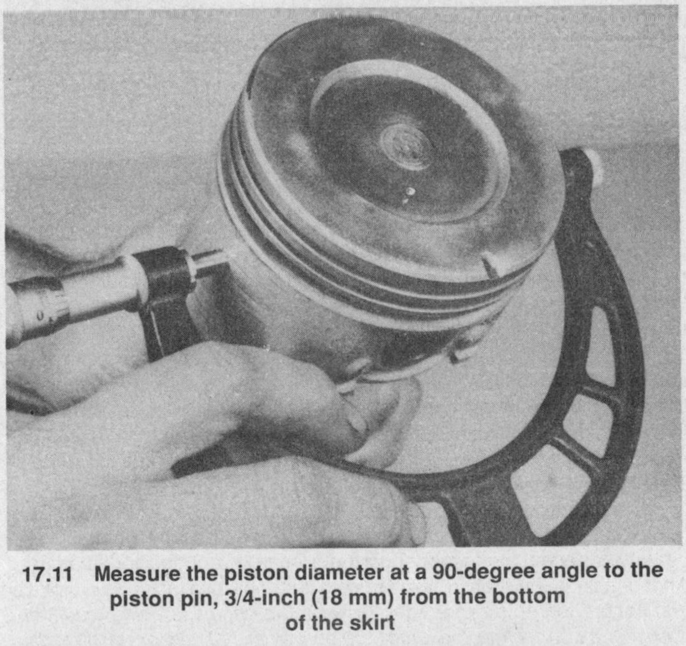

17.11 Measure the piston diameter at a 90-degree angle to the piston pin, 3/4-inch (18 mm) from the bottom of the skirt

18.1 Use a wire or stiff bristle brush to clean the oil holes in the crankshaft

18.3 Rubbing a penny across each journal will reveal their condition – if copper rubs off and adheres to the crankshaft, the journals should be reground

18.4 The oil holes should be chamfered so sharp edges don't gouge or scratch the new bearings

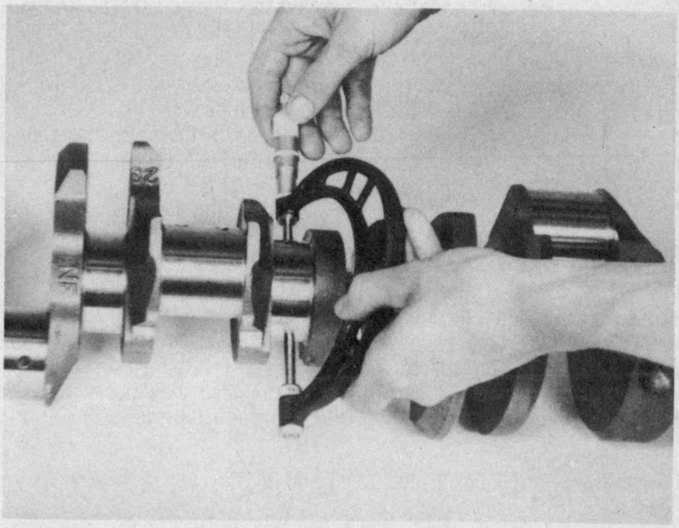

18.6 Measure the diameter of each crankshaft journal at several points to detect taper and out-of-round conditions

12 Check the piston-to-rod clearance by twisting the piston and rod in opposite directions. Any noticeable play indicates excessive wear, which must be corrected. The piston/connecting rod assemblies should be taken to an automotive machine shop to have the pistons and rods resized and new pins installed.

13 If the pistons must be removed from the connecting rods for any reason, they should be taken to an automotive machine shop. While they are there have the connecting rods checked for bend and twist, since automotive machine shops have special equipment for this purpose. **Note:** *Unless new pistons and/or connecting rods must be installed, do not disassemble the pistons and connecting rods.*

14 Check the connecting rods for cracks and other damage. Temporarily remove the rod caps, lift out the old bearing inserts, wipe the rod and cap bearing surfaces clean and inspect them for nicks, gouges and scratches. After checking the rods, replace the old bearings, slip the caps into place and tighten the nuts finger tight. **Note:** *If the engine is being rebuilt because of a connecting rod knock, be sure to install new or rebuilt rods.*

18 Crankshaft – inspection

Refer to illustrations 18.1, 18.3, 18.4, 18.6 and 18.8

1 Clean the crankshaft with solvent and dry it with compressed air (if available). Be sure to clean the oil holes with a stiff brush **(see illustration)** and flush them with solvent.

2 Check the main and connecting rod bearing journals for uneven wear, scoring, pits and cracks.

3 Rub a penny across each journal several times **(see illustration)**. If a journal picks up copper from the penny, it's too rough and must be reground.

4 Remove all burrs from the crankshaft oil holes with a stone, file or scraper **(see illustration)**.

5 Check the rest of the crankshaft for cracks and other damage. It should be magnafluxed to reveal hidden cracks – an automotive machine shop will handle the procedure.

18.8 **If the seals have worn grooves in the crankshaft journals, or if the seal contact surfaces are nicked or scratched, the new seals will leak**

6 Using a micrometer, measure the diameter of the main and connecting rod journals **(see illustration)** and compare the results to the Specifications in this Chapter. By measuring the diameter at a number of points around each journal's circumference, you'll be able to determine whether or not the journal is out-of-round. Take the measurement at each end of the journal, near the crank throws, to determine if the journal is tapered.
7 If the crankshaft journals are damaged, tapered, out-of-round or worn beyond the limits given in the Specifications in this Chapter, have the crankshaft reground by an automotive machine shop. Be sure to use the correct size bearing inserts if the crankshaft is reconditioned.
8 Check the oil seal journals at each end of the crankshaft for wear and damage. If the seal has worn a groove in the journal, or if it's nicked or scratched **(see illustration)**, the new seal may leak when the engine is reassembled. In some cases, an automotive machine shop may be able to repair the journal by pressing on a thin sleeve. If repair isn't feasible, a new or different crankshaft should be installed.
9 Refer to Section 19 and examine the main and rod bearing inserts.

19 Main and connecting rod bearings – inspection and main bearing selection

Inspection

Refer to illustration 19.1

1 Even though the main and connecting rod bearings should be replaced with new ones during the engine overhaul, the old bearings should be retained for close examination, as they may reveal valuable information about the condition of the engine **(see illustration)**.
2 Bearing failure occurs because of lack of lubrication, the presence of dirt or other foreign particles, overloading the engine and corrosion. Regardless of the cause of bearing failure, it must be corrected before the engine is reassembled to prevent it from happening again.
3 When examining the bearings, remove them from the engine block, the main bearing caps, the connecting rods and the rod caps and lay them out on a clean surface in the same general position as their location in the engine. This will enable you to match any bearing problems with the corresponding crankshaft journal.
4 Dirt and other foreign particles get into the engine in a variety of ways. It may be left in the engine during assembly, or it may pass through filters or the PCV system. It may get into the oil, and from there into the bearings. Metal chips from machining operations and normal engine wear are often present. Abrasives are sometimes left in engine components after reconditioning, especially when parts are not thoroughly cleaned using the proper cleaning methods. Whatever the source, these foreign objects often end up embedded in the soft bearing material and are easily recognized. Large particles will not embed in the bearing and will score or gouge the bearing and journal. The best prevention for this cause of bearing failure is to clean all parts thoroughly and keep everything spotlessly clean during engine assembly. Frequent and regular engine oil and filter changes are also recommended.

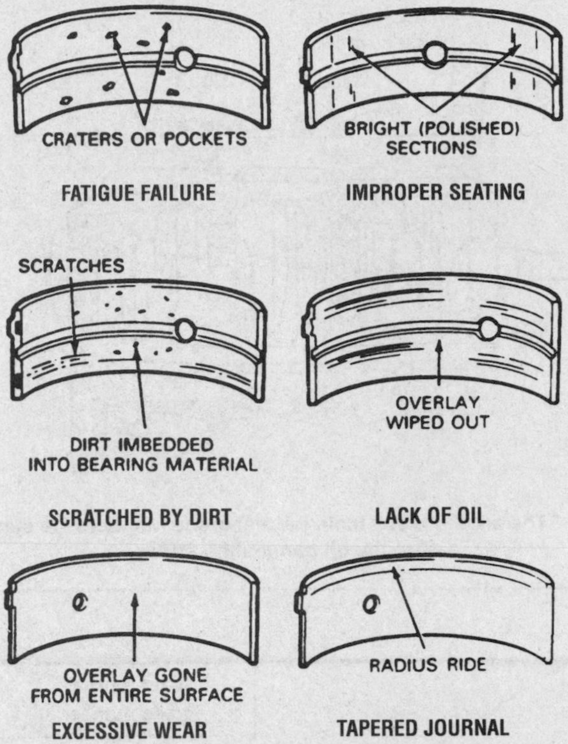

19.1 **Typical bearing failures**

2B

5 Lack of lubrication (or lubrication breakdown) has a number of interrelated causes. Excessive heat (which thins the oil), overloading (which squeezes the oil from the bearing face) and oil leakage or throw off (from excessive bearing clearances, worn oil pump or high engine speeds) all contribute to lubrication breakdown. Blocked oil passages, which usually are the result of misaligned oil holes in a bearing shell, will also oil starve a bearing and destroy it. When lack of lubrication is the cause of bearing failure, the bearing material is wiped or extruded from the steel backing of the bearing. Temperatures may increase to the point where the steel backing turns blue from overheating.
6 Driving habits can have a definite effect on bearing life. Full throttle, low speed operation (lugging the engine) puts very high loads on bearings, which tends to squeeze out the oil film. These loads cause the bearings to flex, which produces fine cracks in the bearing face (fatigue failure). Eventually the bearing material will loosen in pieces and tear away from the steel backing. Short trip driving leads to corrosion of bearings because insufficient engine heat is produced to drive off the condensed water and corrosive gases. These products collect in the engine oil, forming acid and sludge. As the oil is carried to the engine bearings, the acid attacks and corrodes the bearing material.
7 Incorrect bearing installation during engine assembly will lead to bearing failure as well. Tight fitting bearings leave insufficient bearing oil clearance and will result in oil starvation. Dirt or foreign particles trapped behind a bearing insert result in high spots on the bearing which lead to failure.

Selection (main bearings only)

Refer to illustrations 19.9, 19.10 and 19.11

8 If the original main bearings are worn or damaged, or if the oil clearances are incorrect (see Section 22), the following procedure should be

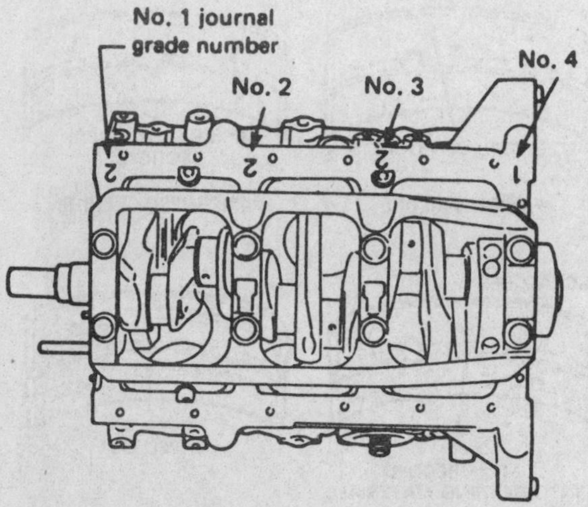

19.9 The engine block main journal grade numbers are stamped into the oil pan mating surface

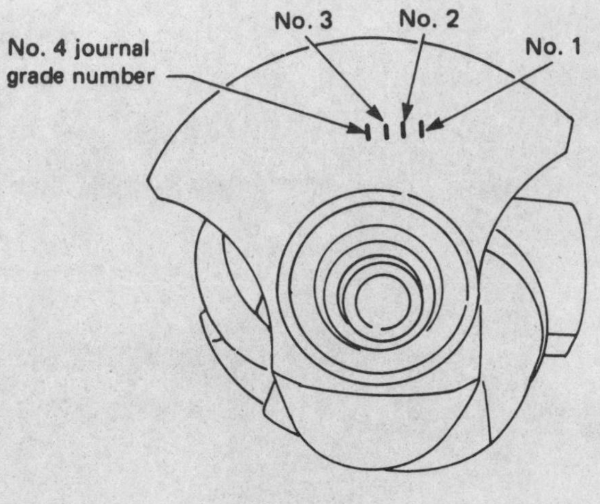

19.10 The crankshaft main journal grade numbers are stamped on the crank counterweight

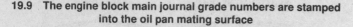

		Main journal grade number		
		0	1	2
		Main bearing grade number		
Crankshaft journal grade number	0	0	1	2
	1	1	2	3
	2	2	3	4

For example:

Main journal grade number: 1

Crankshaft journal grade number: 2

Main bearing grade number = 1 + 2
= 3

19.11 Main bearing selection chart

used to select the correct new main bearings for engine reassembly. However, if the crankshaft has been reground, new undersize bearings must be installed – *the following procedure should not be used if undersize bearings are required.* The automotive machine shop that reconditions the crankshaft will provide or help you select the correct size bearings. Regardless of how the bearing sizes are determined, use the oil clearance, measured with Plastigage (see Section 22), as a guide to ensure the bearings are the right size.

9 Locate the main journal grade numbers stamped into the oil pan mating surface on the engine block **(see illustration)**.

10 Locate the main journal grade numbers on the crankshaft as well **(see illustration)**.

11 Use the accompanying chart to determine the correct bearings for each main journal **(see illustration)**.

12 Remember, the oil clearance is the final judge when selecting new bearing sizes. If you have any questions or are unsure which bearings to use, get help from a Nissan dealer parts or service department.

20 Engine overhaul – reassembly sequence

Refer to illustrations 20.2a and 20.2b

1 Before beginning engine reassembly, make sure you have all the necessary new parts, gaskets and seals as well as the following items on hand:

Common hand tools
A 1/2-inch drive torque wrench
Piston ring installation tool
Piston ring compressor
Short lengths of rubber or plastic hose to fit over connecting rod bolts
Plastigage
Feeler gauges
A fine-tooth file
New engine oil
Engine assembly lube or moly-base grease
Gasket sealant
Thread locking compound

2 In order to save time and avoid problems, engine reassembly must be done in the following general order **(see illustrations)**:

Piston rings
Crankshaft and main bearings
Rear main oil seal and retainer
Piston/connecting rod assemblies
Oil pump
Oil pan
Cylinder heads, camshafts, lifters and rocker arms
Timing belt and sprockets
Timing belt cover
Intake and exhaust manifolds
Rocker arm covers
Engine rear plate
Flywheel/driveplate

21 Piston rings – installation

Refer to illustrations 21.3, 21.4, 21.5, 21.9a, 21.9b and 21.12

1 Before installing the new piston rings, the ring end gaps must be checked. It's assumed that the piston ring side clearance has been checked and verified correct (Section 17).

20.2a Assembled engine prior to installation – timing belt end

20.2b Assembled engine prior to installation – firewall side shown, other side similar

2 Lay out the piston/connecting rod assemblies and the new ring sets so the ring sets will be matched with the same piston and cylinder during the end gap measurement and engine assembly.

3 Insert the top (number one) ring into the first cylinder and square it up with the cylinder walls by pushing it in with the top of the piston **(see illustration)**. The ring should be near the bottom of the cylinder, at the lower limit of ring travel.

4 To measure the end gap, slip feeler gauges between the ends of the ring until a gauge equal to the gap width is found **(see illustration)**. The feeler gauge should slide between the ring ends with a slight amount of drag. Compare the measurement to the Specifications in this Chapter. If the gap is larger or smaller than specified, double-check to make sure you have the correct rings before proceeding.

5 If the gap is too small, it must be enlarged or the ring ends may come in contact with each other during engine operation, which can cause serious damage to the engine. The end gap can be increased by filing the ring ends very carefully with a fine file. Mount the file in a vise equipped with soft jaws, slip the ring over the file with the ends contacting the file face and slowly move the ring to remove material from the ends. When performing this operation, file only from the outside in **(see illustration)**.

6 Excess end gap isn't critical unless it's greater than 0.040-inch. Again, double-check to make sure you have the correct rings for your engine.

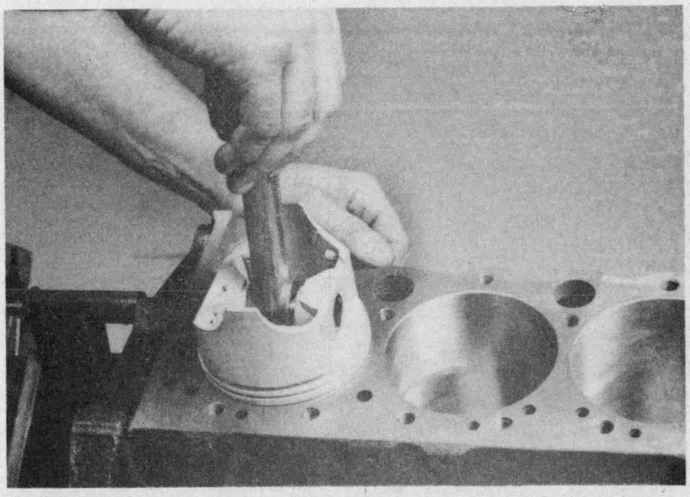

21.3 When checking piston ring end gap, the ring must be square in the cylinder bore (this is done by pushing the ring down with the top of a piston as shown)

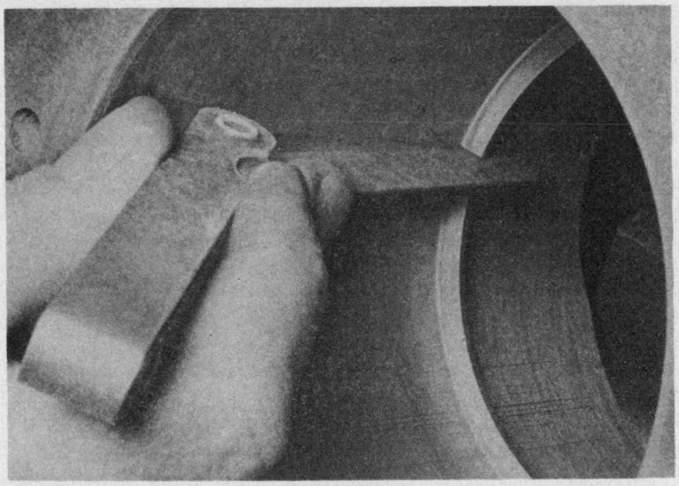

21.4 With the ring square in the cylinder, measure the end gap with a feeler gauge

21.5 If the end gap is too small, clamp a file in a vise and file the ring ends (from the outside in only) to enlarge the gap slightly

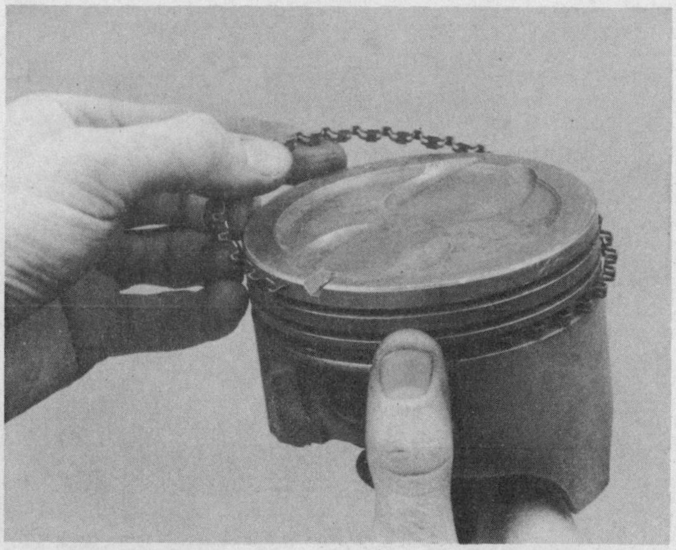

21.9a Installing the spacer/expander in the oil control ring groove

21.9b DO NOT use a piston ring installation tool when installing the oil ring side rails

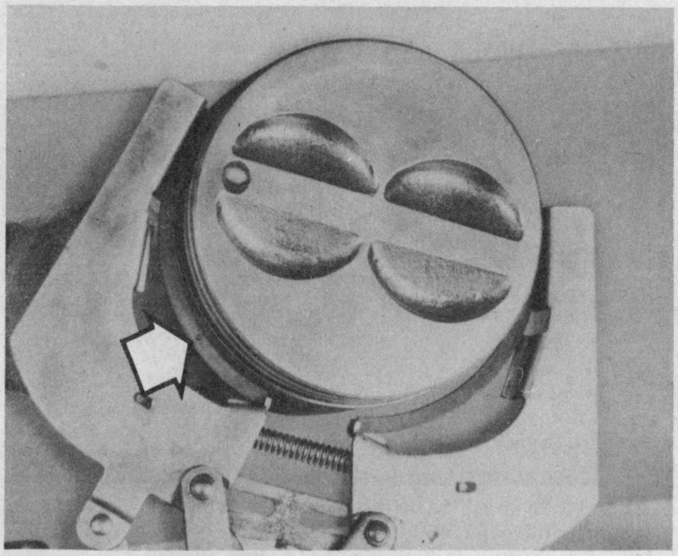

21.12 Installing the compression rings with a ring expander – the mark (arrow) must face up

7 Repeat the procedure for each ring that will be installed in the first cylinder and for each ring in the remaining cylinders. Remember to keep rings, pistons and cylinders matched up.

8 Once the ring end gaps have been checked/corrected, the rings can be installed on the pistons.

9 The oil control ring (lowest one on the piston) is usually installed first. It's composed of three separate components. Slip the spacer/expander into the groove **(see illustration)**. If an anti-rotation tang is used, make sure it's inserted into the drilled hole in the ring groove. Next, install the lower side rail. Don't use a piston ring installation tool on the oil ring side rails, as they may be damaged. Instead, place one end of the side rail into the groove between the spacer/expander and the ring land, hold it firmly in place and slide a finger around the piston while pushing the rail into the groove **(see illustration)**. Next, install the upper side rail in the same manner.

10 After the three oil ring components have been installed, check to make sure that both the upper and lower side rails can be turned smoothly in the ring groove.

11 The number two (middle) ring is installed next. It's usually stamped with a mark which must face up, toward the top of the piston. **Note:** *Always follow the instructions printed on the ring package or box – different manufacturers may require different approaches. Do not mix up the top and middle rings, as they have different cross sections.*

12 Use a piston ring installation tool and make sure the identification mark is facing the top of the piston, then slip the ring into the middle groove on the piston **(see illustration)**. Don't expand the ring any more than necessary to slide it over the piston.

13 Install the number one (top) ring in the same manner. Make sure the mark is facing up. Be careful not to confuse the number one and number two rings.

14 Repeat the procedure for the remaining pistons and rings.

22 Crankshaft – installation and main bearing oil clearance check

Refer to illustrations 22.5, 22.6, 22.11, 22.13 and 22.15

1 Crankshaft installation is the first step in engine reassembly. It's assumed at this point that the engine block and crankshaft have been cleaned, inspected and repaired or reconditioned.

2 Position the engine with the bottom facing up.

3 Remove the main bearing cap bolts and lift out the cap assembly.

4 If they're still in place, remove the original bearing inserts from the block and the main bearing caps. Wipe the bearing surfaces of the block and caps with a clean, lint-free cloth. They must be kept spotlessly clean.

Main bearing oil clearance check

5 Clean the back sides of the new main bearing inserts and lay one in each main bearing saddle in the block. If one of the bearing inserts from each set has a large groove in it, make sure the grooved insert is installed in the block. Lay the other bearing from each set in the corresponding main bearing cap. Make sure the tab on the bearing insert fits into the recess in the block or cap. **Caution:** *The oil holes in the block must line up with the oil holes in the bearing inserts* **(see illustration)**. *Do not hammer the bearing into place and don't nick or gouge the bearing faces. No lubrication should be used at this time.*

6 The flanged thrust bearing must be installed in the fourth (rear) cap and saddle **(see illustration)**.

7 Clean the faces of the bearings in the block and the crankshaft main bearing journals with a clean, lint-free cloth.

8 Check or clean the oil holes in the crankshaft, as any dirt here can go only one way – straight through the new bearings.

9 Once you're certain the crankshaft is clean, carefully lay it in position in the main bearings.

10 Before the crankshaft can be permanently installed, the main bearing oil clearance must be checked.

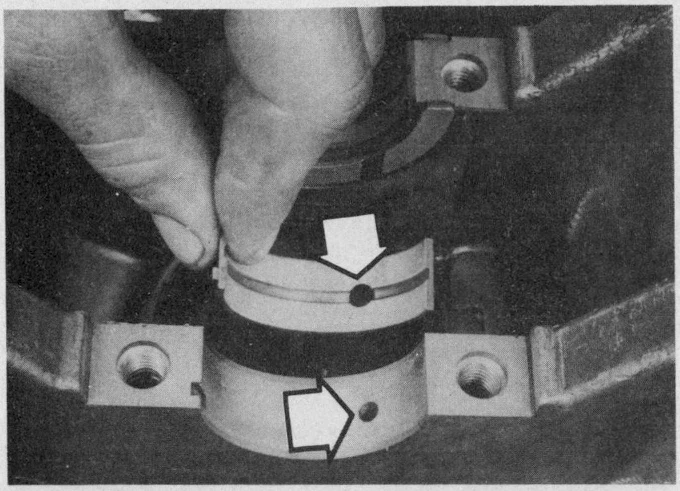

22.5 Make sure the oil holes in the bearings are aligned with the oil holes in the block (arrows)

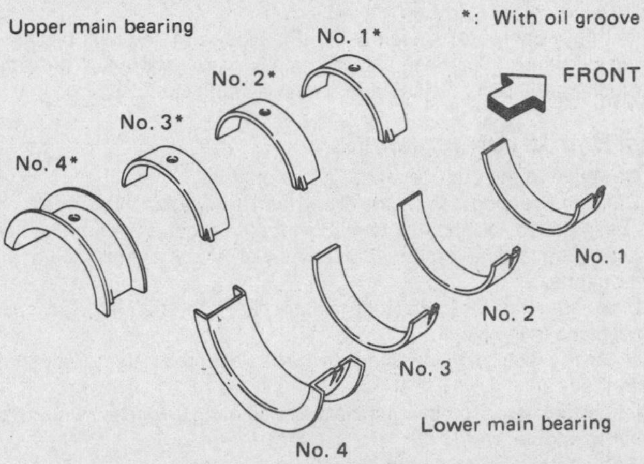

22.6 The main bearing inserts must be installed in this order, with the thrust bearing at the fourth (rear) main journal and the bearings with the oil grooves in the block

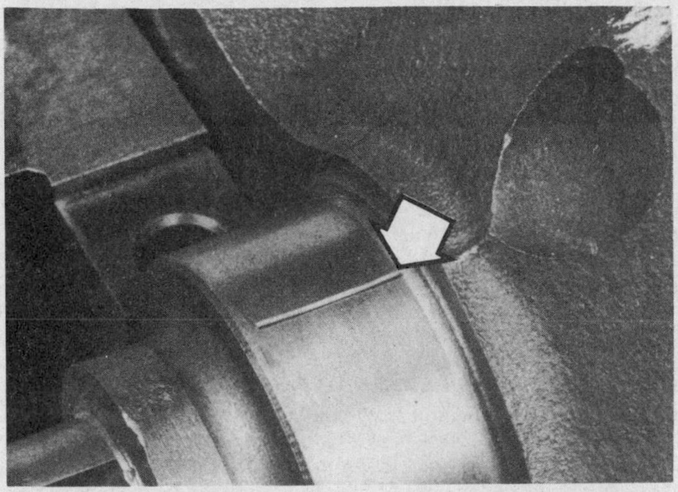

22.11 Lay the Plastigage strips (arrow) on the main bearing journals, parallel to the crankshaft centerline

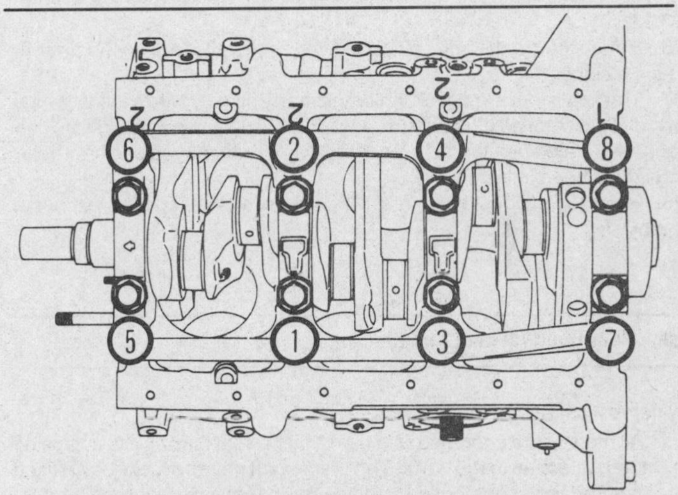

22.13 Tighten the main bearing cap retaining bolts in this sequence

11 Cut several pieces of the appropriate size Plastigage (they must be slightly shorter than the width of the main bearings) and place one piece on each crankshaft main bearing journal, parallel with the journal axis **(see illustration)**.

12 Clean the faces of the bearings in the cap assembly and install it with the arrow pointing toward the timing belt end of the engine. Don't disturb the Plastigage.

13 Starting with the center main and working out toward the ends, tighten the main bearing cap assembly bolts, in three steps, to the torque specified in this Chapter **(see illustration)**. Don't rotate the crankshaft at any time during this operation.

14 Remove the bolts and carefully lift off the main bearing cap assembly. Don't disturb the Plastigage or rotate the crankshaft.

15 Compare the width of the crushed Plastigage on each journal to the scale printed on the Plastigage envelope to obtain the main bearing oil clearance **(see illustration)**. Check the Specifications in this Chapter to make sure it's correct.

16 If the clearance is not as specified, the bearing inserts may be the wrong size (which means different ones will be required). Before deciding that different inserts are needed, make sure that no dirt or oil was between the bearing inserts and the caps or block when the clearance was measured. If the Plastigage was wider at one end than the other, the journal

22.15 Compare the width of the crushed Plastigage to the scale on the container to determine the main bearing oil clearance (always take the measurement at the widest point of the Plastigage); be sure to use the correct scale – standard and metric scales are included

may be tapered (refer to Section 18).
17 Carefully scrape all traces of the Plastigage material off the main bearing journals and/or the bearing faces. Use your fingernail or the edge of a credit card – don't nick or scratch the bearing faces.

Final crankshaft installation

18 Carefully lift the crankshaft out of the engine.
19 Clean the bearing faces in the block, then apply a thin, uniform layer of moly-base grease or engine assembly lube to each of the bearing surfaces. Be sure to coat the thrust faces as well as the journal face of the thrust bearing.
20 Make sure the crankshaft journals are clean, then lay the crankshaft back in place in the block.
21 Clean the faces of the bearings in the cap assembly, then apply lubricant to them.
22 Install the cap assembly with the arrow pointing toward the timing belt end of the engine.
23 Tighten the bearing cap bolts to 10-to-12 ft-lbs.
24 Gently tap the ends of the crankshaft forward and backward with a lead or brass hammer to line up the main bearing and crankshaft thrust surfaces.
25 Retighten all main bearing cap bolts to the specified torque, starting with the center main and working out toward the ends **(see illustration 22.13)**.
26 Rotate the crankshaft a number of times by hand to check for any obvious binding.
27 The final step is to check the crankshaft end play with a feeler gauge or a dial indicator as described in Section 13. The end play should be correct if the crankshaft thrust faces aren't worn or damaged and new bearings have been installed.
28 Refer to Section 23 and install the new seal, then bolt the retainer to the block.

23 Rear main oil seal installation

Refer to illustrations 23.3 and 23.4

1 All models are equipped with a one-piece seal that fits into a housing (retainer) attached to the block. The crankshaft must be installed first and the main bearing caps bolted in place, then the new seal should be installed in the retainer and the retainer bolted to the block.
2 Check the seal contact surface very carefully for scratches and nicks that could damage the new seal lip and cause oil leaks. If the crankshaft is damaged, the only alternative is a new or different crankshaft.
3 The old seal can be removed from the retainer with a hammer and punch by driving it out from the back side **(see illustration)**. Be sure to note how far it's recessed into the retainer bore before removing it; the new seal will have to be recessed an equal amount. Be very careful not to scratch or otherwise damage the bore in the retainer or oil leaks could develop.
4 Make sure the retainer is clean, then apply a thin coat of engine oil to the outer edge of the new seal. The seal must be pressed squarely into the retainer bore, so hammering it into place is not recommended. If you don't have access to a press, sandwich the retainer and seal between two smooth pieces of wood and press the seal into place with the jaws of a large vise. The pieces of wood must be thick enough to distribute the force evenly around the entire circumference of the seal. Work slowly and make sure the seal enters the bore squarely **(see illustration)**.
5 The seal lips must be lubricated with moly-base grease or engine assembly lube before the seal/retainer is slipped over the crankshaft and bolted to the block. Use a new gasket – no sealant is required – and make sure the dowel pins are in place before installing the retainer.
6 Tighten the screws a little at a time until the torque specified in this Chapter is reached.

24 Pistons/connecting rods – installation and rod bearing oil clearance check

Refer to illustrations 24.5, 24.9, 24.11, 24.13 and 24.17

1 Before installing the piston/connecting rod assemblies, the cylinder walls must be perfectly clean, the top edge of each cylinder must be chamfered, and the crankshaft must be in place.
2 Remove the cap from the end of the number one connecting rod (refer to the marks made during removal). Remove the original bearing inserts and wipe the bearing surfaces of the connecting rod and cap with a clean, lint-free cloth. They must be kept spotlessly clean.

Connecting rod bearing oil clearance check

3 Clean the back side of the new upper bearing insert, then lay it in place in the connecting rod. Make sure the tab on the bearing fits into the recess in the rod. Don't hammer the bearing insert into place and be very careful not to nick or gouge the bearing face. Don't lubricate the bearing at this time.

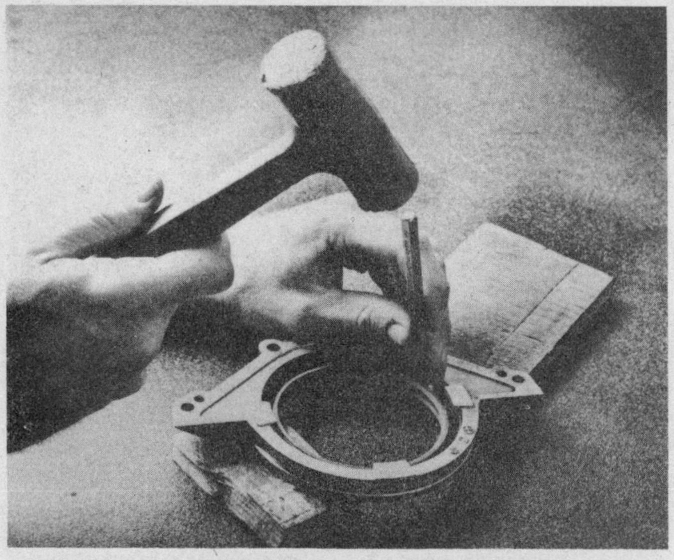

23.3 Place the retainer between two blocks of wood and drive the seal out of the retainer from the rear

23.4 Drive the new seal into the retainer with a block of wood or a section of pipe, if you have one large enough – make sure that you don't cock the seal in the bore

4 Clean the back side of the other bearing insert and install it in the rod cap. Again, make sure the tab on the bearing fits into the recess in the cap, and don't apply any lubricant. It's critically important that the mating surfaces of the bearing and connecting rod are perfectly clean and oil free when they're assembled.
5 Position the piston ring gaps at 120-degree intervals around the piston **(see illustration)**.
6 Slip a section of plastic or rubber hose over each connecting rod cap bolt.
7 Lubricate the piston and rings with clean engine oil and attach a piston ring compressor to the piston. Leave the skirt protruding about 1/4-inch to guide the piston into the cylinder. The rings must be compressed until they're flush with the piston.
8 Rotate the crankshaft until the number one connecting rod journal is at BDC (bottom dead center) and apply a coat of engine oil to the cylinder walls.
9 With the mark on top of the piston **(see illustration)** facing the timing belt end of the engine, gently insert the piston/connecting rod assembly into the number one cylinder bore and rest the bottom edge of the ring compressor on the engine block.
10 Tap the top edge of the ring compressor to make sure it's contacting the block around its entire circumference.
11 Gently tap on the top of the piston with the end of a wooden hammer handle **(see illustration)** while guiding the end of the connecting rod into place on the crankshaft journal. The piston rings may try to pop out of the ring compressor just before entering the cylinder bore, so keep some downward pressure on the ring compressor. Work slowly, and if any resistance is felt as the piston enters the cylinder, stop immediately. Find out what's hanging up and fix it before proceeding. Do not, for any reason, force the piston into the cylinder – you might break a ring and/or the piston.
12 Once the piston/connecting rod assembly is installed, the connecting rod bearing oil clearance must be checked before the rod cap is permanently bolted in place.
13 Cut a piece of the appropriate size Plastigage slightly shorter than the width of the connecting rod bearing and lay it in place on the number one connecting rod journal, parallel with the journal axis **(see illustration)**.
14 Clean the connecting rod cap bearing face, remove the protective hoses from the connecting rod bolts and install the rod cap. Make sure the mating mark on the cap is on the same side as the mark on the connecting rod.
15 Install the nuts and tighten them to the torque specified in this Chapter (work up to it in three steps). **Note:** *Use a thin-wall socket to avoid erroneous torque readings that can result if the socket is wedged between the rod cap and nut. If the socket tends to wedge itself between the nut and the*

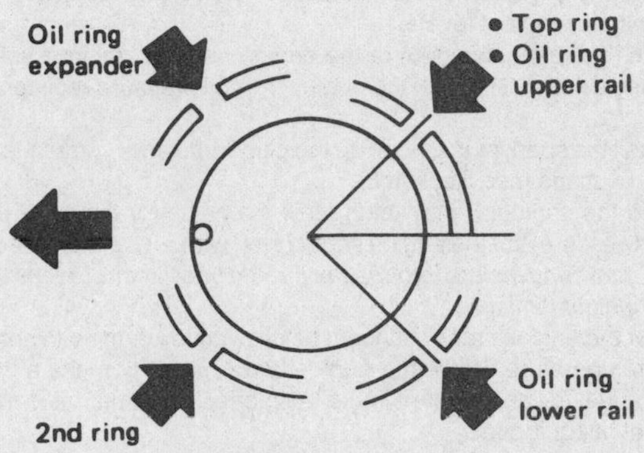

24.5 Stagger the ring end gaps as shown

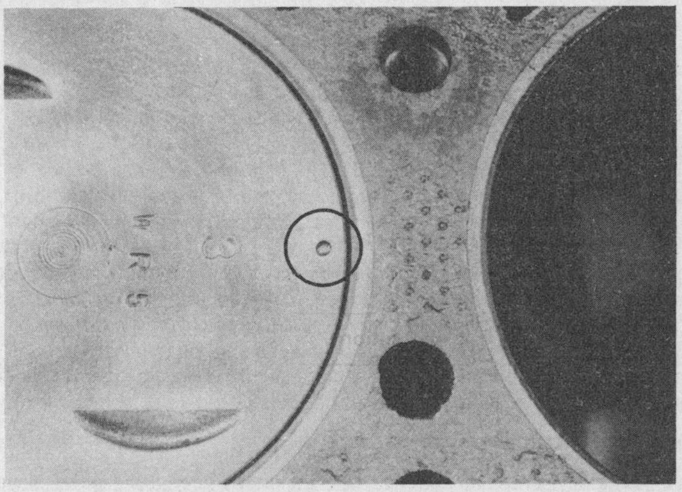

24.9 The dot stamped on the piston should point to the timing belt end of the engine after installation

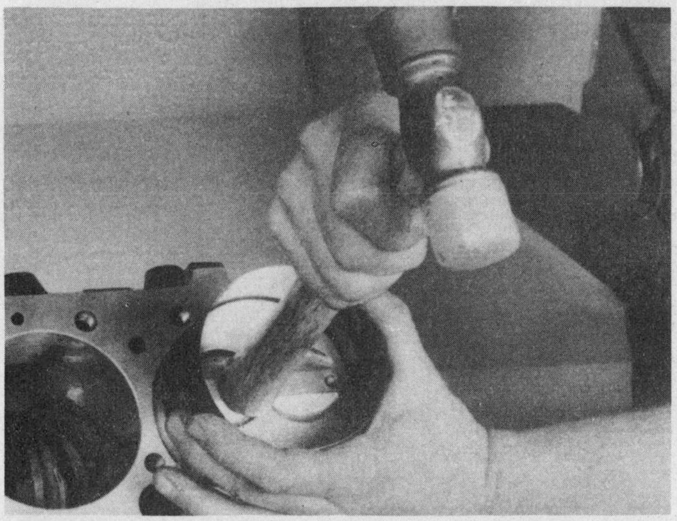

24.11 The piston can be driven (gently) into the cylinder bore with the end of a wooden hammer handle

24.13 Lay the Plastigage strips on each rod bearing journal, parallel to the crankshaft centerline

2B

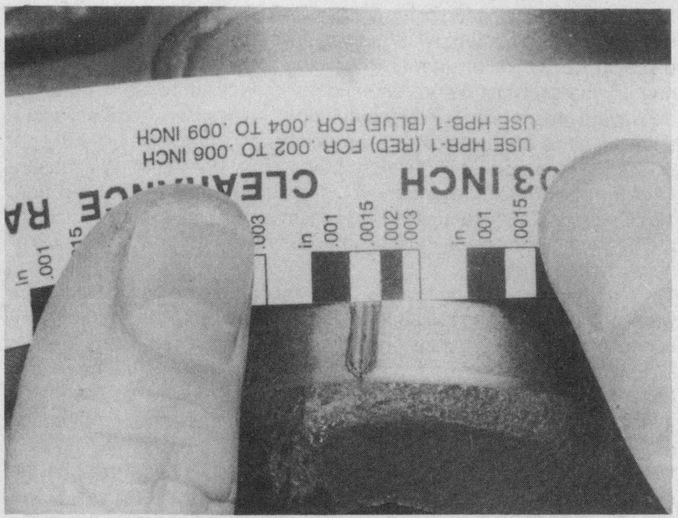

24.17 Measuring the width of the crushed Plastigage to determine the rod bearing oil clearance (be sure to use the correct scale – standard and metric scales are included)

cap, lift up on it slightly until it no longer contacts the cap. Do not rotate the crankshaft at any time during this operation.

16 Remove the nuts and detach the rod cap, being very careful not to disturb the Plastigage.

17 Compare the width of the crushed Plastigage to the scale printed on the Plastigage envelope to obtain the oil clearance **(see illustration)**. Compare it to the Specifications in this Chapter to make sure the clearance is correct.

18 If the clearance is not as specified, the bearing inserts may be the wrong size (which means different ones will be required). Before deciding that different inserts are needed, make sure that no dirt or oil was between the bearing inserts and the connecting rod or cap when the clearance was measured. Also, recheck the journal diameter. If the Plastigage was wider at one end than the other, the journal may be tapered (refer to Section 18).

Final connecting rod installation

19 Carefully scrape all traces of the Plastigage material off the rod journal and/or bearing face. Be very careful not to scratch the bearing – use your fingernail or the edge of a credit card.

20 Make sure the bearing faces are perfectly clean, then apply a uniform layer of clean moly-base grease or engine assembly lube to both of them. You'll have to push the piston into the cylinder to expose the face of the bearing insert in the connecting rod – be sure to slip the protective hoses over the rod bolts first.

21 Slide the connecting rod back into place on the journal, remove the protective hoses from the rod cap bolts, install the rod cap and tighten the nuts to the specified torque. Again, work up to the torque in three steps.

22 Repeat the entire procedure for the remaining pistons/connecting rods.

23 The important points to remember are . . .

a) Keep the back sides of the bearing inserts and the insides of the connecting rods and caps perfectly clean when assembling them.
b) Make sure you have the correct piston/rod assembly for each cylinder.
c) The mark on the piston must face the timing belt end of the engine.
d) Lubricate the cylinder walls with clean oil.
e) Lubricate the bearing faces when installing the rod caps after the oil clearance has been checked.

24 After all the piston/connecting rod assemblies have been properly installed, rotate the crankshaft a number of times by hand to check for any obvious binding.

25 As a final step, the connecting rod end play must be checked. Refer to Section 12 for this procedure.

26 Compare the measured end play to the Specifications to make sure it's correct. If it was correct before disassembly and the original crankshaft and rods were reinstalled, it should still be right. If new rods or a new crankshaft were installed, the end play may be inadequate. If so, the rods will have to be removed and taken to an automotive machine shop for resizing.

25 Initial start-up and break-in after overhaul

Warning: *Have a fire extinguisher ready when starting the engine for the first time.*

1 Once the engine has been installed in the vehicle, double-check the engine oil and coolant levels.

2 With the spark plugs out of the engine and the ignition system disabled (see Section 3), crank the engine until oil pressure registers on the gauge.

3 Install the spark plugs, hook up the plug wires and restore the ignition system functions (see Section 3).

4 Start the engine. It may take a few moments for the fuel system to build up pressure, but the engine should start without a great deal of effort. **Note:** *If backfiring occurs through the throttle body, recheck the valve timing and ignition timing.*

5 After the engine starts, it should be allowed to warm up to normal operating temperature. While the engine is warming up, make a thorough check for fuel, oil and coolant leaks. Also check the automatic transaxle fluid level (if equipped).

6 Shut the engine off and recheck the engine oil and coolant levels.

7 Drive the vehicle to an area with minimum traffic, accelerate at full throttle from 30 to 50 mph, then allow the vehicle to slow to 30 mph with the throttle closed. Repeat the procedure 10 or 12 times. This will load the piston rings and cause them to seat properly against the cylinder walls. Check again for oil and coolant leaks and fluid levels.

8 Drive the vehicle gently for the first 500 miles (no sustained high speeds) and keep a constant check on the oil level. It is not unusual for an engine to use oil during the break-in period.

9 At approximately 500 to 600 miles, change the oil and filter.

10 For the next few hundred miles, drive the vehicle normally. Do not pamper it or abuse it.

11 After 2000 miles, change the oil and filter again and consider the engine broken in.

Chapter 3 Cooling, heating and air conditioning systems

3

Contents

Air conditioning and heater control assembly – removal and installation	12
Air conditioning system – check and maintenance	13
Air conditioning system compressor – removal and installation	15
Air conditioning system condenser – removal and installation	16
Air conditioning system receiver/drier – removal and installation	14
Antifreeze – general information	2
Blower unit – removal and installation	10
Coolant level check	See Chapter 1
Coolant reservoir – removal and installation	6
Coolant temperature sending unit – check and replacement	9
Cooling system check	See Chapter 1
Cooling system servicing (draining, flushing and refilling)	See Chapter 1
Drivebelt check, adjustment and replacement	See Chapter 1
Engine cooling fans – check and replacement	4
General information	1
Heater core removal and installation	11
Radiator – removal and installation	5
Thermostat – check and replacement	3
Underhood hose check and replacement	See Chapter 1
Water pump – check	7
Water pump – replacement	8

Specifications

General

Radiator cap pressure rating	11 to 14 psi
Thermostat rating	
1985 through 1988	170-degrees F (77-degrees C)
1989 on	180-degrees F (82-degrees C)
Cooling system capacity	See Chapter 1
Refrigerant capacity	
1985 through 1988	2.0 lbs
1989 on	0.0 to 2.2 lbs

Torque specifications

	Ft-lbs
Water pump-to-engine block bolts	16 to 21
Thermostat housing cover bolts	12 to 15

1 General information

Engine cooling system

All vehicles covered by this manual employ a pressurized engine cooling system with thermostatically controlled coolant circulation. An impeller type water pump mounted on the front of the block pumps coolant through the engine. The coolant flows around each cylinder and toward the rear of the engine. Cast-in coolant passages direct coolant around the intake and exhaust ports, near the spark plug areas and in close proximity to the exhaust valve guides.

A wax pellet type thermostat is located in a housing near the front of the engine. During warm up, the closed thermostat prevents coolant from circulating through the radiator. As the engine nears normal operating temperature, the thermostat opens and allows hot coolant to travel through the radiator, where it's cooled before returning to the engine.

The cooling system is sealed by a pressure type radiator cap, which raises the boiling point of the coolant and increases the cooling efficiency of the radiator. If the system pressure exceeds the cap pressure relief value, the excess pressure in the system forces the spring-loaded valve inside the cap off its seat and allows the coolant to escape through the overflow tube into a coolant reservoir. When the system cools the excess coolant is automatically drawn from the reservoir back into the radiator.

The coolant reservoir does double duty as both the point at which fresh coolant is added to the cooling system to maintain the proper fluid level and as a holding tank for overheated coolant.

This type of cooling system is known as a closed design because coolant that escapes past the pressure cap is saved and reused.

Heating system

The heating system consists of a blower fan and heater core located in the heater box, the hoses connecting the heater core to the engine cooling system and the heater/air conditioning control head on the dashboard. Hot engine coolant is circulated through the heater core. When the heater mode is activated, a flap door opens to expose the heater box to the passenger compartment. A fan switch on the control head activates the blower motor, which forces air through the core, heating the air.

Air conditioning system

The air conditioning system consists of a condenser mounted in front of the radiator, an evaporator mounted adjacent to the heater core, a compressor mounted on the engine, a receiver-drier which contains a high pressure relief valve and the plumbing connecting all of the above components.

A blower fan forces the warmer air of the passenger compartment through the evaporator core (sort of a radiator-in-reverse), transferring the heat from the air to the refrigerant. The liquid refrigerant boils off into low pressure vapor, taking the heat with it when it leaves the evaporator.

2 Antifreeze – general information

Warning: *Do not allow antifreeze to come in contact with your skin or painted surfaces of the vehicle. Rinse off spills immediately with plenty of water. NEVER leave antifreeze lying around in an open container or in a puddle in the driveway or on the garage floor. Children and pets are attracted by it's sweet smell. Antifreeze is toxic, so use common sense when disposing of it. Many communities maintain toxic material disposal sites and/or offer regular pick-up of hazardous materials. Antifreeze is also flammable, so don't store or use it near open flames.*

The cooling system should be filled with a water/ethylene glycol based antifreeze solution, which will prevent freezing down to at least –20-degrees F, or lower if local climate requires it. It also provides protection against corrosion and increases the coolant boiling point.

The cooling system should be drained, flushed and refilled at the specified intervals (see Chapter 1). Old or contaminated antifreeze solutions are likely to cause damage and encourage the formation of rust and scale in the system. Use distilled water with the antifreeze.

Before adding antifreeze, check all hose connections, because antifreeze tends to search out and leak through very minute openings. Engines don't normally consume coolant, so if the level goes down, find the cause and correct it.

The exact mixture of antifreeze-to-water which you should use depends on the relative weather conditions. The mixture should contain at least 50 percent antifreeze, but should never contain more than 70 percent antifreeze. Consult the mixture ratio chart on the antifreeze container before adding coolant. Hydrometers are available at most auto parts stores to test the coolant. Use antifreeze which meets the vehicle manufacturer's specifications.

3 Thermostat – check and replacement

Warning: *Do not remove the radiator cap, drain the coolant or replace the thermostat until the engine has cooled completely.*

Check

1 Before assuming the thermostat is to blame for a cooling system problem, check the coolant level, drivebelt tension (see Chapter 1) and temperature gauge operation.

2 If the engine seems to be taking a long time to warm up (based on heater output or temperature gauge operation), the thermostat is probably stuck open. Replace the thermostat with a new one.

3 If the engine runs hot, use your hand to check the temperature of the upper radiator hose. If the hose isn't hot, but the engine is, the thermostat is probably stuck closed, preventing the coolant inside the engine from escaping to the radiator. Replace the thermostat. **Caution:** *Don't drive the vehicle without a thermostat. The computer may stay in open loop and emissions and fuel economy will suffer.*

4 If the upper radiator hose is hot, it means that the coolant is flowing and the thermostat is open. Consult the *Troubleshooting* Section at the front of this manual for cooling system diagnosis.

Replacement

Refer to illustrations 3.7, 3.9, 3.10, 3.13 and 3.16

5 Disconnect the negative battery cable from the battery.

6 Drain the cooling system (see Chapter 1). If the coolant is relatively new or in good condition (see Chapter 1), save it and reuse it.

7 Remove the injector blower duct **(see illustration)**, if equipped.

8 Unbolt the cruise control servo (if equipped) and set it aside without

3.7 Remove the two screws and detach the injector blower duct, then remove the cruise control servo (1985 through 1988 models)

1 *Injector blower duct screws*
2 *Cruise control servo mounting screws*

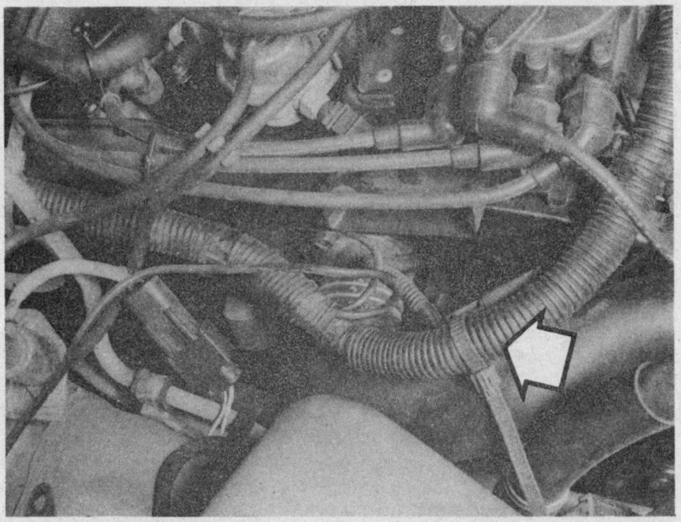

3.9 Detach the wiring harness retaining strap (arrow) and move the harness aside

3.10 On 1989 models, the thermostat housing (arrow) is partially hidden by the radiator hose

disconnecting the cables **(see illustration 3.7)**.

9 Move the wiring aside for access **(see illustration)**.

10 Follow the upper radiator hose to the timing belt end of the engine to locate the thermostat housing **(see illustration)**.

11 Loosen the hose clamp, then detach the hose from the fitting. If it's stuck, grasp it near the end with a pair of adjustable pliers and twist it to break the seal, then pull it off. If the hose is old or deteriorated, cut it off and install a new one.

12 If the outer surface of the large fitting that mates with the hose is deteriorated (corroded, pitted, etc.) it may be damaged further by hose removal. If it is, the thermostat housing cover will have to be replaced.

13 Remove the bolts and detach the housing cover **(see illustration)**. If the cover is stuck, tap it with a soft-face hammer to jar it loose. Be prepared for some coolant to spill as the gasket seal is broken.

14 Note how it's installed (which end is facing out), then remove the thermostat.

15 Stuff a rag into the engine opening, then remove all traces of old gasket material and sealant from the housing and cover with a gasket scraper. Remove the rag from the opening and clean the gasket mating surfaces with lacquer thinner or acetone.

16 Install the new thermostat in the housing. Make sure the correct end faces out – the spring end is normally directed into the engine and the vent valve must be at the top **(see illustration)**.

3.13 Remove the three housing cover bolts (arrows) – 1985 through 1988 models

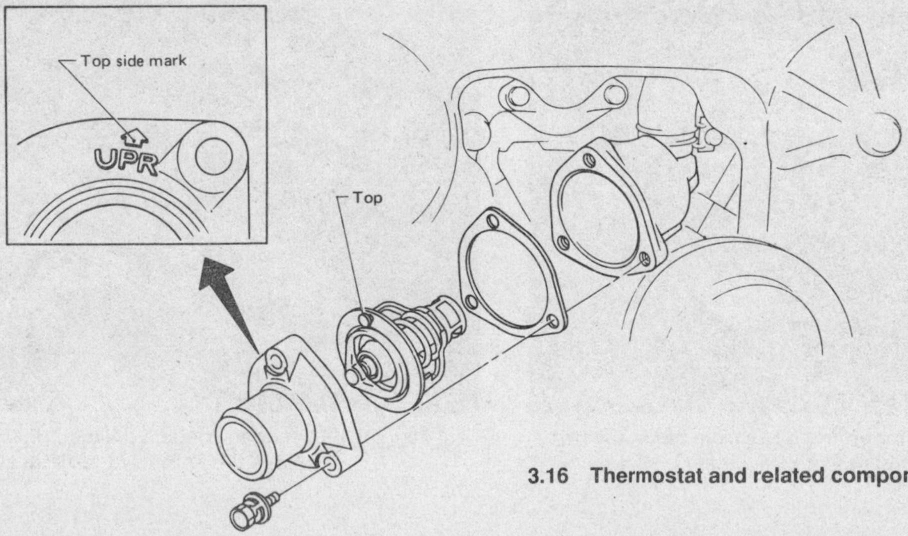

3.16 Thermostat and related components – exploded view

3

4.2 One coolant temperature switch which controls the fan is located in the upper tank portion of the radiator (arrow) – the other switch is located diagonally opposite in the lower tank (1985 through 1989 models)

4.7a Detach the radiator hoses and wiring, then remove the mounting nuts (arrow points to left upper nut) – 1985 through 1988 models

17 Apply a thin, uniform layer of RTV sealant to both sides of the new gasket and position it on the housing.

18 Install the cover and bolts. Tighten the bolts to the torque specified in this Chapter.

19 Reattach the hose to the fitting and tighten the hose clamp securely.

20 Refill the cooling system (see Chapter 1).

21 Start the engine and allow it to reach normal operating temperature, then check for leaks and proper thermostat operation (as described in Steps 2 through 4).

4 Engine cooling fans – check and replacement

Warning: *To avoid possible injury or damage, DO NOT attempt to repair fan blades – replace a damaged fan with a new one.*

Check

Refer to illustration 4.2

1 To test the motor, unplug the electrical connector at the motor and use jumper wires to connect the fan directly to the battery. If the fan still doesn't work, replace the motor.

2 If the motor tested OK, the fault probably lies in the coolant temperature switches **(see illustration)** or the wiring which connects the components. Carefully check all wiring and connections. If no obvious problems are found, further diagnosis should be done by a dealer service department or repair shop.

Removal and installation

Refer to illustrations 4.7a, 4.7b, 4.7c, 4.7d, 4.8 and 4.9

3 Disconnect the negative battery cable from the battery.

4 Drain the coolant from the radiator (see Chapter 1) and remove the radiator hoses.

5 Remove the fan wire harness from the clips.

6 Insert a small screwdriver into the connector to lift the lock tab and un-

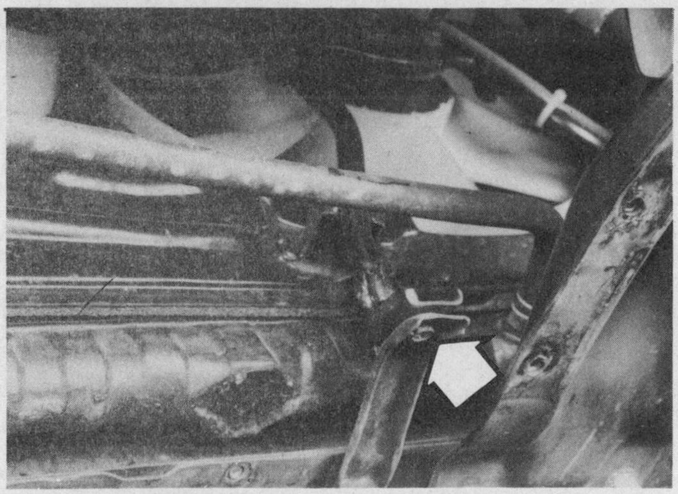

4.7b Remove the lower fan mounting bolts from below (arrow) – 1986 model shown – others similar

4.7c On 1989 models, detach the electrical connectors and remove the shroud-to-radiator bolts

1 Electrical connectors 2 Shroud mounting bolt

4.7d Lift the fan assembly out slowly at an angle until it clears all obstructions

4.8 Remove the screws (arrows) and pull the fan off the motor hub

plug the fan wire harnesses.

7 Unbolt the fan bracket and shroud assembly **(see illustrations)**, then carefully lift it out of the engine compartment **(see illustration)**.

8 To detach the fan from the motor, remove the motor-to-fan screws **(see illustration)** and pull the fan off the hub.

9 To remove the bracket(s) from the fan motor(s), remove the mounting nuts/bolts **(see illustration)**.

10 Installation is the reverse of removal.

5 Radiator – removal and installation

Refer to illustrations 5.5, 5.8a, 5.8b and 5.8c

Warning: *Wait until the engine is completely cool before beginning this procedure.*

1 Disconnect the negative battery cable from the battery.

2 Drain the cooling system (see Chapter 1). If the coolant is relatively new or in good condition, save it and reuse it.

3 Loosen the hose clamps, then detach the radiator hoses from the fittings. If they're stuck, grasp each hose near the end with a pair of adjustable pliers and twist it to break the seal, then pull it off – be careful not to distort the radiator fittings! If the hoses are old or deteriorated, cut them off and install new ones.

4 Disconnect the reservoir hose from the radiator filler neck.

5 Disconnect the cooling fan switch. If the vehicle is equipped with an automatic transmission, disconnect the cooler lines from the bottom of the radiator **(see illustration)**. Use a drip pan to catch spilled fluid.

6 Remove the engine cooling fans (see Section 4 beginning with Step 5).

7 Plug the lines and fittings to prevent the entry of contaminants.

3

4.9 To detach the motor(s), detach the wiring and remove the nuts or bolts (arrows)

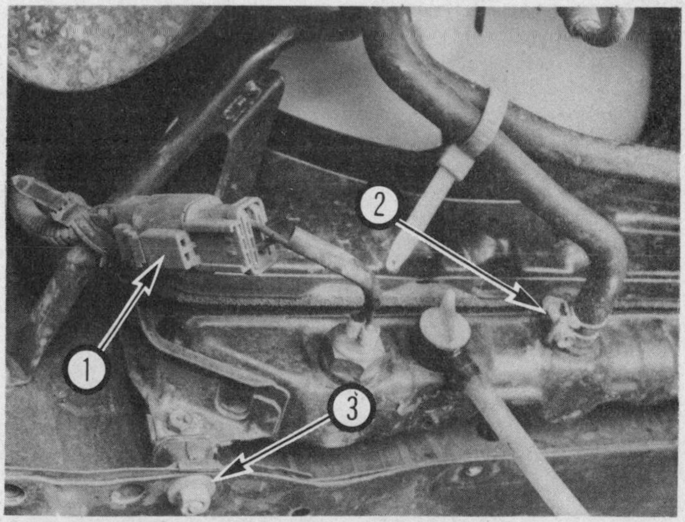

5.5 Typical radiator mounting details – viewed from below

1 Cooling fan switch connector
2 Left transmission cooler line
3 Radiator mounting nut

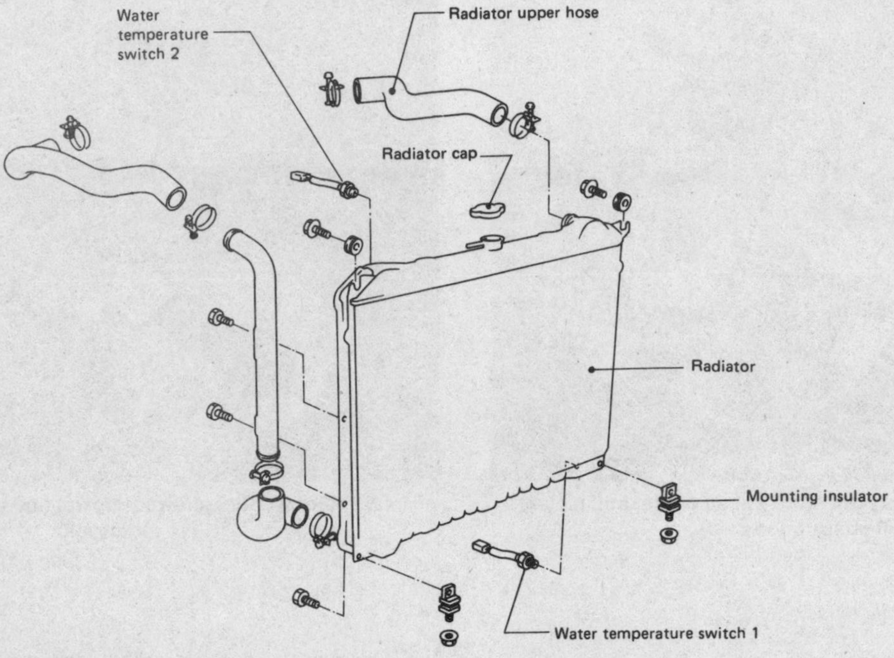

5.8a Typical radiator mounting details (1985 through 1988 models) – exploded view

8 Remove the radiator mounting bolts/nuts **(see illustrations)**.
9 Carefully lift out the radiator. Don't spill coolant on the vehicle or scratch the paint.
10 With the radiator removed, it can be inspected for leaks and damage. If it needs repair, have a radiator shop or dealer service department perform the work as special techniques are required.
11 Bugs and dirt can be removed from the radiator with compressed air and a soft brush. Don't bend the cooling fins as this is done.
12 Check the radiator mounts for deterioration and make sure they seat properly when the radiator is installed.
13 Installation is the reverse of the removal procedure.
14 After installation, fill the cooling system with the proper mixture of antifreeze and water. Refer to Chapter 1 if necessary.
15 Start the engine and check for leaks. Allow the engine to reach normal operating temperature, indicated by the upper radiator hose becoming hot. Recheck the coolant level and add more if required.
16 If you're working on an automatic transmission equipped vehicle, check and add fluid as needed.

6 Coolant reservoir – removal and installation

Refer to illustrations 6.1, 6.2a and 6.2b

Warning: *Wait until the engine is completely cool before beginning this procedure.*

1 Remove the injector cooling fan duct, if equipped **(see illustration)**.

5.8b On 1985 through 1988 models, the top of the radiator is secured with a bolt (arrow) on each side

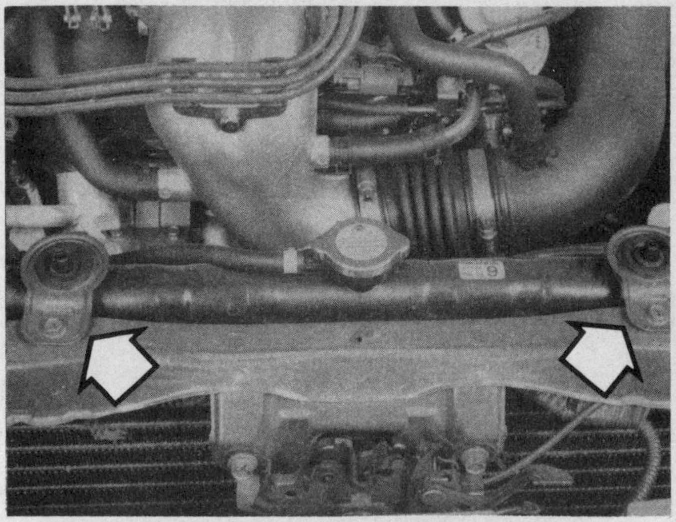

5.8c Radiator on 1989 and later models is secured with mounting brackets on top (arrows)

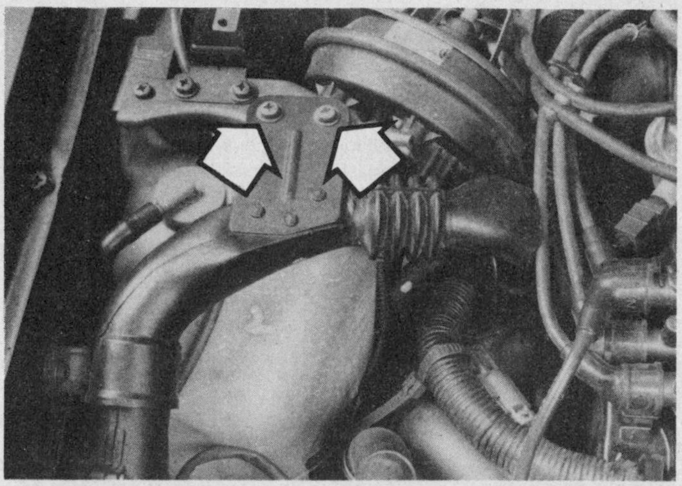

6.1 Remove the two screws (arrows) and lift off the duct

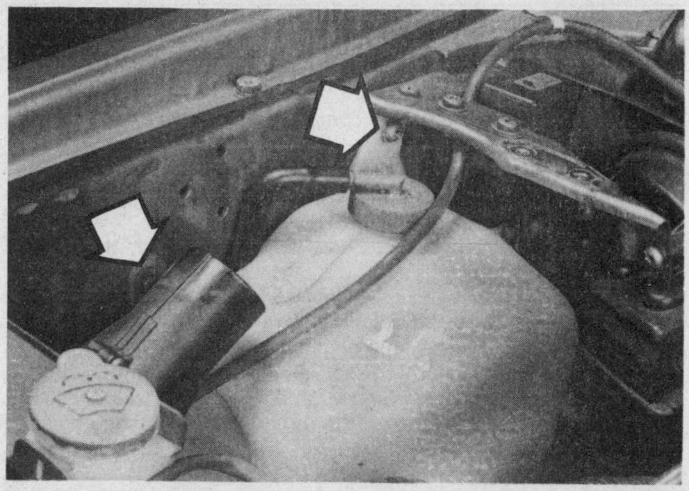

6.2a Detach the hose and remove the mounting screws (arrows) – 1985 through 1988 models

2 Detach the hose at the reservoir and remove the mounting screw(s) **(see illustrations)**.
3 Lift the reservoir from the engine compartment.
4 Installation is the reverse of removal.
5 Refill the cooling system and check for leaks.

7 Water pump – check

Refer to illustrations 7.4 and 7.5

1 A failure in the water pump can cause serious engine damage due to overheating.
2 There are three ways to check the operation of the water pump while it's installed on the engine. If the pump is defective, it should be replaced with a new or rebuilt unit.
3 With the engine running at normal operating temperature, squeeze the upper radiator hose. If the water pump is working properly, a pressure surge should be felt as the hose is released. **Warning**: *Keep your hands away from the fan blades!*
4 Water pumps are equipped with weep or vent holes. If a failure occurs in the pump seal, coolant will leak from the hole. In most cases you'll need a flashlight to find the hole on the water pump to check for leaks **(see illustration)**.
5 If the water pump shaft bearings fail there may be a howling sound at the front of the engine while it's running. Shaft wear can be felt if the water pump pulley is rocked up and down **(see illustration)**. Don't mistake drivebelt slippage, which causes a squealing sound, for water pump bearing failure.

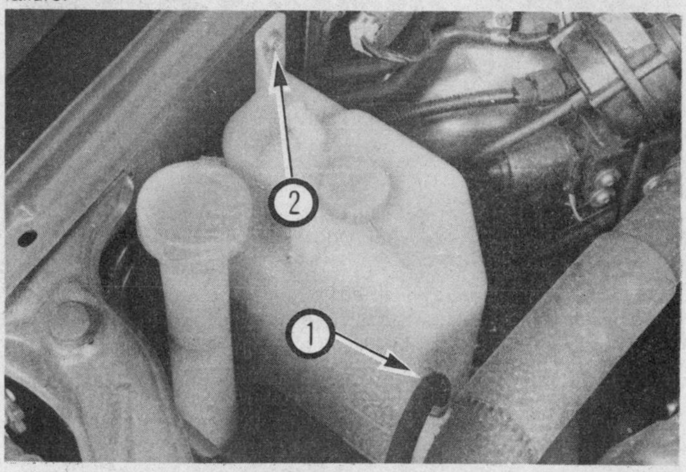

6.2b On later models, remove the hose and mounting screw and lift the reservoir straight up

1 Hose　　*2 Mounting screw*

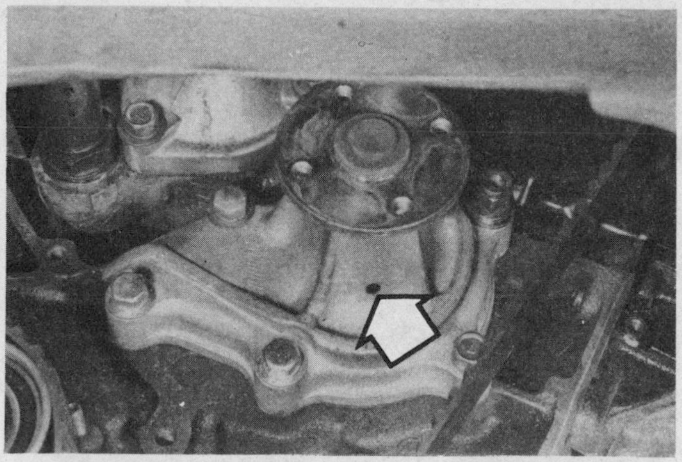

7.4 If coolant is seeping through the weep hole it is an indication that the water pump seal is leaking and the pump will have to be replaced

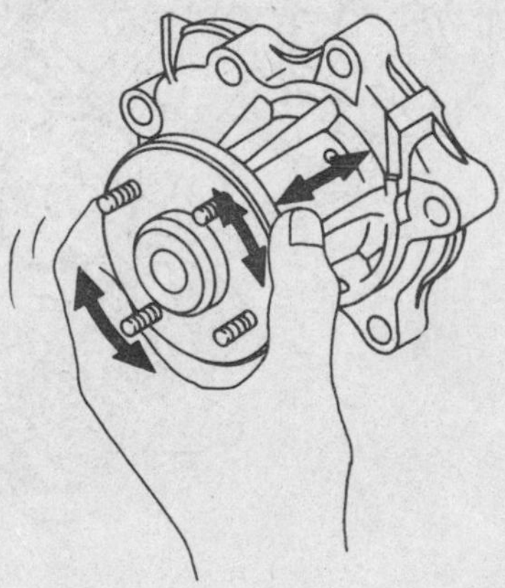

7.5 The pump should turn smoothly with no play in the shaft

3

8 Water pump - replacement

Refer to illustrations 8.5a and 8.5b

Warning: *Wait until the engine is completely cool before beginning this procedure.*

1 Disconnect the negative battery cable from the battery.

2 Drain the cooling system (see Chapter 1). If the coolant is relatively new or in good condition, save it and reuse it.

3 Remove the drivebelts (see Chapter 1) and the pulley at the end of the water pump shaft.

4 Remove the upper and lower timing belt covers (see Chapter 2).

5 Remove the bolts and detach the water pump from the engine. Note the locations of the various lengths and different types of bolts as they're removed to ensure correct installation **(see illustrations)**. Inspect timing belt at this time and replace if necessary (see Chapter 2).

6 Clean the bolt threads and the threaded holes in the engine to remove corrosion and sealant.

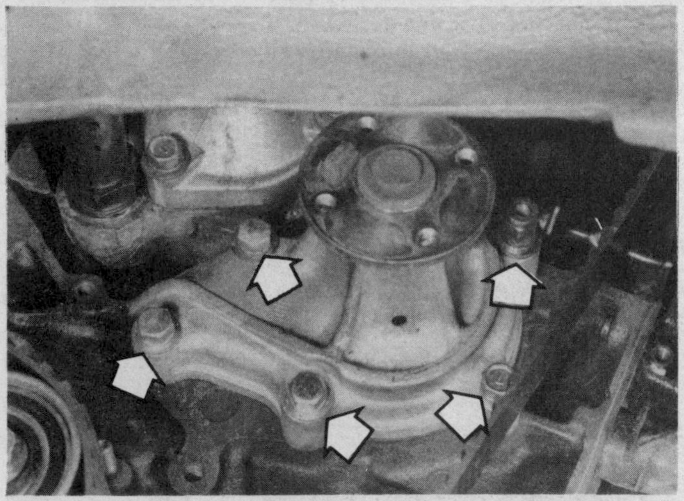

8.5a View of the water pump from below shows the locations of the bolts (arrows)

7 Compare the new pump to the old one to make sure they're identical.

8 Remove all traces of old gasket material from the engine with a gasket scraper.

9 Clean the engine and new water pump mating surfaces with lacquer thinner or acetone.

10 Apply a thin coat of RTV sealant to the engine side of the new gasket.

11 Apply a thin layer of RTV sealant to the gasket mating surface of the new pump, then carefully mate the gasket and the pump. Slip a couple of bolts through the pump mounting holes to hold the gasket in place.

12 Carefully attach the pump and gasket to the engine and thread the bolts into the holes finger tight.

13 Install the remaining bolts. Tighten them to the torque specified in this Chapter in 1/4-turn increments. Don't overtighten them or the pump may be distorted.

14 Reinstall all parts removed for access to the pump.

15 Refill the cooling system and check the drivebelt tension (see Chapter 1). Run the engine and check for leaks.

9 Coolant temperature sending unit – check and replacement

Refer to illustrations 9.1a and 9.1b

Warning: *Wait until the engine is completely cool before beginning this procedure.*

1 The coolant temperature indicator system is composed of a temperature gauge mounted in the instrument panel and a coolant temperature sending unit mounted on the engine **(see illustrations)**. All vehicles covered by this manual have more than one sending unit, but only one is used for the indicator system. **Warning**: *Stay clear of the fan blades, which can come on at any time.*

2 If an overheating indication occurs, check the coolant level in the system and then make sure the wiring between the gauge and the sending unit is secure and all fuses are intact.

3 Test the circuit by momentarily grounding the wire to the sending unit while the ignition is on (engine not running for safety). If the gauge deflects full scale, replace the sending unit.

4 If the sending unit must be replaced, simply unscrew it from the engine and install the replacement. Use sealant on the threads. Make sure the engine is cool before removing the defective sending unit. There will be some coolant loss as the unit is removed, so be prepared to catch it. Check the level after the replacement has been installed.

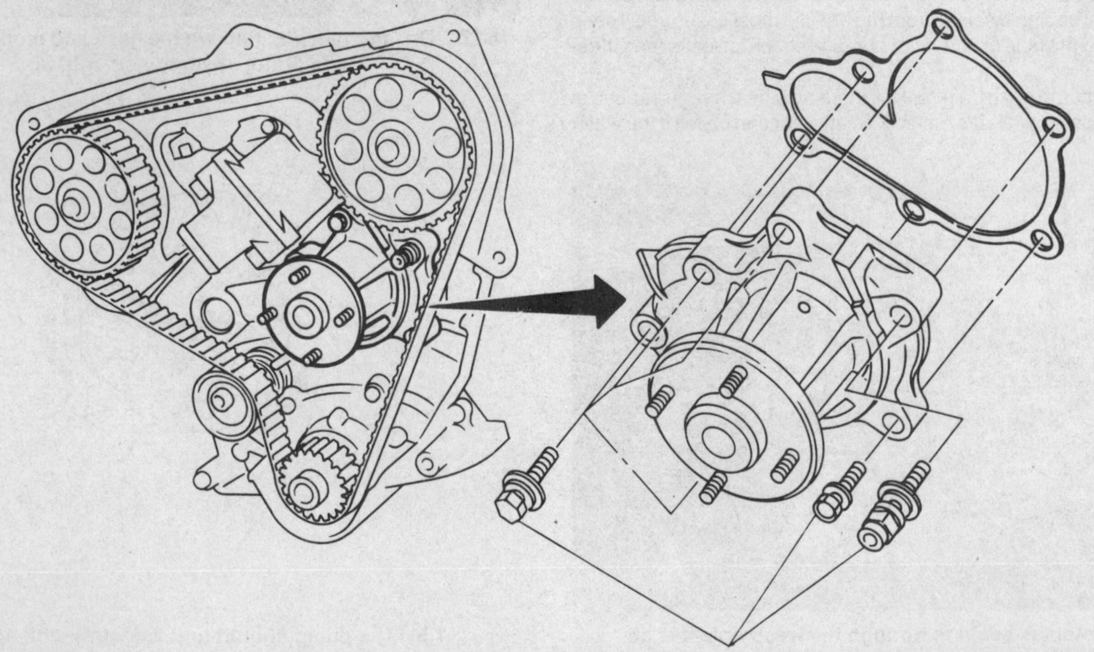

8.5b Water pump mounting details (exploded view) – be sure to reinstall the fasteners in their original locations

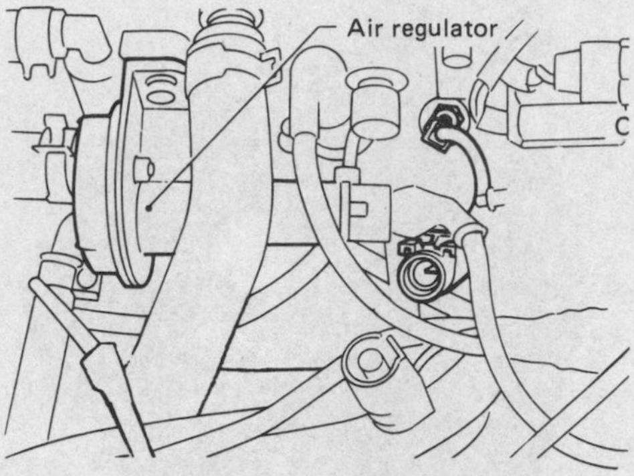

9.1a On 1985 through 1988 models, the coolant temperature sending unit is mounted in the intake manifold adjacent to the air regulator – to test the circuit, unplug the sender and briefly ground the wire while the ignition is on – the needle on the gauge should deflect full scale

10 Blower unit – removal and installation

Refer to illustrations 10.2, 10.4a, 10.4b and 10.5

Warning: *1992 models are equipped with a Supplemental Restraint System (SRS), more commonly known as an airbag. Always disconnect both battery cables and wait ten minutes before working in the vicinity of the impact sensors, steering wheel and column or instrument panel to avoid the possibility of accidental deployment of the air bag, which could cause personal injury (see Chapter 12). The yellow wiring harness and connectors routed through the center console, under hood and right side wheel well are for this system. Do not use electrical test equipment on any of the airbag system wiring or tamper with them in any way.*

1 Disconnect the negative cable from the battery.

2 Remove the right lower dash panel **(see illustration)**.

3 The blower unit is located in the passenger compartment above the right front footwell.

4 Disconnect the flexible tube and wiring connector from the blower unit, then remove the blower unit retaining screws **(see illustrations)** and lower the unit from the housing.

9.1b On later models, the coolant temperature sending unit is located adjacent to the distributor (arrow)

10.2 Remove the screws (arrows) and detach the right lower dash panel

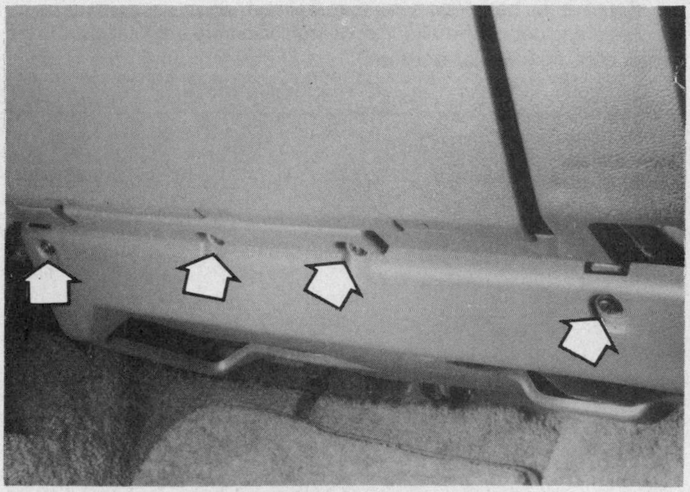

10.4a Disconnect the flexible tube and wiring connector (arrows)

10.4b The blower unit retaining screw holes (arrows) are located at 120-degree intervals around the perimeter – unit removed for clarity

3

5 If the motor is being replaced, transfer the fan to the new motor prior to installation **(see illustration)**.

6 Installation is the reverse of removal. Check for proper operation.

11 Heater core – removal and installation

Refer to illustrations 11.6a and 11.6b

Warning: *1992 models are equipped with a Supplemental Restraint System (SRS), more commonly known as an airbag. Always disconnect both battery cables and wait ten minutes before working in the vicinity of the impact sensors, steering wheel and column or instrument panel to avoid the possibility of accidental deployment of the air bag, which could cause personal injury (see Chapter 12). The yellow wiring harness and connectors routed through the center console, under hood and right side wheel well are for this system. Do not use electrical test equipment on any of the airbag system wiring or tamper with them in any way.*

1 Disconnect the negative cable from the battery.

2 Drain the cooling system (see Chapter 1).

3 Working in the engine compartment, disconnect the heater hoses where they enter the firewall.

4 Remove the instrument panel and the center console (see Chapter 11).

5 Remove the heater controls (see Section 12).

6 Label and detach the air ducts, wiring and controls still attached to the heater housing **(see illustrations)**.

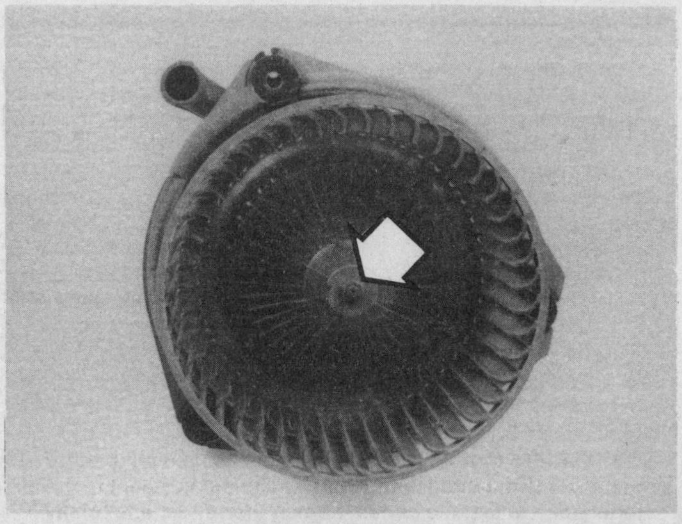

10.5 Remove the nut (arrow) and pull the fan off the motor shaft

7 Unbolt the heater unit and lift it from the vehicle.

8 Remove the screws and clips and separate the two halves of the housing. Take out the old heater core and install the new unit.

9 Reassemble the heater unit and check the operation of the air control flaps. If any parts bind, correct the problem before installation.

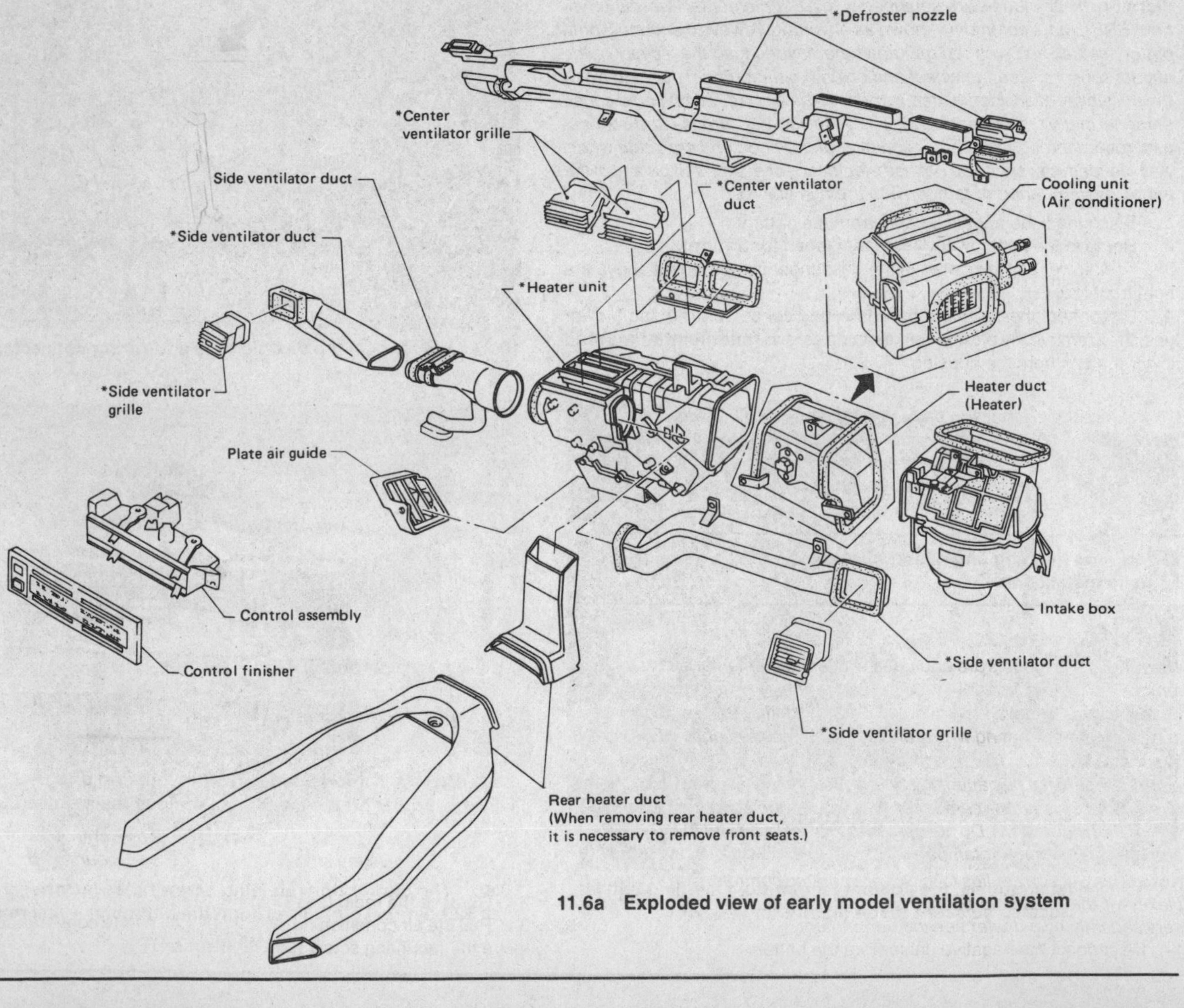

11.6a Exploded view of early model ventilation system

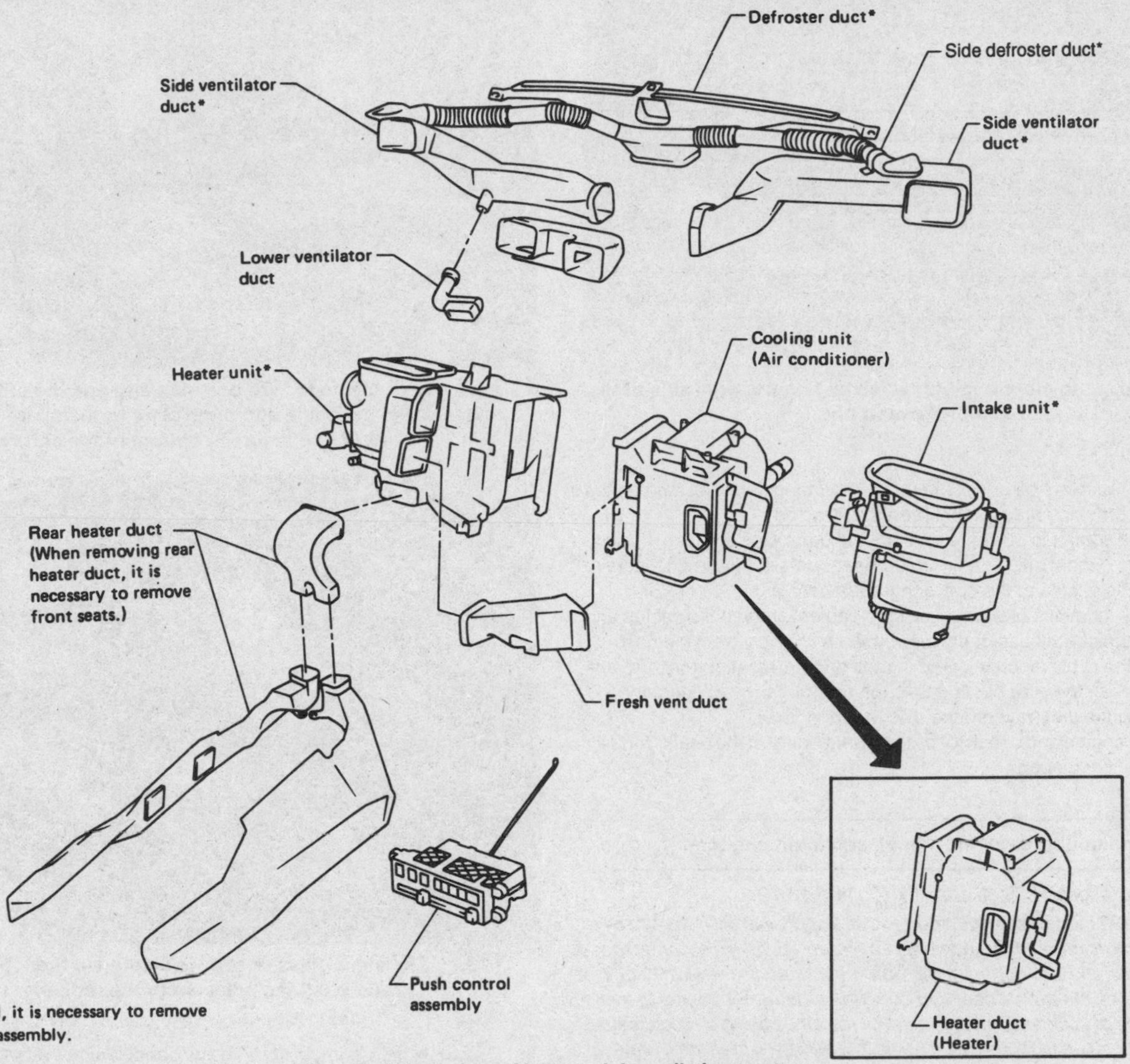

11.6b Exploded view of late model ventilation system

10 Reinstall the remaining parts in the reverse order of removal.
11 Refill the cooling system, reconnect the battery and run the engine. Check for leaks and proper system operation.

12 Air conditioning and heater control assembly – removal and installation

Refer to illustrations 12.3, 12.4 and 12.5

Warning: *1992 models are equipped with a Supplemental Restraint System (SRS), more commonly known as an airbag. Always disconnect both battery cables and wait ten minutes before working in the vicinity of the impact sensors, steering wheel and column or instrument panel to avoid the possibility of accidental deployment of the air bag, which could cause personal injury (see Chapter 12). The yellow wiring harness and connectors routed through the center console, under hood and right side wheel well are for this system. Do not use electrical test equipment on any of the airbag system wiring or tamper with them in any way.*

Note: *This Section applies to the lever operated controls. Due to the complexity of the electronic pushbutton system, we recommend that it be serviced only by a dealer service department.*

1 Disconnect the negative cable from the battery.

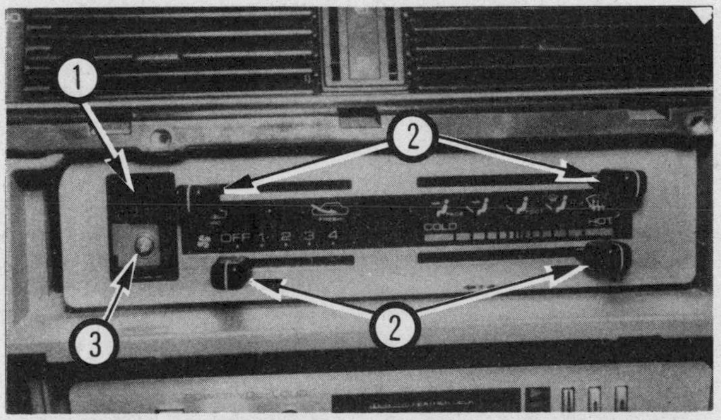

12.3 Pull the air conditioning switch out and unplug it, pull the control knobs off the levers and remove the mounting screw

1 Opening for air conditioning switch
2 Control knobs
3 Mounting screw

2 Remove the radio (see Chapter 12).
3 Pull the air conditioning switch out, pull off the control knobs and remove the mounting screw **(see illustration)**.

12.4 Remove the mounting screw (arrow) on the right side of the control assembly

4 Pull the faceplate off and remove the mounting screw located on the right side of the control assembly **(see illustration)**.

5 Push the control to one side and pull the other side out **(see illustration)**; pull the control out slightly. On some models it will be necessary to disconnect the cables at the operating ends before this is possible.

6 Mark the locations of the clips on the cables. Detach the cables and wiring from the control assembly and lift the assembly from the dash.

7 Fasten the cable mounting clips in their original locations on the cable and check for stiffness or binding through the full range of operation.

8 To install the unit, reverse the above procedure.

9 Run the engine and check for proper functioning of the heater (and air conditioning, if equipped).

13 Air conditioning system – check and maintenance

Refer to illustrations 13.7, 13.10a, 13.10b and 13.12

Warning: *1992 models are equipped with a Supplemental Restraint System (SRS), more commonly known as an airbag. Always disconnect both battery cables and wait ten minutes before working in the vicinity of the impact sensors, steering wheel and column or instrument panel to avoid the possibility of accidental deployment of the air bag, which could cause personal injury (see Chapter 12). The yellow wiring harness and connectors routed through the center console, under hood and right side wheel well are for this system. Do not use electrical test equipment on any of the airbag system wiring or tamper with them in any way.*

Warning: *The air conditioning system is under high pressure. Do not loosen any hose fittings or remove any components until after the system has been discharged by a dealer service department or service station. Always wear eye protection when disconnecting air conditioning system fittings.*

Check

1 The following maintenance checks should be performed on a regular basis to ensure that the air conditioner continues to operate at peak efficiency.

a) Check the compressor drivebelt. If it's worn or deteriorated, replace it (see Chapter 1).
b) Check the drivebelt tension and, if necessary, adjust it (see Chapter 1).
c) Check the system hoses. Look for cracks, bubbles, hard spots and deterioration. Inspect the hoses and all fittings for oil bubbles and seepage. If there's any evidence of wear, damage or leaks, replace the hose(s).
d) Inspect the condenser fins for leaves, bugs and other debris. Use a "fin comb" or compressed air to clean the condenser.
e) Make sure the system has the correct refrigerant charge.

2 It's a good idea to operate the system for about 10 minutes at least once a month, particularly during the winter. Long term non-use can cause hardening, and subsequent failure, of the seals.

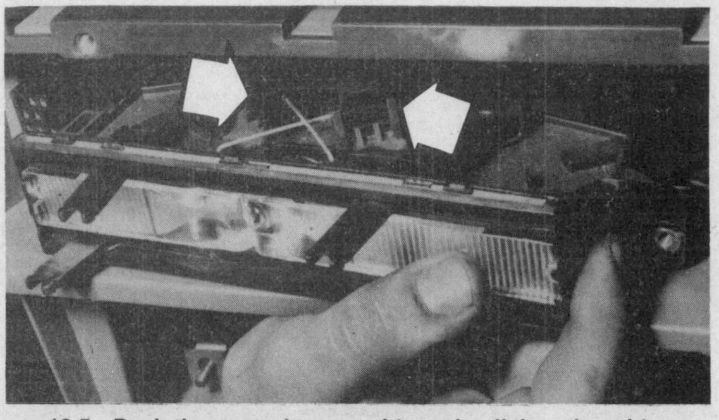

12.5 Push the control to one side and pull the other side out – two of the cable attaching clips (arrows) are on top; the other one is on the bottom of the control

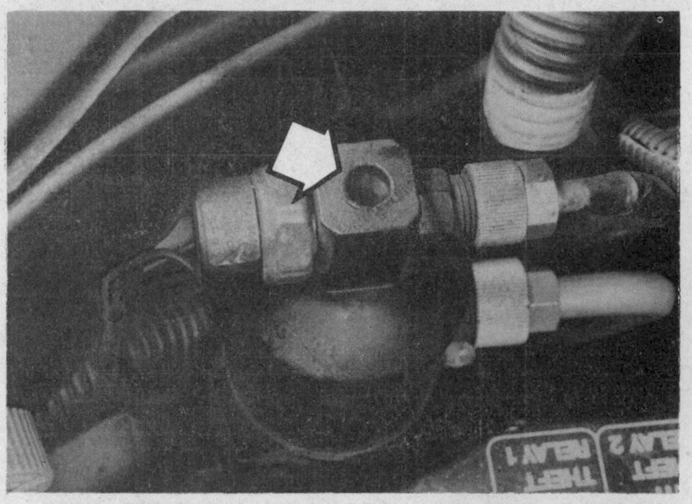

13.7 The sight glass (arrow) is located in the top of the receiver-drier, adjacent to the radiator

3 Because of the complexity of the air conditioning system and the special equipment necessary to service it, in-depth troubleshooting and repairs are not included in this manual. However, simple checks and component replacement procedures are provided in this Chapter.

4 The most common cause of poor cooling is simply a low system refrigerant charge. If a noticeable drop in cool air output occurs, one of the following quick checks will help you determine if the refrigerant level is low.

5 Warm the engine up to normal operating temperature.

6 Place the air conditioning temperature selector at the coldest setting and put the blower at the highest setting. Open the doors (to make sure the air conditioning system doesn't cycle off as soon as it cools the passenger compartment).

7 With the compressor engaged – the clutch will make an audible click and the center of the clutch will rotate – inspect the sight glass, **(see illustration)**. If the refrigerant looks foamy, it's low. Charge the system as described later in this Section.

8 If there's no sight glass, feel the inlet and outlet pipes at the compressor. One side should be cold and one hot. If there's no perceptible difference between the two pipes, there's something wrong with the compressor or the system. It might be a low charge – it might be something else. Take the vehicle to a dealer service department or an automotive air conditioning shop.

Adding refrigerant

9 Buy an automotive charging kit at an auto parts store. A charging kit includes a 14-ounce can of refrigerant, a tap valve and a short section of

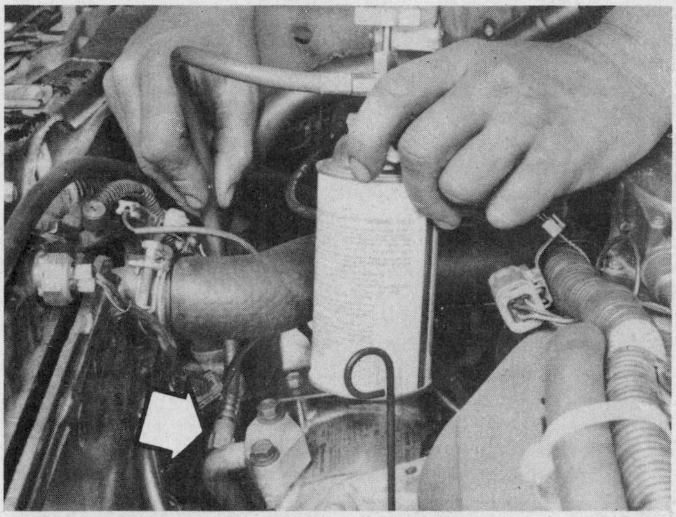

13.10a Refrigerant can be added with a recharge kit, connected to the port (arrow) on the larger diameter line (1985 through 1988 models)

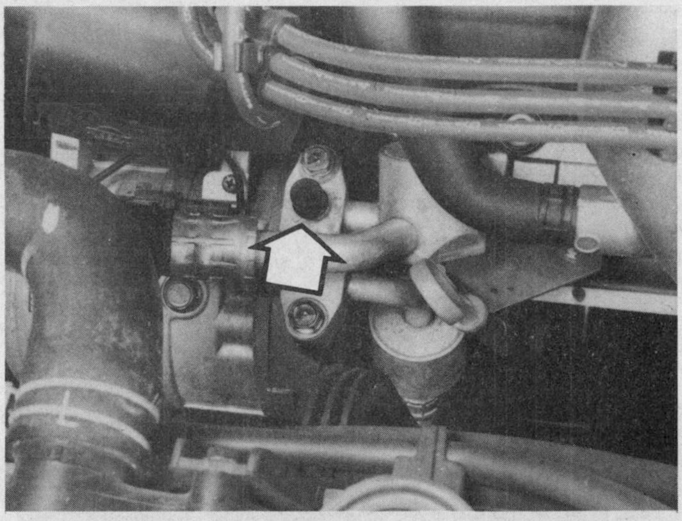

13.10b On later models, remove the cap (arrow) and add refrigerant

hose that can be attached between the tap valve and the system low side service valve. Because one can of refrigerant may not be sufficient to bring the system charge up to the proper level, it's a good idea to buy a few additional cans. Make sure that the first can contains red refrigerant dye. If the system is leaking, the red dye will leak out with the refrigerant and help you pinpoint the location of the leak. **Warning**: *Never add more than three cans of refrigerant to the system.*

10 Hook up the charging kit by following the manufacturer's instructions **(see illustrations)**. **Warning**: *DO NOT hook the charging kit hose to the system high side!*

11 Warm up the engine and turn on the air conditioner. Keep the charging kit hose away from the fan and other moving parts.

12 Place a thermometer in the dashboard vent nearest the evaporator **(see illustration)** and add refrigerant until the indicated temperature is around 40 to 45-degrees F.

14 Air conditioning system receiver/drier – removal and installation

Refer to illustration 14.3

Warning: T*he air conditioning system is under high pressure. DO NOT disassemble any part of the system (hose, compressor, line fittings, etc.) until after the system has been depressurized by a dealer service department or service station.*

1 Have the A/C system discharged (see Warning above).

2 Disconnect the negative battery cable from the battery.

3 Unplug the electrical connector from the pressure switch near the bottom of the receiver-drier **(see illustration)**.

4 Disconnect the refrigerant lines from the receiver-drier. Use a backup wrench to prevent twisting the tubing.

5 Plug the open fittings to prevent entry of dirt and moisture.

6 Loosen the mounting bracket bolt and lift the receiver-drier out.

7 If a new receiver-drier is being installed, remove the Schrader valve and pour the oil out into a measuring cup, noting the amount. Add fresh refrigerant oil to the new receiver-drier equal to the amount removed from the old unit, plus one ounce.

8 Installation is the reverse of removal.

9 Take the vehicle back to the shop that discharged it. Have the A/C system evacuated, charged and leak tested.

13.12 Measure the output air temperature at the center vent

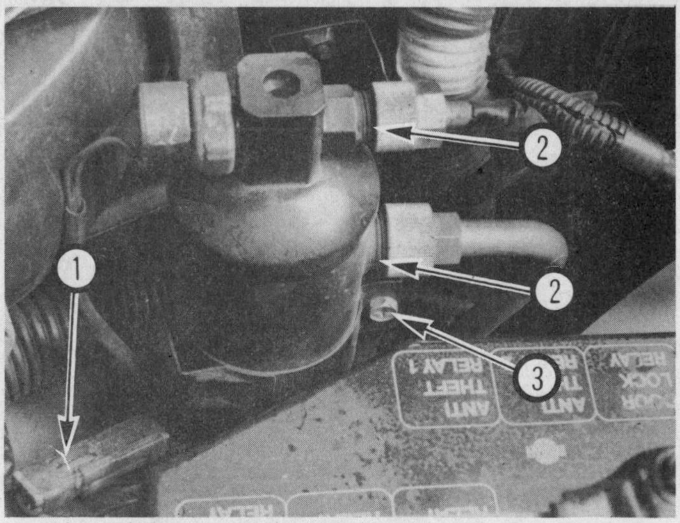

14.3 Receiver-drier mounting details

1 Electrical connector
2 Refrigerant lines
3 Mounting bolt

15 Air conditioning system compressor – removal and installation

Refer to illustrations 15.3 and 15.6

Warning: *The air conditioning system is under high pressure. DO NOT disassemble any part of the system (hoses, compressor, line fittings, etc.) until after the system has been depressurized by a dealer service department or service station.*

Note: *The receiver-drier (see Section 14) should be replaced whenever the compressor is replaced.*

1 Have the air conditioning system discharged (see Warning above).
2 Disconnect the negative battery cable from the battery.
3 Disconnect the compressor clutch wiring harness **(see illustration)**.

15.3 Unplug the compressor electrical connectors (arrows)

4 Remove the drivebelt (Chapter 1).
5 Disconnect the refrigerant lines from the rear of the compressor. Plug the open fittings to prevent entry of dirt and moisture.
6 Unbolt the compressor from the mounting brackets and lift it out of the vehicle **(see illustration)**.
7 If a new compressor is being installed, follow the directions with the compressor regarding the draining of excess oil prior to installation.
8 The clutch may have to be transferred from the original to the new compressor.
9 Installation is the reverse of removal. Replace all O-rings with new ones specifically made for air conditioning system use and lubricate them with refrigerant oil.
10 Have the system evacuated, recharged and leak tested by the shop that discharged it.

16 Air conditioning system condenser – removal and installation

Refer to illustrations 16.5a, 16.5b and 16.6

Warning: *The air conditioning system is under high pressure. DO NOT disassemble any part of the system (hoses, compressor, line fittings, etc.) until after the system has been depressurized by a dealer service department or service station.*

Note: *The receiver-drier (see Section 14) should be replaced whenever the condenser is replaced.*

1 Have the air conditioning system discharged (see Warning above).
2 Disconnect the negative cable from the battery.
3 Drain the cooling system (see Chapter 1).
4 Remove the radiator (see Section 5).
5 Disconnect the refrigerant lines from the condenser **(see illustrations)**. **Note:** *On some models it may be necessary to remove the lower grille to access the fitting at the bottom of the condenser.*
6 Remove the mounting bolts from the condenser brackets **(see illustration)**.

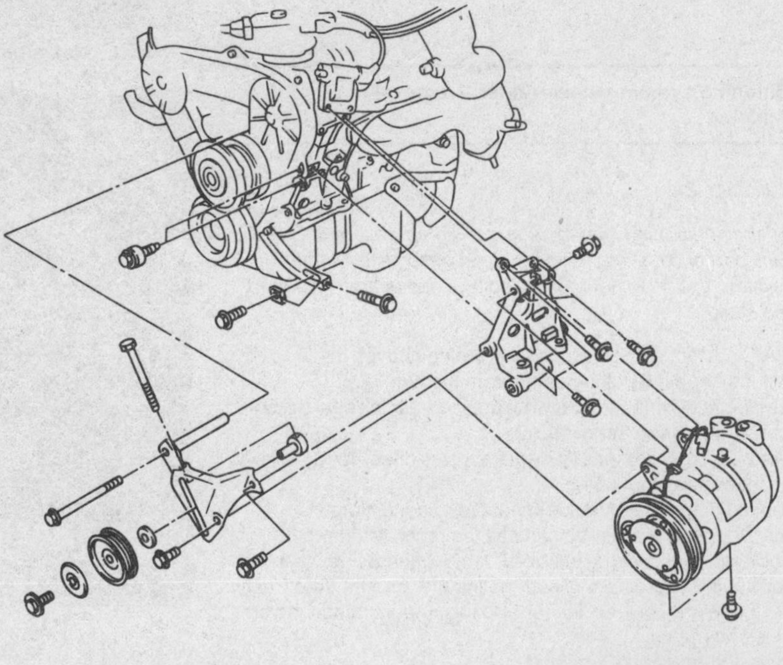

15.6 Compressor mounting details – exploded view

16.5a The upper refrigerant line is connected to the condenser with a through-bolt (arrow)

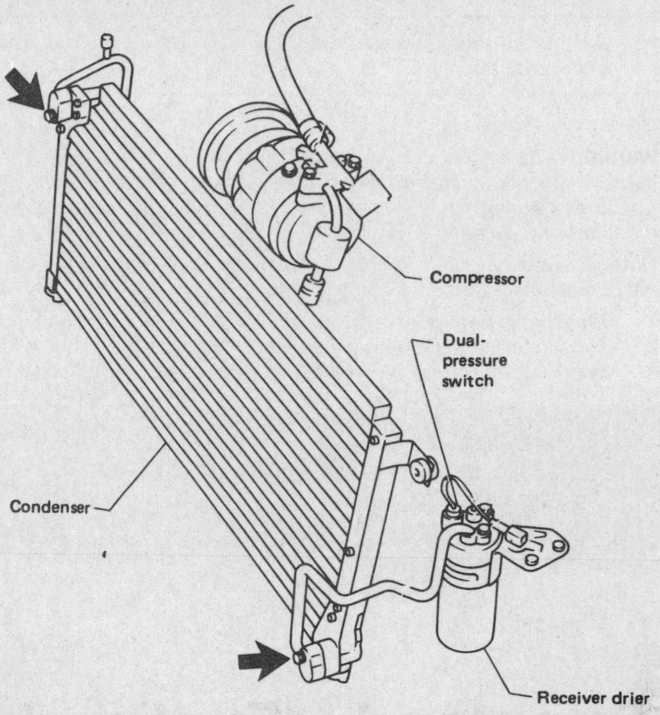

16.5b The refrigerant lines (arrows) connect to the front of the condenser in diagonally opposite corners – some models have a threaded coupling on the bottom instead of the through-bolt shown here

16.6 Remove the mounting bolt (arrow) from each side of the condenser

7 Lift the condenser out of the vehicle and plug the lines to keep dirt and moisture out.

8 If the original condenser will be reinstalled, store it with the line fittings on top to prevent oil from draining out.

9 If a new condenser is being installed, pour one ounce of refrigerant oil into it prior to installation.

10 Reinstall the components in the reverse order of removal. Be sure the rubber grommets are in place on the condenser brackets.

11 Have the system evacuated, recharged and leak tested by the shop that discharged it.

Chapter 4 Fuel and exhaust systems

Contents

Air cleaner assembly/air inlet tubes – removal and installation 2
Air filter replacement .... See Chapter 1
Air flow meter – check, removal and installation 22
Air regulator (1988 and earlier models) – removal, check and installation 12
Cylinder head temperature sensor – check and replacement 14
ECCS components – general information 10
Electronic Fuel Injection (EFI) system – general diagnosis 11
Electronic Fuel Injection (EFI) system – general information 1
Exhaust gas sensor – check 15
Exhaust system check .... See Chapter 1
Exhaust system servicing – general information 24
Fast Idle Control Device (FICD) valve – check, removal and installation 20
Fuel filter replacement .... See Chapter 1
Fuel injectors – check, removal and installation 17
Fuel level sending unit – check, removal and installation 9
Fuel pressure regulator and control solenoid – check, removal and installation 13
Fuel pressure relief procedure 4
Fuel pump/fuel pressure – check 5
Fuel pump relay – general information .... See Chapter 12
Fuel pump – removal and installation 8
Fuel system check .... See Chapter 1
Fuel tank cleaning and repair – general information 7
Fuel tank – removal and installation 6
Fuel temperature sensor – check and replacement 16
Throttle cable – removal and installation 3
Throttle chamber – removal and installation 21
Throttle valve switch – adjustment 19
Throttle valve switch – check 18
Underhood hose check and replacement .... See Chapter 1
Vacuum chamber (1988 and earlier models) – removal and installation 23

Specifications

General

Air regulator resistance	70 ohms
Exhaust gas sensor heater resistance	5 to 6 ohms
Exhaust gas sensor resistance (1989 models)	85.3 ± 8.5 K-ohms
Fuel injector resistance	
1985 and 1986 models	3 ohms
1987 and 1988 models	1.5 ohms
1989 and later models	10 ohms
Air flow meter voltage at terminal B (1989 and later models)	
With ignition On	less than 0.5 volts
At idle	1.0 to 1.3 volts
Throttle valve switch 1989 and later models only (approximate values)	
Accelerator completely released	1 ohm
Accelerator completely depressed	9 ohms

Cylinder head temperature sensor resistance (approximate values)	
At 68-degrees F	2.3 to 2.7 K-ohms
At 122-degrees F	770 to 870 ohms
At 176-degrees F	300 to 330 ohms
Idle-up solenoid resistance	30 ohms
Fuel temperature sensor resistance (approximate values)	
At 68-degrees F	2.3 to 2.7 K-ohms
At 122-degrees F	770 to 870 ohms
At 176-degrees F	300 to 330 ohms
Fuel pressure (with pressure regulator hose connected)	
1988 and earlier models	
At idle	30 psi
At the moment the throttle is opened fully	37 psi
1989 models	
At idle	36 psi
At the moment the throttle is opened fully	43.5 psi
Fuel pressure (with vacuum pump connected to pressure regulator) (1988 and earlier models only)	
With 0 in-Hg of vacuum applied	36 to 37 psi
With 5 in-Hg of vacuum applied	33 to 35 psi
With 10 in-Hg of vacuum applied	31 to 32 psi
With 15 in-Hg of vacuum applied	29 to 30 psi
With 20 in-Hg of vacuum applied	26 to 28 psi

Torque Specifications

	Ft-lbs
Throttle chamber bolts	13 to 16
Air intake collector bolts	13 to 16
Cylinder head temperature sensor	9 to 12
Exhaust gas sensor	30 to 37

1 Electronic Fuel Injection (EFI) system – general information

Refer to illustrations 1.1a, 1.1b, 1.2a and 1.2b

Note: *The underhood photographs show the components typical of 1985 through 1988 models with a separate photograph for 1989 models. When performing procedures in this Chapter, refer to the proper underhood photograph for the location of components.*

The vehicles covered by this manual have an Electronic Fuel Injection (EFI) fuel system **(see illustrations)**. Electronic fuel injection provides optimum mixture ratios, and this, together with the immediate response characteristics of the fuel injection, permits the engine to run on the weakest possible fuel/air mixture. This vastly reduces the exhaust gas toxic emission. The fuel system is interrelated with and works in conjunction with the emissions control and exhaust systems covered in Chapter 6. Thus, some elements that relate directly to the fuel system are covered in that Chapter.

The EFI system consists of three subsystems: The fuel flow system, the air flow system and the electrical signaling system **(see illustrations)**. The various components that make up the entire EFI system are detailed in Section 10.

Fuel from the tank is delivered under pressure by an electric fuel pump. The amount of fuel to be injected is determined by the injection pulse duration as well as by a pressure difference between fuel pressure and intake manifold vacuum pressure. The Electronic Concentrated Control System (ECCS) control unit controls only the injection pulse duration. For this reason, the pressure difference between the fuel pressure and intake manifold vacuum pressure must be maintained at a constant level. Since the intake manifold vacuum pressure varies with engine operating conditions, a pressure regulator is placed in the fuel line to regulate the fuel pressure in response to changes in the intake manifold pressure. Where manifold conditions are such that the fuel pressure could be beyond that specified, the pressure regulator returns surplus fuel to the tank.

An injection of fuel occurs once every rotation of the crankshaft. Because the injection signal comes from the control unit, all six injectors operate simultaneously and independent of the engine stroke. Each injection supplies half the amount of fuel required by the cylinder, and the length of the injection period is determined by information fed to the control unit by various sensors included in the system.

Elements affecting the injection duration include: Engine rpm, quantity and temperature of the intake air, throttle valve opening, temperature of the engine coolant, intake manifold vacuum pressure and amount of oxygen in the exhaust gases.

Because the EFI system operates at high fuel pressure, any leak can affect system efficiency and present a serious fire risk. Also, since the intake air flow is critical to the operation of the system, even a slight air leak will cause an incorrect air/fuel mixture. **Note:** *Certain precautions should be observed when working on the EFI system:*

a) Do not disconnect either battery cable while the engine is running.
b) Prior to any operation in which the fuel line will be disconnected, the high pressure in the system must first be eliminated. This procedure is described in Section 4. Disconnect the negative battery cable to eliminate the possibility of sparks occurring while fuel is present.
c) Prior to removing any EFI component, be sure the ignition switch is Off and the negative battery cable is disconnected.
d) The EFI wiring harness should be kept at least four inches (10 mm) away from adjacent harnesses. This includes a CB antenna feeder cable. This is to prevent electrical pulses in other systems from interfering with EFI operation.
e) Be sure all EFI wiring connections are tight, clean and secure, as a poor connection can cause extremely high voltage surges in the ignition coil which could drain the IC circuit.
f) The accelerator should Not be depressed prior to starting the engine. Immediately after starting, do not rev the engine unnecessarily.

The electric fuel pump uses relays, located in the engine compartment, that are designed so that should the engine stop (causing the alternator to turn off and the oil pressure to drop), the fuel pump will cease to operate.

Some basic checks of the EFI components are included in this Chapter. However, the complexity of the system prevents many problems from being accurately diagnosed by the home mechanic. If a problem develops in the system which cannot be pinpointed by the checks listed here, it is best to take the vehicle to a dealer service department to locate the fault.

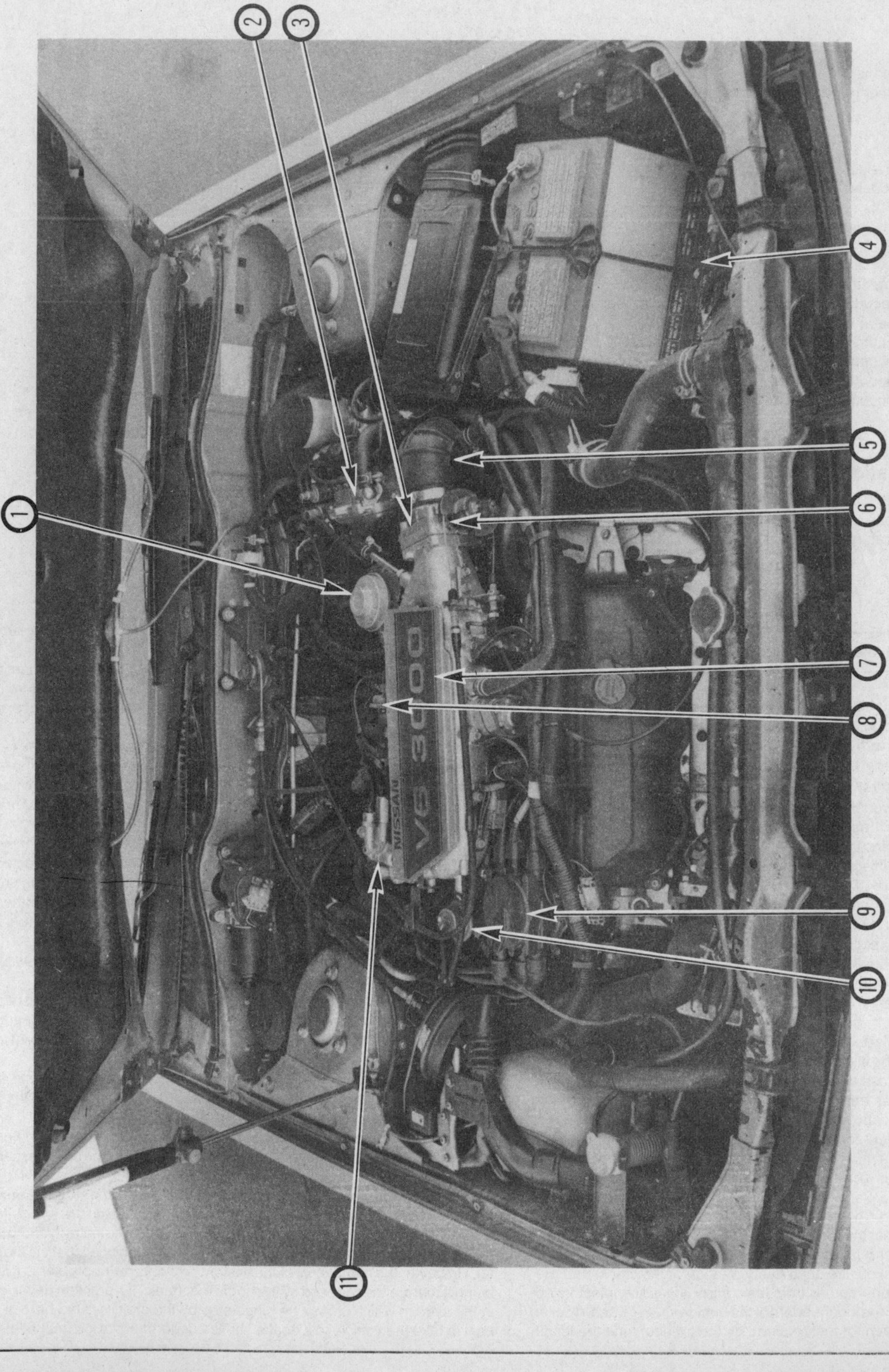

1.1a 1988 and earlier ECCS component locations

1 *EGR valve*
2 *Vacuum chamber*
3 *Throttle switch*
4 *Relay panel*
5 *Air inlet tube*
6 *Throttle chamber*
7 *Air intake collector*
8 *Air regulator*
9 *Distributor*
10 *Fuel pressure regulator*
11 *Fast idle control device*

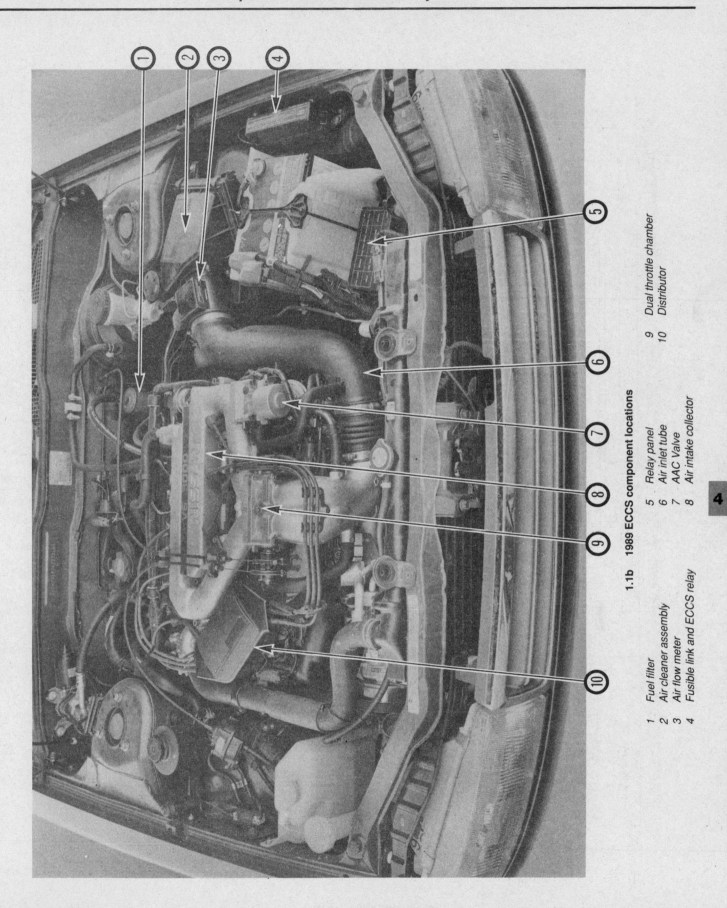

1.1b 1989 ECCS component locations

1 Fuel filter
2 Air cleaner assembly
3 Air flow meter
4 Fusible link and ECCS relay
5 Relay panel
6 Air inlet tube
7 AAC Valve
8 Air intake collector
9 Dual throttle chamber
10 Distributor

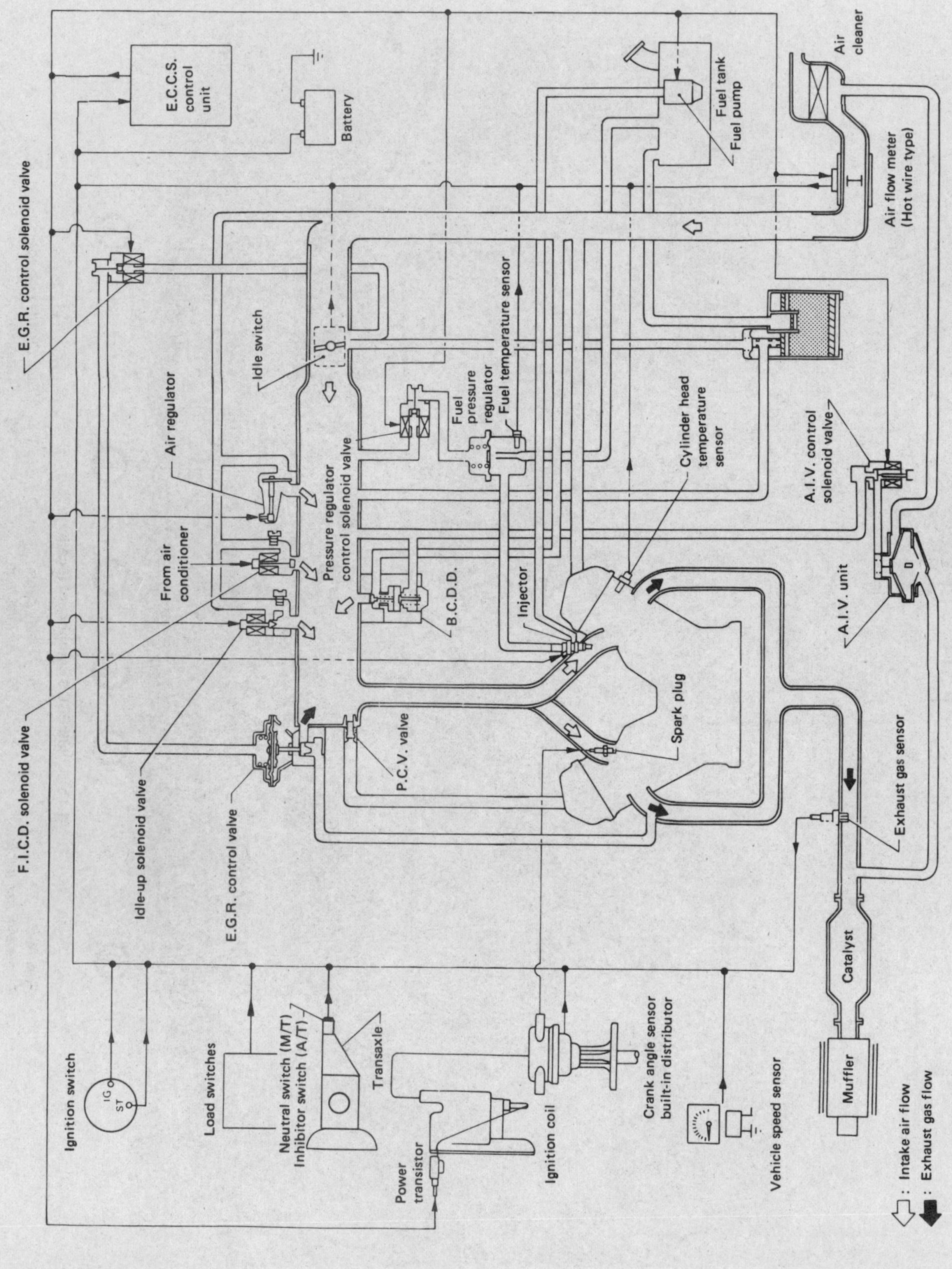

1.2a 1988 and earlier fuel injection system diagram

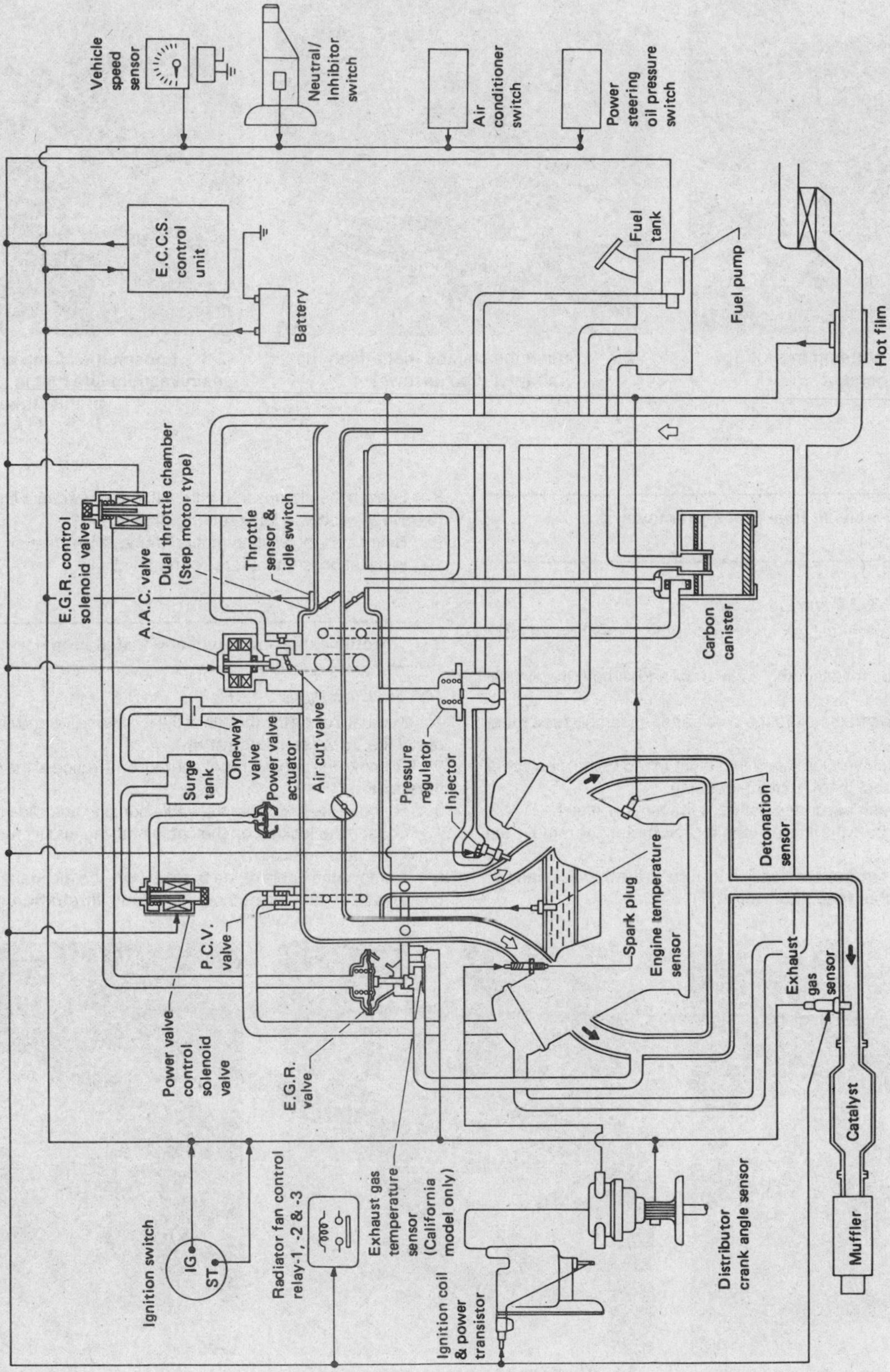

1.2b 1989 and later fuel injection system diagram

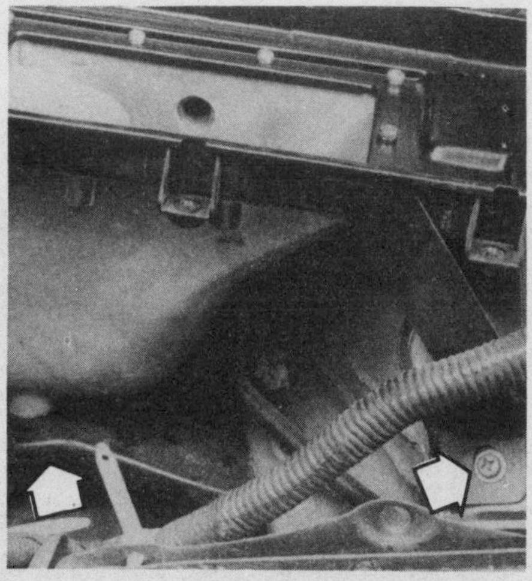

2.3 **Air cleaner housing mounting arrangement**

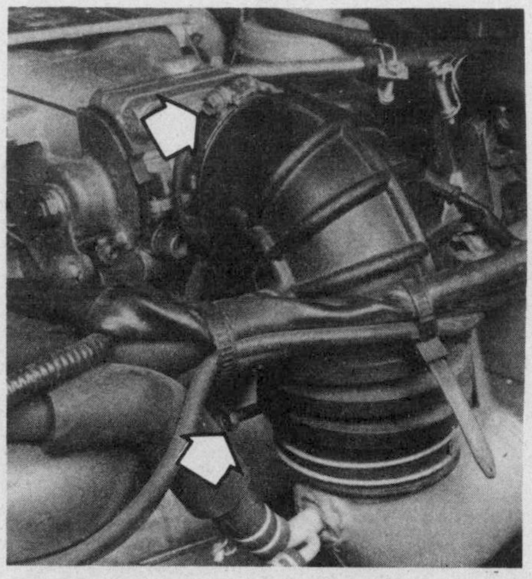

2.7 **Loosen the clamps that attach the air inlet tube (arrows)**

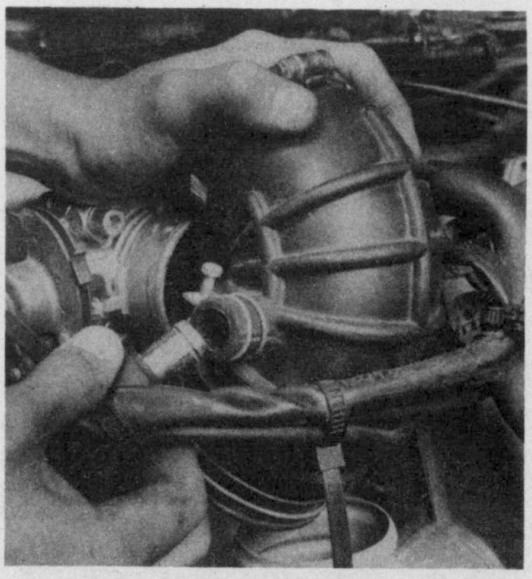

2.8 **Loosen the clamp and remove the main vacuum line that is attached to the air inlet tube**

2 Air cleaner assembly/air inlet tubes – removal and installation

Refer to illustrations 2.3, 2.7 and 2.8

1 Disconnect the battery cables and remove the battery (see Chapter 5).

2 Remove the air cleaner assembly cover bolts and remove the air filter (see Chapter 1).

3 Remove the screws that secure the air cleaner assembly **(see illustration)**.

4 Carefully mark each vacuum hose that is attached to the air cleaner assembly and disconnect them from the housing.

5 Disconnect the electrical connector from the air flow meter.

6 Loosen the clamp from the inlet air tube/air flow meter and remove the air cleaner assembly.

7 Loosen the clamps that attach the air inlet tube to the throttle chamber and the vacuum chamber **(see illustration)**.

8 Loosen the clamps that attach the main vacuum line to the tube and remove the vacuum line **(see illustration)**

9 Using a slight twisting motion, remove the inlet air tube.

10 Installation is the reverse of removal.

3 Throttle cable – removal and installation

Refer to illustrations 3.1, 3.2, 3.5 and 3.6

1 Manually open the throttle at the throttle valve and lift the cable up and out of the track **(see illustration)**.

2 Remove the cable through the slot on the side of the throttle lever **(see illustration)**.

3 Remove the boot from the cable housing and slide it down the cable.

4 Loosen the locknut on the cable housing and lift the cable assembly out of the adjustment bracket.

5 Remove the cable guide bracket from the air intake collector located on the passenger side of the engine **(see illustration)**.

3.1 **Hold the throttle open and lift the cable out of the track**

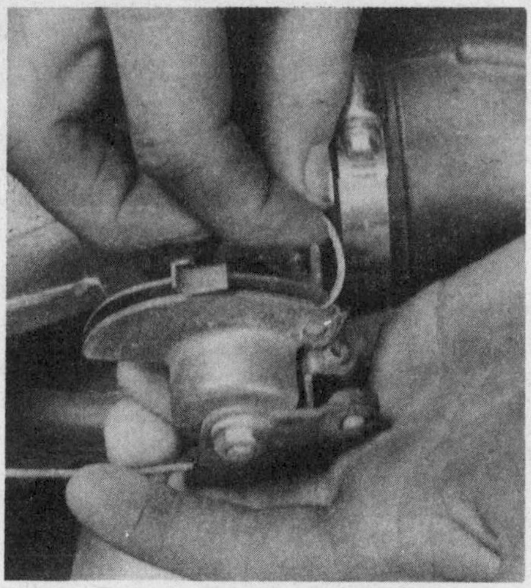

3.2 **Pass the cable through the slot on the side of the throttle lever**

3.5 **Unbolt the cable guide bracket from the right end of the air intake collector**

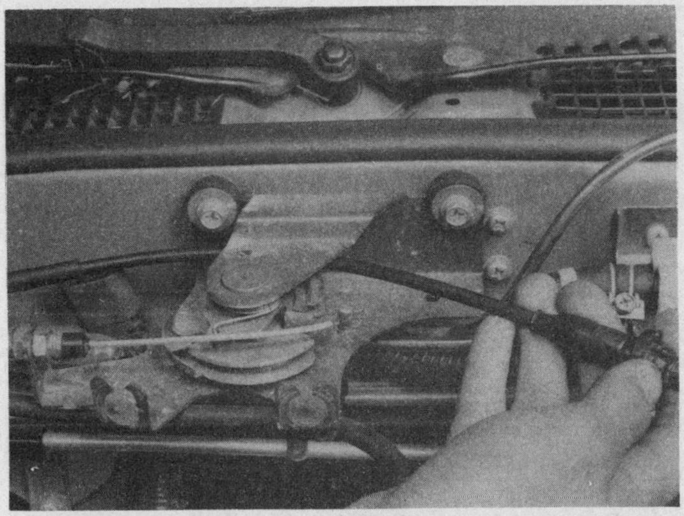

3.6 Disconnect the cruise control cable and pull the throttle cable through the assembly

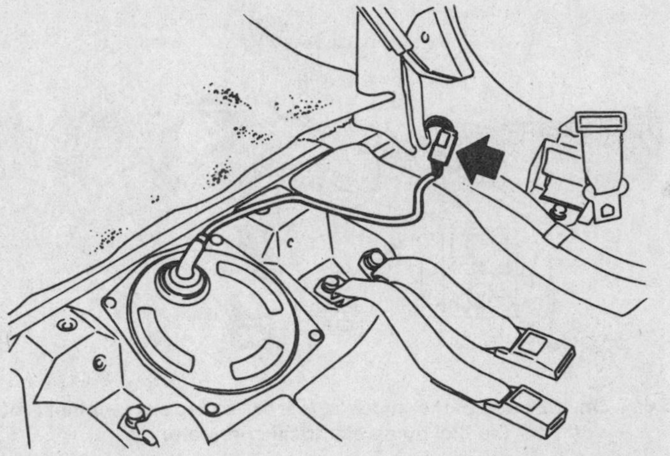

4.2 to relieve the fuel pressure on 1985 models, remove the rear compartment floor mat, start the engine and disconnect the fuel pump electrical connector

6 Disconnect the cruise control cable from its linkage on the firewall and pull the throttle cable through the assembly **(see illustration)**.
7 Disconnect the throttle cable from the accelerator pedal by pulling the cable forward and removing it through the slot on the pedal shaft.
8 Installation is the reverse of removal.

4 Fuel pressure relief procedure

Warning: *Gasoline is extremely flammable, so take extra precautions when working on any part of the fuel system. Don't smoke or allow open flames or bare light bulbs in or near the work area. Also, don't work in a garage if a natural gas appliance such as a water heater or clothes dryer is present.*
1 The fuel system is pressurized, even when the engine is off. Consequently, any time the fuel system is worked on it must be depressurized to avoid the spraying of fuel when a component is disconnected.

1985 models

Refer to illustration 4.2
2 On 1985 models, remove the rear compartment floor mat. Start the engine and disconnect the fuel pump electrical connector with the engine running **(see illustration)**.
3 Allow the engine to run until it stalls.
4 Disconnect the negative battery cable before performing any work on the fuel system.

1986 and later models

Refer to illustrations 4.5a, 4.5b and 4.5c
5 Remove the fuel pump fuse from the fuse panel **(see illustrations)**.
6 Start the engine and let it run until the engine stalls.
7 Crank the engine two or three times to make sure the pressure has been released.
8 Disconnect the negative battery cable before performing any work on the fuel system.

All models

9 When all repairs to the fuel system are complete, turn the ignition switch off and reconnect the fuel pump electrical connector or install the fuse.
10 Erase the memory code (Code 22 of the Self Diagnostic System Mode III) by turning the diagnostic mode selector on the ECU fully clockwise (see Section 11). After the Inspection lights have flashed four times, turn the diagnostic mode selector on the ECU fully counterclockwise.

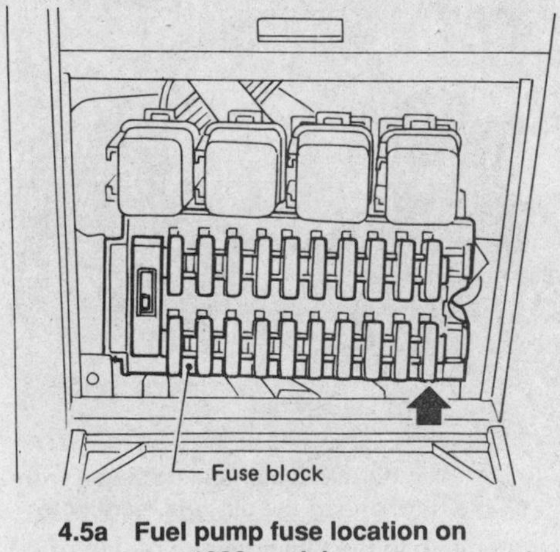

4.5a Fuel pump fuse location on 1986 models

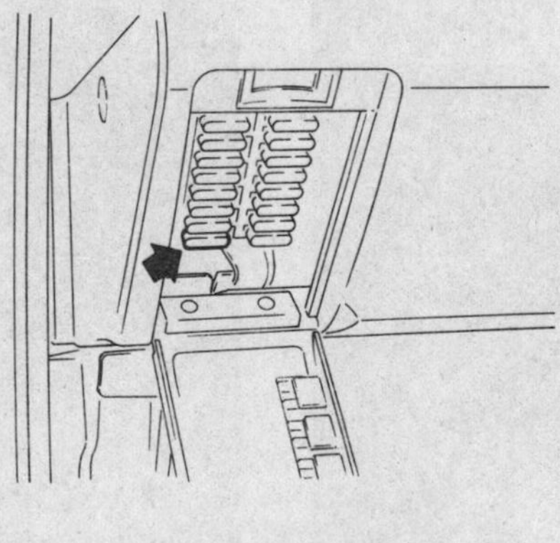

4.5b Fuel pump fuse location on 1987 and 1988 models

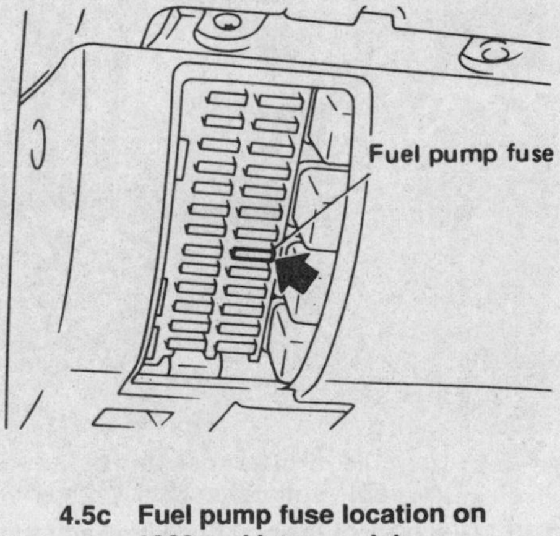

4.5c Fuel pump fuse location on 1989 and later models

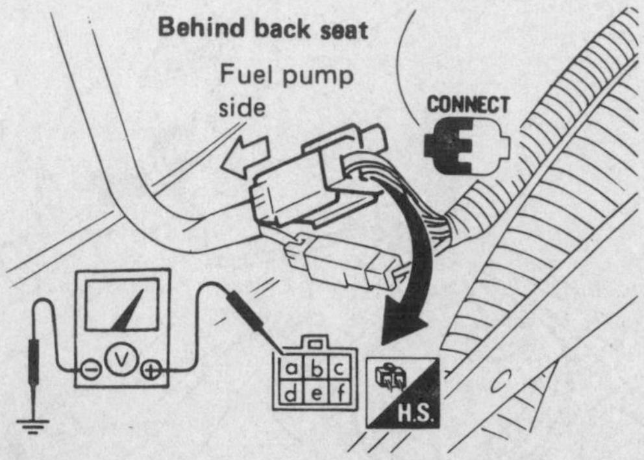

5.6a On 1988 and earlier models, test for voltage at terminal A of the fuel pump electrical connector

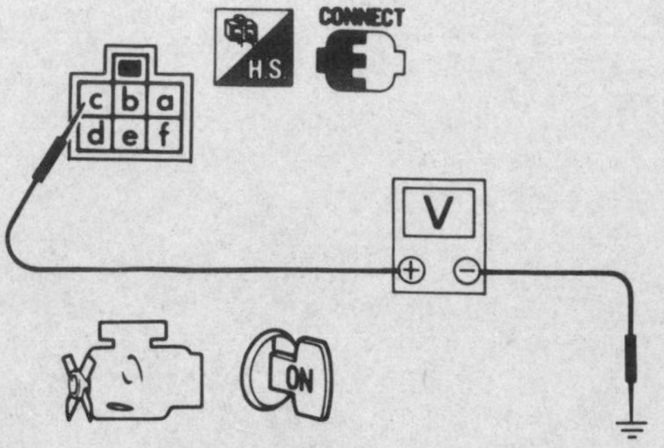

5.6b On 1989 and later models, test for voltage at terminal C of the fuel pump electrical connector under the rear seat

5 Fuel pump/fuel pressure – check

Warning: *Gasoline is extremely flammable, so take extra precautions when working on any part of the fuel system. Don't smoke or allow open flames or bare light bulbs in or near the work area. Also, don't work in a garage if a natural gas appliance such as a water heater or clothes dryer is present.*

Fuel pump check

Refer to illustrations 5.6a and 5.6b

1 If the engine runs poorly or not at all, use the self diagnosis mode (see Section 11) to pinpoint any problems in the vehicle's fuel system.
2 If the ECU flashes 2 red flashes and 2 green flashes, the fuel pump circuit is malfunctioning.
3 Depending on the symptom, the fuel pump and its related circuit have several items that must be checked in order to pinpoint the exact problem.
4 If the engine is impossible to start and there is no sound of combustion, remove the fuel filler cap and listen for the sound of the fuel pump. If the fuel pump is humming, have an assistant crank the engine over and listen carefully for any clicking sounds from the fuel injectors in the engine compartment. If there is no sound from the fuel pump or the fuel injectors, check all the fuses and related wiring harnesses (see Chapter 12).
5 If the engine doesn't run, or if it starts but has poor driveability, check the fuel pressure (see Step 9).
6 Check for voltage to the fuel pump. Turn the ignition switch to the On position and with a voltmeter, check the voltage between terminal A (1988 and earlier models) or terminal C (1989 models) of the fuel pump electrical connector (located behind the rear seat – see Section 8) and ground **(see illustrations)**. The voltage should be 12 volts for 5 seconds after turning the ignition switch to the On position.
7 If there is no voltage, check the continuity of the fuel pump and ECU wiring harness. Also check the fuel pump relay (see Chapter 12 for relay location and wiring diagrams).
8 If voltage is present, check the ground circuit. Turn the ignition switch to Off. Disconnect the fuel pump harness connector behind the rear seat (see Section 8). Check the resistance in the circuit between the fuel pump and ground. The resistance should be 0 ohms. If these tests are all positive, replace the fuel pump.

Fuel pressure check

Refer to illustrations 5.10 and 5.12

Caution: *When reconnecting the fuel line always use new clamps. Check to make sure the clamp screw does not contact adjacent parts.*

Note: *The fuel pressure check requires a special fuel pressure gauge and fittings. If the special tools are not available, have the test performed by a dealership service department.*

9 Relieve the fuel pressure (see Section 4).
10 Disconnect the fuel hose between the fuel filter and the fuel rail (engine side) and install a fuel pressure gauge **(see illustration)**.
11 Start the engine and check for leakage around the gauge connections.
12 Connect a vacuum pump to the fuel pressure regulator **(see illustration)**.

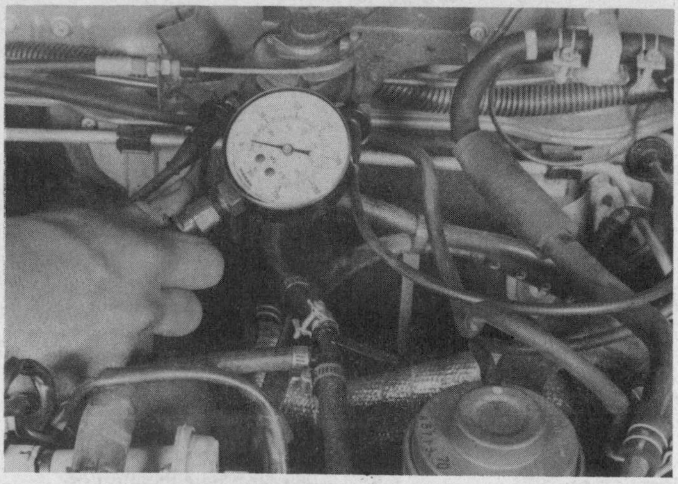

5.10 Disconnect the fuel hose between the fuel filter and fuel rail (engine side) and install a fuel pressure gauge

5.12 Connect a vacuum pump to the fuel pressure regulator

13 Read the fuel pressure gauge with vacuum applied to the pressure regulator and also with no vacuum applied. The fuel pressure should decrease as vacuum increases. Compare your readings with the values listed in this Chapter's Specifications.
14 Reconnect the vacuum hose to the regulator and check the fuel pressure at idle, comparing your reading with the value listed in this Chapter's Specifications. Disconnect the vacuum hose and watch the gauge – the pressure should jump up to the maximum specified pressure as soon as the hose is disconnected. If the pressure at idle was too high (with the hose connected), connect a vacuum gauge to the vacuum hose and check for vacuum. If there isn't any reading on the gauge, check the fuel pressure regulator control solenoid, following the procedure described in Section 13.
15 If the fuel pressure is low, pinch the fuel return line shut and watch the gauge. If the pressure doesn't rise, the fuel pump is defective or there is a restriction in the fuel feed line. If the pressure rises sharply, replace the pressure regulator (see Section 13).
16 If the indicated fuel pressure is too high, disconnect the fuel return line and blow through it to check for a blockage. If there is no blockage, replace the fuel pressure regulator (see Section 13).
17 If the pressure doesn't fluctuate as described in Step 13, replace the fuel pressure regulator (see Section 13).

6 Fuel tank – removal and installation

Refer to illustrations 6.2, 6.4, 6.6 and 6.7

Warning: *Gasoline is extremely flammable, so take extra precautions when working on any part of the fuel system. Don't smoke or allow open flames or bare light bulbs in or near the work area. Also, don't work in a garage if a natural gas appliance such as a water heater or clothes dryer is present.*

1 Disconnect the fuel line and electrical connector from the fuel pump (see Section 8).
2 Disconnect the rear exhaust hanger from the muffler **(see illustration)** and let the exhaust system hang down slightly.
3 Raise the vehicle and support it securely on jackstands.
4 Remove the fuel tank protectors **(see illustration)** to expose some of the fuel tank retaining bolts.
5 Drain the fuel from the tank. If the tank does not have a drain plug, siphon the fuel into an approved gasoline container.

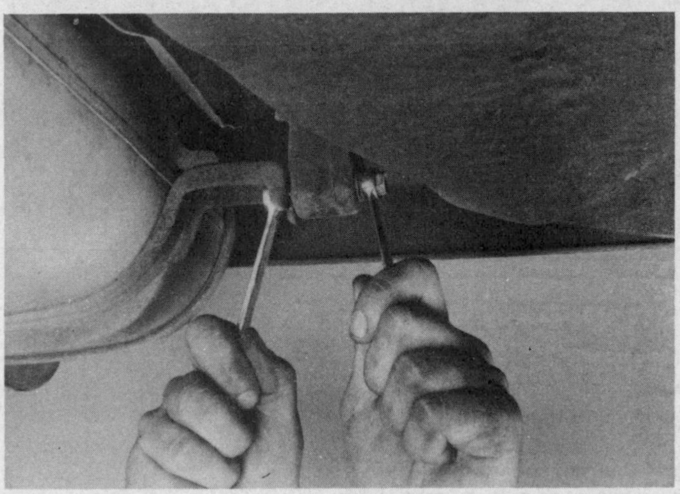

6.2 Disconnect the rear exhaust hanger from the muffler

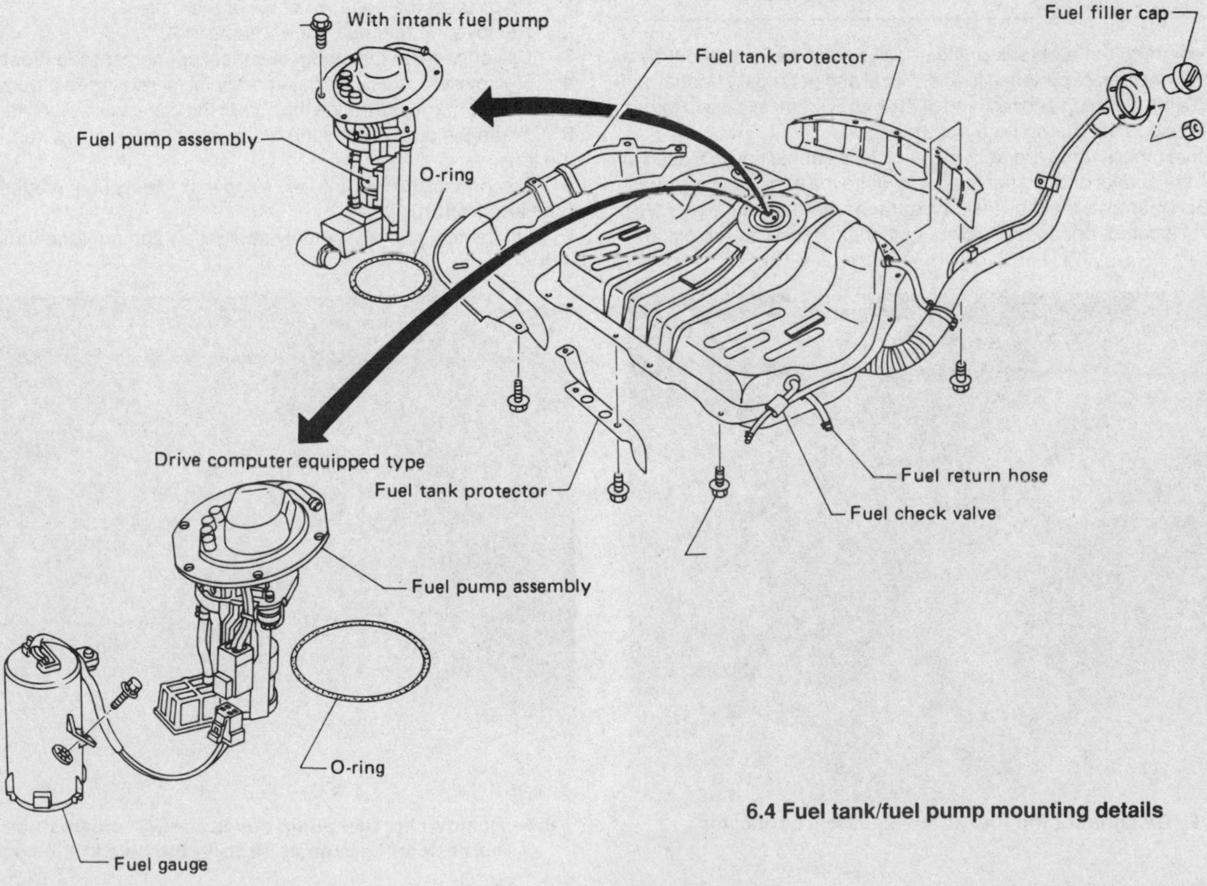

6.4 Fuel tank/fuel pump mounting details

4

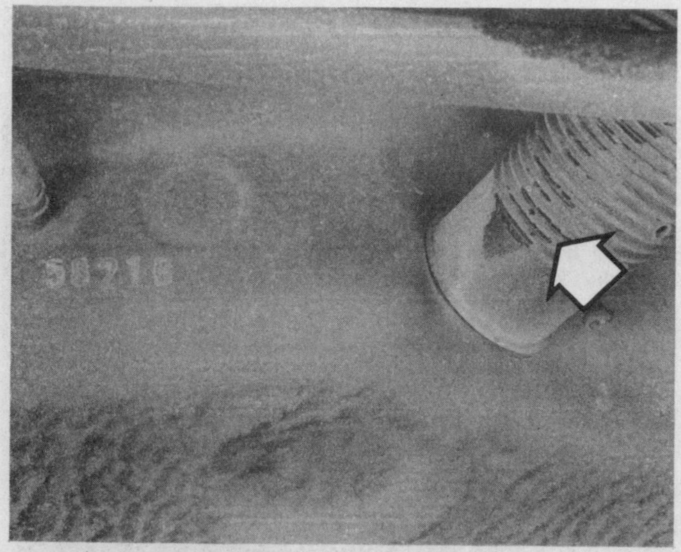

6.6 Remove the fuel tank filler protector and filler (arrow) and any hoses connected to the tank

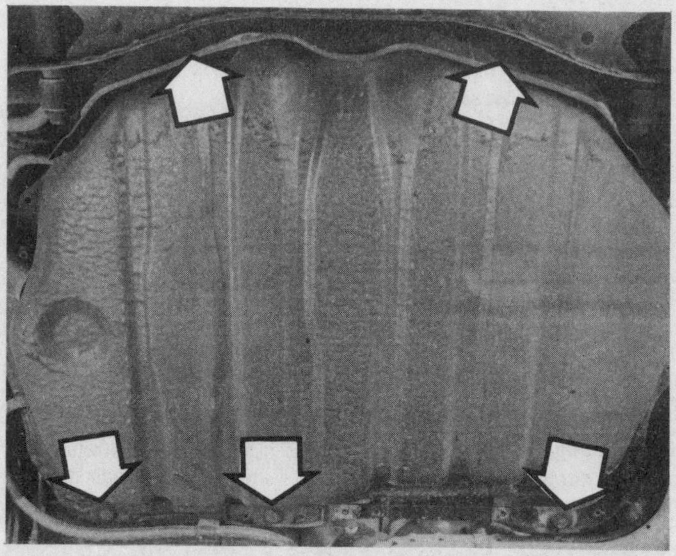

6.7 Remove the mounting bolts and carefully lower the tank

6 Remove the fuel tank filler and any hoses connected to the fuel tank **(see illustration)**.
7 Support the fuel tank with a floor jack. Remove the mounting bolts **(see illustration)** and slowly lower the tank.
8 Installation is the reverse of removal.

7 Fuel tank cleaning and repair – general information

1 Any repairs to the fuel tank or filler neck should be carried out by a professional who has experience in this critical and potentially dangerous work. Even after cleaning and flushing of the fuel system, explosive fumes can remain and ignite during repair of the tank.
2 If the fuel tank is removed from the vehicle, it should not be placed in an area where sparks or open flames could ignite the fumes coming out of the tank. Don't remove the tank inside a garage where a natural gas-type appliance is located, because the pilot light could cause an explosion.

8 Fuel pump – removal and installation

Refer to illustrations 8.3, 8.4, 8.6 and 8.7

Warning: *Gasoline is extremely flammable, so extra precautions must be taken when working on any part of the fuel system. Do not smoke or allow open flames or bare light bulbs near the work area. Also, do not work in a garage if a natural gas type appliance with a pilot light is present.*
1 Disconnect the negative cable at the battery.
2 Remove the rear seat (see Chapter 11).
3 Disconnect the fuel pump electrical connector **(see illustration)**.
4 Remove the fuel pump cover retaining screws **(see illustration)** and slip the wire harness through the hole in the cover while lifting the cover up.
5 Clean the area around the fuel pump to prevent dirt from falling into the tank.
6 Disconnect the fuel line and remove the fuel pump mounting screws **(see illustration)**.
7 Lift the fuel pump assembly straight up and out **(see illustration)**.

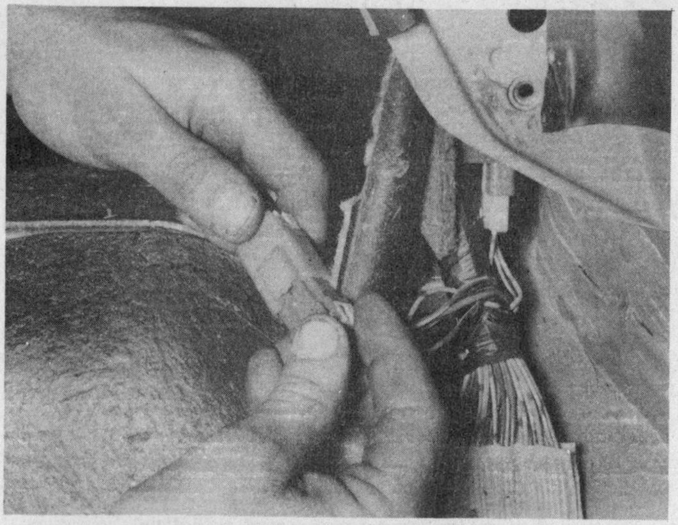

8.3 Disconnect the fuel pump electrical connector

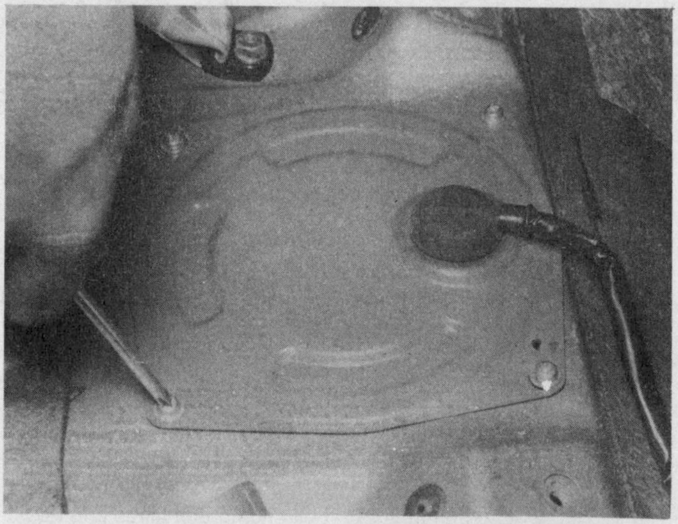

8.4 Remove the fuel pump cover screws and push the wiring harness and grommet through the hole in the cover

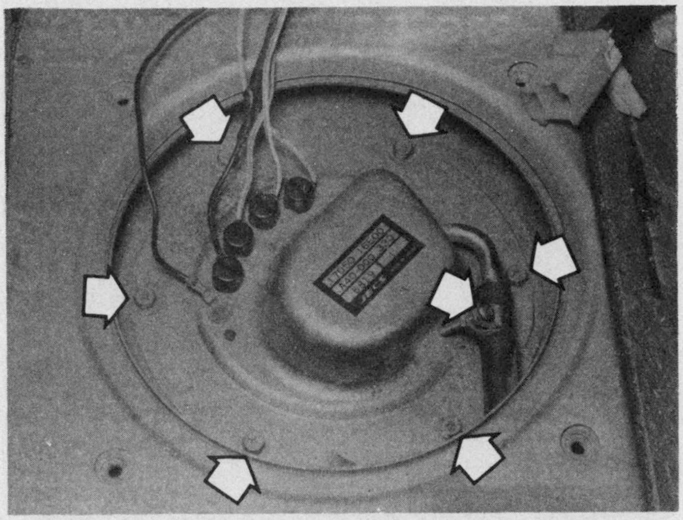

8.6 Disconnect the fuel line and remove the six mounting screws (arrows)

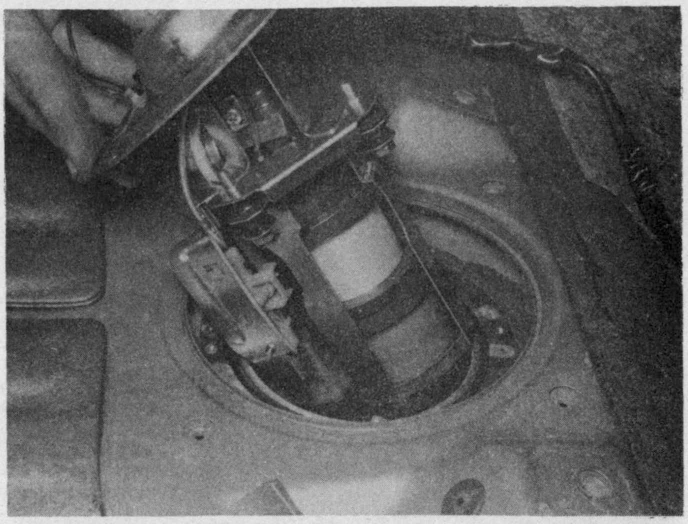

8.7 Lift the fuel pump assembly straight up – be careful not to damage any of the attached components

8 Remove the fuel pump assembly retaining bolts and separate the fuel pump from the fuel level sending unit.

9 Installation is the reverse of the removal procedure, but be sure to use a new rubber O-ring where the pump flange contacts the fuel tank.

9 Fuel level sending unit – check, removal and installation

Refer to illustrations 9.3 and 9.4

Check

1 The fuel level sending unit can be inspected visually for damage and tested with a multimeter for continuity and source voltage.

2 If the fuel gauge does not reach Full, measure the resistance of the fuel level sending unit. Remove the fuel pump/sending unit from the fuel tank (see Section 8).

3 Using an ohmmeter, test the resistance of the fuel level sending unit by raising and lowering the float bowl **(see illustration)**. The resistance value should be approximately 1230 ohms Full and 1325 ohms Empty. Resistance values in-between indicate partially full. If the values are not within range, replace the fuel level sending unit.

4 If the resistance value is acceptable at the fuel level sending unit, check the resistance at the fuel gauge connector. Turn the ignition switch to Off. Remove the instrument cluster (see Chapter 12). Disconnect the electrical connector from the control unit **(see illustration)**, change the position of the float bowl on the fuel level sending unit and measure the resistance between terminals 13 and 15 on the harness side. The resistance should vary from approximately 1230 ohms Full to 1325 ohms Empty.

5 If the resistance values are not within range, check the wiring harness for an open or short-circuit condition.

Removal and installation

6 Remove the fuel pump assembly (see Section 8) and separate the fuel level sending unit from the pump by marking and disconnecting the wires, then removing the retaining screws.

7 Installation is the reverse of removal.

4

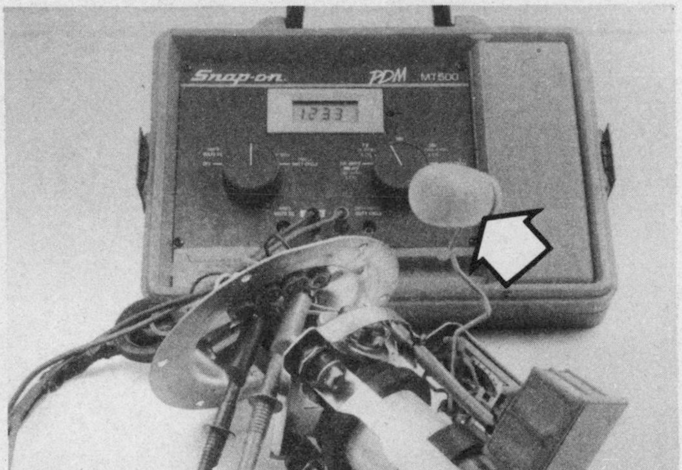

9.3 Connect an ohmmeter to the sending unit leads and raise and lower the float bowl (arrow) to change the resistance

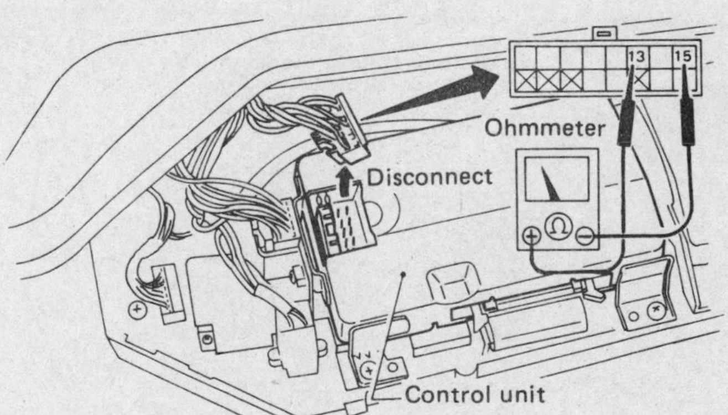

9.4 Disconnect the harness connector from the control unit behind the instrument cluster and measure the fuel level sending unit resistance at the terminals shown

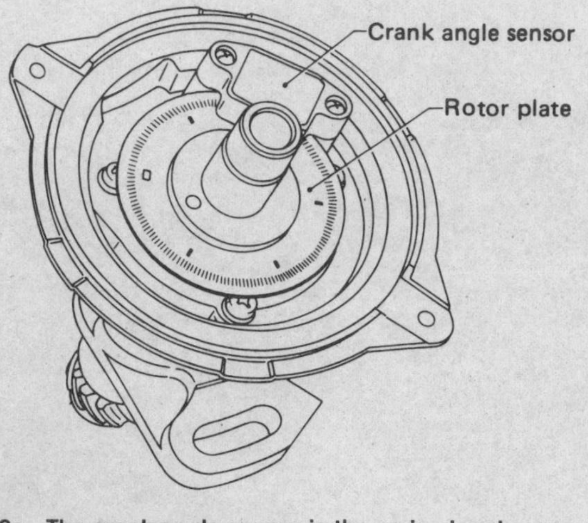

10.2a The crank angle sensor is the main signal sensor for the ECCS

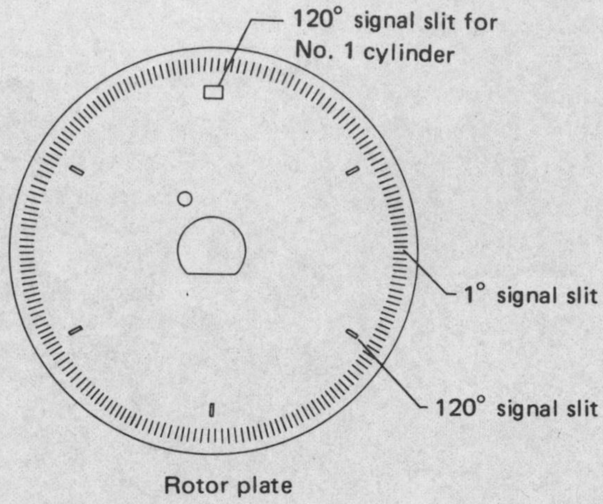

10.2b The rotor plate has 360 slits to indicate engine speed and six slits for crank angle signal

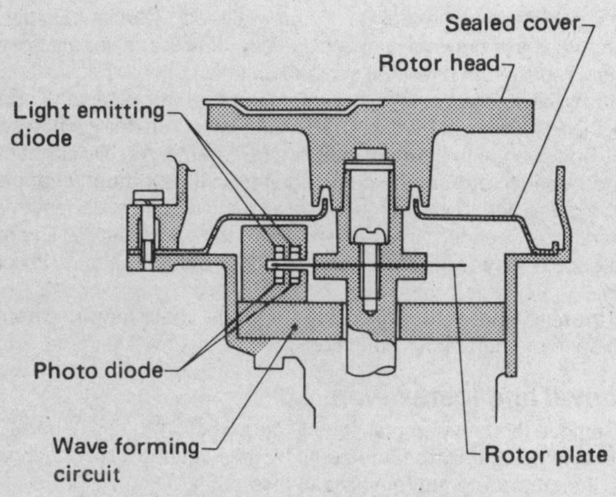

10.2c Light passes through the slits in the rotor plate, sending signals in the form of on-off pulses to the control unit

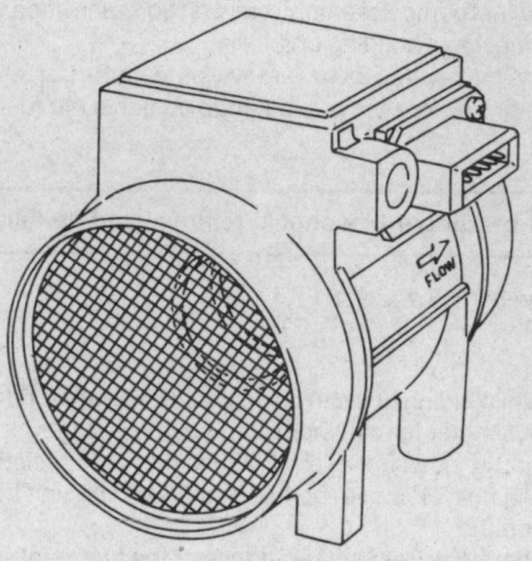

10.3 The air flow meter measures the mass flow rate of intake air

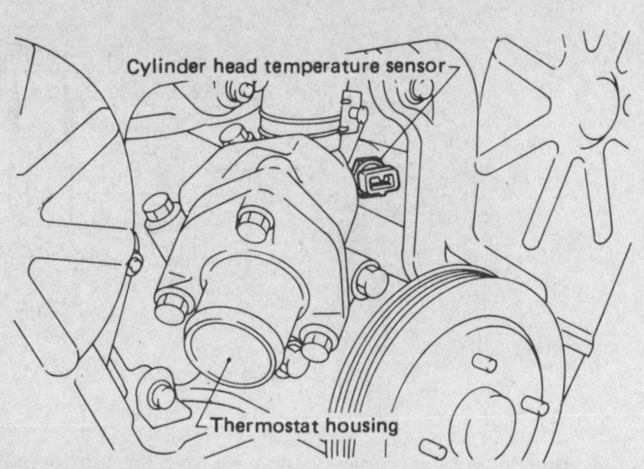

10.4 The cylinder head temperature sensor is located behind the thermostat housing and timing belt cover

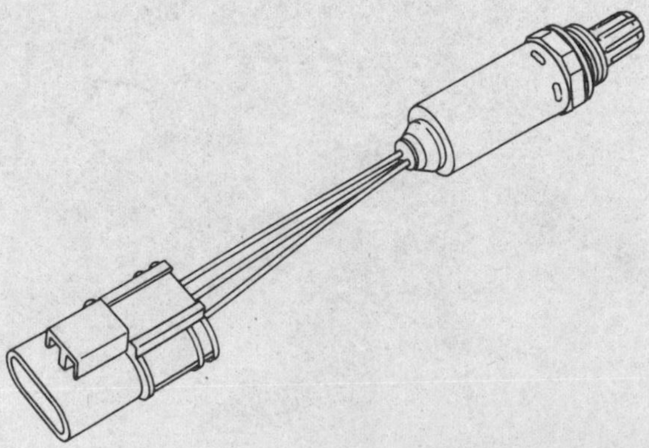

10.5 The exhaust gas sensor monitors the quantity of oxygen in the exhaust gas

10 ECCS components – general information

Refer to illustrations 10.2a, 10.2b, 10.2c, 10.3, 10.4, 10.5, 10.6, 10.8, 10.9, 10.10, 10.11, 10.12, 10.14, 10.15, 10.16, 10.17, 10.18, 10.19, 10.21 and 10.22.

ECCS control unit

1 The Electronic Concentrated Control System (ECCS) control unit, also known as the Engine Control Unit (ECU), is a microcomputer with electrical connectors for receiving input/output signals and for power supply, inspection lamps and a diagnostic mode selector. The control unit regulates the amount of fuel that is injected, as well as the ignition timing, idle speed, fuel pump operation and the feedback of the mixture ratio.

Crank angle sensor

2 The crank angle sensor could be regarded as the right hand to the ECCS control unit, as it is the basic signal sensor for the entire ECCS system. It monitors the engine speed, piston position and it sends signals to the ECCS control unit for control of the fuel injection, ignition timing, idle speed, fuel pump operation and the EGR function **(see illustrations)**.

The crank angle sensor has a rotor plate and a wave forming circuit. The assembly consists of a rotor plate with 360 slits representing 1-degree signals (engine speed signal) and six slits for 120-degree signals (crank angle signal). Light emitting diodes (LED) and photo diodes are built into the wave forming circuit.

In operation, the signal rotor plate passes through the space between the LED and photo diode and the slits in the signal rotor plate intermittantly cut off the light sent to the photo diode from the LED. This causes an alternating voltage and the voltage is converted into an on/off pulse by the wave forming circuit. The on/off signal is sent to the control unit for processing.

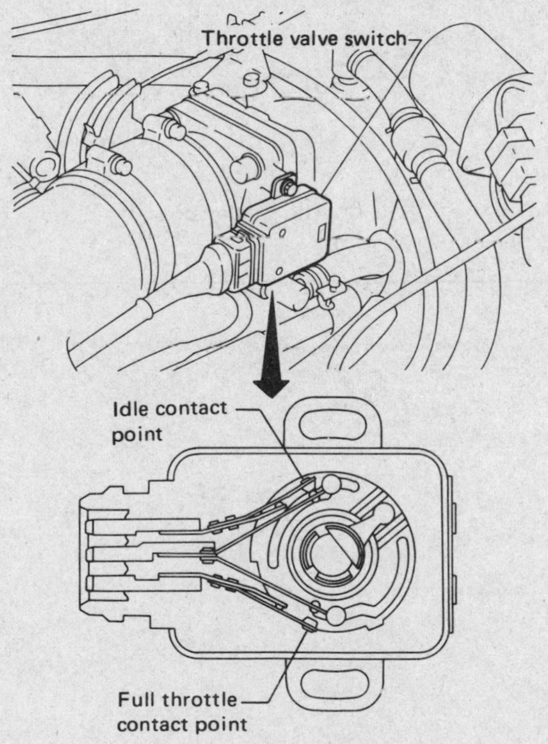

10.6 The throttle switch informs the control unit when the accelerator is at idle, and on electrically controlled automatic transmission equipped models it informs the control unit when the throttle is wide open

Air Flow meter

3 The air flow meter measures the mass flow rate of intake air. The control circuit emits an electrical output signal which varies in relation to the amount of heat dissipated from a hot wire placed in the stream of intake air **(see illustration)**.

Cylinder head temperature sensor

4 The cylinder head temperature sensor is located in the front cylinder head and monitors changes in the cylinder head temperature and transmits a signal to the ECCS control unit **(see illustration)**.

Exhaust gas sensor

5 Mounted in the exhaust manifold, the exhaust gas sensor monitors the quantity of oxygen in the exhaust gases **(see illustration)**.

Throttle valve switch

6 The throttle valve switch is attached to outside of the throttle chamber and actuates in response to accelerator pedal movement. The switch is equipped with two contacts, one for idle and the other for full throttle contact. The idle contact closes when the throttle valve is positioned at idle and opens when it is at any other position. The full throttle contact is used for electronically controlled automatic transmissions only **(see illustration)**.

Vehicle speed sensor

7 The vehicle speed sensor provides a vehicle speed signal to the ECCS control unit. Two types of speed sensors are employed, depending upon the type of speedometer installed. Needle type speedometer models utilize a reed switch, which is installed in the speedometer unit and transforms vehicle speed into a pulse signal which is sent to the control unit. The digital type speedometer consists of an LED, photo diode, shutter and wave forming circuit.

Fuel temperature sensor

8 The fuel temperature sensor is built into the pressure regulator and senses the fuel temperature. When the fuel temperature is higher than the specified level, the ECCS control unit enriches the mixture injected to compensate. The fuel temperature sensor should not be removed from the regulator. Always replace as an assembly **(see illustration)**.

Detonation sensor (1989 and later models)

9 Attached to the cylinder block, the detonation sensor is capable of sensing engine knock conditions. Any knocking vibration from the cylinder

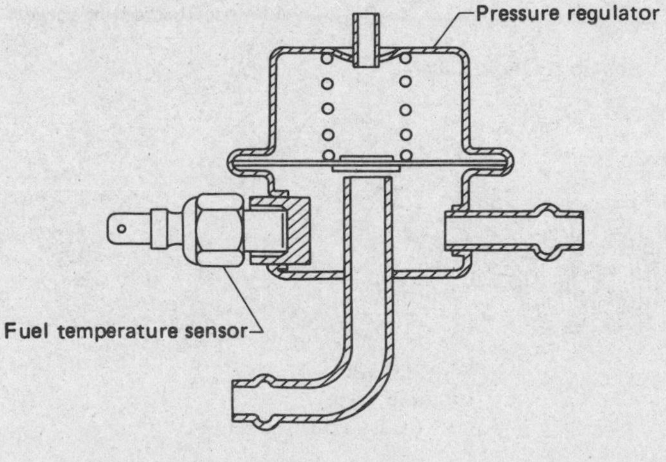

10.8 The fuel temperature sensor lets the ECCS control module know to enrich the mixture when the fuel temperature is too high

4

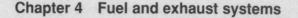

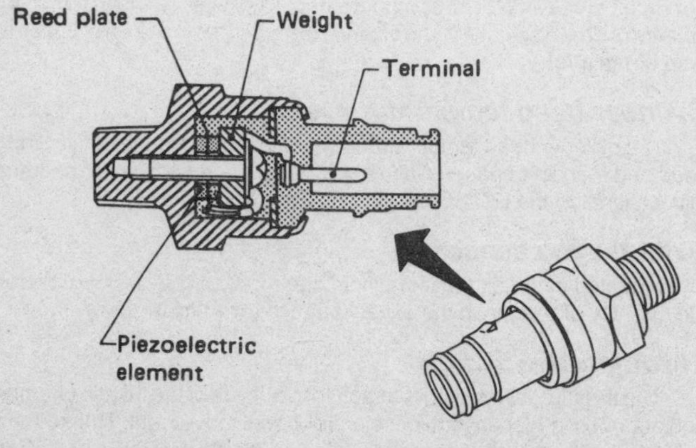

10.9 A detonation sensor is installed on the engine block of later models to sense engine knock conditions

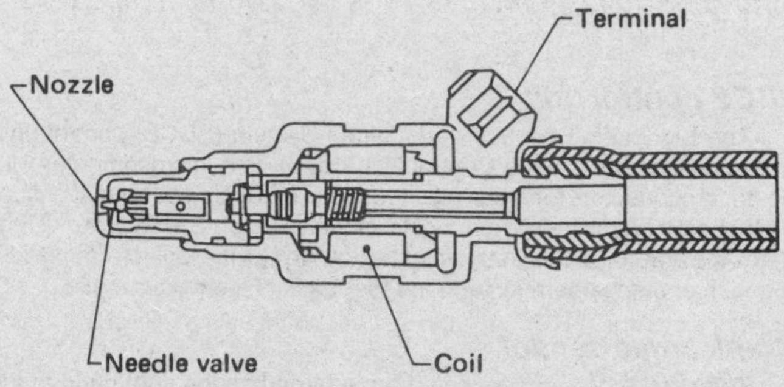

10.10 The fuel injector receives a signal from the control unit and the needle valve opens to inject fuel into the intake manifold – the amount of fuel injected is determined by the pulse duration

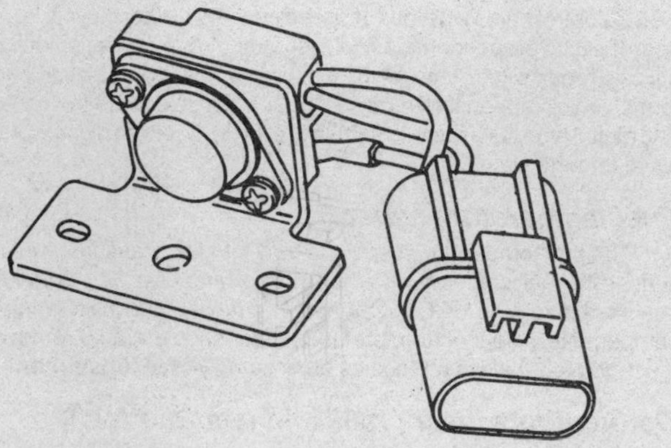

10.11 The ignition signal is amplified by the power transistor, which triggers the proper high voltage in the secondary circuit

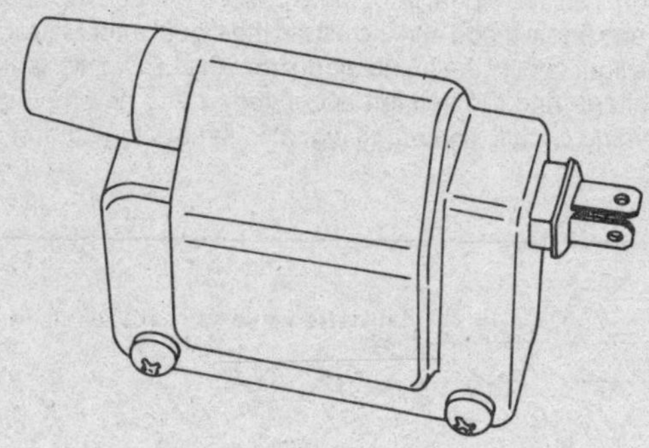

10.12 The ignition coil

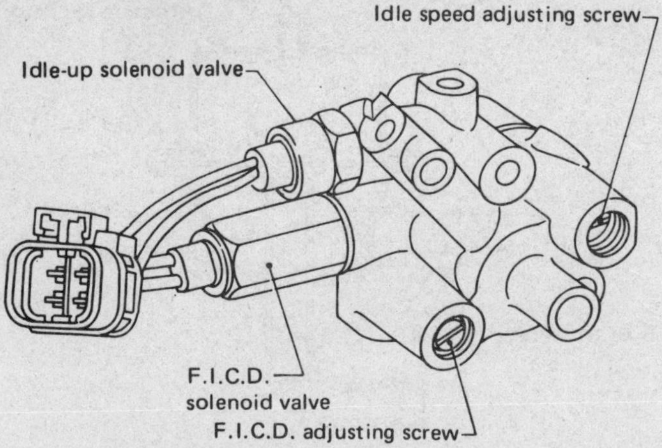

10.14 The idle-up solenoid acts to stabilize idle speed when engine load is heavy

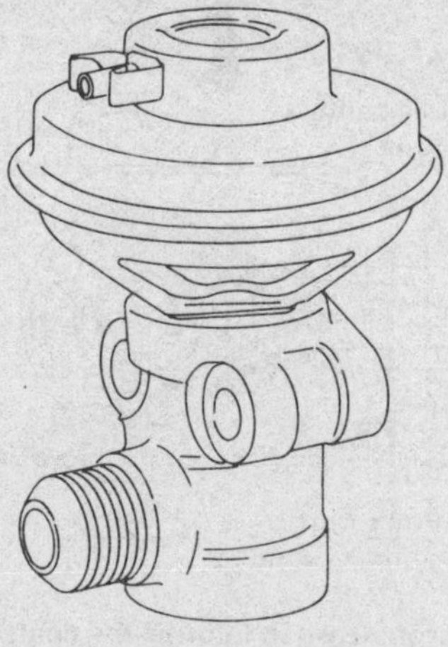

10.15 The EGR valve controls the amount of exhaust gas to be circulated into the intake manifold

block is applied as pressure to the piezoelectric element. This pressure is then converted into a voltage signal which is delivered as output to the control unit **(see illustration)**.

Fuel injector

10 The fuel injector supplies each cylinder with fuel. The injector is a small, precision solenoid valve. As the ECCS control unit outputs an injection signal to each fuel injector, the coil built into the injector pulls the needle valve back and fuel is sprayed through the nozzle into the intake manifold. The amount of fuel injected is controlled by the ECCS control unit by injection pulse duration **(see illustration)**.

Power transistor

11 The ignition signal from the ECCS control unit is amplified by the power transistor, which connects and disconnects the coil primary circuit to induce the proper high voltage in the secondary circuit **(see illustration)**.

Ignition coil

12 The molded type ignition coil provides spark for the combustion process **(see illustration)**.

Auxiliary air control (AAC) valve (1989 and later models)

13 The AAC valve is attached to the intake collector. The ECCS control unit actuates the AAC valve by an on/off pulse. The longer the on-duty signal is left on, the larger the amount of air that will be allowed to flow through the AAC valve.

Idle-up solenoid valve

14 The idle-up solenoid valve is attached to the intake collector. The solenoid is actuated to stabilize idle speed when the engine load is heavy from accessories such as the power steering pump, air conditioning compressor, high draw on the alternator, etc. **(see illustration)**.

EGR control valve

15 The EGR control valve controls the quantity of exhaust gas circulated to the intake manifold through movement of the taper valve connected to the diaphragm, to which vacuum is applied in response to the opening of the throttle valve. **Note:** *When installing the EGR guide tube, be careful of its direction. The outlet faces the rear of the engine. Otherwise the distribution efficiency of the exhaust gas will be reduced* **(see illustration)**.

EGR control solenoid valve

16 The EGR control solenoid valve cuts the intake manifold vacuum signal for EGR control. The solenoid valve actuates in response to the on/off signal from the ECCS control unit. When the solenoid is off, a vacuum signal from the intake manifold is fed into the EGR control valve. As the control unit outputs an on signal, then the coil pulls the plunger downward, and cuts the vacuum signal **(see illustration)**.

Fuel pump

17 The fuel pump, which is located in the fuel tank, is a wet type pump where the vane rollers are directly coupled to a motor which is filled with fuel **(see illustration)**.

Air regulator (1988 and earlier models)

18 The air regulator gives an air bypass when the engine is cold to allow fast idle during warm-up. A bimetal heater and rotary shutter are built into the air regulator. When the bimetal temperature is low, the air bypass post is open. As the engine starts and electric current flows through a heater, the bimetal begins to rotate the shutter to close off the bypass port. The air passage remains closed until the engine is stopped and the bimetal temperature drops **(see illustration)**.

Air injection valve (AIV)

19 The air injection valve sends secondary air to the exhaust manifold by means of a vacuum caused by exhaust pulsation in the exhaust manifold. When the exhaust pressure is below atmospheric pressure (vacuum), secondary air is sent to the exhaust manifold. When the exhaust pressure

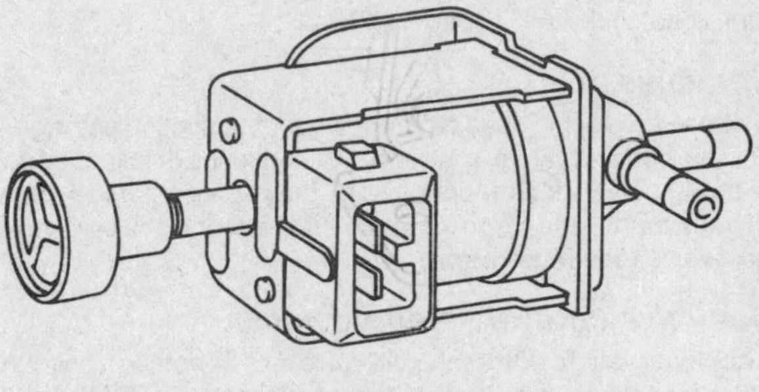

10.16 The EGR control solenoid valve controls the vacuum to the EGR valve

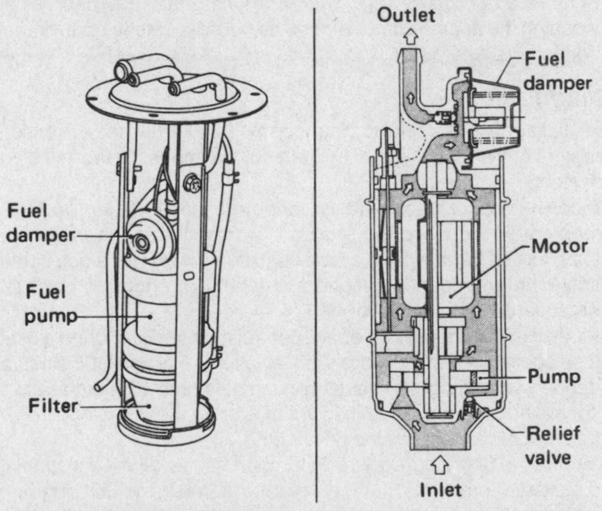

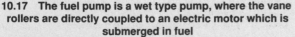

10.17 The fuel pump is a wet type pump, where the vane rollers are directly coupled to an electric motor which is submerged in fuel

10.18 The air regulator bypasses air around the throttle valve into the air intake collector when the engine is cold to provide fast idle during warm-up

4

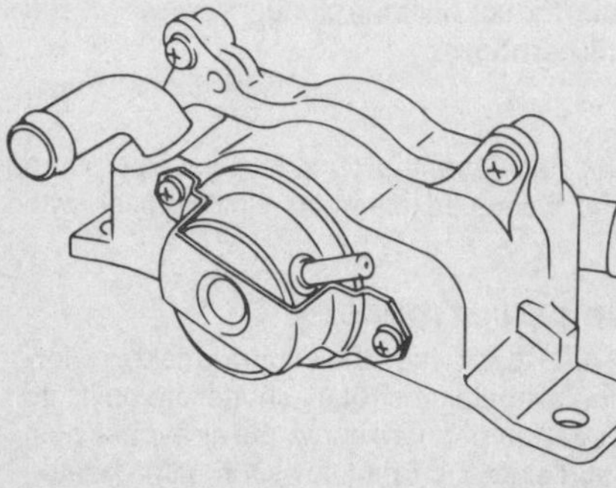

10.19 The air injection valve sends secondary air to the exhaust manifold

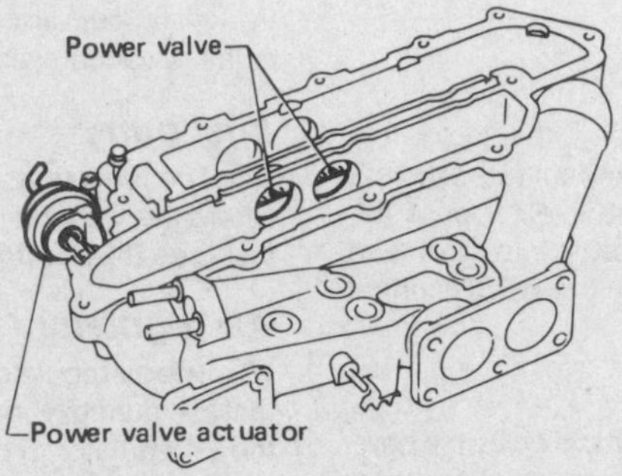

10.21 The power valve is used to regulate the vacuum through the suction passage

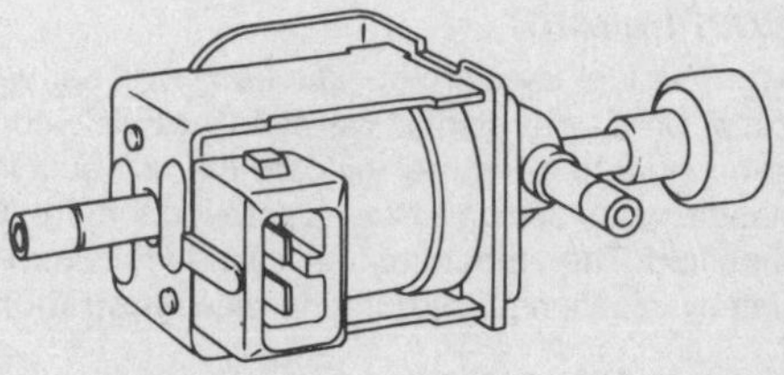

10.22 The power valve control solenoid valve regulates the intake manifold vacuum signal for power valve control

is above the atmospheric pressure the reed valve will prevent the secondary air from being sent back to the air cleaner **(see illustration)**.

AIV control solenoid valve

20 The AIV control solenoid valve controls an intake manifold vacuum signal for the AIV control. The solenoid valve actuates in response to the on/off signal from the ECCS control unit. When the solenoid is Off the vacuum signal from the intake manifold is cut. As this happens the control unit outputs an On signal and the coil pulls the plunger downward, feeding the vacuum signal to the AIV control valve.

Power valve

21 The power valve is used to change over the suction passage of the power valve control system. It is set in the fully closed or fully open position by the power valve actuator operated by the vacuum stored in the surge tank. The vacuum in the surge tank is controlled by the power valve control solenoid valve **(see illustration)**.

Power valve control solenoid valve

22 The power valve control solenoid valve cuts the intake manifold vacuum signal for power valve control. It responds to the ON/OFF signal from the ECU. When the solenoid is cut off, the vacuum signal from the intake manifold is cut. When the ECU sends an ON signal, the coil pull the plunger downward and feeds the vacuum signal to the power valve actuator.

11 Electronic Fuel injection (EFI) system – general diagnosis

General information

The Electronic Concentrated Control System (ECCS) controls the fuel injection system, the spark advance system, the self diagnosis system, the cooling fans, etc. by means of the Engine Control Unit (ECU).

The ECU receives signals from various sensors which monitor changing engine operations such as intake air volume, intake air temperature, coolant temperature, engine RPM, acceleration/deceleration, exhaust temperature, etc. These signals are utilized by the ECU to determine the correct injection duration and ignition timing.

The Sections in this Chapter include general descriptions and checking procedures, within the scope of the home mechanic and component replacement procedures (when possible). Before assuming the fuel and ignition systems are malfunctioning check the emission control system thoroughly (see Chapter 6). The emission system and the fuel system are closely interrelated but can be checked separately. The diagnosis of some of the fuel and emission control devices requires specialized tools, equipment and training. If checking and servicing become too difficult or if a procedure is beyond your ability, consult a dealer service department. Remember, the most frequent cause of fuel and emissions problems is simply a loose or broken vacuum hose or wire, so always check the hose and wiring connections first.

Note: *Because of federally mandated extended warranty which covers the emission control system components (and any other components which have a primary purpose other than emission control but have significant effects on emissions), check with your dealer about warranty coverage before working on any emission related systems. Once the warranty has expired, you may wish to perform some of the component checks and/or replacement procedures in this Chapter to save you money.*

Precautions

a) Always disconnect the power by either turning off the ignition switch or disconnecting the battery terminals before disconnecting EFI wiring connectors.
b) When installing a battery, be particularly careful to avoid reversing the positive and negative cables.
c) Do not subject EFI or emission related components or the ECCS to severe impact during removal or installation.
d) Do not be careless during troubleshooting. Even slight terminal contact can invalidate a testing procedure and even damage one of the numerous transistor circuits.
e) Never attempt to work on the ECU or open the ECU cover. The ECU is protected by a government mandated extended warranty that will be nullified if you tamper with it.
f) If you are inspecting electronic control system components during rainy weather, make sure water does not enter any part. When washing the engine compartment, do not spray these parts or their connectors with water.

Self diagnosis

The self diagnosis is useful to diagnose malfunctions in major sensors and actuators of the ECCS system. There are five modes in the self diagnoses system.

1 Mode I – Mixture ratio feedback control monitor A – During a closed loop condition (when the engine is warm), the green inspection lamp turns ON indicating a lean condition or OFF for a rich condition. During a open loop condition (when the engine is cold) the green lamp remains ON or OFF.

2 Mode II – Mixture ratio feedback control monitor B – During closed loop operation, the red inspection lamp turns ON and OFF simultaneously with the green inspection lamp when the mixture ratio is controlled within the specified value. During the open loop condition, the red lamp remains ON or OFF.

3 Mode III – Self diagnosis – This mode stores all malfunctioning diagnostic items in its memory. It will be stored in the ECU memory until the starter is operated fifty times, or until the power supply to the ECU is interrupted.

4 Mode IV – Switches ON/OFF diagnosis – During this mode, the inspection lamp monitors the idle switch portion of the throttle valve

switch, the starter switch, vehicle speed sensor and other switches with an ON/OFF condition.

5 Mode V – Real time diagnosis – The moment the malfunction is detected, the display will be presented. This is the mode in which the malfunction can be observed during a road test, as it occurs.

Switching modes

Refer to illustration 11.5

Turn the ignition switch to the On position. Turn the diagnostic mode selector on the ECU fully clockwise **(see illustration)** and wait until the inspection lamps flash. Count the number of flashes to find which mode you are in, then turn the diagnostic mode selector fully counterclockwise.

When the ignition switch is turned off during diagnosis, in each mode, and then turned on again after the power to the ECU has dropped off completely, the diagnosis will automatically return to Mode I.

The check engine light on the instrument panel (California models only) comes on when the ignition switch is turned on or in Mode I when the emission system malfunctions (with the engine running).

Malfunctions related to fuel and emission control systems can be diagnosed using the self diagnostic codes of Mode III.

To start the diagnostic procedure, remove the ECU from under the passenger seat (1985 through 1988 models) or under the dash (1989 models). Refer to Chapter 1, Section 28 for location of the ECU. Start the engine and warm it up to normal operating temperature. Turn the diagnostic mode selector on the ECU fully clockwise **(see illustration 11.5)**. After the inspection lamps have flashed 3 times, turn the diagnostic mode selector fully counterclockwise. The ECU is now in Mode III. Check the trouble code chart for the particular malfunction.

After the tests have been performed and the repairs completed, erase the memory by turning the diagnostic mode selector on the ECU fully clockwise. After the inspection lamps have flashed 4 times, turn the mode selector fully counterclockwise. This will erase any signals the ECU has stored concerning a particular component.

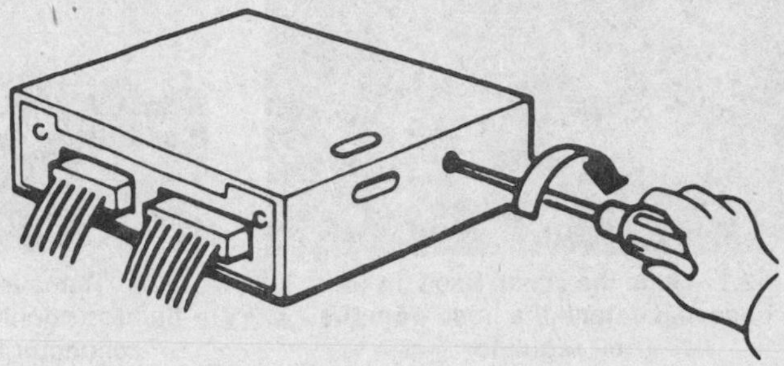

11.5 Turn the mode selector fully clockwise to begin the diagnostic procedure

Trouble codes	Circuit or system	Probable cause
Code 11 (1 red flash, 1 green flash)	Crank angle sensor/circuit	Refer to Chapter 5 for the crank angle sensor check and replacement procedure.
Code 12 (1 red flash, 2 green flashes)	Air flow meter/circuit	The air flow meter source or ground circuit(s) may be shorted or open. Check the air flow meter (Section 22).
Code 13 (1 red flash, 3 green flashes)	Cylinder head temperature sensor	The sensor source or ground circuit(s) may be shorted or open. Check the temperature sensor/circuit(s) (Section 14).
Code 14 (1 red flash, 4 green flashes)	Vehicle speed sensor	The vehicle speed sensor signal circuit is open. This repair must be performed by a dealer service department.
Code 21 (2 red flashes, 1 greeen flash)	Ignition signal	The ignition signal in the primary circuit is not entered during engine cranking or running. This repair must be performed by a dealer service department.
Code 22 (2 red flashes, 2 green flashes)	Fuel pump circuit	The fuel circuit is open or shorted (see section 5).
Code 23 (2 red flashes, 3 green flashes)	Throttle valve switch circuit	The throttle valve switch signal circuit is open (see Section 18).
Code 31 (3 red flashes, 1 green flash)	ECU control unit	The ECU input signal is beyond "normal" range. This repair must be performed by a dealer service department.
Code 32 (3 red flashes, 2 green flashes) (1989 California models only)	EGR Function	The EGR control valve does not operate (see Chapter 6).
Code 33 (3 red flashes, 3 green flashes)	Exhaust gas sensor	The exhaust gas sensor circuit is open (see Section 15).
Code 34 (3 red flashes, 4 green flashes) (1989 Models)	Detonation sensor	The detonation sensor circuit is open or shorted. This repair must be performed by a dealer service department.
Code 41 (4 red flashes, 1 green flashes) (1987 and earlier models – 1988 models)	Fuel temperature sensor	The fuel temperature sensor circuit is open or shorted (see Section 16).
Code 42 (4 red flashes, 2 green flashes) (1988 models)	Fuel temperature sensor	The fuel temperature sensor circuit is open or shorted (see Section 16).
Code 43 (4 red flashes, 3 green flashes) (1989 Models)	Throttle sensor	The throttle sensor circuit is open or shorted. This repair must be performed by a dealer service department.
Code 45 (4 red flashes, 5 green flashes) (1989 California models only)	Injector leak	The injector(s) have fuel leaks (see Section 17)
Code 54 (5 red flashes, 4 green flashes) (1989 Models)	A/T Control Unit	There is a short between the A/T Control unit and the ECU. This repair must be performed by a dealer service department.
Code 55 (5 red flashes, 5 green flashes)	ECCS	Normal operation

4

12.1 **Slide the clamp back on the hose and detach the hose from the air regulator**

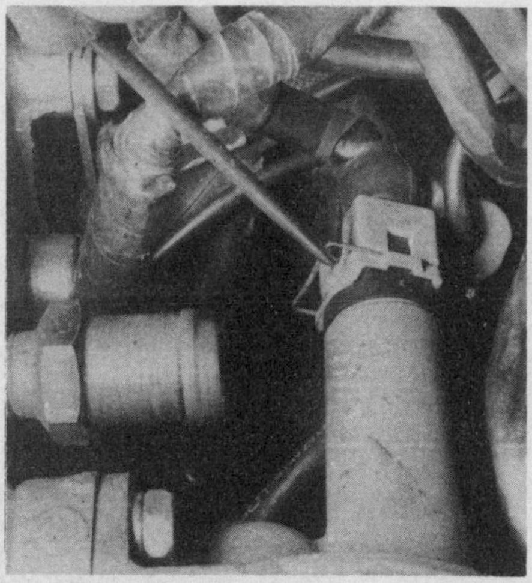

12.2 **Remove the clip that retains the harness connector and disconnect the connector from the air regulator**

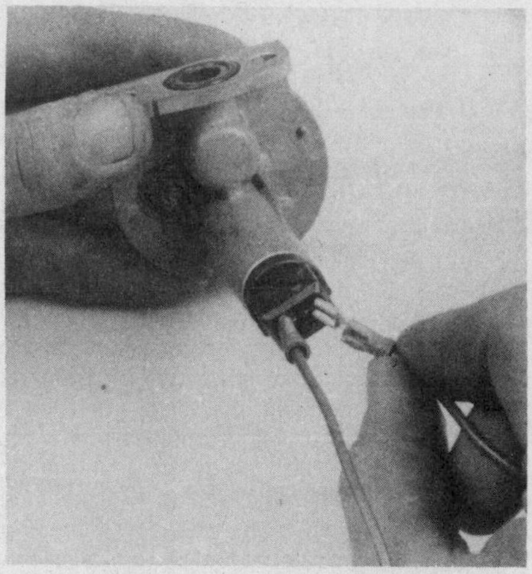

12.6 **Use jumper wires to apply battery voltage to the air regulator (install a fuse in one of the jumper wires to avoid damage to the air regulator in the event the jumper wires contact each other at the terminals)**

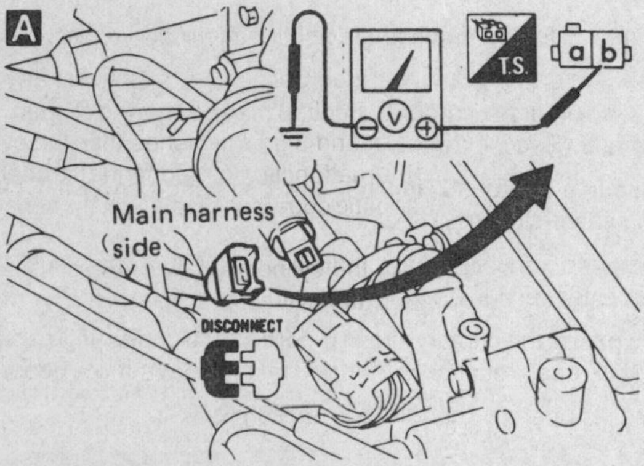

12.10 **Attach the voltmeter positive lead to terminal B (black wire with the white stripe) and ground the voltmeter negative lead**

12 Air regulator (1988 and earlier models) – removal, check and installation

Refer to illustrations 12.1, 12.2, 12.6 and 12.10

Removal

1 Detach the hose from the end of the air regulator **(see illustration)**.
2 Disconnect the electrical connector from the air regulator **(see illustration)**.
3 Remove the two bolts and detach the air regulator from the air intake collector.

Check

4 Due to the complexity of the air regulator control system, the home mechanic is limited to a visual inspection of the valve's operation and resistance and voltage checks, which can be done with a multimeter. If voltage is available to the air regulator and the resistance is correct, but the valve doesn't close as the regulator warms up, take the vehicle to a dealer service department for diagnosis.

5 Look into the end of the regulator and note the position of the shutter. At a temperature of about 65 to 70-degrees F, the shutter should be covering about one-half of the port. At cooler temperatures, the opening will be larger.
6 Use jumper wires to apply battery voltage directly to the air regulator terminals **(see illustration)**. **Caution:** *One of the jumper wires should have an in-line fuse to avoid damage if the wires contact each other at the terminals.*
7 As the air regulator begins to heat up from the applied voltage, the shutter should close off the port (this should occur within five minutes). If it does, the air regulator is functioning correctly – proceed to Step 10.
8 If the shutter takes a very long time to close off the port, or if it doesn't close smoothly, use an ohmmeter to check the resistance of the air regulator by hooking the meter leads to the terminals. The correct resistance is listed in this Chapter's Specifications.
9 If the resistance is incorrect, replace the air regulator.
10 To check for power to the air regulator, attach a voltmeter positive lead to terminal B (black wire with white stripe) in the harness side of the connector and ground the voltmeter negative lead **(see illustration)**.
11 Turn the ignition switch on. The meter should indicate 12-volts (after 5-seconds the voltage will drop to zero). If 12-volts isn't indicated, the wire harness may have an open or short somewhere (such as a disconnected or broken wire). Refer to the wiring diagrams in Chapter 12 and trace the circuit for the problem.
12 Even if voltage is present at terminal B, the air regulator won't operate unless it is grounded through the ECU. If the regulator is good and there is power to it, check the ground wire from the regulator to the ECU for an open or short.

Installation

13 Installation is the reverse of removal, but be sure to use a new O-ring where the air regulator mates to the air intake collector.

13 Fuel pressure regulator and control solenoid – check, removal and installation

Warning: *Gasoline is extremely flammable, so extra precautions must be taken when working on any part of the fuel system. Do not smoke or allow open flames or bare light bulbs near the work area. Also, do not work in a garage if a natural gas type appliance with a pilot light is present.*

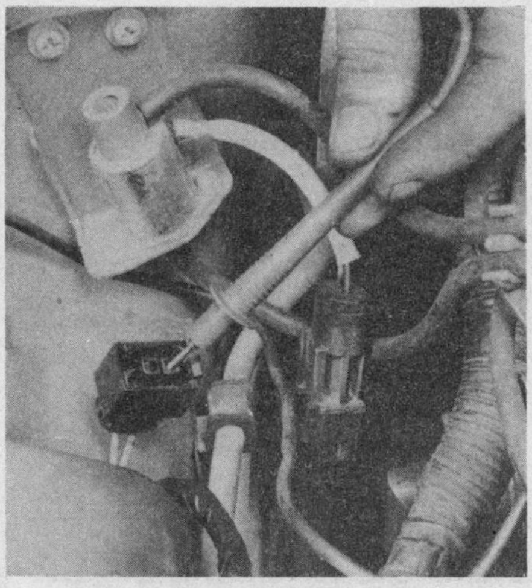

13.3 Check voltage between terminal A (green wire with a black stripe) and ground of the fuel pressure regulator control solenoid

13.11 Loosen the clamps and remove the two top fuel hoses attached to the fuel pressure regulator (arrows)

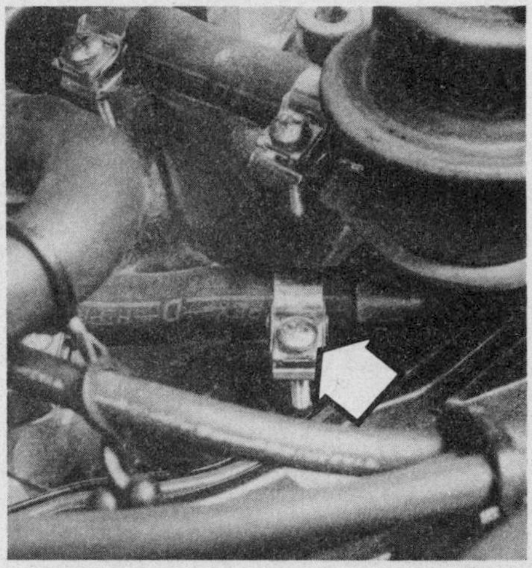

13.13 Disconnect the return line under the fuel pressure regulator

Check

Refer to illustration 13.3

1 The fuel pressure regulator control solenoid cuts the vacuum signal to the pressure regulator during hot start conditions, which will increase the fuel pressure to improve starting during these conditions.

2 If the fuel pressure regulator functions properly when a vacuum pump is connected to it (as described in Section 5) but doesn't work properly when the vacuum control line is connected, check the pressure regulator control solenoid as follows.

3 The fuel pressure regulator control solenoid is located on the right-side inner fenderwell **(see illustration)**. If equipped, remove the cruise control unit for access to the solenoid. Check the power source by disconnecting the electrical connector from the solenoid and turning the ignition switch to the On position. Check the voltage between terminal A (green wire with a black stripe) and ground **(see illustration 13.3)**. The voltmeter should read battery voltage.

4 Disconnect the fuel pressure regulator vacuum line and blow into it – air should pass through the valve when it is not energized.

5 If the fuel pressure control solenoid fails any of these tests, replace it.

Removal and installation

Fuel pressure regulator control solenoid

6 Unbolt the cruise control unit from the inner fender panel for access to the solenoid.

7 Disconnect the vacuum hoses, unplug the electrical connector and unbolt the solenoid from the inner fender panel.

8 Installation is the reverse of the removal procedure.

Fuel pressure regulator

Refer to illustrations 13.11 and 13.13

9 Relieve the fuel system pressure (see Section 4).

10 Disconnect the negative cable at the battery.

11 Loosen the hose clamps and detach the two fuel hoses from the regulator **(see illustration)**. If there is any doubt as to which fittings the hoses are to be connected, mark them with pieces of tape.

12 Disconnect the vacuum line and fuel temperature sensor electrical connector.

13 Loosen the hose clamp and disconnect the fuel return line from the underside of the regulator **(see illustration)**.

14 Remove the two bolts and detach the regulator.

15 Installation is the reverse of the removal procedures. **Note:** *Wet the inside of the fuel hoses with gasoline to facilitate installation.*

14 Cylinder head temperature sensor – check and replacement

Refer to illustrations 14.5 and 14.6

1 Use the self diagnosis mode (see Section 11) to pinpoint any problems in the vehicle's fuel system.

2 If the ECU flashes 1 red flash and 3 green flashes then the cylinder head temperature sensor circuit is malfunctioning. Continue the checks as described below. If the self diagnostic code isn't displayed, the sensor/circuit is functioning properly.

3 Depending on the symptom, the cylinder head temperature sensor and its related circuit have several items that must be checked in order to pinpoint the exact problem.

4 If the engine is impossible to start and there is a sound of partial combustion, disconnect the sensor electrical connector and crank the engine over. If the engine still does not start, check the resistance of the sensor.

5 Remove the cylinder head temperature sensor for testing **(see illustration)**. Refer to the timing belt removal and installation procedure in Chapter 2A for access to the temperature sensor.

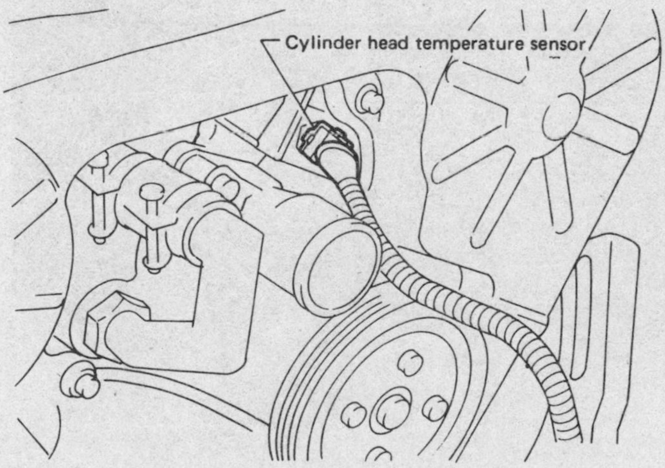

14.5 The cylinder head temperature sensor is located on the cylinder head near the thermostat housing

4

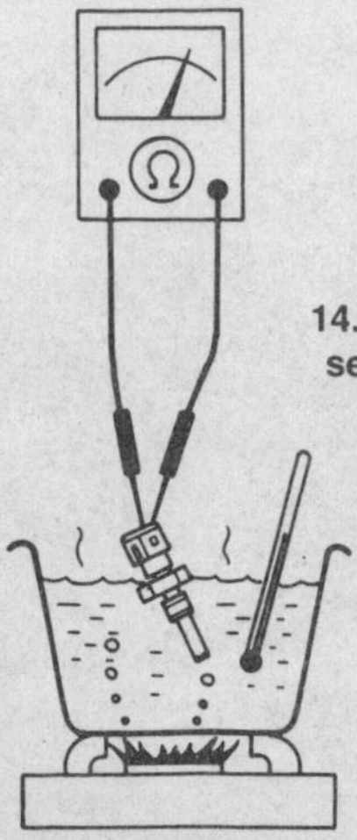

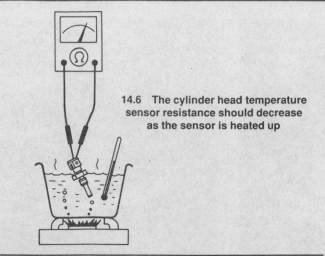

14.6 The cylinder head temperature sensor resistance should decrease as the sensor is heated up

6 Remove the sensor and place it in a pan of lukewarm water. Use a thermometer to monitor the temperature of the water. Use an ohmmeter to check the resistance value of the sensor **(see illustration)**.
7 Place the pan on a heat source (hot plate, stove etc.) and raise the temperature of the water. Carefully monitor the resistance values as the water temperature increases. If the values are not as listed in this Chapter's Specifications, replace the sensor.
8 If the resistance values are acceptable, check the continuity of the cylinder head temperature sensor circuit with an ohmmeter.
9 Installation is the reverse of removal

15 Exhaust gas sensor – check

Refer to illustrations 15.7 and 15.8

1 Use the self diagnosis mode (see Section 11) to pinpoint any problems in the vehicle's fuel system.
2 If the ECU flashes 3 red flashes and 3 green flashes then the exhaust gas sensor circuit is malfunctioning. Continue the check as described below. If the self-diagnostic code isn't displayed, the sensor/circuit is functioning properly.
3 Depending on the symptom, the exhaust gas sensor and its related circuit have several items that must be checked in order to pinpoint the exact problem.

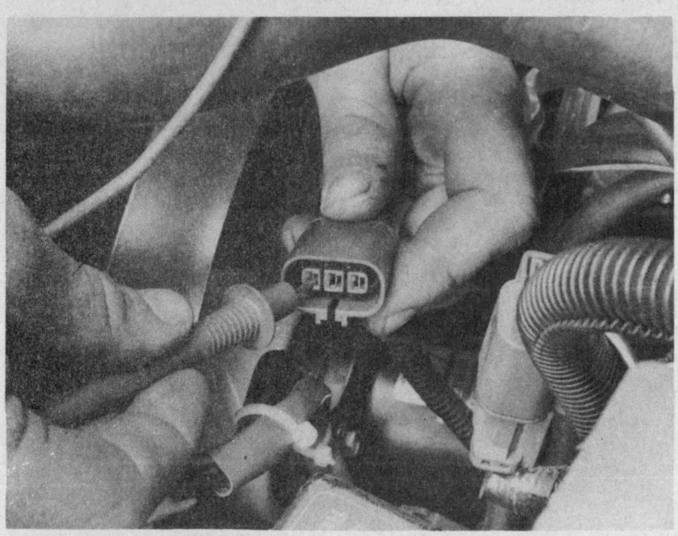

15.7 Turn the ignition switch to the On position and check the voltage between terminal C (black wire with a white stripe) and ground

4 If the vehicle drives poorly and surges while cruising, disconnect the exhaust gas sensor electrical connector (see Chapter 1) and drive the vehicle.
5 If the vehicle's driveability improves, replace the sensor.
6 If there is no improvement, check the power source at the sensor harness connector with it connected.
7 Turn the ignition switch to the On position and check the voltage between terminal C (black wire with a white stripe) and ground **(see illustration)**. The voltmeter should read battery voltage.
8 If the voltage is acceptable, check the exhaust gas sensor heater. Remove the exhaust gas sensor (see Chapter 1, Section 28) and connect an ohmmeter to the two outer leads of the exhaust gas sensor heater **(see illustration)**. The resistance should be as listed in this Chapter's Specifications.
9 If the test results are incorrect, replace the exhaust gas sensor.

16 Fuel temperature sensor – check and replacement

Refer to illustration 16.5

Check

1 Use the self diagnosis mode (see Section 11) to pinpoint any problems in the vehicle's fuel system.
2 If the ECU flashes 4 red flashes and 2 green flashes (1988 models) or 4 red flashes and 1 green flash (1985 through 1987 models) then the fuel temperature sensor circuit is malfunctioning. Continue the check as described below. If the self-diagnostic code isn't displayed, the sensor/circuit is functioning properly.
3 Depending on the symptom, the fuel temperature sensor and its related circuit have several items that must be checked in order to pinpoint the exact problem.
4 If the vehicle is hard to start after warm up, check the fuel temperature sensor resistance.
5 Disconnect the fuel temperature sensor harness connector (the sensor is located on the fuel pressure regulator – see Section 13) and check the resistance between the terminal and ground. The resistance should decrease as the fuel warms up **(see illustration)**. If the resistance values are not as listed in this Chapter's Specifications, replace the sensor.
6 If the sensor tests are correct, check the continuity of the fuel temperature sensor circuit.

Replacement

7 Remove the fuel pressure regulator (see Section 13) and replace the fuel temperature sensor and fuel pressure regulator as a unit.

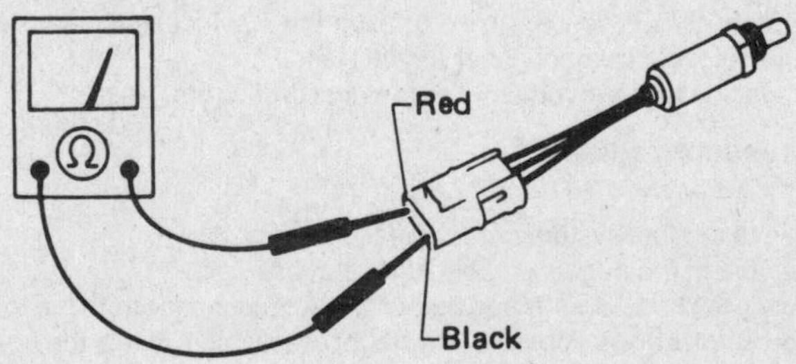

15.8 Use an ohmmeter to measure the resistance of the exhaust gas sensor heater

17 Fuel injectors – check, removal and installation

Warning: *Gasoline is extremely flammable, so extra precautions must be taken when working on any part of the fuel system. Do not smoke or allow open flames or bare light bulbs near the work area. Also, do not work in a garage if a natural gas type appliance with a pilot light is present.*

On-vehicle check

Refer to illustration 17.2

1 With the engine running, or cranking, listen to the sound from each injector with an automotive stethoscope and verify that the injectors sound as if they are operating normally. If you don't have a stethoscope, touch each injector with your finger and, with the engine running, or cranking, try to determine whether the injector feels like it's operating smoothly. What is a "normal" sound or feel for an injector? It should sound/feel smooth and uniform and its sound/feel should rise and fall with engine rpm. If no sound/feel, or an unusual sound/feel, is noted, inspect the wiring connector, the injector resistance, the signal from the computer and the injector itself.

2 To measure the injector resistance, unplug the wiring connector from the injector and, using an ohmmeter, measure the resistance between the two injector terminals **(see illustration)**. Refer to this Chapter's Specifications.

a) If the resistance is within the specified range, but the injector is malfunctioning, remove the injector and have it bench tested by a dealer service department.
b) If the resistance is not within the specified range, replace the injector.

Removal

Refer to illustrations 17.6, 17.7 and 17.12

3 Relieve the fuel pressure (see Section 4).
4 Disconnect the negative cable at the battery.
5 Remove the upper air inlet tube (see Section 2).
6 On the front of the intake air collector, carefully mark all lines and hoses and remove the throttle cable, throttle valve cable (to the transmission), throttle cable brackets and all other vacuum lines and electrical connectors **(see illustration)**.
7 On the rear of the intake air collector, carefully mark all the lines and hoses and disconnect the EGR line, air regulator and all other vacuum lines and electrical connectors **(see illustration)**.

16.5 Connect one lead of the ohmmeter to the fuel temperature sensor and the other lead to ground to check the resistance of the sensor

17.2 Using an ohmmeter, measure the resistance between the two injector terminals

17.6 On the front of the intake air collector, remove the throttle cable (1) throttle valve cable (2), throttle cable brackets (3) and all miscellaneous vacuum lines and electrical connections

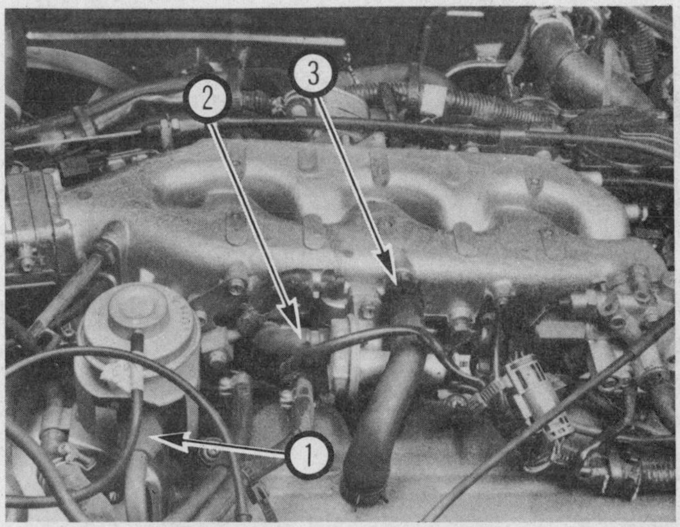

17.7 On the rear of the intake air collector, disconnect the EGR line (1), air regulator (2) PCV vacuum line (3) and all other vacuum lines and electrical connectors

17.12 After removing the fuel lines and injector retaining bolts the injectors will come off as an assembly

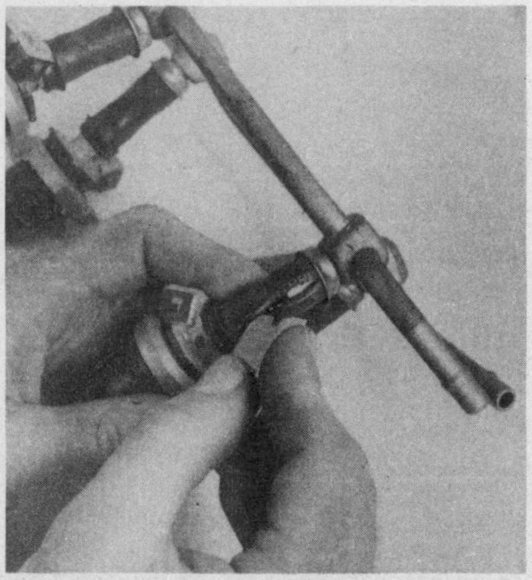

17.13 To replace an injector, carefully cut through the hose

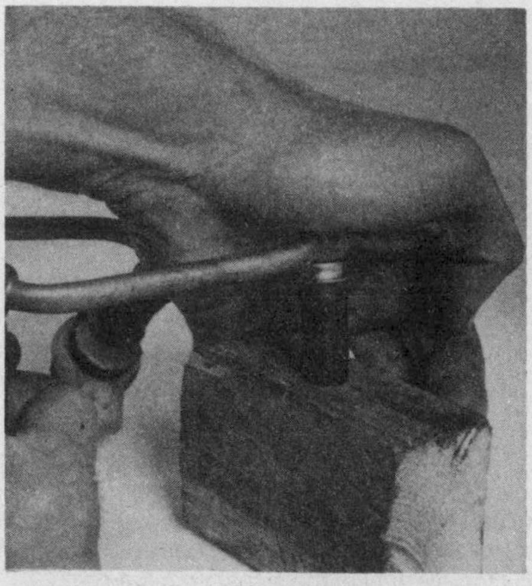

17.14a Be sure the hose seats against the umbrella

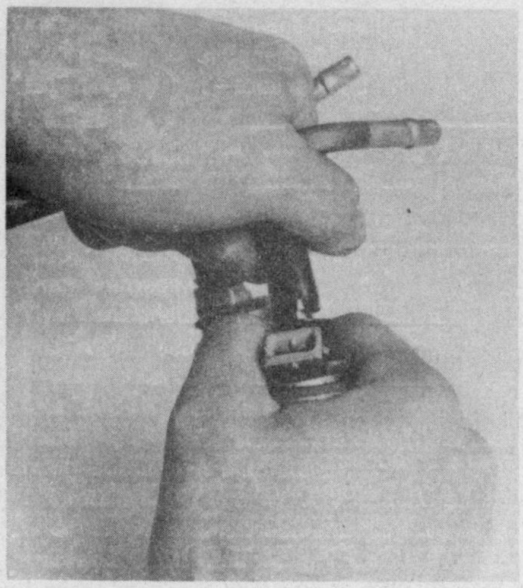

17.14b Even with the hose wet it will take considerable force to seat the injector

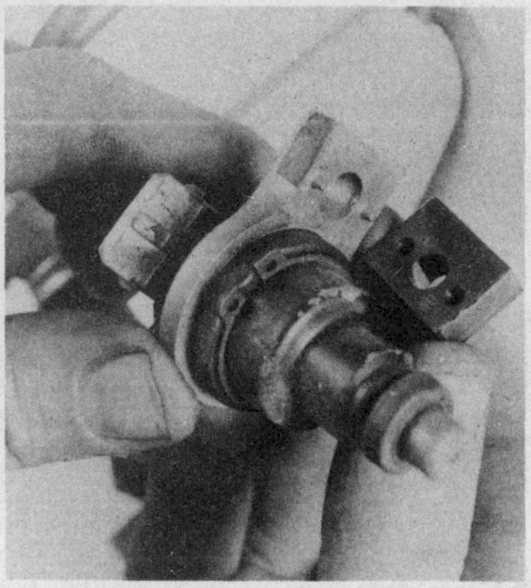

17.16a Make sure the flat spacer is installed properly

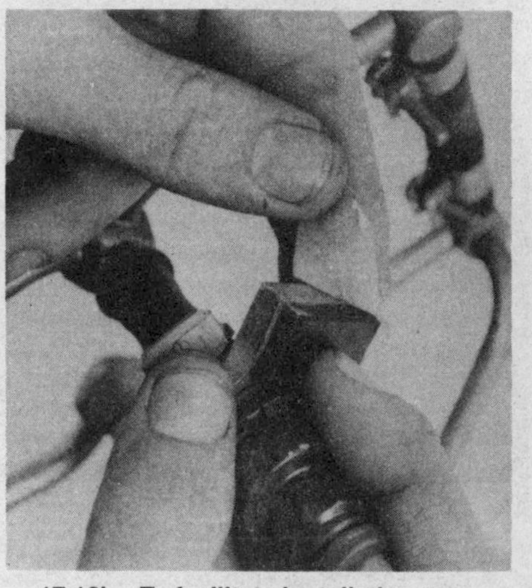

17.16b To facilitate installation, tape the spacer to each injector

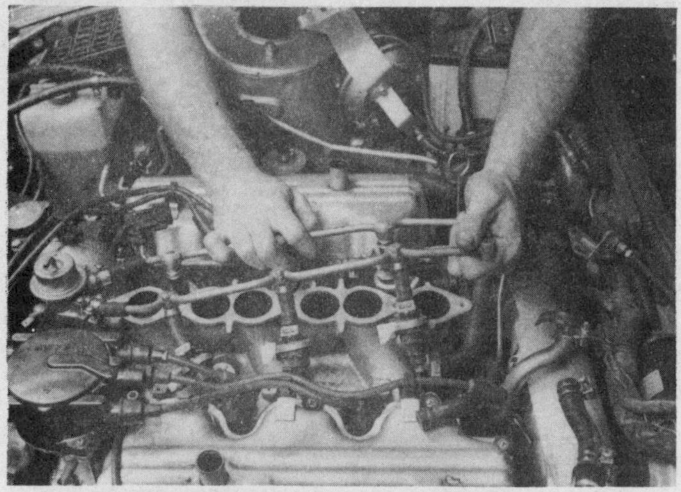

17.16c After lubricating the fuel hoses with gas, lower the fuel rail and injector assembly into place, carefully guiding the injectors into their bores

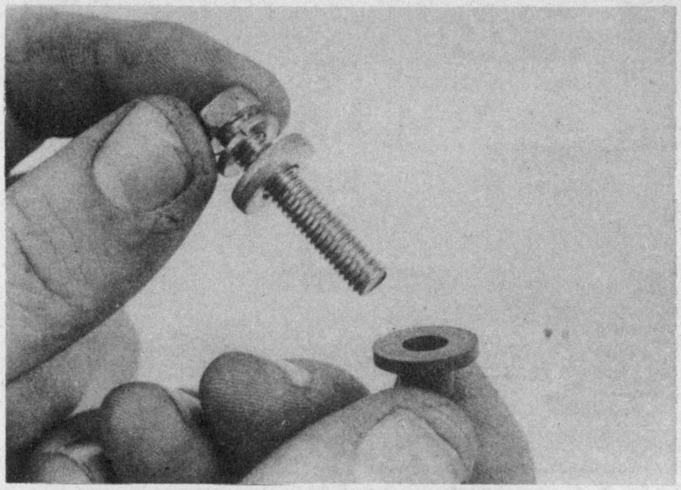

17.17 Proper bolt and washer/spacer installation sequence

8 Drain the coolant (see Chapter 1).
9 Remove the top part of the intake collector with the throttle chamber attached and cover the intake ports with a rag.
10 Disconnect the spark plug wires at the plugs, remove the distributor cap and move the wire assembly out of the work area.
11 Disconnect the fuel rails at the fuel regulator and fuel inlet tubes by loosening the hose clamps and pulling the hoses from the tubing. **Note:** *When disconnecting the fuel lines place a rag around the connection to catch any leaking fuel.*
12 Remove each of the injector retaining bolts and lift off the injector assembly **(see illustration)**.

Injector replacement

Refer to illustrations 17.13, 17.14a and 17.14b

13 If any of the individual injectors are to be replaced, determine the injector to be replaced and carefully cut through the hose to free the injector from the rail assembly **(see illustration)**.
14 To install the new injector, wet the new hose with gasoline, place the umbrella on the fuel rail and press the rubber hose onto the fuel rail. Push the top of the injector onto the hose. Be sure the hose seats against the umbrella **(see illustrations)**.

Installation

Refer to illustrations 17.16a, 17.16b, 17.16c and 17.17

15 Install the fuel line hose clamps about 1/2-inch up the hose.
16 Lubricate the fuel line hoses with gas and attach them to the fuel rail. Position the flat spacers on each injector and tape them in place to facilitate installation **(see illustrations)**. Lower the assembly into place **(see illustration)**.
17 Install and tighten the hold-down bolt for each injector **(see illustration)**.
18 Working on the rear side of the engine, install the metal spring clips onto the injector electrical connector and slip the connector onto each of the injectors on the right side.
19 Clean all traces of old gasket material from the air intake collector and intake manifold. Install a new gasket and set the intake collector in place, routing the rear side wiring harness up on top of the collector.
20 Route the front side wiring harness along the collector.
21 Install the fuel injector electrical connectors onto the injectors on the left side and secure with the metal clips.
22 Install the Allen head bolts that secure the collector to the intake manifold. Tighten the bolts to the torque listed in this Chapter's Specifications.
23 Connect the EGR tube to the air intake collector.
24 Connect all electrical connectors and vacuum/fuel hoses that were disconnected during removal.
25 Connect all wiring harness hold-down straps to the collector.
26 Install the air regulator (see Section 12).
27 The remainder of installation is the reverse of removal.

18 Throttle valve switch – check

Refer to illustration 18.5

1 Use the self diagnosis mode (see Section 11) to pinpoint any problems in the vehicle's fuel system.
2 If the ECU flashes 2 red flashes and 3 green flashes, then the throttle valve switch circuit is malfunctioning. Continue the check as described below. If the self-diagnostic code isn't displayed, the sensor/circuit is functioning properly.
3 Depending on the symptom, the switch and its related circuit have several items that must be checked in order to pinpoint the exact problem.
4 If the vehicle drives poorly and stumbles on acceleration, check the continuity of the switch.
5 Disconnect the throttle valve switch harness connector and position the ohmmeter probes on the upper two terminals (1985, 1986, 1989 and later models). Make sure continuity exists when the throttle is fully closed **(see illustration)**. **Note:** *On 1987 and 1988 models, use the bottom two terminals.*
6 If there is no continuity, adjust the switch (see Section 19).
7 If the adjustment is satisfactory, check to make sure the harness connector is tight and making proper contact.
8 If adjusting the switch doesn't cure the problem and the electrical connector and wiring harness appear to be in good condition, take the vehicle to a dealer service department for further diagnosis.

19 Throttle valve switch – adjustment

Refer to illustration 19.3

1 Unplug both electrical connectors (only one on manual transmission equipped models) attached to the throttle valve switch.
2 With the throttle valve switch electrical connector disconnected, connect an ohmmeter to the terminals indicated in Section 18, Step 5.
3 Loosen the retaining bolts and rotate the throttle valve switch counterclockwise **(see illustration)**. The meter should show no continuity.

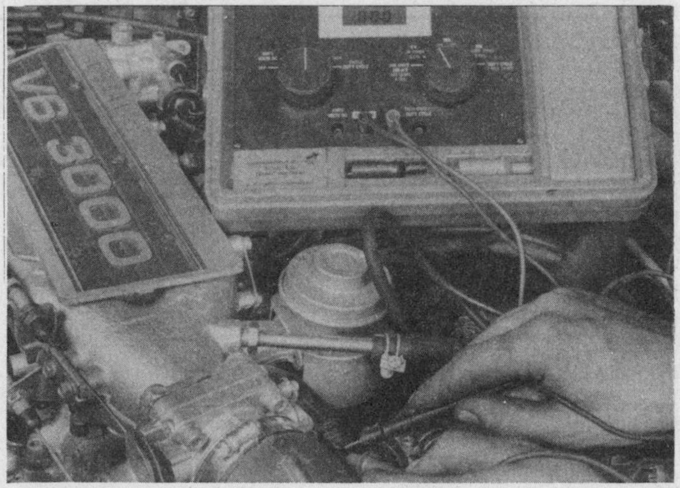

18.5 Place the ohmmeter probes on the upper two terminals of the throttle valve switch (1985, 1986,1989 and later models) and check for continuity when the throttle is fully closed

19.3 Locations of the throttle valve retaining bolts – to adjust the switch, loosen the bolts and rotate the switch

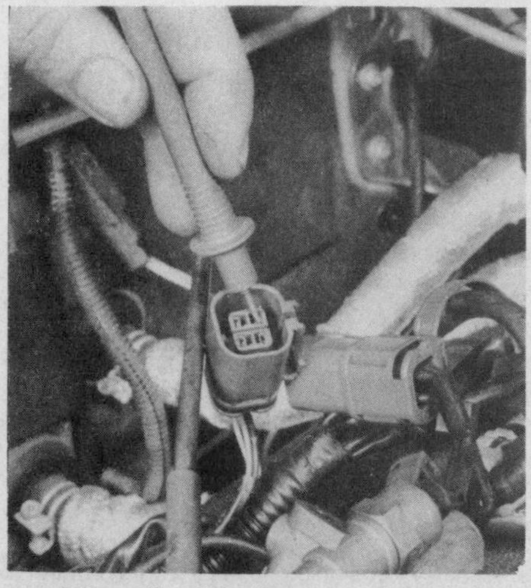

20.2 Check for battery voltage at terminal B on the idle-up control solenoid electrical connector

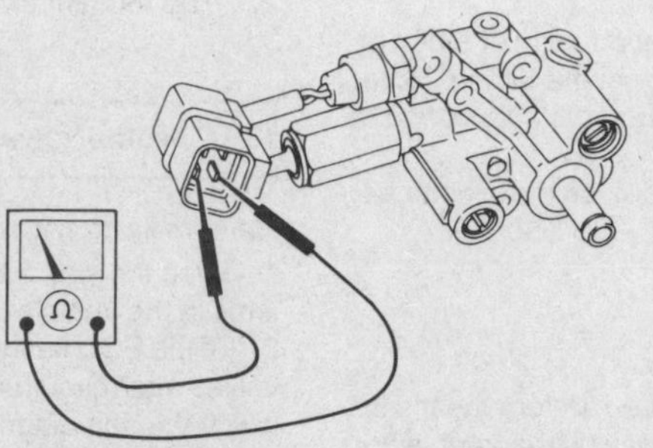

20.3 Check the idle-up solenoid – resistance should be as listed in this Chapter's Specifications

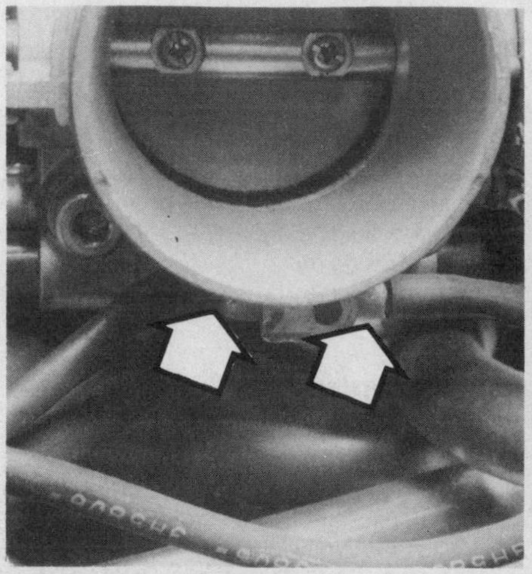

21.3 Disconnect the vacuum lines from both sides of the throttle chamber and mark them with paint or pieces of tape

21.5 Remove the four Allen head bolts that secure the throttle chamber to the air intake collector (arrows)

4 Slowly rotate the throttle valve switch clockwise until continuity is just indicated, then tighten the retaining bolts.
5 Reconnect the electrical connector.
6 If it is necessary to replace the switch, simply remove the two retaining bolts and lift it off. After installing the switch, adjust it using the above procedure.

20 Fast Idle Control Device (FICD) valve – check, removal and installation

Refer to illustrations 20.2 and 20.3

Check

1 Due to the complexity of the FICD and circuit, the home mechanic is limited to a few resistance and voltage checks. The idle-up solenoid (part of the FICD valve, which is mounted to the air intake collector), works in conjunction with the FICD to raise the idle speed of the engine for extra RPM during air conditioning activation or when using headlights, accessories, etc. If the engine continues to idle high without the use of the air conditioning system, check for a possible defective FICD valve.

2 Check the power source on the idle-up control solenoid. Turn the ignition switch On and check the voltage between terminal B and ground on the idle-up control solenoid electrical connector **(see illustration)**. The voltmeter should read battery voltage.
3 If the power source is acceptable, check the resistance of the solenoid valve **(see illustration)** and compare your reading with the resistance value listed in this Chapter's Specifications. If the resistance is as specified, have the vehicle checked by a dealer service department.

Removal and installation

4 Disconnect the negative cable at the battery.
5 To gain access to the FICD remove the upper air inlet tube (see Section 2).
6 Disconnect the electrical connector.
7 Remove the bolt attaching the wiring harness to the FICD valve.
8 Remove the three bolts retaining the FICD valve to the intake collector.
9 Clean off all traces of old gasket material from the mating surfaces.
10 Installation is the reverse of the removal procedure, but be sure to use a new gasket.

21 Throttle chamber – removal and installation

Refer to illustrations 21.3 and 21.5

Removal

1 Disconnect the throttle cable from the throttle lever **(see illustrations 3.1 and 3.2)**.
2 Disconnect the two electrical connectors from the throttle valve switch.
3 Disconnect the vacuum lines from each side of the throttle chamber **(see illustration)**.
4 Use a Phillips screwdriver to loosen the coolant hoses from each side of the throttle chamber. Detach the hoses from the throttle chamber.
5 Remove the four Allen head bolts and separate the throttle chamber from the intake collector **(see illustration)**.

Installation

6 Clean all traces of old gasket material from the air intake collector and throttle chamber mating surfaces.
7 Reverse the removal procedures for installation, but be sure to use a new gasket and tighten the bolts to the torque listed in this Chapter's Specifications.

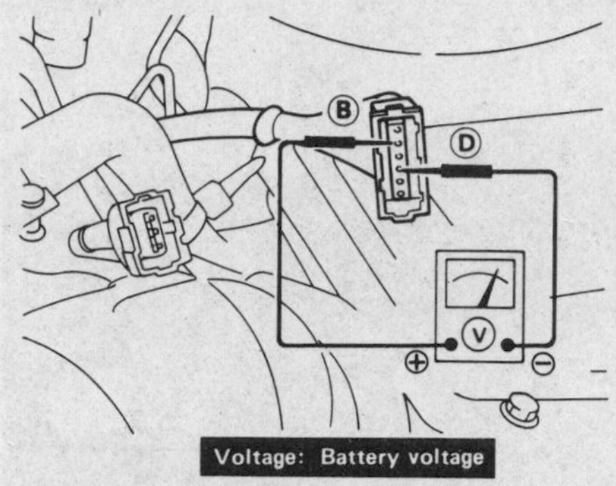

22.5 On 1985 and 1986 models, check for battery voltage at terminal B on the air flow sensor electrical connector

22.6 On 1987 and 1988 models, turn the ignition key to the On position and check for battery voltage at terminal E

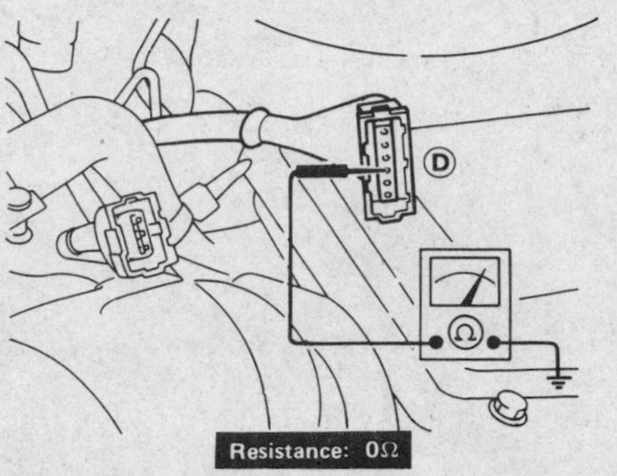

22.7 Check for ground circuit continuity at terminals C and D

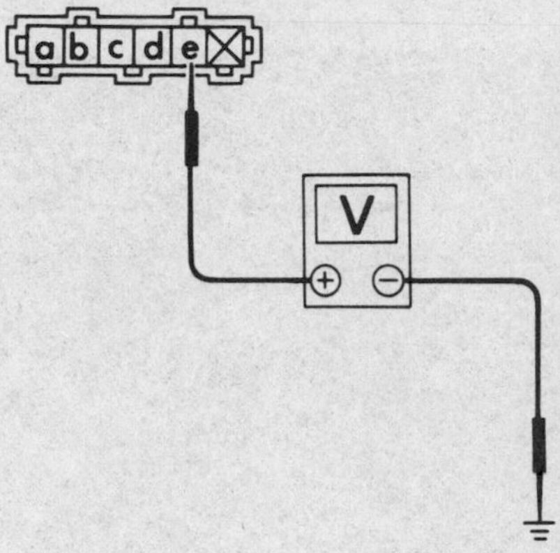

22.9 With the ignition switch in the On position, battery voltage should be present at terminal E of the air flow meter electrical connector (1989 models)

22.13 Remove the bolts that retain the air flow meter to the air cleaner assembly (arrows)

22 Air flow meter – check, removal and installation

Refer to illustrations 22.5, 22.6, 22.7, 22.9 and 22.13

Check

1 Use the self diagnosis mode (see Section 11) to pinpoint any problems in the vehicle's fuel system.

2 If the ECU flashes 1 red flash and 2 green flashes, then the air flow meter circuit is malfunctioning. Continue the check as described below. If the self-diagnostic code isn't displayed, the sensor/circuit is functioning properly.

3 Depending on the symptom, the air flow meter and its related circuit have several items that must be checked in order to pinpoint the problem.

4 If the vehicle drives poorly and stumbles on acceleration, check the power source to the air flow meter as described below.

1988 and earlier models

5 On 1985-86 models, turn the ignition switch to the On position, unplug the electrical connector from the air flow meter and check the voltage between terminal B and ground **(see illustration)**. The voltmeter should read battery voltage.

6 On 1987-88 models, turn the ignition switch to the On position and check voltage between terminal E and ground **(see illustration)**. The volt meter should read battery voltage.

7 If voltage is present, check the ground circuit. Disconnect the air flow meter harness connector and check the resistance between terminals C, D and ground. The resistance should be 0 ohms **(see illustration)**.

8 If there is no resistance, the air flow meter is probably defective, but it would be a good idea to have your findings confirmed by a dealer service department or other repair shop before purchasing a replacement air flow meter.

1989 and later models

9 Turn the ignition key to the On position. With the air flow meter connected, check for voltage at terminal E **(see illustration)**. Battery voltage should be present.

10 Start the engine and warm it up to operating temperature.

11 Check the voltage between terminal B and ground at idle and also check it with the engine off and the ignition key On. Compare your readings to the voltages listed in this Chapter's Specifications.

Removal and installation

12 Remove the air cleaner assembly following the procedure described in Section 2.

13 Remove the air flow meter from the air cleaner assembly **(see illustration)**.

14 Installation is the reverse of removal.

23 Vacuum chamber (1988 and earlier models) – removal and installation

Refer to illustration 23.3

1 Remove the air inlet tube and air cleaner assembly (see Section 2).

2 Disconnect any electrical connectors and vacuum hoses attached to

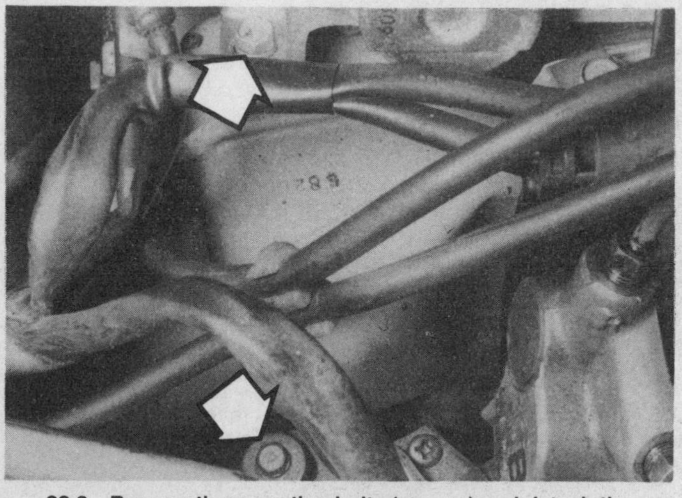

23.3 Remove the mounting bolts (arrows) and detach the vacuum chamber

24.1 The exhaust system is attached to the body with mounting brackets and rubber hangers (arrows)

the vacuum chamber. Disconnect the EGR solenoid and AIV harness connectors.

3 Remove the two mounting bolts that retain the vacuum chamber **(see illustration)**. Remove the vacuum chamber.

4 Installation is the reverse of removal.

24 Exhaust system servicing – general information

Refer to illustrations 24.1 and 24.4

Warning: *The catalytic converter operates at very high temperatures – wait until it is completely cool before attempting to remove it. Failure to do so could result in serious burns.*

1 The exhaust system consists of the exhaust manifold(s), the catalytic converter, the muffler, the tailpipe and all connecting pipes, brackets, hangers and clamps. The exhaust system is attached to the body with mounting brackets and rubber hangers **(see illustration)**. If any of the parts are improperly installed, excessive noise and vibration will be transmitted to the body.

2 Conduct regular inspections of the exhaust system to keep it safe and quiet. Look for any damaged or bent parts, open seams, holes, loose connections, excessive corrosion or other defects which could allow exhaust fumes to enter the vehicle. Deteriorated exhaust system components should not be repaired; they should be replaced with new parts.

3 If the exhaust system components are extremely corroded or rusted together, welding equipment will probably be required to remove them. The convenient way to accomplish this is to have a muffler repair shop remove the corroded sections with a cutting torch. If, however, you want to save money by doing it yourself (and you don't have a welding outfit with a cutting torch), simply cut off the old components with a hacksaw. If you have compressed air, special pneumatic cutting chisels can also be used. Most auto parts stores carry chain-type cutters that wrap around the exhaust pipe and make a clean, straight cut. If you do decide to tackle the job at home, be sure to wear safety goggles to protect your eyes from metal chips and work gloves to protect your hands.

4 Here are some simple guidelines to follow when repairing the exhaust system:

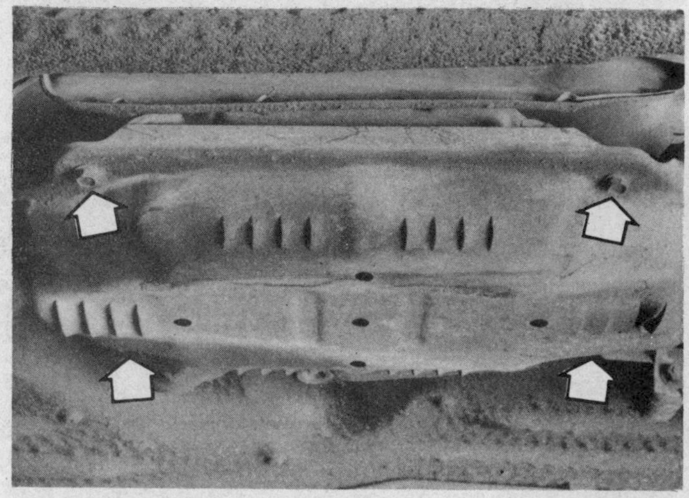

24.4 Remove the heat shield to gain access to the catalytic converter – the heat shield mounting bolts should be soaked with penetrating oil before attempting to remove them

a) Work from the back to the front when removing exhaust system components.
b) Apply penetrating oil to the exhaust system component fasteners to make them easier to remove.
c) Use new gaskets, hangers and clamps when installing exhaust system components.
d) Apply anti-seize compound to the threads of all exhaust system fasteners during reassembly.
e) Be sure to allow sufficient clearance between newly installed parts and all points on the underbody to avoid overheating the floor pan and possibly damaging the interior carpet and insulation. Pay particularly close attention to the catalytic converter and heat shield **(see illustration)**.

Chapter 5 Engine electrical systems

Contents

Alternator – removal and installation 12
Battery cables – check and replacement 4
Battery check and maintenance .... See Chapter 1
Battery – emergency jump starting 3
Battery – removal and installation 2
Charging system – check 11
Charging system – general information and precautions 10
Crank angle sensor – check 9
Distributor – removal and installation 8
Drivebelt check, adjustment and replacement .... See Chapter 1
General information 1
Ignition coil – check and replacement 7
Ignition system – check 6
Ignition system – general information and precautions 5
Ignition timing check and adjustment .... See Chapter 1
Spark plug replacement .... See Chapter 1
Spark plug wire, distributor cap and rotor check and replacement .... See Chapter 1
Starter motor – brush replacement 18
Starter motor – removal and installation 16
Starter motor – testing in vehicle 15
Starter solenoid – removal and installation 17
Starting system – general information and precautions 14
Voltage regulator and brushes – replacement 13

5

Specifications

Ignition coil

Coil primary resistance	1.0 ohms
Coil secondary resistance	10 k-ohms

Charging system

Alternator brush length (minimum)	
1985 through 1987	0.217 in (5.5 mm) or to wear limit line
1988 on	0.276 in (7.0 mm) or to wear limit line

Starting system

Starter brush length (minimum)	
1985 through 1987	0.31 in (8 mm)
1988	0.374 in (9.5 mm)
1989 on	0.472 in (12.0 mm)

1 General information

The engine electrical systems include all ignition, charging and starting components. Because of their engine-related functions, these components are discussed separately from chassis electrical devices such as the lights, the instruments, etc. (which are included in Chapter 12).

Always observe the following precautions when working on the electrical systems:

a) Be extremely careful when servicing engine electrical components. They are easily damaged if checked, connected or handled improperly.
b) Never leave the ignition switch on for long periods of time with the engine off.
c) Don't disconnect the battery cables while the engine is running.
d) Maintain correct polarity when connecting a battery cable from another vehicle during jump starting.
e) Always disconnect the negative cable first and hook it up last or the battery may be shorted by the tool being used to loosen the cable clamps.

It's also a good idea to review the safety-related information regarding the engine electrical systems located in the *Safety first!* section near the front of this manual before beginning any operation included in this Chapter.

2 Battery – removal and installation

Refer to illustration 2.1

1 **Caution:** *Always disconnect the negative cable first and hook it up last or the battery may be shorted by the tool being used to loosen the cable clamps.* Disconnect both cables from the battery terminals **(see illustration)**.

2 Remove the battery hold down bracket.

3 Lift out the battery. Be careful – it's heavy.

4 While the battery is out, inspect the carrier (tray) for corrosion (see Chapter 1).

5 If you are replacing the battery, make sure that you get one that's identical, with the same dimensions, amperage rating, cold cranking rating, etc.

6 Installation is the reverse of removal.

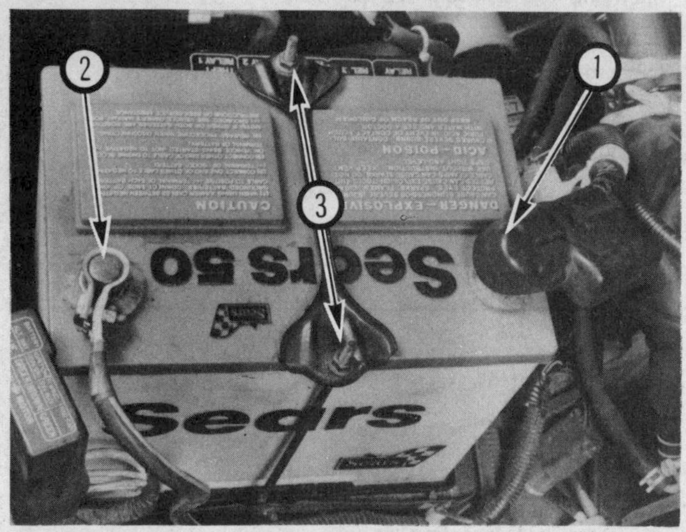

2.1 Pull back the rubber cover on the positive terminal to access the bolt – after the cables are off, remove the nuts and the hold down bracket

1 Positive terminal
2 Negative terminal
3 Hold down bracket nuts

3 Battery – emergency jump starting

Refer to the *Booster battery (jump) starting* procedure at the front of this manual.

4 Battery cables – check and replacement

1 Periodically inspect the entire length of each battery cable for damage, cracked or burned insulation and corrosion. Poor battery cable connections can cause starting problems and decreased engine performance.

2 Check the cable-to-terminal connections at the ends of the cables for cracks, loose wire strands and corrosion. The presence of white, fluffy deposits under the insulation at the cable terminal connection is a sign that the cable is corroded and should be replaced. Check the terminals for distortion, missing mounting bolts and corrosion.

3 When removing the cables, **always disconnect the negative cable first and hook it up last** or the battery may be shorted by the tool used to loosen the cable clamps. Even if only the positive cable is being replaced, be sure to disconnect the negative cable from the battery first (see Chapter 1 for further information regarding battery cable removal).

4 Disconnect the old cables from the battery, then trace each of them to their opposite ends and detach them from the starter solenoid and ground terminals. Note the routing of each cable to ensure correct installation.

5 If you are replacing either or both of the old cables, take them with you when buying new cables. It is vitally important that you replace the cables with identical parts. Cables have characteristics that make them easy to identify: positive cables are usually red, larger in cross-section and have a larger diameter battery post clamp; ground cables are usually black, smaller in cross-section and have a slightly smaller diameter clamp for the negative post.

6 Clean the threads of the solenoid or ground connection with a wire brush to remove rust and corrosion. Apply a light coat of battery terminal corrosion inhibitor, or petroleum jelly, to the threads to prevent future corrosion.

7 Attach the cable to the solenoid or ground connection and tighten the mounting nut/bolt securely.

8 Before connecting a new cable to the battery, make sure that it reaches the battery post without having to be stretched.

9 Connect the positive cable first, followed by the negative cable.

5 Ignition system – general information and precautions

In order for the engine to run correctly, it is necessary for an electrical spark to ignite the fuel/air mixture in the combustion chamber at exactly the right moment in relation to engine speed and load. The ignition system is based on feeding low tension (LT) voltage from the battery to the coil, where it is converted to high tension (HT) voltage. The high tension voltage is powerful enough to jump the spark plug gap in the cylinders many times a second under high compression pressures, providing that the system is in good condition and that all adjustments are correct.

The ignition system is divided into two circuits; the low tension circuit and the high tension circuit.

The low tension (also known as the primary) circuit consists of the ignition switch, ignition and accessory relay, the primary windings of the ignition coil, the transistorized IC ignition unit, the crank angle sensor assembly in the distributor and all connecting wires.

The high tension circuit consists of the high tension or secondary windings of the ignition coil, the heavy ignition lead from the center of the coil to the distributor cap, the rotor, the spark plug wires and spark plugs.

A *crank angle sensor* inside the distributor monitors engine speed and piston position, then sends a signal to the ECCS control unit (ECU). The ECU uses this signal to determine ignition timing, fuel injector duration and other functions. The crank angle sensor assembly consists of a rotor plate, a "wave forming" circuit, a light emitting diode (LED) and a photo diode.

The rotor plate, which is attached to the distributor shaft, is in the base of the distributor housing. There are 360 slits machined into the outer edge of the rotor plate. These slits correspond to each degree of crankshaft rotation. Within this outer row of slits is a series of six slightly larger slits corresponding to each cylinder in the engine. They are spaced 120-degrees apart. The slit for the number one cylinder is slightly larger than the slits for the other cylinders.

The wave forming circuit is positioned underneath the rotor plate. A small housing attached to one side of the wave forming circuit encloses the upper and lower outer edges of the rotor plate. A light emitting diode (LED) is located in the upper half and a photo diode is located in the lower half of the small housing. When the engine is running, the LED emits a continuous beam of light directly at the photo diode. As the outer edge of the rotor plate passes through the housing, the slits allow the light beam to pass through to the photo diode, but the solid spaces between the slits block the light beam. This constant interruption generates pulses which are converted into on-off signals by the wave forming circuit and sent to the ECU. The ECU uses the signal from the outer row of slits to determine engine speed and crankshaft position. It uses the signal generated by the inner, larger slits to determine when to fire each cylinder. This information is then relayed to the coil which builds secondary voltage and sends it to the distributor cap in the conventional manner, where it is distributed by the rotor to the appropriate cylinder.

Warning: *Because of the higher voltage generated by the electronic ignition system, extreme caution should be taken whenever an operation is performed involving ignition components. This not only includes the distributor, coil, control module and ignition wires, but related items which are connected to the system as well, such as the plug connections, tachometer and any testing equipment. Consequently, before any work is performed, such as replacing ignition components or even connecting test equipment, the ignition should be turned off and the battery ground cable disconnected. Never disconnect any of the ignition HT leads when the engine is running or the transistor ignition unit will be permanently damaged.*

6 Ignition system – check

Attach an inductive timing light to each plug wire, one at a time, and crank the engine.

a) If the light flashes, voltage is reaching the plug.
b) If the light does not flash, proceed to the next step.

2 Inspect the spark plug wires, distributor cap, rotor and spark plugs (see Chapter 1).

3 If the engine still won't start, check the ignition coil (see Section 7).

7 Ignition coil – check and replacement

Refer to illustrations 7.3a, 7.3b, 7.3c and 7.6

1 Detach the cable from the negative terminal of the battery.

2 The ignition coil is mounted on the right front inner fender panel, behind the headlight.

3 Pull back the protective cap and unplug the high tension lead from the coil **(see illustrations)**.

7.3a On 1985 through 1988 models pull back the rubber protective cap and unplug the high tension lead located under the cover, then remove the mounting screws (upper screw visible, second screw below)

1 Protective cap *2 Mounting screws*

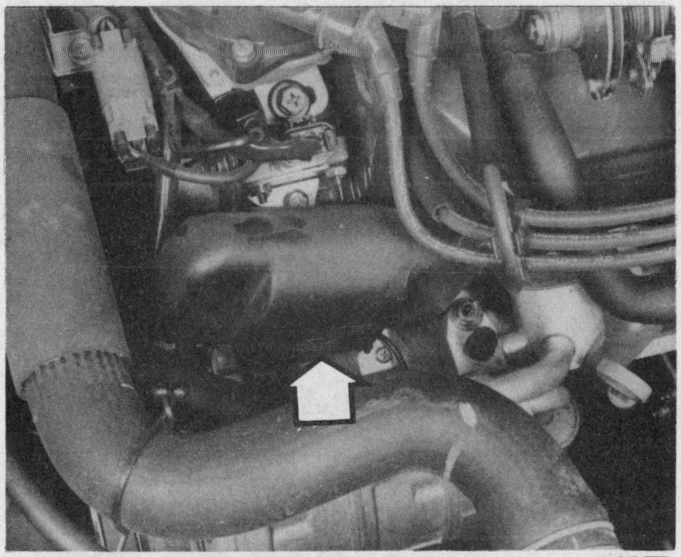

7.3b On 1989 and later models, slip the protective cap (arrow) off . . .

7.3c . . . unplug the high tension lead and connector plug and remove the mounting screws

1 High tension lead
2 Connector plug
3 Mounting screws

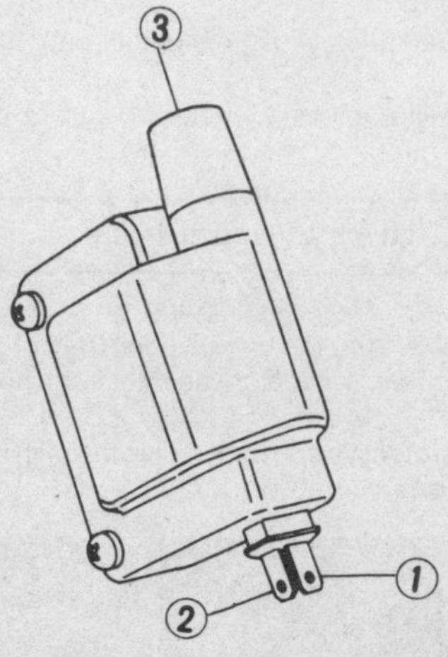

7.6 Measure the resistance between terminals one and two and between one and three

4 On 1985 through 1988 models, remove the two coil bracket-to-body screws and raise the coil enough to reach under it and unplug the electrical connector. Lift the coil from the engine compartment.
5 On 1989 and newer models, unplug the electrical connector and unbolt the coil from its mounting bracket.
6 Using an ohmmeter, check the coil:
a) Measure the resistance between terminals one and two **(see illustration)**. Compare your reading to the coil primary resistance listed in this Chapter's Specifications.
b) Measure the resistance between terminals one and three and compare your reading to the coil secondary resistance listed in this Chapter's Specifications.
7 If either of the above tests yield resistance values other than specified, replace the coil.
8 Reverse the removal procedure for installation.

8 Distributor – removal and installation

Refer to illustrations 8.1, 8.3, 8.5, 8.7a and 8.7b

Removal

1 Disconnect the negative cable from the battery. On later models, remove the distributor cover **(see illustration)**.
2 Unplug the electrical connector for the module. Follow the wires as they exit the distributor to find the connector.
3 Look for a raised "1" on the distributor cap **(see illustration)**. This marks the location for the number one cylinder spark plug wire terminal. If the cap does not have a mark for the number one terminal, locate the number one spark plug and trace the wire back to the terminal on the cap.
4 Remove the distributor cap (see Chapter 1) and turn the engine over until the rotor is pointing toward the number one spark plug terminal inside the cap (see locating TDC procedure in Chapter 2A).
5 Make a mark on the edge of the distributor base directly below the rotor tip and in line with it. Also, mark the distributor base and the cylinder head **(see illustration)** to ensure that the distributor is installed correctly.
6 Remove the distributor hold down bolt and washer, then pull the distributor straight up to remove it. **Caution:** *DO NOT turn the crankshaft while the distributor is out of the engine, or the alignment marks will be useless.*

Installation

Note: *If the crankshaft has been moved while the distributor is out, the number one piston must be repositioned at TDC. This can be done by feeling for compression pressure at the number one plug hole as the crank-*

8.1 On later models, remove the cover for access to the distributor

8.3 The distributor cap should be marked with the cylinder numbers and direction of rotation (1989 model shown, others similar)

8.5 Before removing the distributor, be sure to mark the distributor and cylinder head (arrows) to ensure that the distributor is installed in the same position

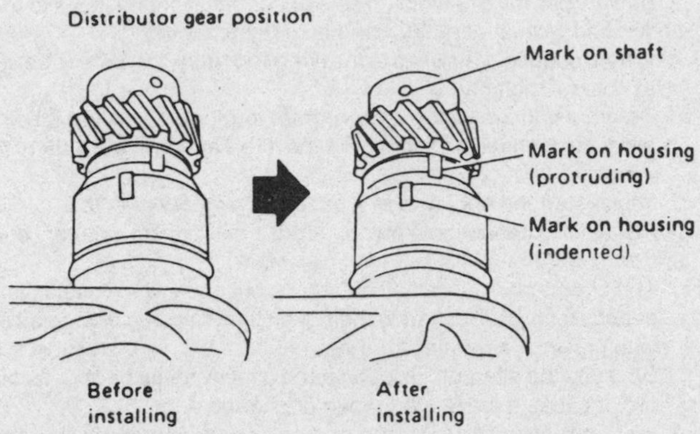

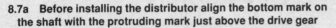

8.7a Before installing the distributor align the bottom mark on the shaft with the protruding mark just above the drive gear

8.7b When the distributor gear engages fully with the drive gear the marks should line up

shaft is turned clockwise. Once compression is felt, align the ignition timing zero mark with the pointer.

7 Insert the distributor into the engine in exactly the same relationship to the head that it was in when removed. To mesh the helical gears on the camshaft and the distributor, it may be necessary to turn the rotor slightly **(see illustrations)**. Recheck the alignment marks between the distributor base and the head to verify that the distributor is in the same position it was in before removal. Also check the rotor to see if it's aligned with the mark you made on the edge of the distributor base.
8 Place the distributor in position and loosely install the bolt.
9 Install the distributor cap.
10 Plug in the module electrical connector.
11 Reattach the spark plug wires to the plugs (if removed).
12 Connect the cable to the negative terminal of the battery.
13 Check the ignition timing (see Chapter 1) and tighten the distributor hold down bolt securely.

9 Crank angle sensor – check

Refer to illustrations 9.3, 9.4 and 9.7
Note: *A description of the crank angle sensor can be found in Section 5.*
1 Remove the distributor (see Section 8).
2 Remove the rotor retaining screw and pull the rotor off the shaft (see Chapter 1).
3 Remove the sensor dust cover retaining screws **(see illustration)** and lift off the cover.
4 Inspect the crank angle signal plate **(see illustration)** for damage and dirt intrusion. Blow any accumulated dust out of the distributor and reinstall the cover and rotor.
5 Inspect the electrical connections for damage and corrosion and correct any defects.
6 With the distributor still removed, reconnect the electrical harness to the crank angle sensor.

5

9.3 Remove the screws retaining the crank angle sensor dust cover (arrows)

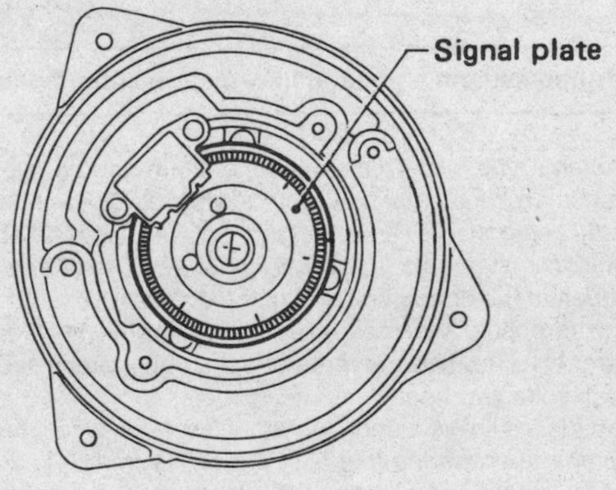

9.4 Inspect the crank angle sensor signal plate for dirt blocking the slits and for damage

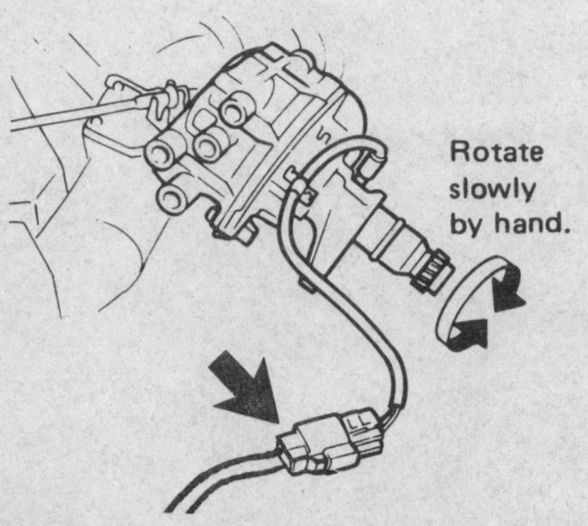

9.7 Insert the test probe into the back of the black wire terminal of the plug (arrow) while it is still connected

7 Attach the ground connector of a high impedance volt-ohm meter to a clean engine ground. Select the ohms scale of approximately 0 to 1,000 ohms and insert the test probe into the black wire terminal in the rear of the distributor connector on the engine side of the harness **(see illustration)**. A reading of approximately zero ohms confirms a good ground connection. **Note:** *Use a thin probe, a stiff wire or a paper clip inserted deeply enough to reach the metal contacts.*

8 Reconnect the battery and turn the ignition to the On position. **Caution:** *Don't activate the starter.*

9 Place the volt-ohm meter on a 0 to 15 volt scale (or closest approximation). Working with the same connector, probe the black and white wire connection for voltage. A reading near battery voltage is normal, if little or no voltage is found, trace and repair the wiring (see Chapter 12).

10 Rotate the distributor shaft very slowly by hand and probe the green/yellow wire for voltage. The voltage should jump from zero to five volts and back again once every revolution. This provides a top dead center indication to the computer.

11 Again rotate the distributor shaft very slowly by hand and probe the green/black wire for voltage. The voltage should jump in steps from zero to five volts and back again six times per revolution. This provides a spark plug firing signal to the computer.

12 Repeat any testing steps that produce inconclusive results to avoid incorrect conclusions. If the voltage pulses fail to occur in Steps 10 and 11, replace the distributor. **Note:** *The crank angle sensor is not available separately.*

13 If you are still unable to find the problem, take the vehicle to a dealer service department for further diagnosis and repair.

10 Charging system – general information and precautions

The charging system includes the alternator, an internal voltage regulator, a charge indicator, the battery, a fusible link and the wiring between all the components. The charging system supplies electrical power for the ignition system, the lights, the radio, etc. The alternator is driven by a drivebelt at the timing belt end of the engine.

The purpose of the voltage regulator is to limit the alternator's voltage to a preset value. This prevents power surges, circuit overloads, etc., during peak voltage output.

The fusible link is a short length of insulated wire integral with the engine compartment wiring harness. The link is smaller in diameter than the circuit it protects. Production fusible links and their identification flags are identified by the flag color. See Chapter 12 for additional information regarding fusible links.

The charging system doesn't ordinarily require periodic maintenance. However, the drivebelt, battery and wires and connections should be inspected at the intervals outlined in Chapter 1.

The dashboard warning light should come on when the ignition key is turned to Start, then go off immediately. If it remains on, there is a malfunction in the charging system (see Section 11). Some vehicles are also equipped with a voltmeter. If the voltmeter indicates abnormally high or low voltage, check the charging system (see Section 11).

Be very careful when making electrical circuit connections to a vehicle equipped with an alternator and note the following:

a) When reconnecting wires to the alternator from the battery, be sure to note the polarity.
b) Before using arc welding equipment to repair any part of the vehicle, disconnect the wires from the alternator and the battery terminals.
c) Never start the engine with a battery charger connected.
d) Always disconnect both battery leads before using a battery charger.
e) The alternator is turned by an engine drivebelt which could cause serious injury if your hands, hair or clothes become entangled in it with the engine running.
f) Because the alternator is connected directly to the battery, it could arc or cause a fire if overloaded or shorted out.
g) Wrap a plastic bag over the alternator and secure it with rubber bands before cleaning the engine.

11 Charging system – check

1 If a malfunction occurs in the charging circuit, don't automatically assume that the alternator is causing the problem. First check the following items:

a) Check the drivebelt tension and condition (Chapter 1). Replace it if it's worn or deteriorated.
b) Make sure the alternator mounting and adjustment bolts are tight.
c) Inspect the alternator wiring harness and the connectors at the alternator. They must be in good condition and tight.
d) Check the fusible link located between the starter solenoid and the alternator. If it's burned, determine the cause, repair the circuit and replace the link (the vehicle won't start and/or the accessories won't work if the fusible link blows). Sometimes a fusible link may look good, but still be bad. If in doubt, check it for continuity.
e) Start the engine and check the alternator for abnormal noises (a shrieking or squealing sound indicates a bad bearing).
f) Check the specific gravity of the battery electrolyte. If it's low, charge the battery (doesn't apply to maintenance free batteries).
g) Make sure the battery is fully charged (one bad cell in a battery can cause overcharging by the alternator).
h) Disconnect the battery cables (negative first, then positive). Inspect the battery posts and the cable clamps for corrosion. Clean them thoroughly if necessary (see Chapter 1). Reconnect the cable to the positive terminal.
i) With the ignition key off, connect a test light between the negative battery post and the disconnected negative cable clamp.
    1) If the test light does not come on, reattach the clamp and proceed to the next step.
    2) If the test light comes on, there is a short (drain) in the electrical system of the vehicle. The short must be repaired before the charging system can be checked.
    3) Disconnect the alternator wiring harness.
        (a) If the light goes out, the alternator is bad.
        (b) If the light stays on, pull each fuse until the light goes out (this will tell you which component is shorted).

2 Using a voltmeter, check the battery voltage with the engine off. If should be approximately 12-volts.

3 Start the engine and check the battery voltage again. It should now be approximately 14-to-15 volts.

4 Turn on the headlights. The voltage should drop, and then come back up, if the charging system is working properly.

5 If the voltage reading is more than the specified charging voltage, replace the voltage regulator (refer to Section 13). If the voltage is less, the alternator diode(s), stator or rectifier may be bad or the voltage regulator may be malfunctioning.

12.4 Unplug the connector near the top and remove the nuts holding the remaining wires (viewed from below)

12.5 Locations of the alternator adjustment and pivot bolts (arrows) (viewed from below)

12 Alternator – removal and installation

Refer to illustrations 12.4 and 12.5

1 Detach the cable from the negative terminal of the battery.
2 Raise the vehicle and support it securely on jackstands.
3 Remove the lower splash pan.
4 Detach the electrical connectors from the alternator **(see illustration)**.
5 Loosen the alternator adjustment and pivot bolts **(see illustration)** and detach the drivebelt.
6 Remove the adjustment and pivot bolts and separate the alternator from the engine.
7 If you are replacing the alternator, take the old one with you when purchasing a replacement unit. Make sure the new/rebuilt unit looks identical to the old alternator. Look at the terminals – they should be the same in number, size and location as the terminals on the old alternator. Finally, look at the identification numbers – they will be stamped into the housing or printed on a tag attached to the housing. Make sure the numbers are the same on both alternators.
8 Many new/rebuilt alternators DO NOT have a pulley installed, so you may have to switch the pulley from the old unit to the new/rebuilt one. When buying an alternator, find out the shop's policy regarding pulleys – some shops will perform this service free of charge.
9 Installation is the reverse of removal.
10 After the alternator is installed, adjust the drivebelt tension (see Chapter 1).
11 Check the charging voltage to verify proper operation of the alternator (see Section 11).

13 Voltage regulator and brushes – replacement

Refer to illustrations 13.3, 13.4, 13.7, 13.10 and 13.11

1 Remove the alternator (see Section 12).
2 Paint or scribe a line along the side of the alternator to ensure proper alignment of the stator with the front and rear covers during reassembly.
3 Remove the four through bolts **(see illustration)**. Don't attempt to pull the alternator apart until you have read the next step.
4 The rear rotor bearing is pressed into the rear cover. Place a 200-watt soldering iron on the bearing box area of the rear end frame for three or four minutes **(see illustration)**. **Warning:** *Wear thick work gloves to protect your hands and avoid the heated area. If you're using an iron with less output, keep it in contact proportionately longer. Don't use a heat gun or torch because the diodes may be damaged.*
5 Pull the alternator halves apart. Pry them apart with a screwdriver if necessary, but don't use excessive force. The rear cover may be hard to remove because a ring is used to lock the outer race of the rear bearing. Be careful not to lose this ring during removal.
6 If the two halves don't come apart fairly easily, the rotor shaft bearing is still stuck in its bore in the rear cover. Put the soldering iron back on the rear cover for a few more minutes.
7 Inspect the brushes for length and condition and replace them if they are worn to near the wear limit line **(see illustration)**.
8 Unsolder the connections and unscrew the brush holder/voltage regulator assembly. **Caution:** *When soldering, apply heat for no more than five seconds at a time – otherwise damage may occur.*
9 Reinstall the regulator/brush holder assembly.
10 Push the brushes into their holders and hold them in place with a straightened paper clip or other thin wire **(see illustration)**.
11 Position the ring in the rear bearing groove at its point of least protrusion **(see illustration)**.
12 Heat the end cover as described in Step 4 and press the rear bearing into place.
13 Remove the wire holding the brushes.
14 Reinstall the remaining components in the reverse order of removal.

14 Starting system – general information and precautions

The sole function of the starting system is to turn over the engine quickly enough to allow it to start.

The starting system consists of the battery, the starter motor, the starter solenoid and the wires connecting them. The solenoid is mounted directly on the starter motor.

The solenoid/starter motor assembly is installed on the front lower part of the engine, on the transaxle bellhousing.

When the ignition key is turned to the Start position, the starter solenoid is actuated through the starter control circuit. The starter solenoid then connects the battery to the starter. The battery supplies the electrical energy to the starter motor, which does the actual work of cranking the engine.

The starter motor on a vehicle equipped with a manual transaxle can only be operated when the clutch pedal is depressed; the starter on a vehicle equipped with an automatic transaxle can only be operated when the transaxle selector lever is in Park or Neutral.

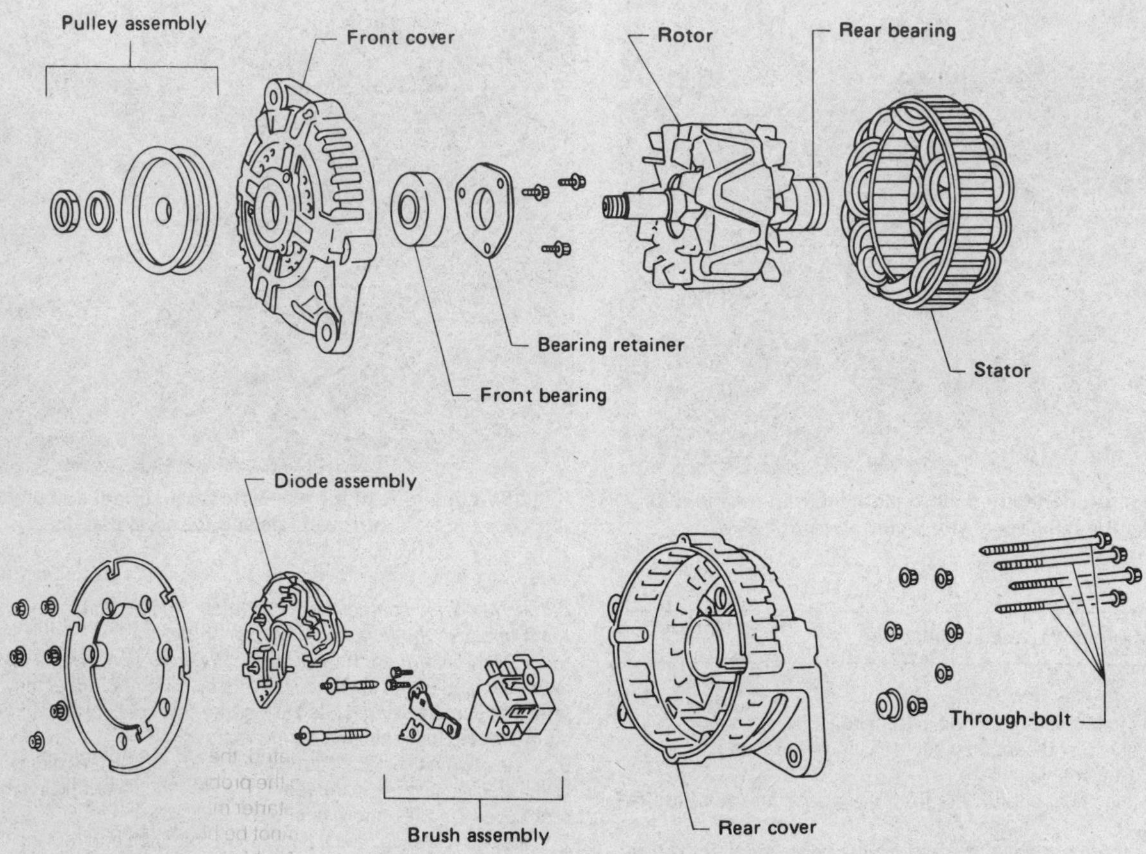

13.3 Alternator components – exploded view

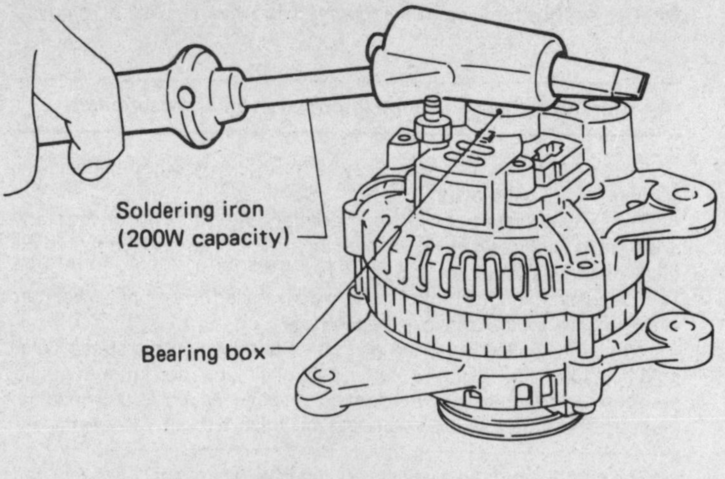

13.4 Heat the rear bearing box with a 200-watt soldering iron for three or four minutes

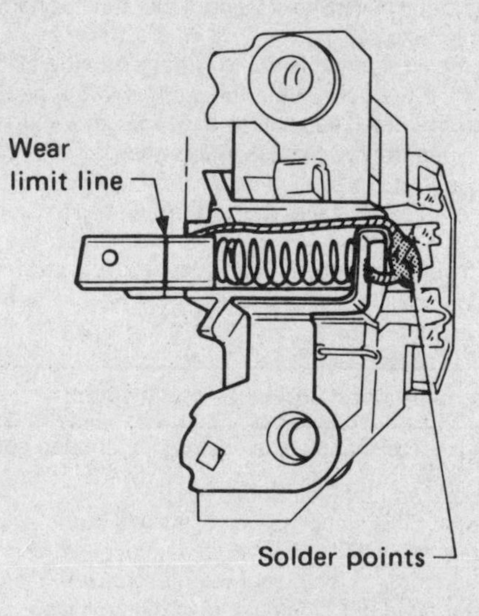

13.7 Inspect the brushes and replace them if they are worn to the wear limit line

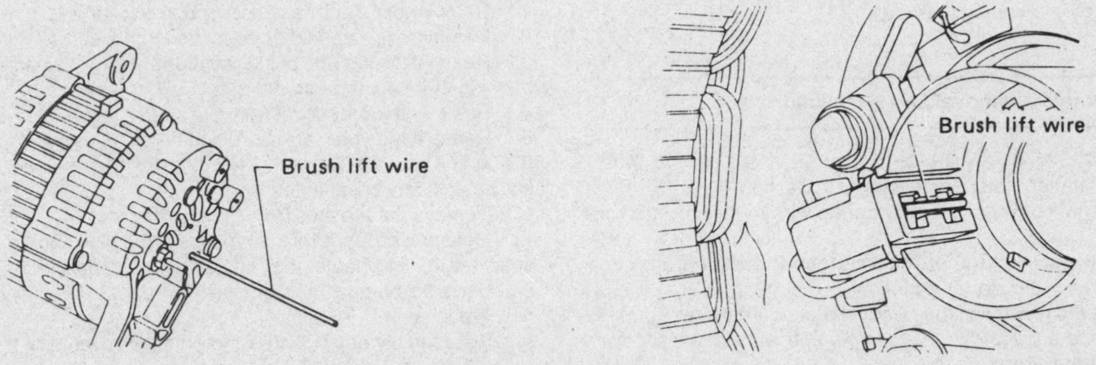

13.10 **Push the brushes into place and hold them with a wire as shown**

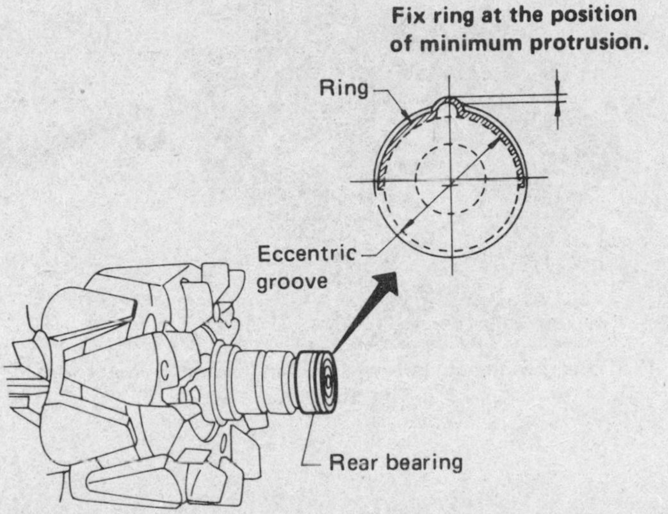

13.11 **Position the ring in the rear bearing groove at its point of least protrusion**

Always observe the following precautions when working on the starting system:

a) Excessive cranking of the starter motor can overheat it and cause serious damage. Never operate the starter motor for more than 15 seconds at a time without pausing to allow it to cool for at least two minutes.
b) The starter is connected directly to the battery and could arc or cause a fire if mishandled, overloaded or shorted out.
c) Always detach the cable from the negative terminal of the battery before working on the starting system.

15 Starter motor – testing in vehicle

Note: *Before diagnosing starter problems, make sure the battery is fully charged.*

1 If the starter motor does not turn at all when the switch is operated, make sure that the shift lever is in Neutral or Park (automatic transaxle) or that the clutch pedal is depressed (manual transaxle).

2 Make sure that the battery is charged and that all cables, both at the battery and starter solenoid terminals, are clean and secure.

3 If the starter motor spins but the engine is not cranking, the overrunning clutch in the starter motor is slipping and the starter motor must be replaced.

4 If, when the switch is actuated, the starter motor does not operate at all but the solenoid clicks, then the problem lies with either the battery, the main solenoid contacts or the starter motor itself (or the engine is seized).

5 If the solenoid plunger cannot be heard when the switch is actuated, the battery is discharged, the fusible link is burned (the circuit is open) or the solenoid itself is defective.

6 To check the solenoid, connect a jumper lead between the battery (+) and the ignition switch wire terminal (the small terminal) on the solenoid. If the starter motor now operates, the solenoid is OK and the problem is in the ignition switch, neutral start switch or the wiring.

7 If the starter motor still does not operate, remove the starter/solenoid assembly for disassembly, testing and repair.

8 If the starter motor cranks the engine at an abnormally slow speed, first make sure that the battery is charged and that all terminal connections are tight. If the engine is partially seized, or has the wrong viscosity oil in it, it will crank slowly.

9 Run the engine until normal operating temperature is reached, then disconnect the coil wire from the distributor cap and ground it on the engine.

10 Connect a voltmeter positive lead to the positive battery post and connect the negative lead to the negative post.

11 Crank the engine and take the voltmeter readings as soon as a steady figure is indicated. Do not allow the starter motor to turn for more than 15 seconds at a time. A reading of 9 volts or more, with the starter motor turning at normal cranking speed, is acceptable. If the reading is 9 volts or more but the cranking speed is slow, the motor is faulty. If the reading is less than 9 volts and the cranking speed is slow, the solenoid contacts are probably burned, the starter motor is bad, the battery is discharged or there is a bad connection.

16 Starter motor – removal and installation

Refer to illustration 16.3

1 Detach the cable from the negative terminal of the battery.

2 Raise the vehicle and support it securely on jackstands.

3 Disconnect the battery positive wire from the terminal on the starter motor solenoid **(see illustration)**. Disconnect the electrical connector in the small gauge wire, a few inches from the solenoid.
4 Remove the mounting bolts and detach the starter.
5 Installation is the reverse of removal.

17 Starter solenoid – removal and installation

Refer to illustrations 17.2, 17.3 and 17.4

1 Remove the starter motor as described in Section 16.
2 Remove the nut holding the heavy gauge wire to the solenoid **(see illustration)**.
3 Remove the two solenoid mounting bolts **(see illustration)** and separate the solenoid from the starter motor.
4 Installation is the reverse of the removal procedure. **Note:** *During installation be sure to engage the solenoid plunger with the starter motor shift lever* **(see illustration)**.

18 Starter motor – brush replacement

Refer to illustration 18.3

1 Remove the starter as described in Section 16.
2 Remove the solenoid as described in Section 17.
3 Remove the through bolts **(see illustration)** by unscrewing them and drawing them out through the rear.
4 Remove the rear cover from the starter motor.
5 Remove the yoke, armature and brush holder as an assembly from the center housing. Be careful not to knock the brushes, commutator or coil against any adjacent part.
6 Remove the brushes from the brush holder.
7 Measure the length of the brushes. If they are shorter than the length specified in this Chapter they should be replaced with new ones.
8 Use a soldering gun to remove the brushes from the yoke and solder new brushes on.
9 Reassembly of the starter motor is the reverse of the disassembly procedure.

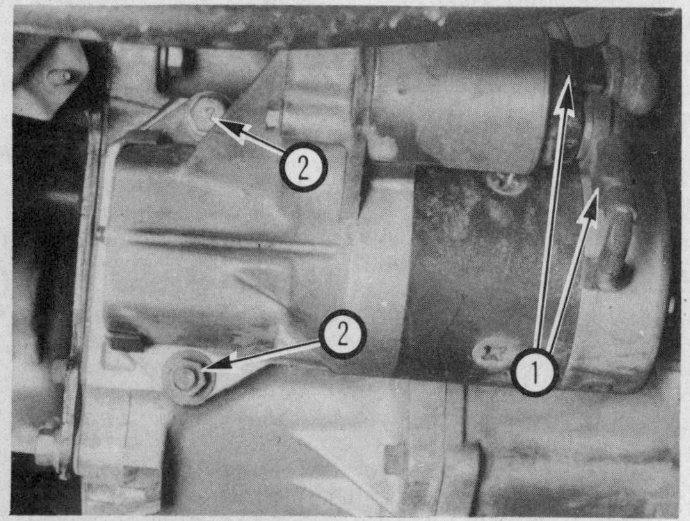

16.3 Pull back the rubber boot to access the starter positive terminal nut – after the wire has been detached, remove the mounting nut and bolt

1 Battery positive terminal *2 Mounting nut/bolt*

17.2 Remove the nut (arrow) securing the starter motor wire to the solenoid

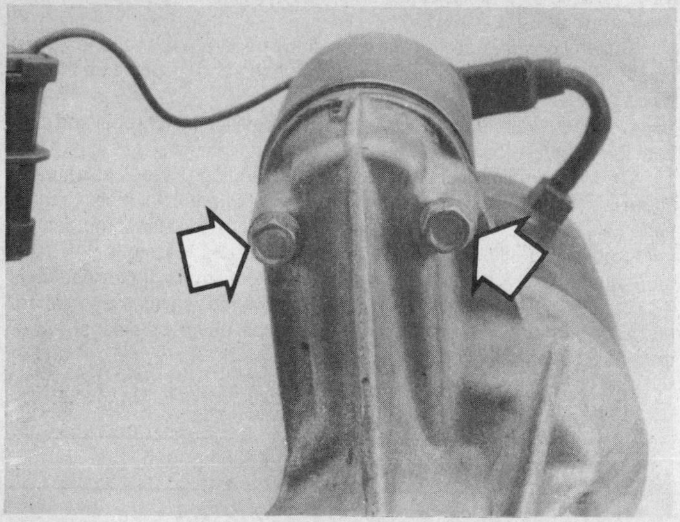

17.3 After removing the two retaining bolts (arrows) the solenoid can be separated from the starter

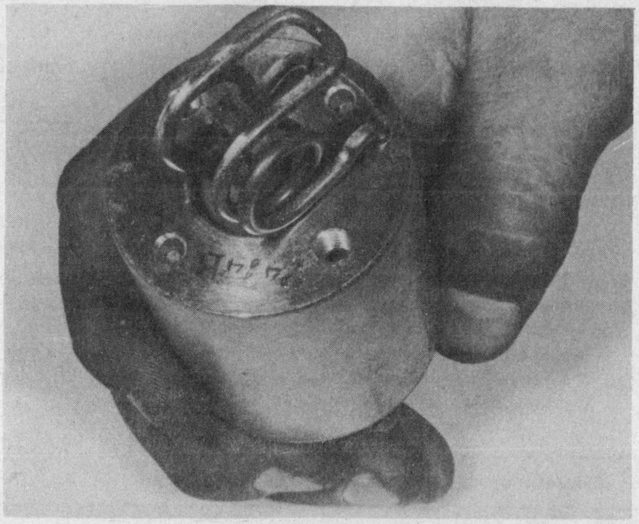

17.4 Assemble the solenoid as shown before installing it on the motor – make sure the solenoid plunger is engaged with the starter motor shift lever

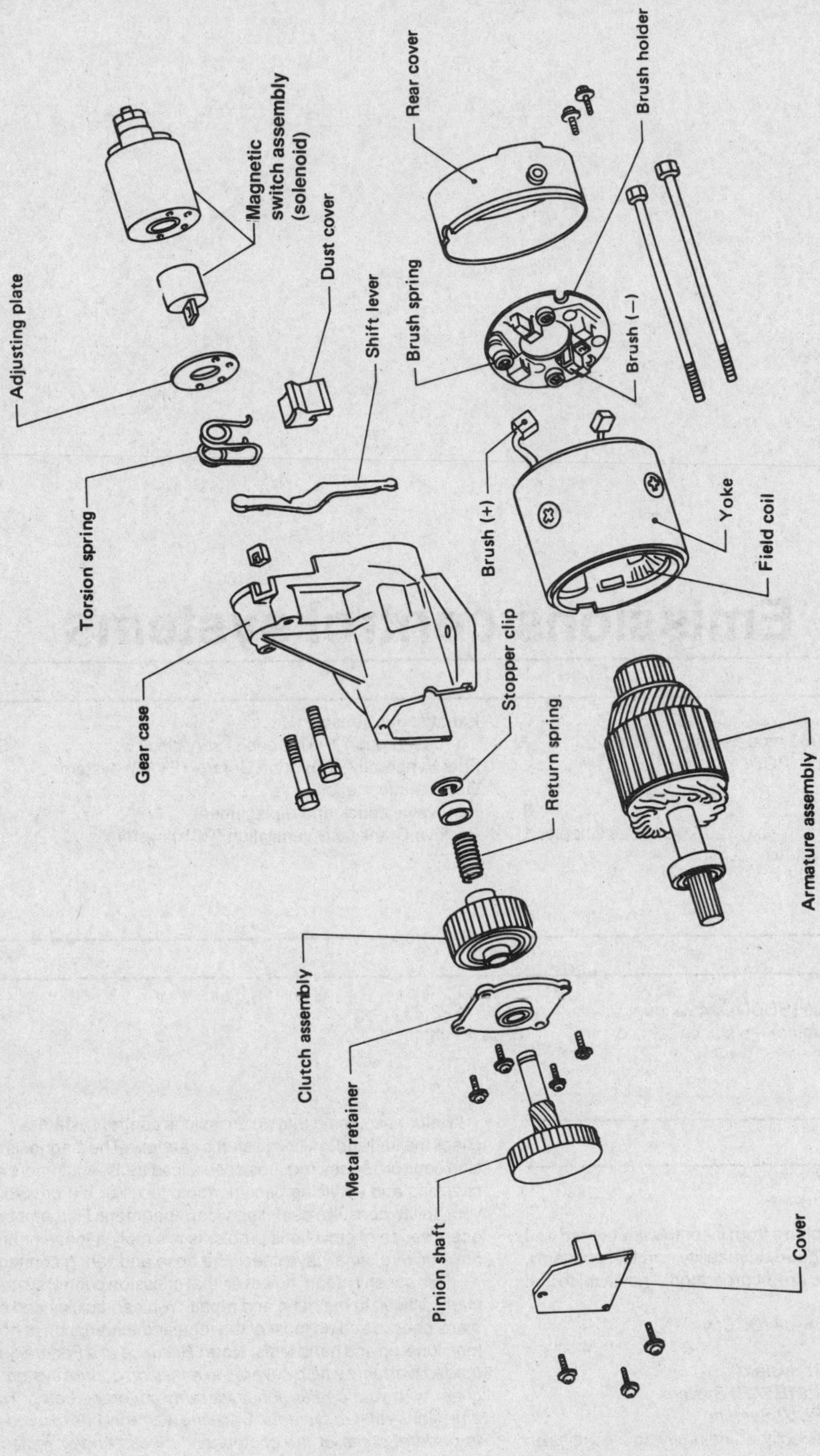

18.3 Starter components – exploded view

Chapter 6 Emissions control systems

Contents

Air Injection Valve (AIV) 6
Auxiliary Air Control (AAC) valve (1989 models only) 7
Boost Controlled Deceleration Device (BCDD)
(1985 through 1988 models only) 4
Catalytic converter 8
EGR valve check .... See Chapter 1
Exhaust Gas Recirculation (EGR) system 5
Exhaust gas sensor
(1985 through 1987 models) servicing .... See Chapter 1
Fuel Evaporative Emission Control (EVAP) system 3
General information 1
PCV valve check and replacement .... See Chapter 1
Positive Crankcase Ventilation (PCV) system 2

Specifications

Boost Controlled Deceleration Device (BCDD) set vacuum	21.65 to 23.23 in-Hg
Auxiliary Air Control (AAC) valve terminal resistance	27 to 40 ohms

1 General information

Refer to illustration 1.7

To prevent pollution of the atmosphere from incompletely burned and evaporating gases, and to maintain good driveability and fuel economy, a number of emission control systems are incorporated. They include the:

Air Injection Valve (AIV)
Boost Controlled Deceleration Device (BCDD)
Catalytic Converter
Exhaust Gas Recirculation (EGR) System
Fuel Evaporative Emission Control (EVAP) System
Positive Crankcase Ventilation (PCV) System

All of these systems are linked, directly or indirectly, to the emission control system.

The Sections in this Chapter include general descriptions, checking procedures within the scope of the home mechanic and component replacement procedures (when possible) for each of the systems listed above.

Before assuming that an emissions control system is malfunctioning, check the fuel and ignition systems carefully. The diagnosis of some emission control devices requires specialized tools, equipment and training. If checking and servicing become too difficult or if a procedure is beyond your ability, consult a dealer service department. Remember, the most frequent cause of emissions problems is simply a loose or broken vacuum hose or wire, so always check the hose and wiring connections first.

This doesn't mean, however, that emission control systems are particularly difficult to maintain and repair. You can quickly and easily perform many checks and do most of the regular maintenance at home with common tune-up and hand tools. **Note:** *Because of a Federally mandated extended warranty which covers the emission control system components, check with your dealer about warranty coverage before working on any emissions-related systems. Once the warranty has expired, you may wish to perform some of the component checks and/or replacement procedures in this Chapter to save money.*

Pay close attention to any special precautions outlined in this Chapter. It should be noted that the illustrations of the various systems may not exactly match the system installed on your vehicle because of changes made by the manufacturer during production or from year-to-year.

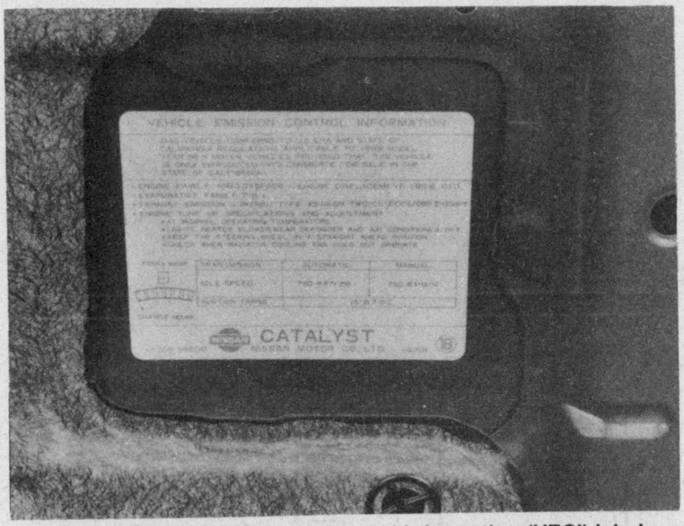

1.7 The Vehicle Emissions Control Information (VECI) label, located under the hood, provides important specifications for tune-ups on your car

A Vehicle Emissions Control Information label is located in the engine compartment **(see illustration)**. This label contains important emissions specifications and adjustment information, as well as a vacuum hose schematic with emissions components identified. When servicing the engine or emissions systems, the VECI label in your particular vehicle should always be checked for up-to-date information.

2 Positive Crankcase Ventilation (PCV) system

Refer to illustration 2.1

1 The Positive Crankcase Ventilation (PCV) system **(see illustration)** reduces hydrocarbon emissions by scavenging crankcase vapors. It does this by circulating fresh air from the air cleaner through the crankcase, where it mixes with blow-by gases and is then rerouted through a PCV valve to the intake manifold.

2 The main components of the PCV system are the PCV valve, a fresh air filtered inlet and the vacuum hoses connecting these two components with the engine.

3 To maintain idle quality, the PCV valve restricts the flow when the intake manifold vacuum is high. If abnormal operating conditions (such as piston ring problems) arise, the system is designed to allow excessive amounts of blow-by gases to flow back through the crankcase vent tube into the air cleaner to be consumed by normal combustion.

4 Checking and replacement of the PCV valve is covered in Chapter 1.

3 Fuel Evaporative Emission Control (EVAP) system

General description

Refer to illustrations 3.1a and 3.1b

1 To reduce hydrocarbon emissions, evaporated fuel from the fuel tank is routed through the charcoal canister to the intake manifold for burning in the cylinders **(see illustrations)**.

Checking and component replacement

Note: *Refer to Chapter 1 for the general system checking procedure.*

Hoses

2 Periodically inspect the fuel vapor lines **(see illustrations 3.1a and 3.1b)** for loose connections, sharp bends and damage. Check the fuel tank plumbing for deformation, cracks or fuel leakage. Check the fuel filler cap for a damaged or deformed gasket.

Canister

Refer to illustrations 3.4, 3.6, 3.10a and 3.10b

3 Remove the three screws and detach the relay box.
4 Detach the upper hoses from the canister **(see illustration)**.
5 Raise the vehicle and place it securely on jackstands.
6 Detach the lower hose **(see illustration)**.
7 Loosen the clamp.
8 Remove the charcoal canister.
9 Inspect the canister for cracks and damage.
10 Using low pressure compressed air, blow into the canister pipe labeled "A" **(see illustrations)** and verify that no air flows from the other pipes. Blow into the hoses labeled "B" and verify that air flows from the other pipes.

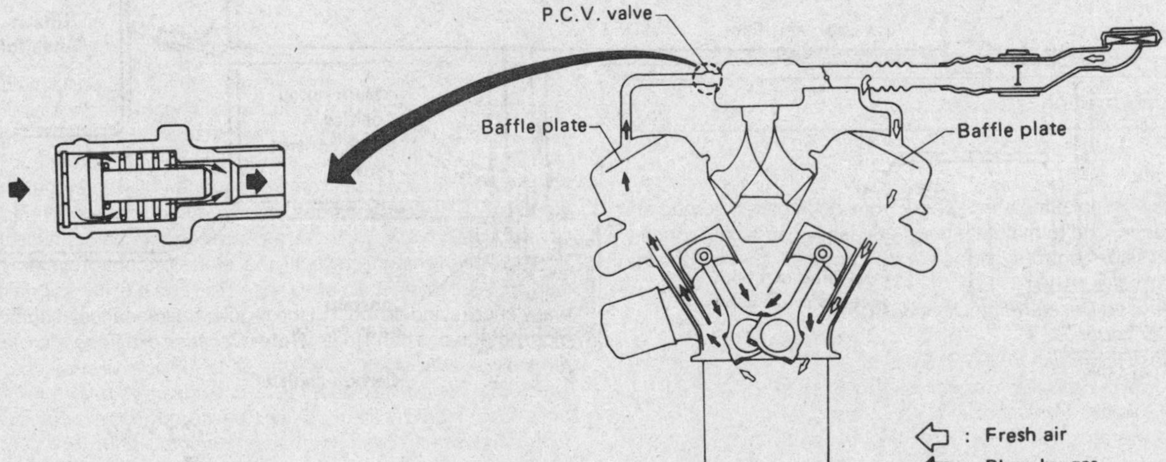

2.1 A typical Positive Crankcase Ventilation (PCV) system

11 If the canister fails to perform as described, replace it.
12 Installation of the canister is the reverse of removal.

Fuel check valve

Refer to illustration 3.14

13 Remove the fuel check valve from the vapor vent line between the fuel tank and the canister. Be sure to note the direction in which the valve is installed. Wipe it off with a clean shop towel.
14 Try to blow through the valve from the fuel tank side. You should feel considerable resistance, but some air should come out the engine side **(see illustration)**.
15 Try to blow air through the valve from the engine side. You should feel no resistance.
16 If the fuel check valve fails either of the above checks, replace it.

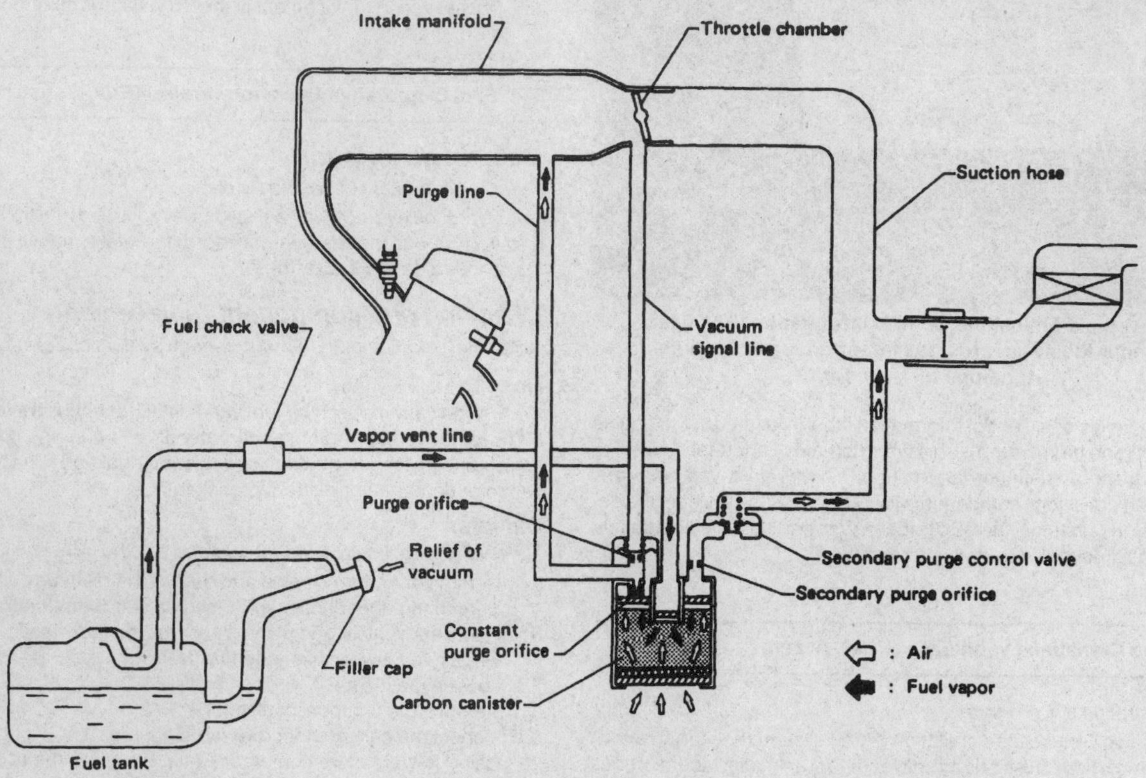

3.1a A typical Fuel Evaporative Emission Control (EVAP) system (1985 through 1988 models)

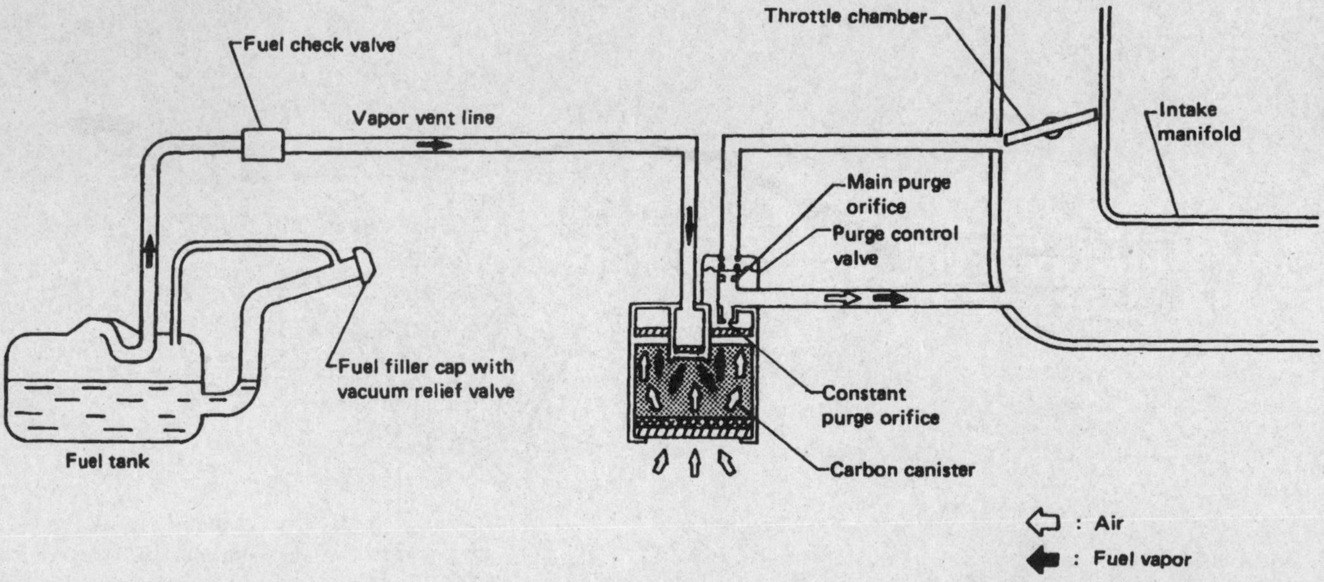

3.1b A typical 1989 and later model Fuel Evaporative Emission Control (EVAP) system

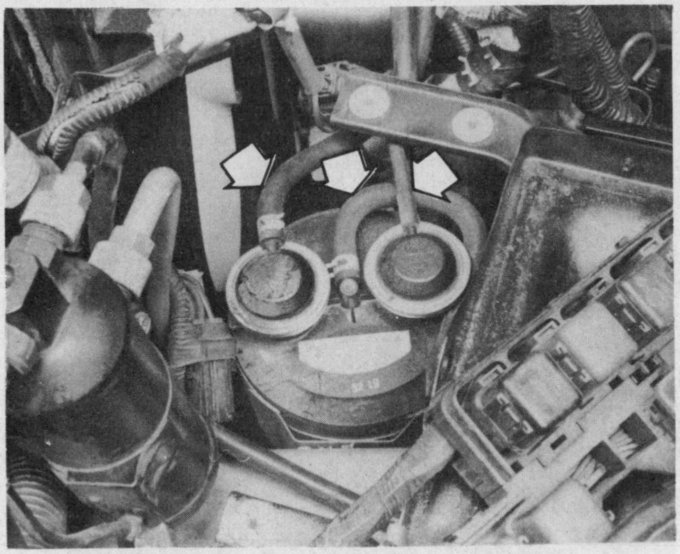

3.4 To remove the canister, first detach these hoses from the top (be sure to label them so you don't mix them up during reassembly)

3.6 Working underneath the vehicle, detach this hose from the bottom of the canister, then reach up the side of the canister and loosen the clamp bolt and slide the canister out

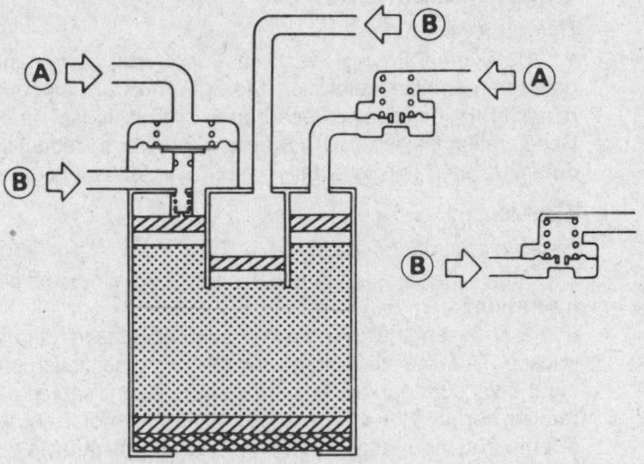

3.10a There are four hoses attached to the charcoal canister on 1985 through 1987 models: when you blow through the hoses labeled A, no leakage should occur; when you blow through the hoses labeled B, there should be air leakage. On 1985 and 1986 models, the secondary purge valve in the hose between the canister and the vacuum chamber must be checked from both sides – again, there should be no leakage when you blow through A, but there should be when you blow through B

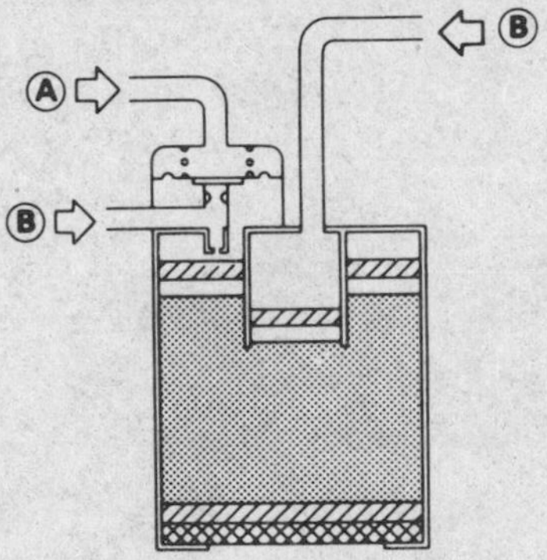

3.10b The canister on 1988 and 1989 models has one less hose than earlier units, but the procedure for checking it is identical to the procedure for earlier models

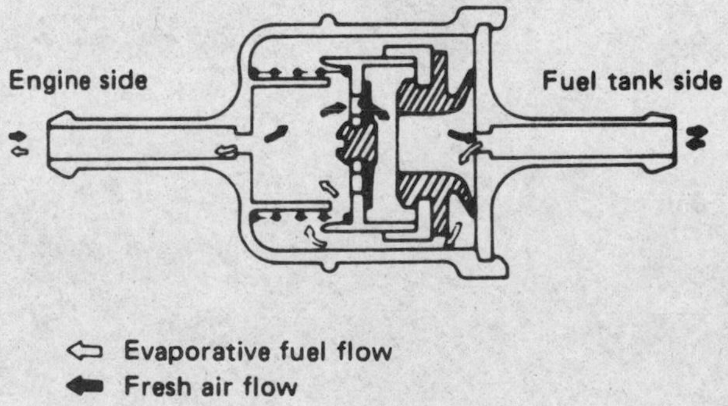

3.14 To test the fuel check valve, first try to blow through the valve from the fuel tank side – you should feel considerable resistance, but some air should get through; then try to blow air through the valve from the engine side – you should feel no resistance

4.1 A typical Boost Controlled Deceleration Device (BCDD)

4.2 Using a T-fitting, attach a vacuum gauge to the intake manifold

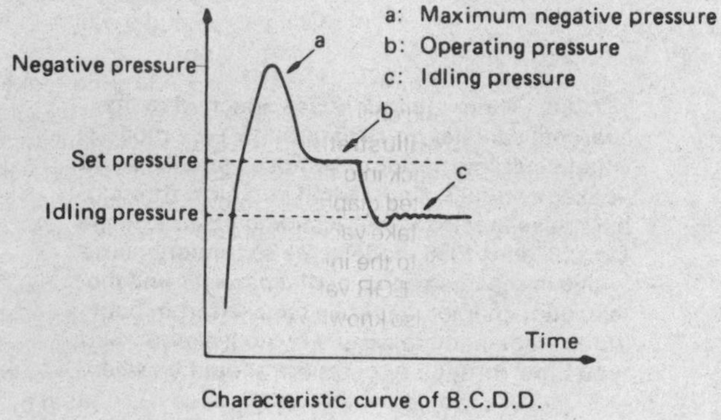

4.3 If you were to plot the relationship of vacuum to time for a properly operating BCDD on a graph, it would look like this

4 Boost Controlled Deceleration Device (BCDD) (1985 through 1988 models only)

General description

Refer to illustration 4.1

1 Because of the high vacuum – and reduced amount of intake air – generated during deceleration, the air/fuel mixture is incompletely burned, resulting in excessive hydrocarbon (HC) emissions. The Boost Controlled Deceleration Device (BCDD) **(see illustration)** reduces HC emissions during deceleration by supplying extra air to the intake.

Checking

Refer to illustrations 4.2 and 4.3

2 Attach a vacuum gauge to the intake manifold with a T-fitting **(see illustration)**.

3 Start the engine and note the vacuum gauge reading while the engine is idling. Then race the engine and abruptly close the throttle while watching the vacuum gauge. The indicated vacuum should attain its highest reading between the moment you shut off the throttle and when the engine returns to its normal operating rpm **(see illustration)**.

4 If the BCDD doesn't react as described above, adjust the operating pressure.

4.5 Using a small screwdriver, pry off the BCDD rubber cap

4.6 Turn the BCDD adjusting screw clockwise to increase the vacuum, or counterclockwise to decrease it

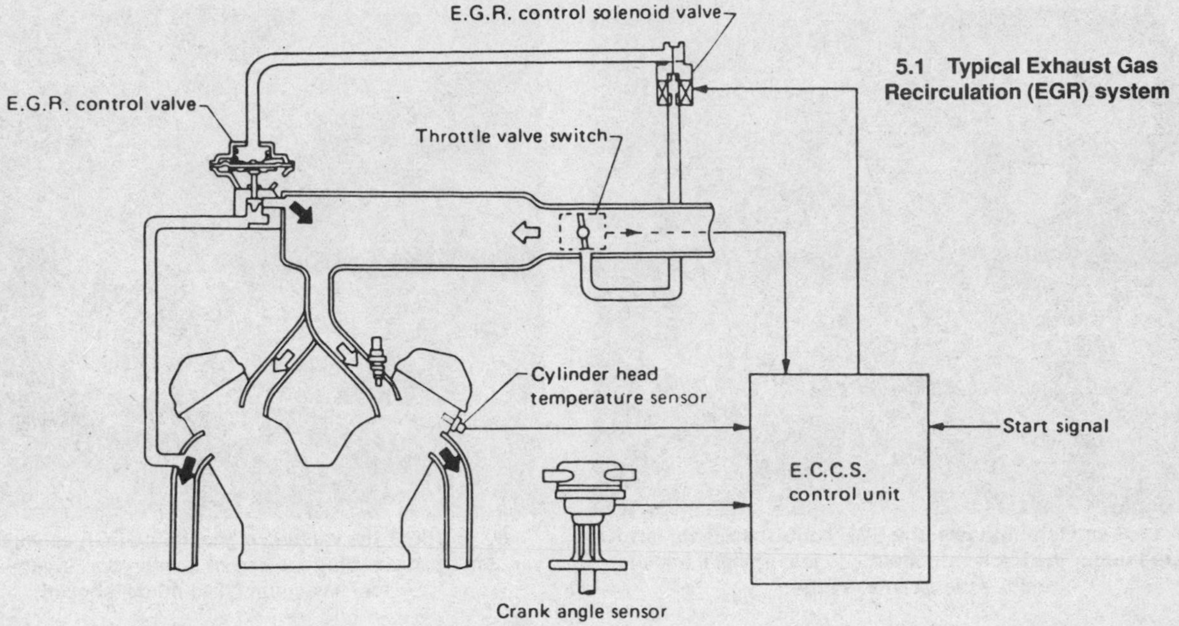

5.1 Typical Exhaust Gas Recirculation (EGR) system

Adjustment

Refer to illustrations 4.5 and 4.6

5 Remove the rubber cap on the BCDD **(see illustration)**.

6 Race the engine and, using a small screwdriver, turn the adjusting screw **(see illustration)** until the set vacuum listed in the Specifications is obtained. Turn the adjusting screw clockwise to increase vacuum; turn the screw counterclockwise to decrease vacuum. Turning the adjusting screw 1/4-turn causes a change in operating vacuum of about 0.79 in Hg (2.7 kPa). **Caution:** *Don't try to jam the screwdriver too tightly into the screw slot or you'll damage it.*

5 Exhaust Gas Recirculation (EGR) system

General description

Refer to illustrations 5.1, 5.2, 5.3a and 5.3b

1 The Exhaust Gas Recirculation (EGR) system **(see illustration)** recirculates a portion of the exhaust gases back through the intake and combustion chamber. This lowers combustion temperatures, which in turn lowers oxides of nitrogen (NOx).

2 The EGR valve is located on the upper left rear corner of the intake on 1986 through 1988 models and on the lower left front corner of the intake on 1989 and later models **(see illustration)**. The EGR valve regulates the quantity of exhaust gas fed back into the intake manifold. A taper valve, connected to a vacuum operated diaphragm, moves up and down in accordance with the amount of intake vacuum applied to the diaphragm, varying the amount of gas fed into the intake manifold.

3 The vacuum signal to the EGR valve diaphragm is regulated by the EGR control solenoid valve, also known as the EGR vacuum cut solenoid valve on later models **(see illustrations)**. The solenoid is turned on and off by the ECCS control unit. When the solenoid is off, vacuum from the intake manifold reaches the EGR valve; when the solenoid is activated by the control unit, it cuts the vacuum to the EGR valve. The solenoid should be on when the engine is being started, the throttle valve switch is On, the engine temperature is low and/or the engine speed is below 900 rpm or above 3200 rpm. At all other times, the solenoid should be Off.

6

5.2 The EGR valve on 1989 models is located at the lower left corner of the intake – you'll want to remove the air intake tube to get at it (the EGR valve on 1986 through 1988 models is shown in illustration 5.8)

5.3a On 1986 through 1988 models, the EGR control solenoid, or EGR vacuum cut solenoid, is on the left – the control solenoid on the right is for the Air Injection Valve (AIV)

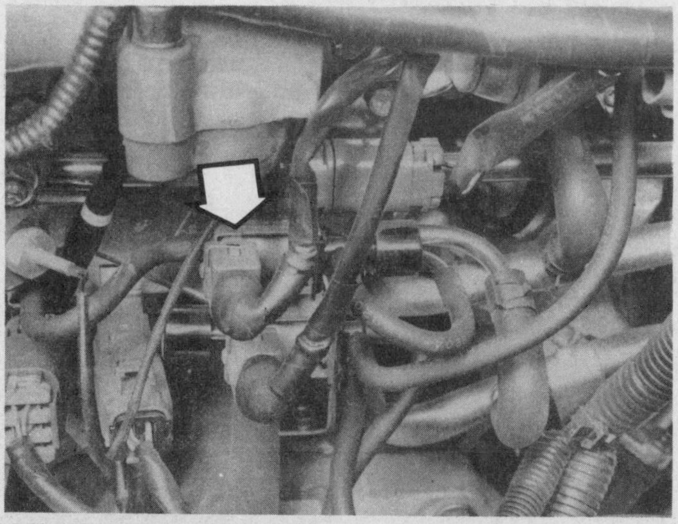

5.3b On 1989 and later models, the EGR control solenoid (arrow) is located under the intake manifold – to test it, you'll have to remove the air intake tube

5.8 To check the vacuum signal to the EGR valve, detach the vacuum hose and plug the end of it with your finger – you should feel a vacuum (1986 model shown)

Checking

4 The most common driveability symptom of a malfunctioning EGR system is a rough engine idle. This problem can be caused by a stuck EGR valve or EGR control solenoid valve, an improperly routed vacuum line (allowing vacuum to the EGR valve under the conditions noted above) or a malfunctioning control unit. If you have already checked the valve for sticking (see Chapter 1), and verified that it's not stuck, the following simple steps will help you locate the problem.

Hoses

5 Inspect the vacuum hoses between the intake manifold, the EGR control solenoid valve and the EGR valve. Look for cracking, hardening, general deterioration and improperly routed hoses (refer to the vacuum hose routing diagram next to the VECI label under the hood). Replace any hoses that are in questionable condition.

Vacuum signal to EGR valve

Refer to illustration 5.8

6 Start the engine and allow it to idle.

7 Detach the vacuum hose from the EGR valve (if the vehicle is a 1989 model, you'll need to remove the air intake tube to detach the hose).

8 With the engine running above 900 rpm (but below 3200 rpm), cover the end of the hose with your finger **(see illustration)**. You should feel a vacuum. If you do, proceed to the next check of the EGR valve itself. If you don't, check the EGR control solenoid valve (see Step 11).

EGR valve

Refer to illustration 5.9

9 Detach the vacuum hose from the EGR valve and attach a hand vacuum pump **(see illustration)**.

10 Apply vacuum with the pump. The engine should run roughly or stall. If the idle does not change, or changes very little, replace the EGR valve.

EGR control solenoid valve

Refer to illustrations 5.14a, 5.14b and 5.17

11 Locate the solenoid **(see illustrations 5.3a and 5.3b)**.

12 Detach the vacuum hose from the top of the solenoid valve.

13 If the vehicle is a 1986 through 1988 model, remove the two solenoid bracket screws and turn the solenoid upside down. If it's a 1989 or later model, remove the air intake tube (see Chapter 4).

14 Detach the vacuum hose from the solenoid. Attach a hand vacuum pump in its place **(see illustrations)**.

15 Start the engine and allow it to idle.

16 Plug the pipe for the upper hose with your finger and apply vacuum

5.9 To check the operation of the EGR valve, detach the vacuum hose, attach a hand vacuum pump in its place and apply vacuum to the valve – the engine should stumble or die (1986 model shown)

5.14a Checking the EGR solenoid valve by applying vacuum – note the solenoid and bracket have been detached and are being held upside down

5.14b 1989 and later models require a similar checking procedure

5.17 To check the voltage to the solenoid, unplug the connector and measure the voltage across the connector terminals – it should be about 12 volts

with the pump. Between 900 and 3200 rpm, you should feel a sucking sensation at the pipe to the EGR valve (the solenoid should hold vacuum). If it doesn't, check the voltage to the solenoid.

17 Unplug the electrical connector from the solenoid and measure the voltage across the connector terminals with a voltmeter **(see illustration)**. It should be about 12 volts. If it is, replace the solenoid. If it isn't, take the vehicle to a dealer and have the control unit checked.

Component replacement

Warning: *Do not attempt to remove the EGR valve right after the engine has been operated. Allow it to cool first.*

18 To replace the EGR valve, detach the vacuum tubes, remove the EGR valve mounting bolts and detach the EGR valve and gasket.

19 Installation is the reverse of removal. Be sure to use a new gasket.

6 Air Injection Valve (AIV)

General description

Refer to illustration 6.1

1 The air injection valve (AIV) **(see illustration)** utilizes the vacuum created by exhaust pulsations in the exhaust manifold to direct additional air into the exhaust manifold when the engine is warming up and during deceleration. Under these conditions, the exhaust pressure is negative (below atmospheric pressure), so extra air is pulled into the exhaust stream; under all other conditions, exhaust pressure is positive and no extra air is needed. Reed valves prevent exhaust gases from escaping back to the air cleaner.

2 The AIV control solenoid valve **(see illustration 5.3a)** controls the intake manifold vacuum signal to the AIV. The solenoid switches on and off in accordance with a voltage signal from the ECCS control unit. When the solenoid is off, the vacuum signal from the intake manifold is cut; when the solenoid is activated by an On signal from the control unit, it directs vacuum to the AIV.

Checking

Refer to illustrations 6.4, 6.6 and 6.8

3 Before performing any of the following tests on the AIV, check for pinched, flattened or disconnected AIV hoses and tubes.

4 Detach the cylinder head temperature sensor harness connector and attach a 2.5 k-ohm resistor between the connector terminals **(see illustration)**.

5 Start the engine and verify that the AIV control solenoid makes a clicking sound. Then detach the vacuum hose from the AIV and put your finger

6

6.1 Typical Air Injection Valve (AIV)

6.4 Unplug the electrical connector to the cylinder head temperature sensor and install a 2.5 k-ohm resistor between the connector terminals

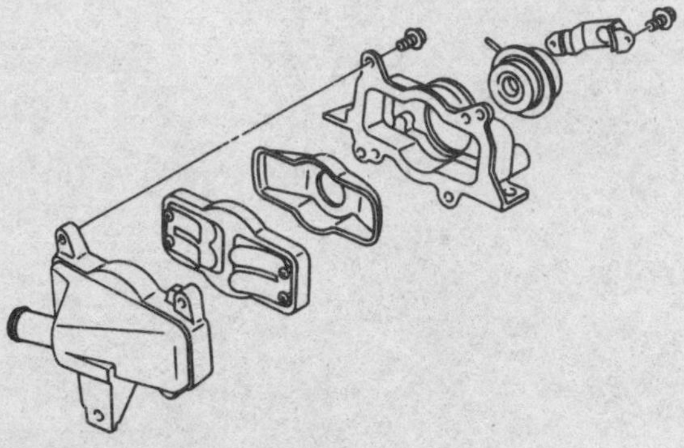

6.6 Exploded view of the AIV

6.8 Check the AIV solenoid control valve by detaching the two hoses and plugging their respective pipes with your fingers – you should feel a slight vacuum at the upper pipe and pressure at the lower one

over the AIV pipe. You should feel a vacuum. If the solenoid clicks, and the AIV produces a vacuum, proceed to the next Step. If the solenoid doesn't click or the AIV fails to produce a vacuum, go to Step 8.

6 Detach the AIV case, remove the case screws, separate the case halves and inspect the AIV control valve and reed valves for binding or damage **(see illustration)**. If the control valve and reed valves are OK, go to the next step. If they're not, replace them. Reassemble the AIV case assembly.

7 Check the cylinder head temperature sensor (see Chapter 4). If it's OK, the AIV system is working properly.

8 Check the operation of the AIV control solenoid by detaching the lower of the two hoses on top and plugging it with your finger **(see illustration)**. You should feel a slight vacuum. If you don't, replace the solenoid valve.

9 If the AIV system still doesn't function properly, take the vehicle to a dealer and have the electrical circuit tested.

7 Auxiliary Air Control (AAC) valve (1989 and later models only)

General description

Refer to illustrations 7.1 and 7.2

1 The Auxiliary Air Control (AAC) valve is located on the intake manifold at the front left corner of the engine **(see illustration)**. The AAC valve is similar in function – but not in operation – to the AIV used on pre-1989 models. The AAC valve is operated by a stepper motor which is controlled by the ECU. The ECU opens and closes the valve in accordance with the need for additional intake air.

2 The air cut valve is located between the AAC valve and intake. As coolant temperature rises, the air cut valve gradually closes. Once the engine has warmed up, the valve restricts auxiliary air flow **(see illustration)**.

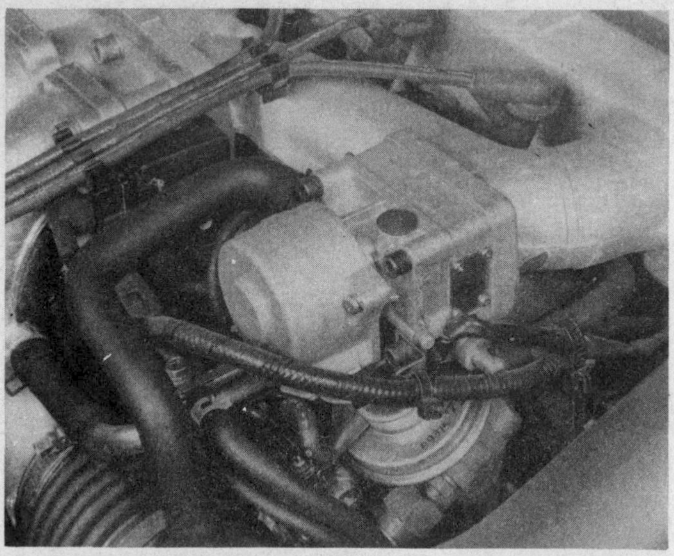

7.1 The Auxiliary Air Control (AAC) valve and air cut valve assembly (1989 and later models)

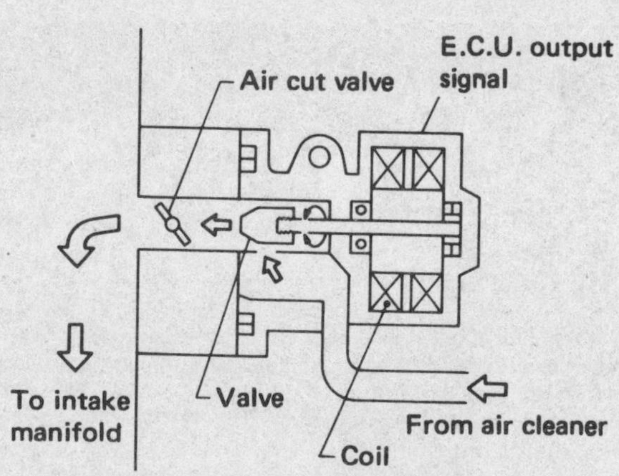

7.2 The air cut valve, located between the AAC valve and the intake, gradually closes as coolant temperature rises (1989 and later models only)

7.4 You'll need to remove the air intake tube to get at the AAC valve electrical connector (arrow), which is located underneath the intake manifold, just behind the EGR – the connector itself is attached to a small bracket from which it must be disconnected for testing: to disconnect it, simply slide the connector toward you

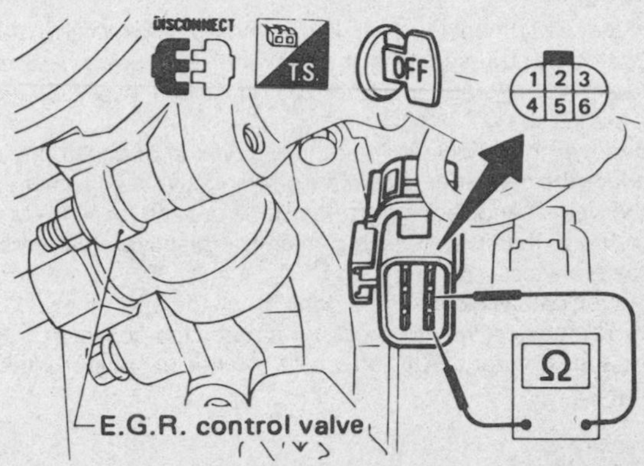

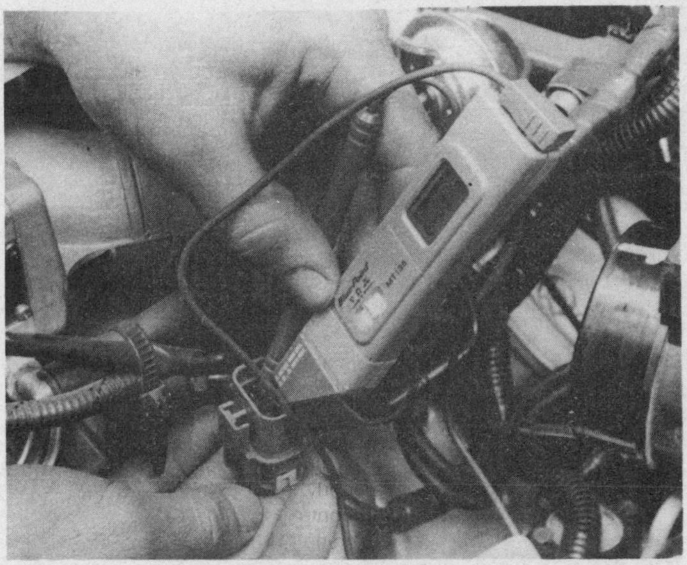

7.5 To check the resistance of the AAC valve, unplug the electrical connector and measure the resistance between terminals 1 and 2, 2 and 3, 3 and 4 and 5 and 6 – it should be 27 to 40 ohms

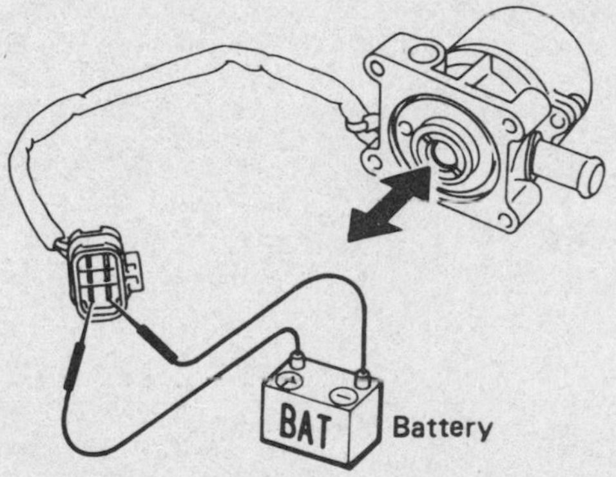

7.7 To check the operation of the AAC valve, remove the valve, apply battery voltage to terminals 3 and 6 and verify that the valve moves in and out

Checking

Refer to illustrations 7.4, 7.5 and 7.7

3 If the engine races, the AAC valve may be faulty. To check the valve, perform the two simple resistance and operation tests below.

4 Remove the air intake tube (see Chapter 4) and unplug the AAC valve harness connector **(see illustration)**.

5 Check the resistance between terminals 1 and 2, 2 and 3, 3 and 4 and 5 and 6 **(see illustration)**. Compare your measurements to the resistance listed in this Chapter's Specifications. If the indicated resistance isn't as specified, replace the AAC valve.

6 Detach the AAC valve assembly from the intake manifold.

7 Apply battery voltage between the terminals **(see illustration)** and verify that the AAC valve moves in and out. If it doesn't, replace the valve. **Note:** *Unless you're watching it very closely, AAC valve movement can be difficult to verify. If you're unable to determine whether the valve is moving in and out by watching it, touch the valve body and note the presence or absence of vibration when the stepper motor is actuated.*

8 When the AAC valve is removed, or replaced, it must be properly seated. To seat the valve, turn the diagnostic mode selector on the ECU fully clockwise (see illustration in Section 11, Chapter 4).

9 If the engine still races after the AAC valve has been replaced and "zeroed" on the computer, the valve opening angle memorized in the ECU may not match the actual valve opening angle. In the unlikely event that this event should occur, take the vehicle to a dealer and have the AAC adjusted.

8 Catalytic converter

Note: *Because of a Federally mandated extended warranty which covers emissions-related components such as the catalytic converter, check with a dealer service department before replacing the converter at your own expense.*

General description

1 The catalytic converter is an emission control device added to the exhaust system to reduce pollutants from the exhaust gas stream. There are two types of converters. The conventional oxidation catalyst reduces the levels of hydrocarbon (HC) and carbon monoxide (CO). The three-way catalyst lowers the levels of oxides of nitrogen (NOx) as well as hydrocarbons (HC) and carbon monoxide (CO).

Checking

2 The test equipment for a catalytic converter is expensive and highly sophisticated. If you suspect that the converter on your vehicle is malfunctioning, take it to a dealer or authorized emissions inspection facility for diagnosis and repair.

3 Whenever the vehicle is raised for servicing of underbody components, check the converter for leaks, corrosion, dents and other damage. Check the welds/flange bolts that attach the front and rear ends of the converter to the exhaust system. If damage is discovered, the converter should be replaced.

4 Although catalytic converters don't break too often, they do become plugged. The easiest way to check for a restricted converter is to use a vacuum gauge to diagnose the effect of a blocked exhaust on intake vacuum.

a) Open the throttle until the engine speed is about 2000 RPM.
b) Release the throttle quickly.
c) If there is no restriction, the gauge will quickly drop to not more than 2 in Hg or more above its normal reading.
d) If the gauge does not show 5 in Hg or more above its normal reading, or seems to momentarily hover around its highest reading for a moment before it returns, the exhaust system, or the converter, is plugged (or an exhaust pipe is bent or dented, or the core inside the muffler has shifted).

Component replacement

5 Refer to the exhaust system removal and installation section in Chapter 4.

Chapter 7 Part A Manual transaxle

Contents

General information	1
Lubricant change	See Chapter 1
Lubricant level check	See Chapter 1
Manual transaxle overhaul – general information	5
Manual transaxle – removal and installation	4
Oil seal replacement	2
Shift lever – removal, installation and free play check	3
Transaxle mount – check and replacement	See Chapter 7B

Specifications

Torque specifications

Torque specifications	Ft-lbs
Gusset to engine	22 to 30
Control rod to transaxle	12 to 16
Support rod to bracket	23 to 30
Support rod bracket to transaxle	20 to 27
Holder bracket fixing bolt	5.8 to 8.0
Holder bracket to support rod	14 to 19
Control lever socket to support rod	5.8 to 8.0
Control lever to control rod	12 to 15

1 General information

The vehicles covered by this manual are equipped with either a five speed manual transaxle or a three speed automatic transaxle. Information on the manual transaxle is included in this Part of Chapter 7. Service procedures for the automatic transaxle are contained in Chapter 7, Part B.

The manual transaxle is a compact, two piece, lightweight aluminum alloy housing containing both the transmission and differential assemblies.

Because of the complexity, unavailability of replacement parts and special tools required, internal repair of the manual transaxle by the home mechanic is not recommended. For readers who wish to tackle a transaxle rebuild, exploded views and a brief *Manual transaxle overhaul – general information* Section are provided. The bulk of information in this Chapter is devoted to removal and installation procedures.

2 Oil seal replacement

Refer to illustrations 2.5, 2.15 and 2.16

1 Oil leaks frequently occur due to wear of the driveaxle oil seals, and/or the speedometer drive gear oil seal and O-ring. Replacement of these seals is relatively easy, since the repairs can usually be performed without removing the transaxle from the vehicle.

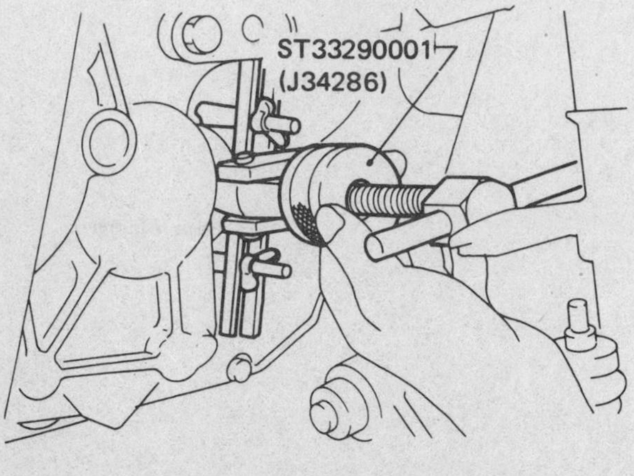

2.5 Remove the driveaxle oil seal with a slide hammer-puller tool if the oil seal cannot easily be removed

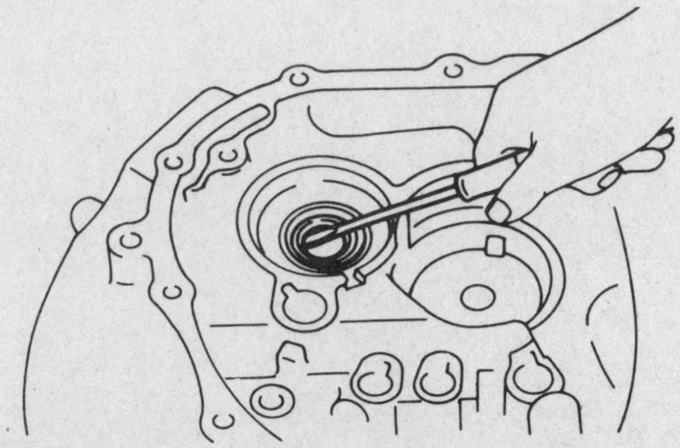

2.15 Pry the front oil seal up, using a screwdriver or seal remover

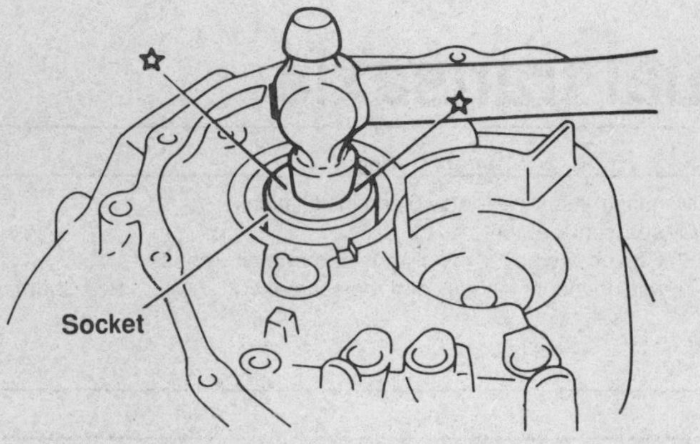

2.16 Install the front oil seal with a large socket and hammer – make sure the seal goes in evenly

Driveaxle oil seals

2 The driveaxle oil seals are located at the side of the transaxle, where the driveaxles are attached. If leakage at the seal is suspected, raise the vehicle and support it securely on jackstands. If the seal is leaking, lubricant will be found on the side of the transaxle.

3 Refer to Chapter 8 and remove the driveaxles.

4 Using a screwdriver or pry bar, carefully pry the oil seal out of the transaxle bore.

5 If the oil seal cannot be removed with a screwdriver or pry bar, a special oil seal removal tool (available at auto parts stores) will be required **(see illustration)**.

6 Using a large section of pipe or a large deep socket as a drift, install the new oil seal. Drive it into the bore squarely and make sure it's completely seated.

7 Install the driveaxle(s). Be careful not to damage the lip of the new seal.

Speedometer cable O-ring

8 The speedometer cable and driven gear housing is located on the transaxle housing. Look for lubricant around the cable housing to determine if the O-ring is leaking.

9 Disconnect the speedometer cable from the transaxle.

10 Using a hook, remove the seal.

11 Using a small socket as a drift, install the new seal.

12 Install the new O-ring on the driven gear housing and reinstall the speedometer cable assembly.

Front oil seal

13 Remove the transaxle (see Section 4).

14 Remove the input shaft cover.

15 Carefully pry the front oil seal up, using a screwdriver or a seal remover **(see illustration)**.

16 Install the new seal by carefully tapping it into place with a large socket and hammer. Make sure the seal goes into the case evenly **(see illustration)**.

3 Shift lever – removal, installation and freeplay check

Refer to illustration 3.2

1 Carefully lift the shift lever boot up and away from the body floor.

2 Remove the control lever socket bolt and lift the socket up **(see illustration)**.

3 Raise the vehicle and support it securely on jackstands.

4 From under the vehicle, remove the control rod/shift lever retaining bolt **(see illustration 3.2)**.

5 Lift the shift lever up and out of the floorboard.

6 Installation is the reverse of removal.

7 There is no adjustment on these types of shift levers. If excess freeplay is felt, replace the control lever upper and lower bearings and the lower bushing as well as the support rod bushing **(see illustration 3.2)**.

4 Manual transaxle – removal and installation

Refer to illustration 4.16

Removal

1 Disconnect the negative cable from the battery.

2 Raise the vehicle and support it securely on jackstands.

3 Drain the transaxle fluid (Chapter 1).

4 Disconnect the shift and clutch linkage from the transaxle.

5 Remove the air cleaner and air flow meter assembly (see Chapter 4).

6 Disconnect the speed sensor and the position switch connector (see Chapter 5).

3.2 Shift lever exploded view

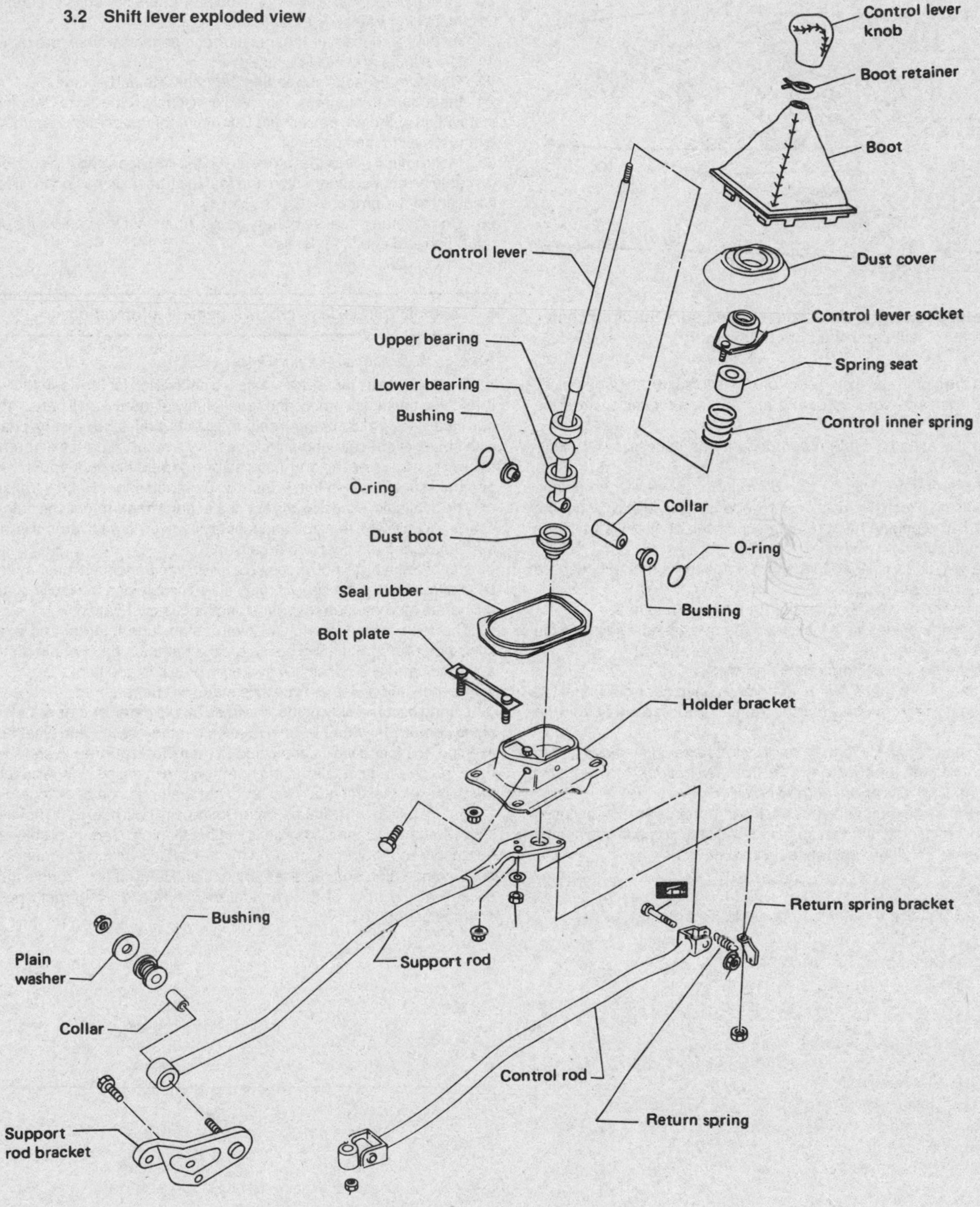
Control lever knob
Boot retainer
Boot
Control lever
Dust cover
Control lever socket
Upper bearing
Spring seat
Lower bearing
Bushing
Control inner spring
O-ring
Collar
Dust boot
O-ring
Seal rubber
Bushing
Bolt plate
Holder bracket
Return spring bracket
Bushing
Plain washer
Support rod
Collar
Control rod
Return spring
Support rod bracket

4.16 Carefully lower the transaxle, making sure the input shaft will clear the clutch assembly

7 Remove the clutch slave cylinder from the transaxle (see Chapter 8).
8 Detach the speedometer cable and wire harness connectors from the transaxle.
9 Remove the exhaust system components as necessary for clearance.
10 Support the engine. This can be done from above with an engine hoist, or by placing a jack (with a block of wood as an insulator) under the engine oil pan. The engine must remain supported at all times while the transaxle is out of the vehicle!
11 Remove any chassis or suspension components that will interfere with transaxle removal (Chapter 10).
12 Disconnect the driveaxles from the transaxle (Chapter 8).
13 Support the transaxle with a jack, then remove the bolts securing the transaxle to the engine.
14 Remove the transaxle mount nuts and bolts.
15 Make a final check that all wires and hoses have been disconnected from the transaxle, then carefully pull the transaxle and jack away from the engine.
16 Once the input shaft is clear, lower the transaxle and remove it from under the vehicle **(see illustration)**. **Caution:** *Do not depress the clutch pedal while the transaxle is out of the vehicle.*
17 With the transaxle removed, the clutch components are now accessible and can be inspected. In most cases, new clutch components should be routinely installed when the transaxle is removed.

Installation

18 If removed, install the clutch components (Chapter 8.)
19 With the transaxle secured to the jack with a chain, raise it into position behind the engine, then carefully slide it forward, engaging the input shaft with the clutch plate hub splines. Do not use excessive force to install the transaxle – if the input shaft does not slide into place, readjust the angle of the transaxle so it is level and/or turn the input shaft so the splines engage properly with the clutch plate hub.
20 Install the transaxle-to-engine bolts. Tighten the bolts securely.
21 Install the transaxle mount nuts or bolts.
22 Install the chassis and suspension components which were removed. Tighten all nuts and bolts securely.
23 Remove the jacks supporting the transaxle and engine.
24 Install the various items removed previously, referring to Chapter 8 for installation of the driveaxles and Chapter 4 for information regarding the exhaust system components.
25 Make a final check that all wires, hoses, linkages and the speedometer cable have been connected and that the transaxle has been filled with lubricant to the proper level (Chapter 1).
26 Connect the negative battery cable. Road test the vehicle for proper operation and check for leaks.

5 Manual transaxle overhaul – general information

Refer to illustrations 5.4a and 5.4b

Overhauling a manual transaxle is a difficult job for the do-it-yourselfer. It involves the disassembly and reassembly of many small parts. Numerous clearances must be precisely measured and, if necessary, changed with select fit spacers and snap-rings. As a result, if transaxle problems arise, it can be removed and installed by a competent do-it-yourselfer, but overhaul should be left to a transmission repair shop. Rebuilt transaxles may be available – check with your dealer parts department and auto parts stores. At any rate, the time and money involved in an overhaul is almost sure to exceed the cost of a rebuilt unit.

Nevertheless, it's not impossible for an inexperienced mechanic to rebuild a transaxle if the special tools are available and the job is done in a deliberate step-by-step manner so nothing is overlooked.

The tools necessary for an overhaul include internal and external snap-ring pliers, a bearing puller, a slide hammer, a set of pin punches, a dial indicator and possibly a hydraulic press. In addition, a large, sturdy workbench and a vise or transaxle stand will be required.

During disassembly of the transaxle, make careful notes of how each piece comes off, where it fits in relation to other pieces and what holds it in place. Exploded views are included **(see illustrations)** to show where the parts go – but actually noting how they are installed when you remove the parts will make it much easier to get the transaxle back together.

Before taking the transaxle apart for repair, it will help if you have some idea what area of the transaxle is malfunctioning. Certain problems can be closely tied to specific areas in the transaxle, which can make component examination and replacement easier. Refer to the *Troubleshooting* section at the front of this manual for information regarding possible sources of trouble.

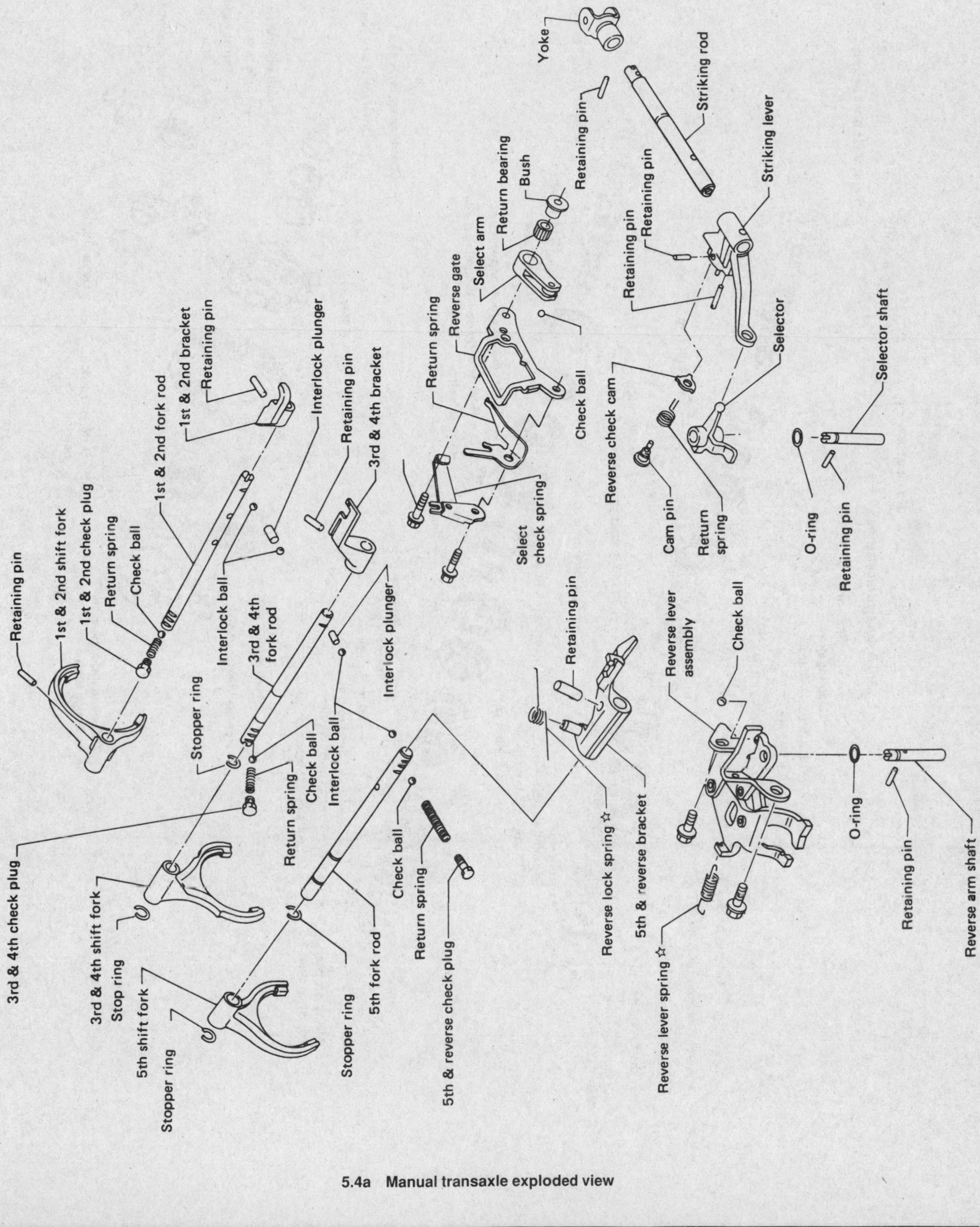

5.4a Manual transaxle exploded view

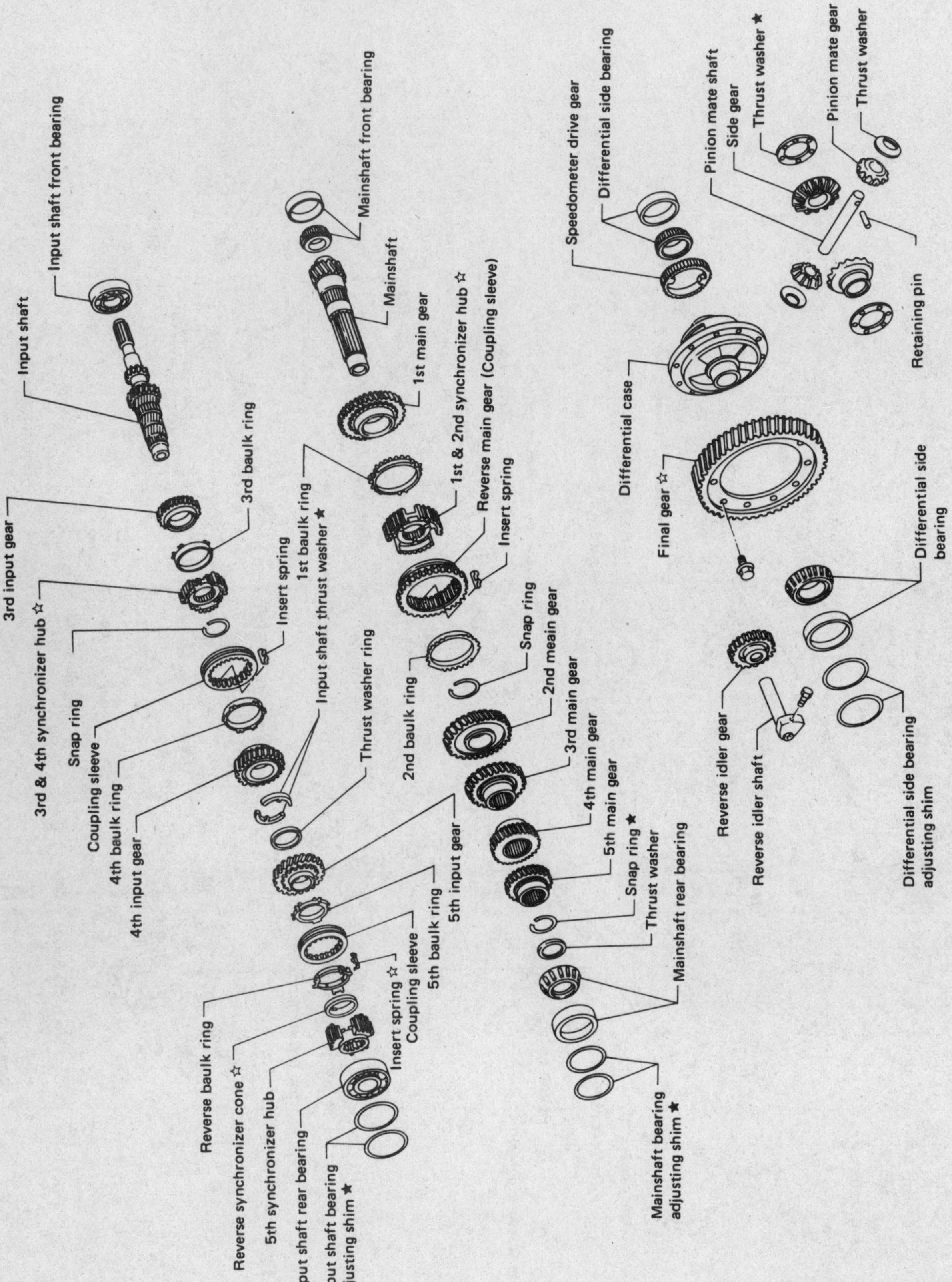

5.4b Manual transaxle exploded view

Chapter 7 Part B Automatic transaxle

Contents

Automatic transaxle fluid change .... See Chapter 1
Automatic transaxle fluid level check .... See Chapter 1
Automatic transaxle – removal and installation 7
Diagnosis – general 2
General information 1
Neutral start switch – check and adjustment 5
Oil seal replacement .... See Chapter 7A
Shift linkage – adjustment 3
Throttle cable adjustment (1985 through 1988 models only) 4
Transaxle mount – check and replacement 6

7B

Specifications

General

Throttle cable stroke	1.54 to 1.69 in
Torque converter/transaxle depth	0.709 in or more

Torque specifications

	Ft-lbs
Driveplate-to-torque converter bolts	29 to 36
Bellhousing-to-engine bolts	29 to 36
Engine-to-bellhousing bolts	22 to 30
Gusset-to-bellhousing bolts	
10 mm bolt	12 to 15
6 mm bolt	4.6 to 6.1
Neutral start switch-to-transmission case	1.4 to 1.9

1 General information

All vehicles covered in this manual come equipped with either a 5-speed manual transaxle or an automatic transaxle. All information on the automatic transaxle is included in this Part of Chapter 7.

Information for the manual transaxle can be found in Part A of this Chapter.

Due to the complexity of the automatic transaxles covered in this manual and the need for specialized equipment to perform most service operations, this Chapter contains only general diagnosis, routine maintenance, adjustment and removal and installation procedures.

If the transaxle requires major repair work, it should be left to a dealer service department or an automotive or transmission repair shop. You can, however, remove and install the transaxle yourself and save the expense, even if the repair work is done by a transmission shop.

2 Diagnosis – general

Note: *Automatic transaxle malfunctions may be caused by five general conditions: poor engine performance, improper adjustments, hydraulic malfunctions, mechanical malfunctions or malfunctions in the computer or its signal network. Diagnosis of these problems should always begin with a check of the easily repaired items: fluid level and condition (Chapter 1), shift linkage adjustment and throttle linkage adjustment. Next, perform a road test to determine if the problem has been corrected or if more diagnosis is necessary. If the problem persists after the preliminary tests and corrections are completed, additional diagnosis should be done by a dealer service department or transmission repair shop. Refer to the Troubleshooting section at the front of this manual for transaxle problem diagnosis.*

Preliminary checks

1 Drive the vehicle to warm the transaxle to normal operating temperature.

2 Check the fluid level as described in Chapter 1:

- a If the fluid level is unusually low, add enough fluid to bring the level within the designated area of the dipstick, then check for external leaks.
- b) If the fluid level is abnormally high, drain off the excess, then check the drained fluid for contamination by coolant. The presence of engine coolant in the automatic transmission fluid indicates that a failure has occurred in the internal radiator walls that separate the coolant from the transmission fluid (see Chapter 3).
- c) If the fluid is foaming, drain it and refill the transaxle, then check for coolant in the fluid or a high fluid level.

3 Check the engine idle speed. **Note**: *If the engine is malfunctioning, do not proceed with the preliminary checks until it has been repaired and runs normally.*

4 Check the throttle valve cable for freedom of movement. Adjust it if necessary (Section 4). **Note:** *The throttle valve cable may function properly when the engine is shut off and cold, but it may malfunction once the engine is hot. Check it cold and at normal engine operating temperature.*

5 Inspect the shift control cable (Section 3). Make sure that it's properly adjusted and that the linkage operates smoothly.

Fluid leak diagnosis

6 Most fluid leaks are easy to locate visually. Repair usually consists of replacing a seal or gasket. If a leak is difficult to find, the following procedure may help.

7 Identify the fluid. Make sure it's transmission fluid and not engine oil or brake fluid (automatic transmission fluid is a deep red color).

8 Try to pinpoint the source of the leak. Drive the vehicle several miles, then park it over a large sheet of cardboard. After a minute or two, you should be able to locate the leak by determining the source of the fluid dripping onto the cardboard.

9 Make a careful visual inspection of the suspected component and the area immediately around it. Pay particular attention to gasket mating surfaces. A mirror is often helpful for finding leaks in areas that are hard to see.

10 If the leak still cannot be found, clean the suspected area thoroughly with a degreaser or solvent, then dry it.

11 Drive the vehicle for several miles at normal operating temperature and varying speeds. After driving the vehicle, visually inspect the suspected component again.

12 Once the leak has been located, the cause must be determined before it can be properly repaired. If a gasket is replaced but the sealing flange is bent, the new gasket will not stop the leak. The bent flange must be straightened.

13 Before attempting to repair a leak, check to make sure that the following conditions are corrected or they may cause another leak.

Note: *Some of the following conditions cannot be fixed without highly specialized tools and expertise. Such problems must be referred to a transmission shop or a dealer service department.*

Gasket leaks

14 Check the pan periodically. Make sure the bolts are tight, no bolts are missing, the gasket is in good condition and the pan is flat (dents in the pan may indicate damage to the valve body inside).

15 If the pan gasket is leaking, the fluid level or the fluid pressure may be too high, the vent may be plugged, the pan bolts may be too tight, the pan sealing flange may be warped, the sealing surface of the transaxle housing may be damaged, the gasket may be damaged or the transaxle casting may be cracked or porous. If sealant instead of gasket material has been used to form a seal between the pan and the transaxle housing, it may be the wrong sealant.

Seal leaks

16 If a transaxle seal is leaking, the fluid level or pressure may be too high, the vent may be plugged, the seal bore may be damaged, the seal itself may be damaged or improperly installed, the surface of the shaft protruding through the seal may be damaged or a loose bearing may be causing excessive shaft movement.

17 Make sure the dipstick tube seal is in good condition and the tube is properly seated. Periodically check the area around the speedometer gear or sensor for leakage. If transmission fluid is evident, check the O-ring for damage. Also inspect the side gear shaft oil seals for leakage.

Case leaks

18 If the case itself appears to be leaking, the casting is porous and will have to be repaired or replaced.

19 Make sure the oil cooler hose fittings are tight and in good condition.

Fluid comes out vent pipe or fill tube

20 If this condition occurs, the transaxle is overfilled, there is coolant in the fluid, the case is porous, the dipstick is incorrect, the vent is plugged or the drain back holes are plugged.

3 Shift linkage – adjustment

1985 through early 1987 models

Refer to illustrations 3.4, 3.5 and 3.7

1 Slowly move the shift lever from P to 1. You should feel each detent lock into position as you move the lever.

2 If the detents cannot be felt or the pointer is improperly aligned, the shift linkage needs adjustment.

3 Raise the vehicle and support it securely on jackstands.

4 Working under the vehicle, remove the shift cable from the shift lever **(see illustration)**.

5 Pull the shift cable back (towards the rear of the vehicle) to place the transaxle lever in Park **(see illustration)**.

6 Make sure you can't turn the driveaxles.

7 Loosen adjusting nuts A and B **(see illustration)**.

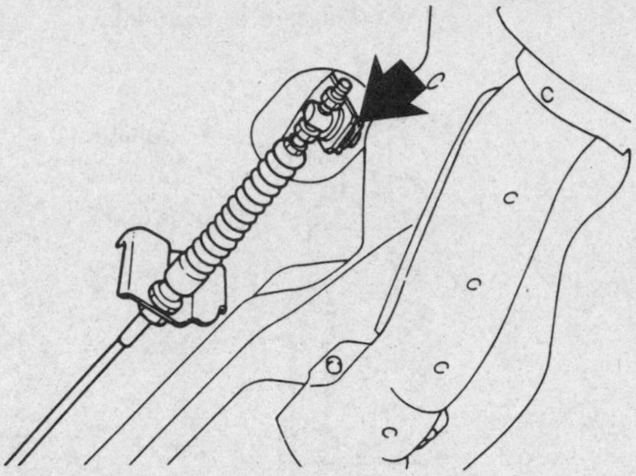

3.4 Working under the vehicle, separate the cable from the gear shift lever by removing the clip (arrow) and pulling the pin out of the lever (1985 through early 1987 models only)

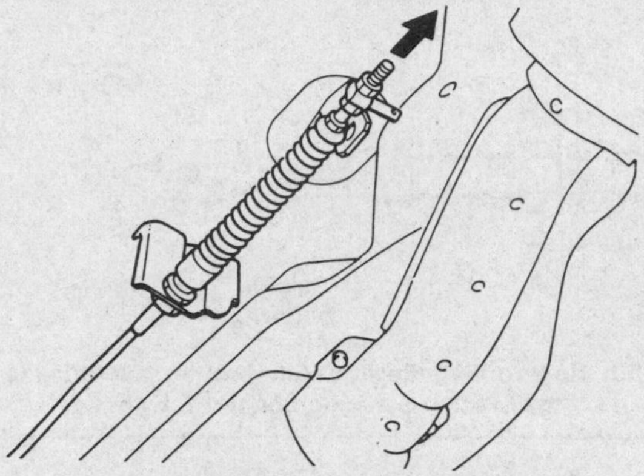

3.5 Pull the shift cable back in order to position the lever on the transaxle in Park

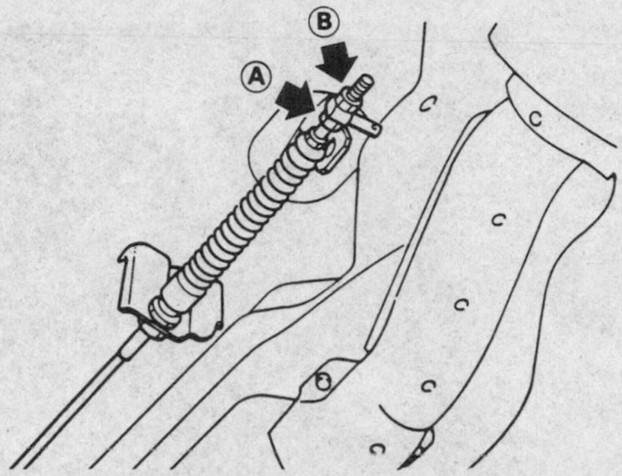

3.7 Loosen the adjusting nuts (A and B) and with both levers securely in Park, insert the pin into the hole (move the pin forward or backward on the cable end as necessary)

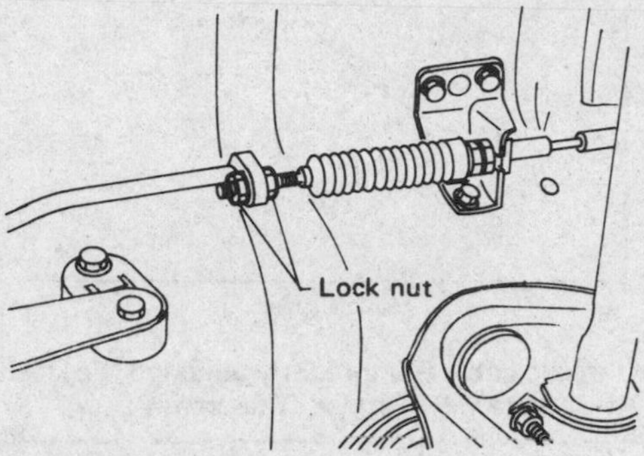

3.12 Loosen the locknuts on the cable end (late 1987 and later models)

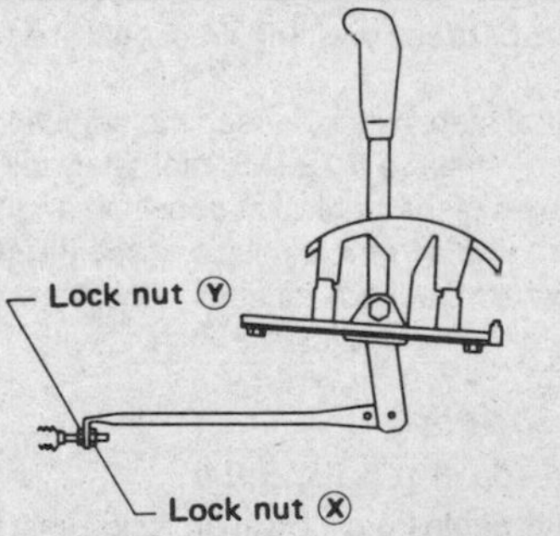

3.13 Turn locknut X until it touches the gear shift rod end – hold the rod horizontal and tighten locknut Y

8 Make sure the gear shift lever (inside the vehicle) moves smoothly and without any noise, then place it in Park.
9 With the transaxle lever securely engaged in the Park detent, move the pin on the end of the cable until it slips freely into the hole in the gear shift lever.
10 Tighten both nuts (A and B) securely (don't move the gear shift lever as the nuts are tightened).

Late 1987 and later models

Refer to illustrations 3.12 and 3.13

11 Place the shift lever in Park.
12 Loosen the locknuts **(see illustration)**.
13 Turn locknut X until it touches the shift rod end while holding the rod horizontal, then tighten locknut Y **(see illustration)**.
14 Move the shift lever from P to 1 and make sure it moves smoothly.

4 Throttle cable adjustment (1985 through 1988 models only)

Refer to illustrations 4.1, 4.2, 4.4 and 4.5

1 Loosen the throttle cable adjustment nuts on the throttle valve side **(see illustration)**.

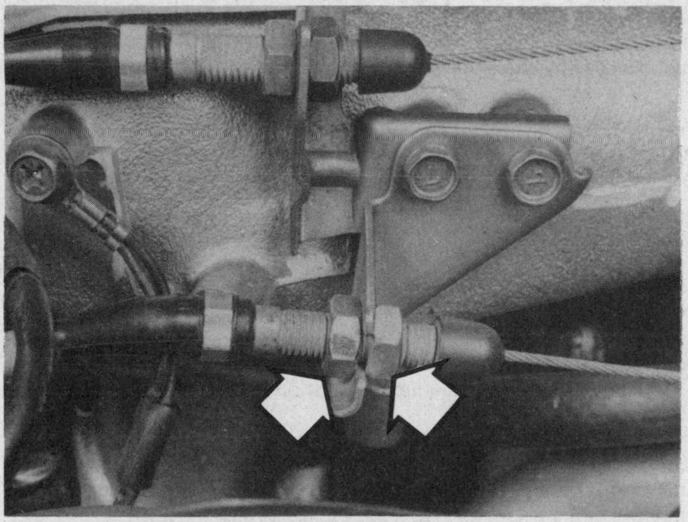

4.1 Loosen the throttle cable adjustment nuts (arrows)

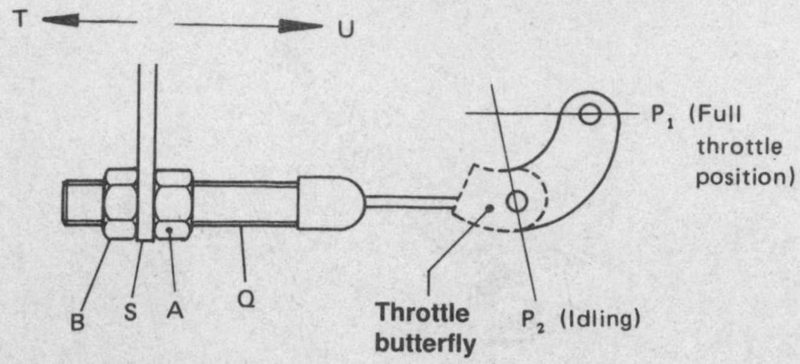

4.2 With the throttle butterfly at full throttle, pull fitting Q toward the bracket S and tighten nut B by hand

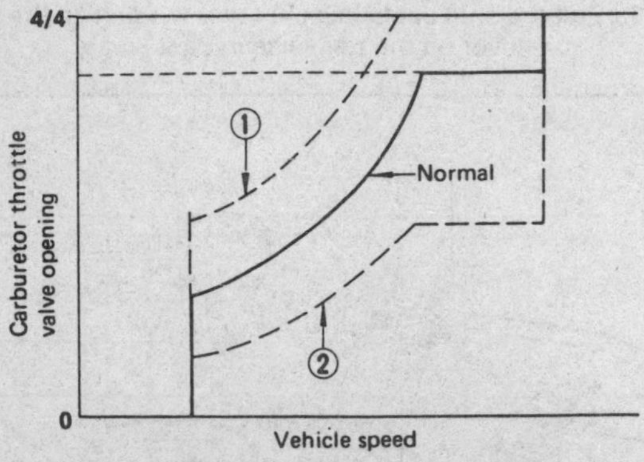

4.5 If the throttle cable is improperly adjusted the kickdown range will increase or decrease

2 With the throttle butterfly set at full throttle (P1), pull fitting Q toward the adjustment bracket (direction T) and tighten nut B by hand until it contacts the bracket S **(see illustration)**.

3 Loosen nut B 3/4 to 1-1/4 revolutions in direction T, then tighten nut A securely. The throttle butterfly should stay at full throttle (P1).

4 Check that the throttle cable stroke L is within the specified limits between full throttle and idle **(see illustration)**. Check the specifications listed in this chapter.

5 If the throttle wire stroke is improperly adjusted then the following problems will arise. When full throttle P1 distance is too close to the bracket (direction T) then the shift schedule will be too quick (2 shown in the illustration) and the kickdown range will greatly increase.

6 When full throttle distance P1 is closer to the throttle butterfly (direction Q) then the shift schedule will be retarded and the kickdown range will not occur **(1 in illustration 4.5)**.

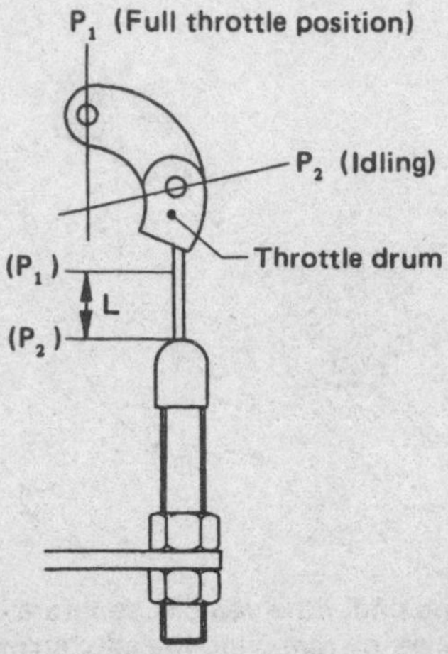

4.4 Check that the throttle cable stroke is within specifications

5.3 Remove the clip from the shift cable (arrow) and separate the cable from the transmission

5 Neutral start switch – check and adjustment

1985 through 1988 models

Refer to illustrations 5.3, 5.4 and 5.6

1 Disconnect the battery cables (negative first, then positive) and remove the battery.

2 Remove the air cleaner assembly and the air flow meter (see Chapter 4).

3 Remove the clip **(see illustration)** and disconnect the shift cable from the transmission.

4 Disconnect the neutral start switch wire harness connector, located on the end of the cylinder head, and check switch continuity with the shift lever in Neutral, Park and Reverse. Place the ohmmeter leads on the designated terminals for each gear position **(see illustration)**.

5 With the shift lever held in Neutral, move it forward and backward in equal amounts and monitor the change in continuity. Continuity should cease at an angle of 1.5 degrees in either direction. If it doesn't, adjust the neutral start switch.

6 To adjust the neutral start switch, loosen the adjusting screws. Place the shift lever in Neutral. Insert a 5/32-inch diameter drill bit (shank end) into the adjustment holes of the neutral start switch and the switch lever and move both of them into a vertical position **(see illustration)**.

7 Tighten the screws and recheck for continuity. If the continuity check is still negative, replace the neutral start switch.

1989 and later models

Refer to illustrations 5.10a, 5.10b and 5.10c

8 Disconnect the shift cable from the transmission shift lever **(see illustration 5.3)**

9 Disconnect the neutral start switch electrical connector.

10 Using an ohmmeter or self-powered test light, check for continuity between the terminals of the neutral start switch connector while moving the shift lever on the transaxle through each position **(see illustrations)**.

11 If continuity is not as shown on the accompanying chart, loosen the switch mounting screws and adjust the switch. If adjustment does not bring the correct continuity, replace the switch. Tighten the switch mounting screws.

12 Re-connect the switch electrical connector.

6 Transaxle mount – check and replacement

Refer to illustrations 6.4a and 6.4b

1 Raise the vehicle and support it securely on jackstands. Remove the front wheels. Remove the fender apron (see Chapter 11).

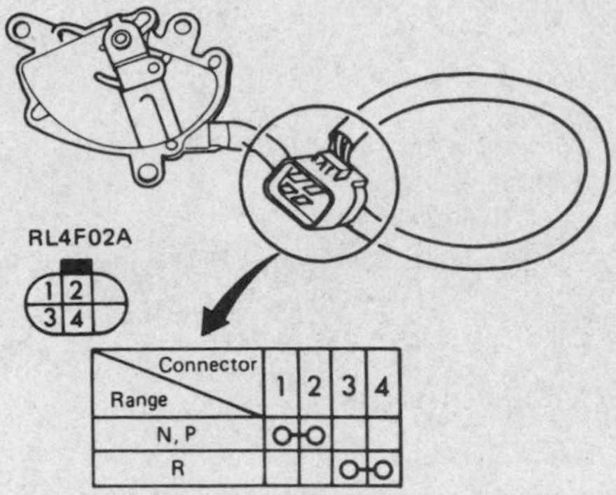

5.4 Connect the ohmmeter leads to the designated terminals and check for continuity in P, N and R

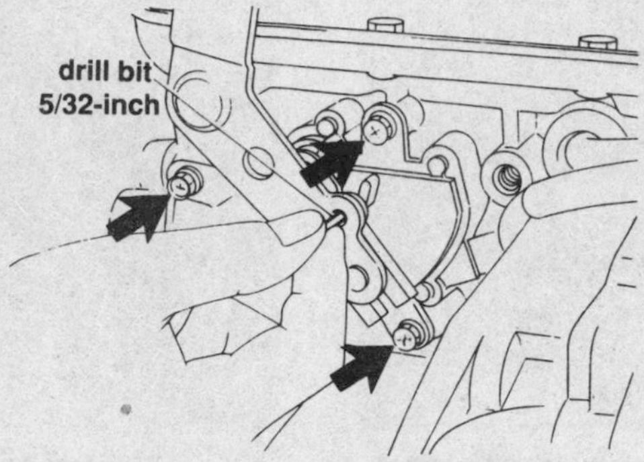

5.6 Loosen the adjusting screws (arrows), insert a 5/32-inch drill bit shank into the neutral start switch and switch lever and move them into a vertical position

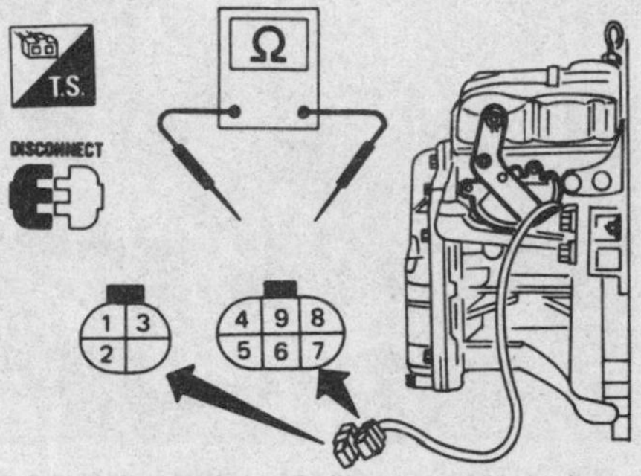

5.10a Check for continuity between the terminals of the neutral start switch electrical connector, . . .

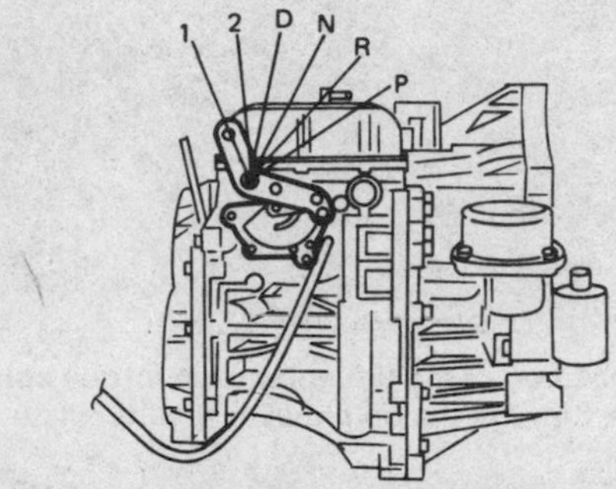

5.10b . . . while moving the shift lever on the transaxle through each position

Lever position \ Terminal No.	①	②	③	④	⑤	⑥	⑦	⑧	⑨
P	O——		——O	O——		——O			
R				O——			——O		
N	O——	O——	——O	——O					
D				O——	——O				
2				O——				——O	
1				O——					——O

5.10c Continuity should be as shown on this chart – for example, in Park (P), there should be continuity between terminals 1 and 3 and between terminals 4 and 6

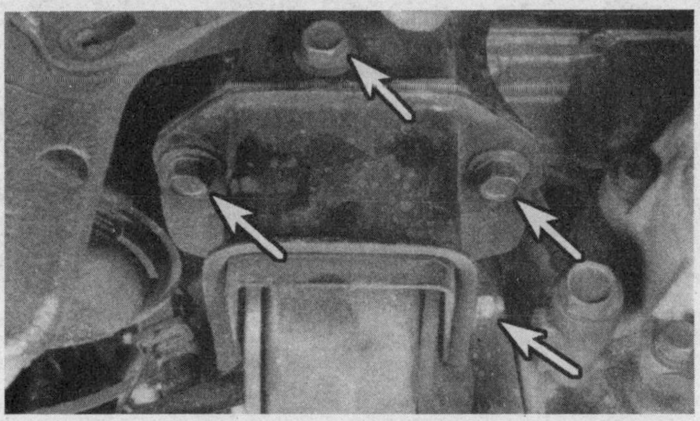

6.4a Remove the lower transaxle mount bolts (arrows) and remove the mount

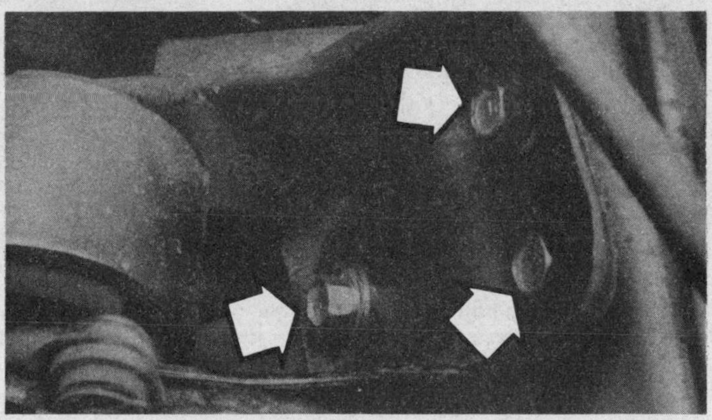

6.4b Remove the upper transaxle mount bolts (arrows) and remove the mount

2 Insert a large screwdriver or prybar between the mount and the transaxle and pry up.
3 The transaxle should not move more than about 1/2 to 3/4-inch away from the mount. If it does, replace the mount.
4 To replace the mount, support the transaxle with a jack, remove the nuts and bolts and remove the mount **(see illustrations)**. It may be necessary to raise the transaxle slightly to provide enough clearance to remove the mount.
5 Installation is the reverse of removal.

7 Automatic transaxle – removal and installation

Refer to illustrations 7.1, 7.2, 7.3, 7.4, 7.5, 7.6 and 7.8

Removal

1 Remove the transaxle with the engine (see Chapter 2B, Section 5). The engine/transaxle is removed as a unit **(see illustration)**.
2 Remove the gusset on each side of the engine oil pan **(see illustration)**.

7B

7.1 Remove the engine and transaxle as a single unit – lower them onto two dollies to move the engine and transaxle after they are separated

7.2 Remove the gusset on each side of the oil pan

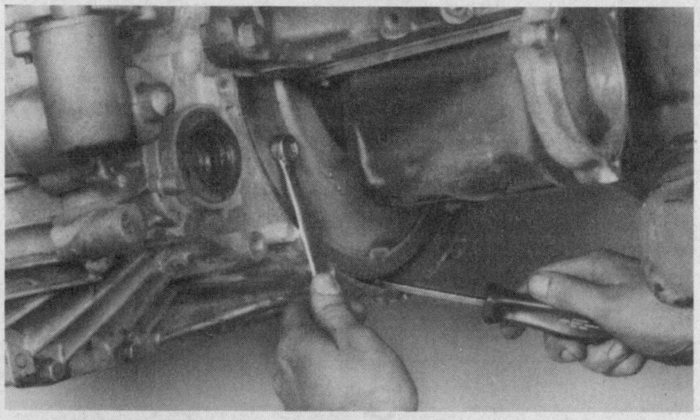

7.3 Use a screwdriver to lock the automatic transaxle driveplate, then remove the driveplate-to-torque converter bolts

7.4 Mark the position of the driveplate and torque converter by painting a line through the bolt hole to thedriveplate surface

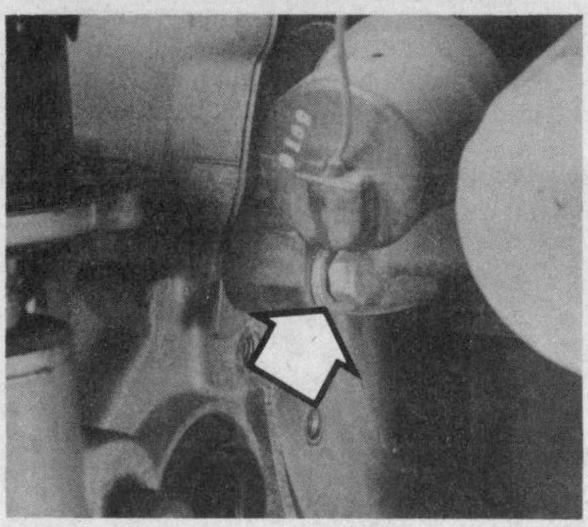

7.5 Remove the bolt directly under the oil pressure switch (arrow)

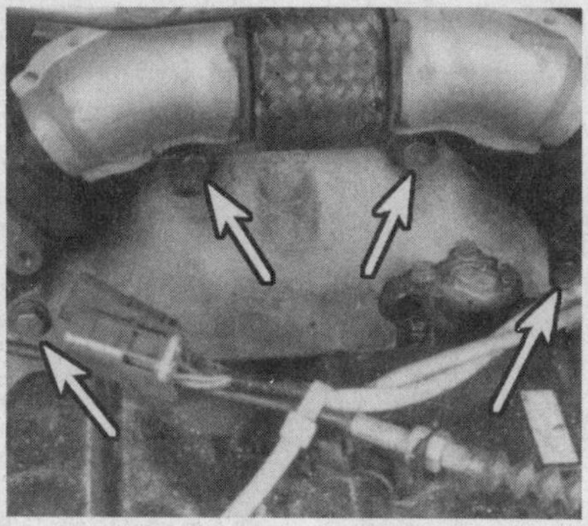

7.6 Remove the remaining bellhousing bolts (arrows)

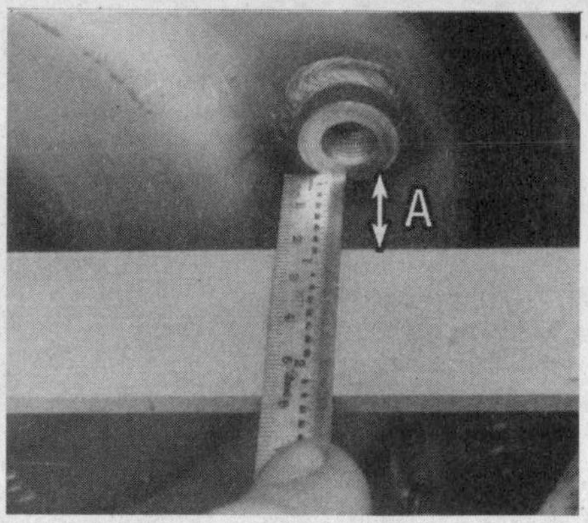

7.8 Make sure the torque converter is properly set on the input shaft and measure the depth – distance A should be 0.709-inch or more

3 Use a screwdriver to lock the automatic transaxle driveplate and remove the torque converter bolts **(see illustration)**.

4 Carefully mark the driveplate by painting a line inside the threaded hole of the torque converter and up onto the driveplate **(see illustration)**.

5 Remove the bellhousing bolt directly under the oil pressure switch **(see illustration)**.

6 Remove the remaining bellhousing bolts from the transaxle **(see illustration)**.

7 Use a large screwdriver to carefully pry the transaxle away from the engine.

Installation

8 Connect the torque converter to the transaxle and measure distance A **(see illustration)**. Refer to this Chapter's specifications. Simultaneously spin and push the torque converter to be sure it has seated itself on the input shaft and recheck the measurement.

9 Reattach the transaxle to the engine.

10 Bolt the torque converter to the driveplate. Make sure the marks are correctly aligned.

11 After the transaxle has been installed, rotate the crankshaft to make sure the transaxle and torque converter do not bind.

12 Install the engine/transaxle in the vehicle (see Chapter 2, Part B).

13 Fill the transaxle with fluid and check the level (see Chapter 1).

Chapter 8 Clutch and driveaxles

Contents

Clutch components – removal, inspection and installation 3
Clutch – description and check 2
Clutch fluid level check .... See Chapter 1
Clutch hydraulic system – bleeding 7
Clutch interlock switch – inspection and adjustment 8
Clutch master cylinder – removal, overhaul and installation 5
Clutch pedal free play check and adjustment .... See Chapter 1
Clutch release bearing and lever – removal, inspection and installation 4
Clutch release cylinder – removal, overhaul and installation 6
Driveaxle boot check .... See Chapter 1
Driveaxle boot replacement and constant velocity (CV) joint overhaul 11
Driveaxle oil seal replacement .... See Chapter 7
Driveaxles – general information and inspection 9
Driveaxles – removal and installation 10
Flywheel – removal and installation .... See Chapter 2A
General information 1

Specifications

Clutch

Pedal free play	See Chapter 1
Clutch disc lining minimum thickness	1/16 in (1.58 mm) above rivet heads
Clutch interlock switch clearance "C"	0.004 to 0.040 in (0.1 to 1.0 mm)

Driveaxles

Inner CV joint boot length (L2)	3.82 to 3.90 in (97 to 99 mm)
Outer CV joint boot length (L1)	3.78 to 3.86 in (96 to 98 mm)
Grease capacity	
Inner joint	5.64 to 6.35 oz. (160 to 180 grams)
Outer joint	7.23 to 7.94 oz. (205 to 225 grams)

Torque specifications

Torque specifications	Ft-lbs
Pressure plate-to-flywheel bolts	16 to 22
Driveaxle hub nut	174 to 231
Wheel lug nuts	See Chapter 1

1 General information

The information in this Chapter deals with the components from the rear of the engine to the drive wheels, except for the transaxle, which is dealt with in the previous Chapter. For the purposes of this Chapter, these components are grouped into two categories: Clutch and driveaxles. Separate Sections within this Chapter offer general descriptions and checking procedures for components in each of the two groups.

Since nearly all the procedures covered in this Chapter involve working under the vehicle, make sure it's securely supported on sturdy jackstands or on a hoist where the vehicle can be easily raised and lowered.

2 Clutch – description and check

Refer to illustration 2.1

1 All vehicles with a manual transmission use a single dry plate, diaphragm spring type clutch **(see illustration)**. The clutch disc has a splined hub which allows it to slide along the splines of the transmission input shaft. The clutch and pressure plate are held in contact by spring pressure exerted by the diaphragm in the pressure plate.

2 The clutch release system is operated by hydraulic pressure. The hydraulic release system consists of the clutch pedal, a master cylinder and fluid reservoir, the hydraulic line, a release (or slave) cylinder which actuates the clutch release lever and the clutch release (or throwout) bearing.

3 When pressure is applied to the clutch pedal to release the clutch, hydraulic pressure is exerted against the outer end of the clutch release lever. As the lever pivots the shaft fingers push against the release bearing. The bearing pushes against the fingers of the diaphragm spring of the pressure plate assembly, which in turn releases the clutch plate.

4 Terminology can be a problem when discussing the clutch components because common names are in some cases different from those used by the manufacturer. For example, the driven plate is also called the clutch plate or disc, the clutch release bearing is sometimes called a throwout bearing and the release cylinder is sometimes called the operating or slave cylinder.

5 Other than to replace components with obvious damage, some preliminary checks should be performed to diagnose clutch problems.

a) The first check should be of the fluid level in the clutch master cylinder. If the fluid level is low, add fluid as necessary and inspect the hydraulic system for leaks. If the master cylinder reservoir has run dry, bleed the system as described in Section 7 and retest the clutch operation.

b) To check "clutch spin down time," run the engine at normal idle speed with the transmission in Neutral (clutch pedal up – engaged). Disengage the clutch (pedal down), wait several seconds and shift the transmission into Reverse. No grinding noise should be heard. A grinding noise would most likely indicate a problem in the pressure plate or the clutch disc.

c) To check for complete clutch release, run the engine (with the parking brake applied to prevent movement) and hold the clutch pedal approximately 1/2-inch from the floor. Shift the transmission between 1st gear and Reverse several times. If the shift is hard or grinds, component failure is indicated, check the release cylinder pushrod travel. With the clutch pedal depressed completely, the release cylinder pushrod should extend substantially. If it doesn't, check the fluid level in the clutch master cylinder and bleed the system (see Section 7).

d) Visually inspect the pivot bushing at the top of the clutch pedal to make sure there is no binding or excessive play.

e) Check under the hood and make sure the clutch release lever is solidly mounted on the ball stud.

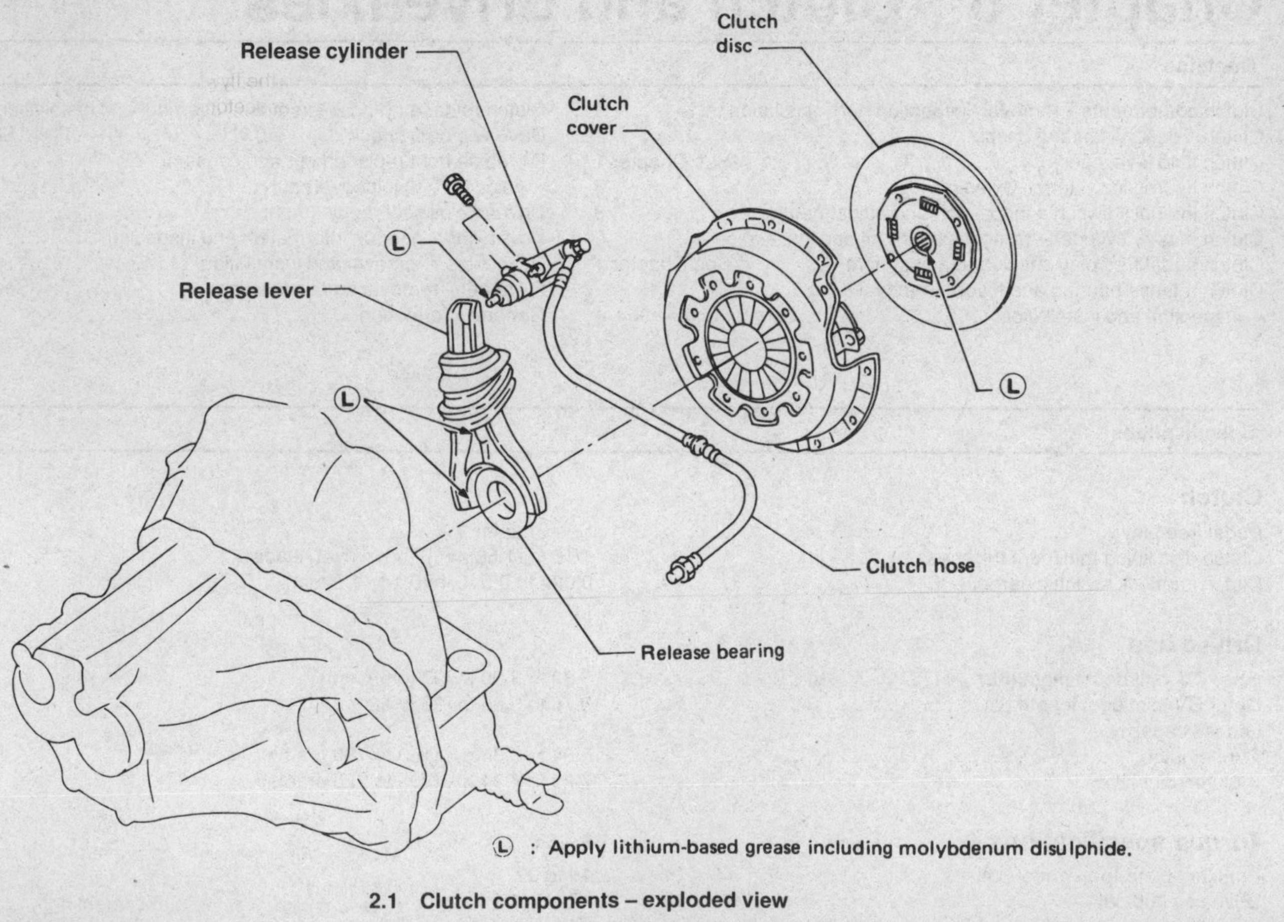

2.1 Clutch components – exploded view

3 Clutch components – removal, inspection and installation

Warning: *Dust produced by clutch wear and deposited on clutch components may contain asbestos, which is hazardous to your health. DO NOT blow it out with compressed air and DO NOT inhale it. DO NOT use gasoline or petroleum-based solvents to remove the dust. Brake system cleaner should be used to flush the dust into a drain pan. After the clutch components are wiped clean with a rag, dispose of the contaminated rags and cleaner in a covered, marked container.*

Removal

Refer to illustration 3.6

1 Access to the clutch components is normally accomplished by removing the transaxle, leaving the engine in the vehicle. If, of course, the engine is being removed for major overhaul, then check the clutch for wear and replace worn components as necessary. However, the relatively low cost of the clutch components compared to the time and trouble spent gaining access to them warrants their replacement anytime the engine or transaxle is removed, unless they are new or in near perfect condition. The following procedures are based on the assumption the engine will stay in place.

2 Referring to Chapter 7 Part A, remove the transaxle from the vehicle. Support the engine while the transaxle is out. Preferably, an engine hoist should be used to support it from above. However, if a jack is used underneath the engine, make sure a piece of wood is positioned between the jack and oil pan to spread the load. **Caution:** *The pickup for the oil pump is very close to the bottom of the oil pan. If the pan is bent or distorted in any way, engine oil starvation could occur.*

3 Remove the release (slave) cylinder (see Section 6).

4 The clutch fork and release bearing can remain attached to the housing for the time being.

5 To support the clutch disc during removal, install a clutch alignment tool through the clutch disc hub.

6 Carefully inspect the flywheel and pressure plate for indexing marks. The marks are usually an X, an O or a white letter. If they cannot be found, scribe marks yourself so the pressure plate and the flywheel will be in the same alignment during installation **(see illustration)**.

7 Turning each bolt only 1/4-turn at a time, loosen the pressure plate-to-flywheel bolts. Work in a criss-cross pattern until all spring pressure is relieved. Then hold the pressure plate securely and completely remove the bolts, followed by the pressure plate and clutch disc.

Inspection

Refer to illustrations 3.11, 3.13a and 3.13b

8 Ordinarily, when a problem occurs in the clutch, it can be attributed to wear of the clutch driven plate assembly (clutch disc). However, all components should be inspected at this time. **Note:** *If the clutch components are contaminated with oil, there will be shiny, black, glazed spots on the clutch disc lining, which will cause the clutch to slip. Replacing clutch components won't completely solve the problem – be sure to check the rear crankshaft oil seal and the transaxle input shaft seal for leaks. If it looks like a seal is leaking, be sure to install a new one to avoid the same problem with a new clutch.*

9 Inspect the flywheel for cracks, heat checking, grooves and other obvious defects. If the imperfections are slight, a machine shop can machine the surface flat and smooth, which is highly recommended regardless of the surface appearance. Refer to Chapter 2A for the flywheel removal and installation procedure.

10 Inspect the splines on the transaxle input shaft.

11 Inspect the lining on the clutch disc. There should be at least 1/16-inch of lining above the rivet heads. Check for loose rivets, distortion, cracks, broken springs and other obvious damage **(see illustration)**. As mentioned above, ordinarily the clutch disc is routinely replaced, so if in doubt about the condition, replace it with a new one.

12 The release bearing should also be replaced along with the clutch disc (see Section 4).

13 Check the machined surfaces and the diaphragm spring fingers of the pressure plate **(see illustrations)**. If the surface is grooved or otherwise damaged, replace the pressure plate. Also check for obvious damage, distortion, cracking, etc. Light glazing can be removed with medium grit emery cloth. If a new pressure plate is required, new and factory-rebuilt units are available.

Installation

Refer to illustration 3.15

14 Before installation, clean the flywheel and pressure plate machined surfaces with lacquer thinner or acetone. It's important that no oil or grease is on these surfaces or the lining of the clutch disc. Handle the parts only with clean hands.

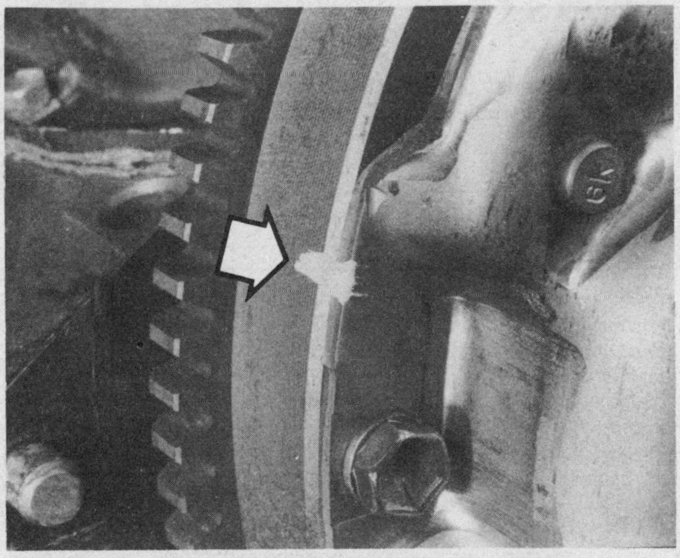

3.6 Make an index mark across the pressure plate and flywheel (just in case you're going to reuse the same pressure plate)

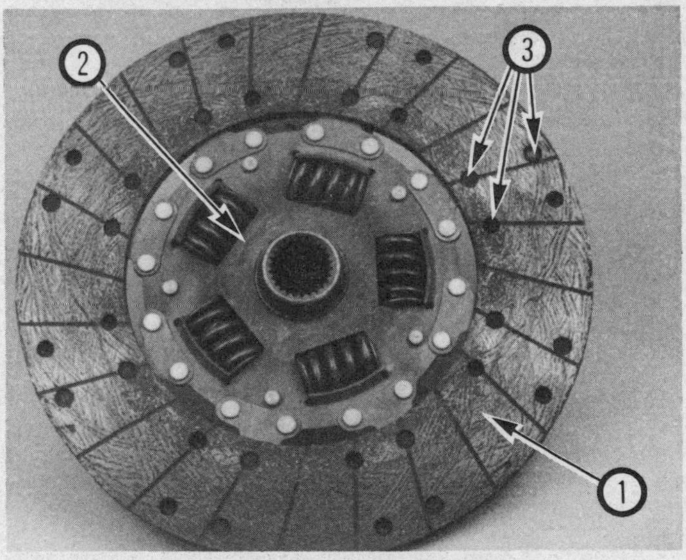

3.11 The clutch disc

1 *Lining – this will wear down in use*
2 *Marks – "Flywheel side" or something similar*
3 *Rivets – secure the lining and will damage the pressure plate if allowed to contact it*

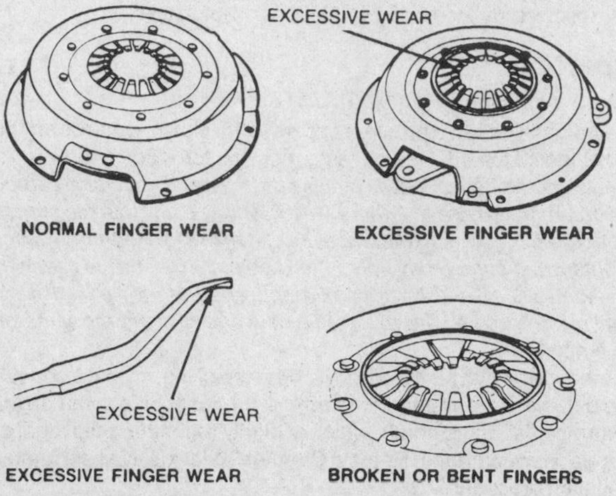

3.13a Replace the pressure plate if the fingers are worn excessively, broken or bent

3.13b Also examine the pressure plate friction surface for score marks, cracks and evidence of overheating (blue discolored areas)

3.15 Center the clutch disc in the pressure plate with a clutch alignment tool

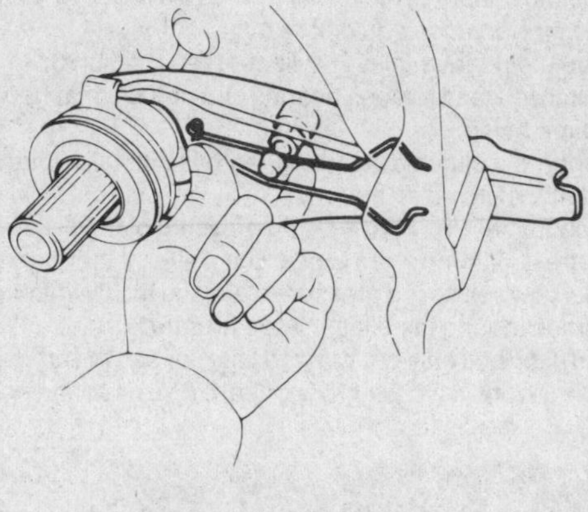

4.3 Reach behind the release lever and disengage the lever from the ball stud by pulling on the retention spring, then remove the lever and bearing

15 Position the clutch disc and pressure plate against the flywheel with the clutch held in place with an alignment tool **(see illustration)**. Make sure it's installed properly (most replacement clutch plates will be marked "flywheel side" or something similar – if not marked, install the clutch disc with the damper springs toward the transaxle).

16 Tighten the pressure plate-to-flywheel bolts only finger tight, working around the pressure plate.

17 Center the clutch disc by ensuring the alignment tool extends through the splined hub and into the recess in the crankshaft. Wiggle the tool up, down or side-to-side as needed to bottom the tool. Tighten the pressure plate-to-flywheel bolts a little at a time, working in a criss-cross pattern to prevent distorting the cover. After all of the bolts are snug, tighten them to the specified torque. Remove the alignment tool.

18 Using high temperature grease, lubricate the inner groove of the release bearing (refer to Section 4). Also place grease on the release lever contact areas and the transaxle input shaft bearing retainer.

19 Install the clutch release bearing as described in Section 4.

20 Install the transaxle, release (slave) cylinder and all components removed previously. Tighten all fasteners to the proper torque specifications.

4 Clutch release bearing and lever – removal, inspection and installation

Refer to illustrations 4.3, 4.4, 4.5a, 4.5b and 4.6

Warning: *Dust produced by clutch wear and deposited on clutch components may contain asbestos, which is hazardous to your health. DO NOT blow it out with compressed air and DO NOT inhale it. DO NOT use gasoline or petroleum-based solvents to remove the dust. Brake system cleaner should be used to flush the dust into a drain pan. After the clutch components are wiped clean with a rag, dispose of the contaminated rags and cleaner in a covered, marked container.*

Removal

1 Disconnect the negative cable from the battery.

2 Remove the transaxle (see Chapter 7).

3 Remove the clutch release lever from the ball stud, then remove the bearing from the lever **(see illustration)**.

Inspection

4 Hold the center of the bearing and rotate the outer portion while apply-

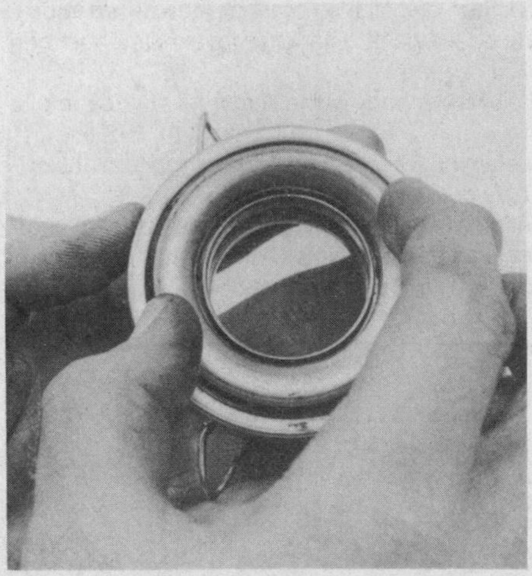

4.4 To check the operation of the bearing, hold it by the outer cage (hub) and rotate the inner race while applying pressure – the bearing should turn smoothly – if it doesn't, replace it

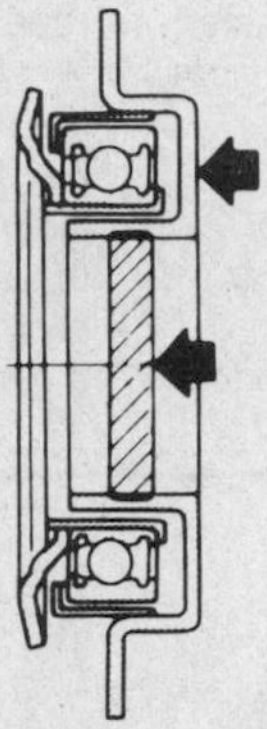

4.5a Fill the groove and contact surfaces (arrows) of the release bearing with high temperature grease

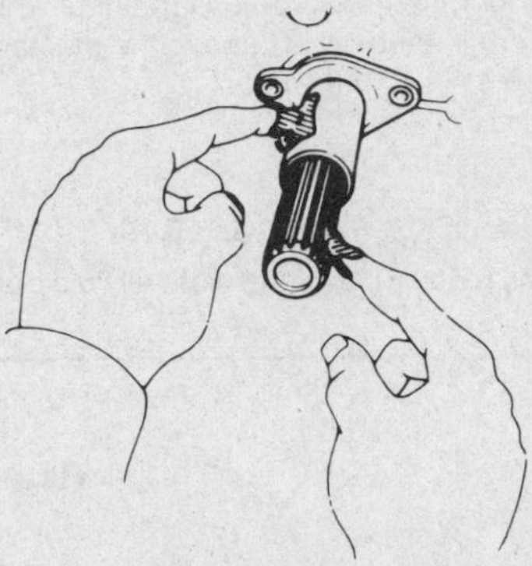

4.5b Apply a light coat of high temperature grease to the transaxle bearing retainer

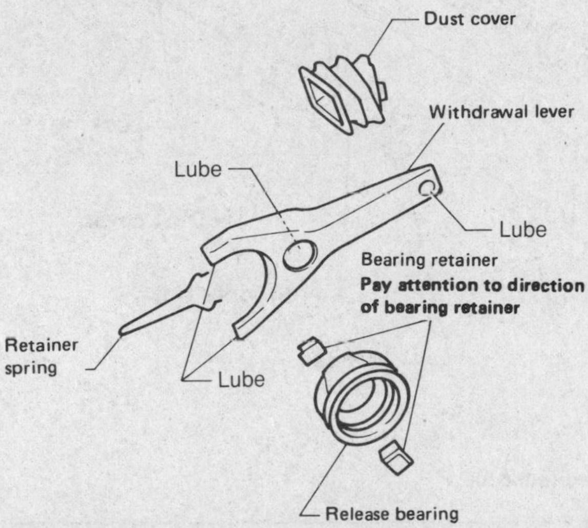

4.6 Lubricate the places indicated

ing pressure **(see illustration)**. If the bearing doesn't turn smoothly or if it's noisy, replace the bearing/hub assembly with a new one. Wipe the bearing with a clean rag and inspect it for damage, wear and cracks. Don't immerse the bearing in solvent – it's sealed for life and to do so would ruin it. Also check the release lever for cracks and distortion.

Installation

5 Fill the inner groove of the release bearing with high-temperature lithium-based grease. Also apply a light coat of the same grease to the transaxle input shaft splines and the front bearing retainer **(see illustrations)**.

6 Lubricate the release lever ball socket, fork ends and release cylinder pushrod socket with high-temperature grease **(see illustration)**.

7 Attach the release bearing to the clutch lever. Slide the release bearing onto the transaxle input shaft front bearing retainer while passing the end of the release lever through the opening in the clutch housing. Push the clutch release lever onto the ball stud until it's firmly seated.

8 Apply a light coat of high-temperature grease to the face of the release bearing, where it contacts the pressure plate diaphragm fingers.

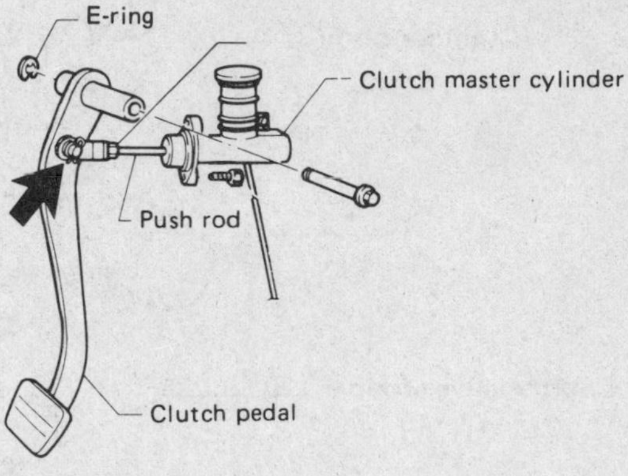

5.2 Clutch actuating components – exploded view (the arrow indicates the clevis pin)

9 The remainder of installation is the reverse of the removal procedure. Tighten all bolts securely.

8

5 Clutch master cylinder – removal, overhaul and installation

Note: *Before beginning this procedure, contact local parts stores and dealer service departments concerning the purchase of a rebuild kit or a new master cylinder. Availability and cost of the necessary parts may dictate whether the cylinder is rebuilt or replaced with a new one. If it's decided to rebuild the cylinder, inspect the bore as described in Step 13 before purchasing parts.*

Removal

Refer to illustration 5.2

1 Disconnect the negative cable from the battery.

2 Working under the dashboard, disconnect the pushrod from the top of the clutch pedal. It's held in place with a clevis pin **(see illustration)**.

3 Disconnect the hydraulic line at the clutch master cylinder. If available, use a flare nut wrench on the fitting, which will prevent the fitting from being rounded off. Have rags handy as some fluid will be lost as the line is

removed. **Caution:** *Don't allow the fluid to come into contact with paint, as it will damage the finish.*

4 Working under the hood, remove the nuts which secure the master cylinder to the engine firewall. Remove the master cylinder, again being careful not to spill any of the fluid.

Overhaul

Refer to illustrations 5.5, 5.6, 5.9 and 5.19

5 Remove the reservoir cap and drain all fluid from the master cylinder. Remove the reservoir band, then pull off the reservoir **(see illustration)**.

6 Pull back the dust cover on the pushrod and remove the stopper ring **(see illustration)**.

7 Push the piston into the cylinder body with a screwdriver and remove the valve stopper.

8 Remove the stopper (retaining washer) and the pushrod from the cylinder.

9 Tap the master cylinder on a block of wood to eject the piston assembly from inside the bore **(see illustration)**. **Note:** *If the rebuild kit supplies a complete piston assembly, ignore the appropriate Steps.*

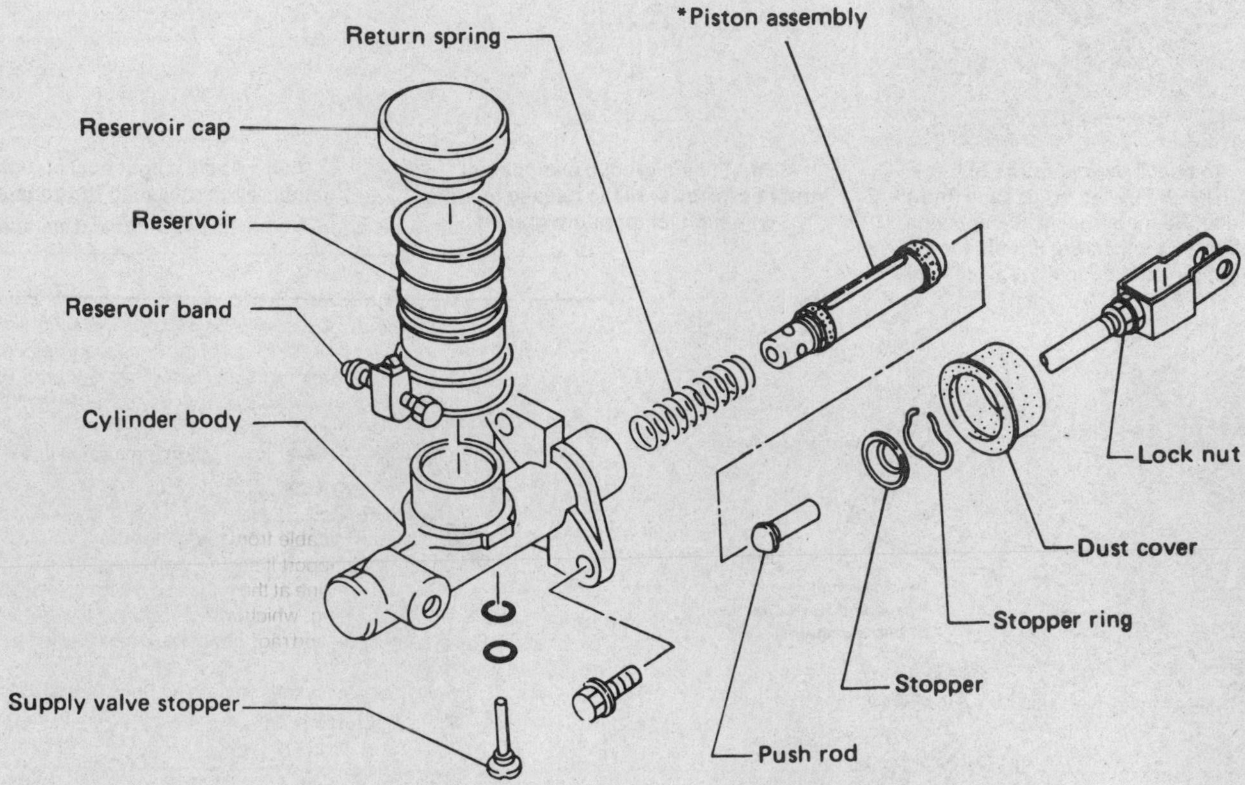

5.5 Clutch master cylinder – exploded view

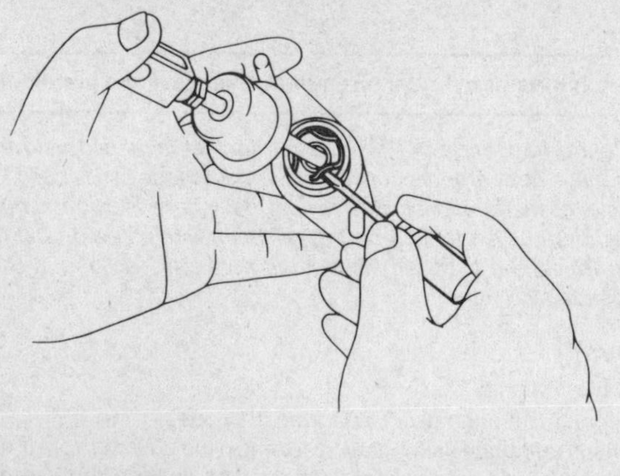

5.6 Use a small screwdriver to pry the stopper ring from the cylinder bore

5.9 Invert the cylinder and tap it against a block of wood to eject the piston

10 Separate the spring from the piston.
11 Remove the spring support, seal and shim from the pushrod.
12 Carefully remove the seal from the piston.
13 Inspect the bore of the master cylinder for deep scratches, score marks and ridges. The surface must be smooth to the touch. If the bore isn't perfectly smooth, the master cylinder must be replaced with a new or factory rebuilt unit.
14 If the cylinder will be rebuilt, use the new parts contained in the rebuild kit and follow any specific instructions which may have accompanied the rebuild kit. Wash all parts to be re-used with brake cleaner, denatured alcohol or clean brake fluid. DO NOT use petroleum-based solvents.
15 Attach the seal to the piston. The seal lips must face away from the pushrod end of the piston.
16 Assemble the shim, spring support and spring on the other end of the piston.
17 Lubricate the bore of the cylinder and the seal with plenty of fresh brake fluid (DOT 3).
18 Carefully guide the piston assembly into the bore, being careful not to damage the seals. Make sure the spring end is installed first, with the pushrod end of the piston closest to the opening.
19 Align the groove of the piston assembly and the valve stopper and install the valve stopper while holding the piston in place with a screwdriver **(see illustration)**.

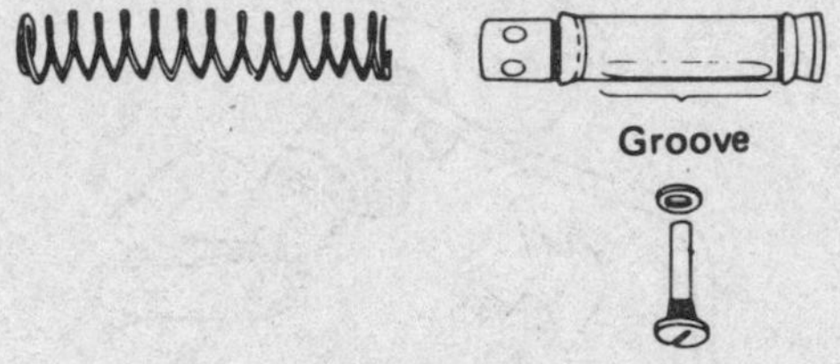

5.19 Align the groove in the piston with the valve stopper

20 Position the pushrod and stopper in the bore, compress the spring and install a new stopper ring.
21 Apply a liberal amount of Girling Rubber Grease or equivalent to the inside of the dust cover and attach it to the master cylinder.

Installation

22 Position the master cylinder on the firewall, installing the mounting nuts finger-tight.
23 Connect the hydraulic line to the master cylinder, moving the cylinder slightly as necessary to thread the fitting properly into the bore. Don't cross-thread the fitting as it's installed.
24 Tighten the mounting nuts securely, then tighten the hydraulic line fitting.
25 Working inside the vehicle, connect the pushrod to the clutch pedal.
26 Fill the clutch master cylinder reservoir with brake fluid conforming to DOT 3 specifications and bleed the clutch system as outlined in Section 7.
27 Check the clutch pedal height and freeplay and adjust if necessary, following the procedure in Chapter 1.

6 Clutch release cylinder – removal, overhaul and installation

Note: *Before beginning this procedure, contact local parts stores and dealer service departments concerning the purchase of a rebuild kit or a new release cylinder. Availability and cost of the necessary parts may dictate whether the cylinder is rebuilt or replaced with a new one. If it's decided to rebuild the cylinder, inspect the bore as described in Step 8 before purchasing parts.*

Removal

Refer to illustration 6.4

1 Disconnect the negative cable from the battery.
2 Raise the vehicle and support it securely on jackstands.
3 Disconnect the hydraulic line at the release cylinder. If available, use a flare nut wrench on the fitting, which will prevent the fitting from being rounded off. Have a small can and rags handy, as some fluid will be spilled as the line is removed.
4 Remove the two release cylinder mounting bolts **(see illustration)**.
5 Remove the release cylinder and heat insulator, if equipped.

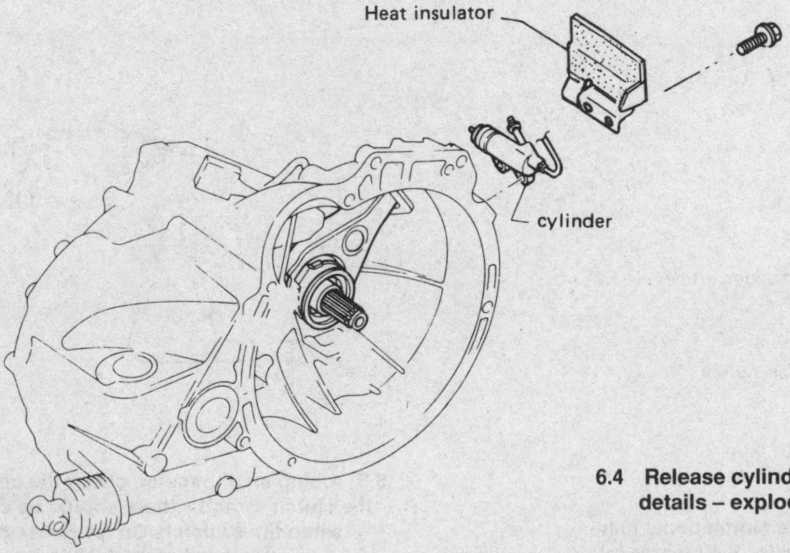

6.4 Release cylinder mounting details – exploded view

8

Overhaul

Refer to illustration 6.6

6 Remove the pushrod and the dust cover (boot) **(see illustration)**.
7 Tap the cylinder on a block of wood to eject the piston and piston cup. Also remove the spring from inside the cylinder.
8 Carefully inspect the bore of the cylinder. Check for deep scratches, score marks and ridges. The bore must be smooth to the touch. If any imperfections are found, the release cylinder must be replaced with a new one.
9 Using the new parts in the rebuild kit, assemble the components using plenty of fresh brake fluid for lubrication. Note the installed direction of the spring and the cup.

Installation

10 Install the release cylinder on the clutch housing. Make sure the pushrod is seated in the release fork pocket.
11 Connect the hydraulic line to the release cylinder. Tighten the fitting.
12 Fill the clutch master cylinder with brake fluid conforming to DOT 3 specifications.
13 Bleed the system as described in Section 7.
14 Lower the vehicle and connect the negative battery cable.

7 Clutch hydraulic system – bleeding

Refer to illustration 7.4

1 The hydraulic system should be bled to remove all air whenever any part of the system has been removed or if the fluid level has been allowed to fall so low that air has been drawn into the master cylinder. The procedure is very similar to bleeding a brake system.
2 Fill the master cylinder with new brake fluid conforming to DOT 3 specifications. **Caution:** *Do not re-use any of the fluid coming from the system during the bleeding operation or use fluid which has been inside an open container for an extended period of time.*
3 The release cylinder is located on the forward (radiator) side of the clutch housing.
4 Remove the dust cap which fits over the bleeder screw and push a length of plastic hose over the screw. Place the other end of the hose into a clear container with about two inches of brake fluid. The hose end must be in the fluid at the bottom of the container **(see illustration)**.
5 Have an assistant depress the clutch pedal and hold it. Open the bleeder screw on the release cylinder, allowing fluid to flow through the hose. Close the bleeder screw when your assistant signals that the clutch

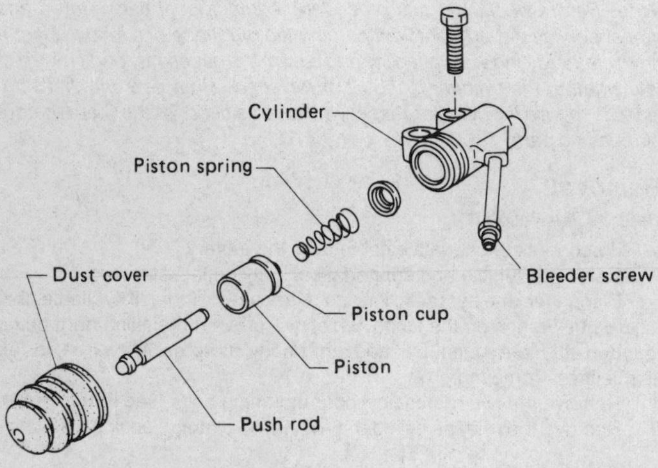

6.6 Clutch release cylinder – exploded view

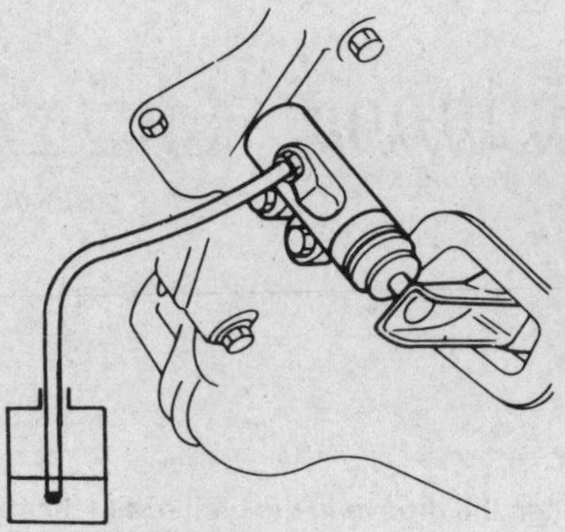

7.4 Connect a hose to the bleeder screw and run it into a clear container

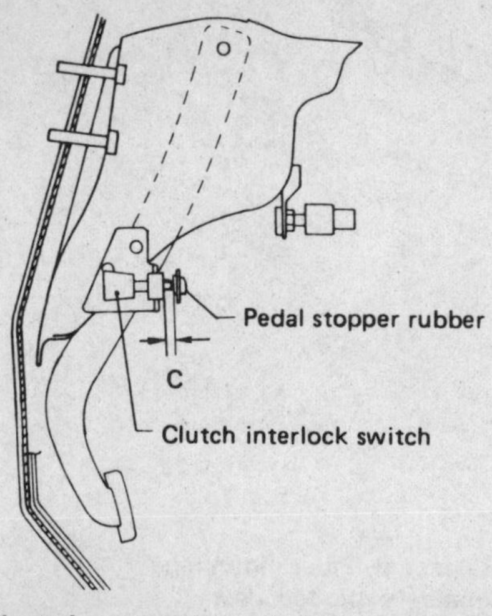

8.4 Adjust clearance "C" with the clutch pedal fully depressed (see the Specifications for the clearance)

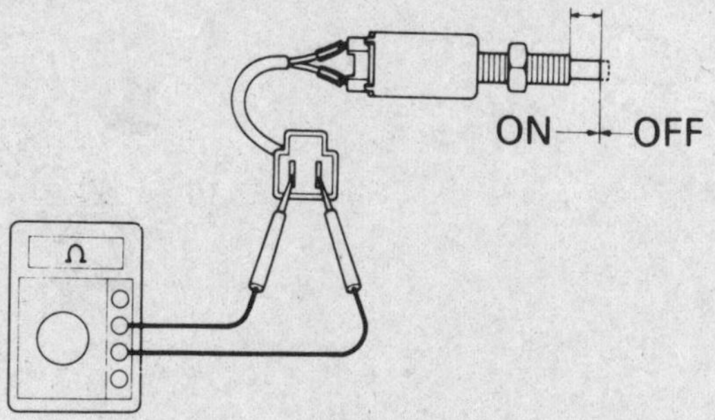

8.6 Using an ohmmeter, check the continuity of the clutch switch – there should be continuity when the switch is On (pushed), but no continuity when it is Off (released)

pedal is at the bottom of its travel. Once closed, have your assistant raise the pedal.

6 Continue this process until all air is evacuated from the system, indicated by a solid stream of fluid being ejected from the bleeder screw each time with no air bubbles in the hose or container. Keep a close watch on the fluid level inside the clutch master cylinder reservoir – if the level drops too low, air will be sucked back into the system and the process will have to be started all over again.

7 Install the dust cap. Check carefully for proper operation before placing the vehicle in normal service.

8 Clutch interlock switch – inspection and adjustment

Refer to illustrations 8.4 and 8.6

1 Check the pedal height, pedal free play and pushrod play (refer to Chapter 1).

2 Verify that the engine will not start when the clutch pedal is released.

3 Verify that the engine will start when the clutch pedal is fully depressed.

4 Fully depress the clutch pedal and measure the clearance "C" **(see illustration)**. It must be as indicated in this Chapter's Specifications. If it is not, adjust or replace the clutch interlock switch.

5 Verify again that the engine does not start when the clutch pedal is released.

6 Verify that there is continuity between the clutch interlock switch terminals when the switch is On **(see illustration)**.

7 Check that there is no continuity between the clutch interlock switch terminals when the switch is Off.

8 If the clutch interlock switch fails either of the above two tests, replace it. This is accomplished by removing the nut nearest the plunger end of the switch and sliding it from its bracket. Disconnect the electrical connector. Installation is the reverse of the removal procedure.

9 Driveaxles – general information and inspection

Power is transmitted from the transaxle to the wheels through a pair of driveaxles. The inner end of each driveaxle is splined to the differential. The outer ends of the driveaxles are splined to the axle hubs and locked in place by a hub nut.

The inner ends of the driveaxles are equipped with sliding double offset joints, which are capable of both angular and axial motion. Each inner joint assembly consists of an inner race, ball bearing and cage assembly and an outer race (housing) in which the inner bearing assembly is free to slide in and out as the driveaxle moves up and down with the wheel. The inner joints are rebuildable (Section 11).

Each outer joint, which consists of ball bearings running between an inner race and an outer cage, is capable of angular but not axial movement. The outer joints are not rebuildable. Should one of them fail, a new joint assembly must be installed.

The boots should be periodically inspected for damage, leaking lubricant and cuts. Damaged CV joint boots must be replaced immediately or the joints can be damaged. Boot replacement involves removal of the driveaxle (Section 10). **Note:** *Some auto parts stores carry "split" type replacement boots, which can be installed without removing the driveaxle from the vehicle. This is a convenient alternative; however, it's recommended that the driveaxle be removed and the CV joint disassembled and cleaned to ensure that the joint is free from contaminants such as moisture and dirt, which will accelerate CV joint wear.*

The most common symptom of worn or damaged CV joints, besides lubricant leaks, is a clicking noise in turns, a clunk when accelerating from a coasting condition or vibration at highway speeds.

To check for wear in the CV joints and driveaxle shafts, grasp each axle (one at a time) and rotate it in both directions while holding the CV joint housings, inspecting for movement, indicating worn splines or sloppy CV joints. Also check the driveaxle shafts for cracks, dents, twisting and bending.

10 Driveaxles – removal and installation

Refer to illustrations 10.2, 10.5a, 10.5b, 10.7, 10.8, 10.9, 10.12 and 10.14

Removal

1 Loosen the wheel lug nuts, raise the front of the vehicle and support it securely on jackstands. Apply the parking brake. Remove the front wheel.

2 Remove the cotter pin and adjusting cap and loosen the driveaxle hub nut. To prevent the hub from turning, place a pry bar between two of the wheel studs, then loosen the nut **(see illustration)**.

3 Remove the splash pan from the inner fender.

4 Drain the lubricant from the transaxle (see Chapter 1).

5 Remove the three balljoint-to-control arm nuts and separate the balljoint from the control arm **(see illustrations)**. Refer to Chapter 10 if necessary.

6 Detach the tie rod end from the steering knuckle (see Chapter 10).

7 Back the axle nut off until it has about ten threads still engaged with the axle (to protect the threads). Gently tap on the nut with a soft-face hammer **(see illustration)** while pulling out on the strut/spindle assembly to break the axle loose from the hub. Remove the nut.

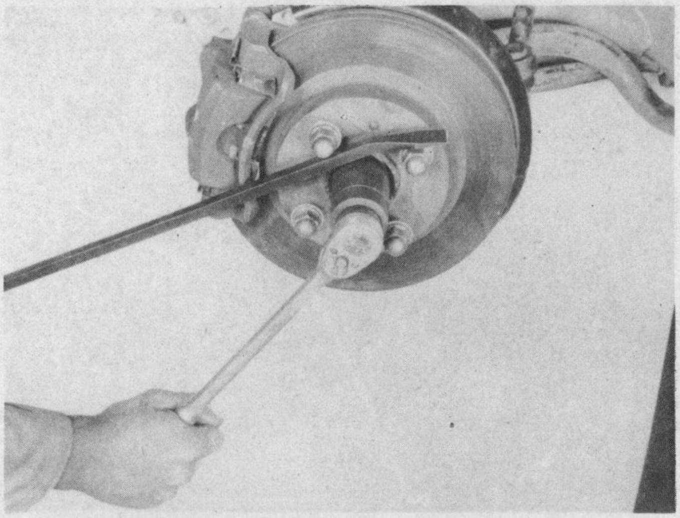

10.2 Install lug nuts to protect the threads, then use a large prybar to immobilize the hub while loosening the hub nut

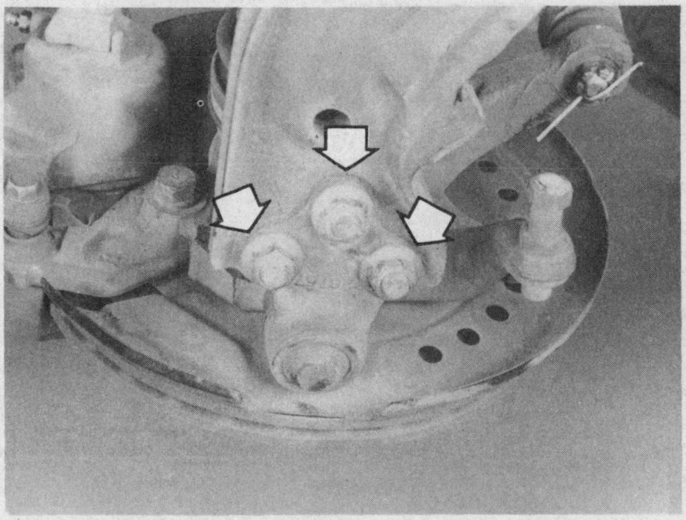

10.5a Remove the three nuts (arrows) . . .

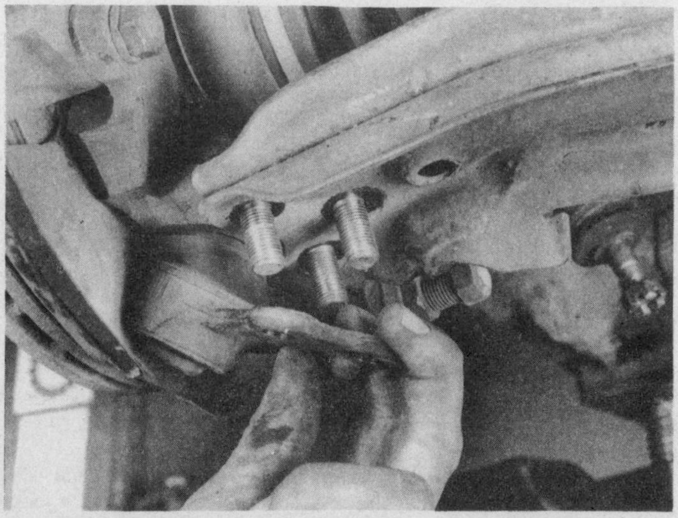

10.5b ... and separate the balljoint from the control arm

10.7 Gently tap on the nut with a soft-face hammer to break the axle loose from the hub

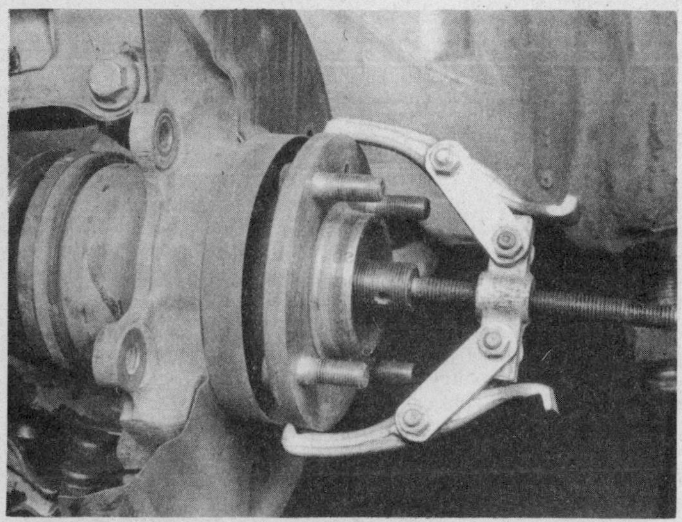

10.8 If the driveaxle won't slide out of the hub easily, remove the brake rotor and use a jaw-type puller to push it out

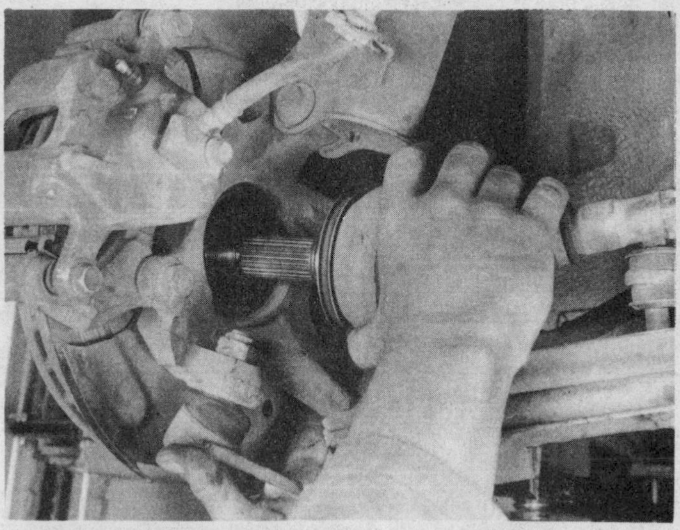

10.9 Pull out on the strut assembly – once the axle is out of the steering knuckle it may be carefully slipped out of the transaxle

10.12 Remove the three bolts (arrows) from the support bearing holder on the right axle

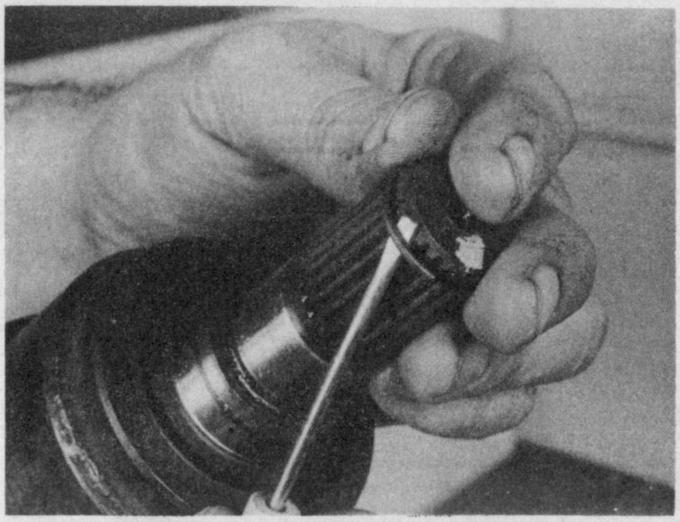

10.14 Always replace the circlip on the left inner CV joint stub shaft before reinstalling the driveaxle

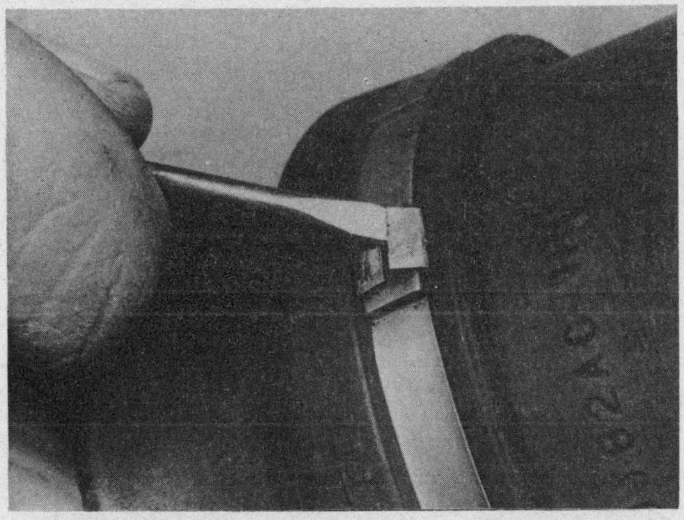

11.3 **Pry the boot clamp retaining tabs up with a small screwdriver and slide the clamps off the boot**

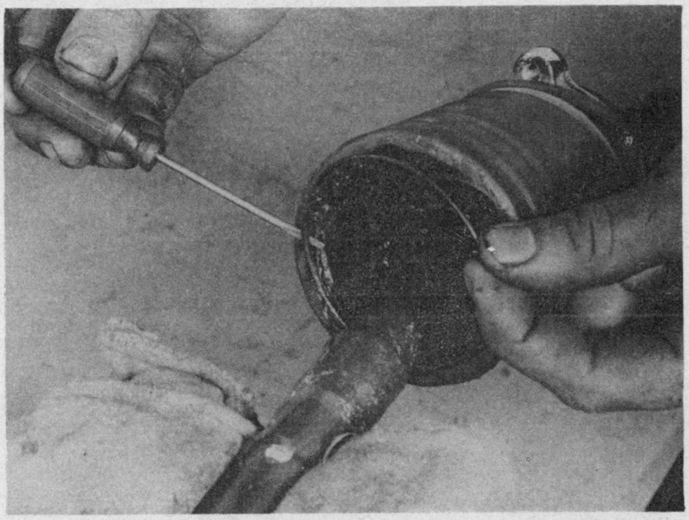

11.4a **Pry the wire ring ball retainer out of the slide joint housing**

8 If the axle is stuck, remove the brake rotor as described in Chapter 9 and push the driveaxle from the hub with a puller **(see illustration)**.
9 Once the axle is broken loose from the hub, pull the strut assembly out enough to clear the end of the driveaxle **(see illustration)**.
10 Temporarily support the outer end of the driveaxle with a piece of rope or wire to prevent damage to the inner CV joint.
11 Left side only – carefully pry the inner end of the axle from the transaxle, using a pry bar positioned between the transaxle housing and the CV joint housing.
12 Right side only – remove the three bolts from the support bearing holder **(see illustration)**.
13 Support the CV joints and carefully remove the driveaxle from the vehicle.

Installation

14 Left side only – pry the old circlip off the inner end of the driveaxle and install a new one **(see illustration)**.
15 Lubricate the differential seal with multi-purpose grease. Raise the driveaxle into position while supporting the CV joints and insert the splined end of the inner CV joint/axle shaft into the transaxle.
16 The right side axle should slip in by hand. The left side must be driven into place. Temporarily install the nut on the left axle to protect the threads. Hold the CV joints straight and tap on the nut with a soft-face hammer to seat the circlip. **Note:** *The axle should seat easily, if it doesn't, check to see if it's going in crooked. After the axle goes in, pull out on it by hand to ensure that it's seated properly.*
17 Apply a light coat of multi-purpose grease to the outer CV joint splines, pull out on the strut/steering knuckle and install the outer end of the axle into the hub.
18 Reinstall the remaining parts in the reverse order of removal. Be sure to tighten the hub nut to the torque specified in this Chapter and insert a new cotter pin into the axle end.
19 Refill the transaxle with lubricant (see Chapter 1).
20 Reinstall the wheel and lower the vehicle.

11 Driveaxle boot replacement and constant velocity (CV) joint overhaul

Refer to illustrations 11.3, 11.4a, 11.4b, 11.5, 11.6, 11.7, 11.9, 11.10a, 11.10b, 11.11a, 11.11b, 11.13, 11.14, 11.17, 11.19, 11.20, 11.21a, 11.21b, 11.25, 11.28 and 11.34

1 Remove the driveaxle from the vehicle (Section 10).

Inner CV joint and boot

Disassembly

2 Mount the driveaxle in a vise. The jaws of the vise should be lined with wood or rags to prevent damage to the axleshaft.
3 Pry the boot clamp retaining tabs up with a small screwdriver and slide the clamps off the boot **(see illustration)**.
4 Slide the boot back on the axleshaft and pry the wire ring retainer (snap-ring A) from the outer race **(see illustrations)**.
5 Pull the slide joint housing off the cage and race assembly **(see illustration)**.
6 Remove the snap-ring ("C" in illustration 11.4b) from the groove in the axleshaft with a pair of snap-ring pliers **(see illustration)**.
7 Mark the inner race and cage to ensure that they are reassembled with the correct sides facing out **(see illustration)**.
8 Slide the inner race and cage assembly off the axleshaft and then remove snap-ring "B" and the boot.
9 Using a screwdriver or piece of wood, pry the balls from the cage **(see illustration)**. Be careful not to scratch the inner race, the balls or the cage.
10 Align the inner race lands with the cage windows and pull the race out of the cage **(see illustrations)**.

Inspection

11 Clean the components with solvent to remove all traces of grease. Inspect the cage and races for pitting, score marks, cracks and other signs of wear and damage. Shiny, polished spots are normal and will not adversely affect CV joint performance **(see illustrations)**.

Reassembly

12 Insert the inner race into the cage. Verify that the matchmarks are on the same side. However, it's not necessary for them to be in direct alignment with each other.
13 Press the balls into the cage windows with your thumbs **(see illustration)**.
14 Wrap the axleshaft splines with tape to avoid damaging the boot. Slide the small boot clamp and boot onto the axleshaft, then remove the tape **(see illustration)**. Install snap ring "B".
15 Install the inner race and cage assembly on the axleshaft with the larger diameter side or "bulge" of the cage (and the previously applied marks) facing the axleshaft end.
16 Install the snap-ring in the groove. Make sure it's completely seated by pushing on the inner race and cage assembly.
17 Fill the outer race and boot with the specified type and quantity of CV joint grease (normally included with the new boot kit). Pack the inner race and cage assembly with grease, by hand, until grease is worked completely into the assembly **(see illustration)**.

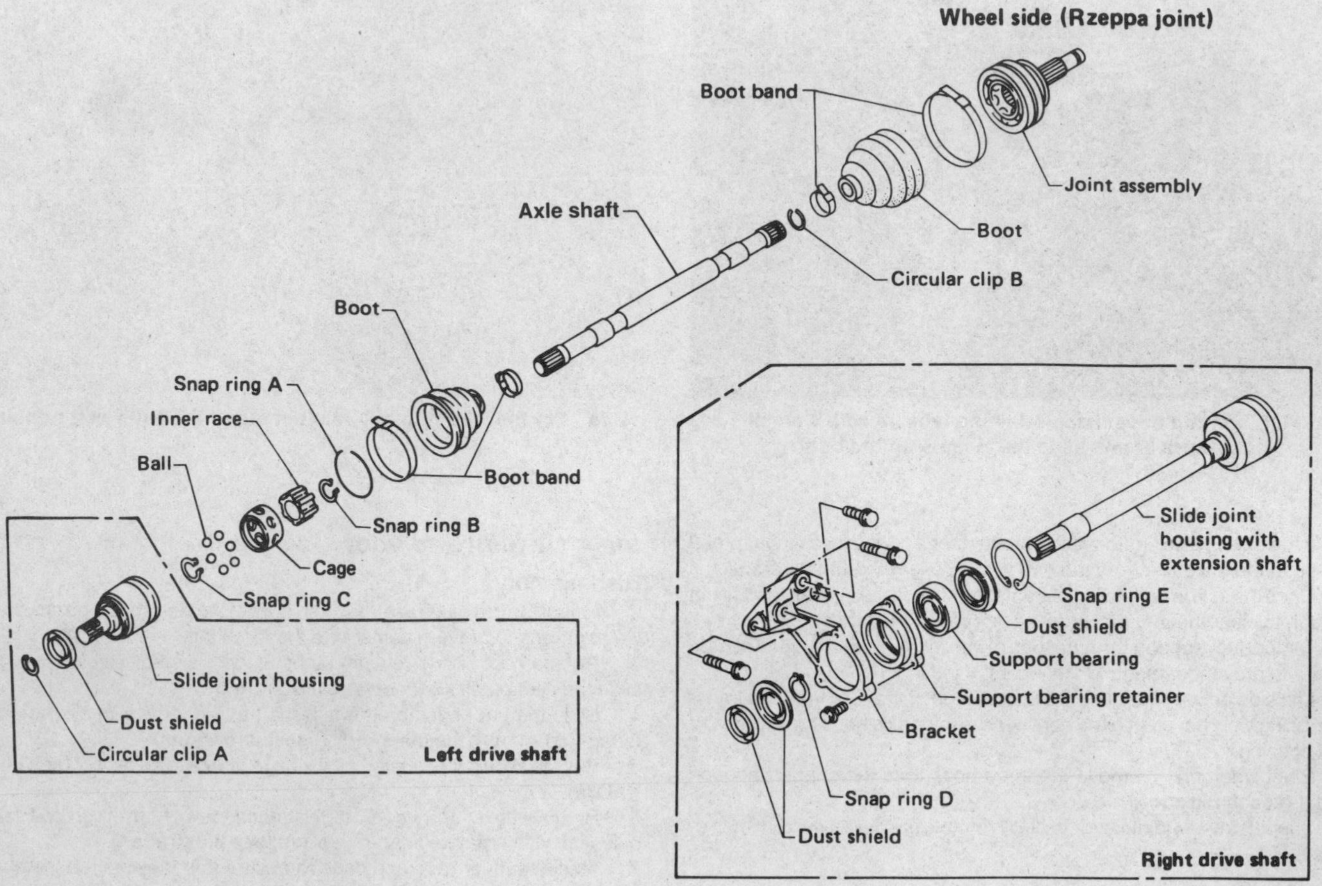

11.4b Driveaxle components – exploded view

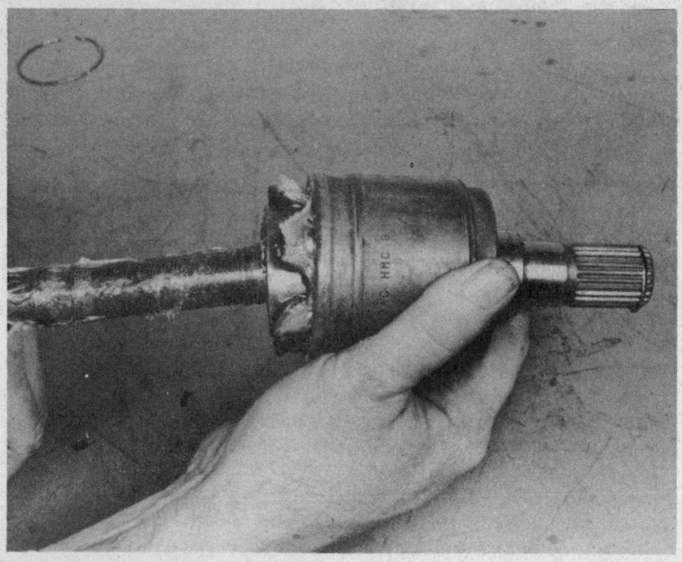

11.5 Pull the slide joint housing off the cage and race assembly (left side shown)

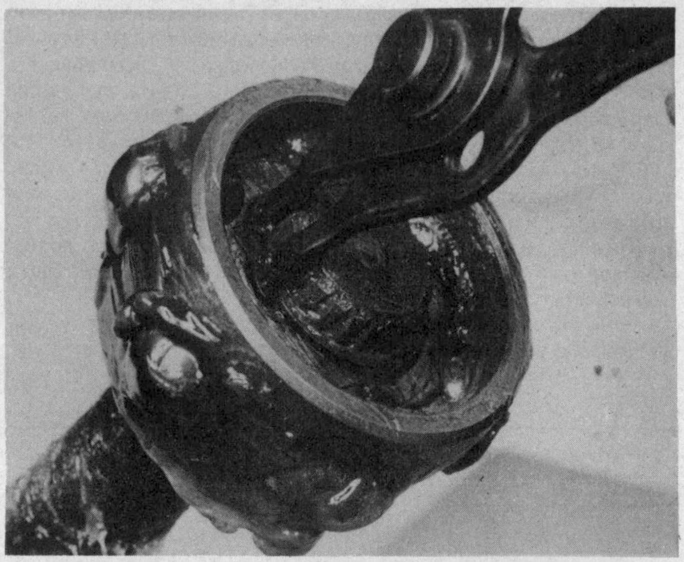

11.6 Remove the snap-ring from the end of the axle

11.7 Place match marks on the inner race and cage to identify which side must face the end of the shaft during reassembly

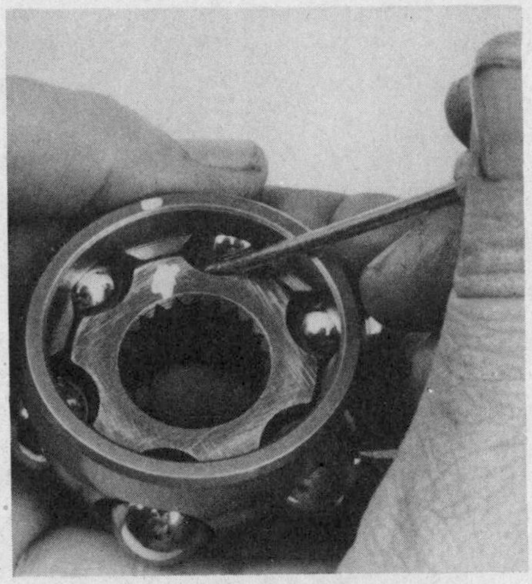

11.9 Pry the balls out of the cage with a screwdriver – be careful not to nick or scratch them

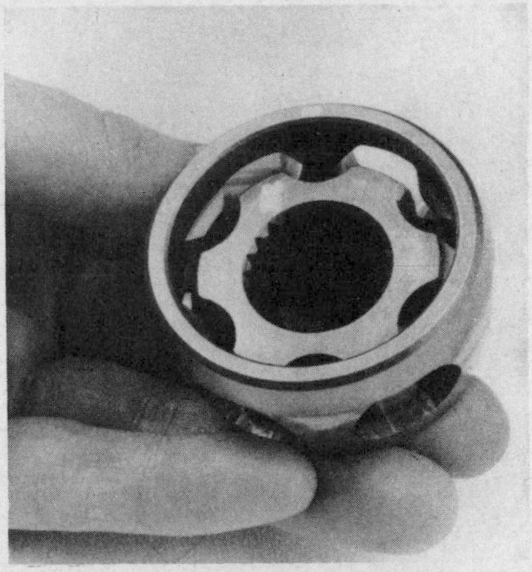

11.10a Align the lands of the inner race with the windows of the cage . . .

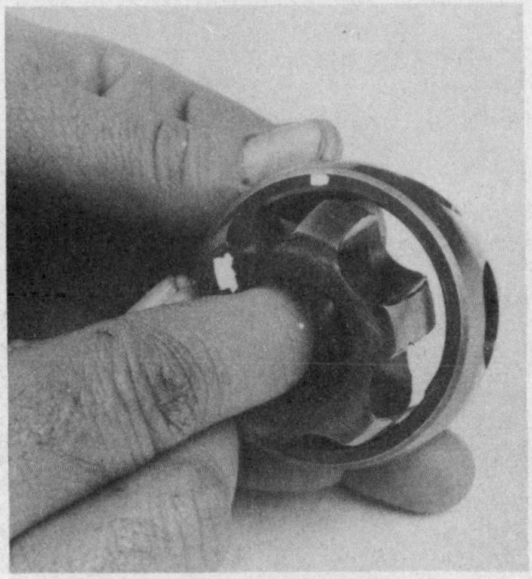

11.10b . . . then remove the inner race from the cage

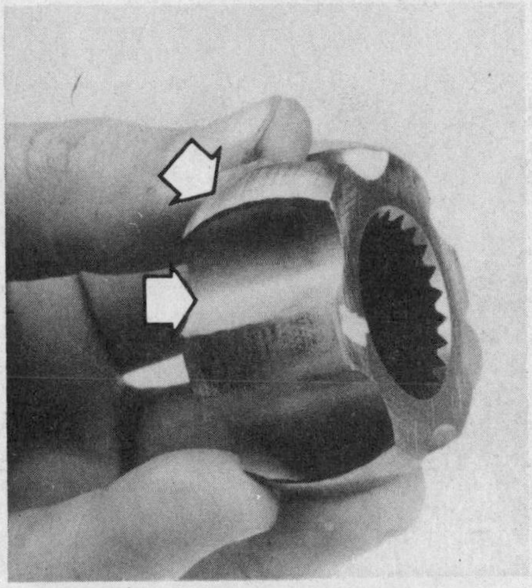

11.11a Check the inner race lands and grooves for pitting and score marks

11.11b Check the cage for cracks, pitting and score marks (shiny spots are normal and don't affect operation)

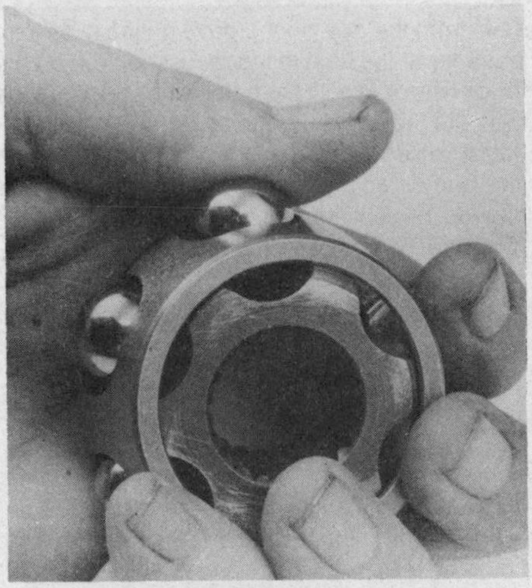

11.13 Press the balls into the cage through the windows using thumb pressure only

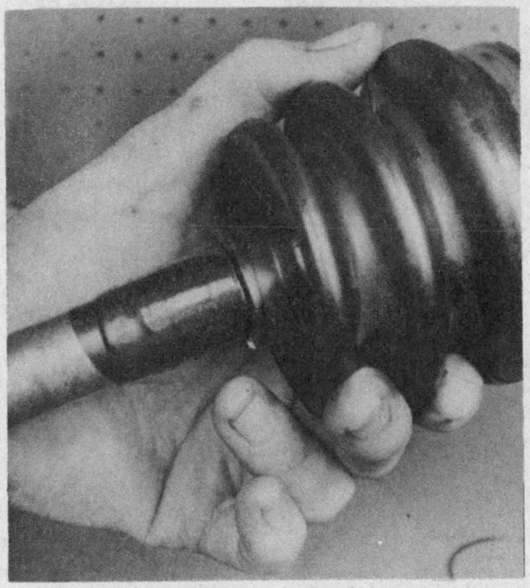

11.14 Wrap the splined area of the axle with tape to prevent damage to the boot when installing it

11.17 Pack the inner race and cage assembly full of CV joint grease (also note that the larger diameter side or "bulge", is facing the axleshaft end)

8

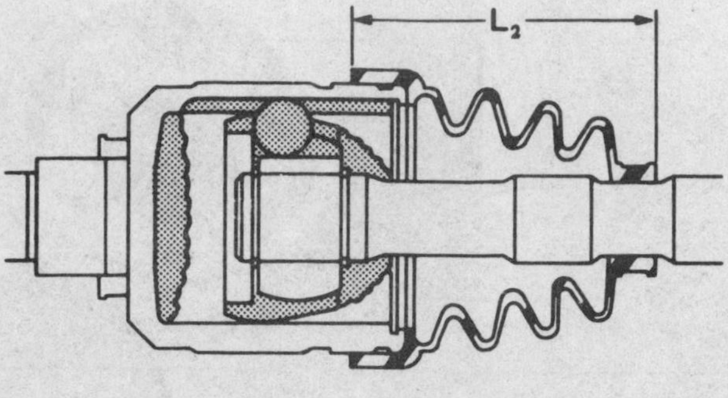

11.19 Adjust the boot length (L2) as specified

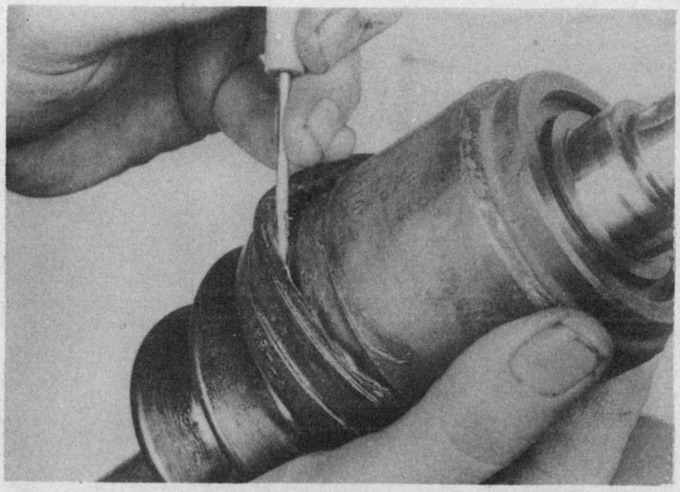

11.20 Equalize the pressure inside the boot by inserting a small, dull screwdriver between the boot and outer race

11.21a To install the new clamps, bend the tang down and . . .

11.21b . . . fold the tabs over to hold it in place

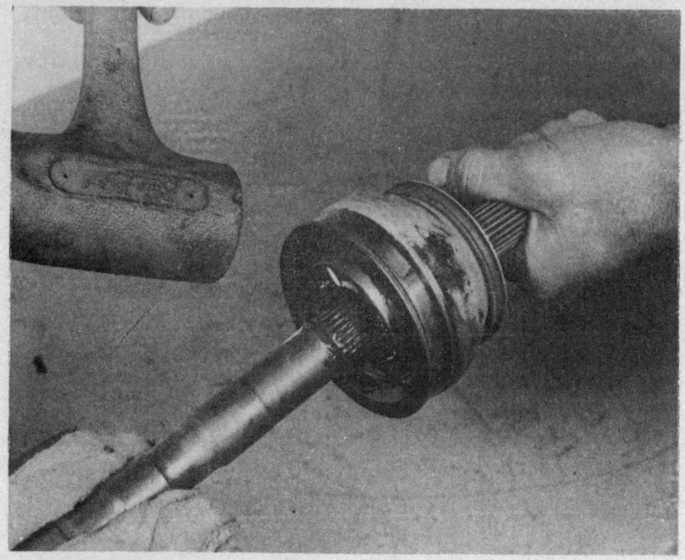

11.25 Drive the outer CV joint off the end of the axle with a soft-face hammer

18 Install the slide joint housing down onto the inner race assembly and install the wire ring retainer.

19 Wipe any excess grease from the axle boot groove on the slide joint housing. Seat the small diameter of the boot in the recessed area on the axleshaft. Push the other end of the boot onto the outer race and move the race in or out to adjust the joint to the proper length as listed in this Chapter's Specifications **(see illustration)**.

20 With the axle set to the proper length, equalize the pressure in the boot by inserting a dull screwdriver between the boot and the outer race **(see illustration)**. Don't damage the boot with the tool.

21 Install the boot clamps **(see illustrations)**.

22 Install a new circlip on the left inner CV joint stub axle **(see illustration 10.14)**.

23 Install the driveaxle as described in Section 10.

Outer CV joint and boot

Disassembly

24 Remove the outer CV joint boot clamps, using the technique described in Step 3. Slide the boot along the axleshaft toward the inner joint.

25 The outer CV joint is held on the axleshaft by a circular ring (circlip) ("B" in illustration 11.4b) similar to the one shown in illustration 10.14. Using a soft-face hammer, tap the inside edge of the joint to drive it off the end of the axle **(see illustration)**.

26 Pry the circlip ("B" in illustration 11.4b) out of the axle shaft groove, then pull the boot off the shaft.

11.28 **After the old grease has been rinsed away and the solvent has been blown out with compressed air, rotate the outer joint housing through its full range of motion and inspect the bearing surfaces for wear and damage – if any of the balls, the race or the cage look damaged, replace the driveaxle and outer joint assembly**

Inspection

27 Thoroughly wash the outer CV joint(s) in clean solvent and blow them dry with compressed air, if available. **Note:** *Because the outer joint cannot be disassembled, it is difficult to wash away all the old grease and to rid the bearing of solvent once it's clean. But it is imperative that the job be done thoroughly, so take your time and do it right.*

28 Bend the outer CV joint housing at an angle to the driveaxle to expose the bearings, inner race and cage **(see illustration)**. Inspect the bearing surfaces for signs of wear. If the bearings are damaged or worn, replace the CV joint.

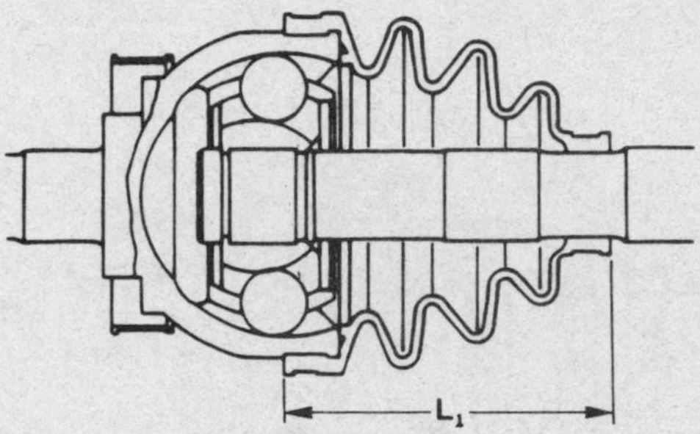

11.34 **Adjust the boot to the specified length L1**

Reassembly

29 Slide the new outer boot onto the axle shaft. It's a good idea to wrap vinyl tape around the splines to prevent damage to the boot **(see illustration 11.14)**.

30 Install a new circlip ("B") in the axle shaft groove.

31 Add the specified amount of grease (included in the boot replacement kit) to the outer joint and the boot (pack the joint with as much grease as it will hold and put the rest into the boot).

32 Drive the outer CV joint housing onto the axleshaft until circlip "B" is engaged to hold it on the shaft.

33 Position the boot over the outer joint housing and make sure the inner end of the boot is seated in the axle shaft groove.

34 Adjust the boot length (L1) to the figure listed in this Chapter's Specifications, then equalize the pressure as described in Step 20 **(see illustration)**.

35 Install the new clamps **(see illustrations 11.21a and 11.21b)**.

36 Install the driveaxle as outlined in Section 10.

Support bearing replacement

37 Replacement of the right axle support bearing requires a hydraulic press. Take the axle assembly to a Nissan dealer or an automotive machine shop for bearing replacement.

Chapter 9 Brakes

Contents

Anti-lock Brake System (ABS) – general information 2
Brake disc – inspection, removal and installation 5
Brake fluid level check .... See Chapter 1
Brake hoses and lines – inspection and replacement 11
Brake hydraulic system – bleeding 12
Brake light switch – removal, installation and adjustment 16
Brake pedal height adjustment .... See Chapter 1
Brake system check .... See Chapter 1
Front brake caliper – removal, overhaul and installation 4
Front brake pads – replacement 3
General information 1
Master cylinder – removal, overhaul and installation 10
Parking brake – adjustment 14
Parking brake cables – replacement 15
Power brake booster – check, removal and installation 13
Rear brake caliper – removal and installation 7
Rear brake pads – replacement 6
Rear brake shoes – replacement 8
Rear hub and wheel bearing – check, repack and adjustment .... See Chapter 10
Wheel cylinder – removal, overhaul and installation 9

Specifications

General

Brake fluid type	See Chapter 1
Brake pedal free height	See Chapter 1
Brake light switch clearance	0.012 to 0.039 in
Brake booster push rod length	0.4045 to 0.4144 in
Parking brake adjustment	
1985 through 1988	7 to 8 clicks
1989 on	9 to 11 clicks

Disc brakes

Front brake disc	
Minimum thickness*	0.787 in
Runout limit	0.0028 in
Rear brake disc minimum thickness*	
1985 through 1988	0.354 in
1989	0.315 in
1990	0.39 in
1991 and 1992	0.35 in
Rear disc runout limit	0.0028 in
Minimum brake pad thickness	See Chapter 1

** Refer to marks stamped on the disc (they supercede information printed here)*

Drum brakes

Drum diameter	
Standard	9.000 in
Maximum*	9.060 in

** Refer to marks cast into the drum (they supercede information printed here)*

Torque specifications

	Ft-lbs
Caliper brake hose bolt	12 to 14
Front disc brake caliper bolts	16 to 23
Rear disc brake caliper bolts	16 to 23
Front torque member bolts	53 to 72
Rear torque member bolts	28 to 38
Master cylinder-to-booster nuts	6 to 8

Power brake booster nuts	
1985 through 1991	6 to 8
1992	9 to 12
Wheel cylinder bolts	5 to 7
Wheel lug nuts	See Chapter 1

1 General information

The vehicles covered by this manual are equipped with hydraulically operated front and rear brake systems. The front brakes are disc type and the rear brakes are disc or drum type. Both the front and rear brakes are self adjusting. The front or rear disc brakes automatically compensate for pad wear, while the rear drum brakes incorporate an adjustment mechanism which is activated as the brakes are applied when the vehicle is driven in reverse.

Hydraulic system

The hydraulic system consists of two separate circuits. The master cylinder has separate reservoirs for the two circuits and in the event of a leak or failure in one hydraulic circuit, the other circuit will remain operative. Some later models are equipped with an anti-lock braking system (ABS).

Power brake booster

The power brake booster, utilizing engine manifold vacuum and atmospheric pressure to provide assistance to the hydraulically operated brakes, is mounted on the firewall in the engine compartment.

Parking brake

The parking brake operates the rear brakes only, through cable actuation. It's activated by a lever mounted in the center console.

Service

After completing any operation involving disassembly of any part of the brake system, always test drive the vehicle to check for proper braking performance before resuming normal driving. When testing the brakes, perform the tests on a clean, dry flat surface. Conditions other than these can lead to inaccurate test results.

Test the brakes at various speeds with both light and heavy pedal pressure. The vehicle should stop evenly without pulling to one side or the other. Avoid locking the brakes because this slides the tires and diminishes braking efficiency and control of the vehicle.

Tires, vehicle load and front-end alignment are factors which also affect braking performance.

2 Anti-lock Brake System (ABS) – general information

The anti-lock brake system was introduced in 1989 and is designed to maintain vehicle steerability, directional stability and optimum deceleration under severe braking conditions and on most road surfaces. It does so by monitoring the rotational speed of each wheel and controlling the brake line pressure to each wheel during braking. This prevents the wheel from lock up.

Components

Actuator assembly

Refer to illustrations 2.2a and 2.2b

The actuator assembly consists of the master cylinder, an electric hydraulic pump and four solenoid valves **(see illustrations)**.

a) The electric pump provides hydraulic pressure to charge the reservoirs in the actuator, which supply pressure to the braking system. The pump and reservoirs are housed in the actuator assembly.
b) The solenoid valves modulate brake line pressure during ABS operation. The valve body contains four valves – one for each wheel.

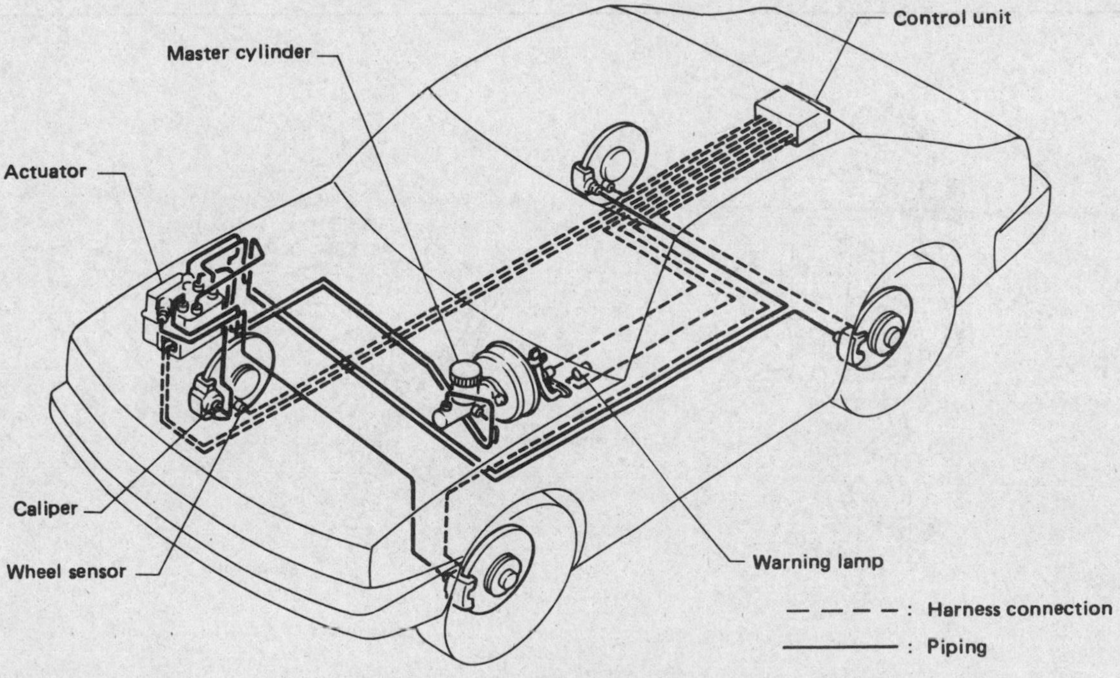

2.2a Locations of the ABS system components

9

Speed sensors

Refer to illustrations 2.4 and 2.5

These sensors are located at each wheel and generate small electrical pulsations when the toothed sensor rings are turning, sending a signal to the electronic controller indicating wheel rotational speed.

The front wheel sensors **(see illustration)** are mounted to the steering knuckle in close relationship to the toothed sensor rings, which are integral with the driveaxles.

The rear wheel sensors are bolted to the brake backing plates **(see illustration)**. The sensor rings are integral with the rear hub assemblies.

Twin Load Sensing Valve

Refer to illustration 2.6

The Twin Load Sensing Valve (TLSV) **(see illustration)** is designed to prevent the rear wheels from locking under severe braking conditions. The valve operates by changing the front and rear brake fluid pressure distribution in response to vehicle loading **(see illustration 2.6)**.

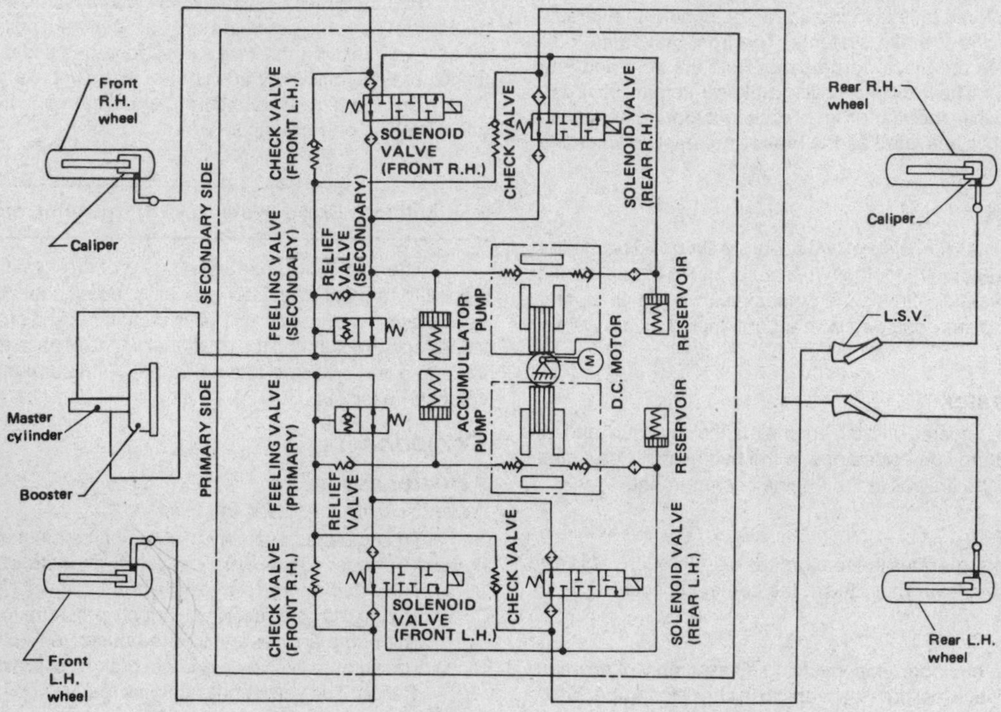

2.2b Schematic of the ABS hydraulic system

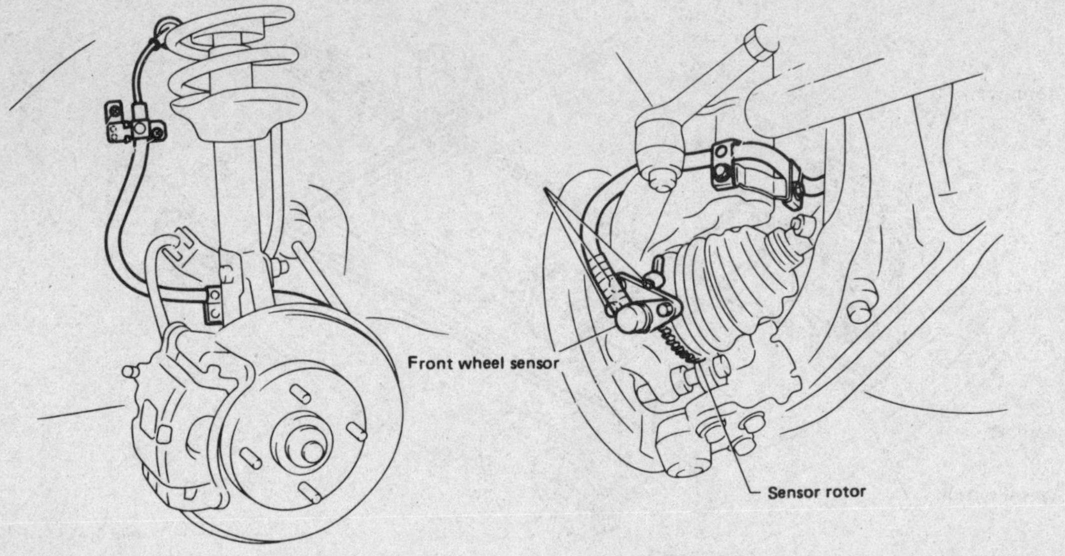

2.4 The front speed sensors bolt to the steering knuckle

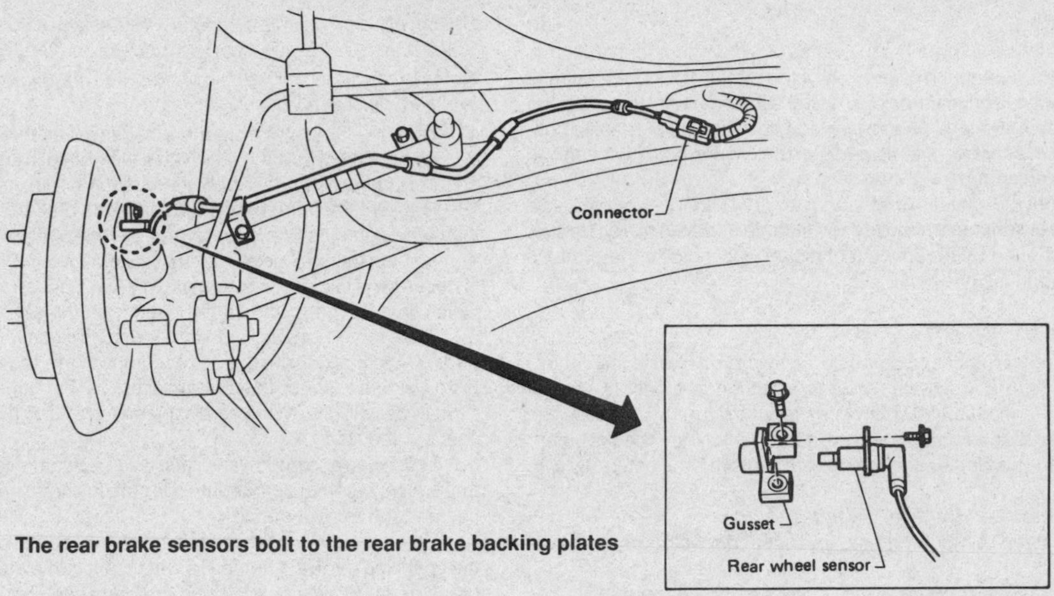

2.5 The rear brake sensors bolt to the rear brake backing plates

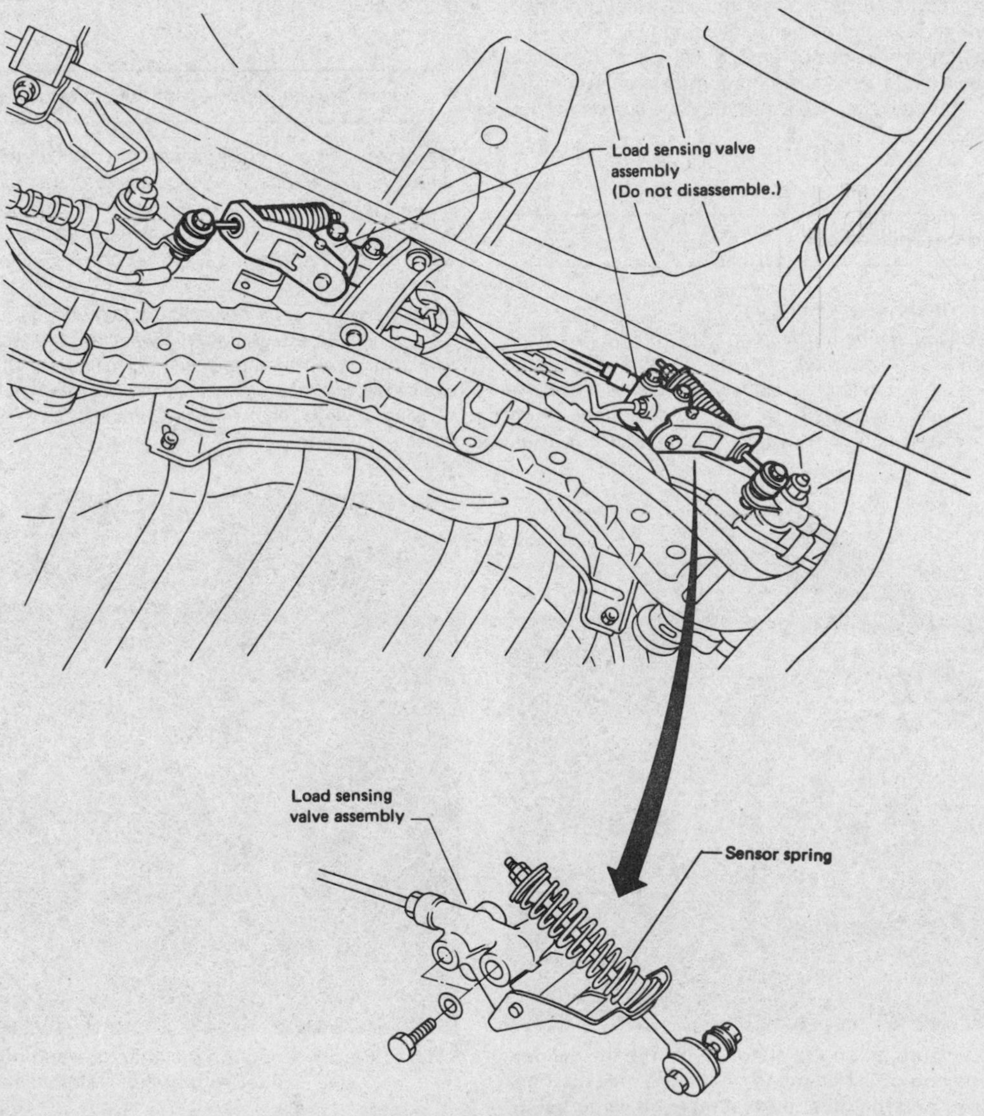

2.6 Location of twin load sensing valves

ABS computer

The ABS computer is mounted in the luggage compartment and is the "brain" for the ABS system. The function of the computer is to accept and process information received from the wheel speed sensors to control the hydraulic line pressure, avoiding wheel lock up. The computer also constantly monitors the system, even under normal driving conditions, to find faults within the system.

If a problem develops within the system, an "ANTILOCK" light will glow on the dashboard. A diagnostic code will also be stored in the computer, which, when retrieved by a service technician, will indicate the problem area or component.

Diagnosis and repair

If a dashboard warning light comes on and stays on while the vehicle is in operation, the ABS system requires attention. Although a special electronic ABS diagnostic tester is necessary to properly diagnose the system, the home mechanic can perform a few preliminary checks before taking the vehicle to a dealer service department which is equipped with this tester.

a) Check the brake fluid level in the reservoir.
b) Check that the computer master cylinder connectors are securely connected.
c) Check the electrical connectors at the actuator assembly.
d) Check the fuses.
e) Follow the wiring harness to each wheel and check that all connections are secure and that the wiring is not damaged.

If the above preliminary checks do not rectify the problem, the vehicle should be diagnosed by a dealer service department. Due to the complex nature of this system, all actual repair work must be done by a dealer service department.

3 Front brake pads – replacement

Refer to illustrations 3.5 and 3.6a through 3.6g

Warning: *Disc brake pads must be replaced on both front wheels at the same time – never replace the pads on only one wheel. Also, the dust created by the brake system may contain asbestos, which is harmful to your health. Never blow it out with compressed air and don't inhale any of it. An approved filtering mask should be worn when working on the brakes. Do not, under any circumstances, use petroleum based solvents to clean brake parts. Use brake cleaner or denatured alcohol only!*

Note: *When servicing the disc brakes, use only high quality, nationally recognized name brand pads.*

1 Remove the cover from the brake fluid reservoir.

2 Loosen the wheel lug nuts, raise the front of the vehicle and support it securely on jackstands. Apply the parking brake.

3 Remove the front wheels. Work on one brake assembly at a time, using the assembled brake for reference if necessary.

4 Inspect the brake disc carefully as outlined in Section 5. If machining is necessary, follow the information in that Section to remove the disc, at which time the pads can be removed from the calipers as well.

5 Push the piston back into the bore to provide room for the new brake pads. A C-clamp can be used to accomplish this **(see illustration)**. As the piston is depressed to thecbottom of the caliper bore, the fluid in the master cylinder will rise. Make sure it doesn't overflow. If necessary, siphon off some of the fluid.

6 Follow the accompanying illustrations, beginning with 3.6a, for the actual pad replacement procedure. Be sure to stay in order and read the caption under each illustration.

7 When reinstalling the caliper, be sure to tighten the mounting bolts to the specified torque. After the job has been completed, firmly depress the brake pedal a few times to bring the pads into contact with the disc.

8 Check for fluid leakage and make sure the brakes operate normally before driving in traffic.

4 Front brake caliper – removal, overhaul and installation

Warning: *Dust created by the brake system may contain asbestos, which is harmful to your health. Never blow it out with compressed air and don't inhale any of it. An approved filtering mask should be worn when working on the brakes. Do not, under any circumstances, use petroleum-based solvents to clean brake parts. Use brake cleaner or denatured alcohol only!*

Note: *If an overhaul is indicated (usually because of fluid leakage) explore all options before beginning the job. New and factory rebuilt calipers are available on an exchange basis, which makes this job quite easy. If it's decided to rebuild the calipers, make sure a rebuild kit is available before proceeding. Always rebuild the calipers in pairs – never rebuild just one of them.*

3.5 Using a large C-clamp, push the piston back into the caliper bore – note that one end of the clamp is on the flat area on the backside of the caliper and the other end (screw-end) is pressing against the outer brake pad

3.6a Before removing the caliper, wash off all traces of brake dust with brake system cleaner

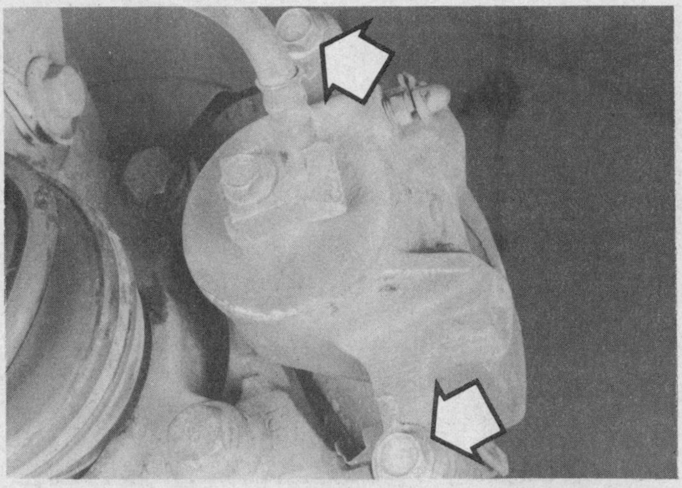

3.6b The brake caliper is secured by two mounting bolts (arrows) – when replacing the front brake pads it is only necessary to remove the lower bolt – then swing the caliper up and tie it securely to the coil spring

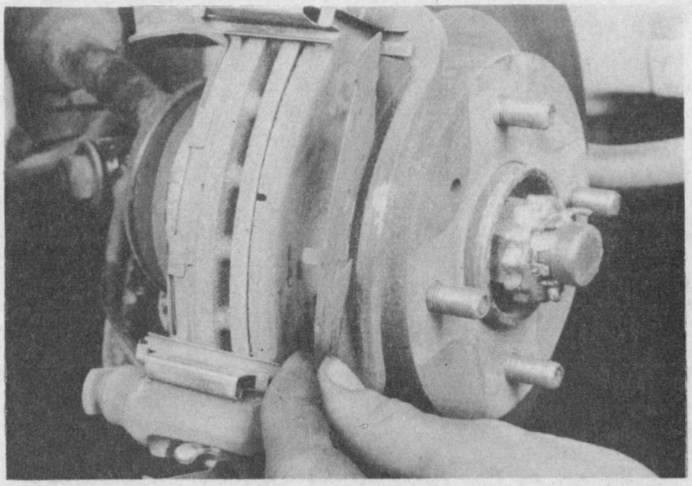

3.6c Remove the shims from the pads and note how they are positioned

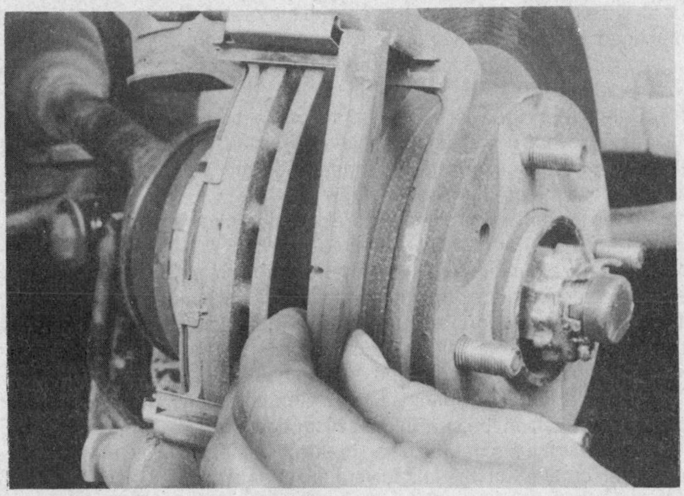

3.6d To remove the pads, slide them straight out of the torque member

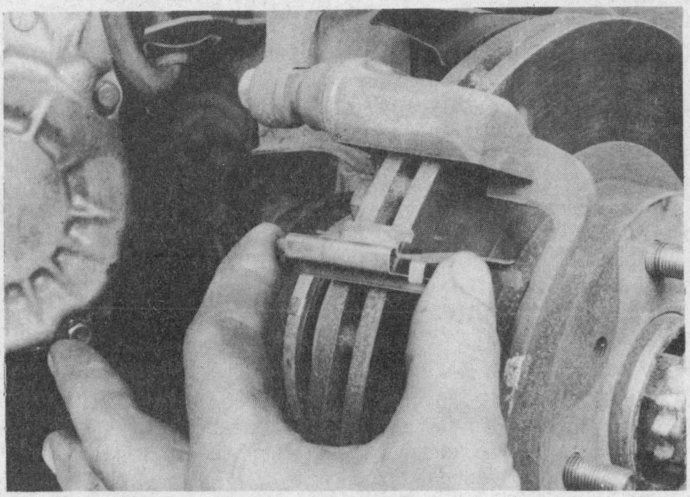

3.6e Remove the pad retainers from the torque member – they should be replaced with new ones if distorted in any way

3.6f Remove the main pins, check the pin boots for cracks or damage and then lubricate the pins with high temperature grease – make sure that they slide freely

3.6g Install the new pads, making sure the pad with the wear indicator (arrow) is installed in the inner position – the remainder of the replacement procedure is the reverse of removal

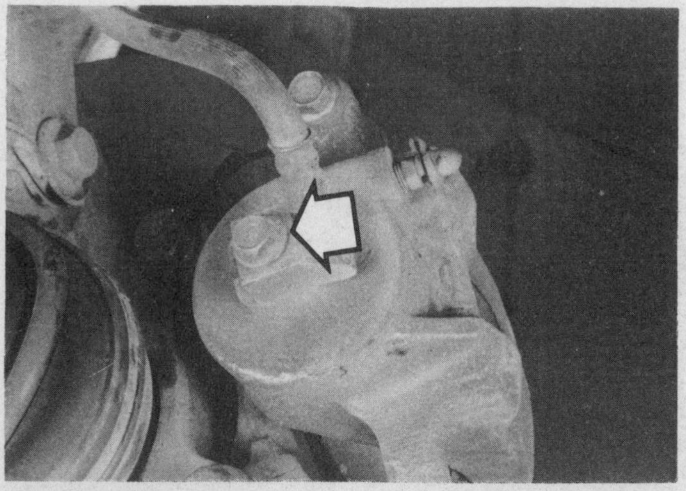

4.4a Location of the brake hose inlet fitting bolt (arrow) – when reinstalling the bolt, be sure to use new sealing washers on each side of the fitting to prevent leaks

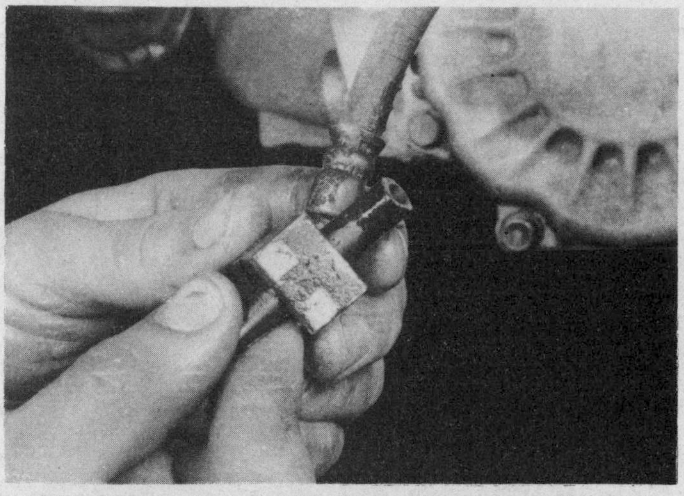

4.4b Using a piece of rubber hose of the appropriate size, plug the brake line

Removal

Refer to illustrations 4.4a and 4.4b

1 Remove the cover from the brake fluid reservoir, siphon off two-thirds of the fluid into a container and discard it.

2 Loosen the wheel lug nuts, raise the front of the vehicle and support it securely on jackstands. Remove the front wheels.

3 Bottom the piston in the caliper bore **(see illustration 3.5)**.

4 Disconnect the brake line from the caliper **(see illustration)**, plug it to keep contaminants out of the brake system and to prevent losing any more brake fluid than is necessary **(see illustration)**.

5 Remove the two mounting bolts and detach the caliper from the vehicle (refer to Section 3 if necessary).

Overhaul

Refer to illustrations 4.8, 4.9a, 4.9b, 4.10 and 4.17

6 Refer to Section 3 and remove the brake pads from the caliper.

7 Clean the exterior of the caliper with brake cleaner or denatured alcohol. Never use gasoline, kerosene or petroleum-based cleaning solvents. Place the caliper on a clean workbench.

8 Position a wooden block or several shop rags in the caliper as a cushion, then use compressed air to remove the piston from the caliper **(see illustration)**. Use only enough air pressure to ease the piston out of the bore. If the piston is blown out, even with the cushion in place, it may be damaged. **Warning:** *Never place your fingers in front of the piston in an attempt to catch or protect it when applying compressed air, as serious injury could occur.*

9 Carefully pry the dust boot out of the caliper bore **(see illustrations)**.

10 Using a wood or plastic tool, remove the piston seal from the groove in the caliper bore **(see illustration)**. Metal tools may cause bore damage.

11 Remove the caliper bleeder screw.

12 Clean the remaining parts with brake system cleaner or denatured alcohol then blow them dry with compressed air.

13 Carefully examine the piston for nicks and burrs and loss of plating. If surface defects are present, the parts must be replaced.

14 Check the caliper bore in a similar way. Light polishing with crocus cloth is permissible to remove light corrosion and stains. Discard the mounting bolts if they're corroded or damaged.

15 When assembling, lubricate the piston bores and seal with clean brake fluid. Position the seal in the caliper bore groove.

16 Lubricate the piston with clean brake fluid, then install a new boot in the piston groove with the fold toward the open end of the piston.

17 Insert the piston squarely into the caliper bore, then apply force to bottom it **(see illustration)**.

4.8 With the caliper padded to catch the piston, use compressed air to force the piston out of its bore – make sure your hands or fingers are not between the piston and caliper frame!

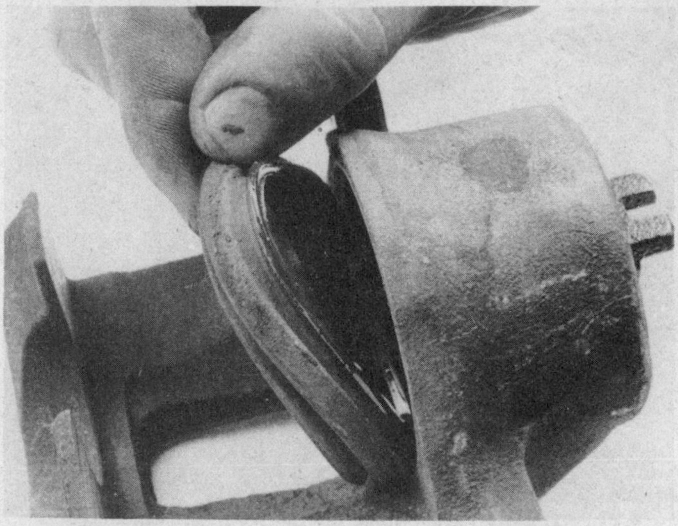

4.9a Carefully remove the dust boot from the caliper

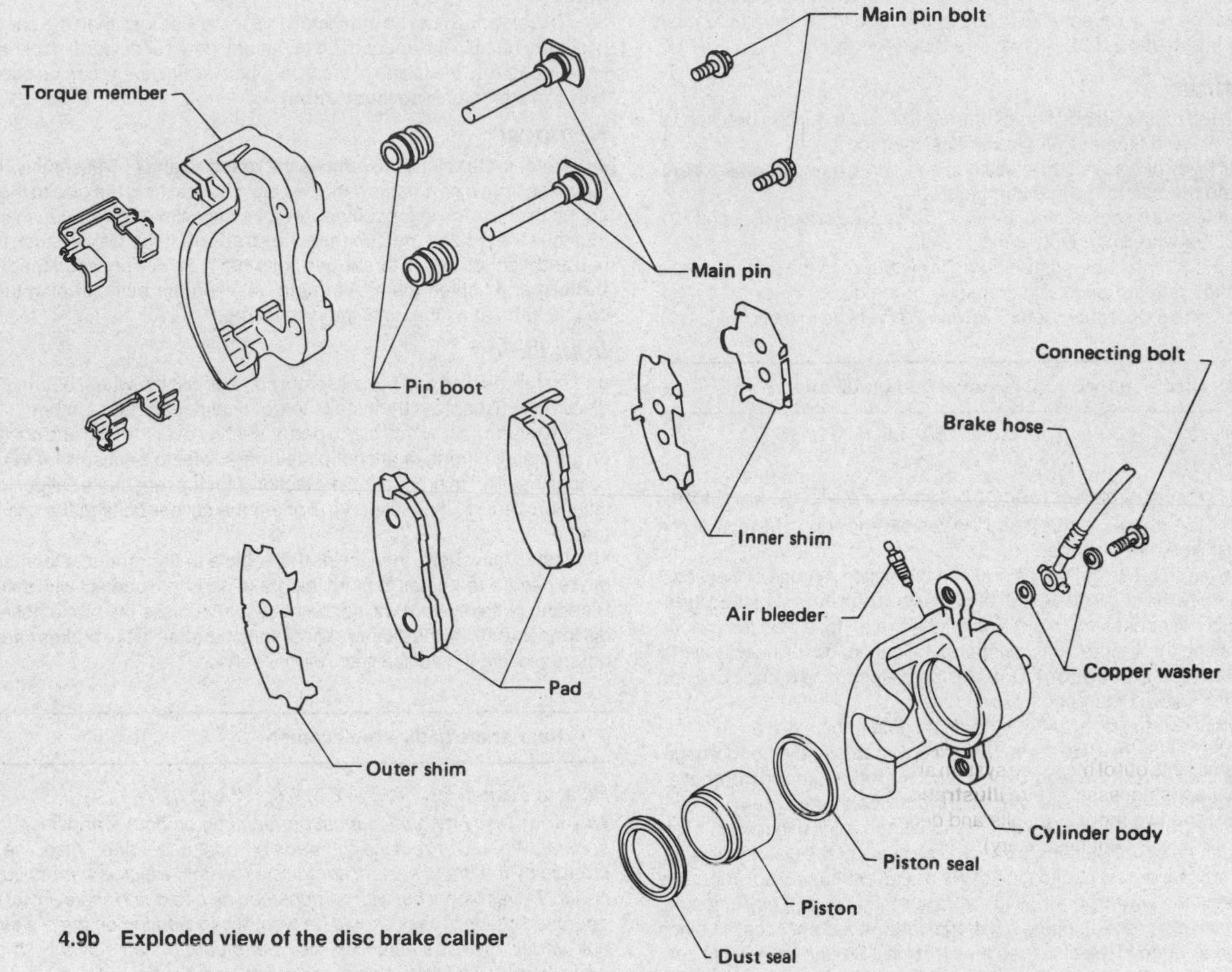

4.9b Exploded view of the disc brake caliper

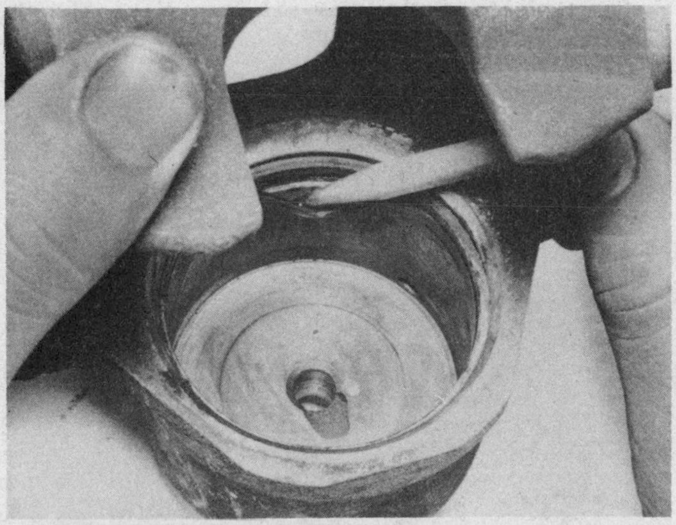

4.10 The piston seal should be removed with a plastic or wooden tool to avoid damage to the bore and seal groove – a pencil will do the job

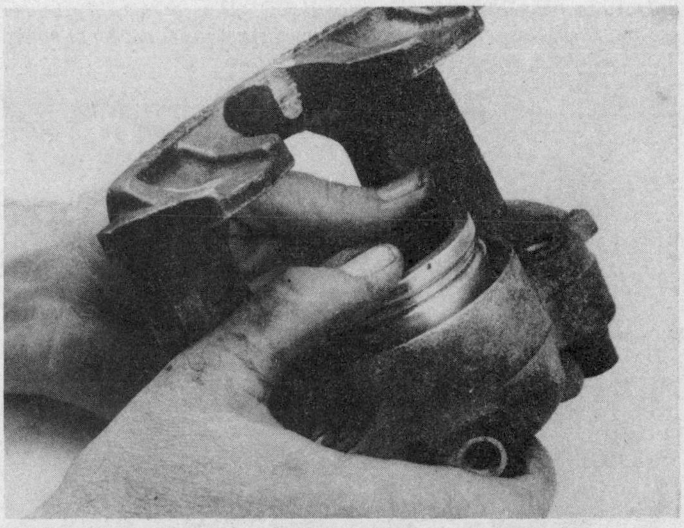

4.17 When installing the piston, make sure it doesn't become cocked in the caliper bore while pushing it down

9

18 Install the bleeder screw.
19 Install new pin boots in the mounting bolt holes and fill the area with the high temperature grease supplied in the rebuild kit. Install the main pins **(see illustration 3.6f)**. Make sure they slide freely.

Installation

20 Place the caliper in position over the rotor and mounting bracket, install the bolts and tighten them to the specified torque.
21 Install the brake hose and inlet fitting bolt, using new copper washers, then tighten the bolt to the specified torque.
22 If the line was disconnected, be sure to bleed the brakes (Section 12).
23 Install the wheels and lower the vehicle.
24 After the job has been completed, firmly depress the brake pedal a few times to bring the pads into contact with the disc.
25 Check brake operation before driving the vehicle in traffic.

5 Brake disc – inspection, removal and installation

Refer to illustrations 5.2a, 5.2b, 5.5a, 5.5b, 5.6, 5.7a and 5.7b

Inspection

Note: *This procedure applies to both front and rear disc brake assemblies.*

1 Loosen the wheel lug nuts, raise the vehicle and support it securely on jackstands. Remove the wheel.
2 Remove the brake caliper as outlined in Section 4 (front) or Section 7 (rear). Remove the U-clip to detach the hose from the front strut **(see illustration)**. It's not necessary to disconnect the brake hose from the caliper. After removing the caliper bolts, suspend the caliper out of the way with a piece of wire **(see illustration)**. Don't let the caliper hang by the hose and don't stretch or twist the hose.
3 Reinstall two lug nuts to hold the disc against the axle flange.
4 Visually check the disc surface for score marks and other damage. Light scratches and shallow grooves are normal after use and may not always be detrimental to brake operation, but deep score marks – over 0.015-inch (0.38 mm) – require disc removal and refinishing by an automotive machine shop. Be sure to check both sides of the disc. If pulsating has been noticed during application of the brakes, suspect disc runout. Be sure to check the wheel bearings to make sure they're properly adjusted.
5 To check disc runout, place a dial indicator at a point about 1/2-inch from the outer edge of the disc **(see illustration)**. Set the indicator to zero and turn the disc. The indicator reading should not exceed the specified allowable runout limit. If it does, the disc should be refinished by an automotive machine shop. **Note:** *Professionals recommend resurfacing of brake discs regardless of the dial indicator reading (to produce a smooth, flat surface that will eliminate brake pedal pulsations and other undesirable symptoms related to questionable discs). At the very least, if you elect not to have the discs resurfaced, deglaze them with sandpaper or emery cloth (use a swirling motion to ensure a nondirectional finish)* **(see illustration)**.
6 The disc must not be machined to a thickness less than the specified minimum refinish thickness. The minimum wear (or discard) thickness is usually cast into the inside of the disc. The disc thickness can be checked with a micrometer **(see illustration)**.

Removal

7 Refer to Chapter 10 to remove the rear disc and hub assembly. To remove the front disc, unscrew the two lug nuts that held the disc to the axle during the inspection procedure, remove the caliper and torque member then pull the disc off the hub **(see illustration)**. If the disc is stuck to the hub and won't come off, thread two bolts into the holes provided **(see illustration)** and tighten them. Alternate between the bolts, turning them a couple turns at a time, until the disc is free.

Installation

8 Install the disc and hub assembly and adjust the wheel bearing (rear discs only) (Chapter 10). Install the front caliper torque member.
9 Install the caliper and brake pad assembly over the disc and position it on the spindle (front) or anchor plate (rear) (refer to Section 4 for the front caliper installation procedure, or Section 7 for the rear brake caliper installation procedure, if necessary). Tighten the caliper bolts to the specified torque.
10 Install the wheel, then lower the vehicle to the ground. Depress the brake pedal a few times to bring the brake pads into contact with the disc. Bleeding of the system will not be necessary unless the brake hose was disconnected from the caliper. Check the operation of the brakes carefully before placing the vehicle into normal service.

6 Rear brake pads – replacement

Refer to illustrations 6.2, 6.4, 6.5, 6.6, 6.7 and 6.8

Warning: *Disc brake pads must be replaced on both rear wheels at the same time – never replace the pads on only one wheel. Also, the dust created by the brake system contains asbestos, which is harmful to your health. Never blow it out with compressed air and don't inhale any of it. An approved filtering mask should be worn when working on the brakes. Do not, under any circumstances, use petroleum-based solvents to clean brake parts. Use brake cleaner or denatured alcohol only!*

Note: *When servicing the disc brakes, use only high quality, nationally recognized brand name pads.*

1 Block the front wheels. Loosen the wheel lug nuts, raise the rear of the vehicle and support it securely on jackstands. Remove the wheel.
2 Before removing the caliper, wash off all traces of brake dust with brake system cleaner **(see illustration)**.

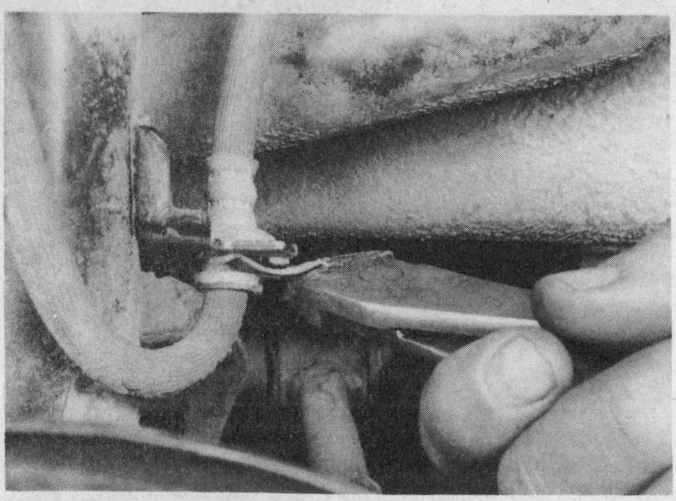

5.2a Remove the U-clip with a pair of pliers to detach the hose from the front strut

5.2b Suspend the caliper with a piece of wire after it's removed – don't let it hang by the brake hose

5.5a Use a dial indicator to check disc runout – if the reading exceeds the maximum allowable runout limit, the rotor will have to be machined or replaced

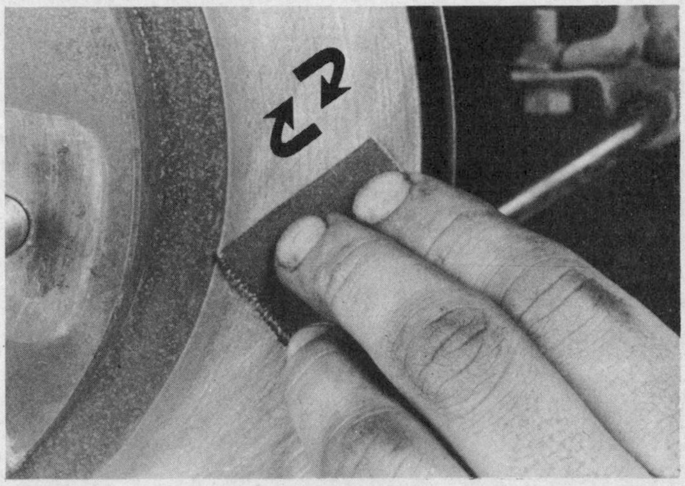

5.5b Using a swirling motion, remove the glaze from the disc surface with medium-grit emery cloth

5.6 Use a micrometer to measure disc thickness at several points near the edge

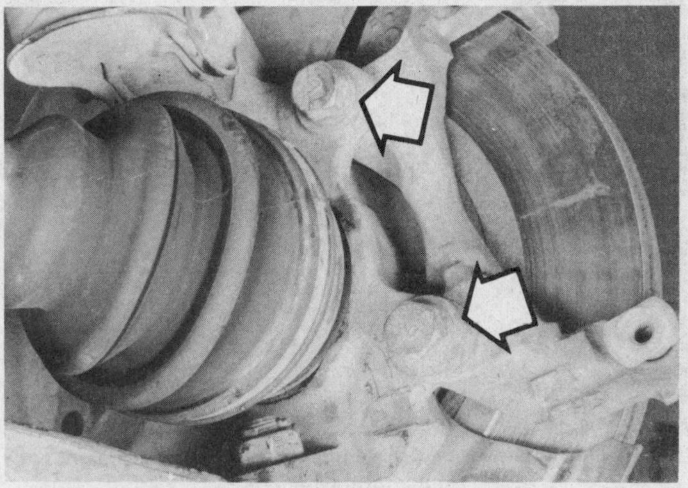

5.7a The torque member (caliper mounting bracket) is secured to the steering knuckle with two bolts (arrows)

5.7b To help free the disc, thread bolts of the appropriate size into the two holes provided in the disc – alternate between the bolts, turning them a little at a time, until the disc is free

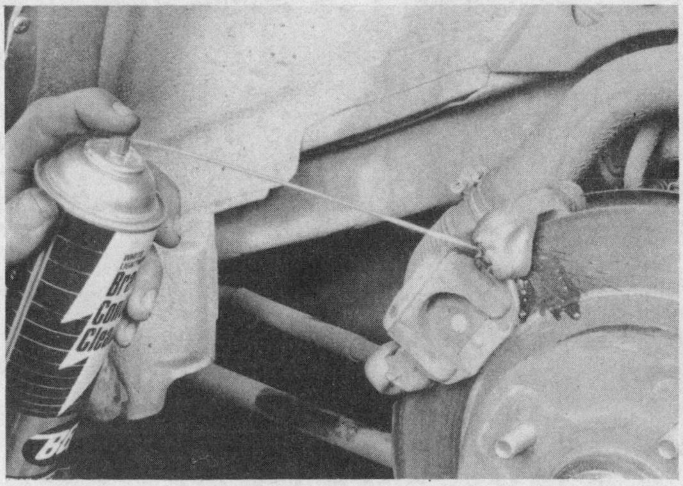

6.2 Before removing the caliper, wash off all traces of brake dust with brake system cleaner

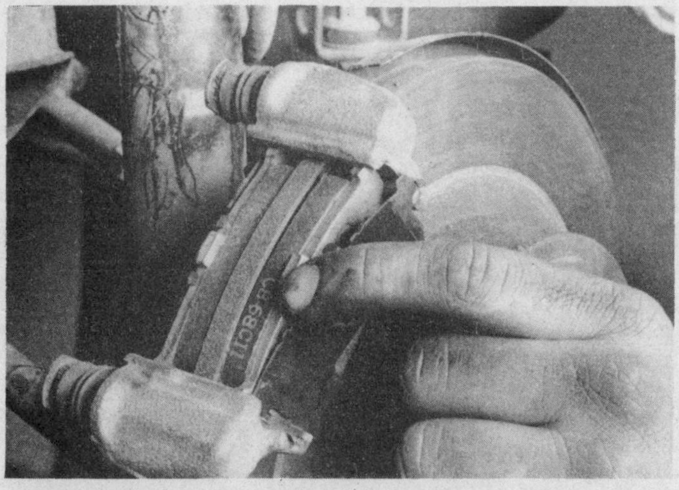

6.4 Note how they are positioned, then remove the shims from the pads.

3 Remove the brake caliper (see Section 7).
4 Remove the inner and outer shims **(see illustration).**
5 Slide the brake pads out of the torque member **(see illustration).**
6 Detach the pad retainers **(see illustration).**
7 Remove the main pins and pin boots **(see illustration).**
8 Using a pair of needle-nose pliers, engage the tips of the pliers in the two slots in the caliper piston face. Turn the piston clockwise until it is completely seated in the caliper. Position the piston in such a way that one of the slots will be aligned with the locating nib on the brake pad when the caliper is installed **(see illustration).**
9 Install the pad retainers. Insert the brake pads into the torque member. Install the inner and outer shims.
10 Swing the caliper into position, making sure the nib on the pad meshes with a slot in the caliper piston.
11 Tighten both bolts to the specified torque.
12 Install the wheel, lower the vehicle and tighten the lug nuts to the specified torque.
13 Depress the brake pedal a few times to bring the pads into contact with the rotor. Bleeding of the system will not be necessary unless the hose was disconnected from the caliper. Check the operation of the brakes carefully before placing the vehicle into normal service.

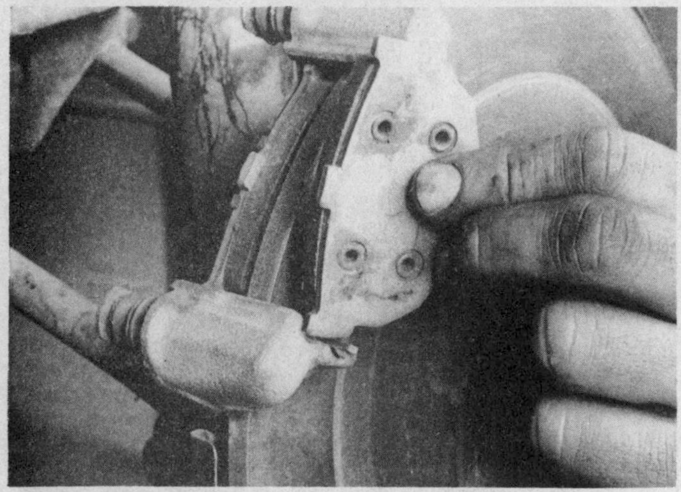

6.5 To remove the pads, slide them to the side then straight out of the torque member

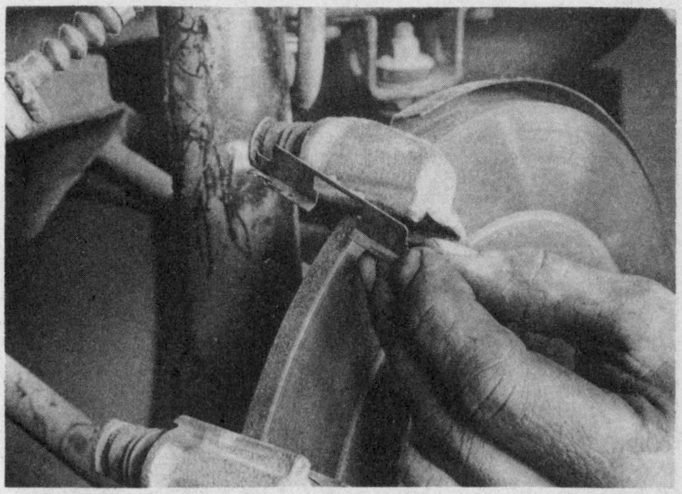

6.6 Remove the pad retainers from the torque member – they should be replaced with new ones if distorted in any way

6.7 Remove the main pins, check the pin boots for cracks or damage and then lubricate the pins with high temperature grease – make sure that they slide freely

6.8 Using a pair of needle-nose pliers, turn the piston clockwise until it is completely seated in the caliper – position the piston in such a way that one of the slots will be aligned with the locating nib on the brake pad when the caliper is installed

7 Rear brake caliper – removal and installation

Note: *Due to the relatively complex design of the rear brake caliper/parking brake actuator assembly, all service procedures requiring disassembly and reassembly should be left to a professional mechanic. The home mechanic can, however, remove the caliper and take it to a repair shop or Nissan dealer service department for repair, thereby saving the cost of removal and installation.*

Removal

Refer to illustrations 7.2 and 7.3

1 Block the front wheels. Loosen the wheel lug nuts, raise the rear of the vehicle and support it securely on jackstands. Remove the wheel.
2 Remove the caliper mounting bolts **(see illustration)**.
3 If the caliper is being removed for access to other components only, removing the hose won't be necessary. If this is the case, hang the caliper out of the way with a piece of wire **(see illustration).**
4 If the caliper is being removed for service, disconnect the brake hose from the caliper. Wrap a plastic bag tightly around the end of the hose to prevent fluid loss and contamination.
5 Lift the caliper away from the torque member.

Installation

6 Installation is the reverse of the removal procedure. Follow the procedure outlined in Section 6 to ensure correct installation of the caliper over the brake pads.
7 Bleed the brakes as outlined in Section 12.

8 Rear brake shoes – replacement

Refer to illustration 8.4

Warning: *Drum brake shoes must be replaced on both wheels at the same time – never replace the shoes on only one wheel. Also, the dust created by the brake system contains asbestos, which is harmful to your health. Never blow it out with compressed air and don't inhale any of it. An approved filtering mask should be worn when working on the brakes. Do not, under any circumstances, use petroleum-based solvents to clean brake parts. Use brake cleaner or denatured alcohol only!*

Caution: *Whenever the brake shoes are replaced, the retractor and hold-down springs should also be replaced. Due to the continuous heating/cooling cycle that the springs are subjected too, they lose their tension over a period of time and may allow the shoes to drag on the drum and wear at a much faster rate than normal. When replacing the rear brake shoes, use only high quality nationally recognized brand-name parts.*

1 Block the front wheels. Loosen the wheel lug nuts, raise the rear of the vehicle and support it securely on jackstands. Remove the rear wheel.
2 Remove the brake drum (see Chapter 10).
3 Thoroughly clean the brake assembly with brake cleaner.
4 Remove the brake shoe return springs **(see illustration)**. Do not mix up the springs.
5 On the front shoe, use pliers or a brake spring tool to depress the anti-rattle spring and retainer and turn them 90-degrees to remove them from the pin.
6 Remove the front shoe and adjuster from the backing plate.
7 Remove the anti-rattle spring from the rear shoe.
8 Disconnect the parking brake cable from the lever.
9 Do not depress the brake pedal while the shoes are off, otherwise the pistons will be forced from the cylinder.
10 Check that the pistons are free to move in the cylinder, that the rubber dust covers are undamaged and in position, and that there are no hydraulic fluid leaks. **Note:** *If there are signs of fluid leakage or the wheel cylinders are to be overhauled for any reason, perform this operation now, before the new linings are installed. Refer to Section 9.*
11 Apply a little brake grease to the adjuster threads.
12 Prior to reassembly, smear a little brake grease on the platforms and shoe locations on the cylinder and adjuster. Do not allow any grease to come into contact with the linings or rubber parts.
13 Remove the clip holding the parking brake lever, and transfer it to the new rear shoe. The rest of reassembly is the reverse of disassembly.
14 Install the brake drum and wheel.
15 Adjust the brake and lower the vehicle to the ground. If there is any chance that air has entered the system, bleed the brakes as described in Section 12. Test the braking capabilities carefully before placing the vehicle into normal operation.

9 Wheel cylinder – removal, overhaul and installation

Note: *If an overhaul is indicated (usually because of fluid leakage or sticky operation) explore all options before beginning the job. New wheel cylinders are available, which makes this job quite easy. If it's decided to rebuild the wheel cylinder, make sure that a rebuild kit is available before proceeding. Never overhaul only one wheel cylinder – always rebuild both of them at the same time.*

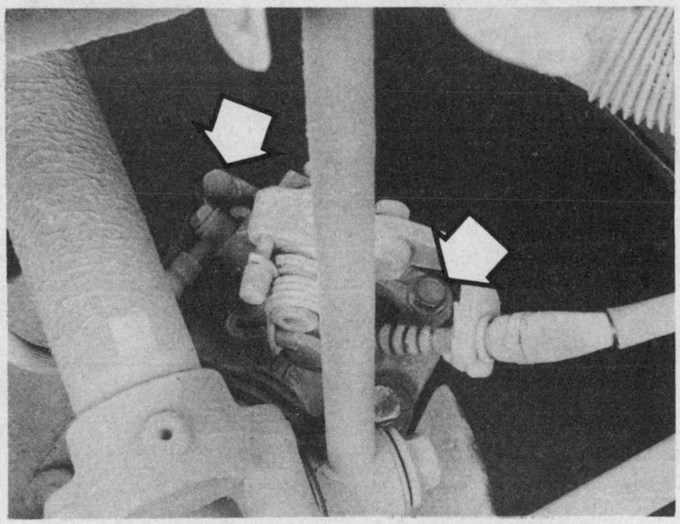

7.2 Remove the two caliper mounting bolts (arrows)

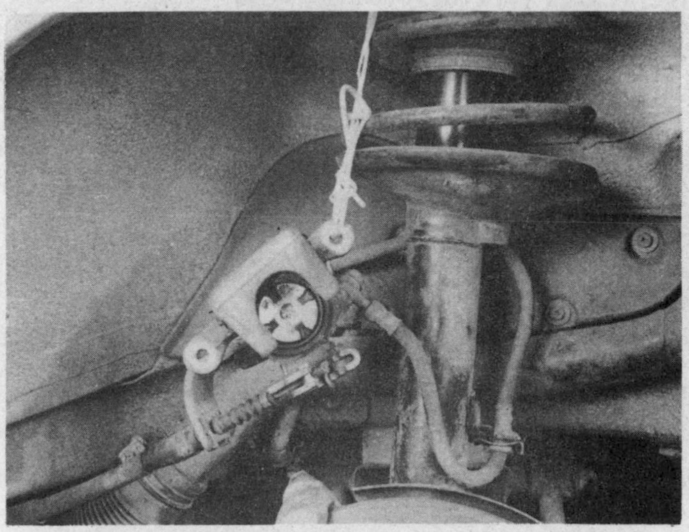

7.3 Once the caliper is removed from the torque member, hang it from the coil spring with a piece of wire – don't let it hang by the brake hose!

9

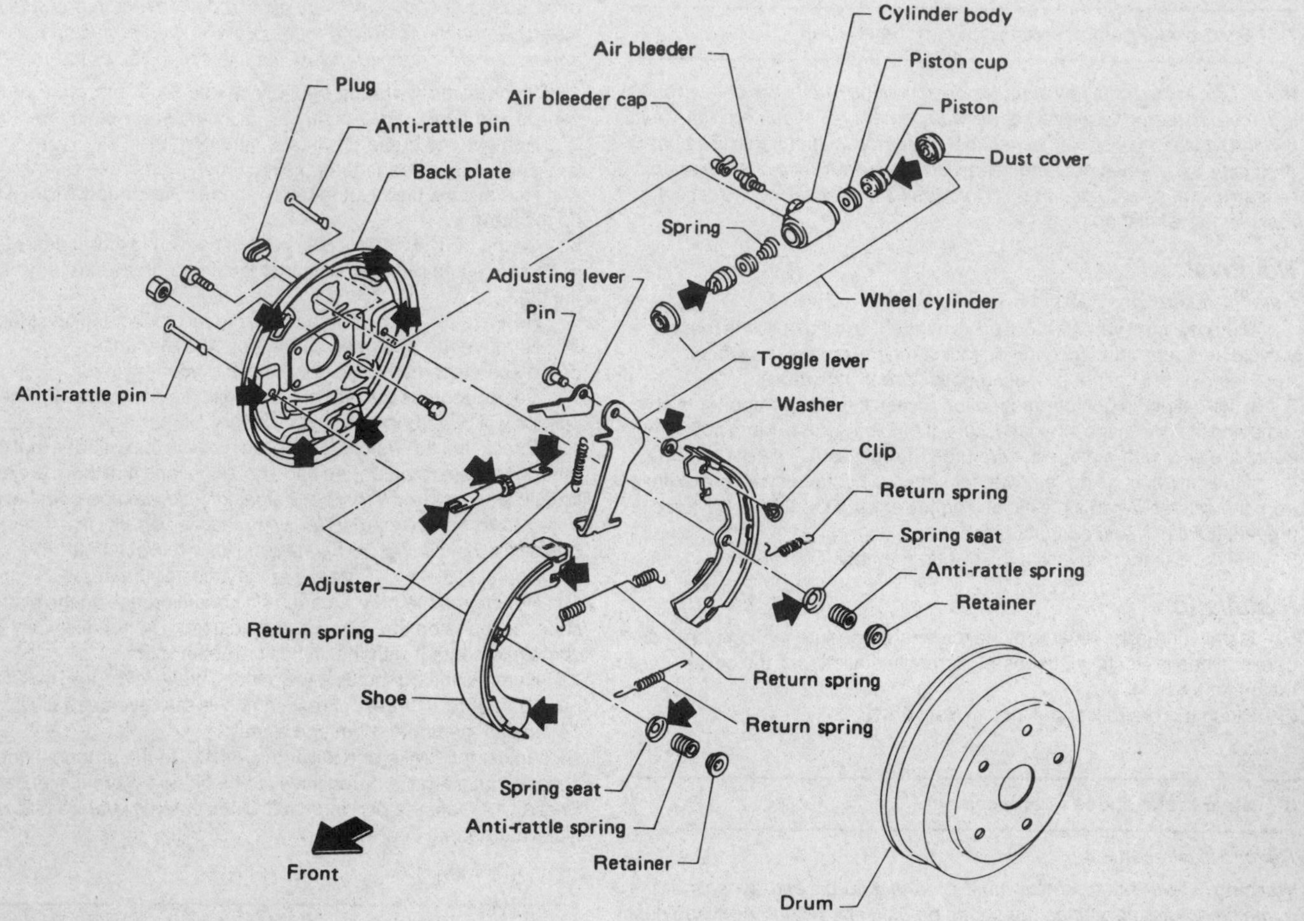

8.4 Exploded view of the rear drum brake assembly – 1989 models

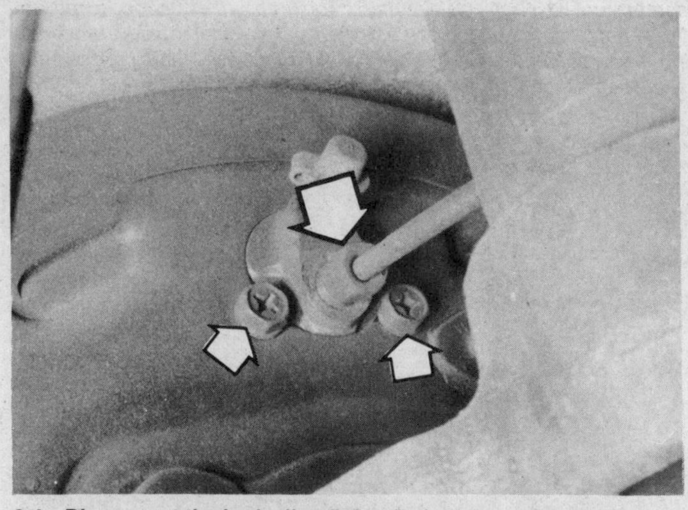

9.4 Disconnect the brake line fitting (arrow) then remove the two wheel cylinder bolts (arrows)

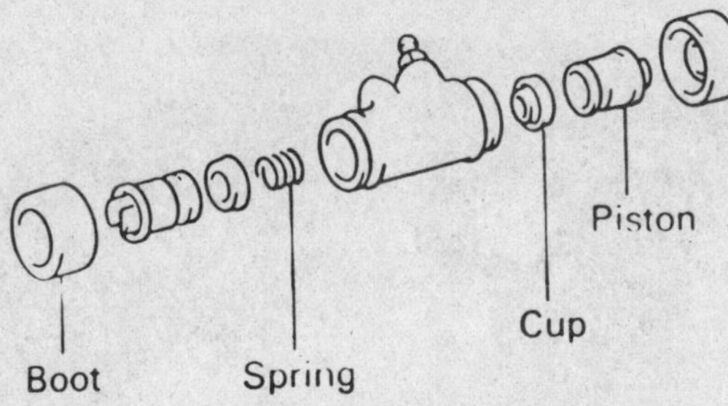

9.7 Exploded view of the wheel cylinder

Removal

Refer to illustration 9.4

1 Raise the rear of the vehicle and support it securely on jackstands. Block the front wheels to keep the vehicle from rolling.
2 Remove the brake shoe assembly (Section 8).
3 Remove all dirt and foreign material from around the wheel cylinder.
4 Unscrew the brake line fitting **(see illustration).** Don't pull the brake line away from the wheel cylinder.
5 Remove the wheel cylinder mounting bolts.
6 Detach the wheel cylinder from the brake backing plate and place it on a clean workbench. Immediately plug the brake line to prevent fluid loss and contamination. **Note:** *If the brake shoe linings are contaminated with brake fluid, install new brake shoes.*

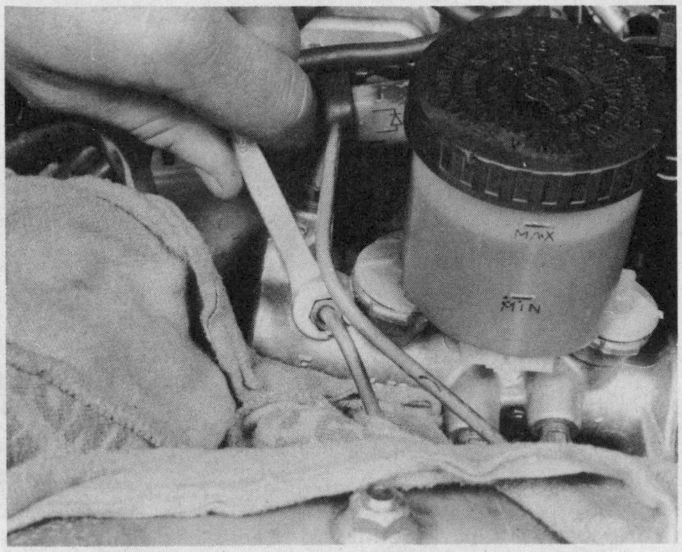

10.4 Unscrew the brake line fitting tube nuts with a flare nut wrench

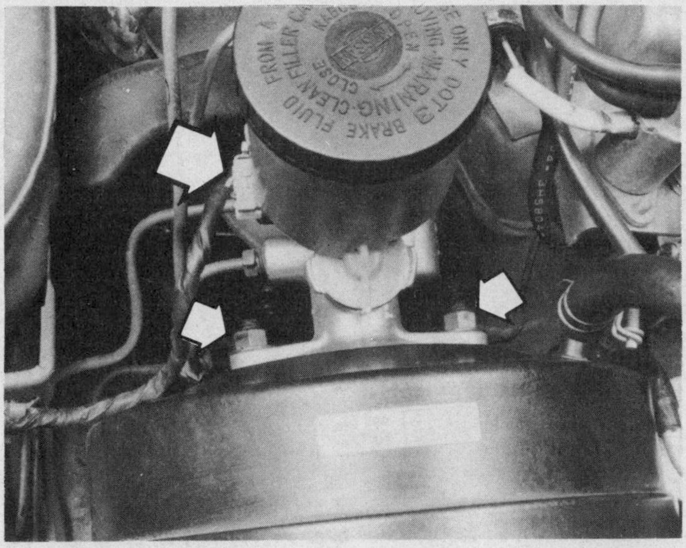

10.6 Unplug the brake fluid level indicator electrical connector, then remove the two master cylinder mounting nuts (arrows)

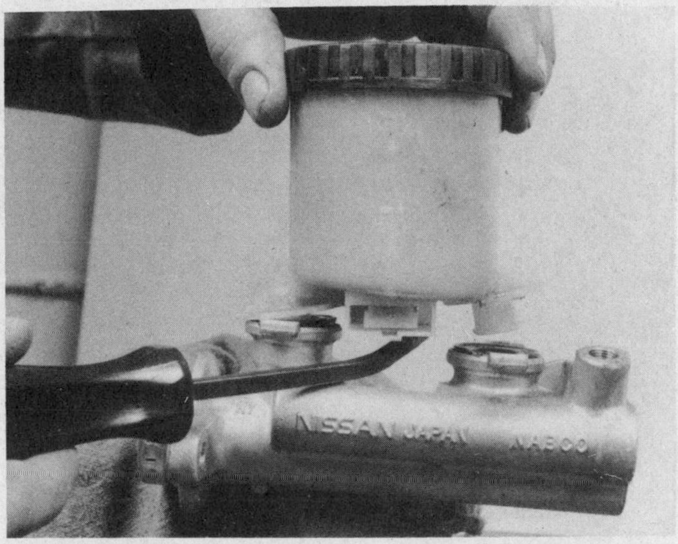

10.8a Pry the plastic reservoir from the cylinder body

Overhaul

Refer to illustration 9.7

7 Remove the bleeder screw, cups, pistons, boots and spring assembly from the wheel cylinder body **(see illustration)**.

8 Clean the wheel cylinder with brake fluid, denatured alcohol or brake system cleaner. **Warning:** *Do not, under any circumstances, use petroleum based solvents to clean brake parts!*

9 Use compressed air to remove excess fluid from the wheel cylinder and to blow out the passages.

10 Check the cylinder bore for corrosion and score marks. Crocus cloth can be used to remove light corrosion and stains, but the cylinder must be replaced with a new one if the defects cannot be removed easily, or if the bore is scored.

11 Lubricate the new cups with brake fluid.

12 Assemble the wheel cylinder components. Make sure the cup lips face in.

Installation

13 Place the wheel cylinder in position and install the bolts.

14 Connect the brake line and tighten the fitting. Install the brake shoe assembly.

15 Bleed the brakes (Section 12).

16 Check brake operation before driving the vehicle in traffic.

10 Master cylinder – removal, overhaul and installation

Refer to illustrations 10.4, 10.6, 10.8a, 10.8b, 10.9, 10.10a, 10.10b and 10.10c

Note: *Before deciding to overhaul the master cylinder, check on the availability and cost of a new or factory rebuilt unit and also the availability of a rebuild kit.*

Removal

1 The master cylinder is located in the engine compartment, mounted to the power brake booster.

2 Remove as much fluid as you can from the reservoir with a syringe.

3 Place rags under the fluid fittings and prepare caps or plastic bags to cover the ends of the lines once they are disconnected. **Caution:** *Brake fluid will damage paint. Cover all body parts and be careful not to spill fluid during this procedure.*

4 Loosen the tube nuts at the ends of the brake lines where they enter the master cylinder **(see illustration)**. To prevent rounding off the flats on these nuts, the use of a flare nut wrench, which wraps around the nut, is preferred.

5 Pull the brake lines slightly away from the master cylinder and plug the ends to prevent contamination.

6 Disconnect the electrical connector at the master cylinder, then remove the two nuts attaching the master cylinder to the power booster **(see illustration)**. Pull the master cylinder off the studs and out of the engine compartment. Again, be careful not to spill the fluid as this is done.

Overhaul

7 Before attempting the overhaul of the master cylinder, obtain the proper rebuild kit, which will contain the necessary replacement parts and also any instructions which may be specific to your model.

8 Place the cylinder in a vise and remove the reservoir **(see illustration)**. Then remove the grommets **(see illustration)**.

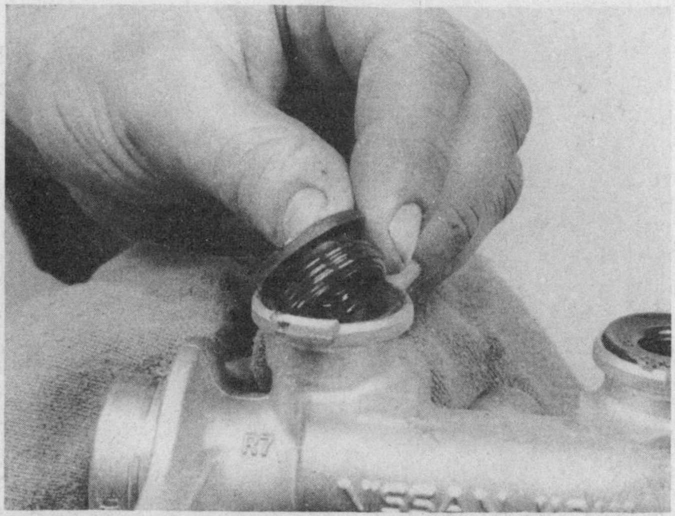

10.8b After the reservoir has been removed, pull the grommets from the cylinder body (do not reuse the grommets – always use new ones)

10.9 Use a Phillips screwdriver to depress the pistons – use a hook to bend the tang up to remove the stopper cap

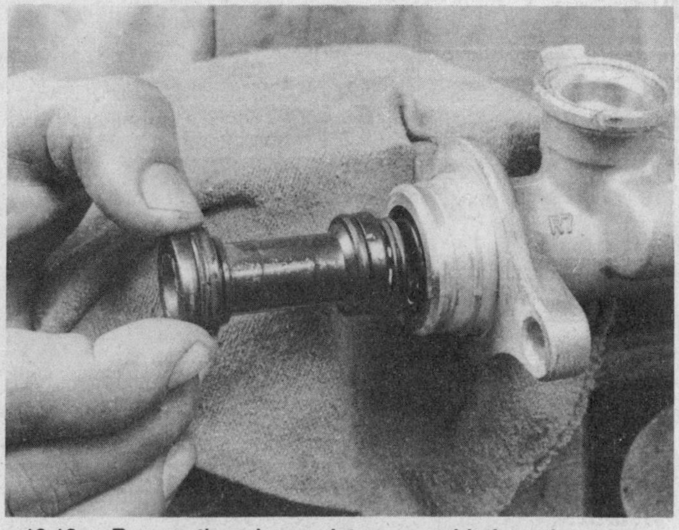

10.10a Remove the primary piston assembly from the master cylinder bore

10.10b To remove the secondary piston assembly, tap the master cylinder firmly against a block of wood

9 Use a punch or Phillips screwdriver to depress the pistons until they bottom against the other end of the master cylinder **(see illustration)**. Hold the pistons in this position and remove the stopper cap.

10 The internal components can now be removed from the cylinder bore **(see illustrations)**. Make a note of the proper order of the components so they can be returned to their original locations. **Note:** *The two springs are of different tension, so pay particular attention to their order. Also, do not disassemble the piston components – they are serviced as an assembly.*

11 Carefully inspect the bore of the master cylinder. Any deep scoring or other damage will mean a new master cylinder is required.

12 Replace all parts included in the rebuild kit, following any instructions in the kit. Clean all reused parts with clean brake fluid or denatured alcohol. Do not use any petroleum-based cleaners. During assembly, lubricate all parts liberally with clean brake fluid.

13 Always use new grommets and a stopper cap.

14 Push the assembled components into the bore, bottoming them against the end of the master cylinder, then install the stopper cap.

15 Before installing the master cylinder it should be bench bled. Because it will be necessary to apply pressure to the master cylinder piston and, at the same time, control flow from the brake line outlets, it is recommended that the master cylinder be mounted in a vise, with the jaws of the vise clamping on the mounting flange. The master cylinder is aluminum, so be careful not to damage it.

16 Insert threaded plugs into the brake line outlet holes and snug them down so that there will be no air leakage past them, but not so tight that they cannot be easily loosened.

17 Fill the reservoir with brake fluid of the recommended type (see Chapter 1).

18 Remove one plug and push the piston assembly into the master cylinder bore to expel the air from the master cylinder. A large Phillips screwdriver can be used to push on the piston assembly.

19 To prevent air from being drawn back into the master cylinder the plug must be replaced and snugged down before releasing the pressure on the piston assembly.

20 Repeat the procedure until only brake fluid is expelled from the brake line outlet hole. When only brake fluid is expelled, repeat the procedure with the other outlet hole and plug. Be sure to keep the master cylinder reservoir filled with brake fluid to prevent the introduction of air into the system.

21 Since high pressure is not involved in the bench bleeding procedure, an alternative to the removal and replacement of the plugs with each stroke of the piston assembly is available. Before pushing in on the piston

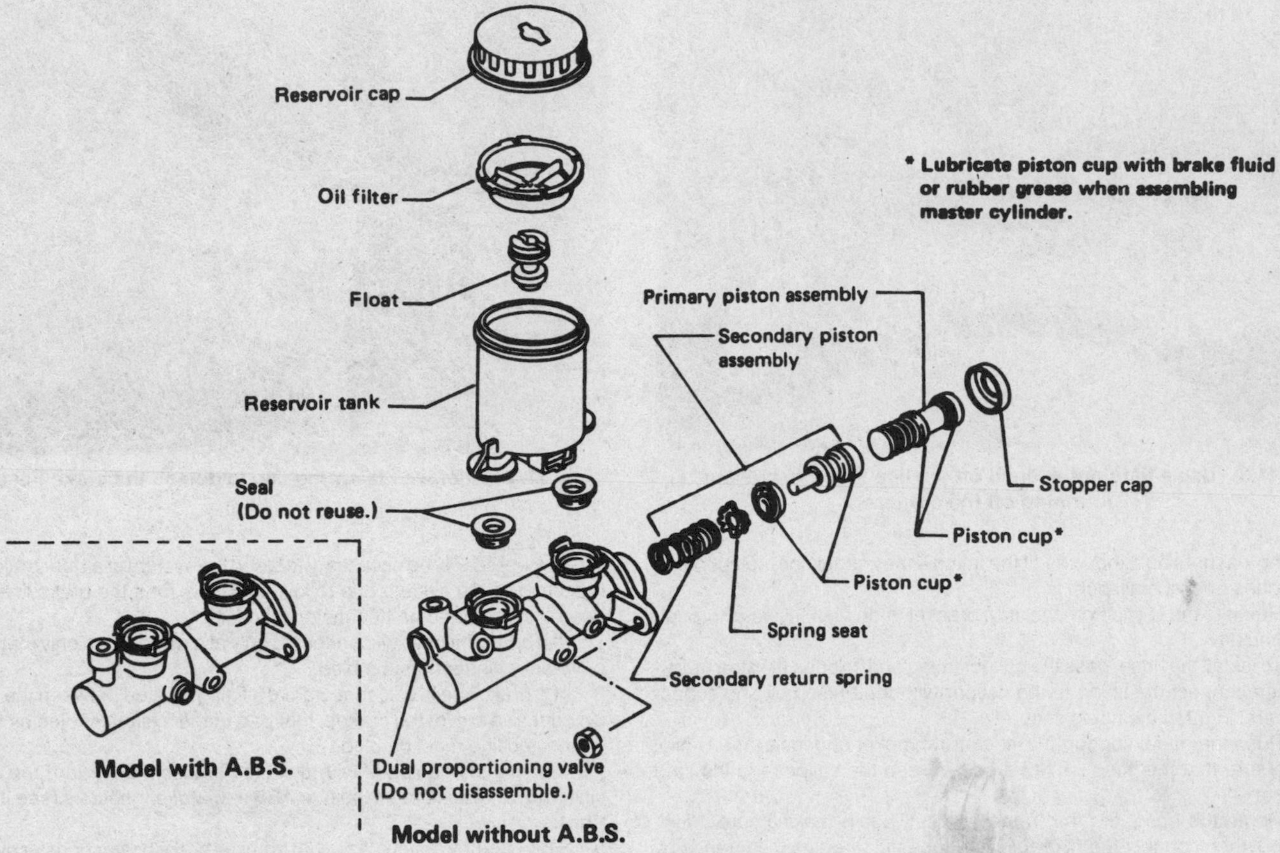

10.10c Exploded view of the master cylinder components

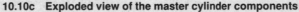

assembly, remove the plug as described in Step 18. Before releasing the piston, however, instead of replacing the plug, simply put your finger tightly over the hole to keep air from being drawn back into the master cylinder. Wait several seconds for brake fluid to be drawn from the reservoir into the piston bore, then depress the piston again, removing your finger as brake fluid is expelled. Be sure to put your finger back over the hole each time before releasing the piston, and when the bleeding procedure is complete for that outlet, replace the plug and snug it before going on to the other port.

Installation

22 Install the master cylinder over the studs on the power brake booster and tighten the attaching nuts only finger tight at this time.
23 Thread the brake line fittings into the master cylinder. Since the master cylinder is still a bit loose, it can be moved slightly for the fittings to thread in easily. Do not strip the threads as the fittings are tightened.
24 Fully tighten the mounting nuts and the brake fittings.
25 Fill the master cylinder reservoir with fluid, then bleed the master cylinder (only if the cylinder has not been bench bled) and the brake system as described in Section 12. To bleed the cylinder on the vehicle, have an assistant pump the brake pedal several times and then hold the pedal to the floor. Loosen the fitting nut to allow air and fluid to escape. Repeat this procedure on both fittings until the fluid is clear of air bubbles. Test the operation of the brake system carefully before placing the vehicle into normal service.

11 Brake hoses and lines – inspection and replacement

Inspection

1 About every six months, with the vehicle raised and supported securely on jackstands, the rubber hoses which connect the steel brake lines with the front and rear brake assemblies should be inspected for cracks, chafing of the outer cover, leaks, blisters and other damage. These are important and vulnerable parts of the brake system and inspection should be complete. A light and mirror will be helpful for a thorough check. If a hose exhibits any of the above conditions, replace it with a new one.

Replacement

Front brake hose

Refer to illustrations 11.3 and 11.4

2 Loosen the wheel lug nuts, raise the vehicle and support it securely on jackstands. Remove the wheel.
3 At the frame bracket, unscrew the tube nut from the hose **(see illustration)**. Use a flare nut wrench on the tube nut to prevent rounding off the corners.
4 Remove the U-clip from the female fitting at the bracket with a pair of pliers, then pass the hose through the bracket **(see illustration)**.
5 At the caliper end of the hose, remove the union bolt from the fitting, then separate the hose from the caliper. Note that there are two copper

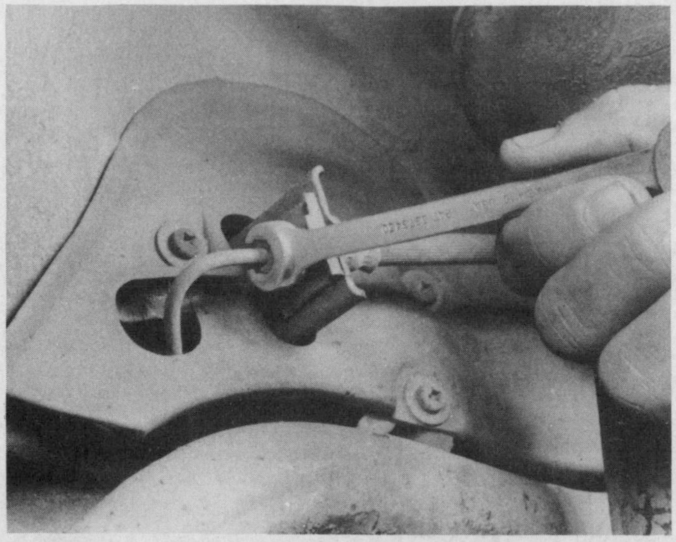

11.3 Use a flare nut wrench on the line fitting to prevent rounding off the corners

11.4 Remove the spring clip to detach the brake hose

sealing washers on either side of the fitting – they should be replaced with new ones upon installation.

6 Remove the U-clip from the strut bracket, then feed the hose through the bracket.

7 To install the hose, pass the caliper fitting end through the strut bracket, then connect the fitting to the caliper with the union bolt and copper washers. Tighten the fitting securely.

8 Push the metal support into the strut bracket and install the U-clip. Make sure that the hose isn't twisted between the caliper and the strut bracket.

9 Route the hose into the frame bracket, again making sure it isn't twisted, then connect the hydraulic line tube nut, starting the threads by hand. Install the U-clip then tighten the fitting securely.

10 Bleed the caliper as described in Section 12.

11 Install the wheel and lug nuts, lower the vehicle and tighten the lug nuts to the specified torque.

Rear brake hose

12 Perform Steps 2, 3 and 4 above, then repeat Steps 3 and 4 to the other end of the hose. Be sure to bleed the wheel cylinder (or caliper) as described in Section 12.

Metal brake lines

13 When replacing brake lines be sure to use the correct parts. Don't use copper tubing for any brake system components. Purchase steel brake lines from a dealer or auto parts store.

14 Prefabricated brake line, with the tube ends already flared and fittings installed, is available at auto parts stores and dealers. These lines are also bent to the proper shapes.

15 When installing the new line make sure it's securely supported in the brackets and has plenty of clearance between moving or hot components.

16 After installation, check the master cylinder fluid level and add fluid as necessary. Bleed the brake system as outlined in the next Section and test the brakes carefully before driving the vehicle in traffic.

12 Brake hydraulic system – bleeding

Refer to illustrations 12.4 and 12.9

Warning: *Wear eye protection when bleeding the brake system. If the fluid comes in contact with your eyes, immediately rinse them with water and seek medical attention.*

Note: *Bleeding the hydraulic system is necessary to remove any air that manages to find its way into the system when it's been opened during removal and installation of a hose, line, caliper or master cylinder.*

1 It will probably be necessary to bleed the system at all four brakes if air has entered the system due to low fluid level, or if the brake lines have been disconnected at the master cylinder.

2 If a brake line was disconnected only at a wheel, then only that caliper or wheel cylinder must be bled.

3 If a brake line is disconnected at a fitting located between the master cylinder and any of the brakes, that part of the system served by the disconnected line must be bled.

4 On models equipped with anti-lock brakes (ABS), turn the ignition switch off and disconnect the four ABS actuator connectors **(see illustration)**.

5 Remove any residual vacuum from the brake power booster by applying the brake several times with the engine off.

6 Remove the master cylinder reservoir cover and fill the reservoir with brake fluid. Reinstall the cover. **Note:** *Check the fluid level often during the bleeding operation and add fluid as necessary to prevent the fluid level from falling low enough to allow air bubbles into the master cylinder.*

7 Have an assistant on hand, as well as a supply of new brake fluid, a clear container partially filled with clean brake fluid, a length of 3/16-inch plastic, rubber or vinyl tubing to fit over the bleeder valve and a wrench to open and close the bleeder valve.

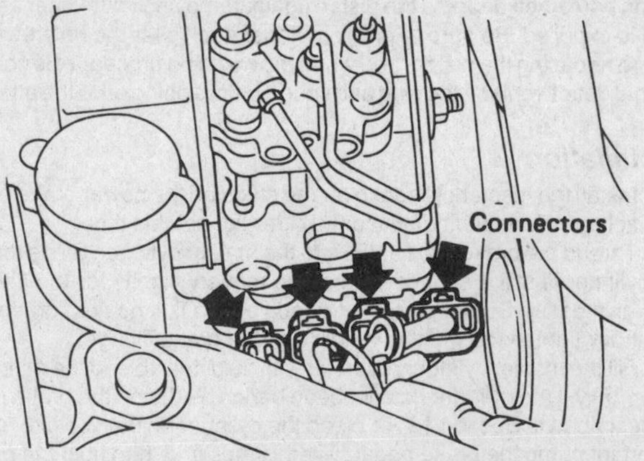

12.4 On models equipped with anti-lock brakes (ABS), when bleeding the brakes, turn the ignition switch off and disconnect the four ABS actuator connectors

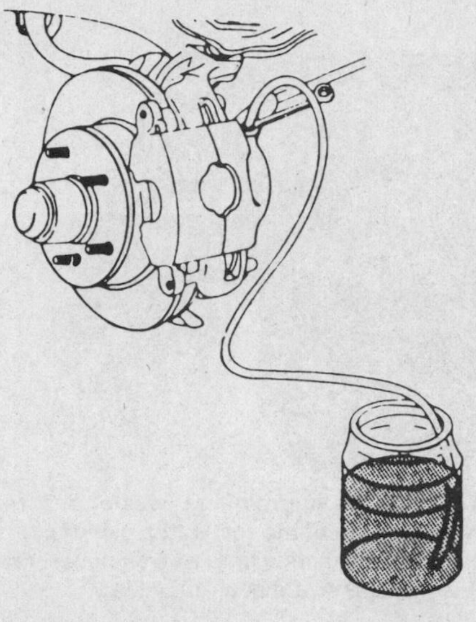

12.9 **When bleeding the brakes, a hose is connected to the bleeder valve at the caliper or wheel cylinder and then submerged in brake fluid. Air will be seen as bubbles in the tube and container. All air must be expelled before moving to the next wheel**

8 Beginning at the left rear wheel, loosen the bleeder valve slightly, then tighten it to a point where it is snug but can still be loosened quickly and easily.
9 Place one end of the tubing over the bleeder valve and submerge the other end in brake fluid in the container **(see illustration)**.
10 Have the assistant pump the brakes slowly a few times to get pressure in the system, then hold the pedal firmly depressed.
11 While the pedal is held depressed, open the bleeder valve just enough to allow a flow of fluid to leave the valve. Watch for air bubbles to exit the submerged end of the tube. When the fluid flow slows after a couple of seconds, close the valve and have your assistant release the pedal.
12 Repeat Steps 10 and 11 until no more air is seen leaving the tube, then tighten the bleeder valve and proceed to the right front wheel, the right rear wheel and the left front wheel, in that order, and perform the same procedure. Be sure to check the fluid in the master cylinder reservoir frequently.
13 Never use old brake fluid. It contains moisture which will deteriorate the brake system components.
14 On models with ABS, reconnect the four ABS actuator connectors.
15 Refill the master cylinder with fluid at the end of the operation.
16 Check the operation of the brakes. The pedal should feel solid when depressed, with no sponginess. If necessary, repeat the entire process. **Warning:** *Do not operate the vehicle if you are in doubt about the effectiveness of the brake system.*

13 Power brake booster – check, removal and installation

Refer to illustrations 13.7, 13.13a and 13.13b

Operating check

1 Depress the brake pedal several times with the engine off and make sure that there is no change in the pedal reserve distance.
2 Depress the pedal and start the engine. If the pedal goes down slightly, operation is normal.

Air tightness check

3 Start the engine and turn it off after one or two minutes. Depress the brake pedal several times slowly. If the pedal goes down farther the first time but gradually rises after the second or third depression, the booster is air tight.
4 Depress the brake pedal while the engine is running, then stop the engine with the pedal depressed. If there is no change in the pedal reserve travel after holding the pedal for 30 seconds, the booster is air tight.

Removal

5 Power brake booster units should not be disassembled. They require special tools not normally found in most service stations or shops. They are fairly complex and because of their critical relationship to brake performance it is best to replace a defective booster unit with a new or rebuilt one.
6 To remove the booster, first remove the brake master cylinder as described in Section 10.
7 Locate the pushrod clevis connecting the booster to the brake pedal **(see illustration)**. This is accessible from the interior in front of the driver's seat.
8 Remove the clevis pin retaining clip with pliers and pull out the pin.
9 Disconnect the hose leading from the engine to the booster. Be careful not to damage the hose when removing it from the booster fitting.

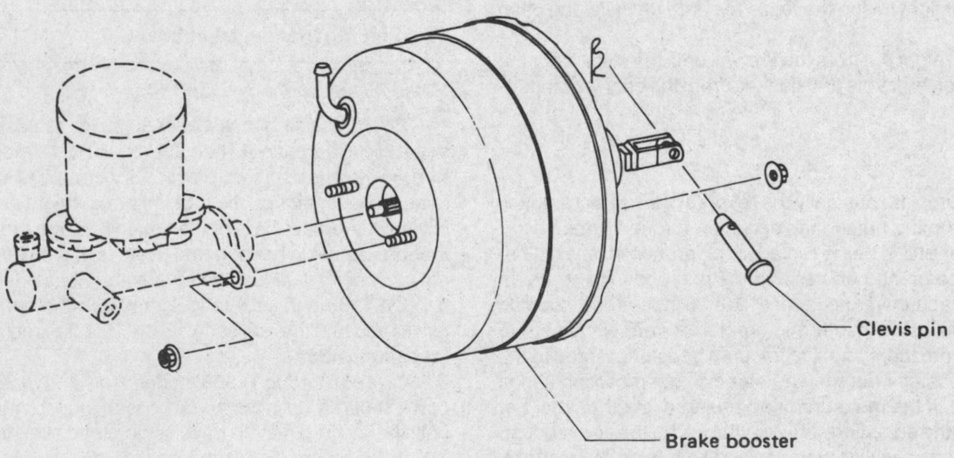

13.7 **Power brake booster details**

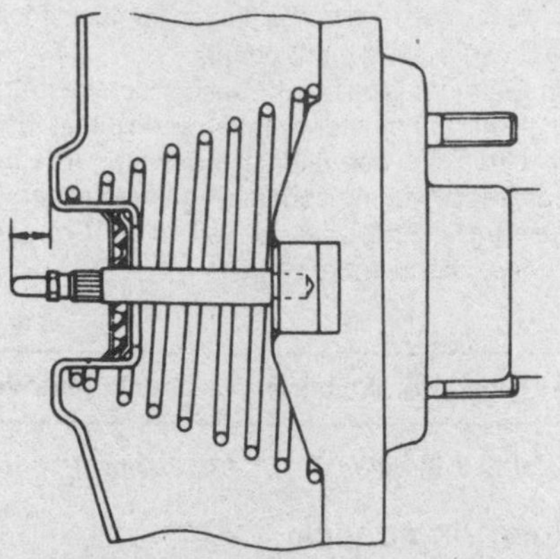

13.13a The booster pushrod length must be as specified – if there is interference between the master cylinder and the end of the pushrod, the brakes may drag; if there is too much clearance, there will be excessive brake pedal travel

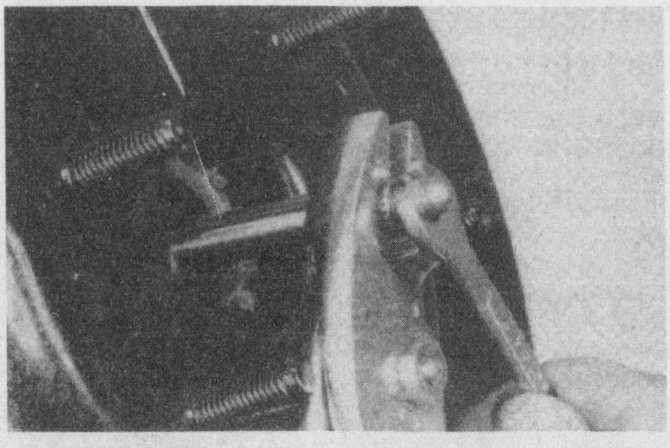

13.13b To adjust the length of the booster pushrod, hold the serrated portion of the rod with a pair of pliers and turn the adjusting screw in or out, as necessary, to achieve the desired setting

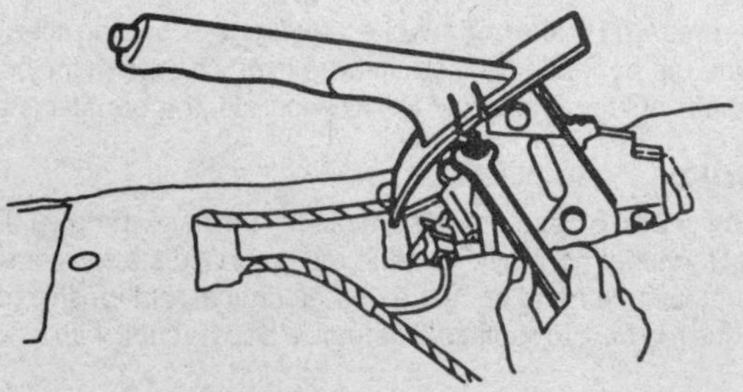

14.2 On 1989 and later models, turn the adjusting nut until the desired handle travel is obtained

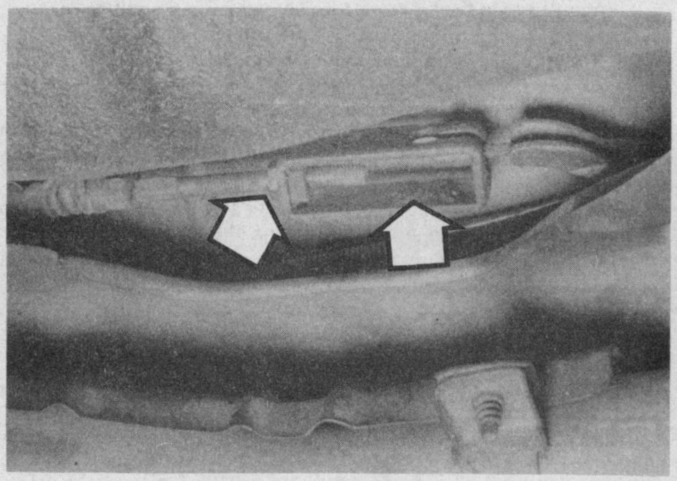

14.3 To adjust the parking brake on 1985 through 1988 models, loosen the lock nut (arrow) then turn the adjuster (arrow) until the desired handle travel is obtained

10 Remove the four nuts and washers holding the brake booster to the firewall. You may need a light to see these, as they are up under the dash area.

11 Slide the booster straight out from the firewall until the studs clear the holes and pull the booster, brackets and gaskets from the engine compartment area.

Installation

12 Installation procedures are basically the reverse of those for removal. Tighten the booster mounting nuts to the specified torque figures.

13 If the power booster unit is being replaced, clearance must exist between the mounting face of the booster and the pushrod in the vacuum booster. Using a hand vacuum pump, apply 19 to 20 inches of vacuum to the brake booster. Then use a depth micrometer or vernier calipers to measure the distance from the end of the vacuum booster pushrod to the mounting face of the booster where the master cylinder mounting flange seats **(see illustration)**. If the measurement (pushrod length) is more or less than specified, turn the adjusting screw on the end of the power booster pushrod until the length is within the specified limit **(see illustration)**.

14 After the final installation of the master cylinder and brake hoses and lines, the brake pedal height must be adjusted and the system must be bled. See the appropriate Sections in this Chapter and Chapter 1 for the procedures.

14 Parking brake – adjustment

Refer to illustrations 14.2 and 14.3

1 Pull the parking brake lever up as far as possible, counting the number of clicks as you go. The travel should be seven to eight clicks on 1985 to 1988 models or nine to eleven clicks on 1989 models. If you are able to raise the lever higher, the parking brake might not hold the vehicle on an incline. If the travel is less than specified, the automatic adjusters on the rear brakes could be rendered useless. If the parking brake lever travel is not as specified, adjust the parking brake, as described below.

2 On 1989 and later models, remove the center console (see Chapter 11) and turn the adjusting nut until the desired handle travel is obtained **(see illustration)**.

3 On 1985 through 1988 models, raise the rear of the vehicle and support it securely on jackstands. Loosen the lock nut, then turn the adjuster until the desired handle travel is obtained **(see illustration)**.

4 If necessary, adjust the parking brake indicator light switch so the Brake light on the instrument panel is off when the parking brake lever is all the way down. To adjust the switch, bend the switch plate as necessary.

5 Check to make sure the rear brakes don't drag when the vehicle is driven.

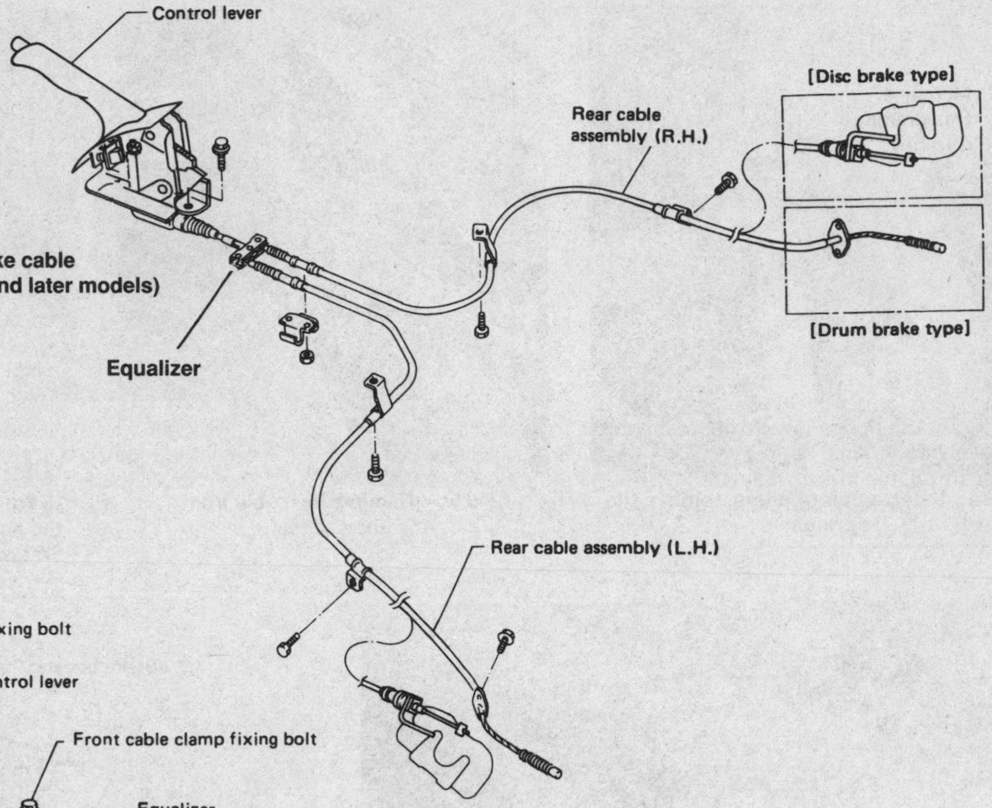

15.1 Parking brake cable installation details (1989 and later models)

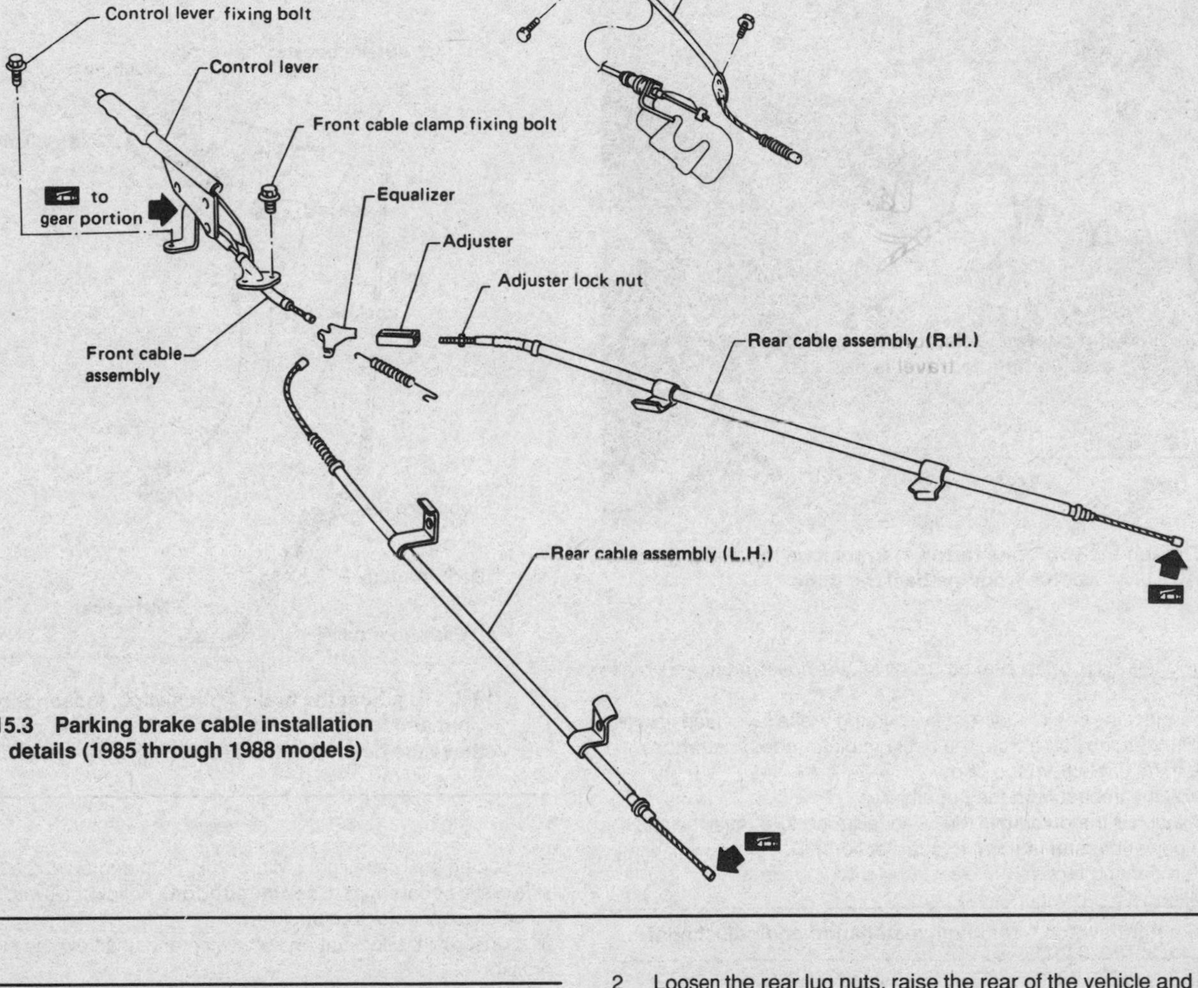

15.3 Parking brake cable installation details (1985 through 1988 models)

15 Parking brake cables – replacement

Refer to illustrations 15.1, 15.3, 15.5a, 15.5b, 15.7a and 15.7b

Note: *This procedure applies to both right and left cables.*

1 On 1989 and later models, remove the center console (see Chapter 11) and completely unscrew the cable adjusting nut **(see illustration)**.

2 Loosen the rear lug nuts, raise the rear of the vehicle and support it securely on jackstands. Place blocks in front of the front wheels and remove the wheel.

3 On 1985 through 1988 models, Loosen the adjuster lock nut and completely unscrew the adjuster **(see illustration)**.

4 On models with disc brakes, remove the caliper (see Section 7).

5 Remove the parking brake cable spring clip **(see illustration)** and detach the cable from the caliper **(see illustration)**.

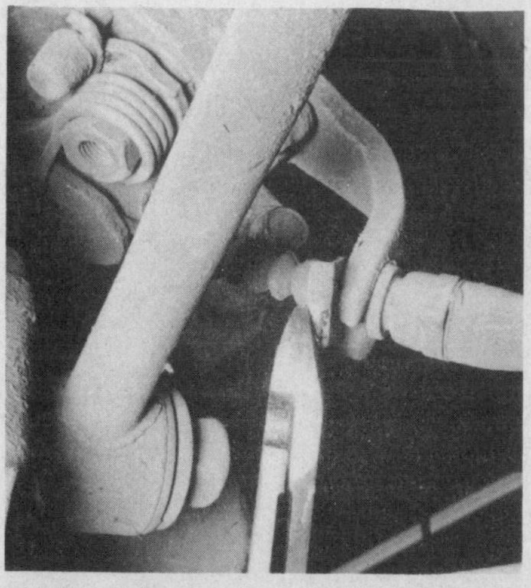

15.5a Using a pair of pliers, remove the spring clip

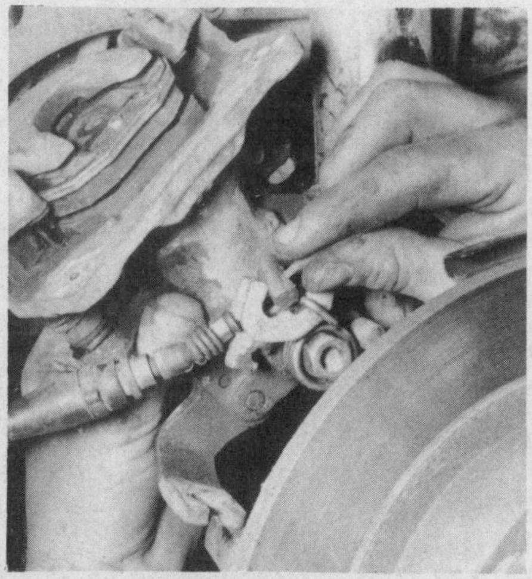

15.5b Remove the cable from the caliper

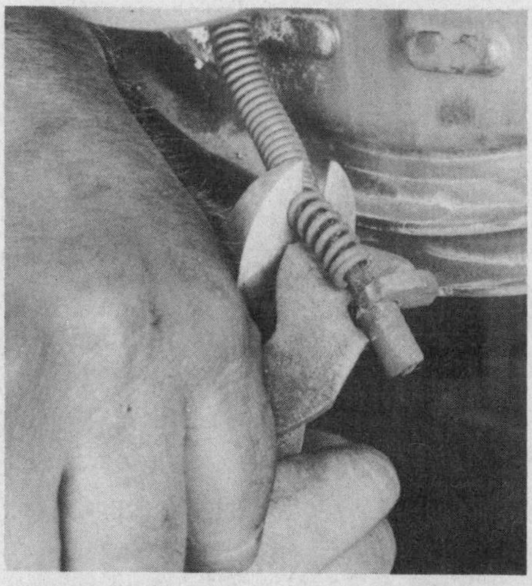

15.7a To disconnect the cable end from the parking brake lever, pull back on the return spring and maneuver the cable out of the slot in the lever

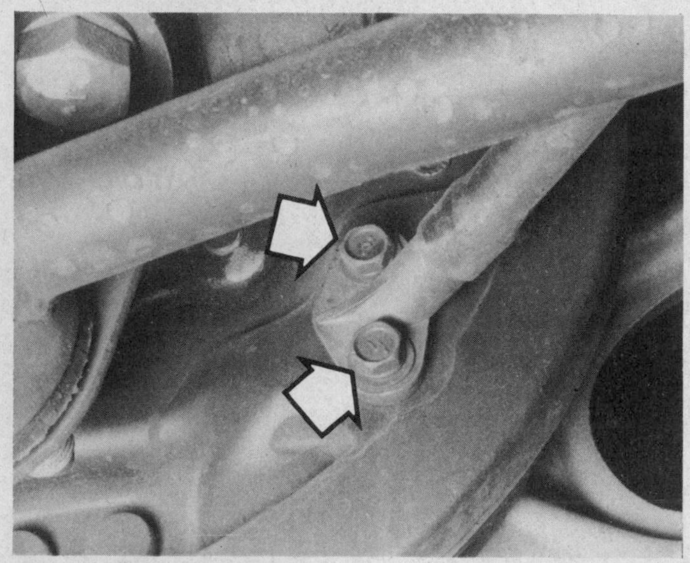

15.7b Detach the two bolts (arrows) to remove the parking brake cable from the backing plate

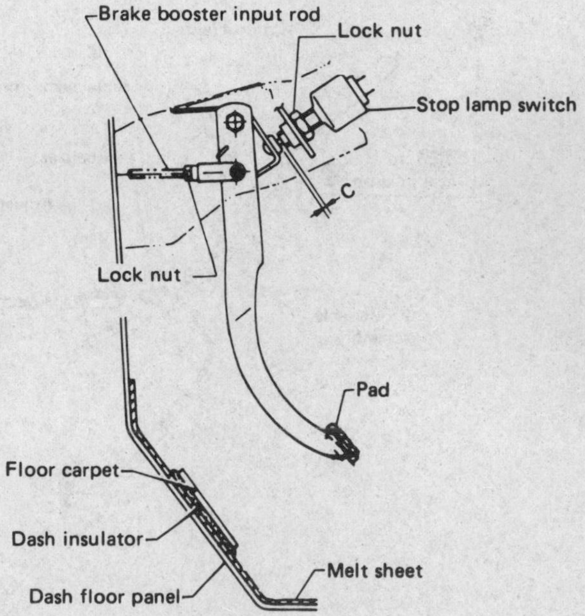

16.2 To adjust the brake light switch, loosen the locknut and turn the switch in or out, as necessary, to achieve the desired setting (brake light switch clearance)

6 On models with drum brakes, remove the brake drum and brake shoes (see Section 8).

7 Disconnect the cable end from the parking brake lever **(see illustration)** and unbolt the cable from the backing plate **(see illustration)**.

8 Unbolt the cable from the body.

9 Detach the cables from the equalizer

10 Installation is the reverse of the removal procedure. After the cable is installed, adjust the parking brake (see Section 14).

16 Brake light switch – removal, installation and adjustment

Refer to illustration 16.2

1 Remove the lower dash panel trim under the steering column (Chapter 11).

2 Locate the brake light switch, which is mounted at the top of the left side brake pedal support **(see illustration)**. Follow the switch wiring to the electrical connector and unplug it.

3 Unscrew the locknut on the switch and unscrew the switch from its bracket.

4 Installation is the reverse of removal. To adjust the switch, loosen the locknut and turn the switch in or out to obtain the correct clearance. Tighten the locknut when the correct adjustment is obtained.

Chapter 10
Suspension and steering systems

Contents

Adjustable Shock Absorber and Sonar Suspension systems – general information 2
Balljoints – replacement 7
Control arm – removal, inspection and installation 6
Front end alignment – general information 23
Front hub and bearing assembly – removal and installation 9
Front stabilizer bar and bushings – removal and installation 3
Front strut/shock absorber and coil spring assembly – removal, inspection and installation 4
Front strut/shock absorber or coil spring – replacement 5
General information 1
Parallel links – removal and installation 12
Power steering fluid level check .... See Chapter 1
Power steering pump – removal and installation 20
Power steering system – bleeding 21
Radius rod – removal and installation 13
Rear hub and wheel bearing – check, repack and adjustment 10
Rear stabilizer bar and bushings – removal and installation 11
Rear strut/shock absorber, coil spring and wheel spindle assembly – inspection, removal, overhaul and installation 14
Steering and suspension check .... See Chapter 1
Steering gear boots – replacement 19
Steering gear – removal and installation 17
Steering knuckle and hub – removal and installation 8
Steering system – general information 15
Steering wheel – removal and installation 16
Tire and tire pressure checks .... See Chapter 1
Tire rotation .... See Chapter 1
Tie-rod ends – removal and installation 18
Wheels and tires – general information 22

Specifications

General

Power steering fluid type	See Chapter 1
Strut fluid type	Nissan strut fluid or equivalent
Strut fluid capacity	
Adjustable	
1985 through 1988	11.0 oz
1989 on	12.0 oz
Non-adjustable	
1985 through 1988	11.2 oz
1989 on	12.0 oz

Torque specifications

	Ft-lbs
Front suspension	
Control arm shaft nut	65 to 87
Control arm shaft bracket to body bolts	87 to 108
Balljoint to control arm nuts	56 to 80
Balljoint stud nut	52 to 64
Steering knuckle to strut bolt/nuts	
1985 through 1988	82 to 91
1989 on	116 to 137
Strut upper mounting nuts	
1985 through 1988	23 to 31
1989 on	29 to 40

Torque specifications

	Ft-lbs
Front suspension (continued)	
Strut damper shaft locknut	
Non-adjustable	43 to 58
Adjustable	51 to 65
Stabilizer bracket to body bolts	23 to 31
Stabilizer connecting rod nut (1989 and later models)	30 to 35
Rear suspension	
Parallel link adjusting locknut	58 to 72
Parallel link bolts/nuts	65 to 87
Radius rod bolts/nuts	65 to 80
Strut to body nuts	
1985 through 1988	23 to 31
1989 on	31 to 40
Strut damper shaft locknut	
Non-adjustable	43 to 58
Adjustable	
1985 through 1988	51 to 65
1989 on	43 to 58
Stabilizer bar bracket bolts	23 to 31
Stabilizer bar mounting bolts	43 to 58
Steering system	
Airbag module Torx bolts	11 to 18
Front wheel bearing locknut	174 to 231
Steering wheel nut	22 to 29
Steering gear mounting bolts	54 to 72
Steering shaft universal joint to steering gear	17 to 22
Tie-rod end to steering knuckle jam nut	22 to 29
Tie-rod to steering knuckle locknut	
1985 through 1988	27 to 34
1989 on	22 to 29
Rear wheel spindle nut	
1985 through 1988	
Initial	18 to 25
Final	6.5 to 8.7
1989 on	137 to 188
Wheel lug nuts	See Chapter 1

1 General information

Refer to illustrations 1.1 and 1.2

The front suspension is a MacPherson strut design. The steering knuckle is located by a lower control arm, and both front control arms are connected by a stabilizer bar, which also controls fore-and-aft movement of the control arms **(see illustration)**.

The rear suspension also utilizes MacPherson struts. Lateral movement is controlled by two parallel links on each side, with longitudinally mounted radius rods between the body and the rear axle carriers **(see illustration)**.

Some models may be equipped with "sonar" suspension or adjustable suspension beginning in 1986. This feature automatically or manually adjusts the suspension to suit road conditions and driving style by changing the shock absorber damping characteristics. These systems will be described in greater detail in the next Section.

The rack-and-pinion steering gear is located behind the engine/transaxle assembly on the firewall and actuates the steering arms, which are integral with the steering knuckles. Most vehicles are equipped with power steering. The steering column is designed to collapse in the event of an accident.

Frequently, when working on the suspension or steering system components, you may come across fasteners which seem impossible to loosen. These fasteners on the underside of the vehicle are continually subjected to water, road grime, mud, etc., and can become rusted or "frozen," making them extremely difficult to remove. In order to unscrew these stubborn fasteners without damaging them (or other components), be sure to use lots of penetrating oil and allow it to soak in for a while. Using a wire brush to clean exposed threads will also ease removal of the nut or bolt and prevent damage to the threads. Sometimes a sharp blow with a hammer and punch is effective in breaking the bond between a nut and bolt threads, but care must be taken to prevent the punch from slipping off the fastener and ruining the threads. Heating the stuck fastener and surrounding area with a torch sometimes helps too, but isn't recommended because of the obvious dangers associated with fire. Long breaker bars and extension, or "cheater," pipes will increase leverage, but never use an extension pipe on a ratchet – the ratcheting mechanism could be damaged. Sometimes, turning the nut or bolt in the tightening (clockwise) direction first will help to break it loose. Fasteners that require drastic measures to unscrew should always be replaced with new ones.

Since most of the procedures that are dealt with in this Chapter involve jacking up the vehicle and working underneath it, a good pair of jackstands will be needed. A hydraulic floor jack is the preferred type of jack to lift the vehicle, and it can also be used to support certain components during various operations. **Warning:** *Never, under any circumstances, rely on a jack to support the vehicle while working on it. Whenever any of the suspension or steering fasteners are loosened or removed they must be inspected and, if necessary, replaced with new ones of the same part number or of original equipment quality and design. Torque specifications must be followed for proper reassembly and component retention. Never attempt to heat or straighten any suspension or steering components. Instead, replace any bent or damaged part with a new one.*

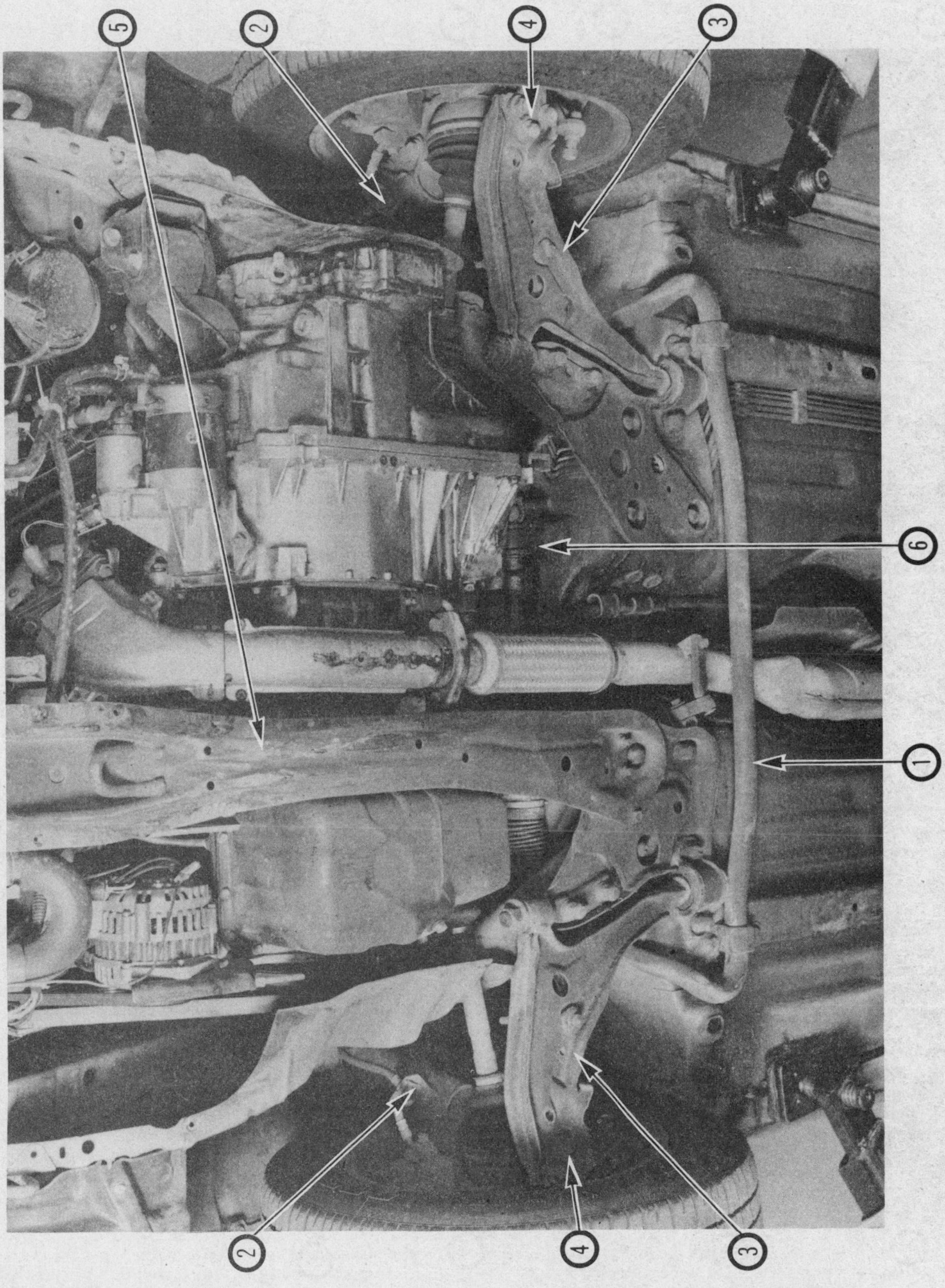

1.1 Typical underside view of front suspension and steering components

1 Stabilizer bar
2 Strut/shock absorber and coil spring assembly
3 Control arm
4 Balljoint
5 Engine crossmember
6 Steering gear

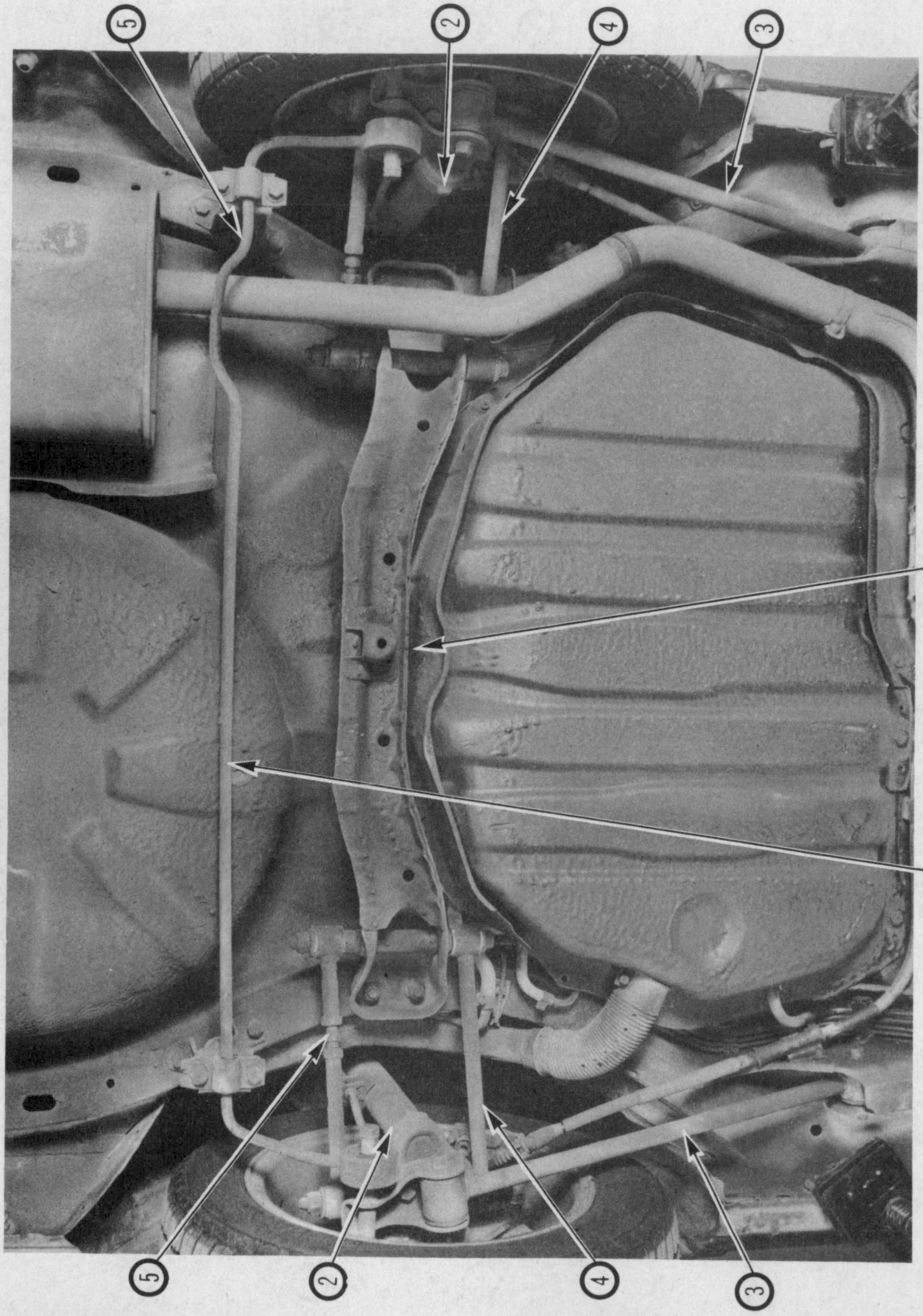

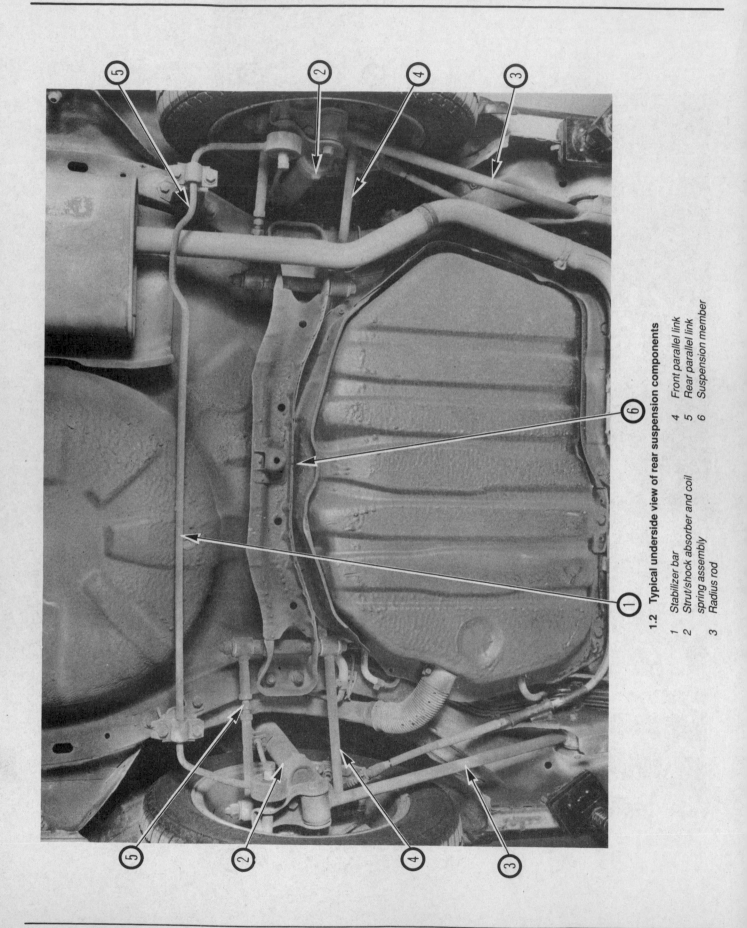

1.2 Typical underside view of rear suspension components

1 Stabilizer bar
2 Strut/shock absorber and coil spring assembly
3 Radius rod
4 Front parallel link
5 Rear parallel link
6 Suspension member

2 Adjustable Shock Absorber and Sonar Suspension systems – general information

Refer to illustrations 2.2a and 2.2b

The Adjustable Shock Absorber system, installed on 1985 through 1988 models and the Sonar Suspension system installed on 1988 and later models automatically or manually changes the shock absorber valving to firm-up the suspension to suit road conditions and driving style. The system incorporates a switch, mounted on the center console, which allows the driver to select three different positions – soft, firm or neutral.

The Sonar suspension system receives information from various sensors located throughout the vehicle. These sensors send inputs to the control module, which in turn decides whether or not to adjust the shock absorbers **(see illustration)**. The Adjustable Shock Absorber system does not have sensors and is controlled by the driver and the switch selection **(see illustration)**.

Due to the rather complex nature of these systems, all troubleshooting and repairs, with the exception of searching for loose connectors, wires and blown fuses, should be left to a qualified dealer service department technician.

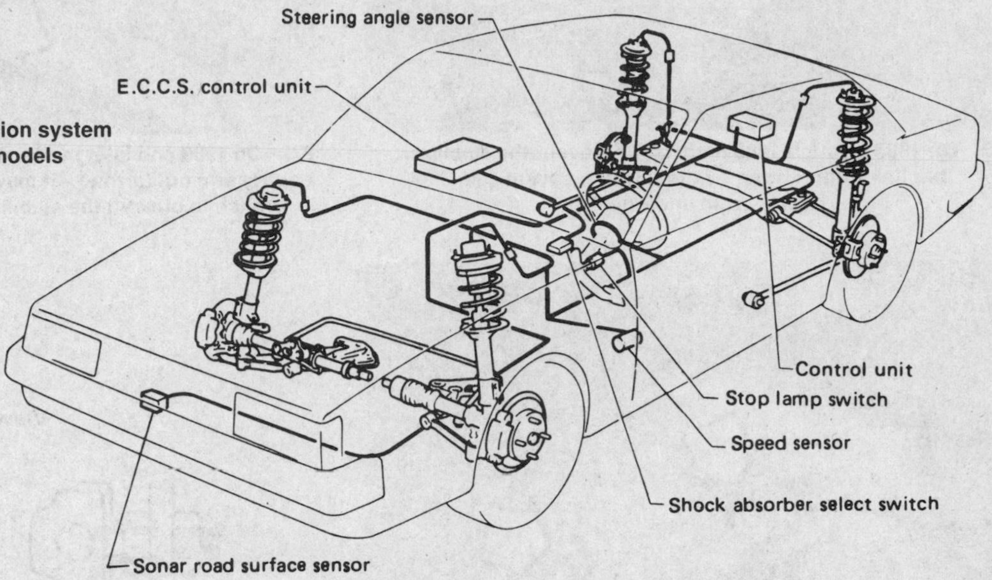

2.2a Details of the Sonar Suspension system used on some 1988 and later models

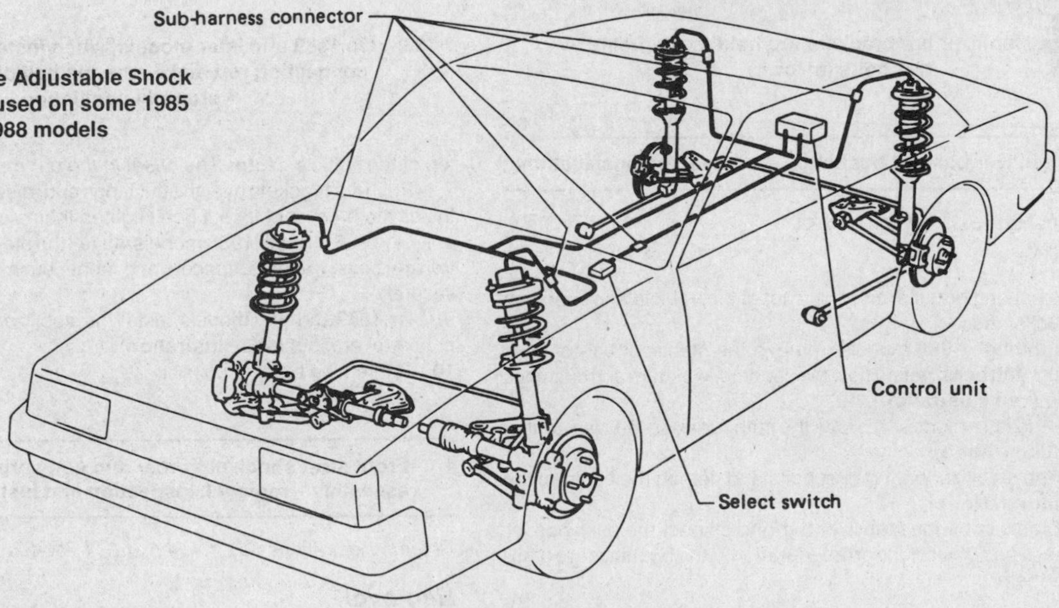

2.2b Details of the Adjustable Shock Absorber system used on some 1985 through 1988 models

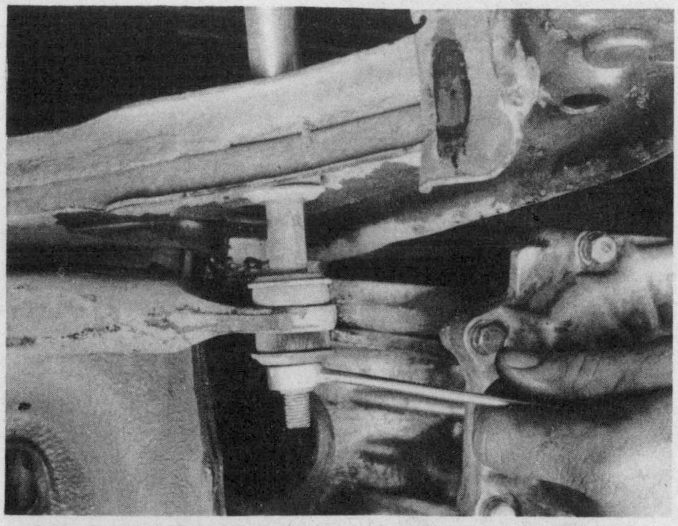

3.2 On 1985 through 1988 models, to prevent the stabilizer bar link from turning – hold it with a socket and ratchet from underneath

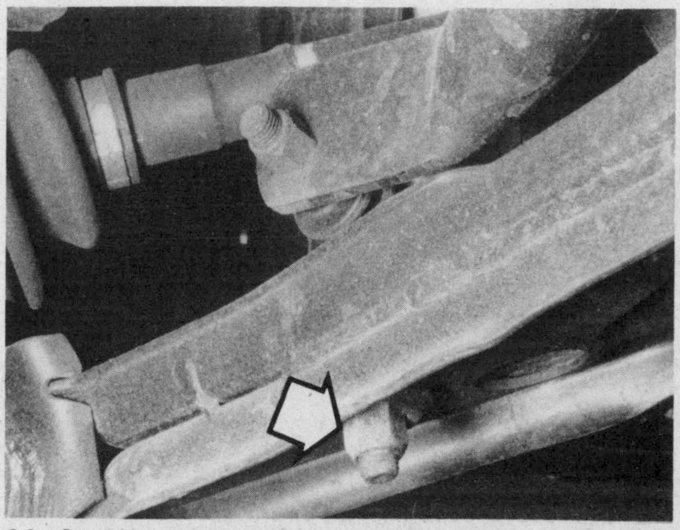

3.3 On 1989 and later models, remove the stabilizer bar-to-lower control arm nut (arrow) – it may be necessary to use an open end wrench to prevent the stabilizer connecting rod from turning

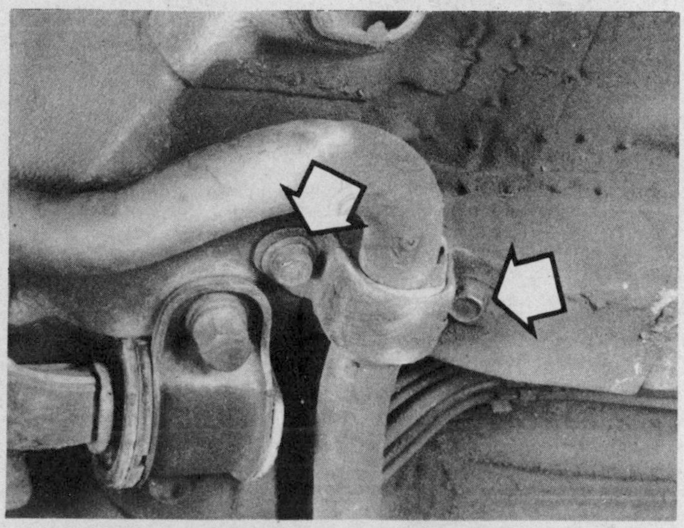

3.4 The stabilizer bar brackets are held to the frame by two bolts (arrows)

3.9 On 1989 and later models, when installing the stabilizer connecting rod make sure the balljoint socket is properly positioned

3 Front stabilizer bar and bushings – removal and installation

Refer to illustrations 3.2, 3.3, 3.4 and 3.9

Removal

1 Apply the parking brake. Raise the front of the vehicle and support it securely on jackstands.

2 On 1985 through 1988 models, remove the stabilizer bar-to-lower control arm nuts and bolts, noting how the spacers, washers and bushings are positioned **(see illustration)**.

3 On 1989 and later models, remove the stabilizer bar-to-lower control arm nut **(see illustration)**.

4 Remove the stabilizer bar bracket bolts and detach the bar from the vehicle **(see illustration)**.

5 Pull the brackets off the stabilizer bar and inspect the bushings for cracks, hardness and other signs of deterioration. If the bushings are damaged, replace them.

Installation

6 Position the stabilizer bar bushings on the bar with the slits facing the top of the vehicle. **Note:** *The offset in the bar must face down.*

7 Push the brackets over the bushings and raise the bar up to the frame. Install the bracket bolts but don't tighten them completely at this time.

8 On 1985 through 1988 models, install the stabilizer bar-to-lower control arm bolts, washers, spacers and rubber bushings and tighten the nuts securely.

9 On 1989 and later models, install the stabilizer connecting rod-to-lower control arm nut **(see illustration)**.

10 Tighten the bracket bolts.

4 Front strut/shock absorber and coil spring assembly – removal, inspection and installation

Refer to illustrations 4.2, 4.4, 4.5, 4.6, 4.7a, 4.7b and 4.15

Removal

1 Loosen the wheel lug nuts, raise the front of the vehicle and support it securely on jackstands. Apply the parking brake. Remove the wheel.

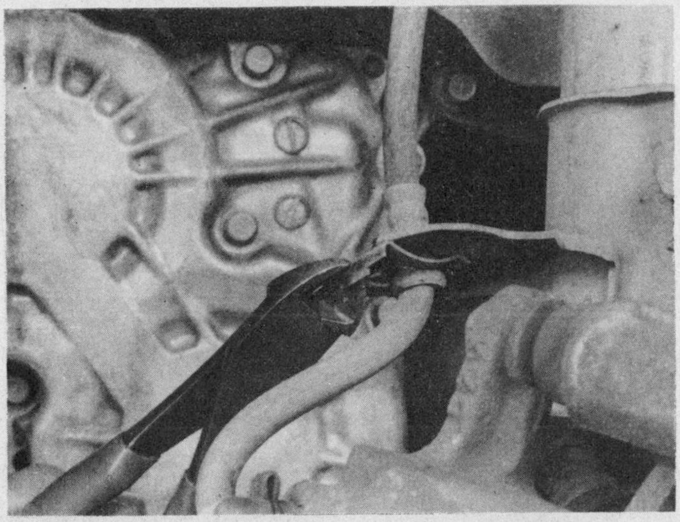

4.2 Pull the brake hose-to-strut bracket clip off

4.4 Remove the nuts from the steering strut-to-knuckle bolts and drive the bolts out with a hammer and punch

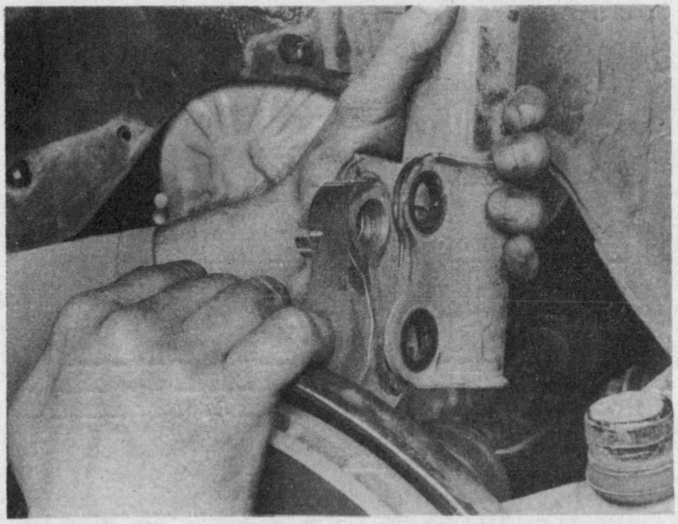

4.5 Pull the steering knuckle out of the strut bracket – be careful not to pull it out too far, though, as the driveaxle inner CV joint may be overextended

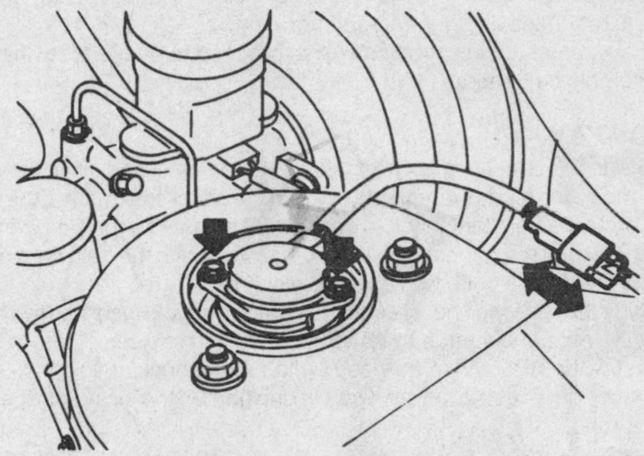

4.6 Disconnect the Sonar Suspension connector, remove the two retaining screws and separate the actuator from the strut/shock absorber

2 Unclip the brake hose from the strut bracket and push it through **(see illustration)**.
3 If equipped with anti-lock brakes (ABS), unbolt the wiring harness from the strut (see Chapter 9).
4 Remove the strut-to-knuckle nuts and knock the bolts out with a hammer and punch **(see illustration)**.
5 Separate the strut from the steering knuckle **(see illustration)**. Be careful not to overextend the inner CV joint. It's a good idea to wire the top of the steering knuckle to the body (where the tie-rod comes through) to prevent this from happening.
6 If equipped with Sonar Suspension or Adjustable Shock Absorber systems, unbolt the actuator from the strut/shock absorber **(see illustration)**.
7 Support the strut and spring assembly with one hand and remove the three strut-to-shock tower nuts **(see illustrations)**. Remove the assembly out from the fender well.

Inspection

8 Check the strut body for leaking fluid, dents, cracks and other obvious damage which would warrant repair or replacement.

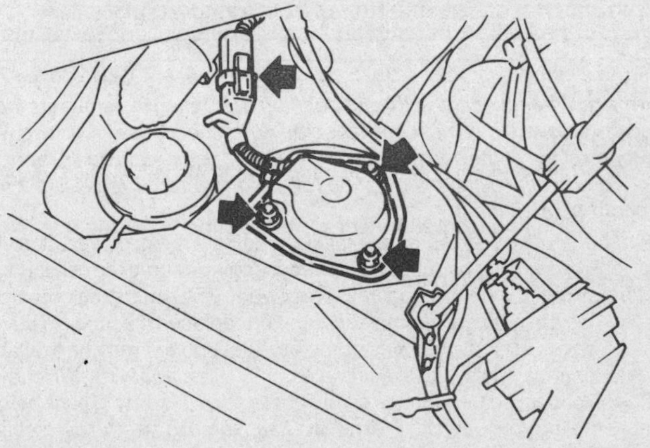

4.7a On models equipped with the Adjustable Shock Absorber system, disconnect the electrical connector and then remove the three nuts (arrows) that fasten the strut to the shock tower

10

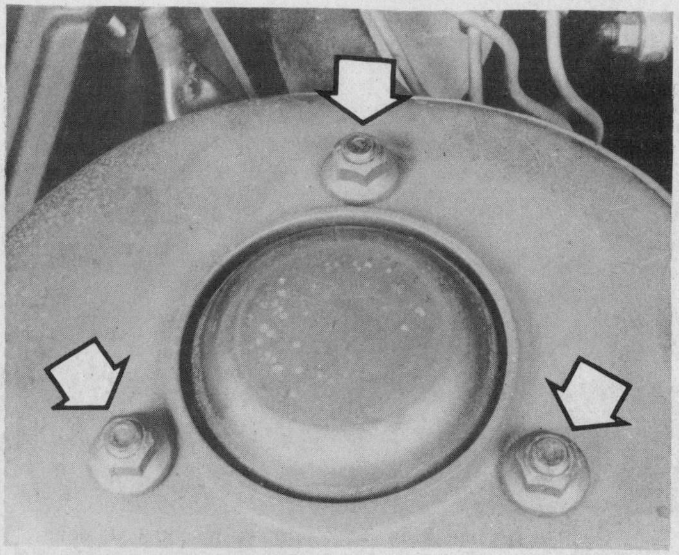

4.7b The upper end of the strut assembly is fastened to the shock tower with three nuts (arrows)

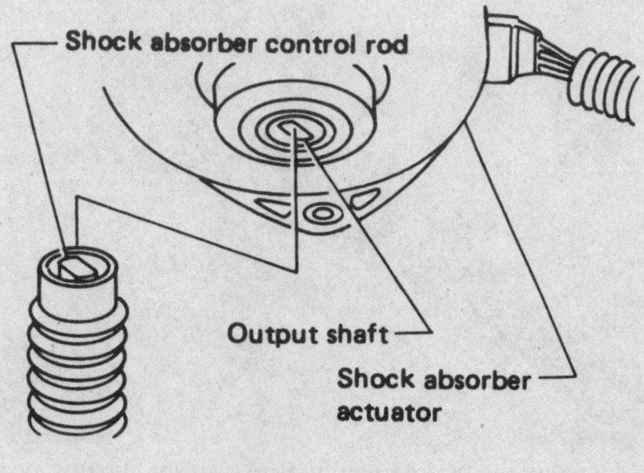

4.15 Align the slot on the output shaft with the shock absorber control rod when installing the actuator or damage could occur

9 Check the coil spring for chips or cracks in the spring coating (this will cause premature spring failure due to corrosion). Inspect the spring seat for cuts, hardness and general deterioration.
10 If any undesirable conditions exist, proceed to Section 5 for the strut disassembly procedure.

Installation

11 Guide the strut assembly up into the fender well and insert the three upper mounting studs through the holes in the shock tower. Once the three studs protrude from the shock tower, install the nuts so the strut won't fall back through. This is most easily accomplished with the help of an assistant, as the strut is quite heavy and awkward.
12 Slide the steering knuckle into the strut flange and insert the two bolts. Install the nuts and tighten them to the specified torque.
13 Install the ABS wiring harness on the strut/shock absorber.
14 Install the wheel, lower the vehicle and tighten the lug nuts to the specified torque.
15 Install the shock/strut actuator making sure the slot and the rod are aligned **(see illustration)**.
16 Tighten the three upper mounting nuts to the specified torque.
17 Drive the vehicle to an alignment shop to have the front end alignment checked and, if necessary, adjusted.

5 Front strut/shock absorber or coil spring – replacement

Refer to illustrations 5.3a, 5.3b, 5.3c, 5.4, 5.5, 5.6, 5.7, 5.11 and 5.12

Warning: *Whenever any of the suspension or steering fasteners are loosened or removed they must be inspected and, if necessary, replaced with new ones of the same part number or of original equipment quality and design. Torque specifications must be followed for proper reassembly and component retention.*

1 If the struts or coil springs exhibit the telltale signs of wear (leaking fluid, loss of damping capability, chipped, sagging or cracked coil springs) explore all options before beginning any work. The strut/shock absorber assemblies are not serviceable and must be replaced if a problem develops. However, strut assemblies complete with springs may be available on an exchange basis, which eliminates much time and work. Whichever route you choose to take, check on the cost and availability of parts before disassembling your vehicle. **Warning:** *Disassembling a strut assembly is a potentially dangerous undertaking and utmost attention must be directed to the job at hand, or serious bodily injury may result. Use only a high quality spring compressor and carefully follow the manufacturer's instructions furnished with the tool. After removing the coil spring from the strut assembly, set it aside in a safe, isolated area (a steel cabinet is preferred).*

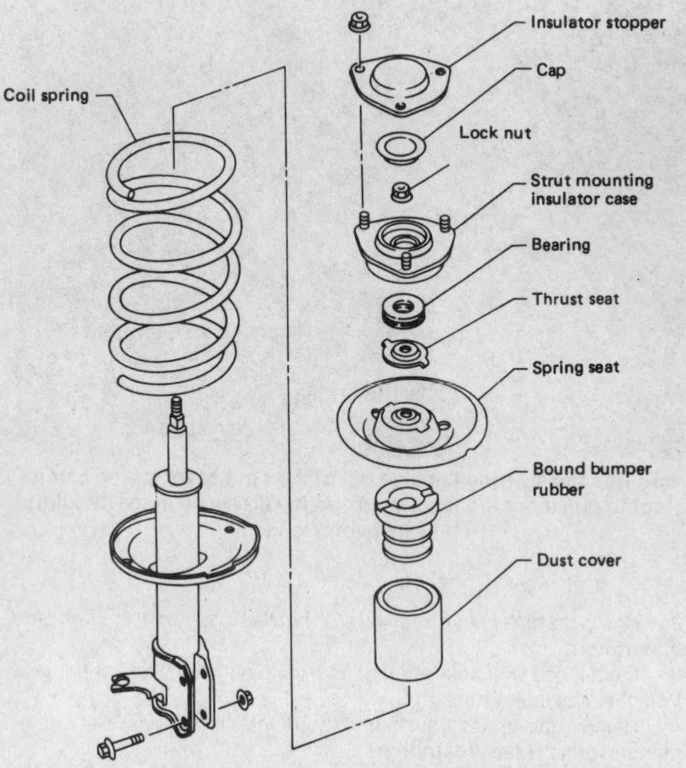

5.3a Exploded view of a non-adjustable strut/shock absorber and coil spring assembly

2 Remove the strut and spring assembly following the procedure described in the previous Section. Mount the strut assembly in a vise. Line the vise jaws with wood or rags to prevent damage to the unit and don't tighten the vise excessively.
3 Following the tool manufacturer's instructions, install the spring compressor (which can be obtained at most auto parts stores or equipment yards on a daily rental basis) on the spring and compress it sufficiently to relieve all pressure from the suspension support **(see illustrations)**. This can be verified by wiggling the spring. Remove the insulator stopper.

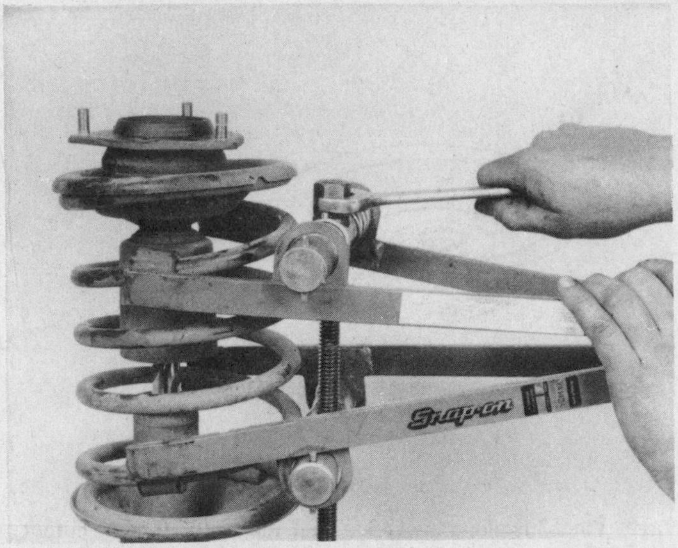

5.3b Install the spring compressor according to the tool manufacturer's instructions and compress the spring until all pressure is relieved from the upper spring seat

5.3c Lift the insulator stopper off the insulator case

5.4 Remove the damper shaft nut

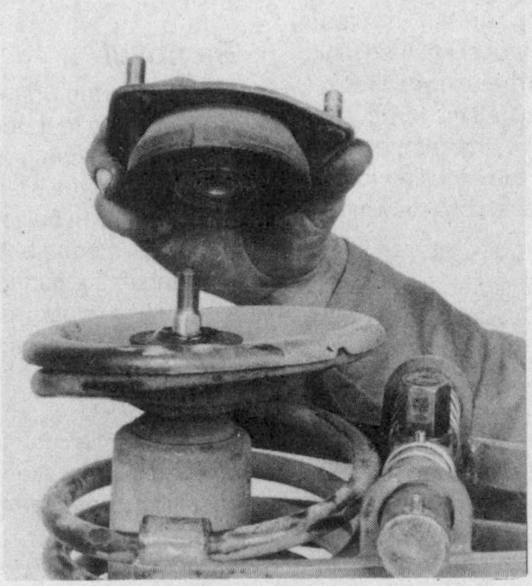

5.5 Lift the insulator case off the damper shaft

5.6 Lift the thrust seat from the spring seat

4 Loosen the damper shaft locknut with a socket wrench **(see illustration)**. To prevent the insulator case and damper shaft from turning, wedge a screwdriver or pry bar between one of the upper mounting studs and the socket.

5 Remove the nut and insulator case **(see illustration)**. Inspect the bearing in the insulator case for smooth operation. If it doesn't turn smoothly, replace the suspension support. Check the rubber portion of the suspension support for cracking and general deterioration. If there is any separation of the rubber, replace it.

6 Lift the thrust seat from the spring seat **(see illustration)**.

7 Lift the spring seat and upper insulator from the damper shaft **(see illustration)**.

8 Carefully lift the compressed spring from the assembly and set it in a safe place, such as a steel cabinet. **Warning:** *Never place your head near the end of the spring!*

9 Slide the rubber bumper and dust boot off the damper shaft.

10 Assemble the strut beginning with the dust boot and rubber bumper – extend the damper rod as far as it will go and slide the boot and bumper down to the strut body.

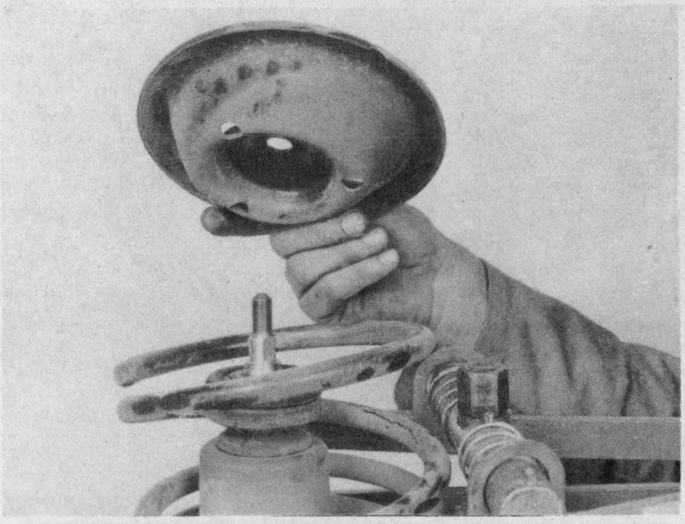

5.7 Remove the spring seat from the damper shaft

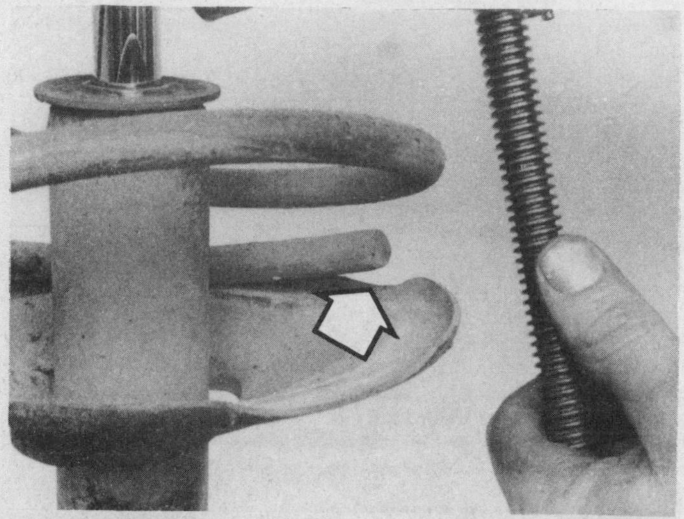

5.11 When installing the spring, make sure that the lower end of the spring fits into the recessed portion of the lower seat (arrow)

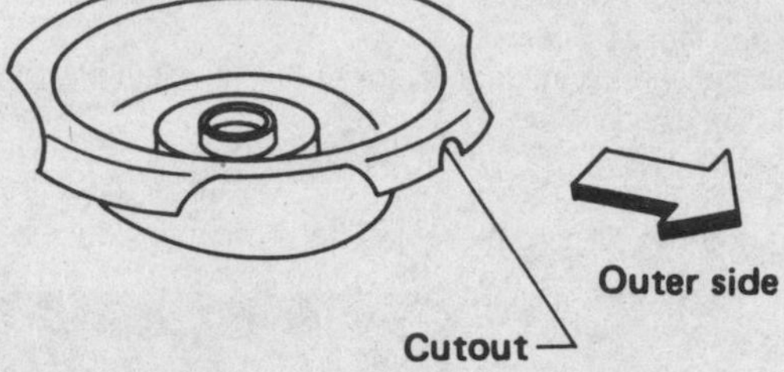

5.12 When installing the spring seat, make sure that the cutout faces the outside of the vehicle

11 Carefully place the coil spring onto the lower insulator, with the end of the spring resting in the lowest part of the insulator **(see illustration)**.
12 Install the upper insulator and spring seat, making sure that the flats in the hole in the seat match up with the flats on the damper shaft. Also make sure that the cutout on the spring seat faces toward the lower bracket, where the steering knuckle fits **(see illustration)**. Install the thrust seat.
13 Install the insulator case and insulator stopper over the damper shaft.
14 Install the damper shaft locknut and tighten it to the specified torque.
15 Install the strut/shock absorber and coil spring assembly following the procedure outlined in the previous Section.

6 Control arm – removal, inspection and installation

Refer to illustrations 6.2 and 6.4

Warning: *Whenever any of the suspension or steering fasteners are loosened or removed they must be inspected and, if necessary, replaced with new ones of the same part number or of original equipment quality and design. Torque specifications must be followed for proper reassembly and component retention.*

Removal

1 Loosen the wheel lug nuts on the side to be dismantled, raise the front of the vehicle, support it securely on jackstands and remove the wheel. Apply the parking brake.
2 Remove the stabilizer bar-to-control arm nut and retainer, then remove the three balljoint nuts **(see illustration)**.
3 Separate the balljoint from the control arm.
4 Unbolt the control arm from the body **(see illustration)**.
5 Pull the control arm off the stabilizer bar and remove it from the vehicle (be careful not to lose the stabilizer bar spacer, if equipped).

Inspection

6 Check the control arm for distortion and the bushings for wear, damage and deterioration. Replace a damaged or bent control arm with a new one. If the control arm bushings are worn, the arm must be replaced as an assembly.

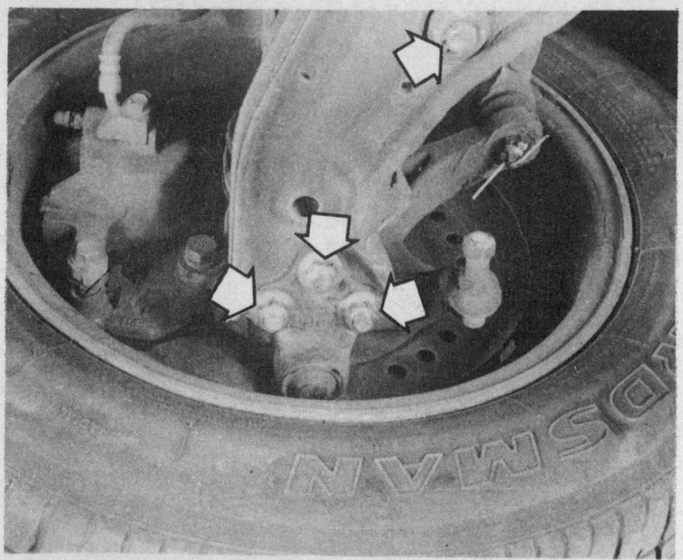

6.2 The balljoint is fastened to the control arm by three nuts (arrows) – the stabilizer bar is fastened by a nut or bolt (arrow)

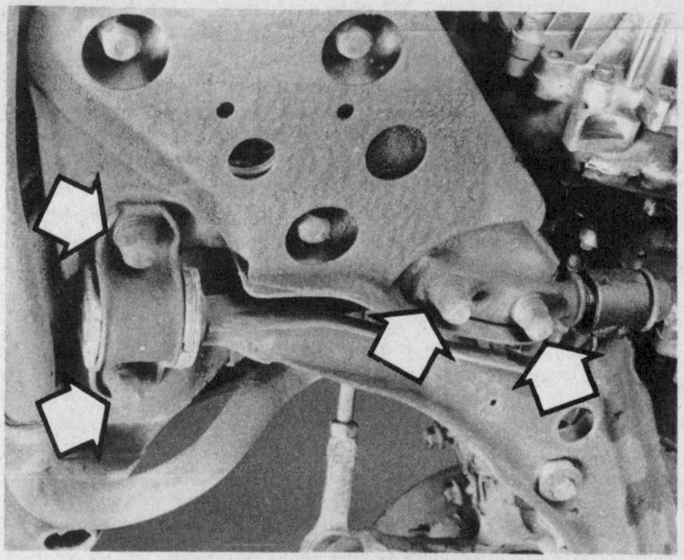

6.4 The control arm is fastened to the body by four nuts (arrows)

Installation

7 Place the control arm balljoint studs into the balljoint. Install the nuts but don't tighten fully yet.
8 Push the stabilizer bar spacer (if equipped) and retainer onto the control arm. Tighten the nut or bolt securely.
9 Attach the control arm to the body. Slightly tighten all the nuts and bolts, but don't fully tighten yet.
10 Install the wheel and lug nuts, lower the vehicle and tighten the lug nuts to the specified torque.
11 Tighten all nuts and bolts to the specified torque at curb weight with the tires on the ground.
12 It's a good idea to have the front wheel alignment checked and, if necessary, adjusted after this job has been performed.

7 Balljoints – replacement

Refer to illustration 7.7

Warning: *Whenever any of the suspension or steering fasteners are loosened or removed, they must be inspected and, if necessary, replaced with new ones of the same part number or of original equipment quality and design. Torque specifications must be followed for proper reassembly and component retention.*

1 Loosen the wheel lug nuts, raise the front of the vehicle and support it securely on jackstands. Apply the parking brake. Remove the wheel.
2 Remove the brake caliper and torque member and hang it out of the way (see Chapter 9).
3 Remove the tie rod end from the steering knuckle (see Section 18).
4 Loosen, but do not remove, the three strut mounting nuts from the strut tower.
5 Remove the three mounting nuts securing the balljoint to the control arm **(see illustration 6.2)**.
6 Remove the driveaxle from the steering knuckle (see Chapter 8).
7 Loosen the balljoint stud nut a couple of turns. Separate the balljoint from the steering knuckle **(see illustration)**, then remove the nut.
8 To install the balljoint, position it on the control arm and install the three bolts, but don't tighten them yet.
9 Insert the balljoint stud into the steering knuckle and install the nut, tightening it to the specified torque.
10 Tighten the balljoint-to-control arm nuts to the specified torque.

7.7 Loosen the balljoint-to-steering knuckle nut a couple of turns and push the balljoint stud from the steering knuckle with a two-jaw puller – DON'T hit the end of the stud with a hammer

11 Install all other components removed previously, tightening all fasteners to the specified torque.
12 Install the wheel and lug nuts. Lower the vehicle and tighten the lug nuts to the specified torque.

8 Steering knuckle and hub – removal and installation

Warning: *Whenever any of the suspension or steering fasteners are loosened or removed they must be inspected and, if necessary, replaced with new ones of the same part number or of original equipment quality and design. Torque specifications must be followed for proper reassembly and component retention. Dust created by the brake system may contain asbestos, which is harmful to your health. Never blow it out with compressed air and don't inhale any of it. Do not, under any circumstances, use petroleum-based solvents to clean brake parts. Use brake cleaner or denatured alcohol only.*

Removal

1 Loosen the wheel lug nuts, raise the front of the vehicle and support it securely on jackstands. Apply the parking brake. Remove the wheel. Remove the brake caliper and support it with a piece of wire as described in Chapter 9.
2 Remove the driveaxle from the steering knuckle and support the end of the driveaxle with a piece of wire (see Chapter 8).
3 Loosen, but do not remove the strut-to-steering knuckle bolts/nuts.
4 Separate the tie-rod from the steering knuckle (see Section 18).
5 Remove the three balljoint-to-control arm nuts (see Section 7). The strut-to-knuckle bolts can now be removed.
6 Remove the steering knuckle and hub assembly from the strut and balljoint.

Installation

7 Push the knuckle into the strut flange and install the bolts/nuts, but don't tighten them yet.
8 Insert the balljoint into the control arm and install the nuts, but don't tighten them yet.
9 Attach the tie-rod to the steering knuckle arm as described in Section 18. Tighten the strut bolt nuts, the balljoint nut and the tie-rod nut to the specified torque.
10 Install the caliper as outlined in Chapter 9.
11 Install the wheel and lug nuts.
12 Lower the vehicle and tighten the lug nuts to the specified torque.

9 Front hub and bearing assembly – removal and installation

Due to the special tools and expertise required to press the hub and bearing from the steering knuckle, this job should be left to a professional mechanic. However, the steering knuckle and hub may be removed and the assembly taken to a local dealer service department or repair shop. Refer to section 8 for steering knuckle and hub removal.

10 Rear hub and wheel bearing – check, repack and adjustment

Check

Refer to illustration 10.1

1 In most cases the rear wheel bearings will not need servicing until the brake pads or shoes are changed. However, the bearings should be checked whenever the rear of the vehicle is raised for any reason. Several items, including a torque wrench and special grease, are required for this procedure **(see illustration)**.
2 With the vehicle securely supported on jackstands, spin each wheel and check for noise, rolling resistance and free play.

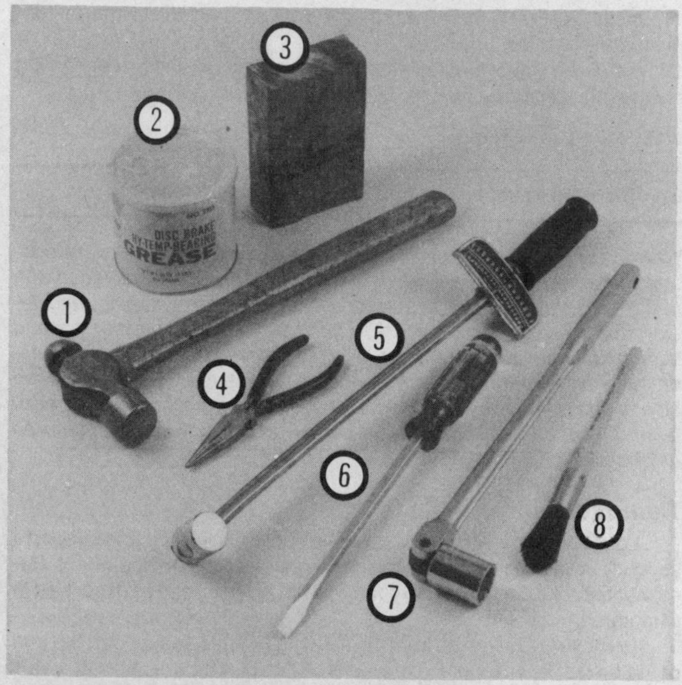

10.1 Tools and materials needed for rear wheel bearing maintenance

1 ***Hammer*** *– A common hammer will do just fine*
2 ***Grease*** *– High-temperature grease which is formulated specially for wheel bearings should be used*
3 ***Wood block*** *– If you have a scrap piece of 2x4, it can be used to drive the new seal into the hub*
4 ***Needle-nose pliers*** *– Used to straighten and remove the cotter pin in the spindle*
5 ***Torque wrench*** *– This is very important in this procedure; if the bearing is too tight, the wheel won't turn freely – if it's too loose, the wheel will "wobble" on the spindle. Either way, it could mean extensive damage.*
6 ***Screwdriver*** *– Used to remove the seal from the hub (a long screwdriver would be preferred)*
7 ***Socket/breaker bar*** *– Needed to loosen the nut on the spindle if it's extremely tight*
8 ***Brush*** *– Together with some clean solvent, this will be used to remove old grease from the hub and spindle*

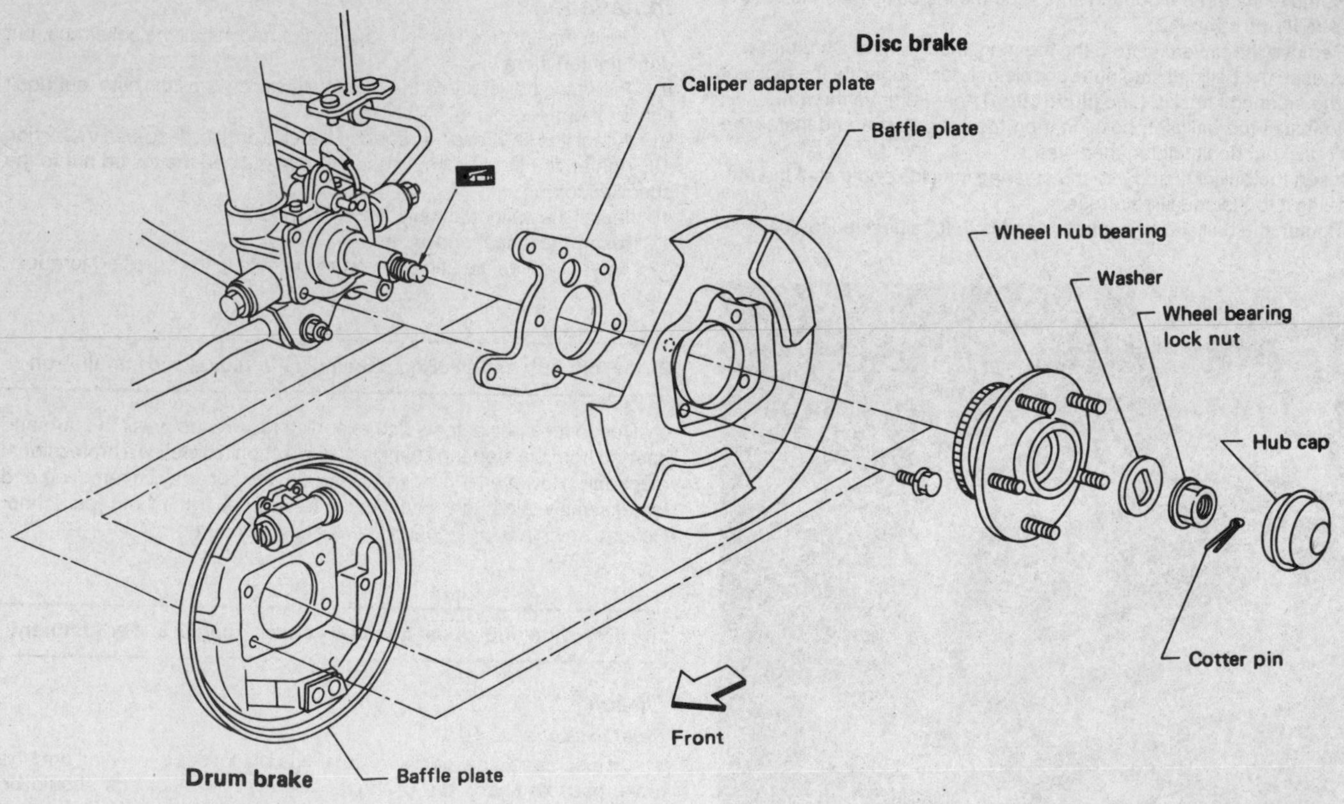

10.4 Exploded view of 1989 and later model rear hub and bearing assembly

10.6 Pry the dust cap out of the hub

10.7a Wire cutters are useful for gripping the greasy cotter pin and pulling it out

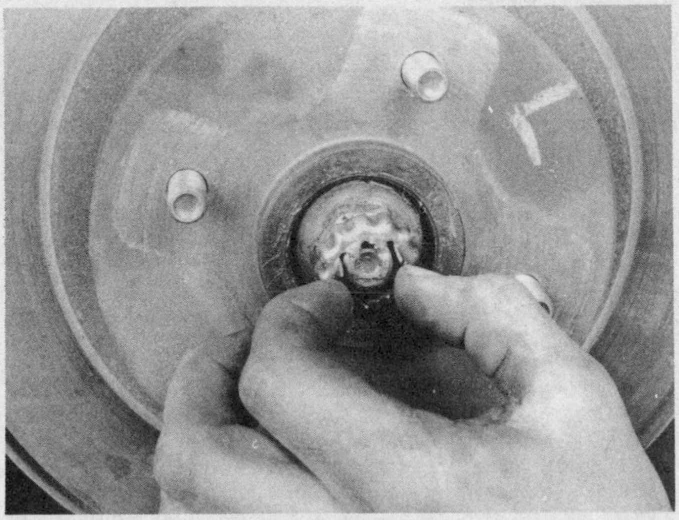

10.7b Pull the nut lock off the spindle nut

10.8 After the spindle nut has been removed, remove the washer

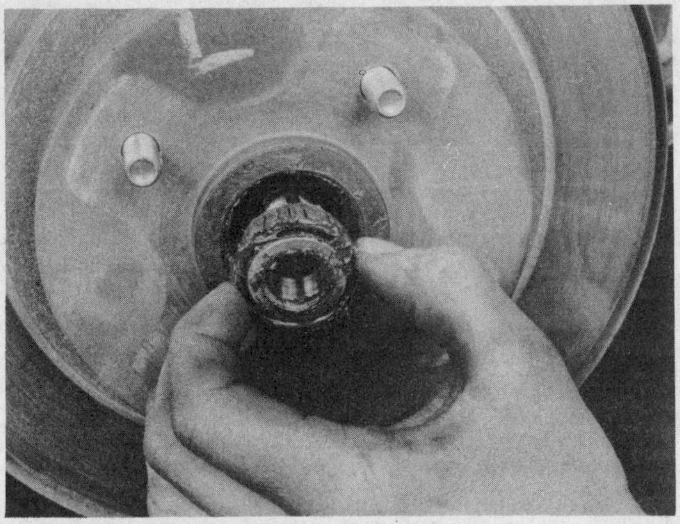

10.9 Remove the outer wheel bearing after pulling the drum or disc/hub out slightly to dislodge it

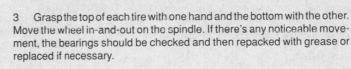

3 Grasp the top of each tire with one hand and the bottom with the other. Move the wheel in-and-out on the spindle. If there's any noticeable movement, the bearings should be checked and then repacked with grease or replaced if necessary.

Repack

Refer to illustrations 10.4, 10.6, 10.7a, 10.7b, 10.8, 10.9, 10.11 and 10.15

4 **Note:** *On 1989 and later models, the rear hub and bearing assembly does not require regular maintenance. If the bearings are defective, it must be replaced as a unit* **(see illustration)**. *Thus, the following procedure applies only to 1988 and earlier models.*

5 Remove the tire/wheel assembly. If necessary, back off the parking brake adjuster (Chapter 9).

6 Pry the dust cap out of the hub assembly using a screwdriver or hammer and chisel **(see illustration)**.

7 Straighten the bent ends of the cotter pin, then pull the cotter pin out of the nut lock **(see illustration)**. Discard the cotter pin and use a new one during reassembly. Remove the nut lock **(see illustration)**.

8 Remove the spindle nut and washer from the end of the spindle **(see illustration)**.

9 Pull the hub assembly out slightly, then push it back into its original position. This should force the outer bearing off the spindle enough so it can be removed **(see illustration)**.

10.11 Pry the seal out of the hub with a screwdriver or hooked seal puller

10.15 Work the grease into the bearing rollers from the back side of the bearing race

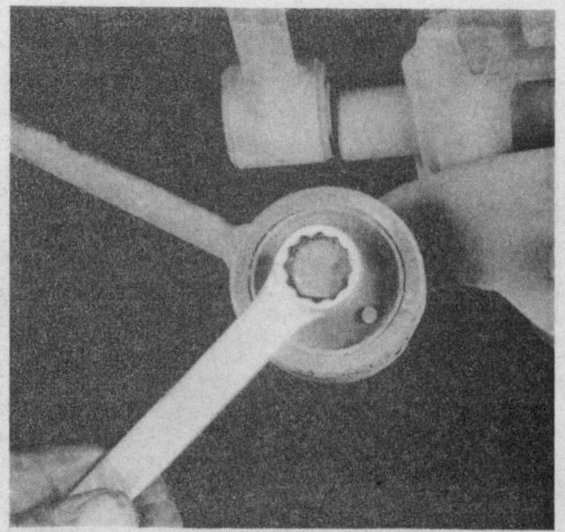

11.2 Remove the stabilizer bar-to-radius rod bracket bolt

10 Pull the drum or disc/hub off the spindle.
11 Use a seal puller or screwdriver to pry the seal out of the rear of the hub **(see illustration)**. As this is done, note how the seal is installed.
12 Remove the inner wheel bearing from the hub.
13 Use solvent to remove all traces of the old grease from the bearings, hub and spindle. A small brush may prove helpful; however make sure no bristles from the brush embed themselves inside the bearing rollers. Allow the parts to air dry.
14 Carefully inspect the bearings for cracks, heat discoloration, worn rollers, etc. Check the bearing races inside the hub for wear and damage. If the bearing races are defective, the hubs should be taken to a machine shop with the facilities to remove the old races and press new ones in. Note that the bearings and races come as matched sets and old bearings should never be installed on new races.
15 Use wheel bearing grease to pack the bearings. Work the grease completely into the bearings, forcing it between the rollers, cone and cage from the back side **(see illustration)**.
16 Apply a thin coat of grease to the spindle at the outer bearing seat, inner bearing seat, shoulder and seal seat.
17 Put a small quantity of grease inboard of each bearing race inside the hub. Using your finger, form a dam at these points to provide extra grease availability and to keep thinned grease from flowing out of the bearing.
18 Place the grease-packed inner bearing into the rear of the hub and put a little more grease outboard of the bearing.
19 Place a new seal over the inner bearing and tap the seal evenly into place with a hammer and block of wood until it's flush with the hub.
20 Carefully place the hub assembly onto the spindle and push the grease-packed outer bearing into position.

Adjustment

21 Install the washer and spindle nut. Tighten the nut to the *initial* specified torque.
22 Spin the hub in both directions to seat the bearings and remove any grease or burrs which could cause excessive bearing play later.
23 Loosen the spindle nut until it's just loose, no more. There should be zero hub axial play.
24 Tighten the spindle nut to the *final* specified torque.
25 Spin the hub in both directions several times, then recheck the nut to make sure it's still at the *final* specified torque.
26 Install the nut lock, then install a new cotter pin through the hole in the spindle and the slots in the nut lock. If the slots don't line up, loosen the nut slightly until they do. The nut should not be loosened more than 15-degrees to install the cotter pin.
27 Bend the ends of the cotter pin until they're flat against the nut. Cut off any extra length which could interfere with the dust cap.
28 Install the dust cap, tapping it into place with a hammer and a large punch.
29 Install the tire/wheel assembly on the drum/hub and tighten the lug nuts.
30 Grasp the top and bottom of the tire and check the bearings in the manner described earlier in this Section.
31 Lower the vehicle.

11 Rear stabilizer bar and bushings – removal and installation

Refer to illustrations 11.2 and 11.3

1 Raise the rear of the vehicle and support it securely on jackstands. Block the front wheels.
2 Remove the stabilizer bar bolt-to-radius rod bracket **(see illustration)**.
3 Unbolt the stabilizer bar bushing U-brackets from the stabilizer link **(see illustration)**.
4 The stabilizer bar can now be removed from the vehicle. Pull the U-brackets off the stabilizer bar (if they haven't fallen off already) using a rocking motion.
5 Check the bushings for wear, hardness, distortion, cracking and other signs of deterioration, replacing them if necessary. Also check the link bushings for these signs.
6 Using a wire brush, clean the areas of the bar where the bushings ride. Installation is the reverse of the removal procedure. If necessary, use a light coat of vegetable oil to ease bushing and U-bracket installation (don't use petroleum based products or brake fluid, as these will damage the rubber).

12 Parallel links – removal and installation

Removal

Refer to illustrations 12.3 and 12.6

Warning: *Whenever any of the suspension or steering fasteners are loosened or removed they should be inspected, and if necessary, replaced with new ones of the same part number or of original equipment quality and design. Torque specifications must be followed for proper reassembly and component retention.*

Note: *The bushings are not serviceable and the links must be replaced in pairs.*

1 Raise the rear of the vehicle and support it securely on jackstands. Block the front wheels.
2 Using two box-end wrenches break the bolt and nut loose. It may be necessary to use a hammer and a punch to drive the bolt out of the mounting brackets.
3 Remove the links. Note that the link with the toe adjustment faces the rear of the vehicle. If this link will be replaced or disassembled, first measure the distance between locknuts **(see illustration)** in order to maintain the same rear wheel alignment.

11.3 The stabilizer bar brackets are retained by two bolts (arrows) – inspect the stabilizer bar link bushings for wear or defects (arrow)

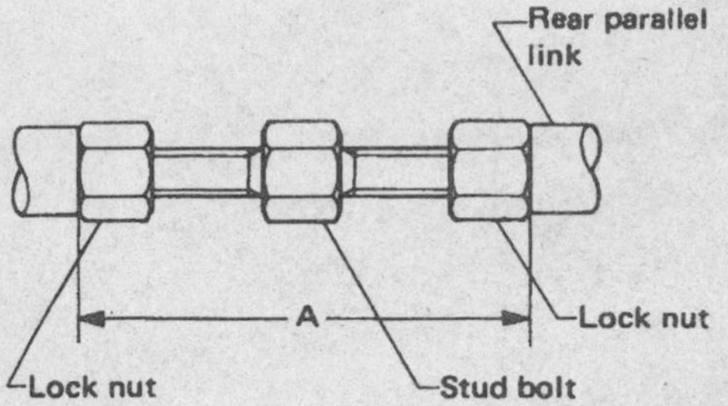

12.3 Because rear wheel alignment is set by the rear parallel link length, carefully measure the distance "A" before parallel link replacement in order to return the alignment to the same position

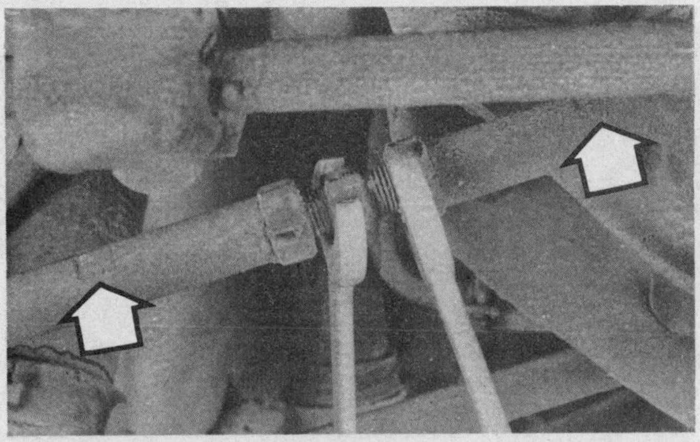

12.6 In order to alter the length of the links, use two open-end wrenches to break the locknuts loose – then adjust the link to the length as measured prior to disassembly. To keep the link bushings from moving when tightening the locknuts, insert one of the wrenches in the slots provided on the link (arrows)

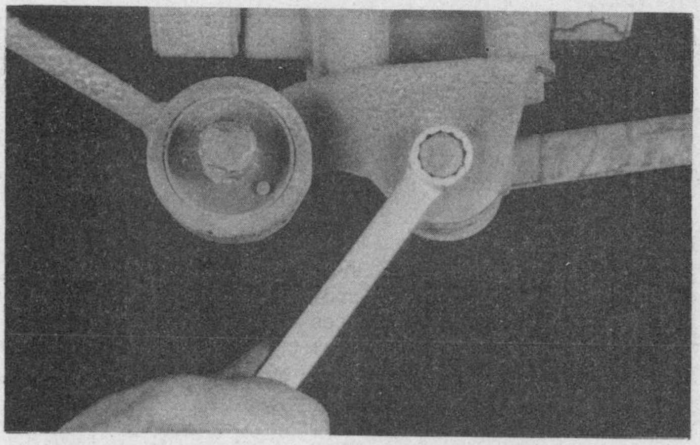

13.2 Remove the radius rod-to-bracket bolt

Installation

4 Installation is the reverse of removal
5 Tighten the bolts and nuts to the specified torque.
6 The rear link sets the rear alignment toe-in by its length. Set the overall length to the measurement obtained prior to disassembling the link (see Step 3 above). This length can be altered by loosening the locknuts and turning the link in or out as necessary **(see illustration)**.
7 Have the rear wheel alignment checked by a dealer service department or an alignment shop as soon as possible.

13 Radius rod – removal and installation

Refer to illustrations 13.2 and 13.3

Warning: *Whenever any of the suspension or steering fasteners are loosened or removed they should be inspected, and if necessary, replaced with new ones of the same part number or of original equipment quality and design. Torque specifications must be followed for proper reassembly and component retention.*

1 Loosen the wheel lug nuts, raise the rear of the vehicle and support it securely on jackstands. Block the front wheels. Remove the wheel.
2 Remove the radius rod-to-strut bracket bolt **(see illustration)**.

13.3 Using two box end wrenches, remove the radius rod-to-body bolt/nut

3 Remove the radius rod-to-body bolt and nut **(see illustration)**.
4 Installation is the reverse of the removal procedure. Be sure to tighten the bolts to the specified torque.

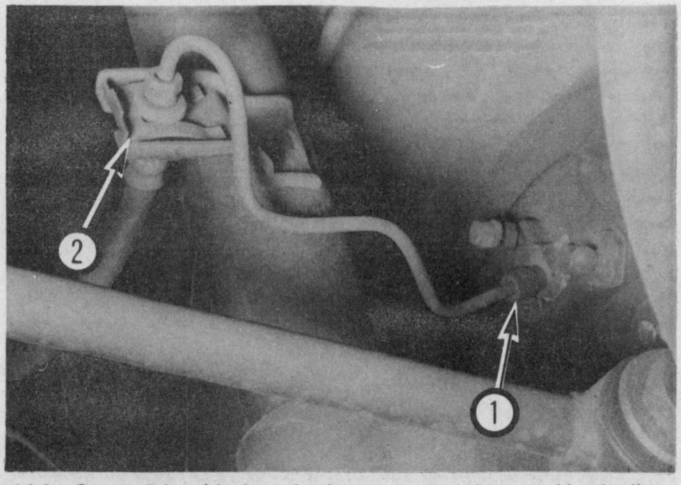

14.2 On models with drum brakes, unscrew the metal brake line (1) from the wheel cylinder then remove the clip (2) and detach the line from the strut – be sure to plug the line to prevent leakage

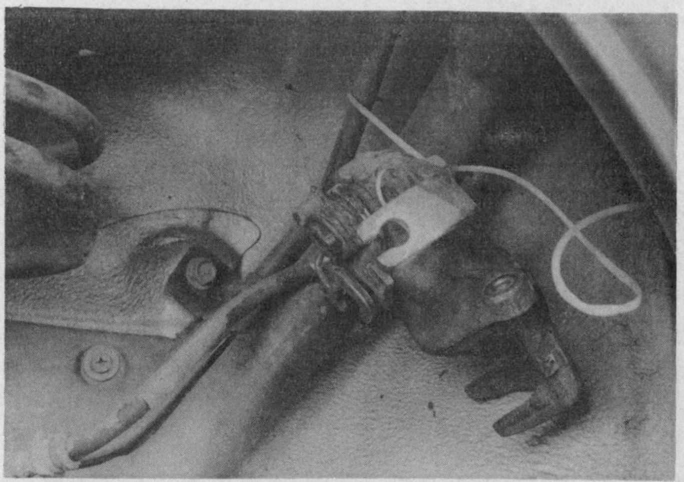

14.3 On models with disc brakes, remove the caliper, parking brake cable and the brake line from the strut and hang it on the fuel tank filler neck – it is not necessary to disconnect the brake line from the caliper

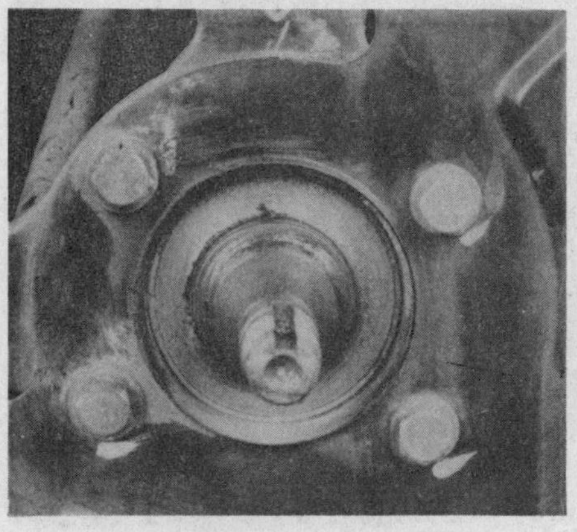

14.5 The brake backing plate is attached to the spindle by four bolts

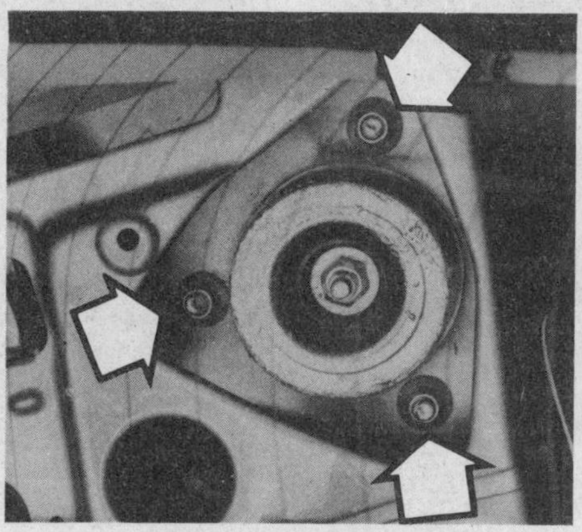

14.8 The upper end of the strut assembly is fastened to the shock tower with three nuts (arrows) – *do not* loosen the center nut!

14.10 Mark the relationship of the mounting insulator and the upper spring seat before beginning overhaul procedures

14 Rear strut/shock absorber, coil spring and wheel spindle assembly – inspection, removal, overhaul and installation

Warning: *Whenever any of the suspension or steering fasteners are loosened or removed they must be inspected and, if necessary, replaced with new ones of the same part number or original equipment quality and design. Torque specifications must be followed for proper reassembly and component retention.*

Inspection

Note: *If the struts or coil springs exhibit the telltale signs of wear (leaking, loss of fluid, loss of damping capability, chipped, snagging or cracked coil springs) explore all options before beginning any work. The strut/shock absorber assemblies are serviceable. However, strut assemblies complete with springs may be available on an exchange basis, which eliminates much time and work. Whichever route you choose to take, check on the cost and availability of parts before disassembling the vehicle.*

Warning: *Disassembling a strut assembly is a potentially dangerous undertaking and utmost attention must be directed to the job at hand, or serious bodily injury may result. Use only a high quality spring compressor and carefully follow the manufacturer's instructions furnished with the tool. After removing the coil spring from the strut assembly, set it aside in a safe, isolated area (a steel cabinet is preferred).*

Removal

Refer to illustrations 14.2, 14.3, 14.5 and 14.8

1 Loosen the wheel lug nuts, raise the rear of the vehicle and support it securely on jackstands. Block the front wheels. Remove the wheel.

2 On vehicles with rear drum brakes, remove the drum, brake shoes and parking brake cable (see Chapter 9). Then remove the rear hub and bearing assembly (see section 10). Unscrew the metal brake line from the wheel cylinder. Use a flare nut wrench to avoid rounding off the corners of the nut. Then remove the line from the strut and plug the line or wrap a plastic bag tightly around the end of the line to prevent leakage and contamination **(see illustration)**.

3 On vehicles with rear disc brakes, remove the caliper, parking brake cable and the brake line from the strut (See Chapter 9) and hang it on the fuel tank filler neck **(see illustration)**.Then remove the brake disc (see section 10).

4 On models with anti-lock brakes (ABS), unbolt the sensor from the brake backing plate (see Chapter 9).

5 Remove the brake backing plate and, if equipped, caliper support bracket **(see illustration)**.

6 Remove the radius rod-to-strut bracket bolt, the parallel link-to-strut bracket bolt and the stabilizer bar-to-strut bracket bolt.

7 Support the strut with a floor jack.

8 Following the procedure outlined in Chapter 11 remove the rear seat and the parcel shelf to gain access to the strut upper mounting bolts **(see illustration)**.

14.12 Install a spring compressor according to the tool manufacturer's instructions and compress the spring until all pressure is relieved from the upper spring seat

14.13 Remove the damper shaft nut

14.14 Remove the lock washer, flat washer and spacer

14.19 Remove the gland packing with a pair of locking pliers

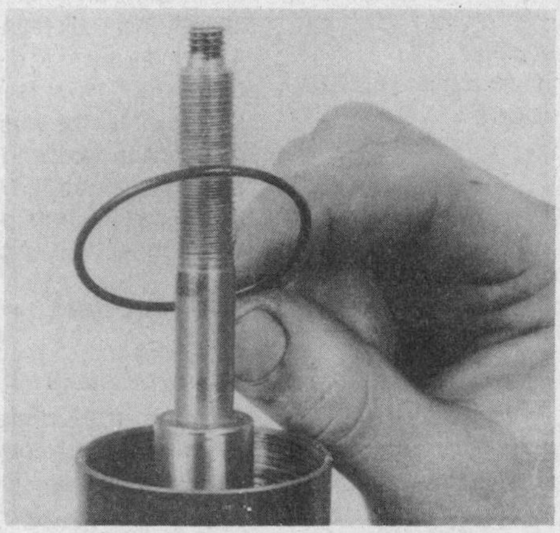

14.20 Lift the O-ring out of the strut

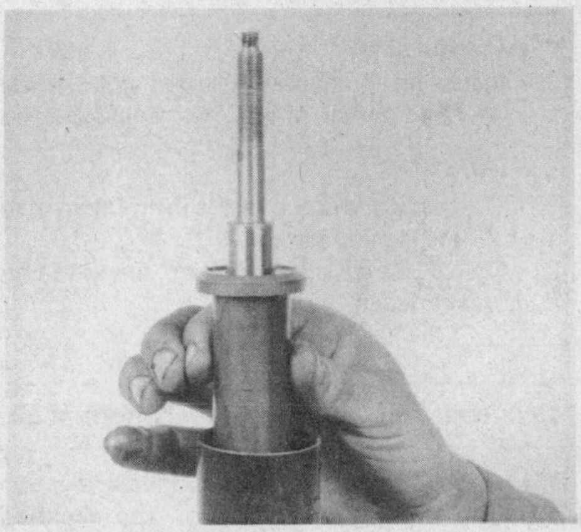

14.21 Lift the piston assembly slowly out of the strut

9 Remove the three mounting nuts and carefully lower the strut out of the fender well.

Overhaul

Refer to illustrations 14.10, 14.12, 14.13, 14.14, 14.19, 14.20, 14.21, 14.25 and 14.29

10 Mark the relationship of the mounting insulator and the upper spring seat before beginning overhaul procedures **(see illustration)**.

11 Mount the strut in a vise. Line the vise jaws with wood or rags to prevent damage to the unit and do not tighten the vise excessively.

12 Following the manufacturer's instructions, install the spring compressor (which can be obtained at most auto parts stores or equipment yards on daily rental basis) on the spring and compress it sufficiently to relieve all pressure from the suspension support **(see illustration)**. This can be verified by wiggling the spring.

13 Remove the damper shaft nut and remove the rebound stopper **(see illustration)**.

14 Then remove the piston rod self-locking nut, lock washer and spacer and the strut insulator **(see illustration)**.

15 Lift the upper spring seat off the shaft.

16 Carefully lift the compressed spring from the damper shaft and set it in a safe place, such as a steel cabinet. **Warning:** *Never place your head near the end of the spring!*

17 Slide the rubber dust cover off the shaft.

18 Retract the piston by pushing it down until it bottoms.

19 Remove the gland packing with a pair of locking pliers **(see illustration)**.

20 Lift the O-ring out of the strut **(see illustration)**.

21 Slowly lift the piston assembly out of the strut **(see illustration)**.

22 Wash all parts with solvent and dry with compressed alr.

23 Install the new piston assembly and add the specified amount of Nissan strut fluid or equivalent.

24 Lubricate the gland packing with grease.

25 Tape the end of the strut shaft to help prevent damaging the gland packing seal **(see illustration)**.

14.25 Tape the end of the strut shaft to help prevent damaging the gland packing

14.29 When installing the spring, make sure that the lower end of the spring fits into the recessed portion of the lower seat

26 Install the gland packing and tighten it securely.
27 Move the piston shaft rod up and down several times to bleed air from the strut.
28 Pull the shaft all the way up and install the dust cover.
29 Install the spring making sure that the lower end of the spring fits into the recessed portion of the lower seat **(see illustration)**.

Installation

30 The rest of the procedure is the reverse of removal. Tighten all fasteners to the specified torque.
31 On models with drum brakes, bleed the brakes following the procedure described in Chapter 9.

15 Steering system – general information

Warning: *1992 models are equipped with a Supplemental Restraint System (SRS), more commonly known as an airbag. Always disconnect both battery cables and wait ten minutes before working in the vicinity of the impact sensors, steering wheel and column or instrument panel to avoid the possibility of accidental deployment of the air bag, which could cause personal injury (see Chapter 12). The yellow wiring harness and connectors routed through the center console, under hood and right side wheel well are for this system. Do not use electrical test equipment on any of the airbag system wiring or tamper with them in any way.*

All models are equipped with rack-and-pinion steering. The steering gear is bolted to the crossmember at the firewall and operates the steering arms via tie-rods. The inner ends of the tie-rods are protected by rubber boots which should be inspected periodically for secure attachment, tears and leaking lubricant.

The power assist system consists of a belt-driven pump and associated lines and hoses. The power steering pump reservoir fluid level should be checked periodically (Chapter 1).

The steering wheel operates the steering shaft, which actuates the steering gear through universal joints. Looseness in the steering can be caused by wear in the steering shaft universal joints, the steering gear, the tie-rod ends and loose retaining bolts.

16 Steering wheel – removal and installation

1985 through 1991 models

Refer to illustrations 16.2, 16.3 and 16.4

1 Disconnect the cable from the negative terminal of the battery.
2 Detach the horn pad from the steering wheel **(see illustration)**.
3 Remove the steering wheel retaining nut then mark the relationship of the steering shaft to the hub (if marks don't already exist or don't line up) to simplify installation and ensure steering wheel alignment **(see illustration)**.
4 Use a puller to detach the steering wheel from the shaft **(see illustration)**. Don't hammer on the shaft to dislodge the steering wheel.
5 To install the wheel, align the mark on the steering wheel hub with the mark on the shaft and slip the wheel onto the shaft. Install the nut and tighten it to the specified torque.
6 Install the horn pad.
7 Connect the negative battery cable.

1992 Models

Removal

Refer to illustrations 16.10, 16.11, 16.12 and 16.15

Warning: *1992 models are equipped with a Supplemental Restraint System (SRS), more commonly known as an airbag. Always disconnect both battery cables and wait ten minutes before working in the vicinity of the impact sensors, steering wheel and column or instrument panel to avoid the possibility of accidental deployment of the air bag, which could cause personal injury (see Chapter 12). The yellow wiring harness and connectors routed through the center console, under hood and right side wheel well are for this system. Do not use electrical test equipment on any of the airbag system wiring or tamper with them in any way.*

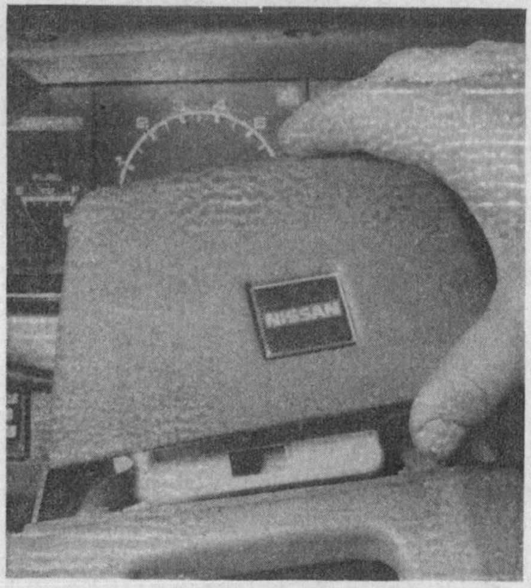

16.2 Pull the horn pad from the steering wheel

16.3 Paint or scribe alignment marks from the steering wheel hub to the steering shaft (arrows)

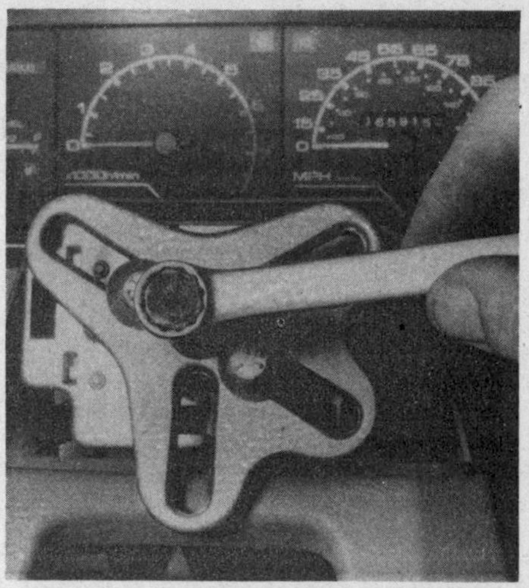

16.4 Use a steering wheel puller to separate the steering wheel from the shaft – DO NOT attempt to remove the wheel with a hammer!

16.10 The airbag module connector is located inside a recess in the underside of the steering wheel; it can be accessed by removing the cover with a small screwdriver

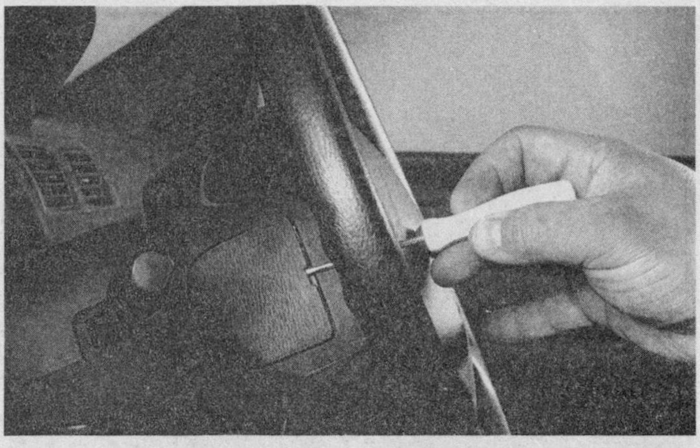

16.11 Use a small screwdriver to remove the plastic covers for access to the airbag module bolts

8 Disconnect the cable from the negative and positive terminals of the battery.

9 Make sure the front wheels are in the straight ahead position.

10 Remove the lower cover from the steering wheel and disconnect the air bag module two-pin electrical connector **(see illustration)**.

11 Remove the side cover on each side of the steering wheel **(see illustration)**.

12 Remove the Torx bolt on each side of the steering wheel securing the airbag module to the steering wheel **(see illustration)**. Discard these bolts as new ones must be installed.

13 Lift the airbag module off the steering wheel. **Warning:** *Carry the airbag module with the trim cover side* ***facing away*** *from your body to minimize injury if the airbag module accidentally deploys. Set the airbag module aside in a safe place, isolated location and set it down with the trim cover side facing up.*

14 Disconnect the horn electrical connector.

15 Remove the steering wheel retaining nut **(see illustration)** .

16 Mark the relationship of the steering wheel to the steering shaft.

17 Use a puller to detach the steering wheel from the shaft. Don't hammer on the shaft to dislodge the steering wheel. Remove the steering wheel.

Installation

18 Make sure the spiral cable is centered properly in the neutral position. **Warning:** *Failure to center the spiral cable could prevent the airbag from deploying in an accident.* To center the spiral cable, perform the following:

a) Make sure the front wheels are still in the straight ahead position. Reposition if necessary.

b) Rotate the spiral cable clockwise until it catches the stopper at the end of its travel (don't try to wind it up beyond the point at which it takes up all of the slack, or you will damage the mechanism).

c) From the end of its travel, rotate the spiral cable counterclockwise approximately two turns until the yellow alignment mark appears on the left gear. Align the arrow mark of the spiral cable with this yellow mark.

19 If removed, install the spiral cable guide pins and pull the spiral cable connectors through the opening in the steering wheel.

20 To install the steering wheel, align the mark on the steering wheel with the mark on the steering shaft and slide the steering wheel onto the shaft. **Caution:** *Make sure the spiral cable doesn't get pinched during steering wheel installation.* Install the nut and tighten to the specified torque.

21 Connect the horn electrical connector.

22 Insert the spiral cable connectors down through the lower opening in the steering wheel.

23 Install the airbag module onto the steering wheel. Use new specially coated Torx bolts and secure the module to the steering wheel. Tighten to the specified torque.

24 Install the side cover on each side of the steering wheel **(see illustration 16.11)**.

25 Connect the air bag module two-pin electrical connector **(see illustration 16.10)**.

26 Install the lower cover onto the steering wheel.

27 When the engine is started, the airbag warning light should come on only momentarily. If the light comes on and remains on after the engine is started, take the vehicle to a dealership service department to have the system checked and reset. Because of the special electronic tester required, this job is impossible at home. **Warning:** *Failure to have the airbag system reset could result in the failure of the airbag to deploy in an accident.*

16.12 The airbag module is attached to the steering wheel with a pair of special coated Torx bolts, located on each side of the steering wheel

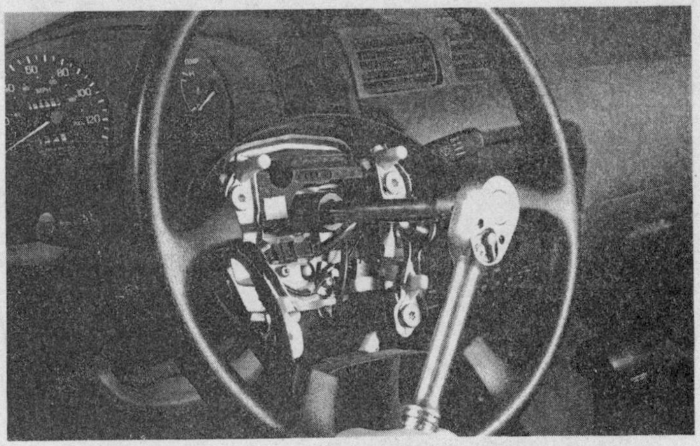

16.15 Remove the steering wheel retaining nut

10

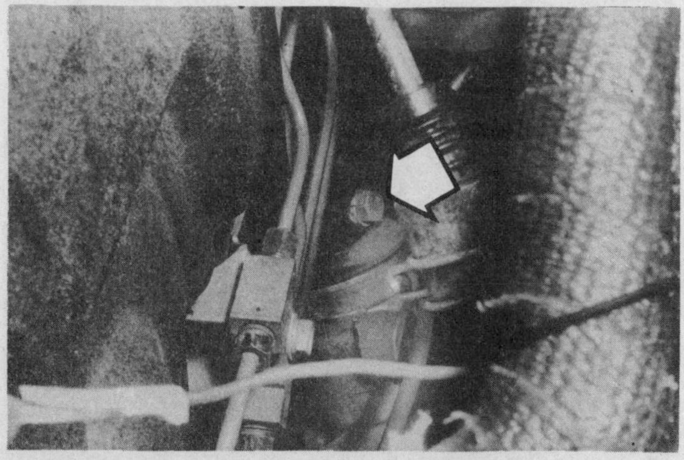

17.5 Before removing the steering shaft pinch bolt (arrow) mark the relationship of the universal joint to the steering gear input shaft

17 Steering gear - removal and installation

Refer to illustrations 17.5, 17.7 and 17.10

Warning: *1992 models are equipped with a Supplemental Restraint System (SRS), more commonly known as an airbag. Always disconnect both battery cables and wait ten minutes before working in the vicinity of the impact sensors, steering wheel and column or instrument panel to avoid the possibility of accidental deployment of the air bag, which could cause personal injury* (see Chapter 12). *The yellow wiring harness and connectors routed through the center console, under hood and right side wheel well are for this system. Do not use electrical test equipment on any of the airbag system wiring or tamper with them in any way.*

Note: *This procedure applies to both power and manual steering gear assemblies. When working on a vehicle equipped with a manual steering gear, ignore any references made to the power steering system.*

Removal

1 Loosen the front wheel lug nuts, raise the front of the vehicle and support it securely on jackstands. Apply the parking brake and remove the wheels. Remove the engine undercovers on models so equipped.

2 Remove the manual transmission linkage or the automatic transmission shift cable (see Chapter 7).

3 Remove the center section of the exhaust system (see Chapter 4).

4 Place a drain pan under the steering gear (power steering only). Remove the power steering pressure and return lines and cap the ends to prevent excessive fluid loss and contamination.

5 Mark the relationship of the universal joint to the steering gear input shaft. Remove the steering shaft pinch bolt **(see illustration)**.

6 Separate the tie-rod ends from the steering knuckle arms (see Section 18).

7 Support the steering gear and remove the steering gear bracket-to-firewall mounting bolts **(see illustration)**. Lower the unit, separate the steering shaft from the steering gear input shaft and remove the steering gear from the vehicle. **Warning:** *Do not allow the steering wheel to turn with the steering gear removed or damage to the airbag spiral cable could occur, resulting in airbag system failure. To prevent the steering wheel from turning, place the ignition switch in the Lock position and remove the key before removing the steering gear.*

8 Check the steering gear mounting insulators for excessive wear or deterioration, replacing them if necessary.

Installation

9 Raise the steering gear into position and connect the U-joint, aligning the marks.

10 Install the mounting brackets and bolts and tighten them to the specified torque. On 1989 and later models, tighten the mounting bolts in the order shown **(see illustration)**.

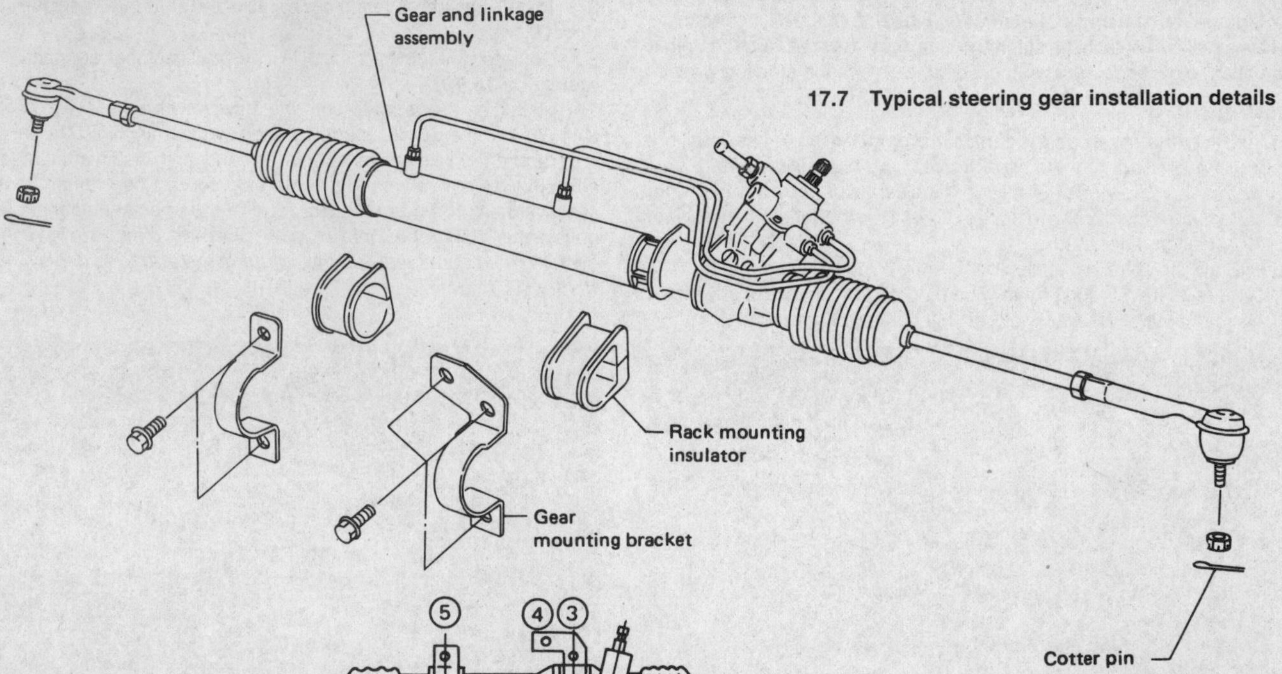

17.7 Typical steering gear installation details

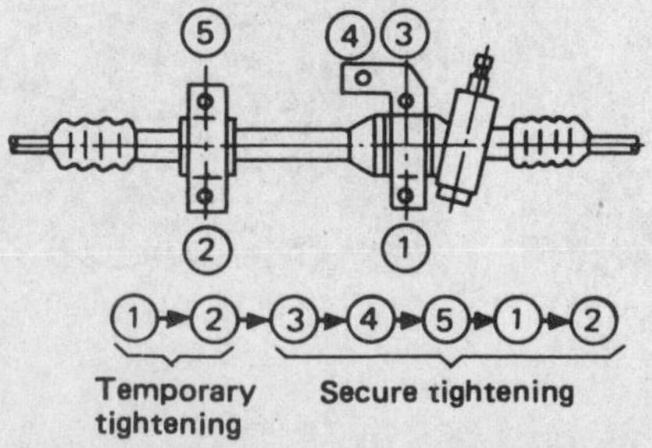

17.10 On 1989 and later models, tighten the mounting bolts in the order shown

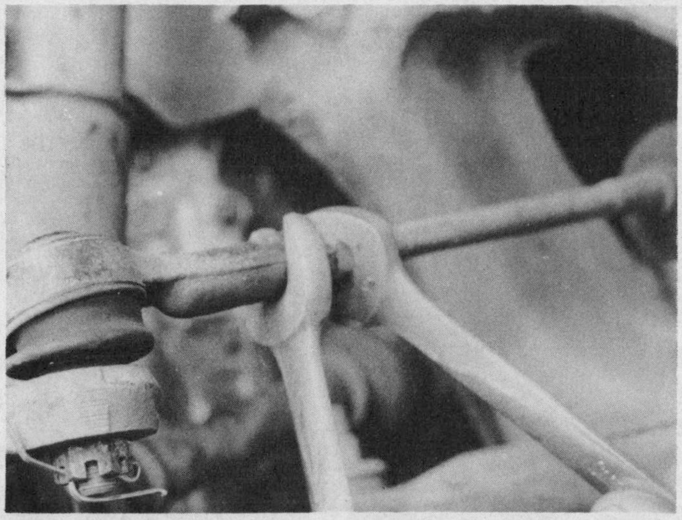

18.2a Loosen the jam nut while holding the tie-rod with a wrench (or pair of locking pliers) on the flat portion of the rod to prevent it from turning

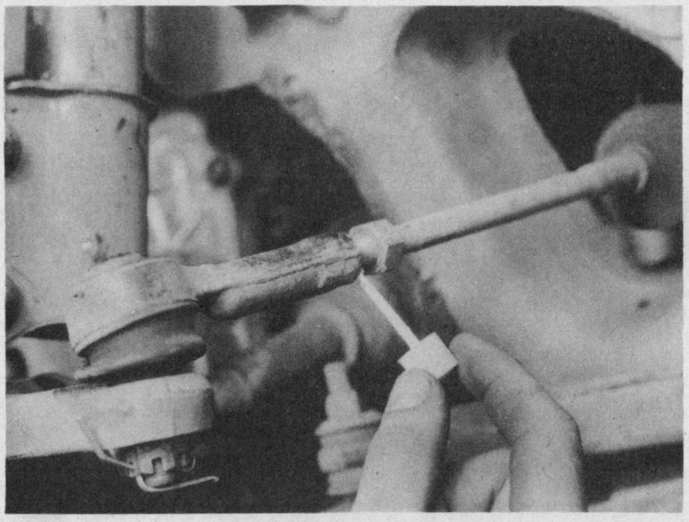

18.2b The relationship of the tie-rod end to the tie-rod can be marked with white paint

11 Connect the tie-rod ends to the steering knuckle arms (Section 18).
12 Install the U-joint pinch bolt and tighten it to the specified torque.
13 Connect the power steering pressure and return hoses to the steering gear and fill the power steering pump reservoir with the recommended fluid (Chapter 1).
14 Install the manual transaxle linkage or the automatic transaxle shift cable (Chapter 7).
15 Install the center section of the exhaust system (Chapter 4).
16 Lower the vehicle and bleed the steering system as outlined in Section 22.

18 Tie-rod ends – removal and installation

Refer to illustrations 18.2a, 18.2b and 18.4

Removal

1 Loosen the wheel lug nuts. Raise the front of the vehicle, support it securely, block the rear wheels and set the parking brake. Remove the front wheel.
2 Hold the tie-rod with a pair of locking pliers or a wrench and loosen the jam nut enough to mark the position of the tie-rod end in relation to the threads **(see illustrations)**.
3 Remove the cotter pin and loosen the nut on the tie-rod end stud. Don't completely remove the nut.
4 Separate the tie-rod from the steering knuckle arm with a puller **(see illustration)**. Remove the nut and detach the tie-rod.
5 Unscrew the tie-rod end from the tie-rod.

Installation

6 Thread the tie-rod end on to the marked position and insert the tie-rod stud into the steering knuckle arm. Tighten the jam nut securely.
7 Install the castellated nut on the stud and tighten it to the specified torque. Install a new cotter pin.
8 Install the wheel and lug nuts. Lower the vehicle and tighten the lug nuts to the specified torque.
9 Have the alignment checked by a dealer service department or an alignment shop.

19 Steering gear boots – replacement

1 Loosen the lug nuts, raise the front of the vehicle and support it securely on jackstands. Apply the parking brake. Remove the wheel.
2 Refer to Section 18 and remove the tie-rod end and jam nut.

18.4 A two-jaw puller works well for separating the tie-rod end from the steering knuckle arm. Note that the nut has not been removed completely – it will prevent the two components from separating violently

3 Remove the steering gear boot clamps and slide the boot off.
4 Before installing the new boot, wrap the threads and serrations on the end of the steering rod with a layer of tape so the small end of the new boot isn't damaged.
5 Slide the new boot into position on the steering gear until it seats in the groove in the steering rod and install new clamps.
6 Remove the tape and install the tie-rod end (Section 18).
7 Install the wheel and lug nuts. Lower the vehicle and tighten the lug nuts to the specified torque.

20 Power steering pump – removal and installation

Refer to illustration 20.7

Warning: *Whenever any of the suspension or steering system components are loosened or removed, they must be inspected and, if necessary, replaced with new ones with the same part number or of original equipment quality and design.*

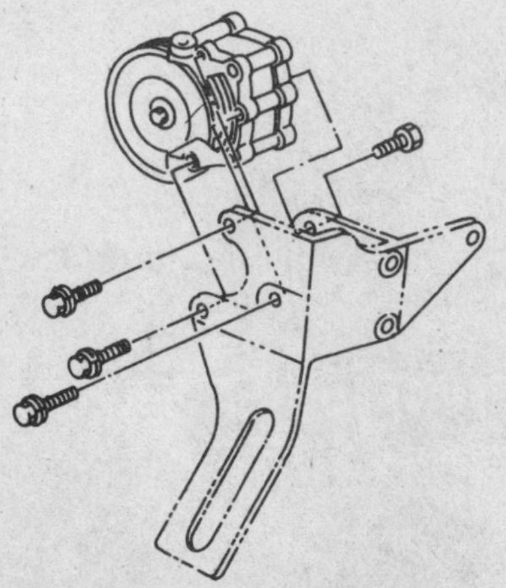

20.7 Power steering pump installation details (1985 through 1988 models shown, others similar)

Removal

1 Disconnect the cable from the negative battery terminal.
2 Using a large syringe or suction gun, suck as much fluid out of the power steering fluid reservoir as possible. Place a drain pan under the vehicle to catch any fluid that spills out when the hoses are disconnected.
3 Loosen the right front wheel lug nuts, raise the front of the vehicle and support it securely on jackstands. Apply the parking brake. Remove the wheel and the fender apron.
4 Remove the power steering drivebelt (see Chapter 1).
5 Loosen the clamp and disconnect the fluid return hose from the pump.
6 Remove the pressure line-to-pump union bolt and separate the line from the pump. **Note:** *A spool and spring may fall out after the union is removed.* Remove the copper sealing washers on each side of the fitting – these should be replaced when installing the pump.
7 The power steering pump is held to the mounting bracket by three bolts in the front and one in the back. Turn the pump pulley so the hole lines up with a bolt, then remove it with a socket. Remove the rear mounting bolt and remove the pump from the vehicle.

Installation

8 To install the pump, reverse the removal procedure. Adjust the drivebelt tension following the procedure described in Chapter 1.
9 Top up the fluid level in the reservoir and bleed the system (see the following Section).

21 Power steering system – bleeding

1 Following any operation in which the power steering fluid lines have been disconnected, the power steering system must be bled to remove all air and obtain proper steering performance.
2 With the front wheels in the straight ahead position, check the power steering fluid level and, if low, add fluid (see Chapter 1).
3 Start the engine and allow it to run at fast idle. Recheck the fluid level and add more if necessary.
4 Bleed the system by turning the wheels from side-to-side, without hitting the stops. This will work the air out of the system. Keep the reservoir full of fluid as this is done.
5 When the air is worked out of the system, return the wheels to the straight ahead position and leave the vehicle running for several more minutes before shutting it off.
6 Road test the vehicle to be sure the steering system is functioning normally and noise free.
7 Recheck the fluid level to be sure it is correct. Add fluid if necessary (see Chapter 1).

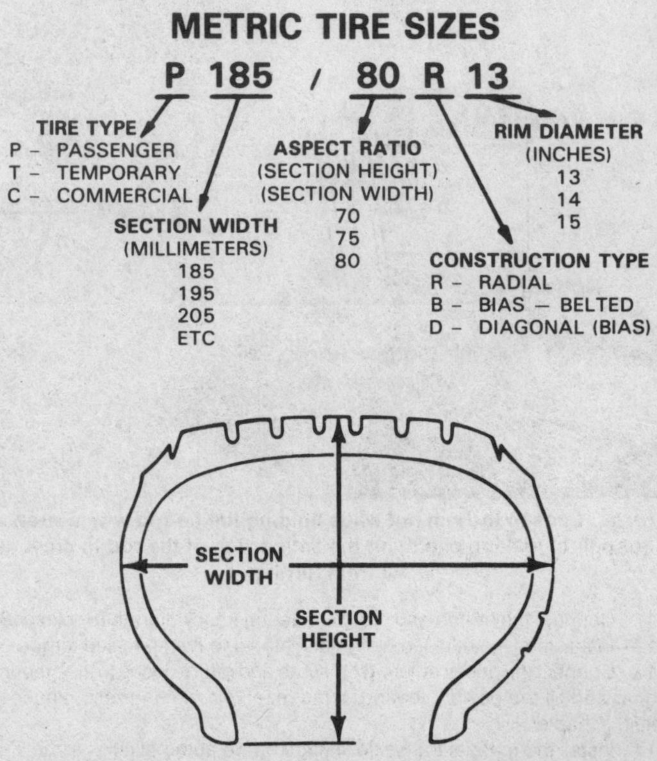

22.1 Metric tire size codes

22 Wheels and tires – general information

Refer to illustration 22.1

All vehicles covered by this manual are equipped with metric-sized fiberglass or steel belted radial tires **(see illustration)**. Use of other size or type of tires may affect the ride and handling of the vehicle. Don't mix different types of tires, such as radials and bias belted, on the same vehicle as handling may be seriously affected. It's recommended that tires be replaced in pairs on the same axle, but if only one tire is being replaced, be sure it's the same size, structure and tread design as the other.

Because tire pressure has a substantial effect on handling and wear, the pressure on all tires should be checked at least once a month or before any extended trips (see Chapter 1).

Wheels must be replaced if they are bent, dented, leak air, have elongated bolt holes, are heavily rusted, out of vertical symmetry or if the lug nuts won't stay tight. Wheel repairs that use welding or peening are not recommended.

Tire and wheel balance is important to the overall handling, braking and performance of the vehicle. Unbalanced wheels can adversely affect handling and ride characteristics as well as tire life. Whenever a tire is installed on a wheel, the tire and wheel should be balanced by a shop with the proper equipment.

23 Front end alignment – general information

Refer to illustration 23.1

A front end alignment refers to the adjustments made to the front wheels so they are in proper angular relationship to the suspension and the ground. Front wheels that are out of proper alignment not only affect steering control, but also increase tire wear. The front end adjustments normally required are camber, caster and toe-in **(see illustration)**.

Getting the proper front wheel alignment is a very exacting process, one in which complicated and expensive machines are necessary to per-

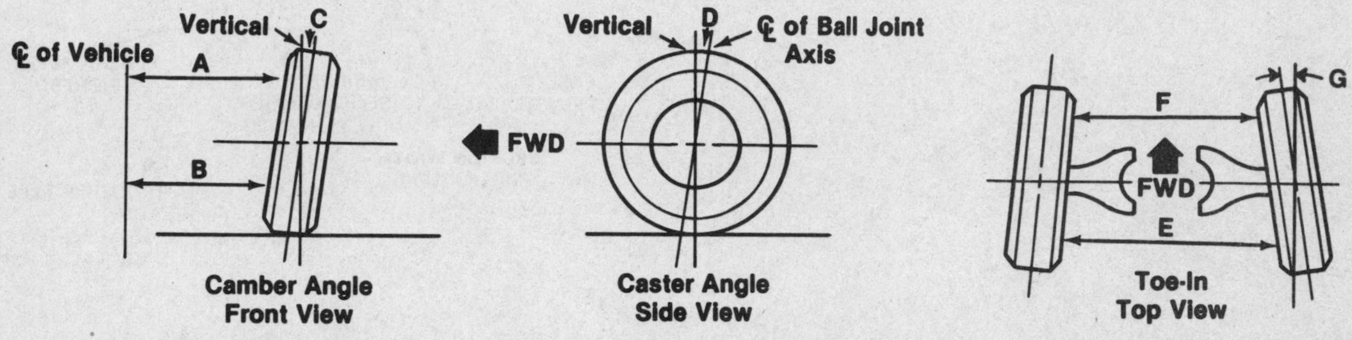

23.1 Front end alignment details – camber (top) and toe-in (bottom). The actual adjustment of these angles is beyond the scope of the home mechanic and must be performed by an alignment shop or service station

A minus B = C (degrees camber)
E minus F = toe-in (measured in inches)
G = toe-in (expressed in degrees)

form the job properly. Because of this, you should have a technician with the proper equipment perform these tasks. We will, however, use this space to give you a basic idea of what is involved with front end alignment so you can better understand the process and deal intelligently with the shop that does the work.

Toe-in is the turning in of the front wheels. The purpose of a toe specification is to ensure parallel rolling of the front wheels. In a vehicle with zero toe-in, the distance between the front edges of the wheels will be the same as the distance between the rear edges of the wheels. The actual amount of toe-in is normally only a fraction of an inch. Toe-in adjustment is controlled by the tie-rod end position on the inner tie-rod. Incorrect toe-in will cause the tires to wear improperly by making them scrub against the road surface.

Camber is the tilting of the front wheels from the vertical when viewed from the front of the vehicle. When the wheels tilt out at the top, the camber is said to be positive (+). When the wheels tilt in at the top the camber is negative (-). The amount of tilt is measured in degrees from the vertical and this measurement is called the camber angle. This angle affects the amount of tire tread which contacts the road and compensates for changes in the suspension geometry when the vehicle is cornering or travelling over an undulating surface.

Caster is the tilting of the top of the front steering axis from the vertical. A tilt toward the rear is positive caster and a tilt toward the front is negative caster.

10

Chapter 11 Body

Contents

Body – maintenance	2
Body repair – major damage	6
Body repair – minor damage	5
Door lock, lock cylinder and handle – removal and installation	16
Door – removal, installation and adjustment	13
Door trim panel – removal and installation	10
Door window glass – removal and installation	17
Fender apron seal – removal and installation	20
Fixed glass – replacement	8
General information	1
Hinges and locks – maintenance	7
Hood – removal, installation and adjustment	9
Instrument panel finish panels – removal and installation	11
Outside mirror – removal and installation	18
Seats – removal and installation	19
Steering column cover – removal and installation	12
Sunroof – lubrication and adjustment	15
Trunk lid – removal, installation and adjustment	14
Upholstery and carpets – maintenance	4
Vinyl trim – maintenance	3

1 General information

These models feature a "unibody" layout, using a floor pan with front and rear frame side rails which support the body components, front and rear suspension systems and other mechanical components.

Certain components are particularly vulnerable to accident damage and can be unbolted and repaired or replaced. Among these parts are the body moldings, bumpers, the hood and trunk lids and all glass.

Only general body maintenance practices and body panel repair procedures within the scope of the do-it-yourselfer are included in this Chapter.

2 Body – maintenance

1 The condition of your vehicle's body is very important, because the resale value depends a great deal on it. It's much more difficult to repair a neglected or damaged body than it is to repair mechanical components. The hidden areas of the body, such as the wheel wells, the frame and the engine compartment, are equally important, although they don't require as frequent attention as the rest of the body.

2 Once a year, or every 12,000 miles, it's a good idea to have the underside of the body steam cleaned. All traces of dirt and oil will be removed and the area can then be inspected carefully for rust, damaged brake lines, frayed electrical wires, damaged cables and other problems. The front suspension components should be greased after completion of this job.

3 At the same time, clean the engine and the engine compartment with a steam cleaner or water soluble degreaser.

4 The wheel wells should be given close attention, since undercoating can peel away and stones and dirt thrown up by the tires can cause the paint to chip and flake, allowing rust to set in. If rust is found, clean down to the bare metal and apply an anti-rust paint.

5 The body should be washed about once a week. Wet the vehicle thoroughly to soften the dirt, then wash it down with a soft sponge and plenty of clean soapy water. If the surplus dirt is not washed off very carefully, it can wear down the paint.

6 Spots of tar or asphalt thrown up from the road should be removed with a cloth soaked in solvent.

7 Once every six months, wax the body and chrome trim. If a chrome cleaner is used to remove rust from any of the vehicle's plated parts, remember that the cleaner also removes part of the chrome, so use it sparingly.

3 Vinyl trim – maintenance

Don't clean vinyl trim with detergents, caustic soap or petroleum based cleaners. Plain soap and water works just fine, with a soft brush to clean dirt that may be ingrained. Wash the vinyl as frequently as the rest of the vehicle.

After cleaning, application of a high quality rubber and vinyl protectant will help prevent oxidation and cracks. The protectant can also be applied to weatherstripping, vacuum lines and rubber hoses, which often fail as a result of chemical degradation, and to the tires.

4 Upholstery and carpets – maintenance

1 Every three months remove the carpets or mats and clean the interior of the vehicle (more frequently if necessary). Vacuum the upholstery and carpets to remove loose dirt and dust.
2 Leather upholstery requires special care. Stains should be removed with warm water and a very mild soap solution. Use a clean, damp cloth to remove the soap, then wipe again with a dry cloth. Never use alcohol, gasoline, nail polish remover or thinner to clean leather upholstery.
3 After cleaning, regularly treat leather upholstery with a leather wax. Never use car wax on leather upholstery.
4 In areas where the interior of the vehicle is subject to bright sunlight, cover leather seats with a sheet if the vehicle is to be left out for any length of time.

5 Body repair – minor damage

See photo sequence

Repair of scratches

1 If the scratch is superficial and does not penetrate to the metal of the body, repair is very simple. Lightly rub the scratched area with a fine rubbing compound to remove loose paint and built up wax. Rinse the area with clean water.
2 Apply touch-up paint to the scratch, using a small brush. Continue to apply thin layers of paint until the surface of the paint in the scratch is level with the surrounding paint. Allow the new paint at least two weeks to harden, then blend it into the surrounding paint by rubbing with a very fine rubbing compound. Finally, apply a coat of wax to the scratch area.
3 If the scratch has penetrated the paint and exposed the metal of the body, causing the metal to rust, a different repair technique is required. Remove all loose rust from the bottom of the scratch with a pocket knife, then apply rust inhibiting paint to prevent the formation of rust in the future. Using a rubber or nylon applicator, coat the scratched area with glaze-type filler. If required, the filler can be mixed with thinner to provide a very thin paste, which is ideal for filling narrow scratches. Before the glaze filler in the scratch hardens, wrap a piece of smooth cotton cloth around the tip of a finger. Dip the cloth in thinner and then quickly wipe it along the surface of the scratch. This will ensure that the surface of the filler is slightly hollow. The scratch can now be painted over as described earlier in this section.

Repair of dents

4 When repairing dents, the first job is to pull the dent out until the affected area is as close as possible to its original shape. There is no point in trying to restore the original shape completely as the metal in the damaged area will have stretched on impact and cannot be restored to its original contours. It is better to bring the level of the dent up to a point which is about 1/8-inch below the level of the surrounding metal. In cases where the dent is very shallow, it is not worth trying to pull it out at all.
5 If the back side of the dent is accessible, it can be hammered out gently from behind using a soft-face hammer. While doing this, hold a block of wood firmly against the opposite side of the metal to absorb the hammer blows and prevent the metal from being stretched.
6 If the dent is in a section of the body which has double layers, or some other factor makes it inaccessible from behind, a different technique is required. Drill several small holes through the metal inside the damaged area, particularly in the deeper sections. Screw long, self tapping screws into the holes just enough for them to get a good grip in the metal. Now the dent can be pulled out by pulling on the protruding heads of the screws with locking pliers.
7 The next stage of repair is the removal of paint from the damaged area and from an inch or so of the surrounding metal. This is easily done with a wire brush or sanding disk in a drill motor, although it can be done just as effectively by hand with sandpaper. To complete the preparation for filling, score the surface of the bare metal with a screwdriver or the tang of a file or drill small holes in the affected area. This will provide a good grip for the filler material. To complete the repair, see the Section on filling and painting.

Repair of rust holes or gashes

8 Remove all paint from the affected area and from an inch or so of the surrounding metal using a sanding disk or wire brush mounted in a drill motor. If these are not available, a few sheets of sandpaper will do the job just as effectively.
9 With the paint removed, you will be able to determine the severity of the corrosion and decide whether to replace the whole panel, if possible, or repair the affected area. New body panels are not as expensive as most people think and it is often quicker to install a new panel than to repair large areas of rust.
10 Remove all trim pieces from the affected area except those which will act as a guide to the original shape of the damaged body, such as headlight shells, etc. Using metal snips or a hacksaw blade, remove all loose metal and any other metal that is badly affected by rust. Hammer the edges of the hole inward to create a slight depression for the filler material.
11 Wire brush the affected area to remove the powdery rust from the surface of the metal. If the back of the rusted area is accessible, treat it with rust inhibiting paint.
12 Before filling is done, block the hole in some way. This can be done with sheet metal riveted or screwed into place, or by stuffing the hole with wire mesh.
13 Once the hole is blocked off, the affected area can be filled and painted. See the following subsection on filling and painting.

Filling and painting

14 Many types of body fillers are available, but generally speaking, body repair kits which contain filler paste and a tube of resin hardener are best for this type of repair work. A wide, flexible plastic or nylon applicator will be necessary for imparting a smooth and contoured finish to the surface of the filler material. Mix up a small amount of filler on a clean piece of wood or cardboard (use the hardener sparingly). Follow the manufacturer's instructions on the package, otherwise the filler will set incorrectly.
15 Using the applicator, apply the filler paste to the prepared area. Draw the applicator across the surface of the filler to achieve the desired contour and to level the filler surface. As soon as a contour that approximates the original one is achieved, stop working the paste. If you continue, the paste will begin to stick to the applicator. Continue to add thin layers of paste at 20-minute intervals until the level of the filler is just above the surrounding metal.
16 Once the filler has hardened, the excess can be removed with a body file. From then on, progressively finer grades of sandpaper should be used, starting with a 180-grit paper and finishing with 600-grit wet or dry paper. Always wrap the sandpaper around a flat rubber or wooden block, otherwise the surface of the filler will not be completely flat. During the sanding of the filler surface, the wet-or-dry paper should be periodically rinsed in water. This will ensure that a very smooth finish is produced in the final stage.
17 At this point, the repair area should be surrounded by a ring of bare metal, which in turn should be encircled by the finely feathered edge of good paint. Rinse the repair area with clean water until all of the dust produced by the sanding operation is gone.

18 Spray the entire area with a light coat of primer. This will reveal any imperfections in the surface of the filler. Repair the imperfections with fresh filler paste or glaze filler and once more smooth the surface with sandpaper. Repeat this spray-and-repair procedure until you are satisfied that the surface of the filler and the feathered edge of the paint are perfect. Rinse the area with clean water and allow it to dry completely.
19 The repair area is now ready for painting. Spray painting must be carried out in a warm, dry, windless and dust free atmosphere. These conditions can be created if you have access to a large indoor work area, but if you are forced to work in the open, you will have to pick the day very carefully. If you are working indoors, dousing the floor in the work area with water will help settle the dust which would otherwise be in the air. If the repair area is confined to one body panel, mask off the surrounding panels. This will help minimize the effects of a slight mismatch in paint color. Trim pieces such as chrome strips, door handles, etc., will also need to be masked off or removed. Use masking tape and several thicknesses of newspaper for the masking operations.
20 Before spraying, shake the paint can thoroughly, then spray a test area until the spray painting technique is mastered. Cover the repair area with a thick coat of primer. The thickness should be built up using several thin layers of primer rather than one thick one. Using 600-grit wet-or-dry sandpaper, rub down the surface of the primer until it is very smooth. While doing this, the work area should be thoroughly rinsed with water and the wet-or-dry sandpaper periodically rinsed as well. Allow the primer to dry before spraying additional coats.
21 Spray on the top coat, again building up the thickness by using several thin layers of paint. Begin spraying in the center of the repair area and then, using a circular motion, work out until the whole repair area and about two inches of the surrounding original paint is covered. Remove all masking material 10 to 15 minutes after spraying on the final coat of paint. Allow the new paint at least two weeks to harden, then use a very fine rubbing compound to blend the edges of the new paint into the existing paint. Finally, apply a coat of wax.

6 Body repair – major damage

1 Major damage must be repaired by an auto body shop specifically equipped to perform unibody repairs. These shops have the specialized equipment required to do the job properly.
2 If the damage is extensive, the body must be checked for proper alignment or the vehicle's handling characteristics may be adversely affected and other components may wear at an accelerated rate.
3 Due to the fact that all of the major body components (hood, fenders, etc.) are separate and replaceable units, any seriously damaged components should be replaced rather than repaired. Sometimes the components can be found in a wrecking yard that specializes in used vehicle components, often at considerable savings over the cost of new parts.

7 Hinges and locks – maintenance

Once every 3000 miles, or every three months, the hinges and latch assemblies on the doors, hood and trunk should be given a few drops of light oil or lock lubricant. The door latch strikers should also be lubricated with a thin coat of grease to reduce wear and ensure free movement. Lubricate the door and trunk locks with spray-on graphite lubricant.

8 Fixed glass – replacement

Replacement of the windshield and fixed glass requires the use of special fast-setting adhesive/caulk materials and some specialized tools and techniques. These operations should be left to a dealer service department or a shop specializing in glass work.

9 Hood – removal, installation and adjustment

Refer to illustrations 9.2, 9.3 and 9.11

Note: *The hood is heavy and somewhat awkward to remove and install – at least two people should perform this procedure.*

Removal and installation

1 Use blankets or pads to cover the cowl area of the body and the fenders. This will protect the body and paint as the hood is lifted off.
2 Scribe or paint alignment marks around the bolt heads to insure proper alignment during installation **(see illustration)**.
3 Disconnect any cables or wire harnesses which will interfere with removal. Remove the front hood support shock **(see illustration)**.

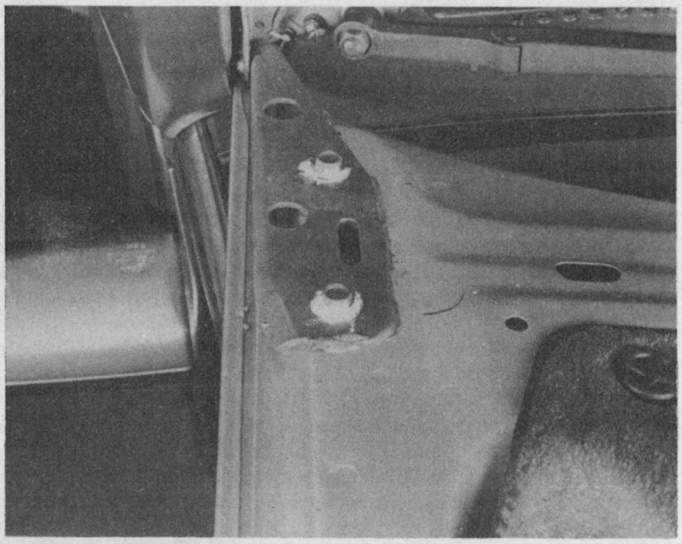

9.2 Make marks around the hood hinge bolts before loosening them

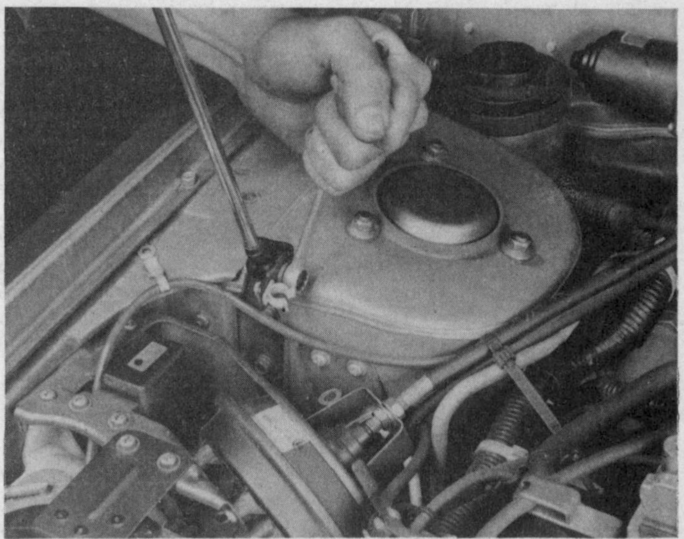

9.3 Loosen the bolts and remove the front hood support shock. Have an assistant hold the hood during the removal

4 Have an assistant support the weight of the hood. Remove the hinge-to-hood nuts or bolts.
5 Lift off the hood.
6 Installation is the reverse of removal.

Adjustment

7 Fore-and-aft and side-to-side adjustment of the hood is done by moving the hood in relation to the hinge plate after loosening the bolts or nuts.
8 Scribe a line around the entire hinge plate so you can judge the amount of movement.
9 Loosen the bolts or nuts and move the hood into correct alignment. Move it only a little at a time. Tighten the hinge bolts or nuts and carefully lower the hood to check the alignment.
10 If necessary after installation, the entire hood latch assembly can be adjusted up-and-down as well as from side-to-side on the radiator support so the hood closes securely and is flush with the fenders. To do this, scribe a line around the hood latch mounting bolts to provide a reference point. Then loosen the bolts and reposition the latch assembly as necessary. Following adjustment, retighten the mounting bolts.
11 Adjust the front hood latch by loosening the latch retaining bolts and sliding the assembly up or down **(see illustration)**.
12 The hood latch assembly, as well as the hinges, should be periodically lubricated with white lithium-base grease to prevent sticking and wear.
13 Installation is the reverse of removal.

9.11 Adjust the front hood latch by loosening the retaining bolts with a box end wrench and moving the assembly up or down into proper adjustment

10 Door trim panel – removal and installation

Refer to illustrations 10.2, 10.3, 10.4 and 10.7

1 Disconnect the negative cable from the battery.
2 Remove the plug in the armrest to gain access to the armrest retaining screw **(see illustration)**.
3 Remove all door trim panel retaining screws and door pull/armrest assemblies **(see illustration)**.
4 On manual window regulator equipped models, remove the window crank. On power regulator models, pry out the control switch assembly and unplug it **(see illustration)**.
5 Insert a putty knife between the trim panel and the door and disengage the retaining clips. Work around the outer edge until the panel is free.
6 Once all of the clips are disengaged, detach the trim panel, unplug any wire harness connectors and remove the trim panel from the vehicle.

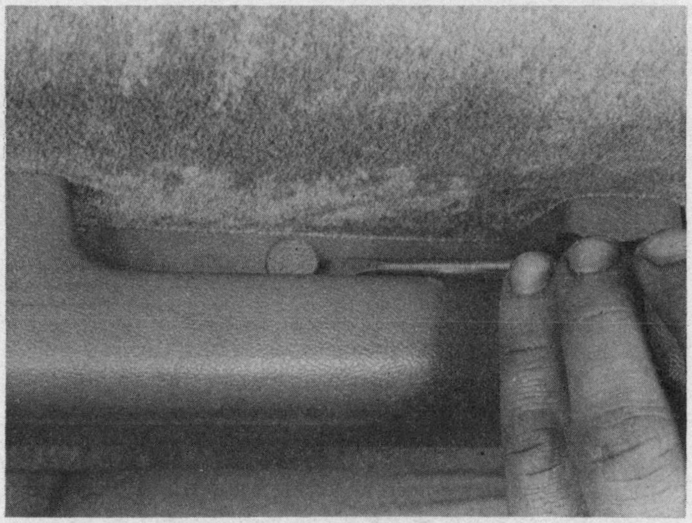

10.2 Remove the plug in the armrest to gain access to the armrest retaining screw

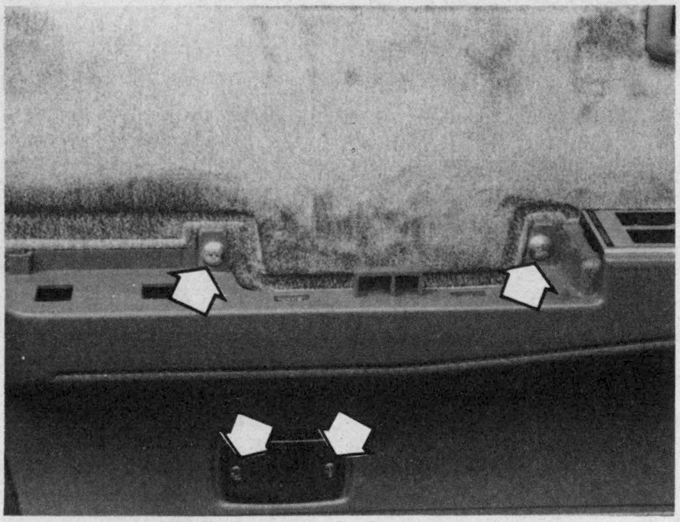

10.3 Remove all the door trim panel retaining screws (arrows)

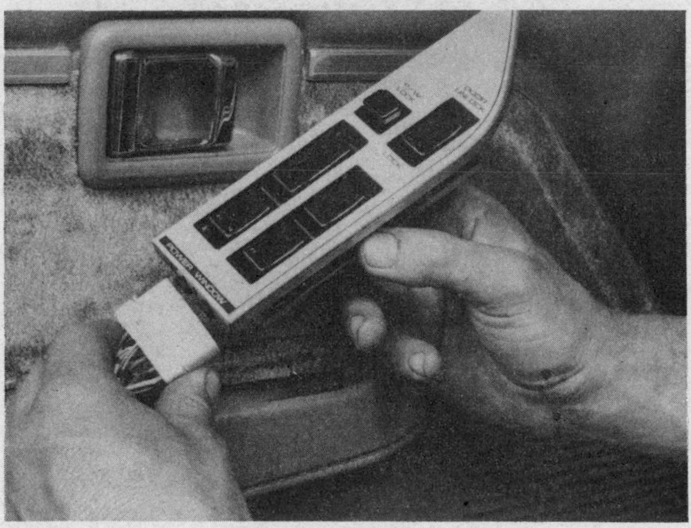

10.4 Pry the power window control switch up and disconnect the electrical connector

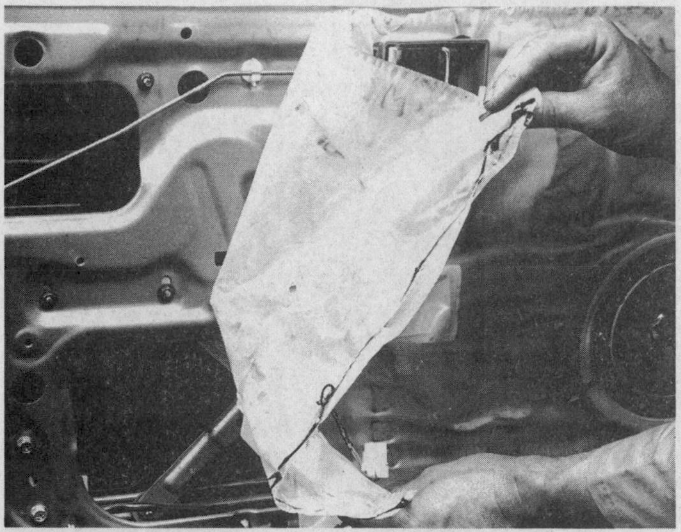

10.7 Carefully peel back the plastic watershield

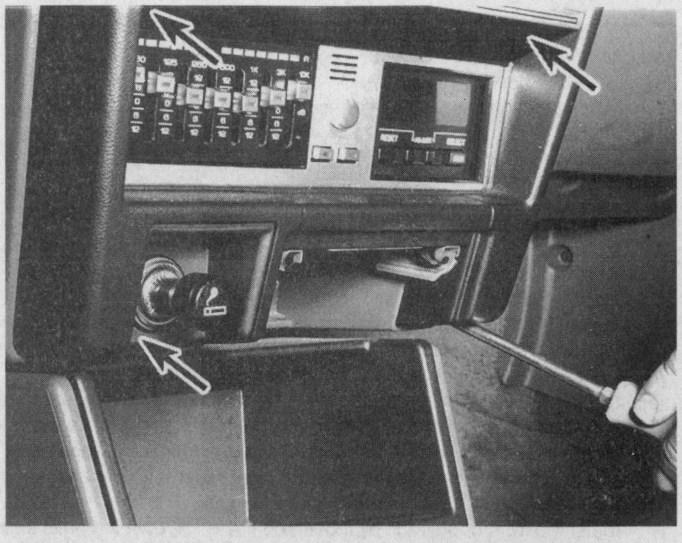

11.1a Remove the screws that retain the finish panel surrounding the radio and ashtray (arrows)

7 For access to the inner door, carefully peel back the plastic watershield **(see illustration)**.

8 Prior to installation of the door panel, be sure to reinstall any clips in the panel which may have come out during the removal procedure and remain in the door itself.

9 Plug in the wire harness connectors and place the panel in position in the door. Press the door panel into place until the clips are seated and install the armrest/door pulls. Install the manual regulator window crank or power window switch assembly.

11 Instrument panel finish panels – removal and installation

Warning: *1992 models are equipped with a Supplemental Restraint System (SRS), more commonly known as an airbag. Always disconnect both battery cables and wait ten minutes before working in the vicinity of the impact sensors, steering wheel and column or instrument panel to avoid the possibility of accidental deployment of the air bag, which could cause personal injury (see Chapter 12). The yellow wiring harness and connectors routed through the center console, under hood and right side wheel well are for this system. Do not use electrical test equipment on any of the airbag system wiring or tamper with them in any way.*

Instrument cluster finish panel

Refer to illustrations 11.1a, 11.1b and 11.1c

1 Remove the retaining screws, rotate the panel up and lift it from the instrument panel **(see illustrations)**. Installation is the reverse of removal.

Lower finish panel

Refer to illustrations 11.2a and 11.2b

2 Remove the retaining screws, pull the panel down, unplug any electrical connectors and detach the panel **(see illustrations)**. Installation is the reverse of removal.

Glove compartment

3 Open the glove compartment for access, remove the retaining screws and pull the assembly down out of the instrument panel **(see illustrations 11.2a and 11.2b)**. Installation is the reverse of removal.

11.1b Remove the screws that retain the finish panel below the instrument cluster (arrows)

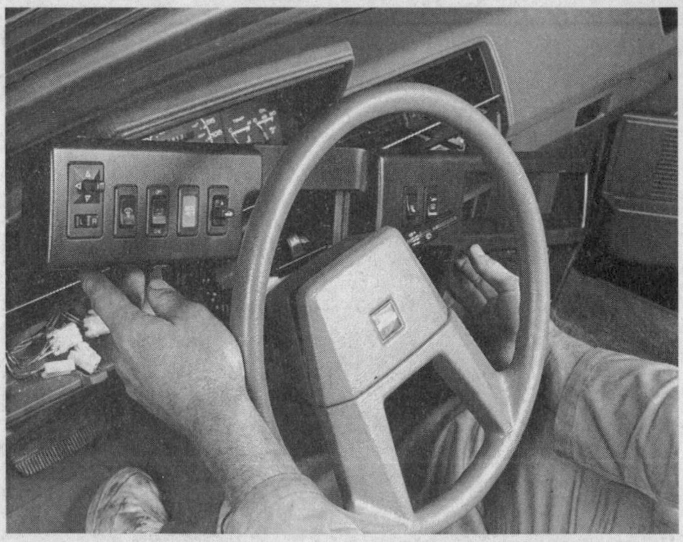

11.1c Pull the panel up and detach it from the instrument panel

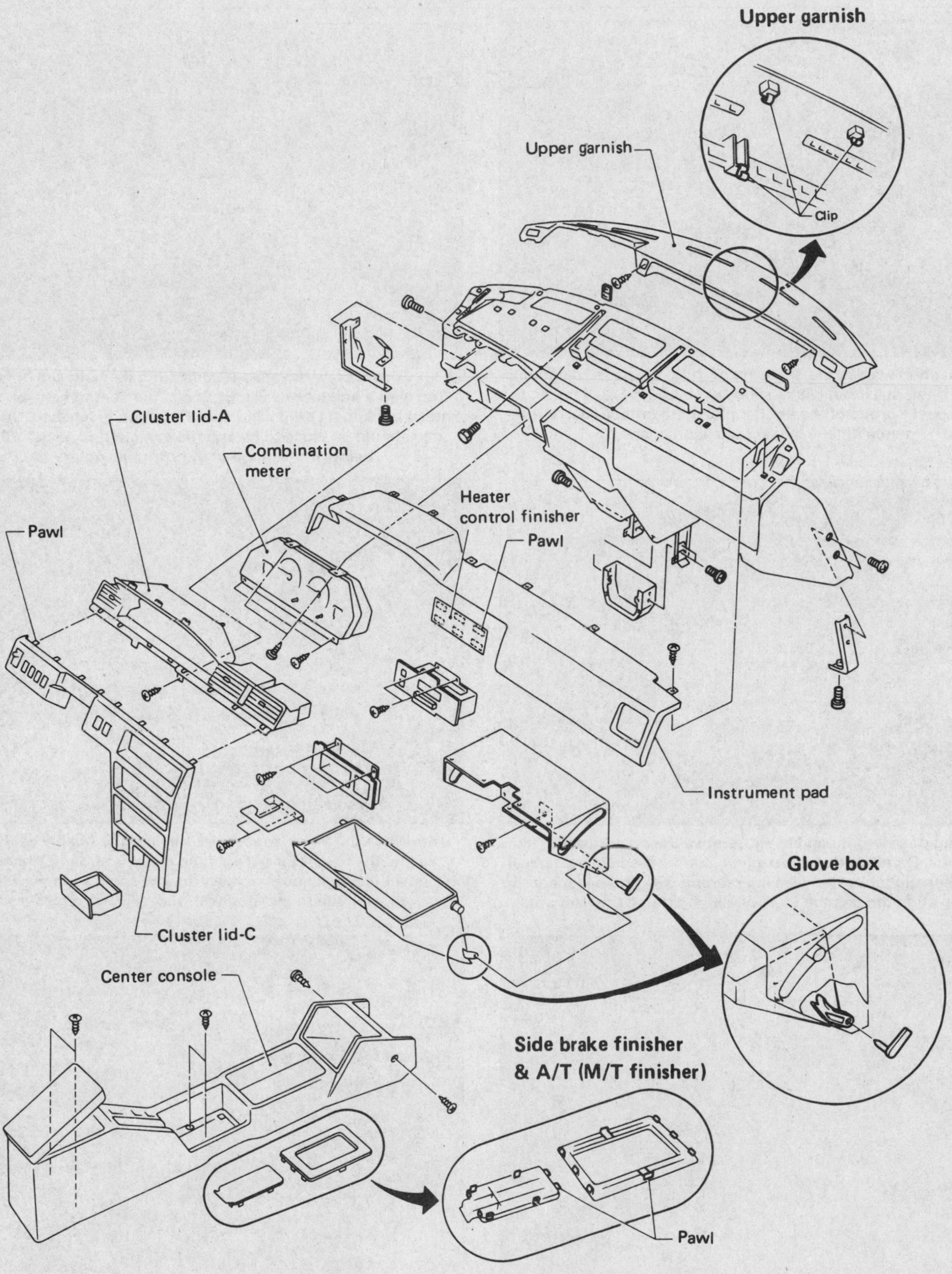

11.2a Instrument panel finish panels on 1985 through 1988 models

These photos illustrate a method of repairing simple dents. They are intended to supplement *Body repair - minor damage* in this Chapter and should not be used as the sole instructions for body repair on these vehicles.

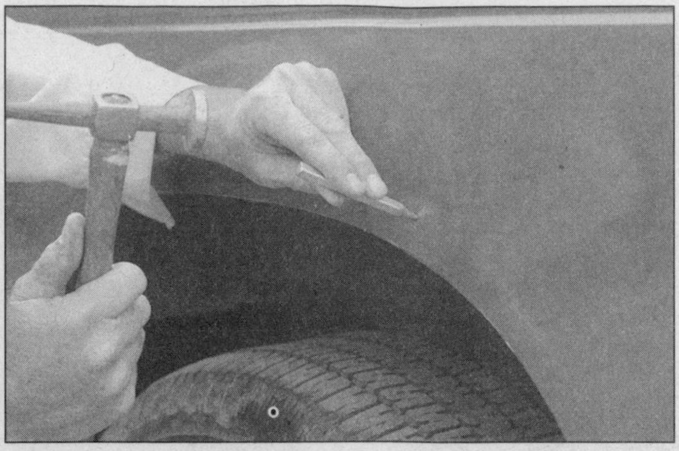

1 If you can't access the backside of the body panel to hammer out the dent, pull it out with a slide-hammer-type dent puller. In the deepest portion of the dent or along the crease line, drill or punch hole(s) at least one inch apart . . .

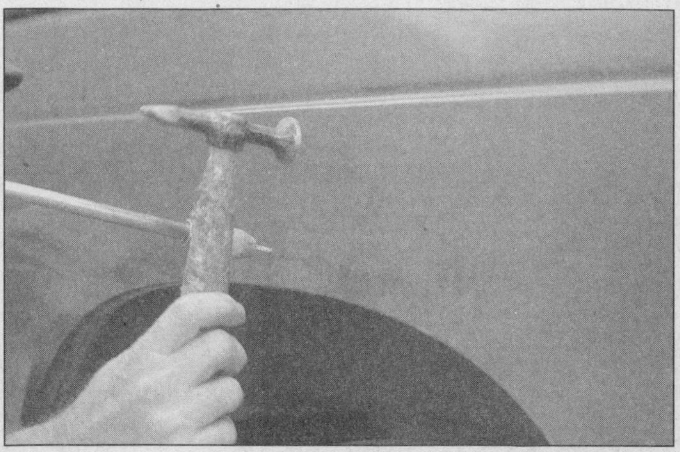

2 . . . then screw the slide-hammer into the hole and operate it. Tap with a hammer near the edge of the dent to help 'pop' the metal back to its original shape. When you're finished, the dent area should be close to its original contour and about 1/8-inch below the surface of the surrounding metal

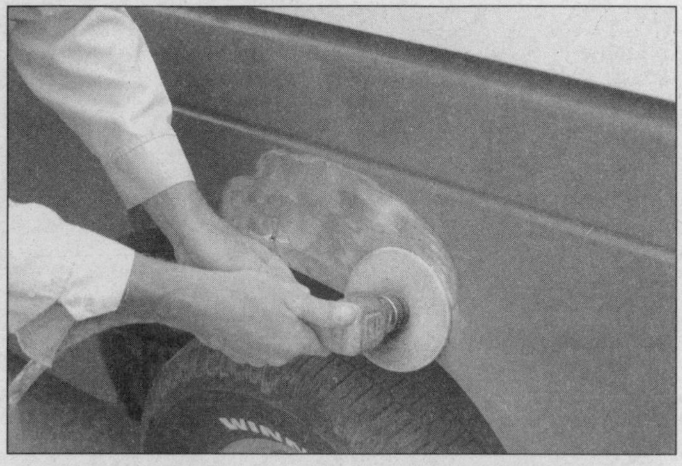

3 Using coarse-grit sandpaper, remove the paint down to the bare metal. Hand sanding works fine, but the disc sander shown here makes the job faster. Use finer (about 320-grit) sandpaper to feather-edge the paint at least one inch around the dent area

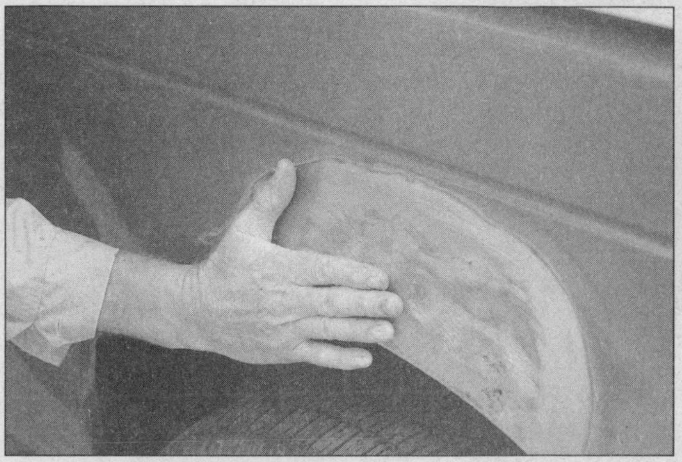

4 When the paint is removed, touch will probably be more helpful than sight for telling if the metal is straight. Hammer down the high spots or raise the low spots as necessary. Clean the repair area with wax/silicone remover

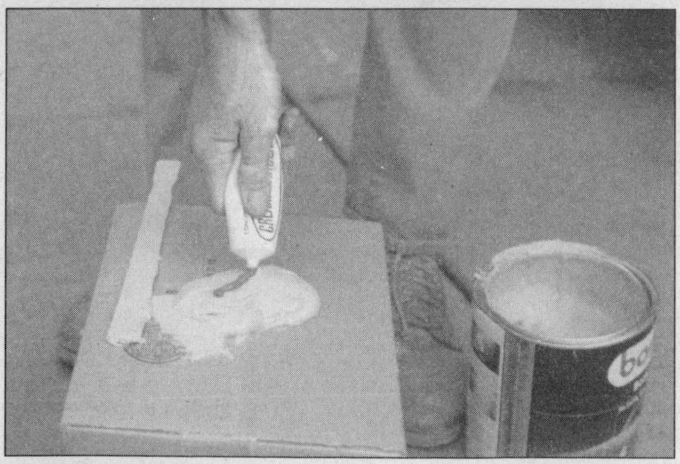

5 Following label instructions, mix up a batch of plastic filler and hardener. The ratio of filler to hardener is critical, and, if you mix it incorrectly, it will either not cure properly or cure too quickly (you won't have time to file and sand it into shape)

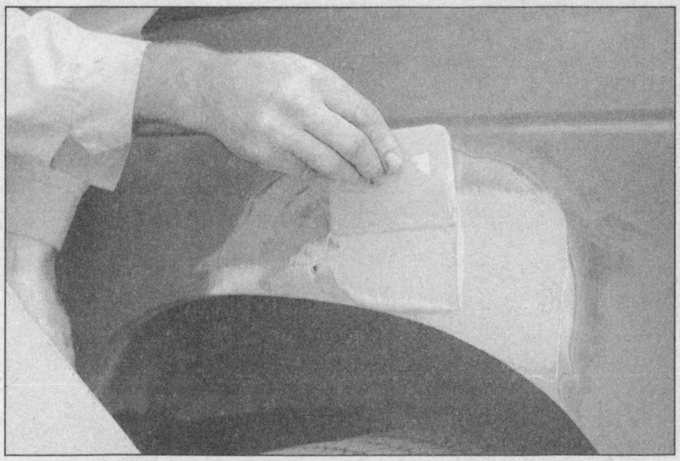

6 Working quickly so the filler doesn't harden, use a plastic applicator to press the body filler firmly into the metal, assuring it bonds completely. Work the filler until it matches the original contour and is slightly above the surrounding metal

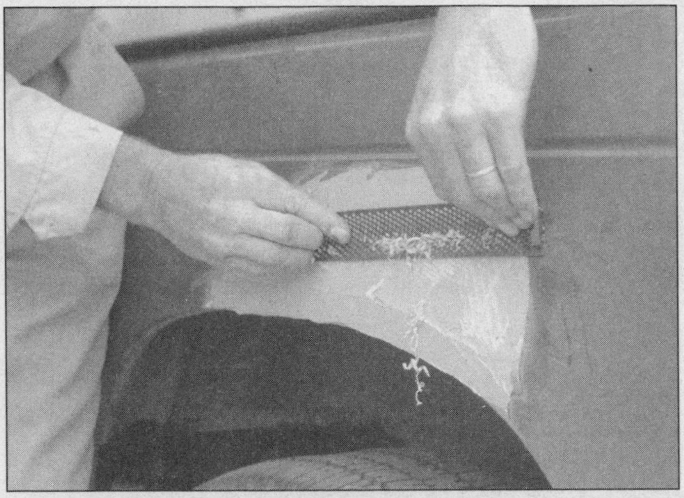

7 Let the filler harden until you can just dent it with your fingernail. Use a body file or Surform tool (shown here) to rough-shape the filler

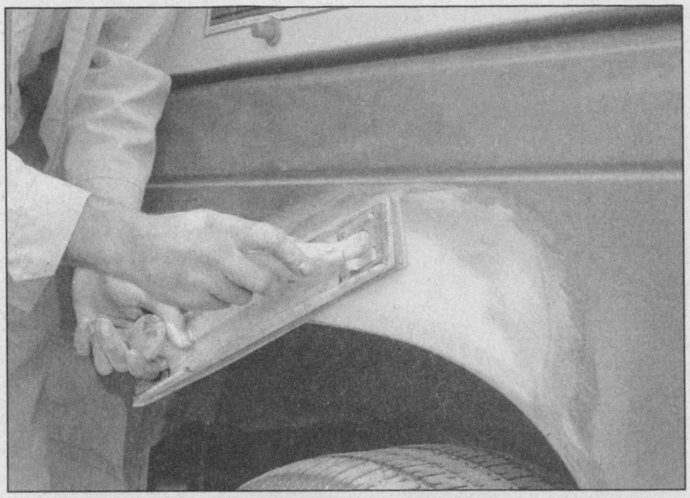

8 Use coarse-grit sandpaper and a sanding board or block to work the filler down until it's smooth and even. Work down to finer grits of sandpaper - always using a board or block - ending up with 360 or 400 grit

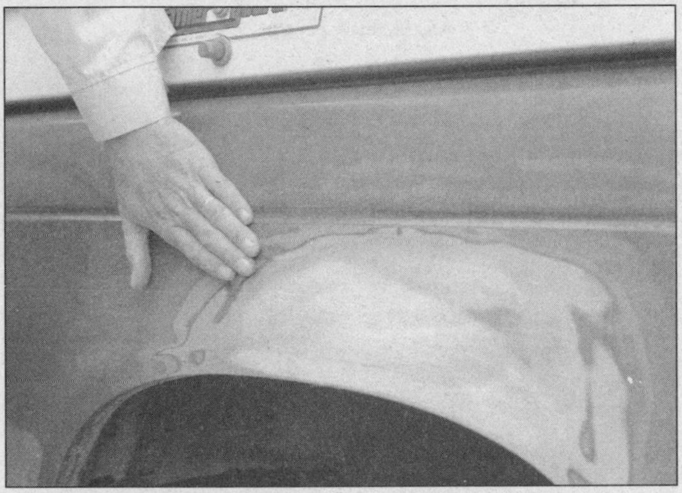

9 You shouldn't be able to feel any ridge at the transition from the filler to the bare metal or from the bare metal to the old paint. As soon as the repair is flat and uniform, remove the dust and mask off the adjacent panels or trim pieces

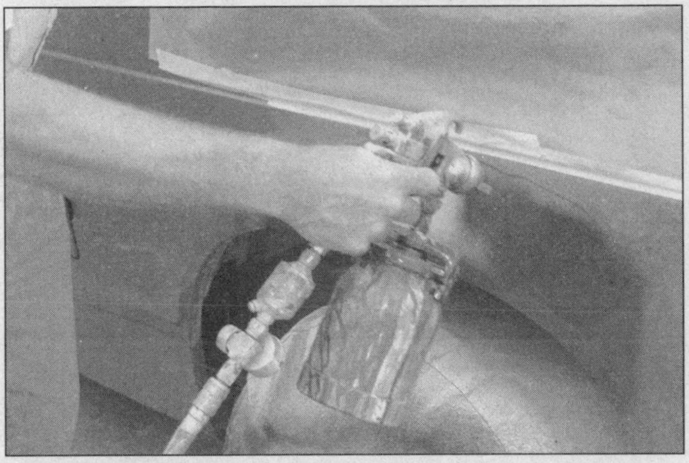

10 Apply several layers of primer to the area. Don't spray the primer on too heavy, so it sags or runs, and make sure each coat is dry before you spray on the next one. A professional-type spray gun is being used here, but aerosol spray primer is available inexpensively from auto parts stores

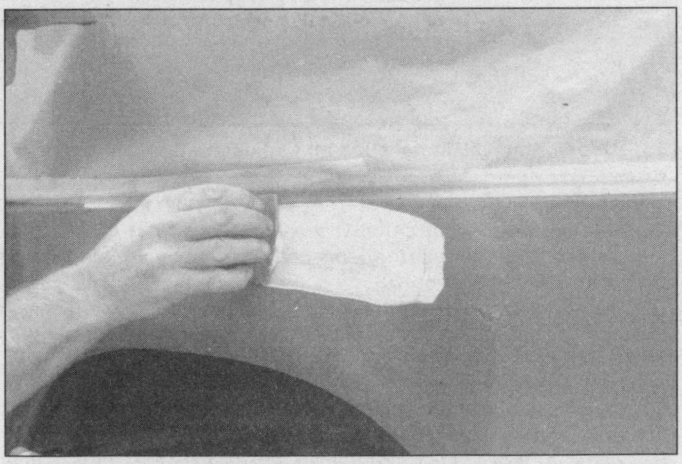

11 The primer will help reveal imperfections or scratches. Fill these with glazing compound. Follow the label instructions and sand it with 360 or 400-grit sandpaper until it's smooth. Repeat the glazing, sanding and respraying until the primer reveals a perfectly smooth surface

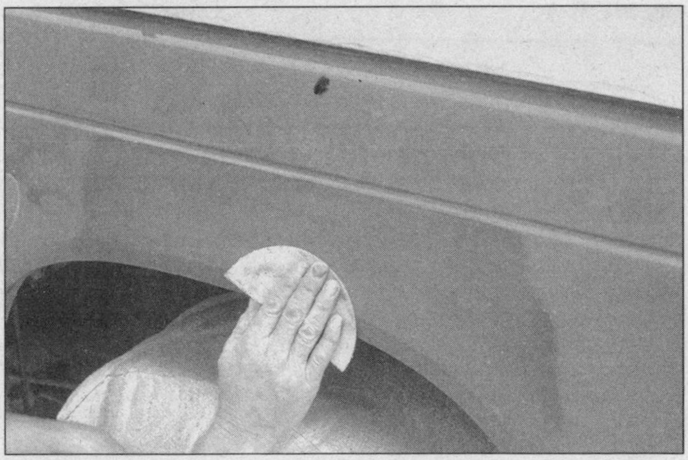

12 Finish sand the primer with very fine sandpaper (400 or 600-grit) to remove the primer overspray. Clean the area with water and allow it to dry. Use a tack rag to remove any dust, then apply the finish coat. Don't attempt to rub out or wax the repair area until the paint has dried completely (at least two weeks)

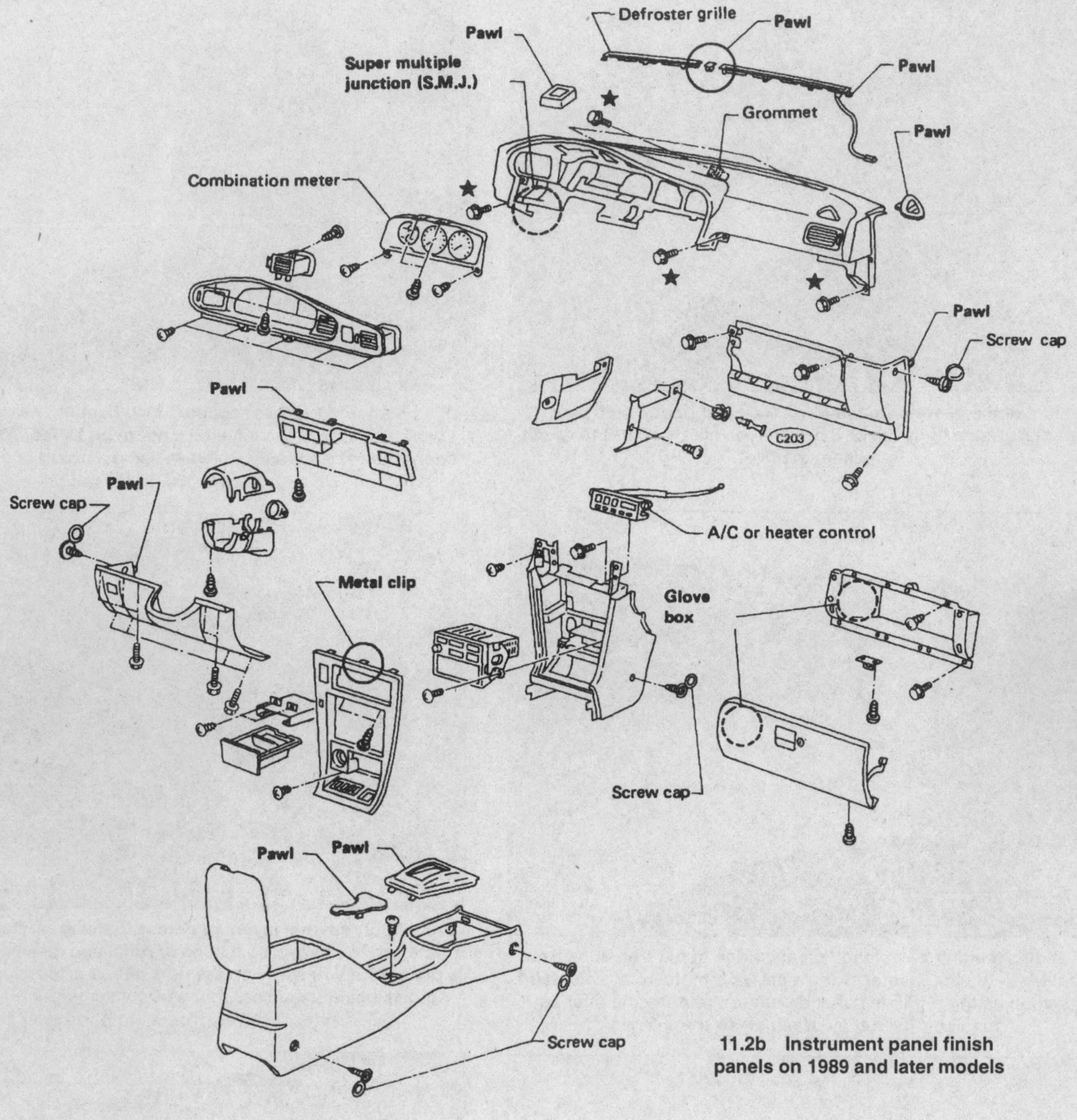

11.2b Instrument panel finish panels on 1989 and later models

12 Steering column cover – removal and installation

Refer to illustration 12.1

Warning: *1992 models are equipped with a Supplemental Restraint System (SRS), more commonly known as an airbag. Always disconnect both battery cables and wait ten minutes before working in the vicinity of the impact sensors, steering wheel and column or instrument panel to avoid the possibility of accidental deployment of the air bag, which could cause personal injury (see Chapter 12). The yellow wiring harness and connectors routed through the center console, under hood and right side wheel well are for this system. Do not use electrical test equipment on any of the airbag system wiring or tamper with them in any way.*

1 Remove the retaining screws **(see illustration)**.
2 Carefully pry the halves of the cover apart. Unplug any electrical connectors and remove the cover halves from the steering column.
3 Installation is the reverse of removal.

13 Door – removal, installation and adjustment

Refer to illustrations 13.2 and 13.5

1 Remove the door trim panel. Disconnect any wire harness connectors and push them through the door opening so they won't interfere with door removal (see Section 10).
2 Place a jack or jackstand under the door or have an assistant on hand to support it when the hinge bolts are removed. **Note:** *If a jack or jackstand is used, place a rag between it and the door to protect the door's painted surfaces* **(see illustration)**.
3 Scribe around the door hinges.
4 Remove the pin in the door safety catch.
5 Remove the door hinge pin retainers and drive out the pins **(see illustration)**.
6 Installation is the reverse of removal.
7 Following installation of the door, check the alignment and adjust it if necessary as follows:

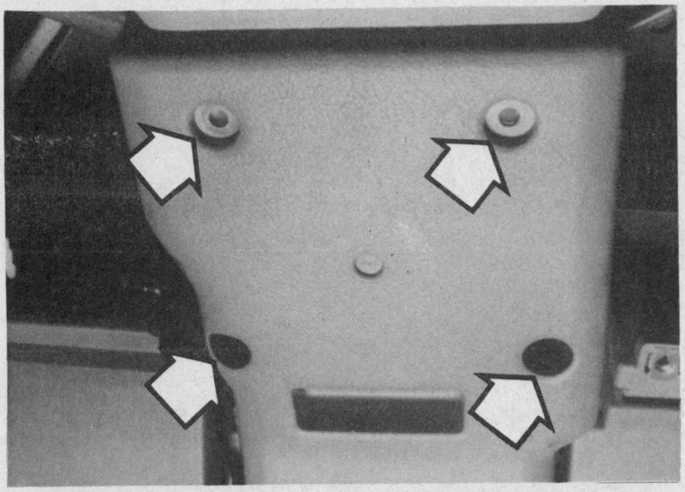

12.1 Remove the steering column cover retaining screws located under the steering column

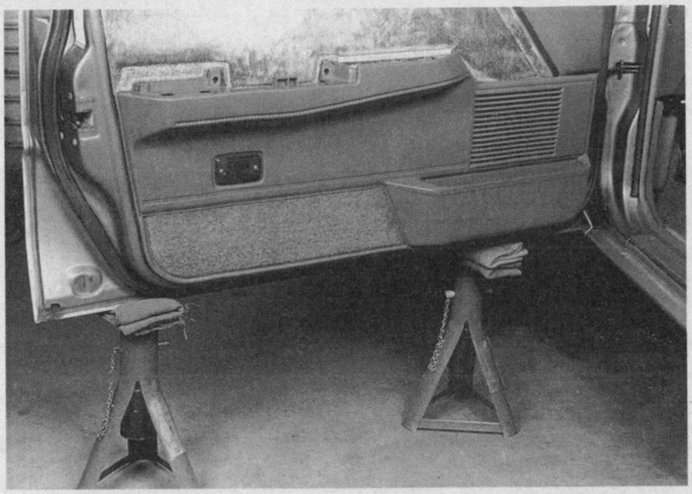

13.2 Place jackstands under the door with rags to protect the paint

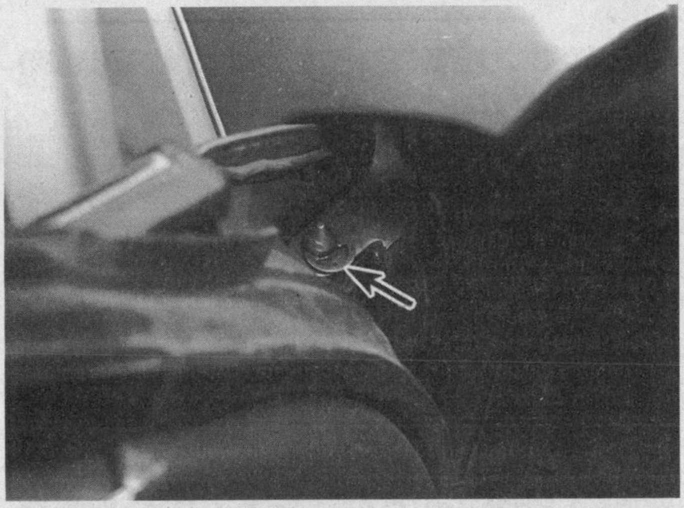

13.5 Remove the door hinge pin retainers (arrow) and drive out the pins

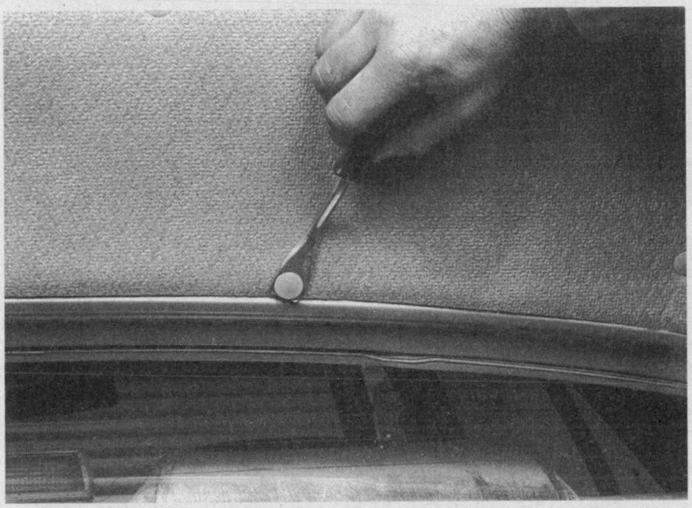

14.3 Remove the trunk pad body clips with an upholstery tool or a wide blade screwdriver

a) Up-and-down and forward-and-backward adjustments are made by loosening the hinge-to-body bolts and moving the door as necessary.
b) The door lock striker can also be adjusted both up-and-down and sideways to provide positive engagement with the lock mechanism. This is done by loosening the mounting bolts and moving the striker as necessary.

14 Trunk lid – removal, installation and adjustment

Refer to illustrations 14.3, 14.4 and 14.7

1 Open the trunk lid and cover the edges of the trunk compartment with pads or cloths to protect the painted surfaces when the lid is removed.
2 Disconnect any cables or wire harness connectors attached to the trunk lid that would interfere with removal.
3 Remove the trunk pad body clips and detach the trunk pad **(see illustration)**.
4 Scribe or paint alignment marks around the hinge mounting flanges **(see illustration)**. While an assistant supports the trunk lid, remove the hinge bolts from both sides and lift it off.
5 Installation is the reverse of removal. **Note:** *When reinstalling the trunk lid, align the hinge flanges with the marks made during removal.*
6 After installation, close the lid and see if it's in proper alignment with the surrounding panels. Fore-and-aft and side-to-side adjustments of the lid are controlled by the position of the hinge bolts in the slots. To adjust it, loosen the hinge bolts, reposition the lid and retighten the bolts.
7 The height of the lid in relation to the surrounding body panels when closed can be adjusted by loosening the lock striker bolts, repositioning the striker and retightening the bolts **(see illustration)**.

15 Sunroof – lubrication and adjustment

Refer to illustrations 15.1, 15.2, 15.3 and 15.4

1 Open the sunroof and lubricate the lower channels of the sunroof rail assembly **(see illustration)**.
2 On 1985 and 1986 models only, locate the rear wedges, one on each side of the sunroof rail assemblies **(see illustration)**.
3 Close the sunroof and carefully observe the roller engage the wedge just before closing. Adjust the wedge to the specifications shown **(see illustration)**.
4 On 1987 through 1989 models, adjust only the sunroof mounting brackets by loosening the bolts and moving the sunroof into correct alignment **(see illustration)**.

16 Door lock, lock cylinder and handle – removal and installation

1 Remove the door trim panel and watershield (Section 10).
2 Remove the door window glass (Section 17).

14.4 Paint around the trunk hinges for alignment purposes

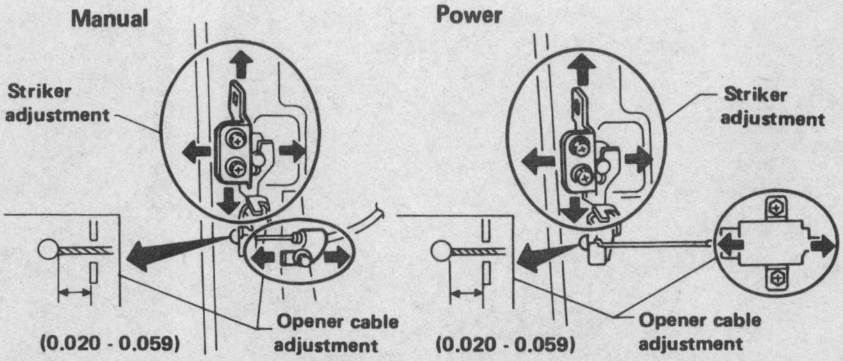

14.7 On 1989 models, adjust the door striker by measuring the travel of the opener cable (it should be 0.020 to 0.059-inch)

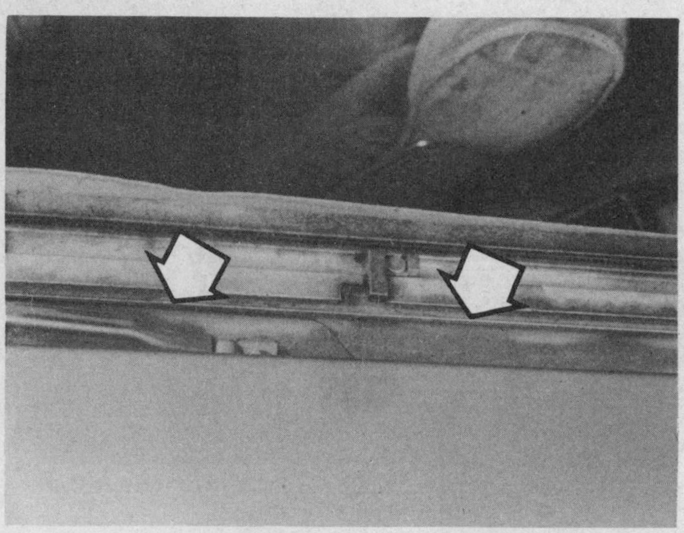

15.1 Be sure to lubricate only the lower channels where the rail travels (arrows)

15.2 Locate the rear wedges on each side of the rail assemblies (arrow)

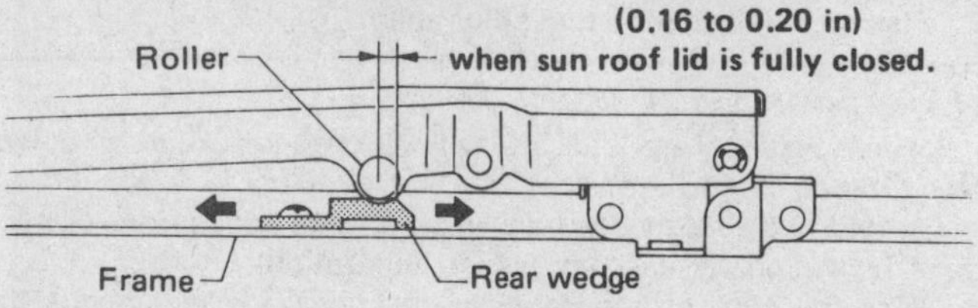

15.3 Adjust the rear wedge so the roller just runs onto the wedge when the sunroof is fully closed (1985 and 1986 models only)

Door lock

Refer to illustration 16.4

3 Reach in through the door service hole and disconnect the control link from the lock.

4 Remove the three door lock retaining screws from the end of the door **(see illustration)**. Remove the door lock.

5 Installation is the reverse of removal.

Inside handle

Refer to illustrations 16.6 and 16.7

6 Remove the retaining screw(s) **(see illustration)**.

7 Lift the handle assembly away from the door and simultaneously pull the handle out and remove the rod from behind the assembly **(see illustration)**.

8 Installation is the reverse of removal.

Outside handle (keyless entry system)

Refer to illustrations 16.9, 16.10 and 16.11

9 Disconnect the control link from the handle **(see illustration)**.

10 Disconnect the four harness connectors through the access hole near the speaker **(see illustration)**.

11 Remove the two inner nuts that retain the outside door handle **(see illustration)**.

12 Installation is the reverse of removal.

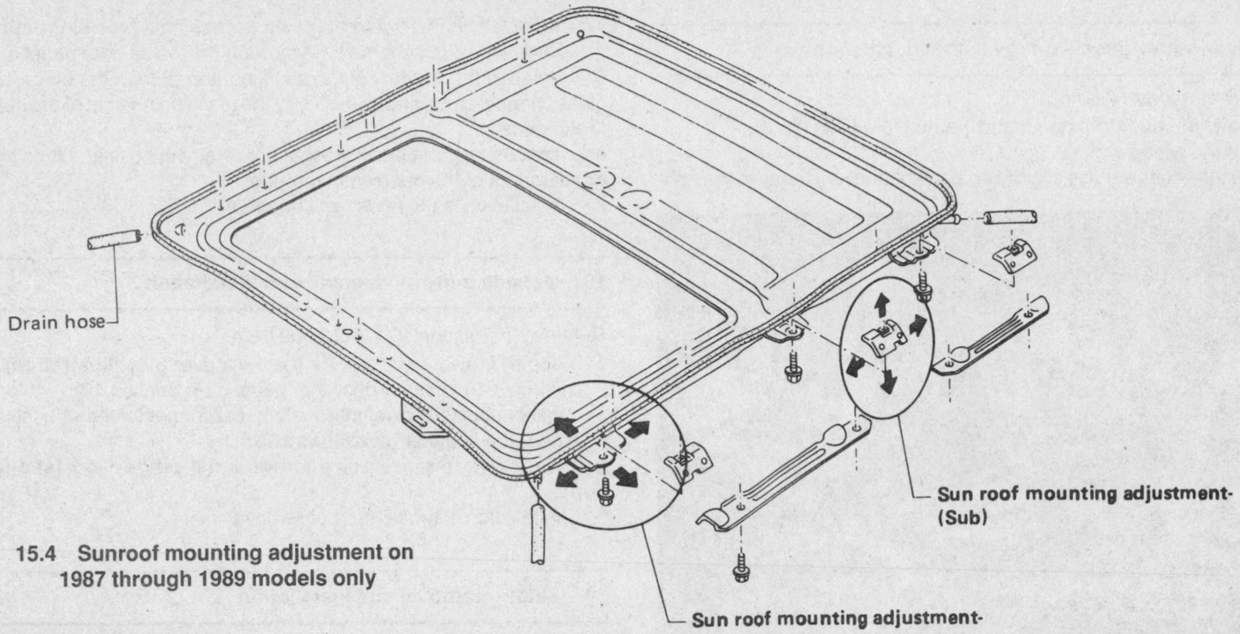

15.4 Sunroof mounting adjustment on 1987 through 1989 models only

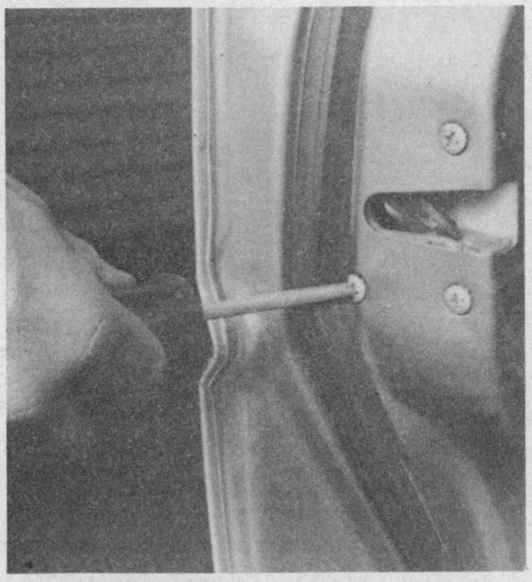

16.4 Remove the three door lock retaining screws

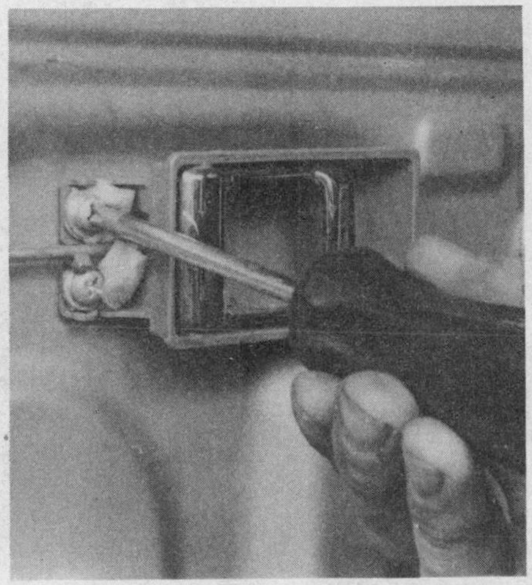

16.6 Remove the inside door handle retaining screws

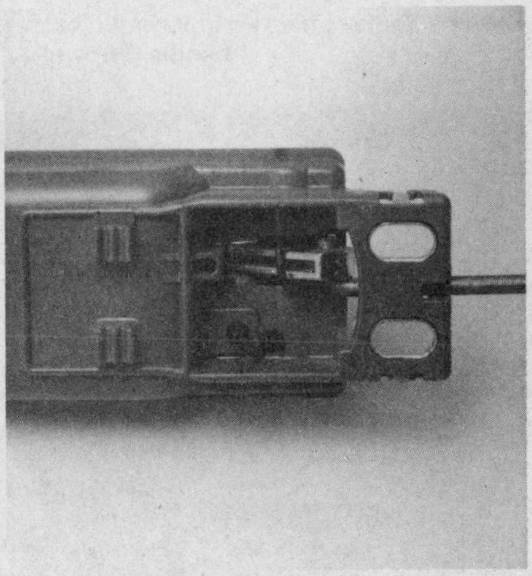

16.7 The handle must pivot out and up in order to release it from the rod (the handle assembly has been removed for viewing the backside of the mechanism)

16.9 Disconnect the control link from the handle by pulling it out of the bushing (arrow)

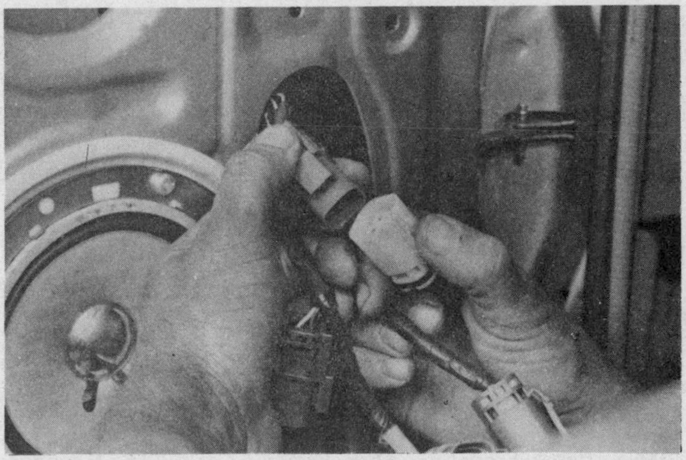

16.10 Disconnect the keyless entry system electrical connectors

17 Door window glass – removal and installation

Refer to illustrations 17.3 and 17.5

1 Remove the door trim panel and watershield (Section 10).
2 Lower the window glass.
3 Raise the window glass slightly from the bottom and remove the right side window channel nut through the access hole **(see illustration)**.
4 Remove the left channel nut through the inside door panel opening.
5 Remove the window glass by tilting it to detach the glass from the glass channel studs and then sliding the glass up and out of the door **(see illustration)**.
6 If necessary, remove the regulator retaining bolts and then slide the regulator out of the opening in the door.
7 Installation is the reverse of removal.

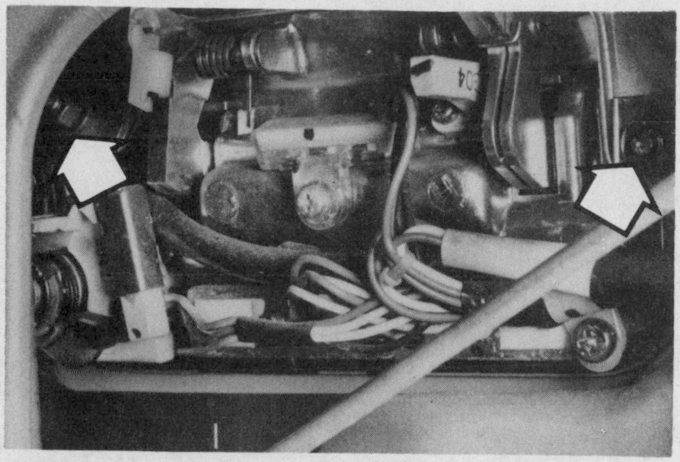

16.11 Remove the two inner nuts that retain the outside door handle (arrows)

18 Outside mirror – removal and installation

Refer to illustrations 18.1, 18.3 and 18.4

1 Use a screwdriver to pry off the trim cover **(see illustration)**.
2 Remove the interior door trim panel (see Section 10).
3 Disconnect the power mirror electrical connector through the access hole near the speaker **(see illustration)**.
4 Remove the three retaining screws and lift off the mirror **(see illustration)**.
5 Installation is the reverse of removal.

19 Seats – removal and installation

Front seat(s)

Refer to illustrations 19.1a and 19.1b

1 Remove the retaining bolts, unplug any electrical connectors and lift

17.3 Raise the window slightly and remove the right side window channel nut through the access hole

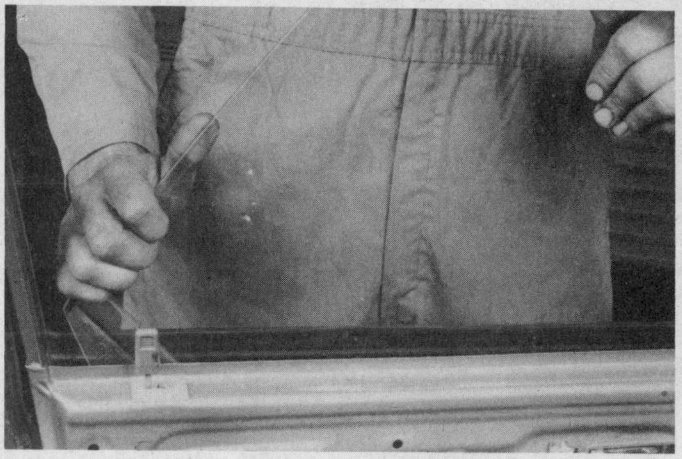

17.5 Tilt the window glass and detach it from the window channels – carefully lift the window glass out

18.1 Carefully pry off the trim cover to expose the outside mirror retaining screws

18.3 Disconnect the power mirror electrical connector through the access hole next to the speaker

18.4 Remove the three retaining screws (arrows) and lift off the mirror

the seats from the vehicle **(see illustrations)**.
2 Installation is the reverse of removal.

Rear seat

Refer to illustrations 19.5, 19.6 and 19.8

3 Pull up on the bottom section of the rear seat and take it out of the vehicle.
4 Pull down the seatback inserts and pull back the carpets to expose the rear seat panel trim.
5 With an upholstery tool or a screwdriver, remove the panel trim that covers the rear seat support brace **(see illustration)**.
6 Remove the rear seat retaining screws **(see illustration)**.
7 Push the rear seat up toward the rear window and lift the seat out.
8 Remove the four bolts that retain the rear seat support brace **(see illustration)** and lift the brace out, along with the seatback inserts.
9 Installation is the reverse of removal.

20 Fender apron seal – removal and installation

Refer to illustration 20.2

Warning: *1992 models are equipped with a Supplemental Restraint System (SRS), more commonly known as an airbag. Always disconnect both battery cables and wait ten minutes before working in the vicinity of the impact sensors, steering wheel and column or instrument panel to avoid the possibility of accidental deployment of the air bag, which could cause personal injury (see Chapter 12). The yellow wiring harness and connectors routed through the center console, under hood and right side wheel well are for this system. Do not use electrical test equipment on any of the airbag system wiring or tamper with them in any way.*

1 Raise the front of the vehicle, support it securely on jackstands and apply the parking brake. Remove the front wheel(s).
2 Pry out the retaining clips with a screwdriver, remove the retaining screws and lower the seal from the fender well **(see illustration)**.
3 Installation is the reverse of removal.

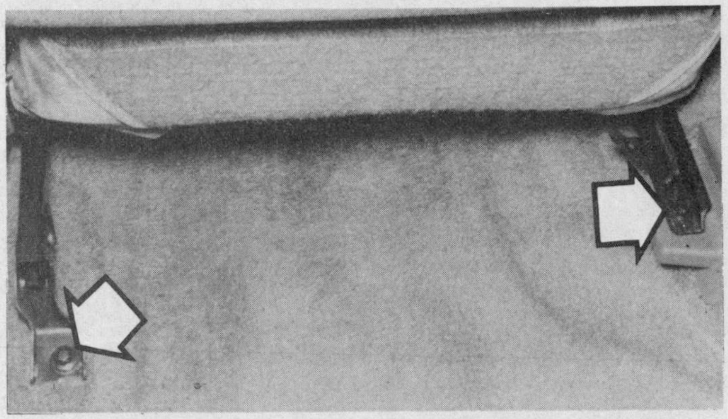

19.1a Move the seat forward and remove the Torx head bolts from the rear of the seat rails (arrows)

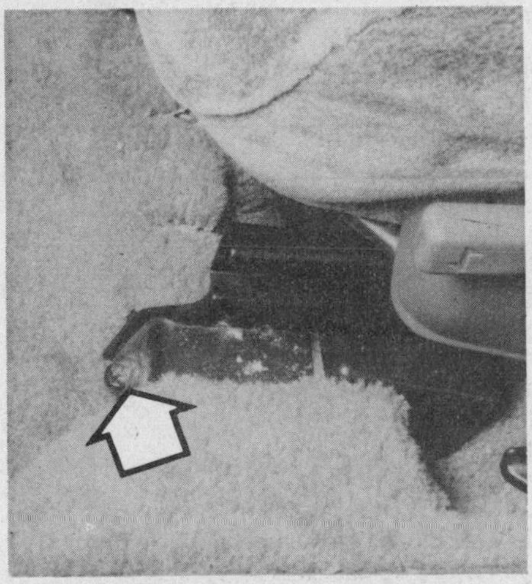

19.1b Move the seat backward and remove the Torx head bolts from the front of the seat rails (arrow)

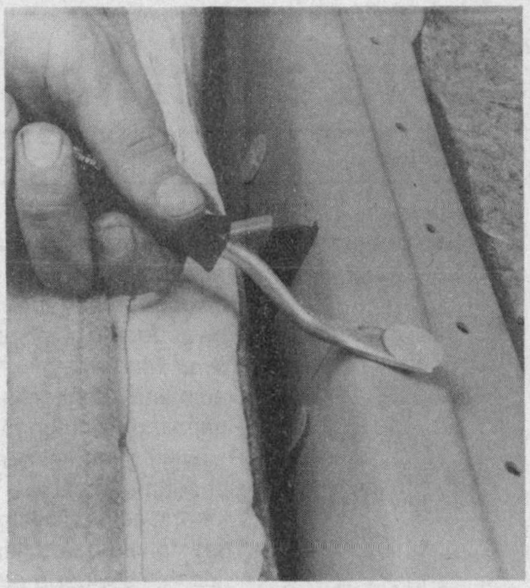

19.5 Use an upholstery tool or a wide blade screwdriver to remove the panel trim clips

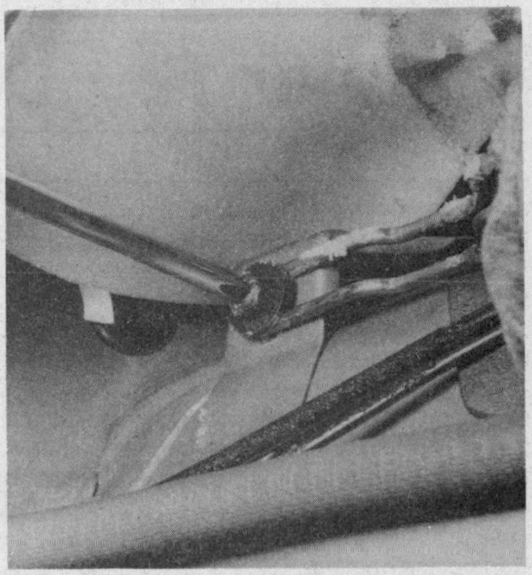

19.6 The rear seatback is retained by a screw on each side

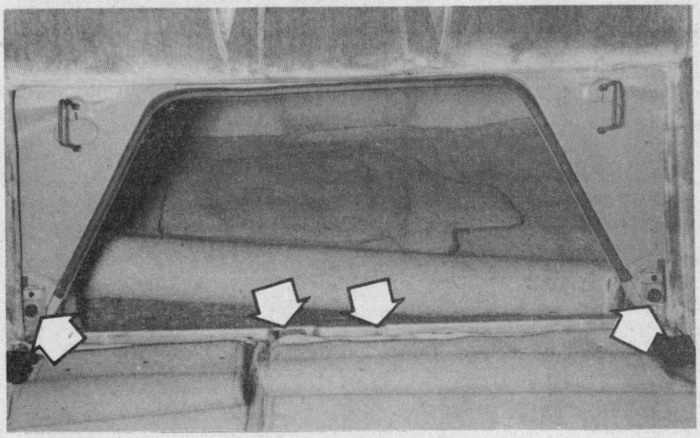

19.8 Remove the four bolts that retain the rear seat support brace (arrows)

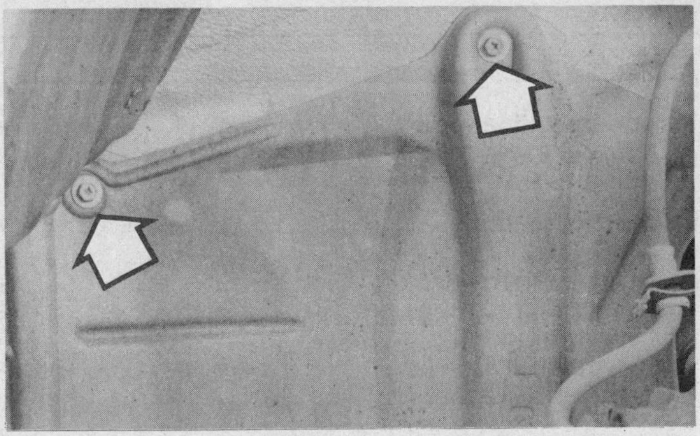

20.2 Remove the retaining screws and detach the fender apron seal from the inner fender (arrows)

Chapter 12 Chassis electrical system

Contents

Airbag system – general information 23
Battery check and maintenance .... See Chapter 1
Battery – removal and installation .... See Chapter 5
Brake light switch – removal, installation and adjustment .... See Chapter 9
Bulb replacement 14
Circuit breakers – general information 5
Combination switch – removal and installation 9
Cruise control system – description and check 18
Electrical troubleshooting – general information 2
Fuses – general information 3
Fusible links – general information 4
General information 1
Headlights – adjustment 13
Headlights – removal and installation 12
Ignition switch – removal and installation 8
Instrument cluster – removal and installation 16
Neutral start switch – replacement and adjustment ... See Chapter 7B
Power antenna – troubleshooting 17
Power door lock system – description and check 19
Power window system – description and check 20
Radio and speakers – removal and installation 11
Rear window defogger – troubleshooting 22
Relays – general information 6
Speedometer cable – removal and installation 21
Steering column switches – removal and installation 10
Turn signal/hazard flashers – check and replacement 7
Windshield wiper motor – removal and installation 15
Wiring diagrams – general information 24

Specifications

Torque specifications	**Ft-lbs**
Super Multiple Junction bolts	2.2 to 3.6

Bulb specifications	**Wattage (W)**
Headlight high/low	65/45
Front clearance light	8
Cornering light	27
Front side marker light	3.8
Front turn signal light	27
Rear combination light	
Turn signal	27
Brake/tail	27/8
Back-up	27
Rear side marker light	3.8

License plate light	
Sedan	8
Wagon	10
Interior light	10
Map light	8
Spot light	8
Step light	3.4
Glove box light	3.4
Trunk light	3.4
Luggage compartment light	10

1 General information

The electrical system is a 12-volt, negative ground type. Power for the lights and all electrical accessories is supplied by a lead/acid-type battery which is charged by the alternator.

This Chapter covers repair and service procedures for the various electrical components not associated with the engine. Information on the battery, alternator, distributor and starter motor can be found in Chapter 5.

It should be noted that when portions of the electrical system are serviced, the negative battery cable should be disconnected from the battery to prevent electrical shorts and/or fires.

2 Electrical troubleshooting – general information

A typical electrical circuit consists of an electrical component, any switches, relays, motors, fuses, fusible links or circuit breakers related to that component and the wiring and connectors that link the component to both the battery and the chassis. To help you pinpoint an electrical circuit problem, wiring diagrams are included at the end of this book.

Before tackling any troublesome electrical circuit, first study the appropriate wiring diagrams to get a complete understanding of what makes up that individual circuit. Trouble spots, for instance, can often be narrowed down by noting if other components related to the circuit are operating properly. If several components or circuits fail at one time, chances are the problem is in a fuse or ground connection, because several circuits are often routed through the same fuse and ground connections.

Electrical problems usually stem from simple causes, such as loose or corroded connections, a blown fuse, a melted fusible link or a bad relay. Visually inspect the condition of all fuses, wires and connections in a problem circuit before troubleshooting it.

If testing instruments are going to be utilized, use the diagrams to plan ahead of time where you will make the necessary connections in order to accurately pinpoint the trouble spot.

The basic tools needed for electrical troubleshooting include a circuit tester or voltmeter (a 12-volt bulb with a set of test leads can also be used), a continuity tester, which includes a bulb, battery and set of test leads, and a jumper wire, preferably with a circuit breaker incorporated, which can be used to bypass electrical components. Before attempting to locate a problem with test instruments, use the wiring diagram(s) to decide where to make the connections.

Voltage checks

Voltage checks should be performed if a circuit is not functioning properly. Connect one lead of a circuit tester to either the negative battery terminal or a known good ground. Connect the other lead to a connector in the circuit being tested, preferably nearest to the battery or fuse. If the bulb of the tester lights, voltage is present, which means that the part of the circuit between the connector and the battery is problem free. Continue checking the rest of the circuit in the same fashion. When you reach a point at which no voltage is present, the problem lies between that point and the last test point with voltage. Most of the time the problem can be traced to a loose connection. **Note:** *Keep in mind that some circuits receive voltage only when the ignition key is in the Accessory or Run position.*

Finding a short

One method of finding shorts in a circuit is to remove the fuse and connect a test light or voltmeter in its place to the fuse terminals. There should be no voltage present in the circuit. Move the wiring harness from side-to-side while watching the test light. If the bulb goes on, there is a short to ground somewhere in that area, probably where the insulation has rubbed through. The same test can be performed on each component in the circuit, even a switch.

Ground check

Perform a ground test to check whether a component is properly grounded. Disconnect the battery and connect one lead of a selfpowered test light, known as a continuity tester, to a known good ground. Connect the other lead to the wire or ground connection being tested. If the bulb goes on, the ground is good. If the bulb does not go on, the ground is not good.

Continuity check

A continuity check is done to determine if there are any breaks in a circuit – if it is passing electricity properly. With the circuit off (no power in the circuit), a self-powered continuity tester can be used to check the circuit. Connect the test leads to both ends of the circuit (or to the "power" end and a good ground), and if the test light comes on the circuit is passing current properly. If the light doesn't come on, there is a break somewhere in the circuit. The same procedure can be used to test a switch, by connecting the continuity tester to the switch terminals. With the switch turned On, the test light should come on.

Finding an open circuit

When diagnosing for possible open circuits, it is often difficult to locate them by sight because oxidation or terminal misalignment are hidden by the connectors. Merely wiggling a connector on a sensor or in the wiring harness may correct the open circuit condition. Remember this when an open circuit is indicated when troubleshooting a circuit. Intermittent problems may also be caused by oxidized or loose connections.

Electrical troubleshooting is simple if you keep in mind that all electrical circuits are basically electricity running from the battery, through the wires, switches, relays, fuses and fusible links to each electrical component (light bulb, motor, etc.) and to ground, from which it is passed back to the battery. Any electrical problem is an interruption in the flow of electricity to and from the battery.

3 Fuses – general information

Refer to illustrations 3.1a, 3.1b and 3.3

The electrical circuits of the vehicle are protected by a combination of fuses, circuit breakers and fusible links. The fuse block is located under the instrument panel on the left side of the dashboard **(see illustration)**. Sometimes fuses are also located on or near the components they protect, i.e. the radio **(see illustration)**.

Each of the fuses is designed to protect a specific circuit, and the various circuits are identified on the fuse panel itself.

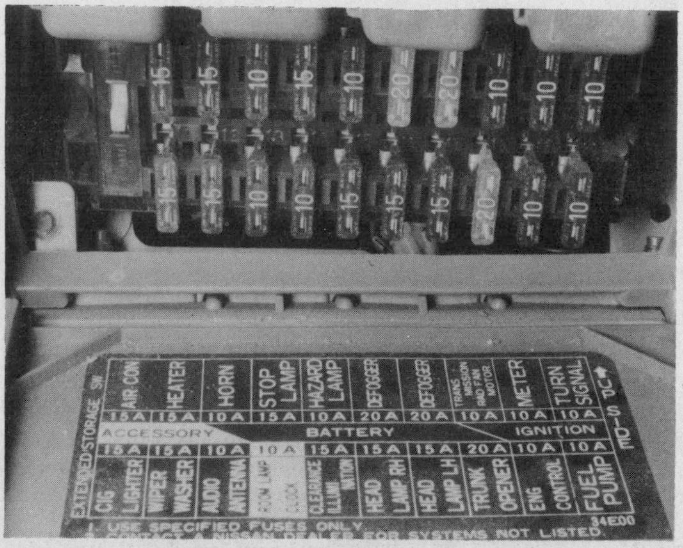

3.1a The fuse block is located under the instrument panel on the left side of the dashboard

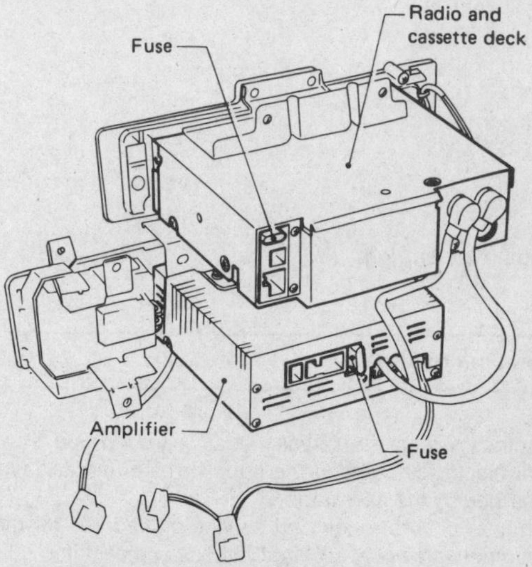

3.1b The radio fuse is located at the rear of the component – the amplifier also is protected with a fuse

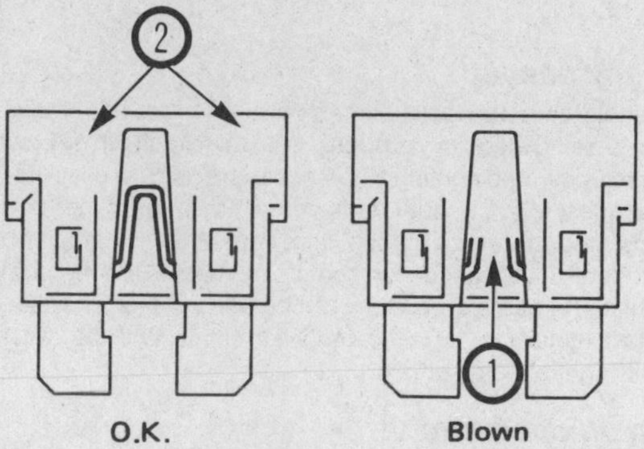

3.3 To test for a blown fuse, pull it out and inspect it for an open (1), then with the fuse installed and the circuit activated, connect a test light across the terminals (2)

4.1 The fusible links are located on the inner fenderwell near the corner of the engine compartment

Miniaturized fuses are employed in the fuse block. These compact fuses, with blade terminal design, allow fingertip removal and replacement. If an electrical component fails, always check the fuse first. A blown fuse is easily identified through the clear plastic body. Visually inspect the element for evidence of damage **(see illustration)**. If a continuity check is called for, the blade terminal tips are exposed in the fuse body.

Be sure to replace blown fuses with the correct type. Fuses of different ratings are physically interchangeable, but only fuses of the proper rating should be used. Replacing a fuse with one of a higher or lower value than specified is not recommended. Each electrical circuit needs a specific amount of protection. The amperage value of each fuse is molded into the fuse body.

If the replacement fuse immediately fails, don't replace it again until the cause of the problem is isolated and corrected. In most cases, the cause will be a short circuit in the wiring caused by a broken or deteriorated wire.

4 Fusible links – general information

Refer to illustration 4.1

Some circuits are protected by fusible links. The links are used in circuits which are not ordinarily fused, such as the ignition circuit **(see illustration)**.

Although the fusible links appear to be a heavier gauge than the wire they are protecting, the appearance is due to the thick insulation. All fusible links are four wire gauges smaller than the wire they are designed to protect.

Fusible links cannot be repaired, but a new link of the same size wire can be put in its place. The procedure is as follows:

a) Disconnect the negative cable from the battery.
b) Disconnect the fusible link from the wiring harness.

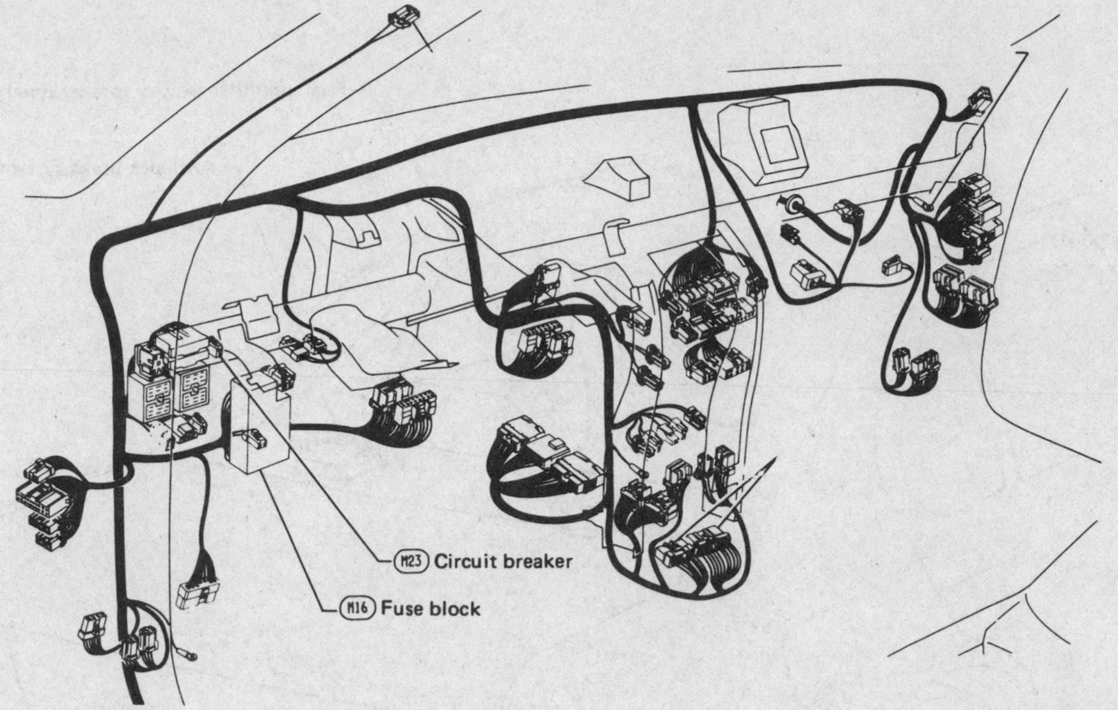

5.1 On 1989 models, the circuit breaker is located near the S.M.J. behind the fuse block

c) Cut the damaged fusible link out of the wiring just behind the connector.
d) Strip the insulation back approximately 1/2-inch.
e) Position the connector on the new fusible link and crimp it into place.
f) Use rosin core solder at each end of the new link to obtain a good solder joint.
g) Use plenty of electrical tape around the soldered joint. No wires should be exposed.
h) Connect the battery ground cable. Test the circuit for proper operation.

5 Circuit breakers – general information

Refer to illustration 5.1

Circuit breakers protect components such as power windows, power door locks and headlights. Some circuit breakers are located in the fuse box **(see illustration)**.

On some models the circuit breaker resets itself automatically, so an electrical overload in a circuit breaker protected system will cause the circuit to fail momentarily, then come back on. If the circuit does not come back on, check it immediately. Once the condition is corrected, the circuit breaker will resume its normal function. Some circuit breakers must be reset manually.

6 Relays – general information

Refer to illustrations 6.2a, 6.2b, 6.2c, 6.2d, 6.2e, 6.2f and 6.2g

Several electrical accessories in the vehicle use relays to transmit the electrical signal to the component. If the relay is defective, that component will not operate properly.

The various relays are grouped together in several locations **(see illustrations)**.

If a faulty relay is suspected, it can be removed and tested by a dealer service department or a repair shop. Defective relays must be replaced as a unit.

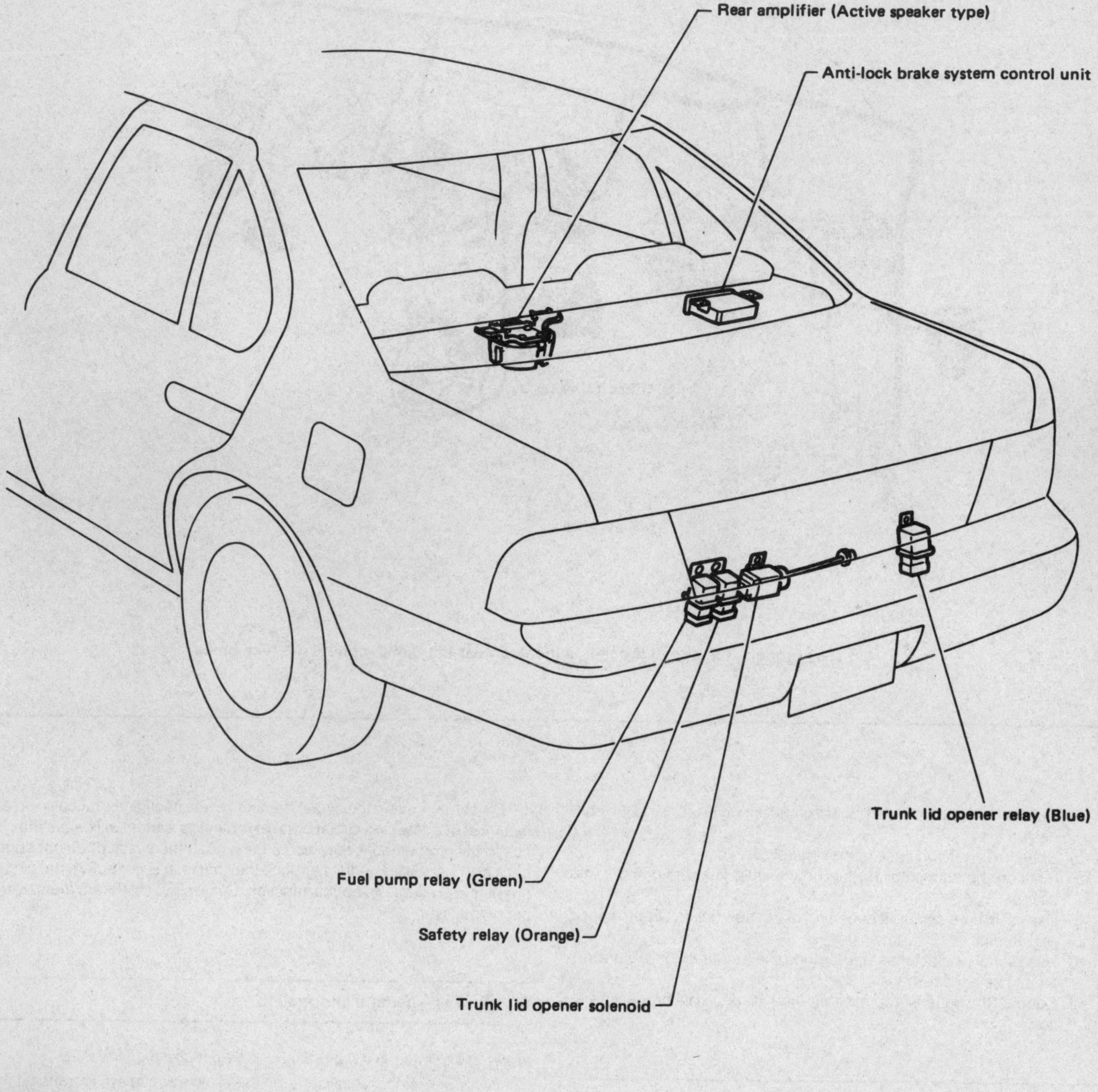

6.2a Relay and component locations on 1989 and later models (in trunk)

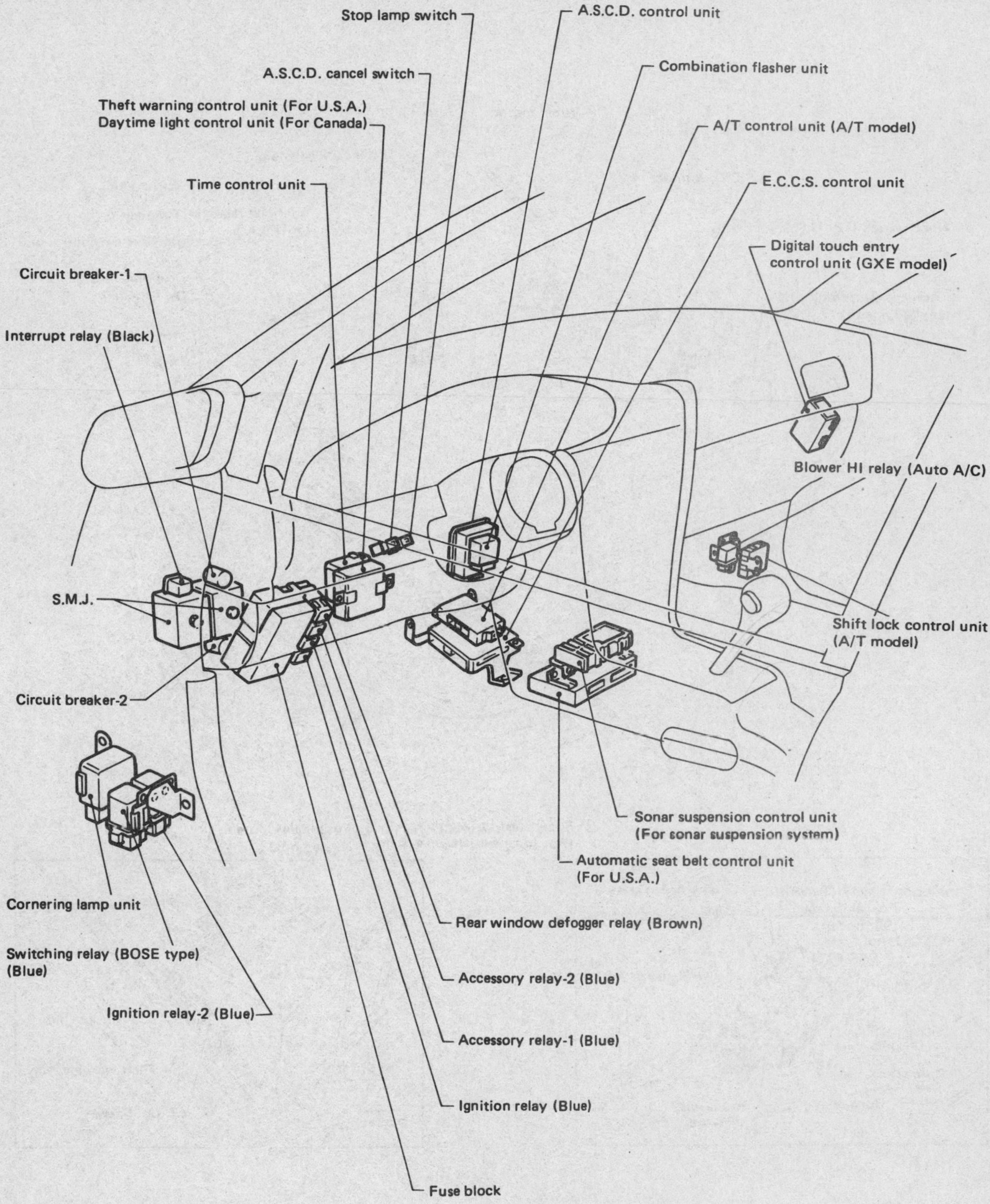

6.2b Relay and component locations on 1989 and later models (in passenger compartment)

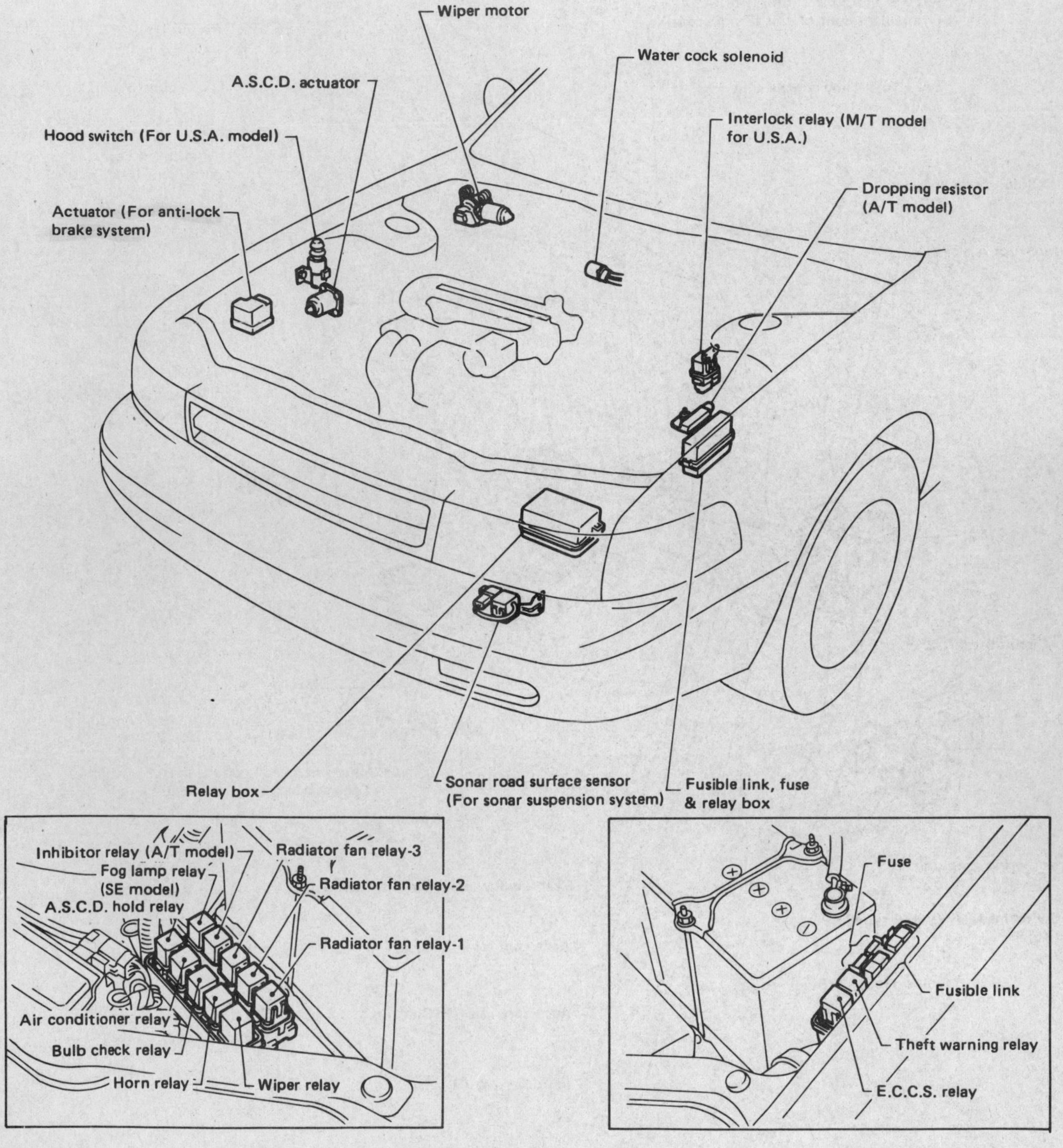

6.2c Relay and component locations on 1989 and later models (under the hood)

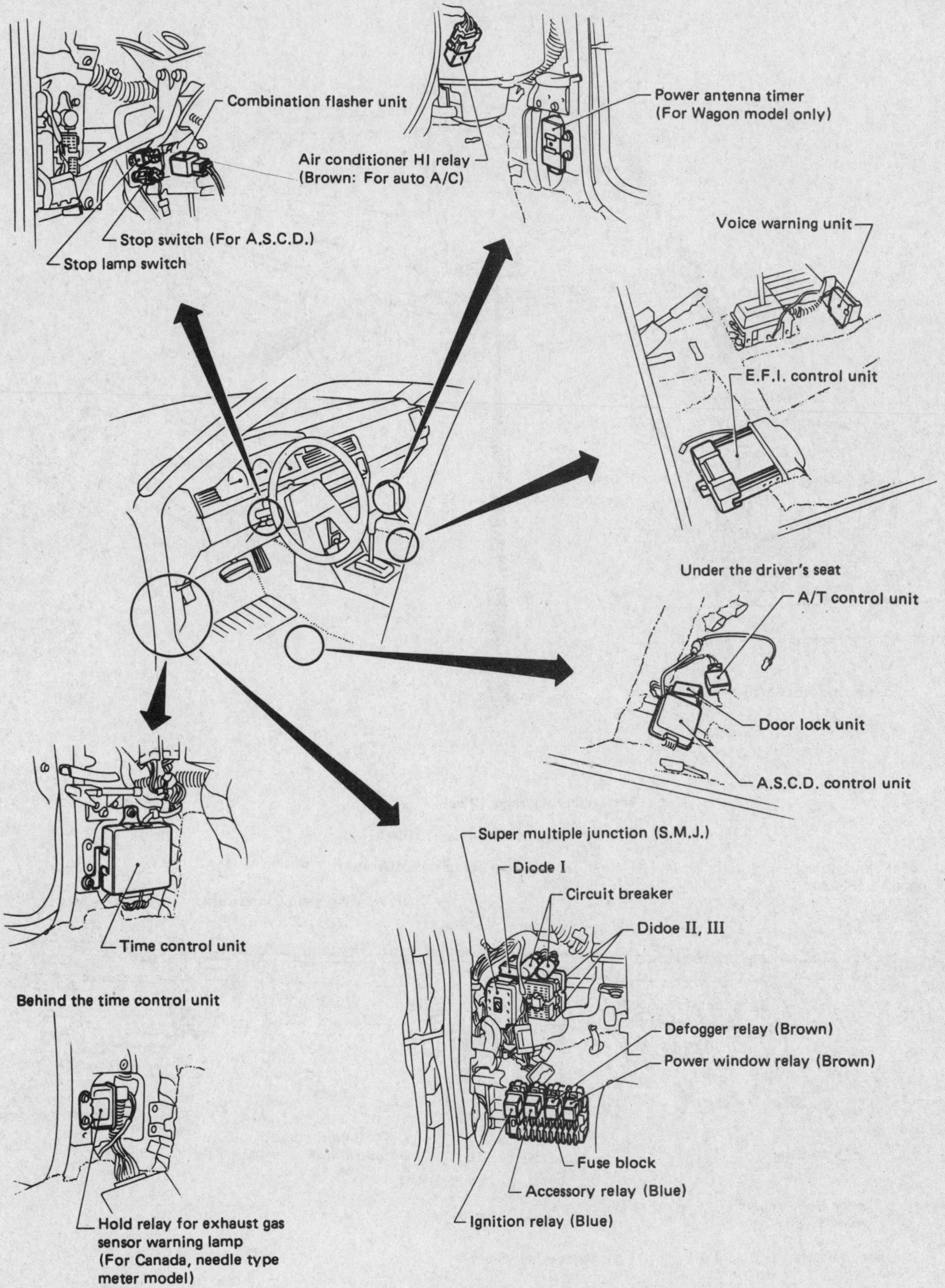

6.2d Relay and component locations on 1985 through 1988 models (in passenger compartment)

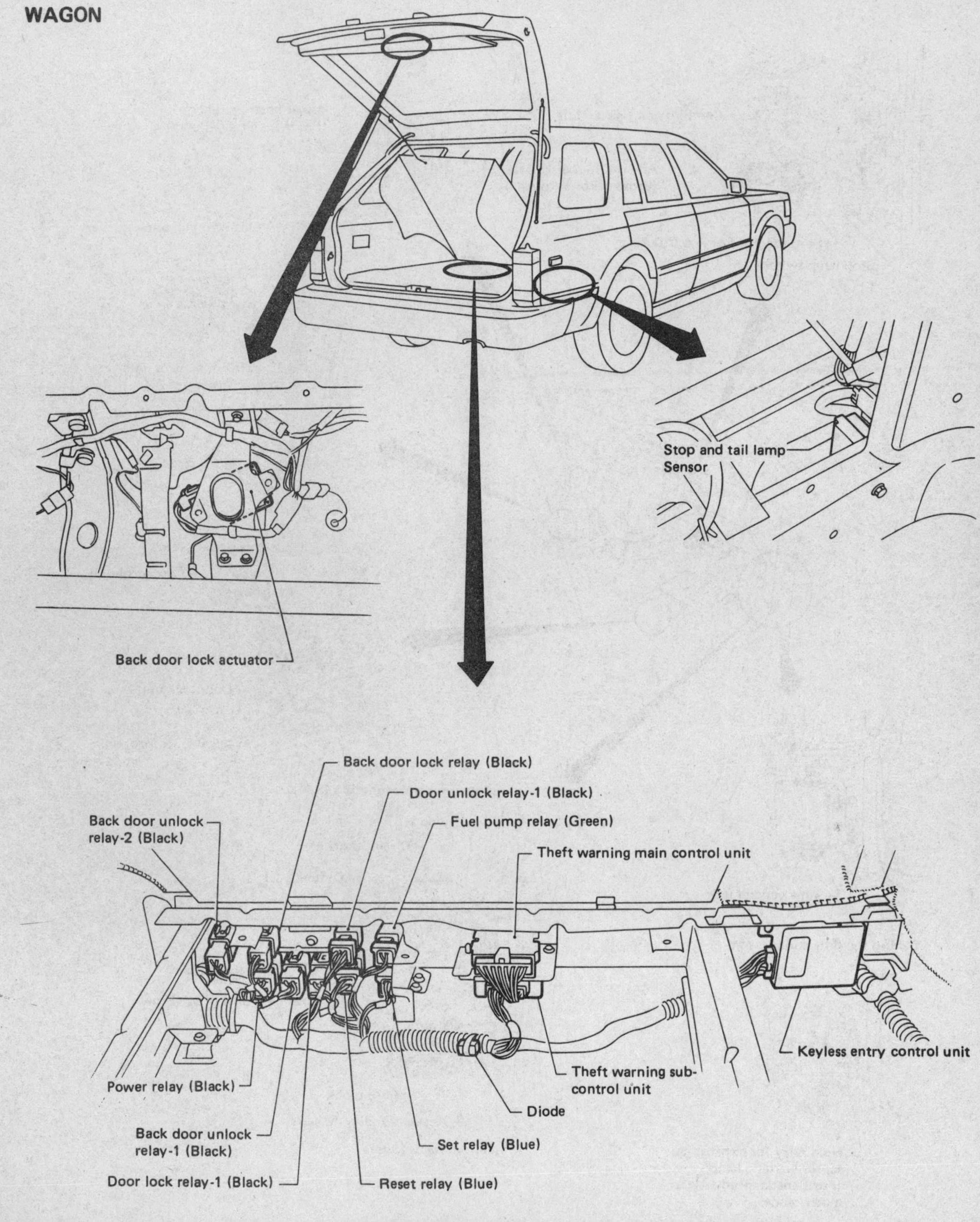

6.2e Relay and component locations on 1985 through 1988 station wagon models

SEDAN

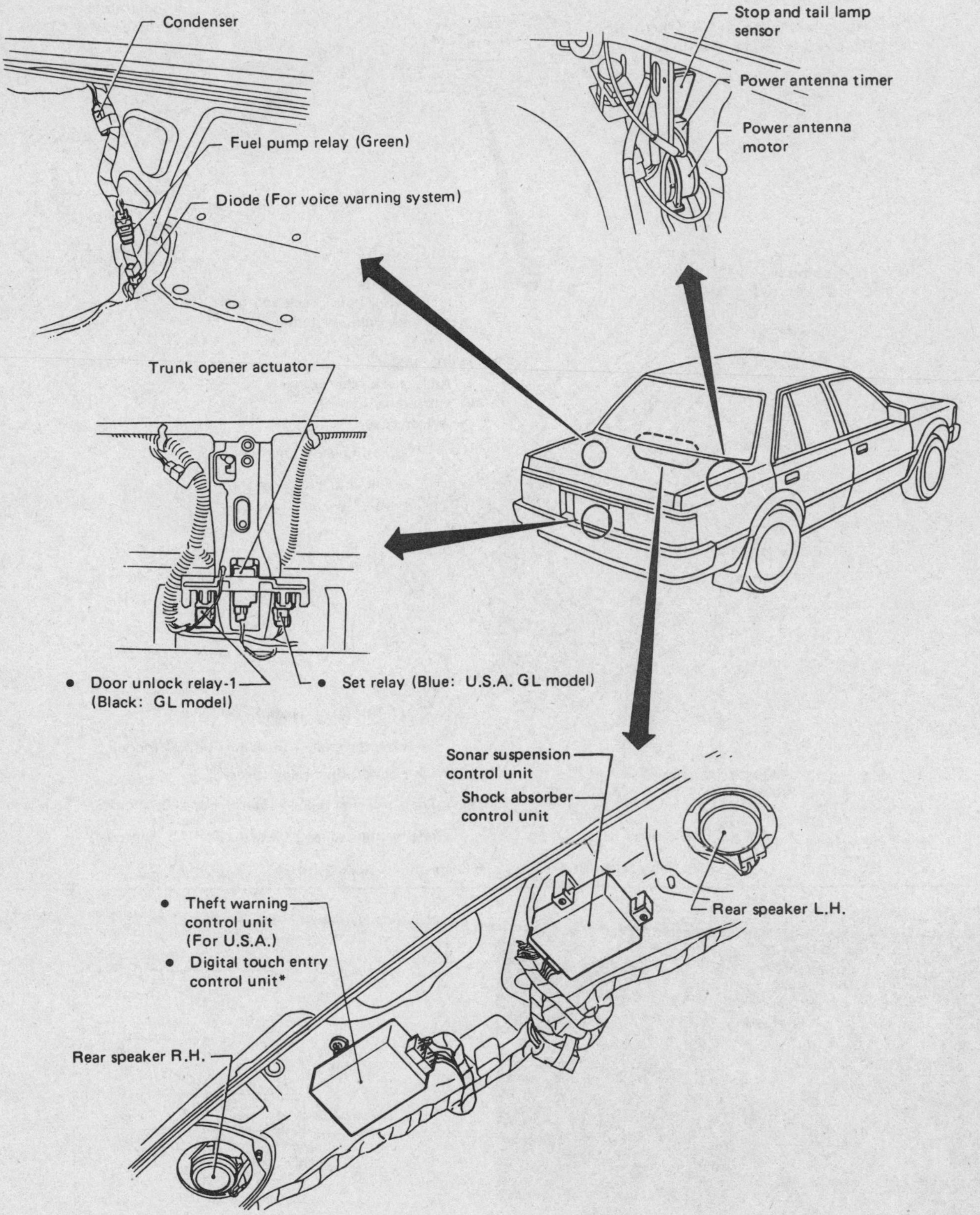

* Digital touch entry control unit for U.S.A. is equipped into theft warning control unit.

6.2f Relay and component locations on 1985 through 1988 models (in trunk)

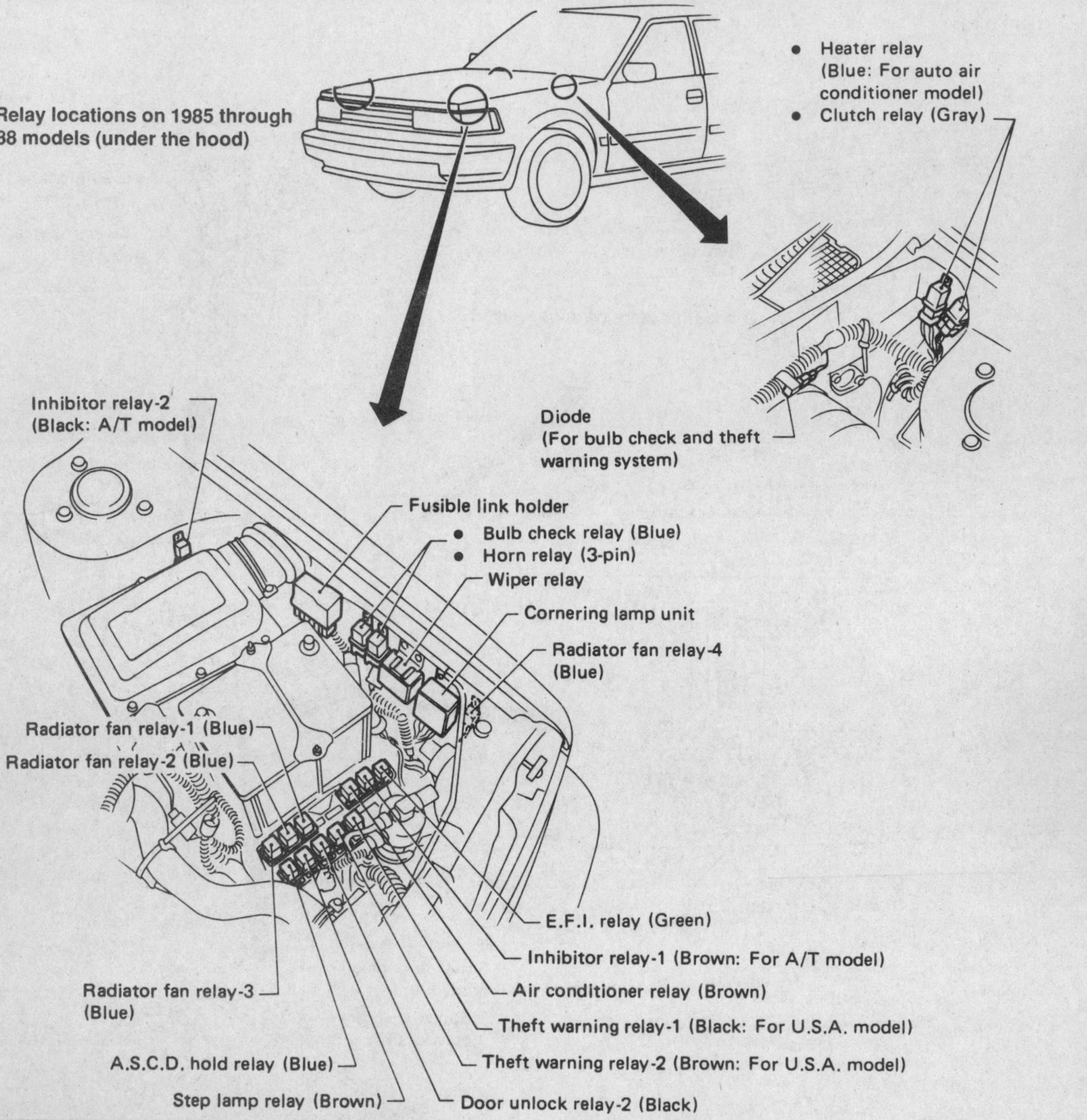

6.2g Relay locations on 1985 through 1988 models (under the hood)

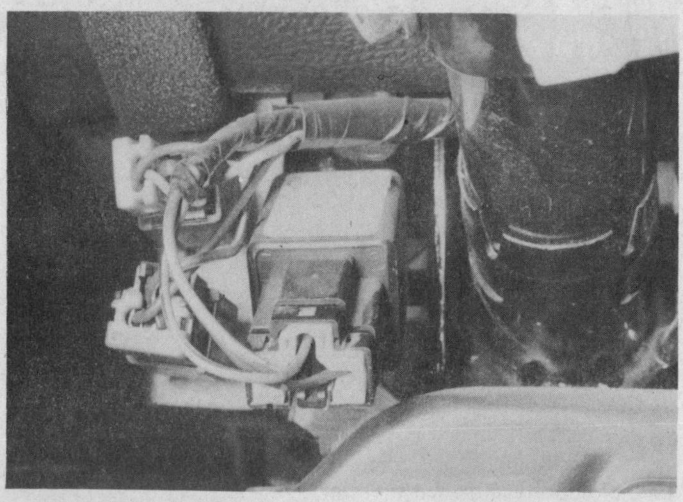

7.1 The turn signal and hazard flasher is located near the steering column under the center kick panel

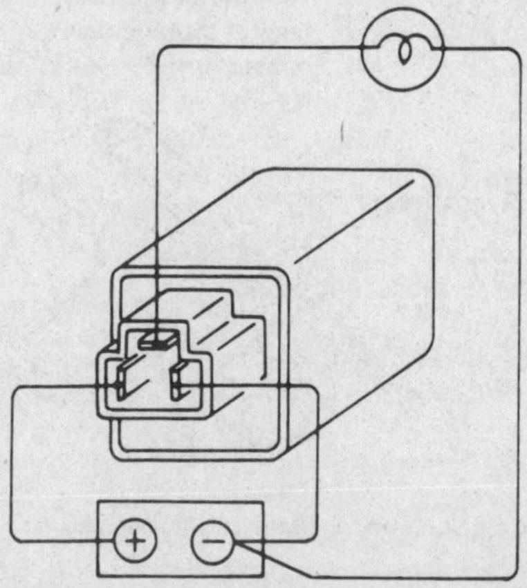

7.3 The flasher unit is working properly if the test light blinks when battery voltage is applied

8.4 Disconnect the electrical harness connector for the ignition switch

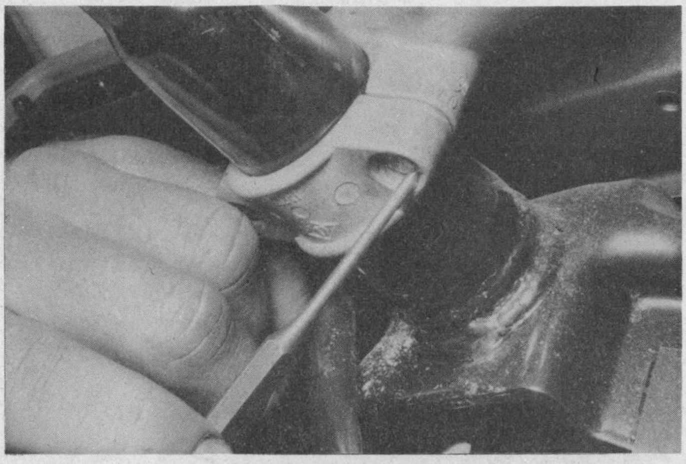

8.5 Use a sharp punch or small chisel to rotate the bolt out

7 Turn signal/hazard flashers – check and replacement

Refer to illustrations 7.1 and 7.3

1 The turn signal flasher, a small canister-shaped unit located under the dash **(see illustration)**, flashes the turn signals.

2 When the flasher unit is functioning properly, an audible click can be heard during its operation. If the turn signals fail on one side or the other and the flasher unit does not make its characteristic clicking sound, a faulty turn signal bulb is indicated.

3 If both turn signals fail to blink, the problem may be due to a blown fuse, a faulty flasher unit **(see illustration)**, a broken switch or a loose or open connection. If a quick check of the fuse box indicates that the turn signal fuse has blown, check the wiring for a short before installing a new fuse.

4 To replace the flasher, simply remove the lower center panel and remove the flasher from the harness.

5 Make sure that the replacement unit is identical to the original. Compare the old one to the new one before installing it.

6 Installation is the reverse of removal.

8 Ignition switch – removal and installation

Refer to illustrations 8.4 and 8.5

Warning: *1992 models are equipped with a Supplemental Restraint System (SRS), more commonly known as an airbag. Always disconnect both battery cables and wait ten minutes before working in the vicinity of the impact sensors, steering wheel and column or instrument panel to avoid the possibility of accidental deployment of the air bag, which could cause personal injury (see Chapter 12). The yellow wiring harness and connectors routed through the center console, under hood and right side wheel well are for this system. Do not use electrical test equipment on any of the airbag system wiring or tamper with them in any way.*

1 Disconnect the negative cable at the battery. Place the cable out of the way so it cannot accidentally come in contact with the negative terminal of the battery, as this would once again allow power into the electrical system of the vehicle.

2 Remove the steering wheel (Chapter 10).

3 Remove the lower finish panel and the steering column cover (Chapter 11).

4 Disconnect the electrical harness connector for the ignition switch behind the lower panel **(see illustration)**.

5 Using a sharp punch or a small chisel, carefully tap the shear bolt to turn it counterclockwise **(see illustration)**. **Note:** *If the shear bolts are very tight, use a drill bit and an easy-out to remove them.*

6 Remove the ignition switch from the steering column assembly.

7 When installing the ignition switch, use new factory shear bolts to secure the ignition switch.

9 Combination switch – removal and installation

Refer to illustrations 9.4, 9.5 and 9.6

Warning: *1992 models are equipped with a Supplemental Restraint System (SRS), more commonly known as an airbag. Always disconnect both battery cables and wait ten minutes before working in the vicinity of the impact sensors, steering wheel and column or instrument panel to avoid the possibility of accidental deployment of the air bag, which could cause personal injury (see Chapter 12). The yellow wiring harness and connectors routed through the center console, under hood and right side wheel well are for this system. Do not use electrical test equipment on any of the airbag system wiring or tamper with them in any way.*

1 Disconnect the negative cable at the battery. Place the cable out of the way so it cannot accidentally come in contact with the negative terminal of the battery, as this would once again allow power into the electrical system of the vehicle.

2 Remove the steering wheel (Chapter 10).

3 Remove the lower finish panel and steering column cover (Chapter 11).

4 Loosen the upper retaining screw **(see illustration)** but do not remove it completely.

5 Disconnect all the connectors at the combination switch **(see illustration)**.

6 Push the combination switch and turn it counterclockwise approximately 30-degrees and remove it from the steering column **(see illustration)**.

7 Installation is the reverse of removal.

9.4 Loosen the upper retaining screw but do not remove it completely

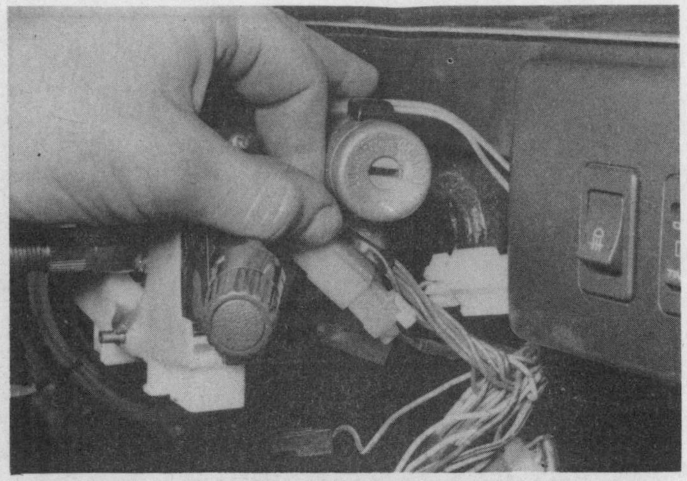

9.5 Mark all the connectors with paint and disconnect them

9.6 Push the combination switch, and turn it counterclockwise approximately 30-degrees to release it from the steering column

10 Steering column switches – removal and installation

Warning: *1992 models are equipped with a Supplemental Restraint System (SRS), more commonly known as an airbag. Always disconnect both battery cables and wait ten minutes before working in the vicinity of the impact sensors, steering wheel and column or instrument panel to avoid the possibility of accidental deployment of the air bag, which could cause personal injury (see Chapter 12). The yellow wiring harness and connectors routed through the center console, under hood and right side wheel well are for this system. Do not use electrical test equipment on any of the airbag system wiring or tamper with them in any way.*

1 Remove the combination switch (Section 9).

Turn signal/headlight control/cruise control switch

Refer to illustration 10.2

2 Remove the retaining screws and lift the switch off the combination switch main body **(see illustration)**.

3 Installation is the reverse of removal.

Wiper/washer switch

Refer to illustration 10.4

4 Remove the retaining screws, detach the switch and lift it off the combination switch **(see illustration)**.

5 Installation is the reverse of removal.

Hazard warning flasher switch

Refer to illustration 10.7

6 Remove the turn signal/headlight control switch.

7 Use a small screwdriver and push the tab down and away from the locking tab **(see illustration)** on the hazard warning switch.

8 Lift the flasher switch up and off the combination switch main body.

9 Installation is the reverse of removal.

11 Radio and speakers – removal and installation

Warning: *1992 models are equipped with a Supplemental Restraint System (SRS), more commonly known as an airbag. Always disconnect both battery cables and wait ten minutes before working in the vicinity of the impact sensors, steering wheel and column or instrument panel to avoid the possibility of accidental deployment of the air bag, which could cause personal injury (see Chapter 12). The yellow wiring harness and connectors routed through the center console, under hood and right side wheel well are for this system. Do not use electrical test equipment on any of the airbag system wiring or tamper with them in any way.*

1 Disconnect the negative cable at the battery. Place the cable out of the way so it cannot accidentally come in contact with the negative terminal of the battery, as this would once again allow power into the electrical system of the vehicle.

10.2 Remove the retaining screws and separate the turn signal/headlight switch from the combination switch

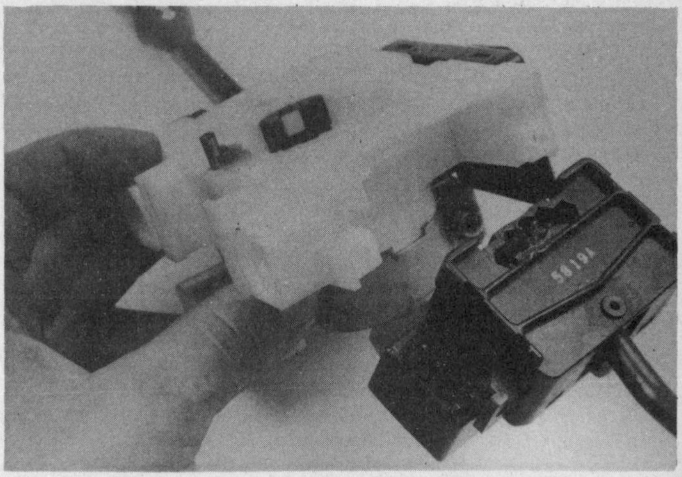

10.4 Remove the wiper/washer switch from the combination switch

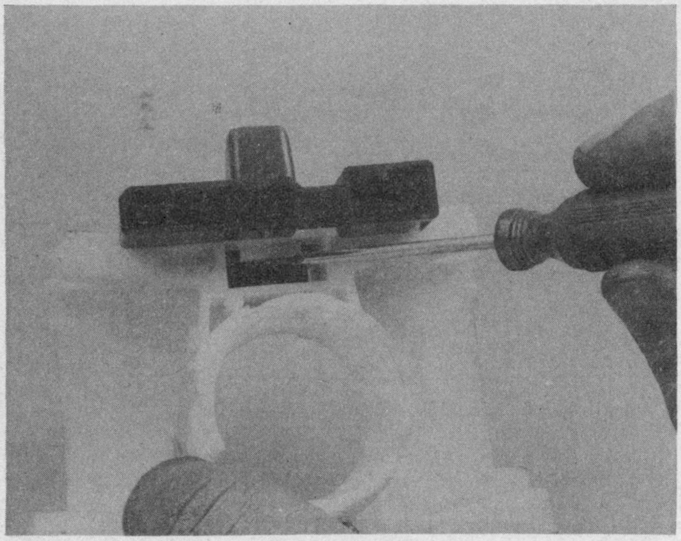

10.7 Use a small screwdriver and push the tab down and away from the locking tab to release the hazard warning switch from the combination switch

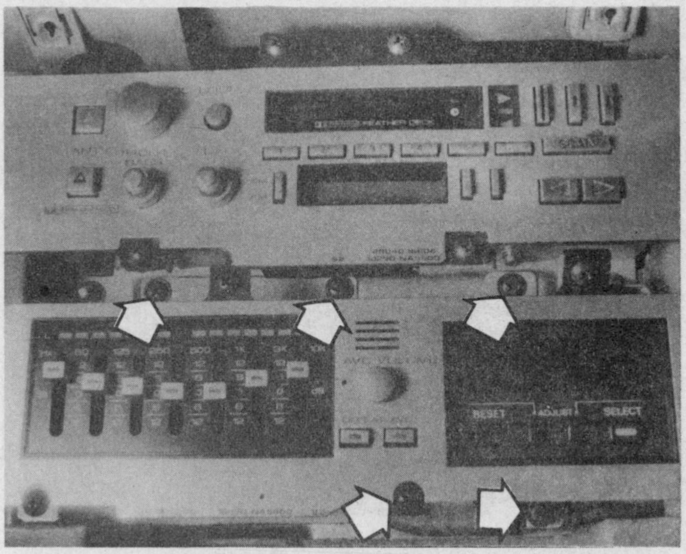

11.3 Remove the inner mounting screws (arrows) and remove the equalizer and radio/tape deck as separate units

Radio

Refer to illustration 11.3

2 Remove the instrument panel center finish panel (Chapter 11) and the ashtray.
3 Remove the radio mounting screws or bolts **(see illustration)**.
4 Pull the radio out, reach behind it and unplug the electrical connector and the antenna lead.
5 Lift the radio from the instrument panel.
6 Installation is the reverse of removal.

Speakers

Refer to illustration 11.8

7 Remove the rear speaker cover(s) (Chapter 11).
8 Remove the retaining screws or bolts, unplug the connector and lift the speaker out of position **(see illustration)**.
9 Installation is the reverse of removal.

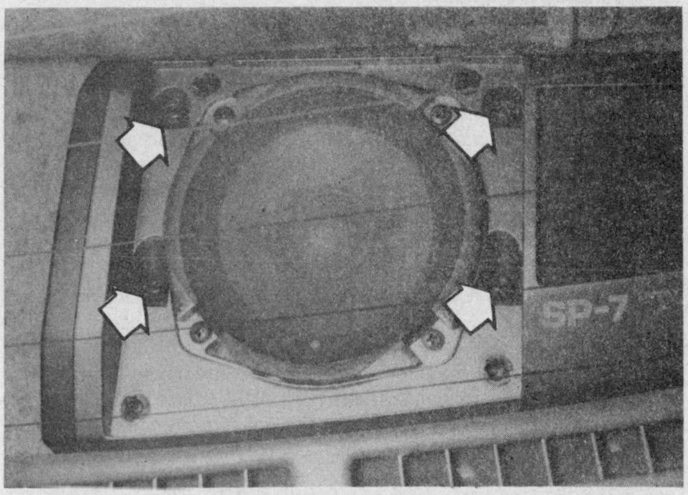

11.8 Remove the mounting screws and lift the rear speaker out

12 Headlights – removal and installation

Refer to illustrations 12.3 and 12.5

Warning: *The halogen gas filled bulbs used on these models are under pressure and may shatter if the surface is scratched or the bulb is dropped. Wear eye protection and handle the bulbs carefully, grasping only the base whenever possible. Do not touch the surface of the bulb with your fingers because the oil from your skin could cause it to overheat and fail prematurely. If you do touch the bulb surface, clean it with rubbing alcohol.*

1 Disconnect the negative cable from the battery. Place the cable out of the way so it cannot accidentally come in contact with the negative terminal of the battery, as this would once again allow power into the electrical system of the vehicle.
2 Open the hood. Unplug the electrical connector.
3 Reach behind the headlight assembly, grasp the bulb holder and turn it counterclockwise to remove it **(see illustration)**. Lift the holder assembly out for access to the bulb.
4 Release the tab on the side of the bulb and separate it from the assembly.
5 Insert the new bulb assembly into the holder **(see illustration)**.
6 Install the bulb holder in the headlight assembly.

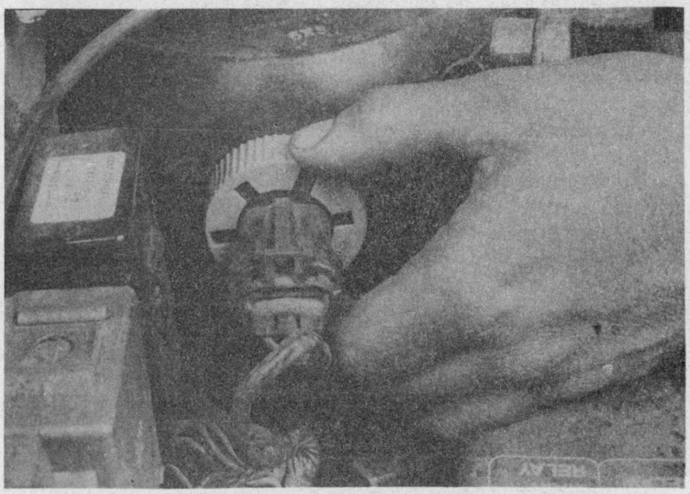

12.3 Reach behind the headlight assembly, grasp the bulb holder and turn it counterclockwise to remove it

12

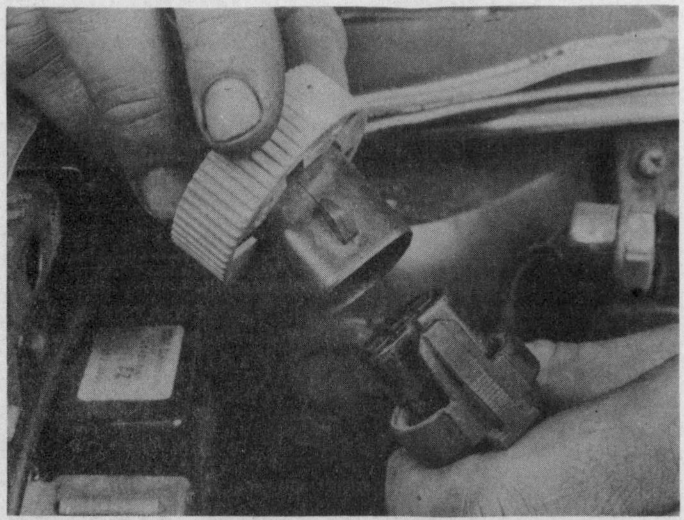

12.5 Insert the new bulb into the holder

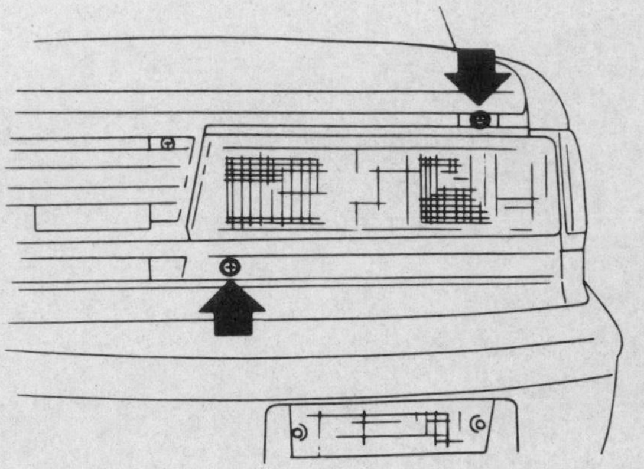

13.1 Remove the headlight covers to expose the adjusting screws

13 Headlights – adjustment

Refer to illustrations 13.1 and 13.3

Note: *The headlights must be aimed correctly. If adjusted incorrectly they could blind the driver of an oncoming vehicle and cause a serious accident or seriously reduce your ability to see the road. The headlights should be checked for proper aim every 12 months and any time a new headlight is installed or front end body work is performed. It should be emphasized that the following procedure is only an interim step which will provide temporary adjustment until the headlights can be adjusted by a properly equipped shop.*

1 Headlights have two spring loaded adjusting screws, one on the top controlling up-and-down movement and one on the side controlling left-and-right movement **(see illustration)**.

2 There are several methods of adjusting the headlights. The simplest method requires a blank wall 25 feet in front of the vehicle and a level floor.

3 Position masking tape vertically on the wall in reference to the vehicle centerline and the centerlines of both headlights **(see illustration)**.

4 Position a horizontal tape line in reference to the centerline of all the headlights. **Note:** *It may be easier to position the tape on the wall with the vehicle parked only a few inches away.*

5 Adjustment should be made with the vehicle sitting level, the gas tank half-full and no unusually heavy load in the vehicle.

6 Starting with the low beam adjustment, position the high intensity zone so it is two inches below the horizontal line and two inches to the right of the headlight vertical line. Adjustment is made by turning the top adjusting screw clockwise to raise the beam and counterclockwise to lower the beam. The adjusting screw on the side should be used in the same manner to move the beam left or right.

7 With the high beams on, the high intensity zone should be vertically centered with the exact center just below the horizontal line. **Note:** *It may not be possible to position the headlight aim exactly for both high and low beams. If a compromise must be made, keep in mind that the low beams are the most used and have the greatest effect on driver safety.*

8 Have the headlights adjusted by a dealer service department or service station at the earliest opportunity.

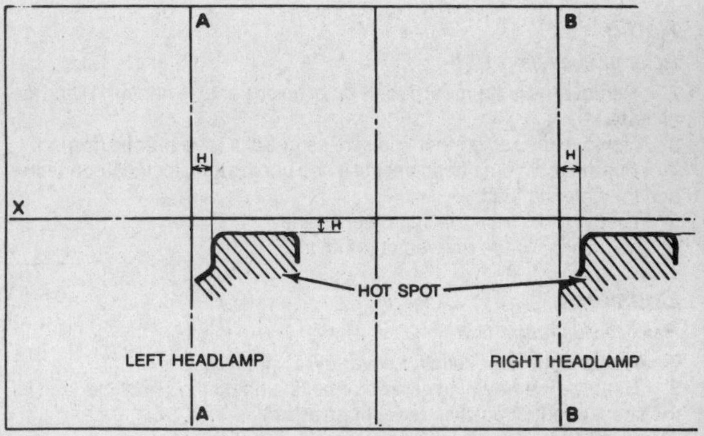

13.3 The vehicle must be on a level surface to get an accurate adjustment

14 Bulb replacement

Refer to illustrations 14.2, 14.3 and 14.4

1 The lenses of many lights are held in place by screws, which makes it a simple procedure to gain access to the bulbs.

2 On some lights the lenses are held in place by clips. The lenses can be removed either by unsnapping them or by using a small screwdriver to pry them off **(see illustration)**.

3 Several types of bulbs are used. Some are removed by pushing in and turning them counterclockwise. Others can simply be unclipped from the terminals or pulled straight out of the socket **(see illustration)**.

4 To gain access to the instrument panel lights, the instrument cluster will have to be removed first (see Section 16). Carefully remove the bulb(s) with the cartridge, located on the rear of the instrument cluster **(see illustration)**.

15 Windshield wiper motor – removal and installation

Refer to illustrations 15.2, 15.3, 15.4, 15.5 and 15.6

1 Disconnect the negative cable at the battery. Place the cable out of the way so it cannot accidentally come in contact with the negative terminal of the battery, as this would once again allow power into the electrical system of the vehicle.

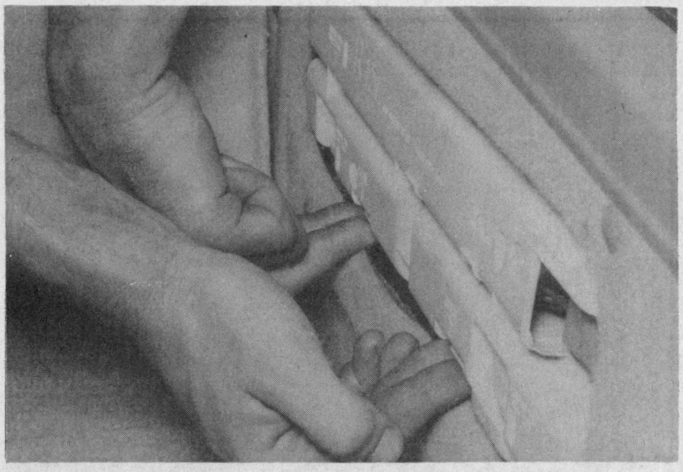

14.2 The rear bulb assembly can be removed by pressing up on the locking tabs and pulling out

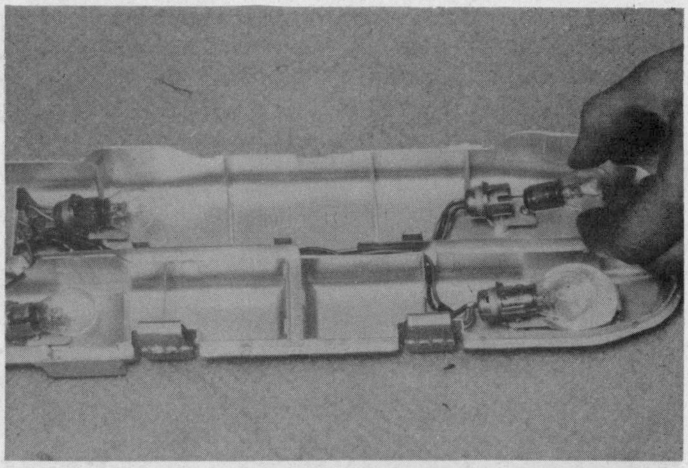

14.3 Carefully remove the bulbs from their sockets by turning them counterclockwise

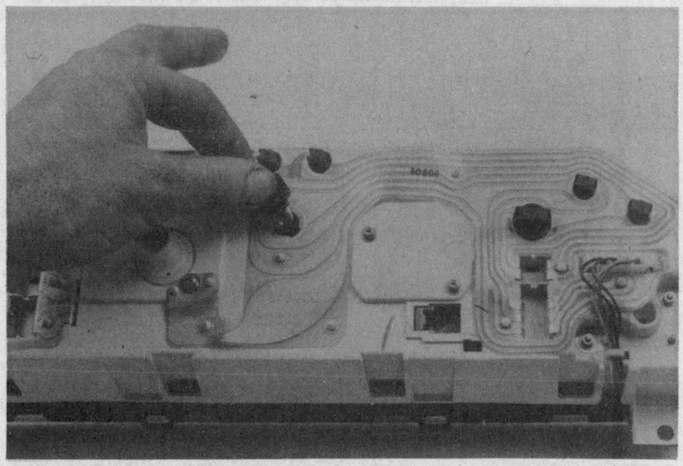

14.4 The bulb cartridge is plugged into the rear face of the instrument cluster directly over the printed circuit (remove it as a single unit)

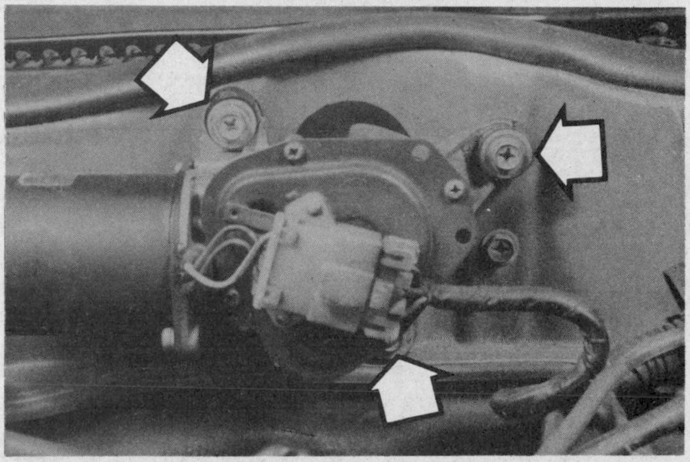

15.2 The windshield wiper motor is located on the engine compartment wall near the power steering reservoir – remove the bolts (arrows) to detach it

2 Unplug the electrical connector and remove the retaining bolts that secure the wiper motor to the engine compartment body (**see Illustration**).

3 Remove the wiper arm nuts from the wiper arm shaft (**see illustration**) and lift the wiper assembly arm up.

4 Remove the front cowl retaining screws (**see illustration**) and lift the cowl up.

5 Remove the weatherstrip directly above the wiper motor access cover and remove the access cover retaining screws (**see illustration**).

6 Disconnect the wiper arm nut directly behind the wiper motor (**see illustration**).

7 Carefully pry the arm off the wiper motor.

8 Installation is the reverse of removal.

16 Instrument cluster – removal and installation

Refer to illustrations 16.5, 16.6, 16.7 and 16.8

Warning: *1992 models are equipped with a Supplemental Restraint System (SRS), more commonly known as an airbag. Always disconnect both battery cables and wait ten minutes before working in the vicinity of the impact sensors, steering wheel and column or instrument panel to avoid the possibility of accidental deployment of the air bag, which could cause personal injury (see Chapter 12). The yellow wiring harness and connectors routed through the center console, under hood and right side wheel well are for this system. Do not use electrical test equipment on any of the airbag system wiring or tamper with them in any way.*

1 Disconnect the negative cable at the battery. Place the cable out of the way so it cannot accidentally come in contact with the negative termi-

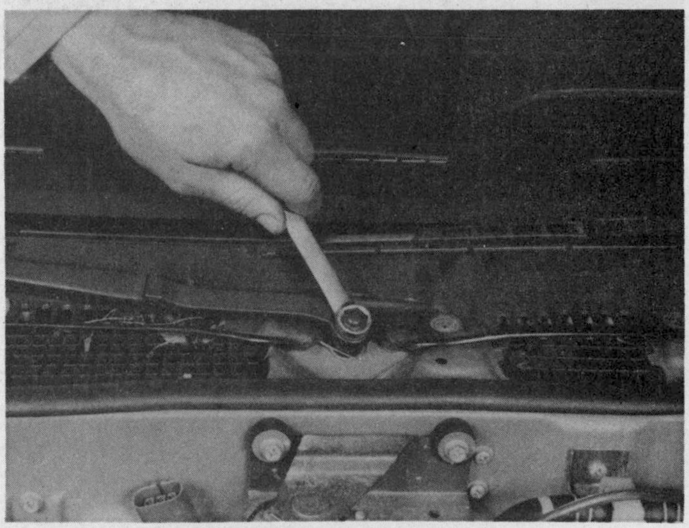

15.3 Remove the wiper arm assemblies

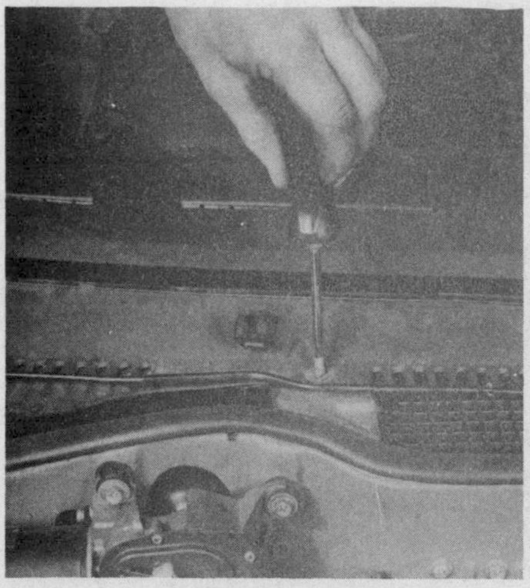

15.4 Remove the front cowl retaining screws and separate the cowl from the body

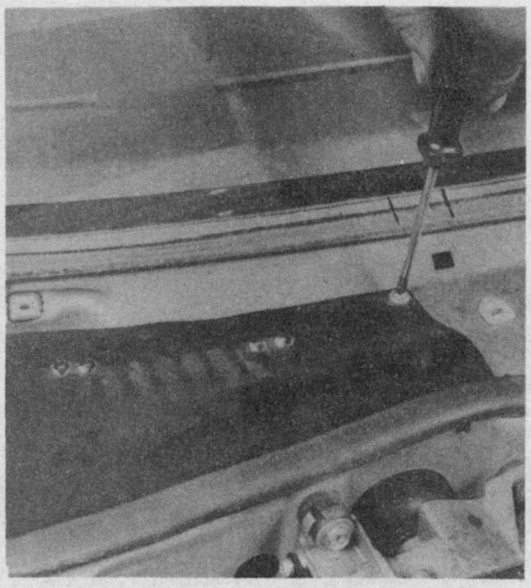

15.5 Remove the wiper motor access cover

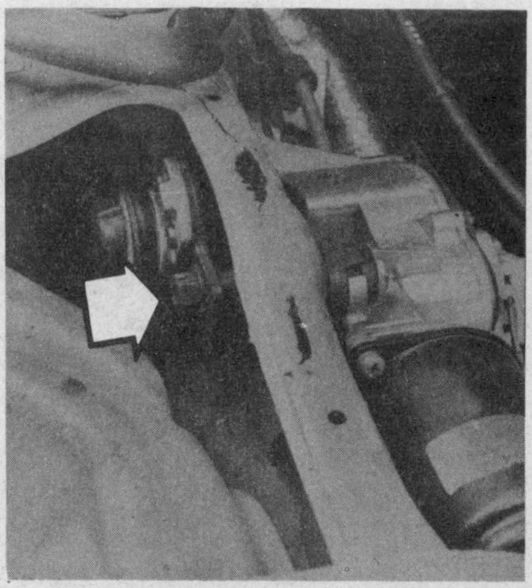

15.6 Remove the wiper motor arm retaining nut (arrow) and carefully take the motor assembly out

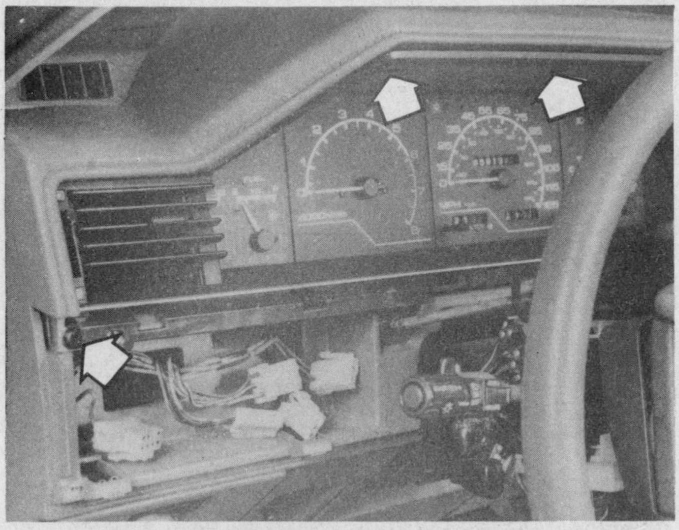

16.5 Remove the instrument cluster finish panel retaining screws (arrows)

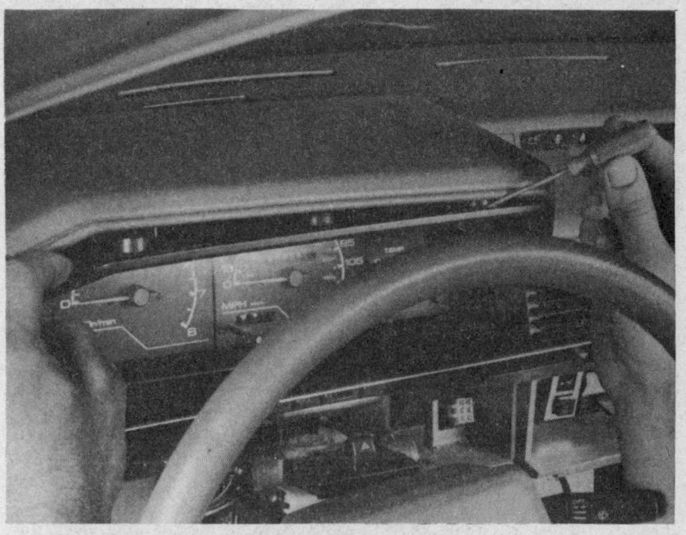

16.6 Carefully pry down the finish panel to unlock it from the dashboard

16.7 Remove the instrument cluster retaining screws (arrows)

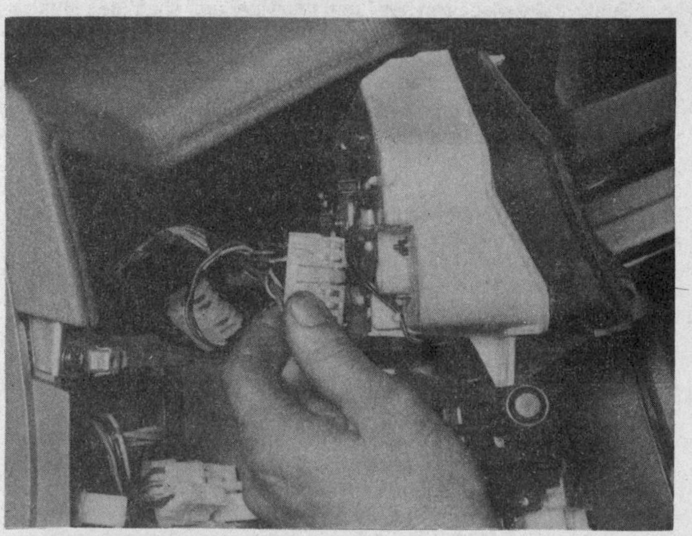

16.8 Disconnect the speedometer cable and any electrical connectors and remove the instrument cluster

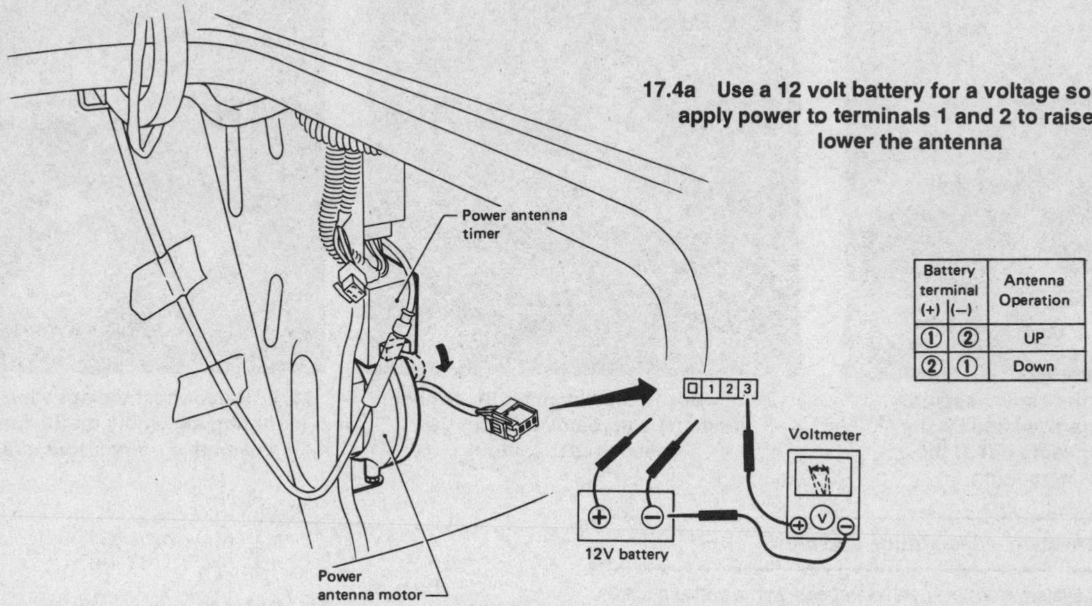

17.4a Use a 12 volt battery for a voltage source and apply power to terminals 1 and 2 to raise and lower the antenna

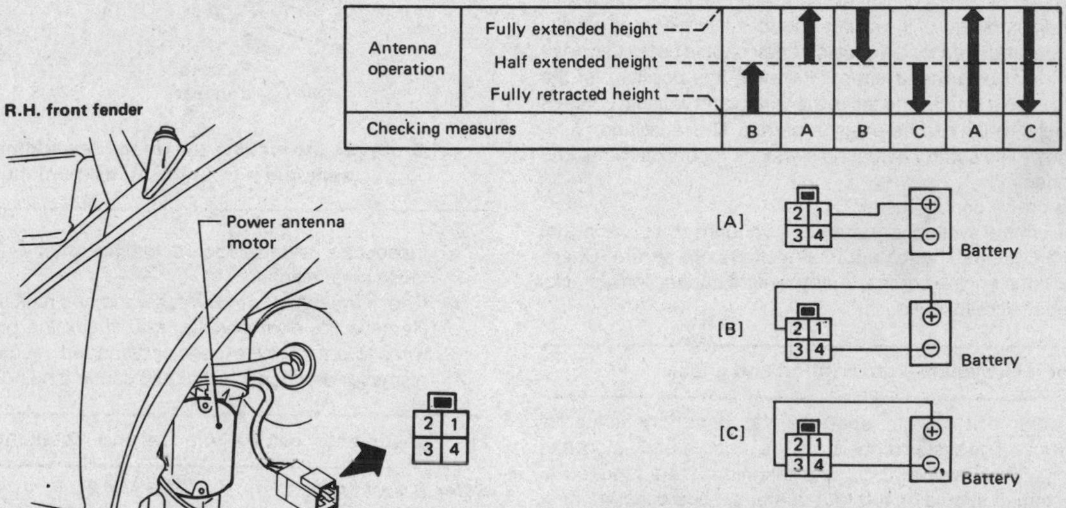

17.4b On station wagons, the antenna motor is located under the right front fender – use a battery to apply power to the different terminals and test for the proper reaction

nal of the battery, as this would once again allow power into the electrical system of the vehicle.

2 Remove the steering column covers (Chapter 11).

3 Remove the screws holding the cluster finish panel in place, then remove the finish panel (Chapter 11).

4 Follow Steps 1 to 3 of Section 21 and push the speedometer cable into the dashboard to allow for slack on the cable.

5 Remove the instrument cluster finish panel retaining screws **(see illustration)**.

6 Carefully pry down the top of the finish panel and make sure not to damage the unit **(see illustration)**.

7 Remove the instrument cluster retaining screws and pull the unit partially out **(see illustration)**.

8 Disconnect the speedometer cable (see Section 21) and the electrical connectors **(see illustration)** and remove the instrument cluster.

9 To replace any faulty components within the cluster, simply unbolt or unscrew them and replace them with new units.

10 Installation is the reverse of removal.

17 Power antenna – troubleshooting

Refer to illustrations 17.4a and 17.4b

1 Remove the two retaining screws and the two panel clips on the right side of the trunk compartment and remove the inner trunk panel.

2 Remove the secondary inner trunk panel clips and lift the panel out.

3 Disconnect the harness connector between the power antenna unit and the antenna timer.

4 Use a 12 volt battery for a voltage source and apply power to terminals 1 and 2 to make sure the antenna rod extends and retracts **(see illustrations)**.

5 Connect a voltmeter across terminal 3 and the ground terminal of the battery **(see illustration 17.4a)**. Raise and lower the antenna and observe the voltage reading.

6 The voltage should not vary more than 1 or 2 volts when power is applied. If the above tests are not satisfactory, replace the antenna motor.

21.1 Remove the cable assembly retaining bolt (arrow) and lift the speedometer cable out of the transaxle housing

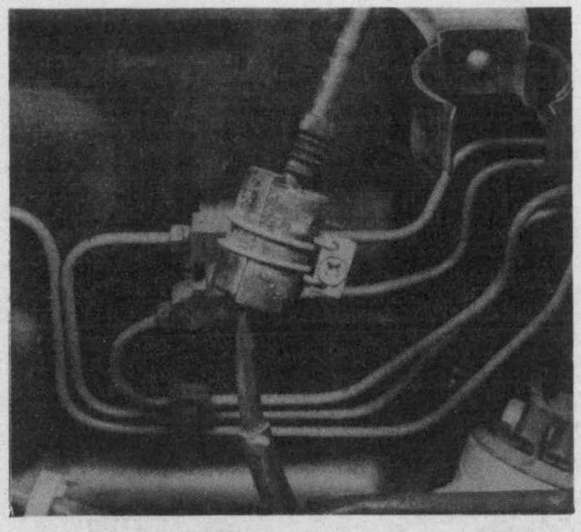

21.2 Loosen the clamp on the rubber grommet and remove it from the speedometer cable

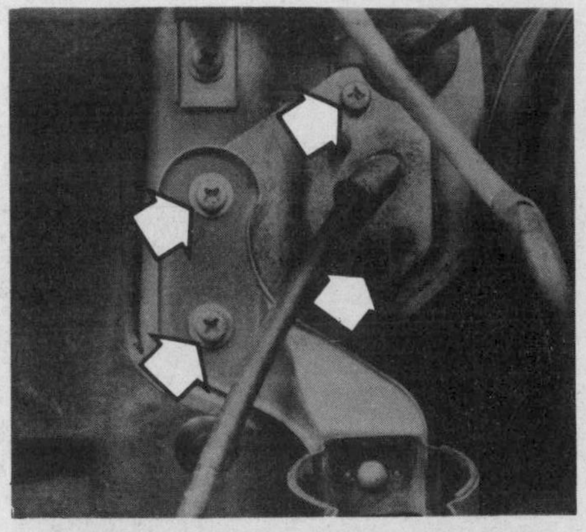

21.3 Disconnect the speedometer cable mounting assembly on the inner wall of the engine compartment (arrows)

18 Cruise control system – description and check

The cruise control system maintains vehicle speed with a vacuum actuated servo motor located in the engine compartment, which is connected to the throttle linkage by a cable. The system consists of the servo motor, clutch switch, brake switch, control switches, a relay and associated vacuum hoses.

Because of the complexity of the cruise control system and the special tools and techniques required for diagnosis, repair should be left to a dealer service department or a repair shop. However, it is possible for the home mechanic to make simple checks of the wiring and vacuum connections for minor faults which can be easily repaired. These include:

a) Inspect the cruise control actuating switches for broken wires and loose connections.
b) Check the cruise control fuse.
c) The cruise control system is operated by vacuum so it's critical that all vacuum switches, hoses and connections are secure. Check the hoses in the engine compartment for tight connections, cracks and obvious vacuum leaks.

19 Power door lock system – description and check

The power door lock system operates the door lock actuators mounted in each door. The system consists of the switches, actuators and associated wiring. Since special tools and techniques are required to diagnose the system, it should be left to a dealer service department or a repair shop. However, it is possible for the home mechanic to make simple checks of the wiring connections and actuators for minor faults which can be easily repaired. These include:

a) Check the system fuse and/or circuit breaker.
b) Check the switch wires for damage and loose connections. Check the switches for continuity.
c) Remove the door panel(s) and check the actuator wiring connections to see if they're loose or damaged. Inspect the actuator rods (if equipped) to make sure they aren't bent or damaged. Inspect the actuator wiring for damaged or loose connections. The actuator can be checked by applying battery power momentarily. A discernible click indicates that the solenoid is operating properly.

20 Power window system – description and check

The power window system operates the electric motors mounted in the doors which lower and raise the windows. The system consists of the control switches, the motors (regulators), glass mechanisms and associated wiring.

Because of the complexity of the power window system and the special tools and techniques required for diagnosis, repair should be left to a dealer service department or a repair shop. However, it is possible for the home mechanic to make simple checks of the wiring connections and motors for minor faults which can be easily repaired. These include:

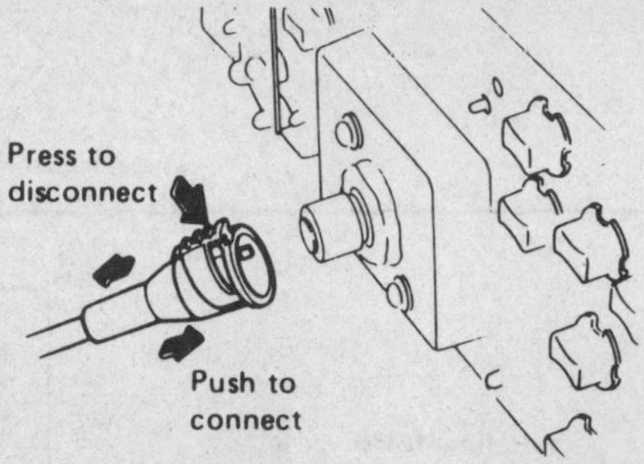

21.5 Press the locking tab on the speedometer cable and separate it from the instrument cluster

a) Inspect the power window actuating switches for broken wires and loose connections.
b) Check the power window fuse/and or circuit breaker.
c) Remove the door panel(s) and check the power window motor wires to see if they're loose or damaged. Inspect the glass mechanisms for damage which could cause binding.

21 Speedometer cable – removal and installation

Refer to illustrations 21.1, 21.2, 21.3 and 21.5

1 Disconnect the speedometer cable from the transaxle. Remove the cable assembly retaining bolt and lift the speedometer cable out of the transaxle housing **(see illustration)**.

2 Loosen the clamp on the rubber grommet assembly on the speedometer cable and remove the grommet **(see illustration)**.

3 Disconnect the speedometer cable mounting assembly on the engine compartment wall **(see illustration)** and push the cable into the dashboard area.

4 Remove the instrument cluster (see Section 16).

5 Press the locking tab on the speedometer cable housing directly behind the instrument cluster and separate the speedometer cable **(see illustration)** from the instrument cluster.

6 Installation is the reverse of removal.

22 Rear window defogger – troubleshooting

Refer to illustrations 22.2, 22.3 and 22.4

1 Turn the ignition switch to the On position and activate the rear window defogger switch.

2 Attach the voltmeter probes to the filaments on the rear window **(see illustration)**. A normal reading should be 6 volts.

3 If a filament is burned out or broken, the voltmeter will read either zero volt or 12 volts but not in between **(see illustration)**.

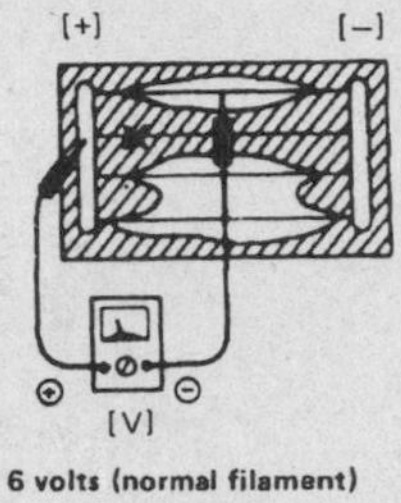

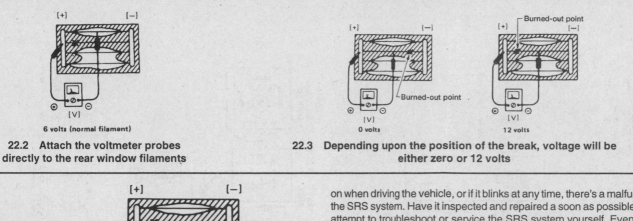

22.2 Attach the voltmeter probes directly to the rear window filaments

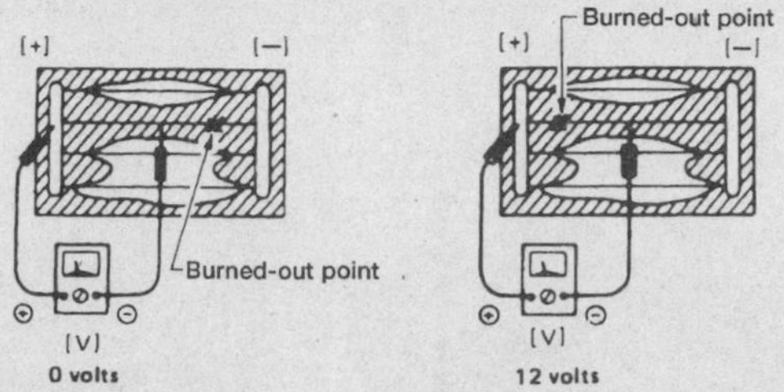

22.3 Depending upon the position of the break, voltage will be either zero or 12 volts

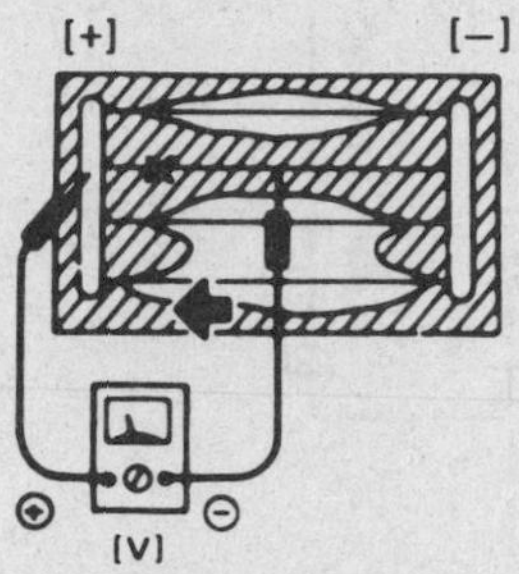

22.4 Move one of the probes along the filaments while the other probe remains stationary – observe the voltmeter for changes

4 To locate a burned or broken filament, move the probe to the left or right along the rows of filaments while the other probe is in a stationary position **(see illustration)**.

5 If there is no power reaching the filaments at any spot, trace the short in the wiring harness of the vehicle.

23 Airbag system – general information

1 The 1992 models are equipped with a Supplemental Restraint System (SRS), more commonly known as an airbag, designed to protect the driver from serious injury in the event of head-on or frontal collision. These models have a diagnostic/control unit inside the passenger compartment.

Airbag module

2 The airbag module consists of a housing incorporating the cushion (airbag) and inflator unit. The inflator assembly is mounted on the back of the housing over a hole through which gas is expelled, inflating the bag almost instantaneously when an electrical signal is sent from the system. The specially wound wire on the steering wheel that carries this signal to the module is called a spiral cable. The spiral cable is a flat, ribbon-like electrically conductive tape that is wound many times so that it can transmit an electrical signal regardless of the steering wheel position.

Diagnostic/control unit

3 The diagnostic/control unit contains an on-board microprocessor which monitors the operation of the system, and also contains a crash sensor. It checks the system every time the vehicle is started, causing the AIRBAG light to go on then off, if the system is operating properly. If there is a fault in the system, the light will go on and stay on and will store fault code(s) indicating the nature of the fault. If the AIRBAG light goes on and stays on, the vehicle should be taken to your dealership immediately for service.

Operation

4 For the airbag to deploy, one or both of the impact sensors must be activated. When this condition occurs, the circuit to the airbag module is closed and the airbag inflates. If the battery is destroyed by the impact, or is too low to power the inflator, a back-up power unit inside the SRS unit provides power.

Self-diagnosis system

5 A self-diagnosis circuit in the SRS unit displays a light on the instrument panel when the ignition switch is turned to the On position. If the system is operating normally, the light should go out after seven seconds. If the light doesn't come on, or doesn't go out after sevens seconds, or if it comes on when driving the vehicle, or if it blinks at any time, there's a malfunction in the SRS system. Have it inspected and repaired a soon as possible. Do not attempt to troubleshoot or service the SRS system yourself. Even a small mistake could cause the SRS system to malfunction when you need it.

Servicing components near the SRS system

6 Nevertheless, there are times when you need to remove the steering wheel, radio or service other components on or near the instrument panel. At these times, you'll be working around components and wire harnesses for the SRS system. The SRS system wiring harnesses are easy to identify: They're bright yellow. Do not unplug the connectors for these wires. And do not use electrical test equipment on the SRS system yellow wires; it could cause the airbag to deploy. **ALWAYS DISABLE THE SRS SYSTEM BEFORE WORKING NEAR THE SRS SYSTEM COMPONENTS OR RELATED WIRING.**

Disabling the SRS system

Warning: *Any time you are working in the vicinity of airbag wiring or components, DISABLE THE SRS SYSTEM.*

7 Disconnect the battery negative and positive cables, then wait ten minutes before proceeding.

8 Remove the access cover panel in the steering wheel below the airbag and unplug the two-pin connector between the airbag and the spiral cable.

Enabling the system

9 After you've disabled the airbag and performed the necessary service, reconnect the two-pin air bag connector into the two-pin spiral cable connector. Reinstall the cover panel on the underside of the steering wheel.

10 Turn the ignition switch to the Off position.

11 Reattach both battery cables (see Chapter 1).

Removal and installation

12 Refer to Chapter 10 for removal and installation of the driver's airbag.

24 Wiring diagrams – general information

Wiring diagrams

1 Since it isn't possible to include all wiring diagrams for every year covered by this manual, the following diagrams are those that are typical and most commonly needed.

2 Prior to troubleshooting any circuits, check the fuse and circuit breakers (if equipped) to make sure they're in good condition. Make sure the battery is properly charged and check the cable connections (Chapter 1).

3 When checking a circuit, make sure that all connectors are clean, with no broken or loose terminals. When unplugging a connector, do not pull on the wires. Pull only on the connector housings themselves.

Super Multiple Junction (S.M.J)

4 These vehicles are equipped with a complete terminal block for testing the circuits within the wiring diagram.

5 Disconnect the negative battery cable and remove the fuse block to gain access to the S.M.J.

6 Slide the fuse block to the side and remove the S.M.J. retaining bolts to gain access to the terminals.

7 Each terminal has a letter and number designation and can be matched with the corresponding wiring diagram.

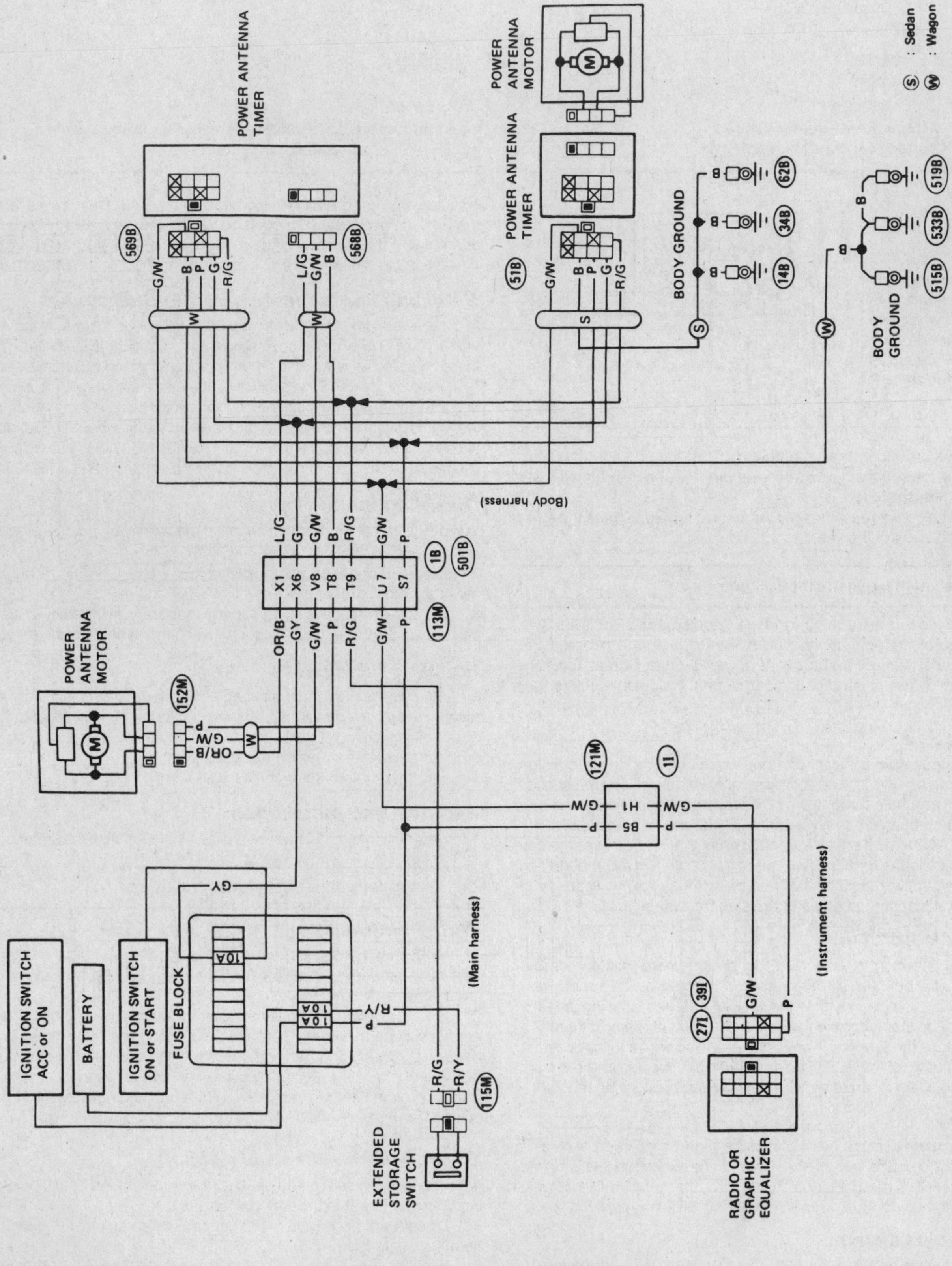

Power antenna wiring diagram (typical)

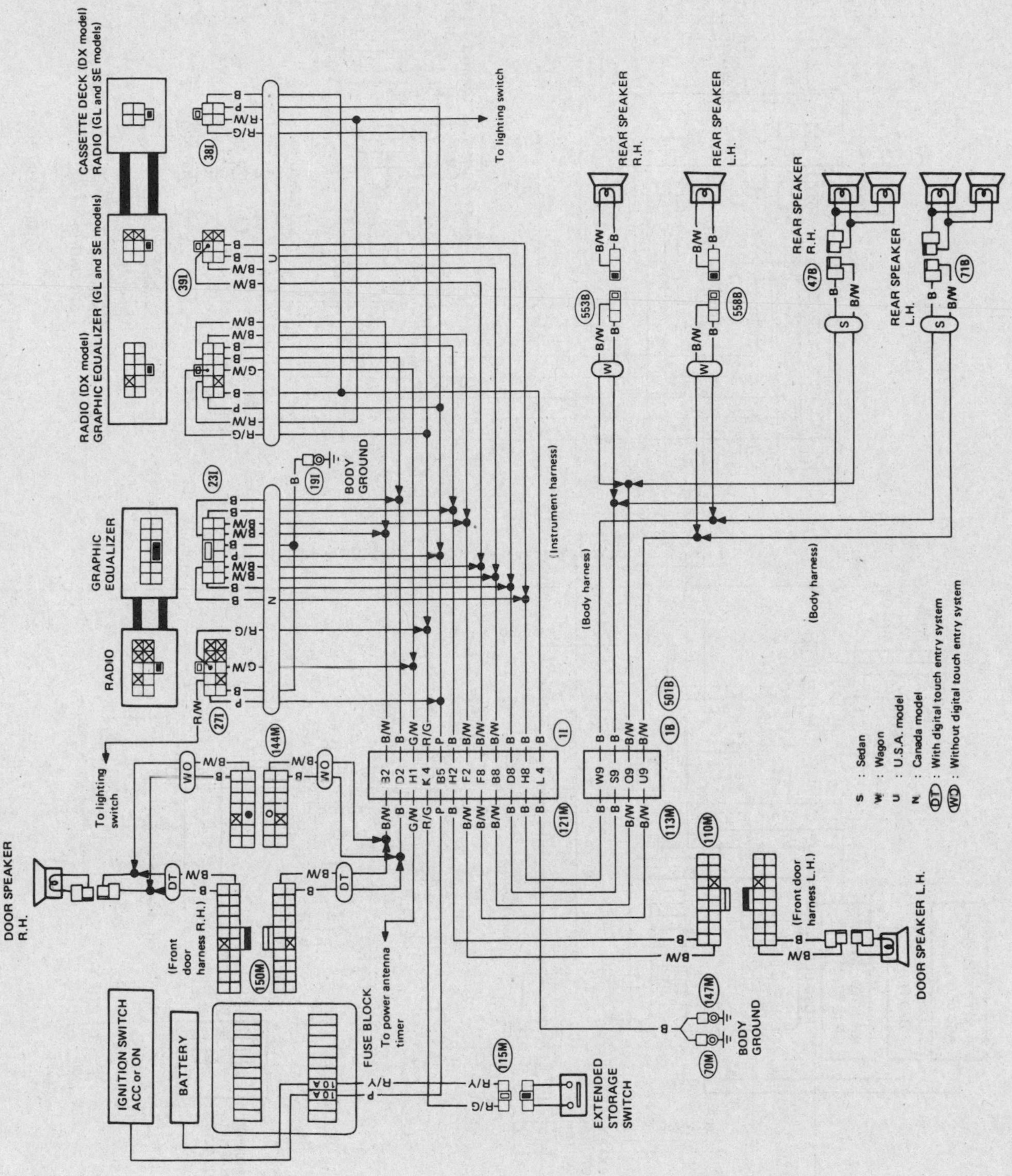

Audio wiring diagram (typical)

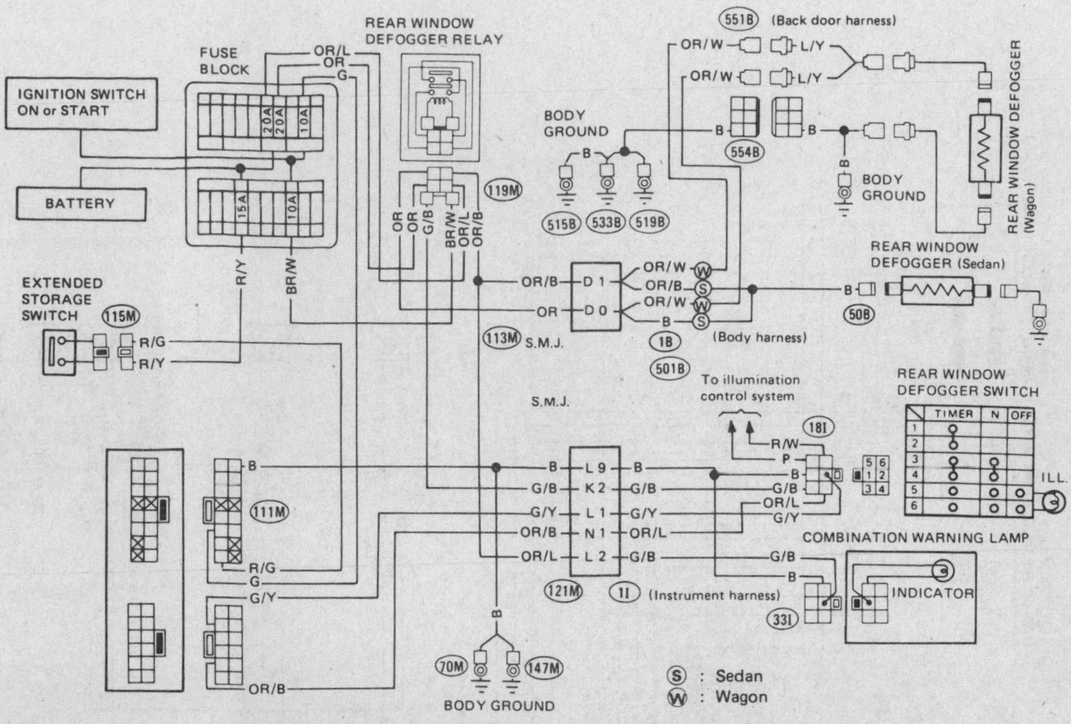

Rear window defogger wiring diagram (1985 models)

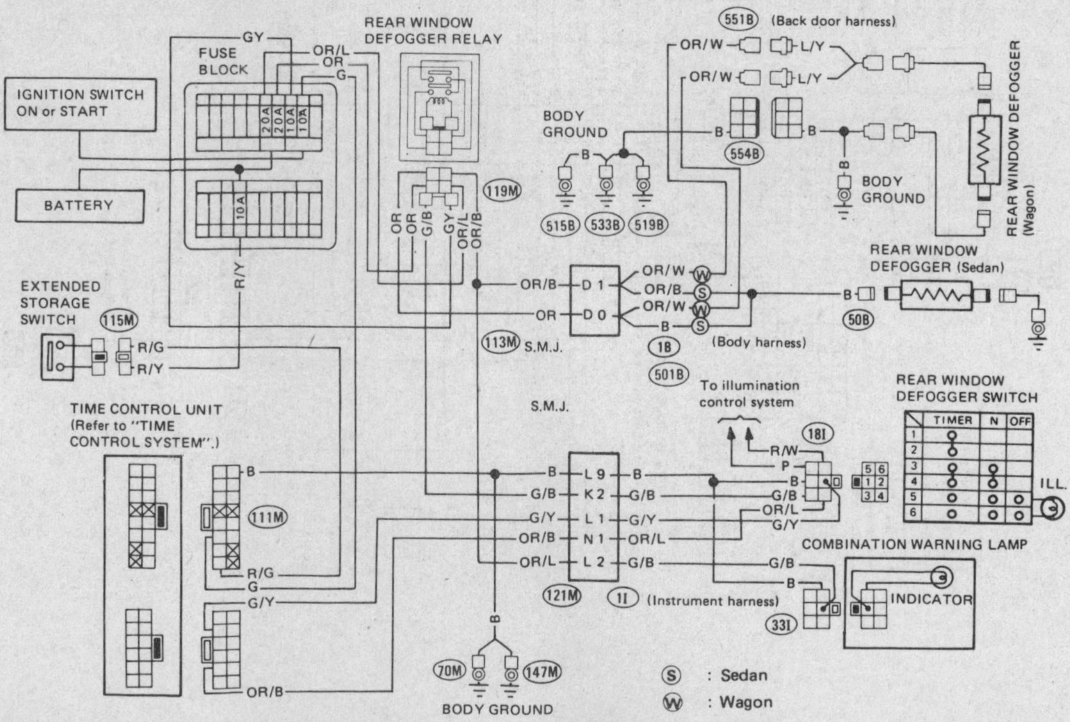

Rear window defogger diagram (1986 through 1988 models)

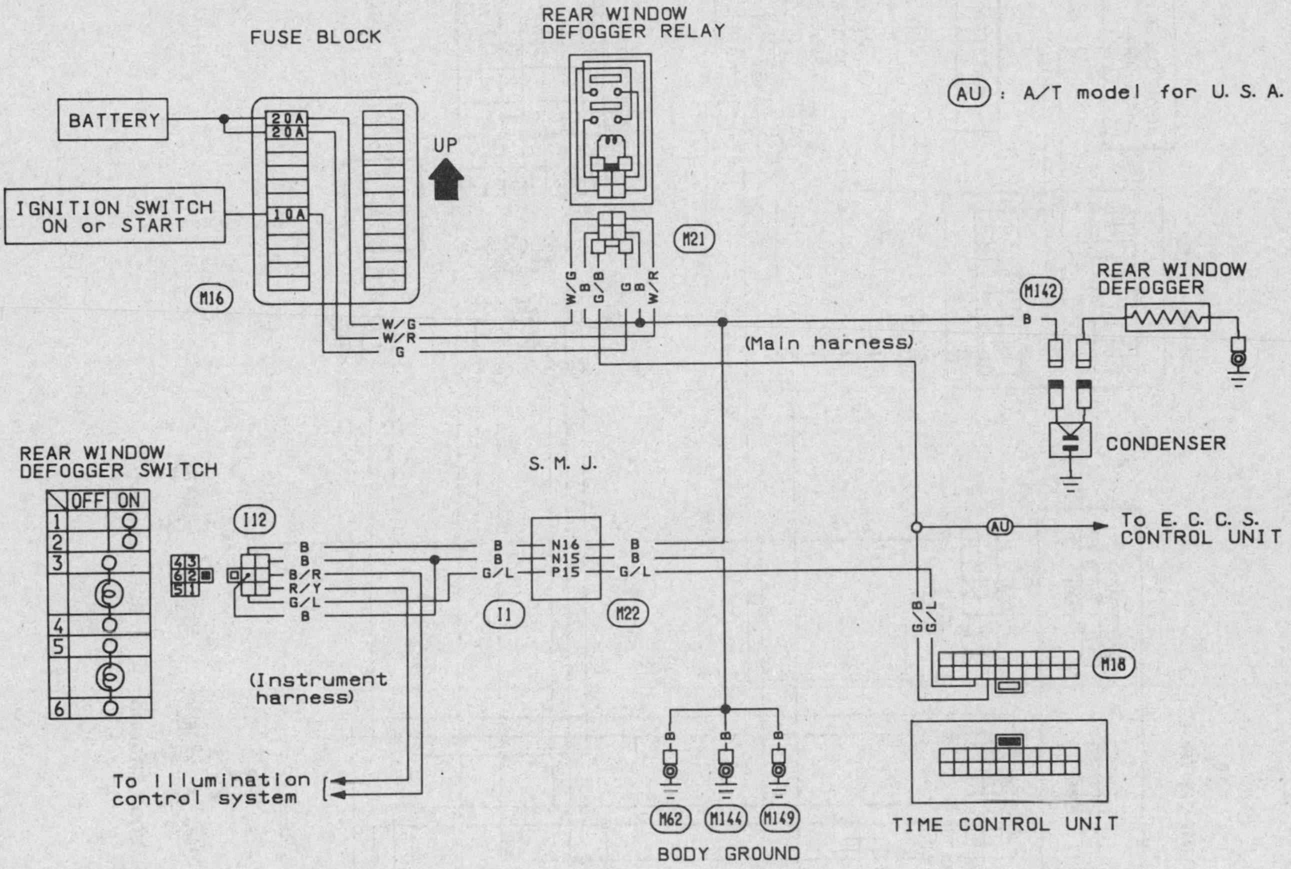

Rear window defogger wiring diagram (later models)

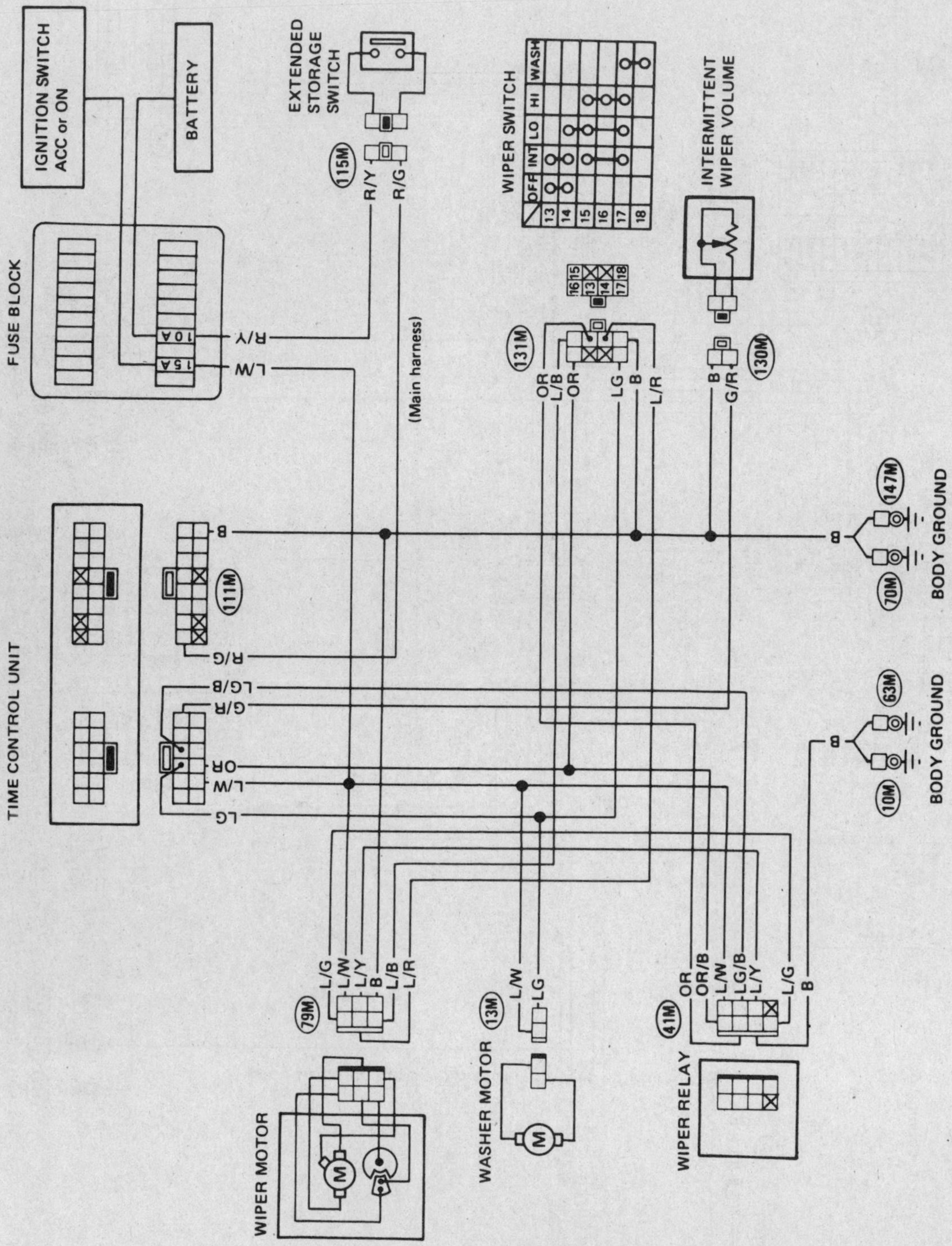

Front wiper and washer wiring diagram (1985 through 1988 models)

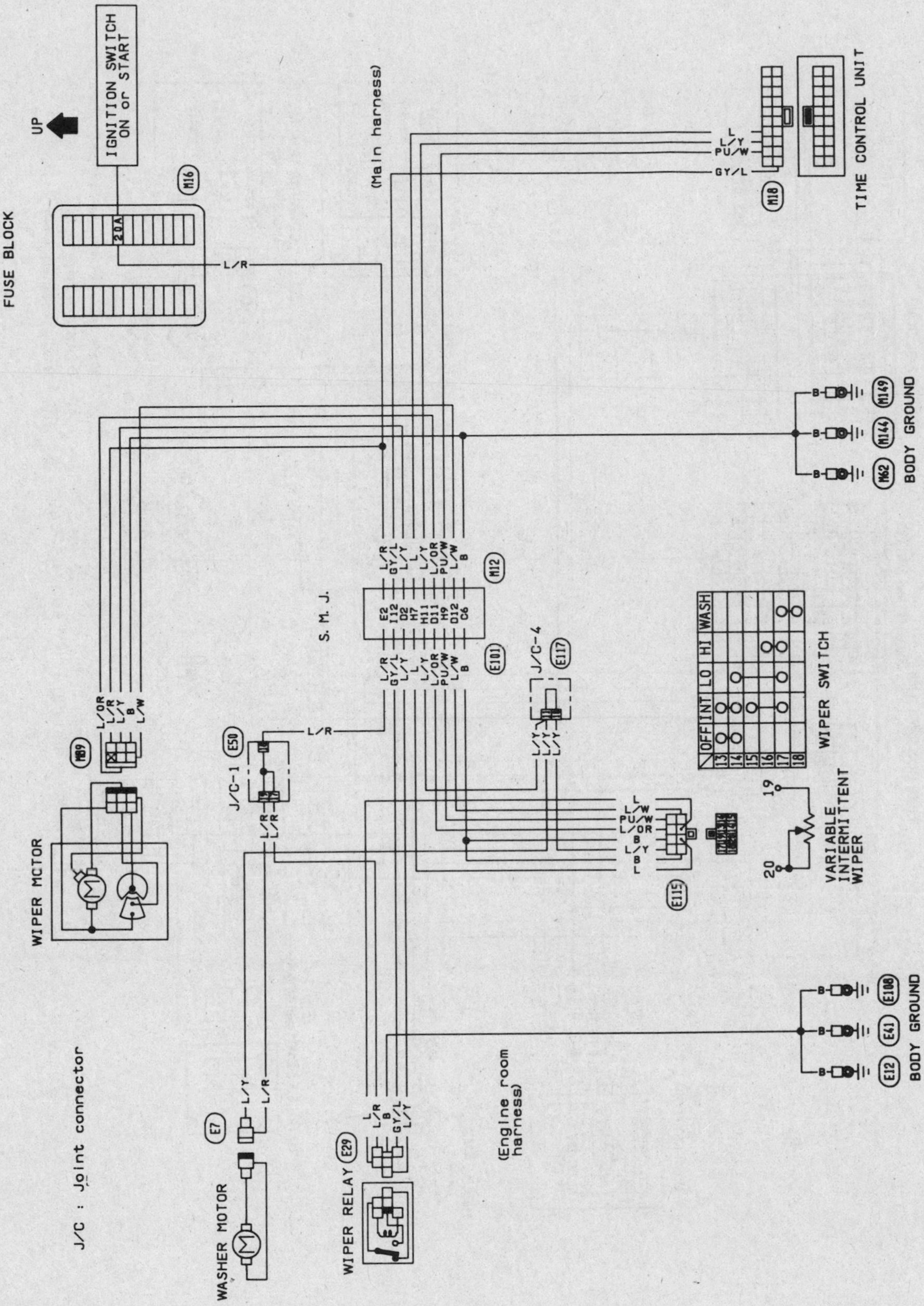

Front wiper and washer wiring diagram (later models)

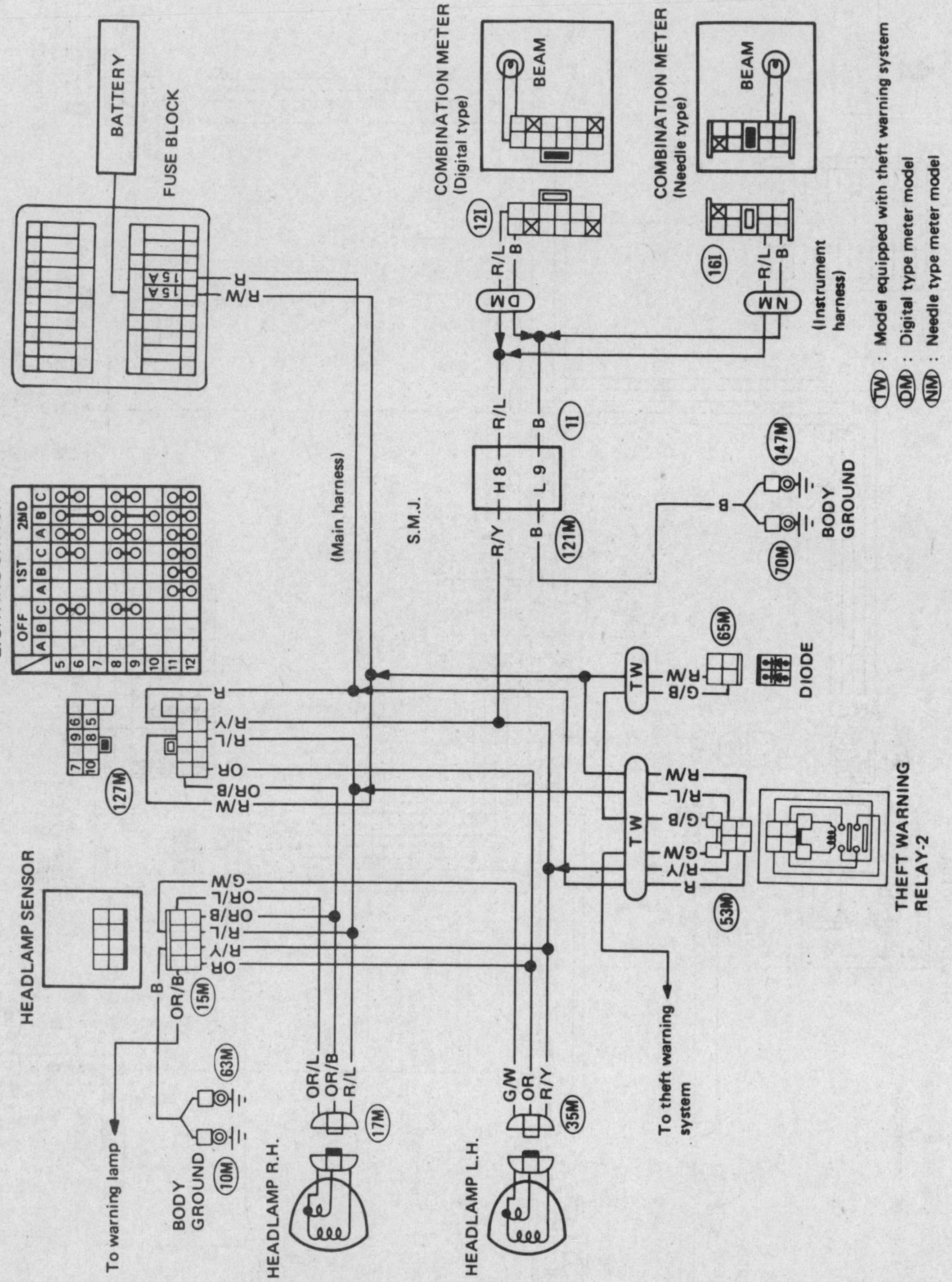

Headlight wiring diagram (1985 through 1988 USA models)

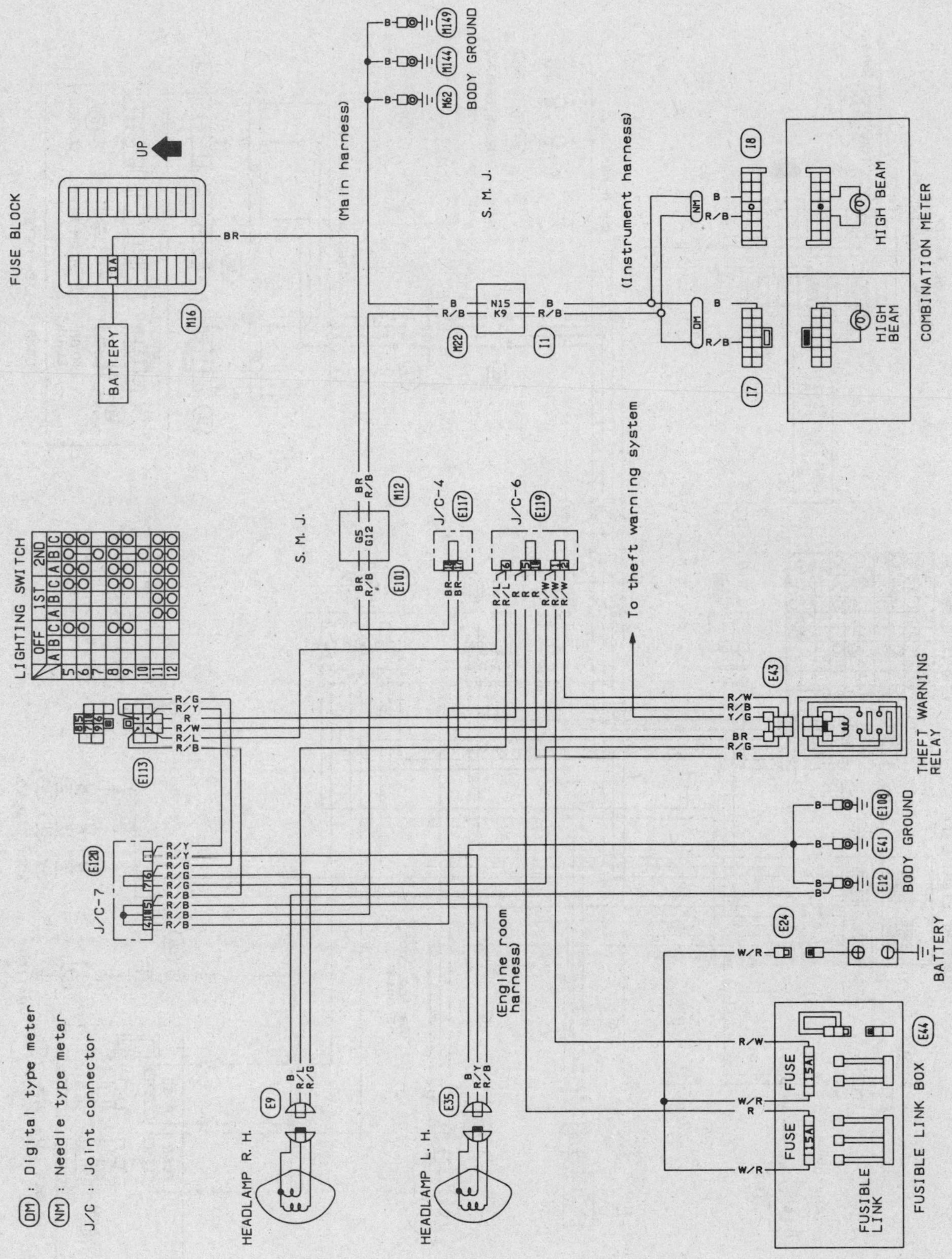

Headlight wiring diagram (later USA models)

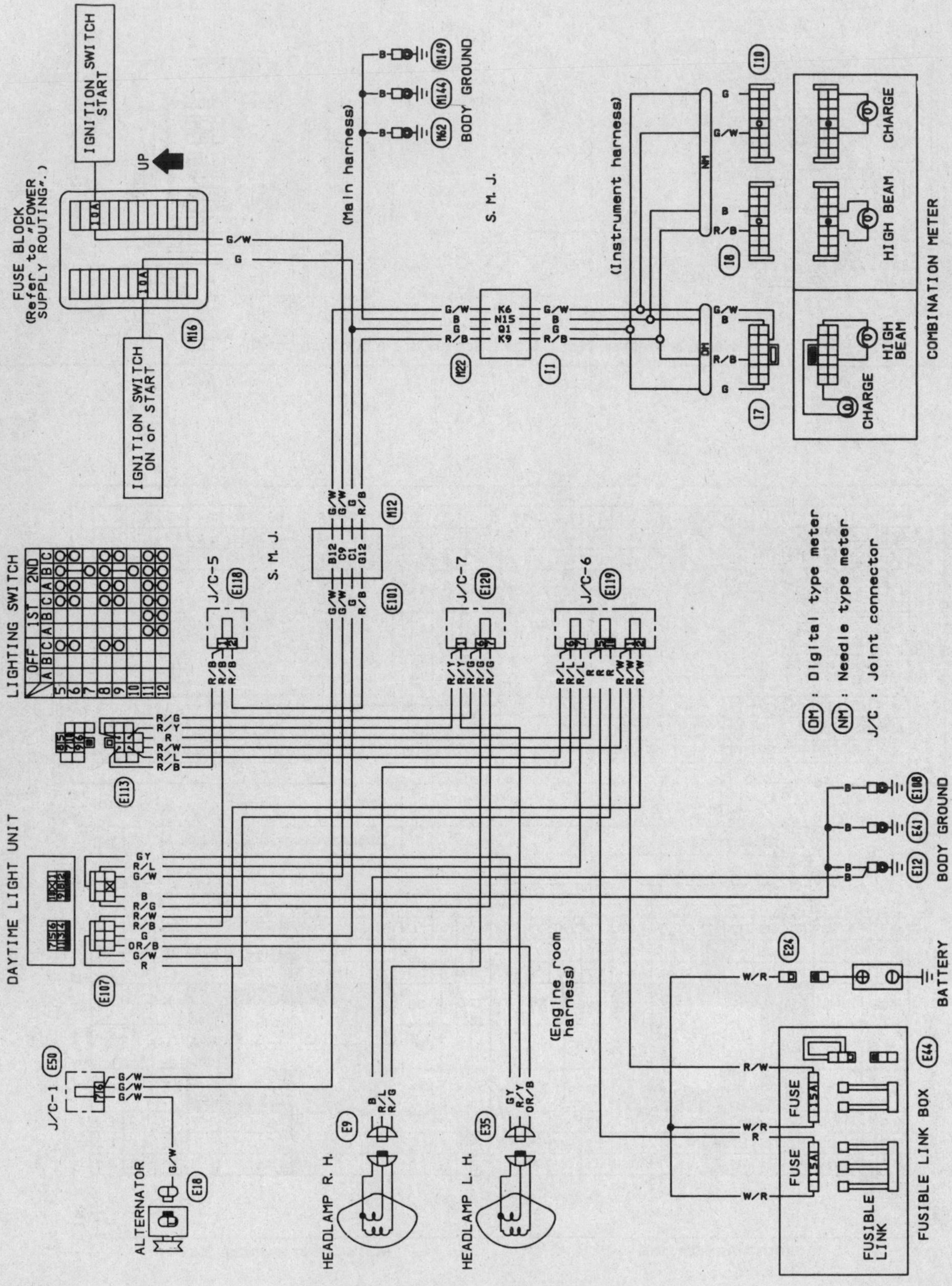

Headlight wiring diagram (typical Canada models)

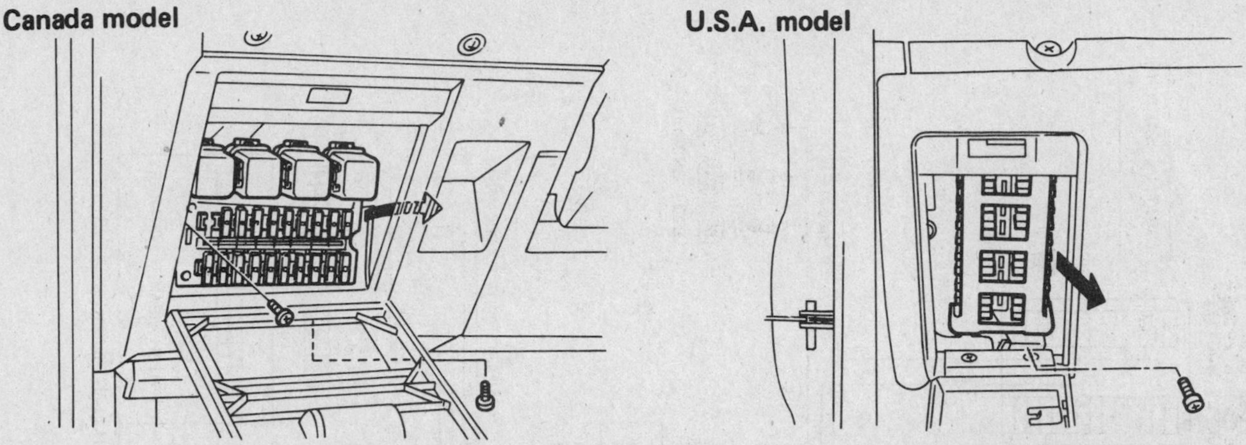

Remove the fuse block to gain access to the S.M.J. (typical)

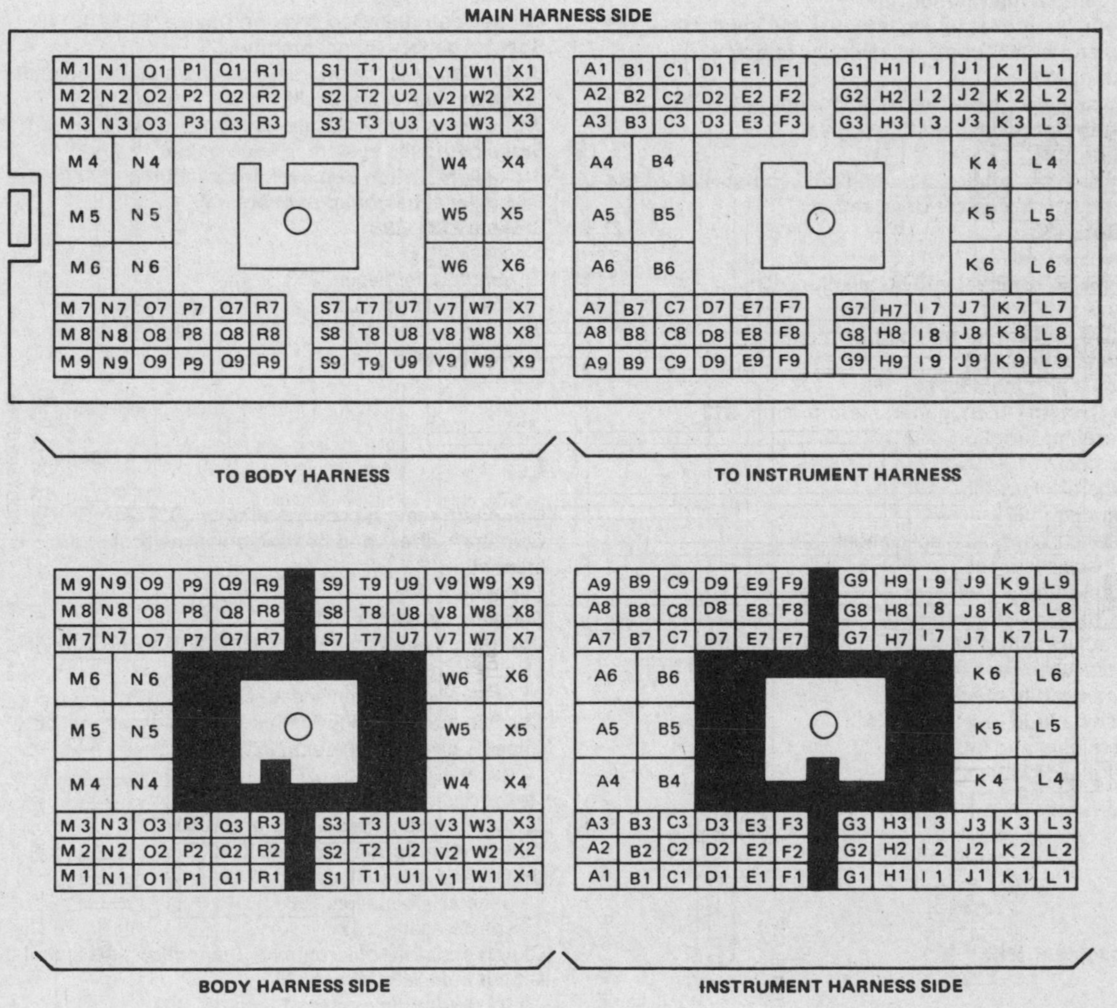

On 1987 models, the S.M.J. can be accessed from the harness side or the terminal side

Index

A

About this manual, 5
Adjustable Shock Absorber and Sonar Suspension systems, general information, 237
Airbag system, general information, 289
Air cleaner assembly/air inlet tubes, removal and installation, 142
Air conditioning and heater control assembly, removal and installation, 131
Air conditioning system, check and maintenance, 132
Air conditioning system compressor, removal and installation, 134
Air conditioning system condenser, removal and installation, 134
Air conditioning system receiver/drier, removal and installation, 133
Air filter, replacement, 46
Air flow meter, check, removal and installation, 161
Air Injection Valve (AIV), 181
Air regulator (1988 and earlier models), removal, check and installation, 154
Alternator, removal and installation, 169
Anti-lock Brake System (ABS), general information, 213
Antifreeze, general information, 122
Automatic transaxle, 191—196
diagnosis, general information, 192
general information, 192
neutral start switch, check and adjustment, 194
removal and installation, 195
shift linkage, adjustment, 192
specifications, 191
throttle cable adjustment, 193
transaxle mount, check and replacement, 195
Automatic transaxle fluid change, 56
Automatic transaxle fluid level check, 41
Automotive chemicals and lubricants, 17
Auxiliary Air Control (AAC) valve, 182

B

Balljoints, replacement, 243
Battery
jump starting, 15
removal and installation, 164
Battery cables, check and replacement, 164
Battery check and maintenance, 41
Battery electrolyte, level check, 36
Blower unit, removal and installation, 129
Body, 256—269
general information, 256
maintenance, 256—269
Body repair
major damage, 258
minor damage, 257
Boost Controlled Deceleration Device (BCDD), 178
Booster battery (jump) starting, 15
Brake disc, inspection, removal and installation, 220
Brake fluid level check, 36
Brake hoses and lines, inspection and replacement, 227
Brake hydraulic system, bleeding, 228
Brake light switch, removal, installation and adjustment, 232
Brake pedal height adjustment, 47
Brakes, 212—232
check, 45
general information, 213
specifications, 212
Bulb replacement, 284
Buying parts, 8

C

Camshaft, removal and installation, 83
Camshaft, lifters and bearing surfaces/rocker arms and shafts, inspection, 84
Capacities, 29
Catalytic converter, 183
Charging system
check, 168
general information and precautions, 168
Chassis and body lubrication and maintenance, 46
Chassis electrical system, 270—299
general information, 271
specifications, 270
Circuit breakers, general information, 273
Clutch, description and check, 198
Clutch and driveaxles, 197—211
general information, 198
specifications, 197
Clutch components, removal, inspection and installation, 199
Clutch fluid level check, 36
Clutch hydraulic system, bleeding, 204
Clutch interlock system, inspection and adjustment, 205
Clutch master cylinder, removal, overhaul and installation, 201
Clutch pedal height and freeplay check and adjustment, 47
Clutch release bearing and lever, removal, inspection and installation, 200

Clutch release cylinder, removal, overhaul and installation, 203
Combination switch, removal and installation, 281
Constant velocity (CV) joint, overhaul, 207
Control arm, removal, inspection and installation, 242
Coolant level check, 35
Coolant reservoir, removal and installation, 126
Coolant temperature sending unit, check and replacement, 128
Cooling system check, 42
Cooling system servicing, 55
Cooling, heating and air conditioning systems, 121—135
 general information, 122
 specifications, 121
Crank angle sensor, check, 167
Crankshaft
 inspection, 112
 installation and main bearing oil clearance check, 116
 removal, 107
Crankshaft front oil seal, replacement, 77
Crankshaft oil seal, replacement, 78
Crankshaft pulley, removal and installation, 72
Crankshaft rear oil seal, replacement, 91
Cruise control system, description and check, 288
Cylinder compression check, 96
Cylinder head
 cleaning and inspection, 104
 disassembly, 103
 reassembly, 106
Cylinder head temperature sensor, check and replacement, 155
Cylinder head(s), removal and installation, 81
Cylinder honing, 110

D

Distributor, removal and installation, 166
Door, removal, installation and adjustment, 264
Door lock, lock cylinder and handle, removal and installation, 265
Door trim panel, removal and installation, 259
Door window glass, removal and installation, 268
Driveaxle boot, replacement, 207
Driveaxle boots, check, 48
Driveaxles, removal and installation, 205
driveaxles, general information and inspection, 205
Drivebelt check, adjustment and replacement, 43

E

ECCS components, general information, 149
Electrical troubleshooting, general information, 271
Electronic Fuel Injection (EFI) system
 general diagnosis, 152
 general information, 137
Emissions control systems, 174—184
 specifications, 174
Engine, 63—92
 general information, 65
 removal and installation, 97
 specifications, 93
Engine block
 cleaning, 108
 inspection, 109
Engine coolant level check, 35
Engine cooling fans, check and replacement, 124
Engine electrical systems, 163—173
 general information, 164
 specifications, 163
Engine mounts, check and replacement, 92
Engine oil and filter change, 39
Engine overhaul
 disassembly sequence, 101
 general information, 95
 reassembly sequence, 114
Engine overhaul procedures, 93—120
Engine rebuilding alternatives, 98
Engine removal, methods and precautions, 97
Engine specifications, 63
Evaporative emissions control system check, 59
Exhaust Gas Recirculation (EGR) system, 179
Exhaust Gas Recirculation (EGR) valve, check, 56
Exhaust gas sensor, check, 156
Exhaust gas sensor servicing, 53
Exhaust manifolds, removal and installation, 70
Exhaust system, check, 48
Exhaust system servicing, general information, 162

F

Fast Idle Control Device (FICD) valve, check and replacement, 160
Fault-finding, 20
Fender apron seal, removal and installation, 269
Fixed glass, replacement, 258
Fluid level checks, 35
Flywheel/driveplate, removal and installation, 90
Front brake caliper, removal, overhaul and installation, 216
Front brake pads, replacement, 216
Front end alignment, general information, 254
Front hub and bearing assembly, removal and installation, 243
Front stabilizer bar and bushings, removal and installation, 238
Front strut/shock absorber and coil spring assembly, removal, inspection and installation, 238
Front strut/shock absorber or coil spring, replacement, 240
Fuel and exhaust system, specifications, 136
Fuel and exhaust systems, 136—162
Fuel Evaporative Emission Control (EVAP) system, 175
Fuel filter replacement, 50
Fuel injectors, check, removal and installation, 157
Fuel level sending unit, check, removal and installation, 147
Fuel pressure regulator and control solenoid, check and replacement, 154
Fuel pressure relief procedure, 143
Fuel pump, removal and installation, 146
Fuel pump/fuel pressure, check, 144
Fuel system check, 54
Fuel tank, removal and installation, 145
Fuel tank cap gasket replacement, 58
Fuel tank cleaning and repair, general information, 146
Fuel temperature sensor, check and replacement, 156
Fuses, general information, 271
Fusible links, general information, 272

H

Headlights
 adjustment, 284
 removal and installation, 283

Heater core, removal and installation, 130
Hinges and locks, maintenance, 258
Hood, removal, installation and adjustment, 258

I

Ignition coil, check and replacement, 165
Ignition switch, removal and installation, 281
Ignition system
  check, 165
  general information and precautions, 164
Ignition timing check and adjustment, 59
Initial start-up and break-in after overhaul, 120
Instrument cluster, removal and installation, 285
Instrument panel finish panels, removal and installation, 260
Intake manifold, removal and installation, 68
Introduction to the Nissan Maxima, 5

J

Jacking, 15
Jump starting, 15

L

Lifters, removal and installation, 68
Lubricants and fluids, 29

M

Main and connecting rod bearings, inspection and main bearing selection, 113
Maintenance, 28—62
Maintenance schedule, 34
Maintenance specifications, 29
Maintenance techniques, tools and working facilities, 8
Manual transaxle, 185—190
  general information, 185
  oil seal replacement, 185
  overhaul, general information, 188
  removal and installation, 186
  shift lever, removal, installation and freeplay check, 186
  specifications, 185
Manual transaxle lubricant change, 56
Manual transaxle lubricant level check, 49
Master cylinder, removal, overhaul and installation, 225

O

Oil and filter change, 39
Oil level check, 35
Oil pan, removal and installation, 86
Oil pump, removal, inspection and installation, 88
Outside mirror, removal and installation, 268

P

Parallel links, removal and installation, 246
Parking brake, adjustment, 230
Parking brake cables, replacement, 231
Piston rings, inspection, 114
Pistons/connecting rods
  inspection, 110
  installation and rod bearing oil clearance check, 118
  removal, 106
Positive Crankcase Ventilation (PCV) system, 175
Positive Crankcase Ventilation (PCV) valve, check and replacement, 58
Power antenna, troubleshooting, 287
Power brake booster, check, removal and installation, 229
Power door lock system, description and check, 288
Power steering fluid, level check, 37
Power steering pump, removal and installation, 253
Power steering system, bleeding, 254
Power window system, description and check, 288

R

Radiator, removal and installation, 125
Radio and speakers, removal and installation, 282
Radius rod, removal and installation, 247
Rear brake caliper, removal and installation, 223
Rear brake pads, replacement, 220
Rear brake shoes, replacement, 223
Rear hub and wheel bearing, check, repack and adjustment, 243
Rear main oil seal installation, 118
Rear stabilizer bar and bushings, removal and installation, 246
Rear strut/shock absorber, coil spring and wheel spindle assembly, inspection, removal, overhaul and installation, 248
Rear window defogger, troubleshooting, 288
Relays, general information, 273
Repair operations possible with the engine in the vehicle, 65
Rocker arm components, removal and installation, 67
Rocker arm covers, removal and installation, 66

S

Safety first, 18
Seatbelt, check, 46
Seats, removal and installation, 268
Spark plug replacement, 52
Spark plug wire, distributor cap and rotor, check and replacement, 50
Speedometer cable, removal and installation, 288
Starter motor
  brush replacement, 172
  removal and installation, 171
  testing in vehicle, 171
Starter solenoid, removal and installation, 172
Starting system, general information and precautions, 169
Steering, specifications, 233
Steering column cover, removal and installation, 264
Steering column switches, removal and installation, 282
Steering gear, removal and installation, 252
Steering gear boots, replacement, 253
Steering knuckle and hub, removal and installation, 243
Steering system, 233—255
  general information, 250

Steering wheel, removal and installation, 250
Sunroof, lubrication and adjustment, 265
Suspension, specifications, 233
Suspension and steering, check, 48
Suspension and steering systems, general information, 234
Suspension system, 233—255

T

Thermostat, check and replacement, 122
Throttle cable, removal and installation, 142
Throttle chamber, removal and installation, 160
Throttle valve switch
- adjustment, 159
- check, 159

Tie-rod ends, removal and installation, 253
Timing belt, removal, installation and adjustment, 73
Tire and tire pressure checks, 37
Tire rotation, 50
Top Dead Center (TDC) for number one piston, locating, 65
Towing, 15
Troubleshooting, 20
Trunk lid, removal, installation and adjustment, 265
Tune-up, general information, 30
Tune-up and routine maintenance, 28—62
- introduction, 30

Tune-up specifications, 29
Turn signal/hazard flashers, check and replacement, 281

U

Underhood hose check and replacement, 46
Upholstery and carpets, maintenance, 257

V

Vacuum chamber, removal and installation, 161
Valve spring, retainer and seals, replacement, 79
Valves, servicing, 105
Vehicle identification numbers, 6
Vinyl trim, maintenance, 257
Voltage regulator and brushes, replacement, 169

W

Warning lights, general information, 61
Water pump
- check, 127
- replacement, 128

Wheel cylinder, removal, overhaul and installation, 223
Wheels and tires, general information, 254
Windshield washer fluid, level check, 36
Windshield wiper motor, removal and installation, 284
Wiper blade inspection and replacement, 39
Wiring diagrams, general information, 289

Haynes Automotive Manuals

NOTE: New manuals are added to this list on a periodic basis. If you do not see a listing for your vehicle, consult your local Haynes dealer for the latest product information.

ACURA
- 12020 Integra '86 thru '89 & Legend '86 thru '90
- 12021 Integra '90 thru '93 & Legend '91 thru '95

AMC
- Jeep CJ - see JEEP (50020)
- 14020 Concord/Hornet/Gremlin/Spirit '70 thru '83
- 14025 (Renault) Alliance & Encore '83 thru '87

AUDI
- 15020 4000 all models '80 thru '87
- 15025 5000 all models '77 thru '83
- 15026 5000 all models '84 thru '88

AUSTIN
- Healey Sprite - see MG Midget (66015)

BMW
- *18020 3/5 Series '82 thru '92
- 18021 3 Series including Z3 models '92 thru '98
- 18025 320i all 4 cyl models '75 thru '83
- 18050 1500 thru 2002 except Turbo '59 thru '77

BUICK
- *19010 Buick Century '97 thru '02
- Century (FWD) - see GM (38005)
- *19020 Buick, Oldsmobile & Pontiac Full-size (Front wheel drive) '85 thru '02
- 19025 Buick Oldsmobile & Pontiac Full-size (Rear wheel drive) '70 thru '90
- 19030 Mid-size Regal & Century '74 thru '87
- Regal - see GENERAL MOTORS (38010)
- Skyhawk - see GM (38030)
- Skylark - see GM (38020, 38025)
- Somerset - see GENERAL MOTORS (38025)

CADILLAC
- 21030 Cadillac Rear Wheel Drive '70 thru '93
- Cimarron, Eldorado & Seville - see GM (38015, 38030, 38031)

CHEVROLET
- 10305 Chevrolet Engine Overhaul Manual
- *24010 Astro & GMC Safari Mini-vans '85 thru '03
- 24015 Camaro V8 all models '70 thru '81
- 24016 Camaro all models '82 thru '92
- Cavalier - see GM (38015)
- Celebrity - see GM (38005)
- 24017 Camaro & Firebird '93 thru '02
- 24020 Chevelle, Malibu, El Camino '69 thru '87
- 24024 Chevette & Pontiac T1000 '76 thru '87
- Citation - see GENERAL MOTORS (38020)
- 24032 Corsica/Beretta all models '87 thru '96
- 24040 Corvette all V8 models '68 thru '82
- 24041 Corvette all models '84 thru '96
- 24045 Full-size Sedans Caprice, Impala, Biscayne, Bel Air & Wagons '69 thru '90
- 24046 Impala SS & Caprice and Buick Roadmaster '91 thru '96
- Lumina '90 thru '94 - see GM (38010)
- *24048 Lumina & Monte Carlo '95 thru '03
- Lumina APV - see GM (38035)
- 24050 Luv Pick-up all 2WD & 4WD '72 thru '82
- Malibu - see GM (38026)
- 24055 Monte Carlo all models '70 thru '88
- Monte Carlo '95 thru '01 - see LUMINA
- 24059 Nova all V8 models '69 thru '79
- 24060 Nova/Geo Prizm '85 thru '92
- 24064 Pick-ups '67 thru '87 - Chevrolet & GMC, all V8 & in-line 6 cyl, 2WD & 4WD '67 thru '87; Suburbans, Blazers & Jimmys '67 thru '91
- 24065 Pick-ups '88 thru '98 - Chevrolet & GMC, all full-size models '88 thru '98; C/K Classic '99 & '00; Blazer & Jimmy '92 thru '94; Suburban '92 thru '99; Tahoe & Yukon '95 thru '99
- *24066 Pick-ups '99 thru '02 - Chevrolet Silverado & GMC Sierra '99 thru '02; Suburban/Tahoe/Yukon/Yukon XL '00 thru '02
- 24070 S-10 & GMC S-15 Pick-ups '82 thru '93
- *24071 S-10, Gmc S-15 & Jimmy '94 thru '01
- *24072 Chevrolet TrailBlazer & TrailBlazer EXT, GMC Envoy & Envoy XL, Oldsmobile Bravada '02 and '03
- 24075 Sprint '85 thru '88, Geo Metro '89 thru '01
- 24080 Vans - Chevrolet & GMC '68 thru '96

CHRYSLER
- 10310 Chrysler Engine Overhaul Manual
- 25015 Chrysler Cirrus, Dodge Stratus, Plymouth Breeze, '95 thru '98
- 25020 Full-size Front-Wheel Drive '88 thru '93
- K-Cars - see DODGE Aries (30008)
- Laser - see DODGE Daytona (30030)
- 25025 Chrysler LHS, Concorde & New Yorker, Dodge Intrepid, Eagle Vision, '93 thru '97
- *25026 Chrysler LHS, Concorde, 300M, Dodge Intrepid '98 thru '03
- 25030 Chrysler/Plym. Mid-size '82 thru '95
- Rear-wheel Drive - see DODGE (30050)
- *25035 PT Cruiser all models '01 thru '03
- *25040 Chrysler Sebring/Dodge Avenger '95 thru '02

DATSUN
- 28005 200SX all models '80 thru '83
- 28007 B-210 all models '73 thru '78
- 28009 210 all models '78 thru '82
- 28012 240Z, 260Z & 280Z Coupe '70 thru '78
- 28014 280ZX Coupe & 2+2 '79 thru '83
- 300ZX - see NISSAN (72010)
- 28016 310 all models '78 thru '82
- 28018 510 & PL521 Pick-up '68 thru '73
- 28020 510 all models '78 thru '81
- 28022 620 Series Pick-up all models '73 thru '79
- 720 Series Pick-up - NISSAN (72030)
- 28025 810/Maxima all gas models, '77 thru '84

DODGE
- 400 & 600 - see CHRYSLER (25030)
- 30008 Aries & Plymouth Reliant '81 thru '89
- 30010 Caravan & Ply. Voyager '84 thru '95
- *30011 Caravan & Ply. Voyager '96 thru '02
- 30012 Challenger/Plymouth Saporro '78 thru '83
- Challenger '67-'76 - see DART (30025)
- 30016 Colt/Plymouth Champ '78 thru '87
- 30020 Dakota Pick-ups all models '87 thru '96
- *30021 Durango '98 & '99, Dakota '97 thru '99
- 30025 Dart, Challenger/Plymouth Barracuda & Valiant 6 cyl models '67 thru '76
- 30030 Daytona & Chrysler Laser '84 thru '89
- Intrepid - see Chrysler (25025, 25026)
- *30034 Dodge & Plymouth Neon '95 thru '99
- *30035 Omni & Plymouth Horizon '78 thru '90
- 30040 Pick-ups all full-size models '74 thru '93
- *30041 Pick-ups all full-size models '94 thru '01
- *30045 Ram 50/D50 Pick-ups & Raider and Plymouth Arrow Pick-ups '79 thru '93
- 30050 Dodge/Ply./Chrysler RWD '71 thru '89
- 30055 Shadow/Plymouth Sundance '87 thru '94
- 30060 Spirit & Plymouth Acclaim '89 thru '95
- *30065 Vans - Dodge & Plymouth '71 thru '03

EAGLE
- Talon - see MITSUBISHI (68030, 68031)
- Vision - see CHRYSLER (25025)

FIAT
- 34010 124 Sport Coupe & Spider '68 thru '78
- 34025 X1/9 all models '74 thru '80

FORD
- 10355 Ford Automatic Transmission Overhaul
- 10320 Ford Engine Overhaul Manual
- 36004 Aerostar Mini-vans '86 thru '97
- Aspire - see FORD Festiva (36030)
- 36006 Contour/Mercury Mystique '95 thru '00
- 36008 Courier Pick-up all models '72 thru '82
- *36012 Crown Victoria & Mercury Grand Marquis '88 thru '00
- 36016 Escort/Mercury Lynx '81 thru '90
- 36020 Escort/Mercury Tracer '91 thru '00
- Expedition - see FORD Pick-up (36059)
- 36022 Ford Escape & Mazda Tribute '01 thru '03
- *36024 Explorer & Mazda Navajo '91 thru '01
- 36025 Ford Explorer & Mercury Mountaineer '02 and '03
- 36028 Fairmont & Mercury Zephyr '78 thru '83
- 36030 Festiva & Aspire '88 thru '97
- 36032 Fiesta all models '77 thru '80
- *36034 Focus all models '00 and '01
- 36036 Ford & Mercury Full-size '75 thru '87
- 36044 Ford & Mercury Mid-size '75 thru '86
- 36048 Mustang V8 all models '64-1/2 thru '73
- 36049 Mustang II 4 cyl, V6 & V8 '74 thru '78
- 36050 Mustang & Mercury Capri '79 thru '86
- *36051 Mustang all models '94 thru '03
- 36054 Pick-ups and Bronco '73 thru '79
- 36058 Pick-ups and Bronco '80 thru '96
- *36059 Pick-ups, Expedition & Lincoln Navigator '97 thru '02
- *36060 Super Duty Pick-up, Excursion '97 thru '02
- 36062 Pinto & Mercury Bobcat '75 thru '80
- 36066 Probe all models '89 thru '92
- 36070 Ranger/Bronco II gas models '83 thru '92
- *36071 Ford Ranger '93 thru '00 & Mazda Pick-ups '94 thru '00
- 36074 Taurus & Mercury Sable '86 thru '95
- *36075 Taurus & Mercury Sable '96 thru '01
- 36078 Tempo & Mercury Topaz '84 thru '94
- 36082 Thunderbird/Mercury Cougar '83 thru '88
- 36086 Thunderbird/Mercury Cougar '89 thru '97
- 36090 Vans all V8 Econoline models '69 thru '91
- *36094 Vans full size '92 thru '01
- *36097 Windstar Mini-van '95 thru '03

GENERAL MOTORS
- 10360 GM Automatic Transmission Overhaul
- 38005 Buick Century, Chevrolet Celebrity, Olds Cutlass Ciera & Pontiac 6000 '82 thru '96
- *38010 Buick Regal, Chevrolet Lumina, Oldsmobile Cutlass Supreme & Pontiac Grand Prix front wheel drive '88 thru '02
- 38015 Buick Skyhawk, Cadillac Cimarron, Chevrolet Cavalier, Oldsmobile Firenza Pontiac J-2000 & Sunbird '82 thru '94
- *38016 Chevrolet Cavalier/Pontiac Sunfire '95 thru '04
- 38020 Buick Skylark, Chevrolet Citation, Olds Omega, Pontiac Phoenix '80 thru '85
- 38025 Buick Skylark & Somerset, Olds Achieva, Calais & Pontiac Grand Am '85 thru '98
- *38026 Chevrolet Malibu, Olds Alero & Cutlass, Pontiac Grand Am '97 thru '00
- 38030 Cadillac Eldorado & Oldsmobile Toronado '71 thru '85, Seville '80 thru '85, Buick Riviera '79 thru '85
- *38031 Cadillac Eldorado & Seville '86 thru '91, DeVille & Buick Riviera '86 thru '93, Fleetwood & Olds Toronado '86 thru '92
- 38032 DeVille '94 thru '02, Seville '92 thru '02
- 38035 Chevrolet Lumina APV, Oldsmobile Silhouette & Pontiac Trans Sport '90 thru '96
- *38036 Chevrolet Venture, Olds Silhouette, Pontiac Trans Sport & Montana '97 thru '01
- General Motors Full-size Rear-wheel Drive - see BUICK (19025)

GEO
- Metro - see CHEVROLET Sprint (24075)
- Prizm - see CHEVROLET (24060) or TOYOTA (92036)
- 40030 Storm all models '90 thru '93
- Tracker - see SUZUKI Samurai (90010)

GMC
- Vans & Pick-ups - see CHEVROLET

HONDA
- 42010 Accord CVCC all models '76 thru '83
- 42011 Accord all models '84 thru '89
- 42012 Accord all models '90 thru '93
- 42013 Accord all models '94 thru '97
- *42014 Accord all models '98 thru '02
- 42020 Civic 1200 all models '73 thru '79
- 42021 Civic 1300 & 1500 CVCC '80 thru '83
- 42022 Civic 1500 CVCC all models '75 thru '79
- 42023 Civic all models '84 thru '91
- 42024 Civic & del Sol '92 thru '95
- *42025 Civic '96 thru '00, CR-V '97 thru '00, Acura Integra '94 thru '00
- Passport - see ISUZU Rodeo (47017)
- 42026 Civic '01 thru '04, CR-V '02 thru '04
- *42040 Prelude CVCC all models '79 thru '89

HYUNDAI
- *43010 Elantra all models '96 thru '01
- 43015 Excel & Accent all models '86 thru '98

ISUZU
- Hombre - see CHEVROLET S-10 (24071)
- *47017 Rodeo '91 thru '02, Amigo '89 thru '02, Honda Passport '95 thru '02
- 47020 Trooper '84 thru '91, Pick-up '81 thru '93

JAGUAR
- 49010 XJ6 all 6 cyl models '68 thru '86
- 49011 XJ6 all models '88 thru '94
- 49015 XJ12 & XJS all 12 cyl models '72 thru '85

JEEP
- 50010 Cherokee, Comanche & Wagoneer Limited all models '84 thru '01
- 50020 CJ all models '49 thru '86
- *50025 Grand Cherokee all models '93 thru '04
- 50029 Grand Wagoneer & Pick-up '72 thru '91
- *50030 Wrangler all models '87 thru '00
- 50035 Liberty '02 thru '04

LEXUS
- ES 300 - see TOYOTA Camry (92007)

LINCOLN
- Navigator - see FORD Pick-up (36059)
- *59010 Rear Wheel Drive all models '70 thru '01

MAZDA
- 61010 GLC (rear wheel drive) '77 thru '83
- 61011 GLC (front wheel drive) '81 thru '85
- 61015 323 & Protegé '90 thru '00
- *61016 MX-5 Miata '90 thru '97
- 61020 MPV all models '89 thru '94
- Navajo - see FORD Explorer (36024)
- 61030 Pick-ups '72 thru '93
- Pick-ups '94 on - see Ford (36071)
- 61035 RX-7 all models '79 thru '85
- 61036 RX-7 all models '86 thru '91
- 61040 626 (rear wheel drive) '79 thru '82
- 61041 626 & MX-6 (front wheel drive) '83 thru '91
- 61042 626 '93 thru '01, & MX-6/Ford Probe '93 thru '97

MERCEDES-BENZ
- 63012 123 Series Diesel '76 thru '85
- 63015 190 Series 4-cyl gas models, '84 thru '88
- 63020 230, 250 & 280 6 cyl sohc '68 thru '72
- 63025 280 123 Series gas models '77 thru '81
- 63030 350 & 450 all models '71 thru '80

MERCURY
- 64200 Villager & Nissan Quest '93 thru '01
- *All other titles, see FORD listing.*

MG
- 66010 MGB Roadster & GT Coupe '62 thru '80
- 66015 MG Midget & Austin Healey Sprite Roadster '58 thru '80

MITSUBISHI
- 68020 Cordia, Tredia, Galant, Precis & Mirage '83 thru '93
- 68030 Eclipse, Eagle Talon & Plymouth Laser '90 thru '94
- *68031 Eclipse '95 thru '01, Eagle Talon '95 thru '98
- 68035 Mitsubishi Galant '94 thru '03
- 68040 Pick-up '83 thru '96, Montero '83 thru '93

NISSAN
- 72010 300ZX all models incl. Turbo '84 thru '89
- 72015 Altima all models '93 thru '04
- 72020 Maxima all models '85 thru '92
- *72021 Maxima all models '93 thru '01
- 72030 Pick-ups '80 thru '97, Pathfinder '87 thru '95
- *72031 Frontier Pick-up '98 thru '01, Xterra '00 & '01, Pathfinder '96 thru '01
- 72040 Pulsar all models '83 thru '86
- 72050 Sentra all models '82 thru '94
- 72051 Sentra & 200SX all models '95 thru '99
- 72060 Stanza all models '82 thru '90

OLDSMOBILE
- *73015 Cutlass '74 thru '88
- *For other OLDSMOBILE titles, see BUICK, CHEVROLET or GM listings.*

PLYMOUTH
- *For PLYMOUTH titles, see DODGE.*

PONTIAC
- 79008 Fiero all models '84 thru '88
- 79018 Firebird V8 models except Turbo '70 thru '81
- 79019 Firebird all models '82 thru '92
- 79040 Mid-size Rear-wheel Drive '70 thru '87
- *For other PONTIAC titles, see BUICK, CHEVROLET or GM listings.*

PORSCHE
- 80020 911 Coupe & Targa models '65 thru '89
- 80025 914 all 4 cyl models '69 thru '76
- 80030 924 all models incl. Turbo '76 thru '82
- 80035 944 all models incl. Turbo '83 thru '89

RENAULT
- Alliance, Encore - see AMC (14020)

SAAB
- *84010 900 including Turbo '79 thru '88

SATURN
- *87010 Saturn all models '91 thru '02
- 87020 Saturn all L-series models '00 thu '04

SUBARU
- 89002 1100, 1300, 1400 & 1600 '71 thru '79
- 89003 1600 & 1800 2WD & 4WD '80 thru '94

SUZUKI
- 90010 Samurai/Sidekick/Geo Tracker '86 thru '01

TOYOTA
- 92005 Camry all models '83 thru '91
- 92006 Camry all models '92 thru '96
- *92007 Camry/Avalon/Solara/Lexus ES 300 '97 thru '01
- 92015 Celica Rear Wheel Drive '71 thru '85
- 92020 Celica Front Wheel Drive '86 thru '99
- 92025 Celica Supra all models '79 thru '92
- 92030 Corolla all models '75 thru '79
- 92032 Corolla rear wheel drive models '80 thru '87
- 92035 Corolla front wheel drive models '84 thru '92
- 92036 Corolla & Geo Prizm '93 thru '02
- 92040 Corolla Tercel all models '80 thru '82
- 92045 Corona all models '74 thru '82
- 92050 Cressida all models '78 thru '82
- 92055 Land Cruiser FJ40/43/45/55 '68 thru '82
- 92056 Land Cruiser FJ60/62/80/FZJ80 '80 thru '96
- 92065 MR2 all models '85 thru '87
- 92070 Pick-up all models '69 thru '78
- 92075 Pick-up all models '79 thru '95
- *92076 Tacoma '95 thru '00, 4Runner '96 thru '00, T100 '93 thru '98
- *92078 Tundra '00 thru '02, Sequoia '01 thru '02
- 92080 Previa all models '91 thru '95
- *92082 RAV4 all models '96 thru '02
- 92085 Tercel all models '87 thru '94

TRIUMPH
- 94007 Spitfire all models '62 thru '81
- 94010 TR7 all models '75 thru '81

VW
- 96008 Beetle & Karmann Ghia '54 thru '79
- *96009 New Beetle '98 thru '00
- 96016 Rabbit, Jetta, Scirocco, & Pick-up gas models '74 thru '91 & Convertible '80 thru '92
- 96017 Golf, GTI & Jetta '93 thru '98, Cabrio '95 thru '98
- *96018 Golf, GTI, Jetta & Cabrio '98 thru '02
- 96020 Rabbit, Jetta, Pick-up diesel '77 thru '84
- 96023 Passat '98 thru '01, Audi A4 '96 thru '01
- 96030 Transporter 1600 all models '68 thru '79
- 96035 Transporter 1700, 1800, 2000 '72 thru '79
- 96040 Type 3 1500 & 1600 '63 thru '73
- 96045 Vanagon air-cooled models '80 thru '83

VOLVO
- 97010 120, 130 Series & 1800 Sports '61 thru '73
- 97015 140 Series all models '66 thru '74
- 97020 240 Series all models '76 thru '93
- 97025 260 Series all models '75 thru '82
- 97040 740 & 760 Series all models '82 thru '88

TECHBOOK MANUALS
- 10205 Automotive Computer Codes
- 10210 Automotive Emissions Control Manual
- 10215 Fuel Injection Manual, 1978 thru 1985
- 10220 Fuel Injection Manual, 1986 thru 1999
- 10225 Holley Carburetor Manual
- 10230 Rochester Carburetor Manual
- 10240 Weber/Zenith/Stromberg/SU Carburetor
- 10305 Chevrolet Engine Overhaul Manual
- 10310 Chrysler Engine Overhaul Manual
- 10320 Ford Engine Overhaul Manual
- 10330 GM and Ford Diesel Engine Repair
- 10340 Small Engine Repair Manual
- 10345 Suspension, Steering & Driveline
- 10355 Ford Automatic Transmission Overhaul
- 10360 GM Automatic Transmission Overhaul
- 10405 Automotive Body Repair & Painting
- 10410 Automotive Brake Manual
- 10415 Automotive Detaiing Manual
- 10420 Automotive Eelectrical Manual
- 10425 Automotive Heating & Air Conditioning
- 10430 Automotive Reference Dictionary
- 10435 Automotive Tools Manual
- 10440 Used Car Buying Guide
- 10445 Welding Manual
- 10450 ATV Basics

SPANISH MANUALS
- 98903 Reparación de Carrocería & Pintura
- 98905 Códigos Automotrices de la Computadora
- 98910 Frenos Automotriz
- 98915 Inyección de Combustible 1986 al 1999
- 99040 Chevrolet & GMC Camionetas '67 al '87
- 99041 Chevrolet & GMC Camionetas '88 al '98
- 99042 Chevrolet Camionetas Cerradas '68 al '95
- 99055 Dodge Caravan/Ply. Voyager '84 al '95
- 99075 Ford Camionetas y Bronco '80 al '94
- 99077 Ford Camionetas Cerradas '69 al '91
- 99088 Ford Modelos de Tamaño Mediano '75 al '86
- 99091 Ford Taurus & Mercury Sable '86 al '95
- 99095 GM Modelos de Tamaño Grande '70 al '90
- 99100 GM Modelos de Tamaño Mediano '70 al '88
- 99110 Nissan Camionetas '80 al '96, Pathfinder '87 al '95
- 99118 Nissan Sentra '82 al '94
- 99125 Toyota Camionetas y 4-Runner '79 al '95

** Listings shown with an asterisk (*) indicate model coverage as of this printing. These titles will be periodically updated to include later model years - consult your Haynes dealer for more information.*

Nearly 100 Haynes motorcycle manuals also available

2-05

Haynes North America, Inc., 861 Lawrence Drive, Newbury Park, CA 91320 • (805) 498-6703